A Companion to Western Historical Thought

WITHDRAWN

BLACKWELL COMPANIONS TO HISTORY

Published

A Companion to Western Historical
Thought
Edited by Lloyd Kramer and Sarah Maza

In preparation

A Companion to Gender History
*Edited by Teresa Meade and
Merry E. Weisner-Hanks*

BLACKWELL COMPANIONS TO BRITISH HISTORY

(Published in association with The Historical Association.)

Published

A Companion to Eighteenth-Century Britain
Edited by H. T. Dickinson

In preparation

A Companion to Roman Britain
Edited by Malcolm Todd

A Companion to Britain in the Later
Middle Ages
Edited by Stephen Rigby

A Companion to Tudor Britain
Edited by Robert Tittler and Norman Jones

A Companion to Stuart Britain
Edited by Barry Coward

A Companion to Nineteenth-Century
Britain
Edited by Chris Williams

A Companion to Early Twentieth-Century
Britain
Edited by Chris Wrigley

A Companion to Contemporary Britain
Edited by Paul Addison and Harriet Jones

BLACKWELL COMPANIONS TO EUROPEAN HISTORY

Published

A Companion to the Worlds of the
Renaissance
Edited by Guido Ruggiero

In preparation

A Companion to the Reformation World
Edited by R. Po-chia Hsia

BLACKWELL COMPANIONS TO AMERICAN HISTORY

Published

A Companion to the American Revolution
Edited by Jack P. Greene and J. R. Pole

A Companion to 19th-Century America
Edited by William L. Barney

A Companion to the American South
Edited by John B. Boles

A Companion to American Indian History
*Edited by Philip J. Deloria and
Neal Salisbury*

A Companion to American Women's
History
Edited by Nancy A. Hewitt

A Companion to Post-1945 America
*Edited by Jean-Christophe Agnew and
Roy Rosenzweig*

In preparation

A Companion to Colonial America
Edited by Daniel Vickers

A Companion to 20th-Century America
Edited by Stephen J. Whitfield

A Companion to the Vietnam War
*Edited by Marilyn Young and
Robert Buzzanco*

A Companion to the American West
Edited by William Deverell

A Companion to American Foreign
Relations
Edited by Robert Schulzinger

BLACKWELL COMPANIONS TO WORLD HISTORY

In preparation

A Companion to the History of Africa
Edited by Joseph Miller

A COMPANION TO WESTERN HISTORICAL THOUGHT

Edited by

Lloyd Kramer and Sarah Maza

Blackwell
Publishers

907.2
C737
2002

Copyright © Blackwell Publishers 2002

First published 2002

2 4 6 8 10 9 7 5 3 1

Blackwell Publishers Inc.
350 Main Street
Malden, Massachusetts 02148
USA

Blackwell Publishers Ltd
108 Cowley Road
Oxford OX4 1JF
UK

Library of Congress Cataloging-in-Publication Data

A companion to Western historical thought / edited by Lloyd Kramer and Sarah Maza.
     p. cm. – (Blackwell companions to history)
   Includes bibliographical references and index.
   ISBN 0–631–21714–2 (alk. paper)
   1. History, Philosophy. 2. History, Ancient – Historiography. 3. History, Modern – Historiography. I. Kramer, Lloyd S. II. Maza, Sarah C., 1953–
III. Series.
   D16.8 .B55 2002
   907'.2 – dc21

                                                   2001037574

British Library Cataloguing in Publication Data

A CIP catalogue record for this book is available from the British Library.

Typeset in 10.5 on 12.5 pt Galliard
by Best-set Typesetter Ltd., Hong Kong
Printed in Great Britain by TJ International Ltd, Padstow, Cornwall

This book is printed on acid-free paper

Contents

List of Contributors   viii

Acknowledgments   xii

Introduction: The Cultural History of Historical Thought
Lloyd Kramer and Sarah Maza   1

PART I   THE PRE-MODERN ORIGINS OF WESTERN HISTORICAL THOUGHT

1   Historiography in Ancient Israel
   John Van Seters   15

2   Historical Thought in Ancient Greece
   Philip A. Stadter   35

3   Historical Thought in Ancient Rome
   J. E. Lendon   60

4   Historical Thought in Medieval Europe
   Gabrielle M. Spiegel   78

5   Historical Thought in the Renaissance
   Paula Findlen   99

PART II   THE SHAPING OF MODERN WESTERN HISTORICAL THOUGHT

6   Historical Thought in the Era of the Enlightenment
   Johnson Kent Wright   123

7   German Historical Thought in the Age of Herder, Kant,
    and Hegel
    Harold Mah   143

8   German Historical Writing from Ranke to Weber: The Primacy
    of Politics
    Harry Liebersohn   166

9   National History in the Age of Michelet, Macaulay,
    and Bancroft
    Thomas N. Baker   185

10 Marxism and Historical Thought
    Walter L. Adamson   205

PART III   PATTERNS IN TWENTIETH-CENTURY WESTERN
           HISTORICAL THOUGHT

11 The Professionalization of Historical Studies and the Guiding
    Assumptions of Modern Historical Thought
    Georg G. Iggers   225

12 The History of Armed Power
    Peter Paret   243

13 Total History and Microhistory: The French and
    Italian Paradigms
    David A. Bell   262

14 Anthropology and the History of Culture
    William M. Reddy   277

15 The History of Science, Or, an Oxymoronic Theory of
    Relativistic Objectivity
    Ken Alder   297

16 Language, Literary Studies, and Historical Thought
    Susan A. Crane   319

17 Psychology, Psychoanalysis, and Historical Thought
    Lynn Hunt   337

18 Redefining Historical Identities: Sexuality, Gender, and
    the Self
    Carolyn J. Dean   357

19 Historicizing Natural Environments: The Deep Roots of
    Environmental History
    Andrew C. Isenberg   372

PART IV CHALLENGES TO THE BOUNDARIES OF WESTERN
HISTORICAL THOUGHT

20 The New World History
    Jerry H. Bentley   393

21 Postcolonial History
    Prasenjit Duara   417

22 The Multicultural History of Nations
    Donna R. Gabaccia   432

23 New Technologies and Historical Knowledge
    James M. Murray   447

24 The Visual Media and Historical Knowledge
    Robert A. Rosenstone   466

Consolidated Bibliography   482

Index   495

Contributors

Walter L. Adamson is Samuel Candler Dobbs Professor of Intellectual History at Emory University. His publications include *Hegemony and Revolution: A Study of Antonio Gramsci's Political and Cultural Theory* (1980), *Marx and the Disillusionment of Marxism* (1985), and *Avant-Garde Florence: From Modernism to Fascism* (1993).

Ken Alder is Associate Professor of History at Northwestern University. His first book, *Engineering the Revolution: Arms and Enlightenment in France, 1763–1815* (1997) won the 1998 Dexter Prize for the best book on the history of technology. He is currently completing a book on the origins of the metric system in Revolutionary France, *The World's Measure*, which will be published by the Free Press in 2002.

Thomas N. Baker is a visiting Assistant Professor in the Program in History at Centre College, Danville, Kentucky. His first book was *Sentiment and Celebrity: Nathaniel Parker Willis and the Trials of Literary Fame* (1999), and he is presently working on a study of deism in the early US republic.

David A. Bell is Professor of History at the Johns Hopkins University. He is the author of *Lawyers and Citizens: The Making of a Political Elite in Old Regime France* (1994), *The Cult of the Nation in France: Inventing Nationalism, 1680–1800* (2001), and co-editor of *Raison universelle et cultures nationales au siècle des lumières* (1999).

Jerry H. Bentley is Professor of History at the University of Hawaii and editor of the *Journal of World History*. Recently his research has concentrated on processes of cross-cultural interaction. His book *Old World Encounters: Cross-Cultural Contacts and Exchanges in Pre-Modern Times* (1993) examines processes of cultural exchange and religious conversion before the modern era, and his pamphlet *Shapes of World History in Twentieth-Century Scholarship* (1996) discusses the historiography of world history. His current interests include processes of cross-cultural interaction and cultural exchanges in modern times.

Susan A. Crane is Associate Professor of Modern European History at the University of Arizona. Her publications include *Collecting and Historical Consciousness in Early 19th-Century Germany* (2000), and (editor) *Museums and Memory* (2000).

Carolyn J. Dean teaches history at Brown University. She is the author of *The Self and its Pleasures: Bataille, Lacan, and the History of the Decentered Subject* (1992), and *The Frail Social Body: Pornography, Homosexuality and Other Fantasies in Interwar France* (2000).

Prasenjit Duara is Professor in the departments of History and East Asian Languages and Civilizations at the University of Chicago. Author of *Culture, Power and the State: Rural Society in North China, 1900–1942* (1988, 1991), and *Rescuing History from the Nation: Questioning Narratives of Modern China* (1995, 1996), he is at present completing another book tentatively entitled *Frontiers of the East Asian Modern: Authenticity and Sovereignty in Manchukuo.*

Paula Findlen, Professor of History at Stanford University, is the author of *Possessing Nature: Museums, Collecting, and Scientific Culture in Early Modern Italy* (1994), and (with Pamela H. Smith) *Merchants and Marvels: Commerce, Science and Art in Early Modern Europe* (2001). She recently completed *A Fragmentary Past: the Making of Museums in Renaissance Italy* (forthcoming) and is completing *The Woman Who Understood Newton: Laura Bassi and Her World.*

Donna R. Gabaccia is Charles H. Stone Professor of American History at the University of North Carolina at Charlotte, where she teaches courses on comparative social history and the twentieth-century world. She is the author of many books and articles on international migration and immigrant life in the Unites States, including *Immigration and American Diversity* (forthcoming), *Italy's Many Diasporas* (2000), and *We Are What We Eat: Ethnic Food and the Making of Americans* (1998).

Lynn Hunt is Eugen Weber Professor of Modern European History at the University of California, Los Angeles. She is the author of *Politics, Culture and Class in the French Revolution* (1984), *The Family Romance of the French Revolution* (1992), and the editor of *The New Cultural History* (1989), and *Beyond the Cultural Turn* (1999). She will be President of the American Historical Association in 2002.

Georg G. Iggers is Distinguished Professor Emeritus, State University of New York at Buffalo. He is the author of *The German Conception of History: the National Tradition of Historical Thought from Herder to the Present* (1968); *New Directions in European Historiography* (1975); and *Historiography in the Twentieth Century* (1997). He was President of the International Commission for the History and Theory of Historiography from 1995 to 2000.

Andrew C. Isenberg completed his doctorate in environmental history, the American West, and American Indian history at Northwestern University and is now an Assistant Professor of History at Princeton University. A former fellow at the Huntington Library, he is currently a Fulbright Senior Scholar at the University of Erfurt in Germany. He is the author of *The Destruction of the Bison: An Environmental Hsitory, 1750–1920* (2000).

Lloyd Kramer is Professor of History at the University of North Carolina, Chapel Hill. His publications include *Threshold of a New World: Intellectuals and the Exile Experience in Paris, 1830–1848* (1988), *Lafayette in Two Worlds: Public Cultures and Personal Identities in an Age of Revolutions* (1996), and *Nationalism: Political Cultures in Europe and America, 1775–1865* (1998).

J. E. Lendon teaches in the history department at the University of Virginia at Charlottesville. His publications include *Empire of Honour: The Art of Government in the Roman World* (1997).

Harry Liebersohn is a Professor of History at the University of Illinois, Urbana-Champaign. He is the author of *Fate and Utopia in German Sociology* (1988) and *Aristocratic Encounters: European Travelers and North American Indians* (1998).

Harold Mah teaches modern European intellectual and cultural history at Queen's University in Canada. He is the author of *The End of Philosophy, the Origin of "Ideology": Karl Marx and the Crisis of the Young Hegelians* (1987) and of articles on French and German cultural history and the theory of historical writing, the most recent of which is "Phantasies of the Public Sphere: Rethinking the Habermas of Historians" in *The Journal of Modern History* 72 (March 2000). A new book on cultural identity, entitled *Phantasies of Identity in France and Germany, Diderot to Nietzsche*, is forthcoming.

Sarah Maza is Jane Long Professor of Arts and Sciences at Northwestern University, where she teaches in the History Department. She is the author of *Servants and Masters in Eighteenth-Century France* (1983), *Private Lives and Public Affairs: The Causes Célèbres of Prerevolutionary France* (1993), and of many articles on the theory and practice of cultural history.

James M. Murray is Professor of History at the University of Cincinnati. As a medieval specialist he has written on the urban and economic history of Europe in the fourteenth century. He is co-author of *A History of Business in Medieval Europe* (1999). A Silicon Valley childhood played some role in an early interest in personal computers. He has used and written about the use of these machines in historical work since the 1980s.

Peter Paret is Professor Emeritus in the School of Historical Studies at the Institute for Advanced Study in Princeton, New Jersey. He has published on the history of art as well as numerous works on diverse aspects of military history. His books include *Clausewitz and the State* (1976), *Understanding War: Essays on Clausewitz and the History of Military Power* (1992), and *Imagined Battles: Reflections of War in European Art* (1997).

William M. Reddy is William T. Laprade Professor of History and Professor of Cultural Anthropology at Duke University. His research and teaching focus on the social and cultural history of France since the eighteenth century and cultural theory in history and anthropology. His most recent books are *The Invisible Code: Honor and Sentiment in Postrevolutionary France, 1815–1848* (1997) and *The Navigation of Feeling: A Framework for the History of the Emotions* (2001).

Robert A. Rosenstone, Professor of History at the California Institute of Technology, has in recent years focused on two related topics: new forms of narrative and the interaction between history and the visual media. His half dozen books include *Romantic Revolutionary: A Biography of John Reed* (1975), *Mirror in the Shrine: American Encounters with Meiji Japan* (1988), and *Visions of the Past: the Challenge of Film to Our Idea of History* (1995).

Gabrielle M. Spiegel is Professor of History at the Johns Hopkins University. She is author of *The Chronicle Tradition of Saint-Denis: A Survey* (1978), *Romancing the Past: The Rise of Vernacular Historiography in Thirteenth-Century France* (1993), and *The Past as Text: The Theory and Practice of Historiography* (1997), as well as numerous articles on medieval historiography and critical theory. She is the recipient of the William J. Koren, Jr. Prize for the best article on French history for 1987 and of the Berkshire Conference of Women Historians' article prize for 1990.

Philip A. Stadter, Eugene H. Falk Professor in the Humanities at the University of North Carolina at Chapel Hill, is author of *Arrian of Nicomedia* (1980), and *A Commentary on Plutarch's Pericles* (1989). He has edited *Speeches in Thucydides* (1973) and *Plutarch and the Historical Tradition* (1992). He has written articles on Herodotus, Thucydides, Xenophon, Plutarch, and Arrian. Recently he provided introductions and commentaries for *Plutarch, Nine Greek Lives* (1998) and *Plutarch, Eight Roman Lives* (1999).

John Van Seters is James A. Gray Professor Emeritus, Department of Religious Studies at the University of North Carolina, Chapel Hill. He currently resides in Waterloo, Ontario, Canada. His publications include *In Search of History: Historiography in the Ancient World and the Origins of Biblical History* (1983), winner of the James H. Breasted Award of the American Historical Association; and *Prologue to History: The Yahwist as Historian in Genesis* (1992).

Johnson Kent Wright is Associate Professor and Director of Graduate Studies in the Interdisciplinary Humanities Program at Arizona State University. He is the author of *A Classical Republican in Eighteenth-Century France: the Political Thought of Mably* (1997), as well as several essays on modern historiography.

Acknowledgments

This book grew out of an initiative by Tessa Harvey of Blackwell Publishers, who suggested that a volume of essays on the history of Western historical thought would be useful for students, history teachers, and other readers who are looking for an accessible introduction to this wide-ranging subject. We therefore thank Tessa for proposing an idea that has now evolved into this book. We have also benefited from the ideas and efficient assistance of other colleagues at Blackwell, including Angela Cohen, Anthony Grahame, Tamsin Smith, and Louise Spencely.

Christopher Beneke, a graduate student in the history department at Northwestern University, used his technological skills to help prepare the manuscript and electronic files for production. We thank him for his excellent contribution to this project. We would also like to thank each of the authors in this collection for their thoughtful, efficient work and for the timely manner in which they wrote their essays. The editors were exceptionally fortunate in working with contributors who were always cooperative, reliable, and knowledgeable. We have learned from reading and editing their essays, and we believe that other readers will learn from their work too.

Finally, we would like to thank Gwynne Pomeroy, Kyle Kramer, Renee Kramer, Sean Shesgreen, and Juliette Maza Shesgreen for their patience and good humor throughout the time we have been working on this book. They all seem to understand that writing and thinking about the past takes a lot of time and attention from our lives in the present. We appreciate their tolerance and support, all of which contributed in various ways to the completion of this book.

Lloyd Kramer   Sarah Maza

Introduction: The Cultural History of Historical Thought

Lloyd Kramer and Sarah Maza

This volume provides an overview of the many forms of historical thought which have flourished in Europe and North America from biblical times and classical antiquity down to the contemporary era of the Internet, television, and the global film industry. In essays that cover more than two thousand years of Western cultural history, the twenty-four contributors to this book examine the evolving theories, methods, and conceptual categories that men and women have used to explain and write about the past. Over the long development of Western historical writing, historians have come from an extraordinary range of social and cultural positions – monks, courtiers and royal scribes, army generals and wealthy aristocrats, prosperous merchants and poor workers, political leaders and statesmen, philosophers, poets, teachers, university professors, artists, and filmmakers. Thinking and writing about history, as the authors of the following essays show, has always been shaped by a host of different and often conflicting ideals, aspirations, and practical objectives, including religious beliefs, political ideologies, propaganda for ruling elites (or for their opponents), literary expression, popular entertainment, academic careerism, and the search for personal or collective identities.

The chapters in this book refer in various ways to all of these historical practices, and they describe specific historians as well as wider historical movements that have influenced both their own era and the historical thought of later generations. The story of historical thought begins in times so remote that their histories survive only in fragments written by nameless chroniclers, but it continues into a twenty-first century whose technologies and mass media are rapidly transforming the oldest traditions of historical work. Previously obscure documents and historical records have become instantly available through the world-wide web of the computer age, yet the readership of academic history-writing is dwindling, and historians are anxiously searching for new ways to communicate with a culture that gives far more value to "speed" and "the present" than to slow-moving commentaries on the people and events of the past.

A survey of historical thought must therefore recognize the ways in which historical understanding both changes and stays the same in the different eras of human history. We asked each of the authors in this book to discuss the origin and legacy of a specific period or form of historical thought and thereby provide a concise summary of often diverse historical texts or historiographical traditions. When and where did a particular style or method of historical thought appear and what were its most distinctive traits? What were its guiding assumptions and what impact did this kind of history have on historical conceptions of human events or human societies? What were its limitations or historical blind spots? Did this form of historical thought produce an enduring legacy that remains relevant or influential in the historical writing and thought of our own era? We asked all of the authors to address such questions in essays that would be accessible to readers who have an interest in history but little or no specialist knowledge of historical thought and philosophies of history.

The following chapters thus emphasize the main themes of different eras and forms of historical thought, but they are also organized roughly in chronological fashion to suggest the development of historical thought across time. We decided to use this mostly linear organization – though the chronology flattens out in later sections that discuss the concurrent themes of contemporary historical thought – in order to show how various aspects of historiography have reappeared in different historical eras or remained influential or changed amid evolving historical contexts. Many of the assumptions we take for granted when we think about history today have origins that can in fact be traced far back into the history of pre-modern Western thought. The idea of a "people" or "nation" as the fundamental unit of historical thought, for example, emerged in some of the earliest biblical narratives and in ancient Greek histories of early Greek wars. Cultural history had its practitioners in ancient Greece, in Renaissance Italy, and in eighteenth-century France long before it took on new philosophical themes in nineteenth-century Germany. Some Renaissance historians were the first to point out that history written from the vantage point of women would look much different from the usual male-centered story. Eighteenth-century thinkers began to divide the sweep of Western history into "stages" whose dominant characteristics were forms of economic activity or social organization. In some periods – the Renaissance and early nineteenth century, for instance – historians focused attention on the importance of original, written documents, while at other times the sources became almost invisible behind the writer's own voice. Such traditions and many others described in this book remain influential in historical thought to this day, though they have also been challenged, criticized, and redefined in the historical debates of almost every generation. Like other forms of human culture, historical thought draws on models or antecedents from the past, but it also transforms, revises, and recreates all the traditions that it uses.

The essays in this volume draw attention not only to the assumptions that have shaped historical thought in a succession of times and places, but also to the different social, political, and cultural contexts in which accounts of the past have been produced. What we see today as the "normal" context for writing history – advanced degrees, university departments, professional meetings, journals, and monographs – took shape little more than a century ago. The professional environment in which most historians now work developed in the new universities, libraries, archives, and publishing systems of the modern nation-state, but these institutions (and the nation-states that supported them) are now undergoing rapid and unpredictable changes. It is difficult to imagine what "doing history" will look like a century from now, though it seems likely that this future world will be increasingly dominated by the visual media, by cyberspace and by the global cultural exchanges that are emerging in this new technological context. Historical thought is shaped by the historian's religious, political, and intellectual commitments, but also by more immediate social and institutional factors such as the need to provide historical legitimacy for powerful persons, to flatter a monarch, to defend the privileges of an institution, to complete an encyclopedic European-style thesis, or to gain the security of a tenured academic job. As these shaping institutional structures change in the coming century, the nature of historical work is bound to change too.

This volume's survey of the leading ideas and influential contexts that have shaped previous centuries and patterns of historical thought deals essentially with developments in what is usually called the "Western World": the ancient Mediterranean, Europe, and modern North America. It does not cover the independent evolution of historical thought in other important civilizations and cultural traditions in Asia, Africa, and Latin America. The book's final section, however, suggests that current intellectual exchanges are making such clearly demarcated cultural distinctions increasingly untenable. Thinkers from other parts of the world have challenged Western historians to recast their histories of both the Western world and the large, diverse world outside the West. The rapid growth of new global and post-colonial histories shows how complex, cross-cultural exchanges have long influenced all parts of the world (including of course the West). One of the main themes of post-colonial history, for instance, stresses the ambiguous, often vexed nature of national identities among the inhabitants of Europe's former colonies. The work of post-colonial historians has in turn influenced historians of Europe and America, leading them to examine the multicultural characteristics of modern nations and to question the very concept of nationhood as it applies to countries like France, Britain or the United States. Historical thought in the contemporary world is therefore becoming global and encouraging new cross-cultural themes that will surely be as influential as new technologies, new media and new social institutions in shaping the future development of historical thought.

The study of historical thought thus could and should move far beyond the Western tradition, but even within the Western tradition itself it would be possible to explore many themes that are not examined in this volume. We could have included more analysis of how social and cultural assumptions about gender affect historical writing, or a survey of how historical novels influence historical understanding, or a detailed discussion of how historical thought appears and disappears in contemporary popular culture. Given the inevitable limits of a single book, however, we have chosen to focus mostly on the long intellectual history of Western historiography.

This overview of the distant and more recent past summarizes what earlier historians have thought and written about the meaning of history, but it is also designed to encourage new critical thinking about contemporary and future historical work. Placing recent historical practice in a wider cultural and temporal context shows both the contingency and the cultural origins of our own historical assumptions. It also provokes questions about the new directions that historical thought could take in the twenty-first century. How long will we continue to think of history as unfolding within the boundaries of nation-states? Will the traditional distinctions between Western and non-Western societies remain important in historical thought? Will we arrive at new understandings of individuals and "selfhood" in history, or grasp the nature of emotions in societies and eras that are far removed from our own culture? Will our longstanding assumptions about the purposes of historical narratives crumble as future generations produce computerized hypertexts instead of bound books and dissertations? Facing such questions about the changes and discontinuities in the theory and practice of historical studies, we need to think again about the enduring characteristics and continuities that have long made historical thought one of the decisive influences in Western intellectual life. But what are the distinctive beliefs and themes of Western historical thought?

The Traditions and Themes of Historical Thought

There is of course no single form of historical "thought" that exists simply as a unified philosophical or cultural tradition. It is thus better to describe historical thought as a collection of related themes, each of which has been important to historical understanding but none of which stands alone as the core of all historical philosophies or theories – except perhaps for the belief that the past has discernible meanings and a significant influence on the present. Almost everyone who has thought about the past in the language of historians has assumed that it is possible to discover and describe significant cultural patterns when we carefully examine past people, events, conflicts, and institutions.

Historical thought thus depends on narratives that tell stories about the past. These narratives can be oral (most historical stories in daily life take this form), or they can appear in writing, or they can emerge in the visual language of films and photographs. The form of a historical narrative affects the message it conveys because oral, written, and visual narratives communicate meanings with different strategies or methods (physical gestures versus prose structures versus visual images, for example). Whatever their form, historical narratives usually describe some kind of change across time. Although historical narratives also typically note structures or ideas that show little change over relatively long historical periods, historians have generally sought to explain how both individuals and social or political systems change over decades, centuries, and even millennia. Historical thought therefore usually assumes that historical research and writing should reveal the relation between historical changes and continuities in past societies. But most historians tend to emphasize one aspect of this historical process over others. Some look constantly for the social, political, and cultural continuities that link each era to previous eras or cultures. Others are much more interested in the ruptures or changes that challenge and displace the ideas, institutions and persons from earlier historical periods. Yet even a radical figure such as the French theorist Michel Foucault, who challenged conventional notions of causality and historical continuity, organized his histories of Western thought and institutions in chronological sequences from the most remote to the most recent times.

The process of analyzing the complex relation between continuities and discontinuities in human societies is thus at the center of much historical thought. Yet there is great diversity in the ways that historians have sought to explain this dynamic process (as the chapters in this book demonstrate), so the broad claim that historians are concerned with the relation between changes and continuities requires more detailed attention to the specific, recurring themes of historical thought. These themes give some limited coherence and a distinctive shape to the intellectual traditions of historical knowledge, but they sometimes express contradictory assumptions, they sometimes defy empirical research, and they frequently provoke vehement debates among historians themselves. The following ideas, however, have reappeared often enough among historians to become important intellectual traditions in the long history of historical studies.

History has meanings, which can be discovered through systematic study and analysis. Most historians from the earliest biblical writers to the modern advocates of social science, biography, or economic determinism assume that they are able to identify significant patterns in individual lives or in the actions of collective social groups. Historical thought is thus a form of creative cultural work that describes the past as a shaping influence on later historical events and people. History is viewed as more than a random, unrelated set of events; rather it is seen as an essential cultural resource for explaining how and why the world came to be as it is. Historians have usually believed that events in human societies and in individual lives have specific causes and that the discovery of patterns of causality gives history its meaning and much of its cultural value.

This belief in recognizable meanings leads, however, in two different directions among students of history. One form of historical thought argues that *the meaning of history appears in recurring, universal patterns or universal truths.* This belief has often appeared in religious conceptions of history (early Jewish and Christian historians, for example, saw the universal purpose and guiding hand of God in all specific historical events), and it has usually carried strong teleological implications. As the advocates of universal history explain it, historical change shows a clear, purposeful direction across time: a progression toward the Second Coming of Christ, the growth of freedom in the world, a progressive expansion in the use of Reason or scientific knowledge, a steady movement toward capitalist or socialist economic systems, an inexorable movement toward "modernization" or nation-states or world government. The precise content of these unfolding, historical patterns thus differs according to the concerns of the historians who interpret them, but all such theories assume that history is moving toward recognizable goals. And the underlying assumption in this view of history suggests that deep similarities in various societies and historical periods are ultimately more significant than apparent cultural differences.

But another account of the meaningful patterns in history argues that *the meaning of history emerges in the distinctive cultural, social, and political characteristics that make each society and historical era unique or different from other cultures.* This emphasis on the distinctiveness or particularity of each culture has become for many thinkers the most important feature of historical thought. History shows how each group of people differs from others, and it helps us avoid the anachronistic belief that people in other eras and cultures thought about the world like we do or acted with the same social and political aspirations. A strong interest in cultural differences has shaped the theoretical assumptions of "historicism" – the belief that each culture inevitably has its own beliefs, institutions, and social mores – and it leads also to the common use of "periodization" in historical thought. The "Middle Ages" differed from the "Renaissance," which differed from the "Enlightenment," which differed, in turn, from the "Age of Romanticism," and so forth. While such labels are always open to challenge, all historical eras, as periodizing historians describe them, embody distinctive values and institutions, which form more or less coherent patterns of social, cultural, and political life, and which historians can explain through the careful discipline of historical research.

Historical research thus becomes a method for uncovering both the universal and distinctive characteristics of past societies, all of which make it possible for historians to *use the past to create collective and personal identities.* Here, too, one sees a recurring cultural use of historical thought, from the identity-shaping historical claims in the cultures of ancient Hebrews and Greeks to the civic humanist claims of Renaissance historians or the nationalist claims of nineteenth-century French historians or the political claims of modern labor historians, feminist historians, post-colonial historians, and environmental historians (all have used history to define the lineage of their causes and the identity of their groups). Historical thought has always helped individuals explain who they are by explaining where they came from; and it has enabled social groups to express collective identities by referring to the past achievements or defeats of specific human communities.

One of the most common historical strategies for defining personal or group identities emerges in *the use of exemplary models from past generations to demonstrate virtuous behavior.* The historical search for courageous military or political heroes – the great men of the past – was a familiar pattern throughout the historical works of antiquity and the Renaissance, but the pattern has by no means vanished from modern historical thought. Historians continue to look for exemplary past figures who can provide a model for later generations: the militant labor leader, the freedom-seeking slave, the independent woman, the militant supporter of national liberation, the critical public intellectual. The belief that history provides models for each rising generation has been a familiar theme in historical thought and historical education across all the centuries of Western cultural life (sometimes the models show negative examples of behaviors that people should avoid).

The importance of moral exemplars in historical writing and thought suggests also *the close connections between history and politics.* Since the time of the ancient Greeks and Romans, historians have often expressed an intense, pragmatic interest in the political lessons of history and in the uses of power that history reveals. The historical meaning of politics extends well beyond specific political institutions such as monarchies, constitutions, government ministries, and republican assemblies to include the wider uses of power, violence, warfare, and social control. Many historians have been active in politics, and they have studied history in order to make sense of their own societies or their own political failures. Here is one of the many places in which historical thought has been influenced by assumptions about gender, because historians traditionally viewed politics as a sphere for male action and male commentary. The political dimensions of historical thought appear also in the many historical works that have been written to justify the power of a king, to explain the legitimacy of a ruling elite or to mobilize popular opposition to reigning powers. Even when the history of political elites has lost favor as the main object for historical analysis (as is the case in much recent historical thought), the close connections between politics, history and power have remained important themes in historical analysis.

One of the patterns that emerges in broadly conceived histories of politics and power concerns *the complex historical connection between the actions of individuals and the social structures in which they live.* Historians have always wanted to explain the actions of specific individuals whose lives and actions seemed to have a major influence on their historical eras, but there has also been a growing historical interest in the ways that each person tries to achieve individual ambitions, overcome anxieties, or protect a sense of "selfhood" within the social and cultural institutions that shape daily life. Where the great ancient Greek biographer Plutarch narrated the lives of famous men and established the historical genre of biography, more recent historians have told the stories of previously unknown women and men who sought to shape a family, a career, a friendship, or a community. Much of this literature is commemorative or admiring as it explores the historical construction of selfhood in different epochs, but this kind of biographical writing often seeks also to explain the nefarious effects of power on individual lives. In all of these cases, ancient and modern, historians have argued that history is a story of individuals and personal identities as well as vast social systems and impersonal collective structures.

No matter what the object of their analysis, however, historians have typically insisted on *the importance of verifiable evidence to support historical claims about what happened in the past.* This insistence on documentary evidence became one of the distinctive intellectual traits of historical thought in the modern era; indeed it gave historians a key criterion for separating themselves from novelists, poets, artists, philosophers, theologians and many other intellectuals in the era after the eighteenth century. Yet even ancient and Renaissance historians frequently buttressed their claims for special knowledge with references to the eyewitnesses they had consulted or the documents they had read. The appeal to empirical evidence has often been interpreted as part of the "science" in historical thought and research, but historians also use their evidence to construct literary narratives about people, events, and social changes. This sophisticated combination of verifiable evidence and artistic, literary prose styles has been regarded as a distinctive hallmark of great historians from the time of Herodotus in ancient Greece to the latest announcement of prizewinning books at the American Historical Association.

Yet historians have usually been expected to do more than simply gather reliable evidence and tell a good story; they are also supposed to *evaluate documents, events, and historical figures with an objective, balanced method.* The concept of objectivity, like the emphasis on evidence, became especially important during the modern professionalization of historical studies in the late nineteenth century, but the desire for balanced, fair-minded historical narratives emerged long before the modern era. Some historians in almost every premodern culture sought to establish the objectivity of their research and writing – whether they were proving the forgery of an old document or establishing a claim for royal genealogy or describing the causes of a deadly war. To be sure, the modern scientific conception of objective knowledge had a decisive, shaping influence on modern historical thought and the conventions of modern historical writing (for example, the use of footnotes, bibliographies, diverse documentation), yet one also finds at least limited concepts of objectivity as far back as Thucydides. In the later twentieth century, some historians strongly challenged the whole concept of objectivity, arguing that it was an impossible goal and that claims to impartiality served to conceal dominant values. Others claimed that the ideal of objective knowledge remained essential, even if it could not be realized in practice. Objectivity, in short, has often been a kind of "noble dream" in historical thought, a dream than never quite disappears and never finally comes true.

The search for reliable knowledge led historians to create their own disciplinary standards or rules for evidence and documentation (which, as noted above, separated them from novelists and artists), but historians have also shown a remarkable *tendency to use other forms of knowledge and other disciplines to develop historical accounts of past societies and people.* The history of human beings encompasses every aspect of human activity, including economics, social rituals, religion, science, warfare, art, music, political institutions, and families. Historians have therefore long seen the relevance of all the humanistic and social scientific approaches to human experience and knowledge. They were at first attracted mostly to economics, political science, and sociology, but in recent decades they have drawn widely on anthropology, psychology, literary theory, linguistics, and geography. Historical thought has thus long been what we now call "interdisciplinary," and interdisciplinary methods have helped renew and expand historical thought in almost all the modern contexts of historical studies. Renaissance historians learned the skills of humanist literary critics; Enlightenment historians drew on early geographers and anthropologists; nineteenth-century German historicists learned to analyze documents like philologists; and modern biographers have explained irrational human behaviors with the insights of clinical psychology.

The openness to diverse disciplines (though often provoking resistance as well as innovations) has also encouraged historians to *examine constantly widening topics and subjects in their search for comprehensive historical understanding.* Although the classic subjects of politics, warfare and diplomacy have never disappeared from historical thought, historians have increasingly explored levels or forms of historical activity that once lay beyond the interest or the reach of historical analysis: the history of work, marriage, gender and racial theories, food, clothing, manners, smells, sexuality, architecture, book production, birth rituals, death, disease, natural environments, criminality, insanity, agriculture, weather, and dozens of other new subjects. Every con-

ceivable sphere of human activity has entered into one of the growing sub-
disciplines of historical thought and widened the meaning of historical knowledge. The ever-expanding thematic interests in historical studies also have
pre-modern antecedents, but the range of historical subjects has grown most
rapidly in the contemporary era.

In addition to the widening subjects of historical thought, historians have
developed a global understanding of human exchanges and world history. There
were always historians who wrote about diverse human cultures (Herodotus
and Tacitus produced such works in antiquity), and Christian historiography
in the Middle Ages provided a universal vision or conception of world history
(always with the Christian teleology as a shaping philosophy). The contemporary concern with "globalization" in almost every realm of economic,
cultural, and political life, however, has pushed historians toward a new recognition of long-developing relations between the diverse regions and cultures
of the world. It has become increasingly important for historians to place
national histories in a wider, global context and to describe the economic or
cultural interactions that flow in all directions in world history – not simply
from the West to the rest. This globalization of historical thought has become
one of the most significant trends in recent historical writing, and it is bound
to continue as global migrations and exchanges expand even more rapidly in
the twenty-first century.

The influence of the new global context on contemporary historians points
finally to another recurring pattern in the long history of historical thought,
which is *the shaping influence of social and historical contexts on the themes and
concerns of historical writing.* Historians in every generation have responded
to the specific problems, controversies, and conflicts of their times by writing
historical accounts that carry the distinctive preoccupations of their own world
and culture. Historians have always described the religious, political, intellectual, and social controversies of the past, but their own historical context gave
urgency to the questions they asked and the historical interpretations they
developed. This complex relation between historical texts and the cultural contexts in which they are produced makes the history of historical thought an
exemplary part of the historical process itself. Reading past historians often
provides a fascinating entry into the many social, cultural and political worlds
that have generated creative historical thought. This book thus offers a kind
of cultural history of Western societies (including our own) by retracing the
thought of historians over the last 2,500 years.

The Changing Contexts of Historical Thought

The themes that we have noted in discussing the evolving traditions of Western
historical thought will reappear often in the chapters that make up the four

parts of this book, but other themes will also emerge as the authors discuss the development of historiographical trends in various cultural contexts. Although each part deals with a specific era of historical thought, the emphasis gradually shifts from chronological periods toward particular topics and interdisciplinary perspectives as the book approaches the contemporary era. All of the chapters refer both to general thematic patterns and to important historians whose work exemplifies these themes (a short bibliography at the end of each chapter lists the most important books). We cannot discuss the content of all the chapters in the introduction, but we want to summarize the volume's overall structure and refer briefly to the ways in which each part examines historical contexts that have influenced the evolution of historical thought.

Part I, "The Pre-Modern Origins of Western Historical Thought," covers the long period from biblical times through the sixteenth century. The essays describe the early uses of history as the chronicle of a people's past and as the source of collective identities. They also discuss the use of the past as an example for moral or religious teachings and as a justification for the exercise of political power. Historians from ancient times through the Renaissance developed an interest in culture as well as politics and warfare, drawing on history for personal consolation or for broad perspectives on the social and political problems of their times. By the era of the Renaissance, we can also see the emergence of historicist thinking and the careful use of source criticism.

Part II, "The Shaping of Modern Western Historical Thought," focuses on the eighteenth and nineteenth centuries. Ranging from the early Enlightenment to the emergence of Marxism and modern social sciences, these chapters discuss the advent of a "philosophical" history that marched humanity through stages of development, the creation of modern nationalist history in its many guises, and the influential work of thinkers such as Karl Marx and Max Weber. This section also analyzes the expanding influence of historicism, of Hegelian philosophy, and of the archival research methods that came to dominate historical studies in the era of Leopold von Ranke.

Part III, "Patterns in Twentieth-Century Western Historical Thought," adopts a more thematic approach to the major developments of the last century. It begins with an overview of the intellectual and institutional transitions that turned historical studies into a modern academic profession, and subsequent chapters discuss the most influential methods and "schools" of historical thought in the twentieth century. These essays chart the successive influence of other disciplines that helped to reshape professional historical research: sociology and statistical methods in the early twentieth century, and psychology, cultural anthropology, and literary criticism after the 1960s. The new disciplinary approaches encouraged the historical study of new subjects such as gender, sexuality, and the construction of "selfhood," but they also transformed and renewed long established sub-fields such as military history and the history of science. Part III also describes some of the schools of thought that have been most influential in recent historical writing, including the important work of the *Annales* journal in France, the new microhistory in Italy, the growing emphasis on sexual, racial, ethnic, and national identities in the United States, and the wide-ranging impact of postmodernism in both Europe and the Americas.

Part IV, "Challenges to the Boundaries of Western Historical Thought," shows how contemporary cultural developments are forcing twenty-first century historians to rethink their categories of knowledge and the research practices they have long taken for granted. In recent years, the conventional unit of historical analysis, the nation-state, has been challenged from without and within traditional national cultures. Many historians now focus on transnational histories of migrations and diasporas, on cross-cultural economic and intellectual exchanges, and on the historical significance of bodies of water such as the Atlantic and Pacific Oceans rather than on continents or landmasses. Others have highlighted the essential instability and racial–ethnic diversity of populations in the oldest and most powerful Western nations, thus stressing the multiculturalism of all modern societies. Meanwhile, even as the content of recent histories makes us question hallowed distinctions between countries, continents, and cultures, the very forms and media of historical knowledge are rapidly shifting into cyberspace and airwaves. The volume therefore concludes with essays on the technologies and mass media which increasingly supplement and could eventually replace the book, the chapter, the page, and the footnote. New technologies may well shape future historical work even more than the printing press shaped the emergence of modern historical studies. In any case, the changing technological and institutional contexts will inevitably affect the production of historical texts and the themes of historical thought in ways that we can still scarcely imagine.

Despite all of the rapid changes in the theory and practice of historical studies, however, historians will retain important links to cultural traditions and aspirations that have characterized historical thought since antiquity. Following the intellectual assumptions of their many predecessors, historians will almost surely continue to believe that history provides distinctive and essential knowledge about the identities and experiences of individual persons, about the social and political systems that control human societies, about the conflicts and power struggles that appear in every century, and about the complex ideas that give coherence to the cultures in which everyone must live. This book thus points to influential continuities in historical thought, but it also shows that historians – like the people and historical worlds they describe – are always changing and always facing an unpredictable future.

PART I

The Pre-Modern Origins of Western Historical Thought

CHAPTER ONE

Historiography in Ancient Israel

JOHN VAN SETERS

Historiography, as reflected in the Old Testament, is a form of narrative that makes reference to past events in the history of the nation in a chronological sequence from the time of human and national origins to the historical period of the author. The purpose of such narratives is to articulate the people's corporate identity, to account for the nature of their present plight and to suggest their ultimate destiny. Although in form, as a narration of the past, it resembles modern historiography, it is fundamentally different in certain important respects. First, Israelite historiography is not critical of its sources of information about the past, which may include myths and legends about origins, however much it reshapes them for its own presentation. In this use of sources it did not yet share the skepticism of folk traditions that one finds within the classical historiography of Herodotus and Thucydides. Second, biblical history strongly reflects the view that Israel's deity plays an active role in the affairs of humanity and in the destiny of the people of Israel in particular; and this deity is the primary cause for historical events. While this religious belief stands in marked contrast with the secularized and humanistic modes of modern historical thought, it still shares much with the many teleological forms of historical thought that have arisen out of biblical historiography. More generally, the widespread modern belief that history is meaningful, that specific events have a reason or purpose, and that history is moving in an important direction can all be linked to themes in biblical historical writings.

Israelite historiography stands in even more marked contrast with the surrounding civilizations of the Near East, the Assyrians and Babylonians, the Hittites and the Egyptians. While these other cultures produced many monumental inscriptions and other forms of written records to memorialize the deeds of kings and to render an account of their actions to the gods, they did not produce narratives of the nation's past to articulate corporate identity. By contrast, the deeds of kings and leaders are rarely celebrated in Israel's history and more is said about their failures than their achievements. Nevertheless, some formal similarities between Near Eastern and Israelite historical genres may be observed at a number of points. One such example lies in the development of a chronology of the past by means of the construction of king-lists, consisting of the sequence of rulers of a nation and the length of each reign, sometimes correlated with that of a neighboring state. However, while such lists may serve the ideological purpose of legitimating the royal authority of a state or serve the practical purpose of facilitating record keeping in other Near Eastern states, in Israelite historiography it became the chronological framework for the ordering and narrating of historical events. Some formal similarities may also be observed between royal annals and chronicles of Near Eastern states and their imitation by Israelite historians in the presentation of events in their histories. This has led some scholars to conjecture the existence of such annals and chronicles within the Israelite and Judean courts. In most cases, however, it is more likely a case of Israelite historians imitating a literary style that is used for quite different purposes in the biblical context. Consequently, the genres of historical writing in other ancient civilizations of the Near East are of only limited assistance in helping us to understand the nature of historical thought in Ancient Israel.

The biblical history of the people of Israel that is contained in the Old Testament from Genesis to 2 Kings and that stretches chronologically from the time of creation to the fall of Jerusalem in 586 BCE is not the work of a single historian or period of time. Rather, it represents the work of three major historians, writing in succession with the later ones supplementing the work of the earlier. There are also some literary additions of more limited scope. I will not present the critical basis for such a literary analysis here; instead I will focus upon the contributions that each of these historians made to Israelite historical thought.

The scope of this aggregate historical work has, in the past, often been obscured by the traditional division between the Pentateuch (Genesis to Deuteronomy) and the historical books (Joshua to 2 Kings). This has led to a quite different approach to the compositional history of the Pentateuch from that of the historical books and to a lively debate about the literary limits of each historian's work and when and by whom the sections of the Old Testament were actually written. The view that has now won broad acceptance is that Deuteronomy belongs to the following historical books (Joshua to 2 Kings) as a kind of ideological introduction to what is called "the Deuteronomistic History" (DtrH),[1] and its author the Deuteronomist (Dtr). This leaves a Tetrateuch (Genesis to Numbers) which is a combination of two basic "documents", one lay or non-priestly (the so-called Yahwist or J) and one priestly (P). How these relate to each other and how the two together relate to Deuteronomy and DtrH is still a matter of scholarly dispute. For the purpose of this essay I will follow my own solution to these issues which is to propose that DtrH is the earliest of these histories, that it was supplemented by J in Genesis to Numbers and that this was further augmented by P.[2] In what follows, I will treat these three anonymous historians in this order, and refer to them with the abbreviated letter by which they are known in modern scholarship. Finally, I will also note the historical tradition of the biblical books of Chronicles, Ezra, and Nehemiah which challenges and revises at least part of the earlier historical narratives in the Hebrew Bible.

The Deuteronomistic History (DtrH)

This earliest Israelite historical narrative presents the whole history of the people from their origin in the wilderness under Moses through the successive stages of conquest of the promised land, settlement and life under the "judges," and the monarchy down to the demise of the two kingdoms of Israel and Judah. The history is treated as an object lesson in obedience and disobedience to the law of Moses and the consequences that result from both. The historical work originated in a religious reform movement in the time of King Josiah of Judah (late 7th century BCE) that was based upon the "discovery" of a "book of the law" (2 Kings 22–23). This lawbook has been identified by scholars as the code of laws in Deuteronomy (Deut. 12–26), together with a prologue of admonitions (chs. 6–8) and a concluding series of blessings and curses (ch. 28). The historian (Dtr) in the early 6th century BCE took up this lawbook, expanded it with historical reflections upon the wilderness period and the circumstances in which the law was given by the god YAHWEH through Moses, and established a link to the conquest and settlement of the promised land through the appointment of Joshua to be the successor of Moses after his death.

Deuteronomy thus served as an exposition on the origin of the nation as a people under a solemn covenant with their god YAHWEH, the terms of which were set forth in the laws of the Decalogue and the Mosaic code. The deity was thereby bound to his promise to give the people of Israel "the land of the Amorites" – the land of the aboriginal population – and to maintain them in it and insure their prosperity in return for obedience to the law. In this way Josiah's reform program was construed as the constitutional basis of the nation beginning with the lawgiver, Moses. What follows in Joshua to 2 Kings is the way that the people and their leaders complied with these laws and the consequences of their obedience or lack of it through the various periods of their history.

The time of Joshua represents a kind of historical golden age in which the people are completely successful in gaining the promised land and at the same time remain faithful to the covenant throughout the lifetime of Joshua (Josh. 1–11). The period ends with a warning about breaking covenant loyalty with

YAHWEH and foreboding about the future (Josh. 23). The period of the Judges that follows illustrates the consequences of not heeding this admonition. The historian has taken up a number of stories about popular local heroes who achieved fame for some brave act of defiance against a tribal enemy or an occasion of charismatic leadership that rallied limited forces and achieved unusual victory over the superior forces of an oppressor (Judg. 3–16). These stories Dtr has put into the conceptual framework of a repetitive pattern with an ideological introduction (Judg. 2:6–3:6) to support his philosophy of history – a philosophy that stresses patterns of human virtues and human failings. Dtr suggests that after the generation of Joshua and his contemporaries the next generation forgot the deeds of YAHWEH and "did what was evil in his sight," namely serving other gods. As a consequence, YAHWEH gave them in submission to their enemies who oppressed them. Only then would they appeal to YAHWEH for help and he would then send them a deliverer who would rescue them. They would remain faithful for that generation only to fall back into their evil ways with the death of the deliverer. The highly diverse and independent stories are made to fit this scheme by assigning a generation of 40 years to each "judge" as the heroes are called, and the story about their act of deliverance is construed as the divine response to the people's repentance and cry for help. Instead of being merely local stories of no fixed date they are fitted into a generational succession of 40 years each and applied to the people as a whole. Thus Dtr has created a "period of the Judges" between the time of the conquest and the rise of the monarchy; and the history of every generation in this period has been given a clear religious meaning.

The account of the rise of the monarchy and the story of the first three kings of a United Monarchy over the whole people of Israel represents the next major phase of this history (1 Sam. 8–1 Kings 11). At the very outset of the monarchy Dtr expresses a deep ambivalence, through Samuel as spokesman for the deity, about this institution that can only succeed to the degree that the king is obedient to YAHWEH's laws and faithful to his covenant. This is in stark contrast to the other major powers of the Near East, where the monarchy seems to represent the only viable form of government instituted by the gods, and all the major historiographic texts of Mesopotamia and Egypt are intended to show how the king is the agent or embodiment of the divine will on earth.

Saul, the first king, begins well as the god's anointed leader to deliver the people from the Philistines, but as a result of disobedience to a divine command his dynasty is rejected and another one, "a person after god's own heart," – David – arises within Saul's own entourage as champion against the Philistines. After Saul's ignominious defeat at the hands of the Philistines, David replaces him and becomes king of the whole land. He is quite successful in subduing all his enemies and bringing peace to the land as well as establishing Jerusalem as the capital city. For Dtr, David is the one exemplary monarch throughout his whole life who completely obeyed the god's laws, as Dtr never tires of repeating. As a reward for this obedience the god promises that his descendants will always sit on the throne in Jerusalem. David, who wishes to build a temple of cedar for the ark, will not do so but his son (Solomon) who will succeed him will do it.

Solomon fulfils David's wish and the god's promise by building the temple for the ark. At the same time the story of Solomon's temple brings to the fore another major Dtr principle, that the temple in Jerusalem should be the one place chosen by YAHWEH to place his Name, and his presence there in the symbolism of the ark makes it the only legitimate sanctuary. This claim was part of Josiah's reform movement in ca. 625 BCE, so that it is entirely anachronistic for the time of Solomon. There were, of course, many YAHWEH temples throughout Israel and Judah until their abolition by Josiah. Furthermore, the temple that Dtr describes as built by Solomon is also largely an ideological construct. It may be reminiscent of the temple at the end of the monarchy, but it has become highly idealized. Furthermore, one would expect from the language of the early prophets and Psalms that the object of veneration in the inner sanctuary is a seated figure of YAHWEH as Israel's divine king, not unlike other Near Eastern temples. Instead, in Dtr's presentation the divine presence is represented by the ark, a box that contains the laws of the covenant as presented in Deuteronomy. It is this constitution, expressing the will of the deity, that is enshrined at the center of the state. In short, Dtr wrote the history of Solomon's temple to establish the historical legitimacy of certain religious themes in the reform movement of a later time (a familiar pattern in the historical literature of most later cultures).

The rest of Dtr's history (1 Kings 12–2 Kings 25) describes successive violations of the covenant and their fateful consequences. This begins with Solomon who, in violation of Deuteronomy, married many foreign princesses who encouraged the worship of foreign gods in Jerusalem. The deity therefore gave the northern ten tribes to Jeroboam after Solomon's death. If Jeroboam had followed the Davidic example of obedience to the law he could have established his dynasty in perpetuity over the Northern Kingdom. But he failed by setting up rival sanctuaries in the north with images of the deity in the form of "calves." Thus his dynasty is doomed, and since all the northern kings followed his bad example the Northern Kingdom itself is likewise doomed. The same fate befell the Kingdom of Judah in the south, in spite of a temporary reprieve for the sake of Josiah, who had reformed the kingdom on the basis of Deuteronomy. The accumulation of guilt, however, eventually led to the destruction of Jerusalem and the temple, harking back to the divine warning at the time the temple was built.

Some general remarks about this history are in order. This is a national history spanning the whole period from the time of Israel's origin in the wilderness to the end of the two monarchies. There is nothing comparable in

Near Eastern historiography that presents the life of a nation in this kind of linear narrative about the moral meaning of historical events. It is true that Dtr can sometimes take up an older Near Eastern form or genre and use it within his work. Thus the conquest of the land of Canaan under Joshua imitates the accounts of the wars of conquest by the Assyrians, even borrowing some quite specific motifs and language. Likewise, the two king-lists of Judah and Israel, similar to those used in Mesopotamia, can be used for the chronological framework of the history of the monarchy. However, neither in Egypt nor in Mesopotamia nor among the Hittites is there a history of the people that goes beyond the records of the deeds of kings or the chronological succession of their reigns. The virtues or failures of the people within these other nations are never mentioned.

The DtrH also articulates a strong and coherent sense of national and corporate identity. The criteria and limits of this identity are the shared history from origin to the end of Israel's national life, its common customs, laws and institutions and what should be avoided as foreign and intrusive, and its religious foundation in a covenant with the one national deity, YAHWEH. The relationship to the land as YAHWEH's land, promised and given as an "inheritance" to the people, is also basic to this sense of identity. Yet it is not just a geographic determination, as when a person from a certain region is known as a "man from x." The land becomes part of the whole ideological construct, so that to step outside of the religious and cultural boundaries of the Israelite identity is to forfeit any right to the land. A major legacy of biblical historiography is the fact that the ideology of identity becomes a fundamental aspect of its narrative structure and presentation of the people's past. There is nothing comparable to this in the rest of Near Eastern historiography,[3] but the creation of a people's identity by an appeal to their past is an aspect of historiography that reappears often in national histories of modern times.

We have noted above in our survey of the DtrH that divine intervention in the affairs of the nations is a major component in the historian's understanding of causality. In this respect biblical historiography is said to differ significantly from the later classical historians, though it is similar to the perspective of many Near Eastern historical texts. Yet this observation needs some qualification. The biblical historian could make a distinction between immediate and apparent causes of events and the final cause in the will or purpose of the deity. Thus the immediate cause of the breakup of the northern and southern tribes into two kingdoms is presented as the foolish decision of Rehoboam, the son of Solomon, but it is said at the same time to have been "a turn of events brought about by YAHWEH" as a consequence of Solomon's sin in the matter of his mixed marriages and in conformity with a prophetic judgment on Solomon. The will of YAHWEH is the final cause determined long before the event itself. This distinction between short-term and long-term levels of causation is not limited to this passage alone, so that the divine intervention in biblical historical narratives may be a little more sophisticated than it is often presented. At the same time classical historians such as Herodotus could also hint at divine intervention in human affairs in a manner not so different from that suggested here.[4]

Prophecy also plays a significant role in Dtr's historiography, especially in the books of Kings. This is not surprising, given the importance of the institution of prophecy during the time of the monarchy. One also finds that the king's consultation of prophets and omens before important military events or the building of temples was a common feature of Mesopotamian court life and historical texts. In Greek historiography, Herodotus likewise uses the warnings of wise counselors, the predictions of mantics, and the consultation of oracles as important structural devices throughout his history. In the biblical book of Kings, the pattern of prophecy and fulfillment always at the instigation of the one deity YAHWEH creates a strong sense of the divine control of events. When a prophecy and its fulfillment embraces several generations rather than simply the evaluation and immediate consequences of a particular event, it may suggest the notion of a larger divine plan and destiny. History as a whole can then be understood as a prophecy or omen that can disclose the future. In later times, as a consequence, prophets were thought of as historians and historians as prophets, so that the biblical history from Joshua to 2 Kings became known as the Former Prophets.

A brief word should also be said about the so-called Court History of David which is a later narrative that was added to Dtr's history of David (2 Sam 2:8–4:12; 8–20; 1 Kings 1–2). In the past some leading historians and biblical scholars regarded this composition as the work of a near contemporary of David or Solomon, based upon his own observations of the court and a piece of historiography rivaling that of Herodotus centuries before his time.[5] However, this cannot be the case because it is clearly dependent upon the information about David supplied by DtrH. It must be a later addition and therefore fiction.[6]

The presentation of David in the Court History is in stark contrast with the idealization of David in DtrH. It is in the Court History that David has an affair with Bathsheba and then has her husband, Uriah, his loyal warrior, murdered to cover up the affair when Bathsheba finds that she is pregnant. Amnon, David's eldest son, rapes his half sister and when David does nothing about it, the girl's full brother Absalom murders Amnon in revenge. Later Absalom leads a rebellion against his father's rule and takes the throne only to be defeated in a final showdown between his own and his father's forces. In the end Solomon, the younger surviving son of David, gains the throne by a palace intrigue and by the murder of his older brother and his other enemies at court.

The Court History, generally regarded as the finest prose in the Hebrew Bible, is pseudo-historiography embedded within the DtrH in the Persian period (5th or 4th century BCE). Many in this period hoped for a revival of the Judean monarchy, a continuation of the house of David. In my view, the object of the Court History was to present an anti-monarchic view of the house of David to discourage any hope of such a revival. It presents David as one who is no better than Ahab and Jeroboam, the most notorious of the kings of Israel. He is one who does "what is evil in the eyes of YAHWEH" and "despises the word of YAHWEH," and his sons are likewise morally corrupt. Solomon was not the true heir to the throne and the fulfillment of divine promise, but became king through the deception of the queen, Solomon's mother, and the prophet Nathan over the claim of the elder brother. The portrayal of this oriental monarchy is much like one finds in Herodotus' presentation of the Persian kings. What the Court History shares with the DtrH, however, is an emphasis on the actions of specific historical figures and a strong desire to draw moral or political lessons from past events.

The Yahwist's History (J)

As indicated above, the Yahwist (J), who wrote his work in the mid-6th century BCE among the exiled Jews in Babylon, supplemented the DtrH by adding his narrative of Genesis – Numbers to Deuteronomy as a historical prologue.[7] By extending the national history of DtrH back into primeval times and the origins of humanity, J transformed the national tradition into universal history. The only way that this could be done was by using myths of origins that were set within a framework of genealogies, creating a temporal sequence down to "historical" times. J shares such origin myths with other peoples of antiquity, from whom some were directly or indirectly adopted. These include accounts of creation, the origins and invention of culture, the age of semi-divine heroes, the great flood, and the building of the first cities. Yet the way in which he orders these materials in his historical scheme of things has great significance for his articulation of universal history.

Mesopotamia had a number of creation traditions which recounted the origins of the cosmos and of humanity to account for the peoples of what is now southern Iraq, their way of life and institutions, and their cities and temples. This primeval age was separated from "historical" time by means of a great flood which resulted in the destruction of this earlier population and a second, more defective, creation of different types of peoples to populate the world. A connection was made between the flood and later times by means of a list of kings beginning with the descent of kingship from heaven and the fiction of one continuous series of dynasties that ruled from various centers in Mesopotamia from the time of the flood to contemporary history. The degree of universality in the Mesopotamian prehistory is limited to etiological explanation for the origins of life in Babylonia (Sumer-Akkad) and the legitimation of the institution of kingship in this area.[8]

By contrast, the Greeks' traditions of primeval times recognize the multiple origins of the various families of peoples within the Greek world and beyond, which are then reflected in parallel genealogies from their heroic and ancestral beginnings to later times. The great divide for them is the Trojan war which brought to an end the heroic age.[9] The continuity with historical times is portrayed by means of aristocratic genealogies from heroes to the leading families of various city states.

In the book of Genesis, J takes up the notion of a single creation of humanity, as in Mesopotamia, but he restricts it to one human pair from whom the rest of humanity is derived and establishes a direct genealogical connection to the time of the flood. Even when this disaster results in a new beginning, as in Mesopotamia, it is not a new creation but the continuation of one family whose members are then presented as the progenitors of all the families of the earth. It is only at several generations removed from this beginning, and in one of the branches of the genealogical tree, that the ancestors of the Israelite people come into focus. This creates quite a remarkable conceptual unity for an understanding of universal history that is entirely lacking in the other origin traditions of antiquity and it has a very powerful influence on later notions of universal history.

To support this universalistic perspective, J has identified the national god of the Israelites, YAHWEH, as the creator god and the only god in control of the affairs of humans and the world. This suggests a common moral order in the world to which all are responsible and a common human experience beyond the peculiar customs and institutions of the one people, Israel. The universal moral order, in the form of stories about crimes and punishment, is the fundamental theme of the primeval history. The universal judgment of the flood, in particular, gives this history an enduring moral, teleological, understanding of the world that supports notions about the end or goal of history. If the DtrH is concerned with the history of one nation whose destiny is determined by a national law code under the aegis of a national god, then J presents a universal moral order under the blessing or judgment of a universal deity.

The stories of the people's ancestors, Abraham, Isaac, Jacob and Jacob's twelve sons (and one daughter),[10] make up the larger part of Genesis (12–50). For the purpose of filling out this period of the nation's pre-history, the historian J has taken up a body of local traditions about ancestors and has arranged them into a genealogical structure of successive generations and by means of an itinerary associated them with the whole region of the land of Israel. In a manner similar to early Greek tradition, the ancestors are set forth in four generations from Abraham to the twelve sons of Jacob and thereby encompass not only the forefathers of the tribes of Israel (= Jacob), but also the closely related neighboring peoples of Aram (Syria), Ammon, Moab, Edom, and the Arabs. The Phoenician/Canaanite peoples are viewed as part of the older indigenous population.

According to J, already during the time of the ancestors the destiny of their offspring was determined by the deity's promises of nationhood, land, and prosperity to the forefathers. These promises are repeated and transmitted to each successive generation, so that they now give historical meaning to the period as a whole and the episodes within it. It is in this way that J has created an important new dimension to the Israelite-Jewish sense of identity, because J adds to Dtr's criteria for national identity that of an ethnic identity based upon the myth of generic descent from a common set of ancestors to whom the deity YAHWEH has given an unconditional promise of peoplehood. Even after the demise of the state and the loss of a land, the people in exile and diaspora (J's own social context) could maintain a sense of identity through their connection to Abraham and the aspirations of the patriarchal promises.

This articulation of ethnic identity in the patriarchal age is tied, by means of the Joseph story and the sojourn in Egypt, to the originally quite separate tradition of the people's origin in Egypt. It is in this period that the group of ancestors grows into a nation within a nation and constitutes a threat that leads to their expulsion. The story of their oppression in Egypt, their deliverance and exodus, their wilderness wanderings and their arrival on the borders of the "promised" land, is construed as a biography of Moses.[11] In almost every episode in J's presentation of the story, Moses plays a dominant role. This is a quite remarkable development of a historiographic form that has no real precedent, except in a limited way in the Babylonian legend of Sargon.[12] The whole of the historical period that forms the "constitutional age" of the people is set within the limits of the lifetime of Moses, the founder and lawgiver. Not only does this allow J to subsume DtrH's prologue – Deuteronomy – within this presentation as a recapitulation, but it gives him the opportunity of modifying and qualifying his understanding of this period and its principles in his own way. Yet this time of Moses, from its beginning (when the god of the forefathers delivers his people from the hands of the Egyptians) to its end (when Moses views from Mount Nebo the land promised to Abraham, Isaac and Jacob), is bound up with the identity and destiny of a people who have descended from a patriarchal history.

The Priestly History (P)

The Priestly historian (P), writing in the period of reconstruction in Judah in the late 5th century BCE, has expanded and modified the earlier history of J in a number of significant ways. To J's primeval history P has added, as a prologue, a cosmology that includes the origins not only of human, animal and plant life as in J, but also the rest of the cosmos. This is done in a series of pronouncements by the one deity distributed over the course of six days. When this basic order has been established and confirmed as "very good," the seventh day is consecrated as a holy day of rest in imitation of the creator's rest.

It has long been observed that P's presentation of creation is greatly at variance with that of J in Gen. 2:4b–3:24, both in the manner of presentation and also in the ordering of the individual acts of creation. This is largely due to the fact that P has taken up the cosmogonic myth of origins and demythologized or rationalized various features of it, so that dividing the waters of the abyss is no longer the mythical slaying of the demonic monster; the word that empowers "earth" to bring forth her fruit is a pale reflection of the great mother goddess; the sun and moon who "rule" the day and night have, in P, become great lamps in place of gods. Thus, the "genealogy of heaven and earth" (2:4) follows the fixed succession of events that one finds in theogonies, but in a rationalized form to make it conform to the monotheistic theology of the P tradition.

P's prologue in this universal history begins with the creation of time itself by virtue of the god's creation of light that makes possible the first day. This creation of time is then used as the temporal measurement for the rest of the days of creation. Furthermore, the primary function of the heavenly bodies is to regulate times and seasons, months, and years. The sacred days, especially the Sabbath, are reckoned as part of this cosmic order. Of course, this legitimizes and upholds the role of the priests as the guardians of this cosmic order. Once this ideological foundation for precise chronology has been established, P attempts to order the rest of the history into a strict chronological scheme.

In the Babylonian antiquarian tradition, the chronology of the world was fixed by the descent of kingship from heaven at the beginning of time, its renewal after the flood and its strict chronological succession to historical times. A later variant of this tradition tells of the creation of the king as a special human being to rule over the rest of ordinary humanity by the transmission of divine attributes from the various deities to equip him for the task of governance. P has taken over this myth, even retaining the hint of the divine council: "Let us make humans in our image and after our likeness and let them have dominion. . . ." Yet the myth has been democratized to apply to all humanity and its relationship to the rest of creation. So universal history is no longer determined by the chronology of a line of Babylonian kings, but by humanity from Adam to his offspring. It is a single history of one humanity under a single unnamed deity who controls the whole of the cosmos.

Moreover, P takes over J's rudimentary scheme of genealogical chronology of seven generations for the antediluvian period from Adam to Noah and from Noah to Abraham and increases these to ten generations each. With these he combines the strict chronological succession of the Babylonian king-lists, but instead of the length of a king's reign he gives the total life-span of the ancestors and their age at the time of the birth of the eldest son to yield a precise chronology. The Babylonian tradition that the antediluvian kings ruled for very long periods, even thousands of years, is reflected in the very long lives of the antediluvian ancestors of Genesis 5. The chronology of the flood story is also modified to make the flood one year in length and fitted into the larger absolute chronology within the life of Noah. The lives of the patriarchs are likewise supplied with a precise chronology for the principal events in their lives, especially as they relate to births and deaths.[13]

Another important aspect of P's historiography is his attempt to periodize history into certain eras. This was already suggested to some extent by J's major divisions, but P heightens these in particular ways. The first period begins with the first human pair to whom the god extends his blessing of fruitfulness and an injunction to rule the earth. Humanity is also given the fruits of the earth to eat, but not meat, and is thus vegetarian. This era extends to the time of the flood. After the flood, the god renews his blessing of fruitfulness to the survivors but now permits them to eat meat. Yet they are under new laws regarding homicide, the violence that led to the flood, and laws concerning the non-consumption of blood with meat. An "eternal" covenant is established with humanity in the form of a divine promise, confirmed by the sign of the rainbow, not to bring another flood on the earth. In both of these periods the term for deity is simply the generic term *Elohim*, "god."

Abraham, at the end of the tenth generation after the flood, begins a new era with a new "eternal covenant" for his descendants. The sign of this covenant is the rite of circumcision for all males, which is an obligation for all those who wish to remain within this covenant. To them are extended the promises of nationhood and land as with J, as well as the blessing of fruitfulness from creation. To Abraham is revealed the divine name of "God Almighty" (*El Shaddai*) and all the patriarchs know the deity by this name and share this covenant.

The time of Moses begins yet another period. To Moses the deity reveals the sacred name of YAHWEH, the name of the god of Israel. Yet P affirms through the words of the deity that this is the same god as El Shaddai of the patriarchs and the covenantal promises to them are assured to the descendants whom he will rescue from Egypt. With Moses there is also an extended body of laws to mark this era. Yet in contrast to both Deuteronomy and J, little is said explicitly about a Sinai covenant and some have denied that there is one in P. However, since I view P as essentially a supplement to both DtrH and J, it seems to me justified to assume that P takes over the notion of such a covenant. He even suggests that the sign of this covenant is the observance of the Sabbath (Exod. 31).

The largest addition that P makes to the prior history of J has to do with priestly matters of temple worship, purity laws, sacrifices, and festival regulations. This is directly related to the reestablishment of the priestly cultus in the Second Temple period. This is in sharp contrast to J (in the Babylonian exile) who lays down a bare minimum of such observances without the need for any priesthood. Thus in J the "tent of meeting" is merely an oracular tent where Moses receives revelations from the deity but it has no priests and no cult and only a lay person, Joshua, associated with it. By contrast, this "tent of meeting" or "tabernacle" in P has become an elaborate portable temple with a large priesthood and cult and forms the center of the people's life. The constitutional understanding of the people is revised again into that of a "theocracy"[14] in which there is a diarchy of a secular leader and a high priest. In the beginning Moses is preeminent over Aaron, the high priest, because he is the medium of divine revelation of the whole system, but after Moses his successors, like Joshua, must take their direction from the high priest. There are various orders of priests and orders of laymen such that the whole community of the people, known as the "congregation of Israel," is an elaborate organism. The social order and the cultic order belong to the cosmic order and the rule of god, all of which means that P's historical narrative gives priests an essential role in all spheres of social life. This is his historical legitimation of the roles of governor and high priest in the Jerusalem temple-community of the Second Temple period.

P, too, adds another dimension to corporate identity beyond that in DtrH and J. Identity not only embraces the national identity of people and land with absolute commitment to YAHWEH as in DtrH and ethnic identity through the forefathers as in J. For P, identity also includes commitment to certain observances, such as circumcision, the keeping of the Sabbath and festivals and the food laws by all Jews, as well as the maintenance of the theocratic structures of the cult. This makes particular allowance for the diaspora Jews who can in this way maintain an identity as a people quite apart from life in the land of Palestine. It is now P's history that ensures the survival of this identity, no matter where Jews may live.

The Chronicler as Historian

Along side of the Primary History in Genesis to 2 Kings is another historical tradition that both supplements and rivals it, the books of 1 and 2 Chronicles (late 4th century BCE). While much is taken over verbatim from the older history, especially from Samuel–Kings, much is omitted or altered, many stories and new information are added and the whole perspective of the earlier history is radically changed. These changes are so blatantly dominated by ideological and theological concerns that many scholars regard the work as pseudo-history or "midrash."[15] Yet the Chronicler (Chr), by his imitation of the earlier history and his frequent citation of sources, presents his work in a form that is clearly intended to be taken as history, and it was so regarded by later generations. To this issue we will return.

The book of 1 Chronicles begins with Adam, the first human, and extends its history to the time of Cyrus and the end of the Babylonian exile of the Jews (538 BCE). The primeval history from the origins of humanity to the time of David is spanned by means of genealogies that have been gleaned largely from the Pentateuch, especially P, but some also from the earlier DtrH. These establish a continuity with humanity in general and then with the patriarchs, Abraham, Isaac, Jacob and the sons of Jacob, the tribal ancestors, with special attention to Judah, as well as to the royal house of David and the Levitical priesthood. In the case of these two institutions, the genealogies are carried beyond the time-frame of the books of Chronicles well into the Persian period. Within the genealogies are anecdotal remarks about the land settlement of the Israelite tribes so that they legitimate a territorial claim far beyond the bounds of the small province of Judah in the time of the historian.

This form of genealogical history is well attested within the classical antiquarian tradition. The Chronicler (Chr) claims to have derived the genealogical history of chapters 1–8 from a "Book of the Kings of Israel" although this does not correspond with any extant biblical book. The function of such genealogies is to fortify ethnic identity, support territorial claims on ancestral lands and legitimate basic social institutions, both political and religious. To support these aims the older genealogies are greatly augmented with names from the families of the post-exilic period. The genealogical series ends with the names of families and of the temple personnel (priests, Levites and others) who returned from exile (ch. 9).

The history proper begins with an account of the death of Saul as a lead up to David and his reign (1 Chron 10–29). All the previous history is omitted, or rather assumed, whereas David is made into the founder of the nation together with its basic political and religious institutions as a kind of second Moses. For this purpose Chr excises from the prior tradition all those elements that might reflect negatively on David's character, in particular virtually the whole of the Court History. Instead, he gives to David the establishing of the whole system of worship outlined by the Priestly Writer within the context of the new state and its capital in Jerusalem, along with all of the later developments of cult personnel and practice of the Second Temple period which he ascribes anachronistically to David. The fact that the first temple did not yet exist in David's time and was only built by his son Solomon leads Chr to suggest that David spent much of his time and effort making preparation for the future temple, setting out the divinely revealed plan and gathering the materials, so that it was left to Solomon merely to execute the plan. The account of Solomon's reign is likewise idealized by the omission of anything derogatory. The result is that with the combined rule of David and Solomon the theocracy of P is embedded in a "Kingdom of God" with a son of David at its head. For Chr there can be only one legitimate kingdom and state centered in Jerusalem under a son of David, just as there can be only one temple of YAHWEH in Jerusalem.

This leads him to focus his entire history on the kingdom of Judah and to regard the Northern Kingdom of Israel as illegitimate and foreign from the start. He omits from his record the fact that the biblical books of Kings represent the inauguration of the Northern Kingdom as an act of YAHWEH through his prophet Ahijah and open to the same possibility of divine approval as the dynasty of David. For Chr all the kings of the north and the people who submit to them are religious rebels, whereas the true Israelites are those who are willing to leave their homeland in the north and settle in Judah. This includes all the true priests and Levites of YAHWEH, so that there are no members of the true religion left in the north. This, of course, contradicts much of the witness of the books of Kings and the prophetic books, which are therefore simply ignored. The term "Israel" does not refer to a political entity in Chronicles but is intended as a religious designation that can be applied to Judah and its kings. Thus Israel may indeed include members of all the twelve tribes, as in the initial genealogy, but only those who have given their allegiance to Jerusalem and abandoned any religious and political claim to a center in the north, including Samaria and the Samaritans of Mount Gerazim. It is this crucial issue of identity in the Persian and Hellenistic periods to which Chr speaks.

This redefinition of Israelite identity comes to the fore most clearly in Chr's treatment of Hezekiah (2 Chron. 29–32). The fall of Samaria and the Northern Kingdom, which receives important attention from Dtr in Kings (2 Kings 17), is ignored by Chr. Instead, Hezekiah, the contemporary Judean king,[16] is presented as a kind of second David who completely purifies and restores the temple worship after a period of neglect by the apostate Ahaz, his father, and then Hezekiah reunites the whole region of Israel from Beersheba to Dan under his control and in common worship at the Jerusalem temple, in a great Passover celebration and in an extensive reform of both Judah and Israel. Chr completely ignores the existence of any other political or religious authority for the north, which had become an Assyrian province. Instead, Hezekiah is seen as reestablishing the Davidic–Solomonic precedent of a unified Israel and building a continuity with the priestly ideology of the Persian period. The portrayal of Hezekiah's reform is an imitation of the Josiah reform in Kings, which is also repeated in Chronicles but on a lesser scale. Yet both reforms in Chronicles are divorced from any connection with the discovery of the book of the law. For Chr the Mosaic law in its most extensive form (including P) was known and in force from the time of David onward, even if it was not always observed by some of the apostate kings. This is a radical departure from the whole ideology and perspective of the books of Kings.

Basic to understanding Chr's historiography is an appraisal of his use of sources. His most important source, if not his only source, for the whole period of the monarchy is the extant books of Samuel–Kings, which was a single work. Large parts of it are cited verbatim, especially as they have to do with David, Solomon, and the kings of Judah. The Northern Kingdom is ignored unless it directly involves a king of Judah. Yet when Chr treats this material from Samuel–Kings, he refers not to a single source but to a large number of different sources by various names. He also cites as sources twelve books that he attributes to prophets, most of whom are mentioned in Samuel–Kings. These books are so obviously spurious (prophets did not actually write books of any kind much before the exilic period) that scholars have dismissed those citations as a quirk of Chr's literary style.

I understand these references to multiple sources in a quite different way. Chr has only one source for the monarchy, Samuel–Kings, as most acknowledge, which he plagiarizes freely. However, to obscure this fact and to justify his radical departures from his source and his numerous fictions he invents multiple sources, viz, numerous histories that did not exist and writings of inspired persons whose authority cannot be questioned. This legitimates the ideology of his history and its political and religious use for his own day. One other term that he uses for his sources is also instructive: he refers to the "Midrash of the Book of Kings." The Hebrew term *midrash* means "investigation" or "inquiry," from the verb *drš* "to search," and as such *midrash* is the direct equivalent of the Greek term *historia*, "history." As Herodotus uses the term, it includes not merely historical narrative but wonders and marvels and colorful stories of past events. This fits very well a feature of Chronicles, which abounds in miraculous events and edifying tales.

All of this – the plagiarism, the use of spurious sources, and the embellishment with stories for entertainment or edification – points strongly to the influence of Hellenistic historiography. It is a kind of bad history against which historians like Polybius protested,[17] but it was still highly influential and very popular. The work became part of the canonical collection as history and, as such, it played an important role in shaping Jewish and Christian historical thought.

A major literary extension to the national historical tradition appears in the book of Ezra–Nehemiah, which carries the history from the edict of Cyrus in 538 BCE, marking the end of the exile, to the rebuilding of the temple under Zerubbabel, down to the reforms of Ezra the scribe and the rebuilding of the walls of Jerusalem by Nehemiah, the Jewish governor appointed by Artaxerxes I, in the mid 5th century BCE. Both Ezra–Nehemiah and Chronicles are to be dated to a century later in the late Persian, or more likely, early Hellenistic period, but there is much debate about whether Ezra–Nehemiah and Chronicles belong to the same author or "school". At the very least a knowledge of and dependence upon Ezra–Nehemiah by the Chronicler may be safely assumed. They share much of the same ideological perspective.

The book of Ezra–Nehemiah, which should be treated as a single work, begins with the decree of Cyrus in 538 BCE that brings to an end the enforced exile of the Jews in Babylon and inaugurates the Persian period of rule over their homeland in Judah. The restoration of the temple under Zerubbabel and the walls of the city of Jerusalem under Nehemiah with the accompanying reforms are attributed to the initiatives of the leaders from the diaspora and the returning exiles. Much is made of the lists of names of the returnees, both lay and priests, as the nucleus of the real people of Israel and their claim to the land. The work reflects an intolerance toward those who reside in the land, but who do not share their form of exclusivist Yahwism and who fraternize with other communities of the region, especially those of the northern region of Samaria. This is similar to the perspective of Chronicles and one reason why they are closely associated.

Unlike Chronicles however, Ezra–Nehemiah appears to be made up of several separate documents and not based upon a prior history. These consist of "official" Aramaic documents – royal edicts and official letters and communications (whether genuine of spurious), numerous lists of priests and lay persons for various purposes, so-called memoirs of Nehemiah and Ezra, and some other possible documents. These have all been combined and set within a narrative by an editor whose style and language is similar to Chr. The documents are used as the basis of authority and validation both of actions within the history and of the historical narrative itself, showing a new consciousness about the importance of historical sources. Nehemiah's memoirs are written for public display to legitimate his actions. Ezra the scribe brings from Babylon the book of the law of Moses which he is authorized to enforce and from which he reads and instructs the people. The royal edicts and official letters, the legal documents and lists of persons and property all carry authority and the legitimation of rights and privileges. Even in the matter of the divorce and expulsion of foreign wives with their children, a list must be compiled of the offenders. The history is thus primarily the presentation and interpretation of these documents, whether real or spurious. They are essential for the identity of the community and for the identity of those who are excluded.

The principal focus of the history is the reestablishment of the temple and the rebuilding of the city of Jerusalem, and the series of events that make Jerusalem the defining center of the community of Israel. The centralization and purification of the temple cultus in Jerusalem according to Deuteronomic principles was already a major theme within the DtrH, especially in Samuel–Kings. This became the case even more so for Chr in his treatment of the Judean monarchy. Ezra–Nehemiah adds to this theme the inauguration of the Second Temple and the restored city after the radical rupture of the Babylonian exile. The fate of the temple and the city becomes the defining theme of Jewish history, as one sees in the later works of Josephus as well. The sacred place offers a religious and historical center for the identity of the Jewish people.

Conclusion

This biblical historiography that I have described was the product of a small state on the periphery of larger civilizations, and it was produced during that period in its history when this state was under foreign subjection by the great powers.[18] Yet there is no evidence that it borrowed its historiography from the Assyrians, Babylonians or Egyptians, even if the biblical historians adopted some of the literary forms from these other ancient civilizations. Hebrew historiography has much more in common with the classical world of the eastern Mediterranean, and yet the historiography of the one is not directly derived from the other; any direct interaction comes about perhaps only with the rise of Hellenism. There may have been important intermediaries, such as the Phoenicians (= biblical Canaanites), but we have few extant Phoenician literary texts to confirm this hypothesis.

As our survey has attempted to show, biblical historiography articulated various understandings of corporate identity for a people in crisis, trying to maintain their cultural and religious heritage by a narration of the past. It established certain themes and perspectives having to do with absolute loyalty to a single national deity expressed in law and covenant, customs and cultic practice, festivals and rites of initiation. It tied identity to a "promised" land and the myth of ethnic descent from primordial ancestors. It created the notion of an absolute center in Jerusalem and the temple, even for those in the diaspora. All of this was supported by a narrative of origins and succession of events in the life of the people of Israel. The several historians that contributed to this narrative often expressed their understanding of the identity of Israel in somewhat different ways, but all became part of a canonical corpus that was the foundation for later Jewish and Christian identities and their subsequent histories. And they initiated a historical literature that emphasized the importance of both specific events and universal principles in the history of human communities.

NOTES

1 This is the thesis advocated by M. Noth. See his *The Deuteronomistic Historian* (JSOTSup. 15; Sheffield: JSOT Press, 1981).

2 These issues are treated more extensively in John Van Seters, *The Pentateuch: A Social-Science Commentary* (Sheffield: Sheffield Academic Press, 1999). Compare also J. Blenkinsopp, *The Pentateuch: An Introduction to the First Five Books of the Bible* (New York: Doubleday, 1992).

3   See the new comprehensive study by K. L. Sparks, *Ethnicity and Identity in Ancient Israel: Prolegomena to the Study of Ethnic Sentiments and their expression in the Hebrew Bible* (Winona Lake, IN: Eisenbrauns, 1998).

4   See the battle of Artemisium, Herod. 8.8–13.

5   So G. von Rad, in "The Beginnings of Historical Writing in Ancient Israel" (1944), in *The Problem of the Hexateuch and Other Essays*, translated by E. W. T. Dicken (Edinburgh and London: Oliver and Boyd, 1966), pp. 166–204.

6   For details of the debate see J. Van Seters, *In Search of History: Historiography in the Ancient World and the Origins of Biblical History* (New Haven and London: Yale University Press, 1983), pp. 277–91.

7   For an extensive discussion of the Yahwist as historian see my books, *Prologue to History: The Yahwist as Historian in Genesis* (Louisville, KY: Westminster/John Knox, 1992), and *The Life of Moses: The Yahwist as Historian in Exodus-Numbers* (Louisville, KY: Westminster/John Knox, 1994).

8   For fuller discussion see John Van Seters, *Prologue to History*, pp. 47–77.

9   See ibid., pp. 86–99.

10 The daughter plays no role as an ancestress of a tribe.

11 For a more extensive discussion of J's treatment of this period see my *Life of Moses*.

12 This is a fictional autobiography about how the Babylonian king, Sargon the Great, was rescued from the Euphrates River as an infant in a basket to become the ruler of an empire.

13 It was this precise chronology of P that permitted Bishop James Ussher in the mid-century to date the creation of the world to 4004 BCE.

14 This is a term invented by the Jewish historian Josephus to describe this priestly law.

15 The term was coined by J. Wellhausen (*Prolegomena to the History of Israel* [1883], New York: Meridian Books, 1957, p. 227) on the model of later Jewish writings to mean the embellishment of biblical writings by means of moralistic and miraculous stories.

16 It is only in Chr's source in 2 Kings 18:1 that this correlation of dating for Hezekiah's reign is noted since Chr snub's any reference to the Northern Kingdom. Yet the correlation is clearly assumed in what follows.

17 Polybius, *Histories*, 9.2.

18 It was once thought by many scholars, including H. Gunkel and G. von Rad, that history writing arose in Israel during the time of David and Solomon as a reflection of historical consciousness at the beginning of its statehood. This view can no longer be supported and is largely abandoned. For a discussion of this see Van Seters, *In Search of History*, pp. 209–48.

REFERENCES AND FURTHER READING

Blenkinsopp, J., *The Pentateuch: An Introduction to the First Five Books of the Bible*, New York: Doubleday, 1992.

Dentan, R. C. ed., *The Idea of History in the Ancient Near East*, New Haven and London, 1955.

Lemche, N. P., *The Israelites In History and Tradition*, Louisville, KY: Westminster/John Knox, 1998.

Mullen, E. T. Jr., *Ethnic Myths and Pentateuchal Foundations: A New Approach to the Formation of the Pentateuch*, Atlanta: Scholars Press, 1997.

Noth, M., *The Deuteronomistic History*, JSOTSup. 15, Sheffield: JSOT Press, 1981 (translated from *Überlieferungsgeschichtliche Studien*, Tübingen: Max Niemeyer, 1957, pp. 1–110).

——, *The Chronicler's History*, translation and introduction by H. G. M. Williamson, JSOTSup. 50, Sheffield: JSOT Press (translated from *Überlieferungsgeschichtliche Studien*, pp. 110–80).

Rad, G. von, "The Beginnings of Historical Writing in Ancient Israel" (1944), in *The Problem of the Hexateuch and Other Essays*, translated by E. W. T. Dicken (Edinburgh and London: Oliver and Boyd, 1966), 166–204.

Sparks, K. L., *Ethnicity and Identity in Ancient Israel: Prolegomena to the Study of Ethnic Sentiments and their expression in the Hebrew Bible*, Winona Lake, IN: Eisenbrauns, 1998.

Van Seters, John, *In Search of History: Historiography in the Ancient World and the Origins of Biblical History*, New Haven and London: Yale University Press, 1983.

——, *Prologue to History: The Yahwist as Historian in Genesis*, Louisville, KY: Westminster/John Knox, 1992.

——, *The Life of Moses: The Yahwist as Historian in Exodus-Numbers*, Louisville, KY: Westminster/John Knox, 1994.

——, "The Historiography of the Ancient Near East," in Jack M. Sasson, *Civilizations of the Ancient Near East*, vol 4 (Macmillan: New York, 1995), 2433–44.

——, *The Pentateuch: A Social-Science Commentary*, Sheffield: Sheffield Academic Press, 1999.

Wellhausen, J., *Prolegomena to the History of Israel* (1883), New York: Meridian Books, 1957.

CHAPTER TWO

Historical Thought in Ancient Greece

PHILIP A. STADTER

Greek historical writing began as a rival to epic poetry, attempting to bring order and meaning to the different views Greek cities had of their past and present. The two fifth-century BC founders, Herodotus and Thucydides, defined two diverse modes of historical writing, one inclusive, examining all of human culture, the other narrowly focused on contemporary military and political events. After these founders, two later historians, Xenophon and Polybius, created consciously didactic histories, both centered in quite different ways on the moral values behind political leadership and failure. Much later, under the Roman empire, two other writers, Arrian and Plutarch, chose historical biography as a means to convey the role of the individual in political history. No thread unites the disparate achievements of the Greek historians beyond the common aim of comprehending the lessons of past and contemporary human events. This essay, then, cannot have an overall theme: rather it addresses the methods, structures, and underlying ideas of each major historian. Each writer must be seen in his own historical and personal situation, which is tied closely to the form and purpose of his work. We cannot speak of a "development" of historiography, rather of different efforts to address the fundamental problems of how to gather reliable information, how to arrange it in a meaningful way, and how to select what is truly significant. In some ways the most successful were the founders, Herodotus and Thucydides, but each author treated here made his own choices and emphases, which have shaped the writing of history for the whole Western tradition.

Beginnings: Epic Poetry and Oral Traditions

As early as Homer, Greek narratives of the past were used to assert one's identity, to influence one's audience, and to convey information, praise, or persuasion. The Homeric epics themselves deployed a legendary history to define identity and values for their audience in the eighth century BC. Achilles, raging in his tent, listened to his mentor Phoenix tell the history of the hero Meleager, who also was angry, but still had to come and defend his city (*Iliad* 9). Odysseus kept the Phaeacians spellbound with the tales of his adventures, but also tricked friends and enemies alike with tales which made his point while concealing his identity (*Odyssey* 9–12, 13, 14, 19).

Although composed as poetry, the *Iliad* and *Odyssey* established modes and themes which profoundly influenced the narratives of the early Greek historians. Homer narrated the deeds of men and women: the gods, though present, represent an enrichment and augmentation of the human action, not the epics' principal focus. A mixed mode of narrative and quoted speech or dialogue allowed the actors themselves to express their thoughts and emotions, set against the action, background information, and occasional authorial comments of the narrative. The narrative is selective: not the Trojan War, but the wrath of Achilles, covering a short period tightly focused on his withdrawal from the war, the ruin it caused for both sides, and his return to battle and to humanity; not the adventures of the returning Greeks, but the sufferings of one man, Odysseus, until his reunion with his wife and son. The epics also pose essential questions concerning the meaning of human life and achievement, the place of suffering and death, and the morality of action. The Greek historians of the classical period incorporated these methods and questions into their histories. Far from seeking a purely objective, "scientific" account of the past, or inartistic chronicles, they wrote what they thought would be useful to their contemporaries and to later readers, alternating narrative and speeches, carefully selecting incident and interpretation. Like Homer, they sought to express the nature of human experience. Desires and fears, suffering and triumph, depravity and justice manifest themselves in the historical narratives of events.

Greek historical writing emerged from the context of the Greek culture and historical changes of the eighth to fifth centuries BC. Before this time the traditional tales, of which the Homeric epics were the most successful, had been told and retold for centuries. The eighth century saw the birth of the *polis*, the individual self-governing city unit so distinctive of Greece. In the society of the polis a culture of song and story evolved, leaving traces in the poetry of the archaic period (725–500 BC). Though some of the lyric poetry has survived, the prose stories of the same period were not recorded. Nevertheless, their vestiges in poetry indicate that the pre-classical Greek society of aristocratic nobles and warrior-farmers used narratives of the past to defend their position in law or in the assembly, to praise themselves, their ancestors, and their polis, and to assert their own sense of community. The stories were narrated orally and used for the purpose of the moment rather than for future generations.

The earliest known prose writers in Greece recorded and organized the myths of the gods and the genealogies of heroes and the ancestors of aristocratic families. The variety of oral traditions encouraged a skeptical attitude. Simultaneously the earliest pre-Socratic philosophers, seeking unifying principles behind the multiplicity of the world, tried to probe beyond surface phenomena. These trends are apparent in the *Genealogies* of Hecataeus of Miletus, ca. 500 BC, which began with the self-conscious declaration: "Hecataeus of Miletus tells in this way. I write what seems to me true, because, as it seems to me, the stories of the Greeks are many and ridiculous." The necessity of differentiating false from true tales in an oral culture was already known to Homer's swineherd Eumaeus, who rejected part of Odysseus' tale, but accepted the rest (*Odyssey* 14.360–389). History arose in Greece from the conscious effort to sort out, evaluate, and record in prose the oral traditions of the poets and storytellers. The development of writing led to the desire to order and solidify the flux of oral traditions, and encouraged new attempts to test the local traditions against each other.

The archaic period saw the growth of wealthy cities, the spread of trade and colonization, and increasingly dynamic contact with non-Greeks. Thus a host of new stories and new information was generated: stories of the foundings of cities, of strange peoples, of the struggles of individual cities. The entry of two eastern empires into Greek affairs provided yet another stimulus toward historiography. The Lydian king Croesus (ca. 560–543) conquered the Greek cities of the Asia Minor coast, only to fall to the Persian Cyrus the Great (d. 528), who conquered both Croesus' Greek subjects and the adjoining Aegean islands. In quick succession, succeeding Persian kings added Egypt and Libya to their empire, sent expeditions into the Ukrainian steppe and the Balkan peninsula, and finally launched a major land and sea expedition against Greece in 480–479. New stories and new poetry burst into life alongside the traditional tales, as each Greek warrior, city, and people recalled how they had collaborated with or triumphed over the Persian invader.

The beginnings of Greek historical writing, then, are found in the desire to organize traditional stories and to examine them skeptically, but had a strong impulse to develop because of two historical factors: the multitude of individual Greek cities with their diverse traditions and the pressure of Lydian and Persian expansion.

The Greek Historians: A Tradition of Elite Literature

The accidents of fate and the selections of Byzantine scholars and teachers have erased the vast preponderance of the Greek historians. The writers of the sixth and fifth century BC were totally eclipsed by the great surviving works of Herodotus and Thucydides. The great historians of the fourth century are represented only by Xenophon. Alexander the Great and his successors attracted numerous contemporary historians, but none survive today. Of the many lost historians, only fragments remain to provide hints of a flourishing tradition that endured until the fall of Byzantium. Greek historiography from the third to the first century BC is represented by the extant first five books of Polybius' massive history of the rise of Roman power in the Mediterranean. From the Roman empire significant portions of a few second- or third-rate histories survive, such as Dionysius of Halicarnassus' *History of Early Rome*, Diodorus of Sicily's *Library of History*, Josephus' *History of the Jewish People* and *Jewish War*, and histories of Rome by Appian, Cassius Dio, and Herodian. Luke's *Acts of the Apostles* inaugurated the new genre of ecclesiastical history. There are only two Greek historians from the Roman imperial period who invite individual attention: Arrian and Plutarch.

Greek historical writing began as an elite pursuit. The wealth and social class of Herodotus, Thucydides, and Xenophon permitted them the leisure and the literacy essential to the task. All three were active in politics until forced to leave their native cities; all lived for many years as exiles. Polybius, a leader in his own city, wrote most of his work while held in forced detention in Rome. For these four, writing history thus became an expression of political involvement by other means, a commentary on the nature of political action. There was a virtue in this necessity: separation allowed them to view their own cities and cultures with a critical eye, and permitted them contact with other societies and other viewpoints. Arrian and Plutarch were distanced in a different way, as men of Greek culture and language in a Roman world. Both sought to influence the administrators of empire through their writings.

Greek historians, who aspired to celebrate great deeds as the epic narrative tradition had and who were eager to influence their contemporaries, composed in the most effective and attractive style they could devise. The histories of Herodotus and Thucydides represent outstanding artistic and stylistic achievements, rivaling the greatest works of poetry. They established a literary standard for historical prose which has influenced historians down to our own times. Xenophon won classic status by the simplicity and charm of his style. Later Greek historians sought to maintain this literary standard, though frequently the desire to entertain overcame the goal of thoughtful and useful analysis of events. Only Polybius among the great historians shows the familiar academic desire to expound even at the expense of dullness, but he too employs superb artistry in particular episodes.

The audience for Greek history formed an elite as well: literacy was limited, so those who could afford books and had the education to enjoy reading lengthy volumes about distant epochs represented the apex of the social pyramid. The audience for Herodotus' or Thucydides' works in their written form might have been counted in the hundreds. In later centuries, even with the spread of schools and rhetorical education, most readers would have pre-

ferred simple summaries and compendiums, but some historians wrote for
more knowledgeable audiences. Arrian and Plutarch, for example, expected
a much greater level of sophistication from their readers than did Appian or
Diodorus.

Greek historical writing thus represented a major branch of Greek literature, parallel to oratory and philosophical prose. In the absence of a separate
genre of the novel, it offered both entertainment and food for thought.

Herodotus: Defining Method, Structure, and Content

Whatever the accomplishments of the lost early writers such as Hecataeus, it
is the *Histories* of Herodotus of Halicarnassus (ca. 480–420) which created
European historiography. This work fuses all the previously separate elements
of narrative, genealogy, Near Eastern king lists, and philosophical investigation into a reasoned and critical narrative which could record, praise, and
explain the meaning of past events.

> This is the exposition of the inquiry of Herodotus of Halicarnassus, that what
> has been done by men might not be washed out by time, nor the great and won-
> derful works displayed, some by Greeks, some by foreigners, be without glory,
> and especially for what reason they fought with each other. (1. proem)

The themes of greatness and glory in Herodotus' initial sentence derive from
Homer, and the last phrase echoes Homer's words at the beginning of the
Iliad (1.6) "from the moment when they first opposed each other in anger."
But Herodotus also challenges Homer: the authority is his own, not that of
the Muse, and it is backed up by his own inquiry (*historiê*, the word which
would give the name to his work, *historiai*, and to the genre of history).
"Works" to Herodotus includes both what men have built and what they have
done. Homer opposed Greeks to Trojans or to the strange peoples of the
Odyssey; Herodotus' vision is even broader. The polar opposition of Greek and
foreigner defines all mankind as he understood it. Finally, "for what reason"
points both to causal analysis and to moral evaluation, since the word translated "reason" carries in Greek also the senses of "responsibility" and "blame."
Herodotus found an epic theme to rival Homer in the generations of conflict
between Greece and Persia which culminated in the heroic battles of 480 and
479, Thermopylae, Salamis, and Plataea. The ambition and scope of his enterprise is breathtaking: his complete work is almost as long as the *Iliad* and the
Odyssey combined.

Herodotus' inclusivity no doubt reflected his own experience. His native
city, Halicarnassus on the coast of Caria in southeast Asia Minor, was populated by both Greek and Carian speakers. His father had a Carian name and

no doubt Carian blood. The city was part of the Persian empire, and after the Persian defeat it joined the Athenian league. Toward the middle of the century Herodotus had to flee because of civil war in Halicarnassus. Herodotus thus knew a multicultural background from childhood, and expanded this by his travels. His history refers to his visits to Greece, Syria, Egypt, Babylon, and the Black Sea, which allowed him to gather first-hand information on different cultures and traditions. Eventually, it is said, he settled in south Italy. He saw for himself the rise and fall of power, which is the focus of his history, and he knew that "human happiness never remains long in the same place" (1.5).

Such an ambitious work required a complex structure. To give form to the wealth of material, Herodotus relied on traditional oral techniques, which he made more flexible and expanded to fit the written medium. A list of Persian kings provides the backbone. Herodotus takes as his starting point the reign of Croesus in Lydia, "the man whom I know first did unjust acts against the Greeks" (1.5). After Croesus is defeated by Cyrus, the first king of Persia, the narrative follows the reigns of the four kings, Cyrus, Cambyses, Darius, and Xerxes, as they successively expanded Persian power and impinged ever more heavily on the Greek world, until Xerxes was defeated by the Greeks. Herodotus considers other peoples, including Greek cities, as they are attacked or conquered by the Persians. Prior to the great campaigns of 480–479, the histories of Athens and Sparta, the two leading Greek cities in his own day, are attached to the Lydian–Persian sequence at only two points, first when Croesus seeks a Greek alliance against Cyrus, and a second time when the Ionian Greeks ask for help in their revolt against Darius. The subject of the *Histories* thus emerges as the expansion of Lydia and Persia from around 550 BC until it was halted by Greek resistance in 480–479. Frequent narrative synchronisms relate events in different areas to one another. In addition, Herodotus situates his inquiries firmly in the framework of Greek legendary history by tracing back his lists of kings and other genealogies to the legendary period.

Within this framework Herodotus provides a bewildering number of individual accounts. The accounts, often nested within each other, fall into a restricted number of categories, such as the rise or collapse of a dynasty, the dialogue of a ruler with his advisor, the speeches in a council, the account of a campaign or a battle, or an ethnography recording the geography, customs, and history of a whole people. The accounts, according to a standard oral technique, regularly begin from a connecting reference to particular individuals or events which had been mentioned in another logos. Herodotus supplements these initial ties with a dense web of common themes and patterns of human behavior and experience. In a technique both powerful and daunting, everything in the *Histories* seems connected to everything else.

Interrelated patterns of action and reaction, injustice and repayment, insult and vengeance emerge as the fundamental explanation for the Persian Wars.

Individuals and peoples are bound in a network of exchanges and obligations, in which willingly or unwillingly a just balance is achieved. Vengeance for injustice is the most prominent pattern of action, found from the first stories of reciprocal kidnappings of women in the preface (1.1–4) to the crucifixion of a Persian satrap in the final chapters. Vengeance motivates Xerxes' attack on Greece, though Herodotus notes that other factors are significant, such as the urge to imperialist aggression, the lust for power or revenge in individuals, and the divine rules of limit and balance. All these factors appear in the Persian debate preceding the expedition (7.8–18). The *History* shows one great wave in a constant cycle of growth and decline, as well as many lesser instances, and it ends at the moment of Persian decline. Herodotus is especially interested in the deep patterns of behavior he finds in events, because he assumes that these patterns explain the course of human history.

These patterns of human behavior – vengeance, imperialism, reassertion of a natural balance – were surely also meant to apply to the two great rival powers of his own day, Athens and Sparta. Herodotus recognizes the glory won by both cities in the Persian Wars, and especially the essential role of Athens and its navy (7.139). Yet he chooses to end the *History* when the Greeks, led by the Athenians, begin their own attack on Asia. In his own day Athens had converted their success against the Persians into domination of the Aegean; the Athenians now collected the tribute once paid the Persians. Sparta is also seen to be self-serving, and not averse to installing tyrants in other cities to maintain control over them (5.91–94). Herodotus does not make the point explicit, but he must have believed that the historical truths of power and domination apparent in his narrative were equally true in his contemporary world.

Herodotus' method is twofold, involving investigation and judgment. Investigation depends on two sources, personal observation and oral report. In a famous passage in his account of Egypt, he stresses the importance of both observation and reports as he moves from describing the land and customs of the Egyptians to their history. "Up to this point," he explains, "my observation, judgment, and inquiry have been speaking; from here on I will give the stories of the Egyptians, adding also something of my own observation" (2.99). After learning the stories told by his informants, Herodotus compared them with the accounts of informants from other cities or countries. In Sparta, for instance, he learned of the Spartan expedition against Samos from Archias, the grandson of a Spartan of the same name who had heroically died there (3.54–55). Earlier he had traced the war to the loss of a valuable wine bowl being sent to Croesus as a gift: the Spartans said that the Samians had captured it; the Samians that the Spartans carrying the bowl had sold it to them. Here Herodotus does not take sides, but records the comment (his own, or the Samians'?) that "those who sold it, when they arrived in Sparta, perhaps would say that it had been taken from them" (1.70). On other occasions he seems to have invented accounts to show how other people might have presented their view of the event. He himself probably originally presented many of the segments of his work as stories recounted to small audiences during his travels. We may imagine him at a communal meal in Sparta, therefore, telling stories, and hearing in turn the story of Archias, which would become the basis of a new story. Only later would the stories have been organized and written down as the book we now possess.

Herodotus' method reflects significant changes from that used by the earlier writers who systematized myths and genealogies. His content is not the legendary past but the period of the three most recent generations before the speaker, a period now recognized as the span for which oral tradition remains most reliable. He concentrates especially on events shared by different populations, such as the Spartan war against Samos. His own observation often confirms a story by reference to some present monument, such as the contested wine bowl, originally Spartan, and now on Samos, or the temple of "Foreign Aphrodite" in Memphis, which he takes as supporting the story that Helen went to Egypt rather than Troy (2.113). Finally, each story is subject to the historian's judgment of its probability. Where there are no alternative stories, and no obvious correction, he renounces judgment: "Whether this is true or not I do not know; I write what is said" (4.195 and often).

Herodotus' efforts at ascertaining the truth were hindered by many factors. He confronts many, but he was not conscious of all of them. We know now that even participants and observers regularly adjust their memories to habitual or fitting narratives; events become mythologized with astounding rapidity. His stories of Croesus' meeting with Solon and his salvation from a burning pyre (1.29–33, 86–87) have clearly been created using folk-tale and fictional motifs, but comparison with an earlier poetic version shows that Herodotus has attempted to keep the stories within the bounds of historical probability. In an oral culture, the difference between fact and fiction is often not easy to establish and for many purposes precision may not be important. Herodotus, conscious of this difficulty, makes the reader aware of his work as a critical investigator by constantly calling attention to his own activity.

Herodotus believed that people were shaped by two fundamental factors: geography and customs. Each nation adapts to its own territory, and assumes customs which are right for it, though Herodotus evaluates some customs as better than others. As an ethnographer, Herodotus goes beyond oddities of behavior to features which shape life and thinking. His ethnographic studies of Egypt and Scythia (the Ukrainian steppe) in books 2 and 4 are justly famous. Egypt is the gift of the Nile, whereas Scythia is a land of rivers and unbounded space: their customs, from funeral and marriage customs to political institutions, vary accordingly. Neither resembles Greece. Structuralist critics have noted that Herodotus presents customs of peoples in terms of polar opposites, especially those of Egypt and Scythia, but much remains to be done to establish the anthropological and historical premises for his treatment. Herodotus is our best informant for the fifth-century Greek discovery that fundamental customs and cultural values vary from people to people. Yet for Herodotus, this does not lead to a relativistic stance. Rather, for him the study of Greeks and non-Greeks is a means to recognize the underlying pattern of human events and furnishes a mirror for Greeks to see themselves.

Above all, Herodotus is a consummate narrator. The stories which he hears he makes his own, and he retells them with charm and insight, revealing themes and patterns that his informants often would have not have recognized. They are marked by a style which ranges from the simple to the sublime, always in perfect harmony with the material. The stories attributed to specific informants, the frequent dialogues, and the longer speeches (which highlight special moments, such as Xerxes' decision to invade Greece) create a rich and suggestive polyphony.

In Herodotus' narrative, oral tradition became history, a history that made critical use of evidence, pointed to fundamental patterns of human behavior, and wove traditions from different cities, nations, and cultures into a coherent, carefully structured narrative. His history is distinguished by its incorporation of the voices of women and of the enemies of the Greeks and by the importance it attributes to geography and ethnography.

Thucydides: Restricting the Focus and Intensifying the Analysis of Human Nature

In the period during which Herodotus was composing his history, ca. 445–425, antagonism between Athens and Sparta came slowly to a head and erupted into the Peloponnesian War (431–404). Thucydides, Herodotus' younger contemporary (ca. 460–395), decided to study the new struggle. He began "from the outbreak of the war" (1.1), since he was convinced that the new war would be even greater than the Persian War. His *History of the Peloponnesian War* makes a number of significant departures from the Herodotean model, which he almost certainly knew, though the older historian is never named.

Thucydides' account focuses narrowly on political and military events in the Greek world during the war, abandoning Herodotus' wide sweep over three continents. Despite the importance of Persia in deciding the war's outcome, Thucydides is silent on its leaders and policies until almost twenty years into the war. He excludes women, family, the gods (including oracles and other manifestations of religion), and ethnography from most of his narrative. Enormous gains balance these losses, most notably in the intensity and depth of his extraordinary analysis of power, reason, and emotion in wartime.

Thucydides came from an aristocratic background, with ties to the royal family of Thrace. His familial connections and his mining concessions in

Thrace made him extremely influential there. He himself is an actor in his history. He notes that he caught the plague which hit Athens in the first years of the war, but survived. Later, as an Athenian fleet commander in 424, he was held responsible for the loss of a major Athenian colony in Thrace to the Spartans, and exiled. Although he lived to see the end of the war and the defeat of Athens, which he mentions in his text, his account is incomplete, ending abruptly in late summer 411. Despite endless scholarly debate, we do not know when he actually composed the different sections of his book, which of the extant portions of his work have reached their intended final state, or how he would have treated the remaining years of the war.

The main narrative is rigidly compartmentalized into years, which are divided into summer (the active campaigning season, from spring to fall) and winter. Each year is formally marked and numbered at its end: e.g. "the winter ended, and the fifth year of this war, which Thucydides composed" (3.88). Within these divisions, he reports individual actions in the different theaters of the war. A single campaign continuing action over two or three years is divided between the separate years, although on rare occasions Thucydides will follow through to a later conclusion. The books into which our modern texts are divided represent much later editorial decisions, as with Herodotus. For Thucydides, the major units of his history were the present first book, which gives the background of the war to the moment of formal disruption of relations, the first period of war, 431–421 BC (marked at 5.24–25 by his polemical assertion that the peace between Athens and Sparta in 421 did not actually end the war), and the remaining years to the history's abrupt termination in 411.

The first book employs a more complex schema, aimed first at explaining Thucydides' reasons for writing (1.1–23) and then the war's long-term and immediate causes (1.24–144), in a tour-de-force display of narrative modes. The innovation of this technique is as important, though less recognized, as his annalistic method in the later books. In treating the causes of the war, he first gives rapid, dramatic narratives of preliminary conflicts between the two rival blocs, then uses four speeches presented at a congress in Sparta in 432 to lay out the characteristics of the combatants and the various emotions and reasons that led to the Spartan decision to go to war. Then, stopping the action, Thucydides rapidly reviews Athens' dynamic drive for power in the years 478–439, the success of which provoked Sparta's decision to oppose Athens. The narrative resumes with accounts of diplomatic maneuvers that the Spartans pursued in order to win time and put the Athenians in a bad light. Two speeches by the Corinthians and by Pericles explore the resources available to each side and confirm the will to war. Between them, Thucydides inserts the enigmatic stories, in almost Herodotean style, of an Athenian would-be tyrant and of the two great commanders of the Persian Wars, Pausanias of Sparta and Themistocles of Athens, both of whom were accused of betraying Greece to Persia. The narrative variety of the first book indicates that the following austere organization by summers and winters represented Thucydides' conscious decision, not a poverty of imagination. The annalistic scheme for Thucydides' extraordinarily long war admirably captures the complexity of the action and the steady pressure of events, as the war ground on year after year.

Thucydides in an important methodological chapter writes that he did not accept chance accounts or his own impressions of the events he describes, but took great pains to achieve accuracy. "Precision could be found out only with difficulty, since those who were present at any given event did not report the same about the same matters, but each spoke according to his bias or memory" (1.22). Unlike Herodotus, he was not searching out traditions going back over one hundred years, but interviewing contemporaries about contemporary events. Nevertheless, like Herodotus, he found it necessary to set stories side by side and evaluate them on the basis of his informants' memory and bias, and (a factor he does not mention) how events actually turned out. Thucydides differs from Herodotus in suppressing his own inquiry and the different voices of his informants. With only a few exceptions, he never gives alternate stories or expresses uncertainty concerning his narrative. His voice is that of a person who has examined the alternatives and discovered the truth. Thucydides occasionally cites documents, such as the texts of the treaties of 421 and 420 (5.18–19, 23–24, 47). Unfortunately, only rarely can the accuracy of his narrative be checked against documents preserved on inscriptions. One controversial case has arisen recently concerning an inscribed text, a copy of an alliance between Athens and Segesta in Sicily that belongs (apparently) to 418. Thucydides, in describing Segesta's role in urging the expedition of 415 against Sicily, makes no allusion to this recent treaty. The modern historian must wonder whether this omission (if real) represents a serious distortion of the record, or exclusion of irrelevant detail.

Thucydides in his preface on early Greek history (1.2–19) employs other tools and sources not explicitly mentioned in the body of his work. In this preface, Thucydides utilizes arguments from probability, comparative ethnography, archaeological discoveries, and a critique of Homer to analyze the growth of power and common action in Greece. The analysis is set into a cogent theoretical framework that sketches the nature of power. The methodology employed and especially the intellectual examination of the foundations of power (stability, money, navy, walls) alert the reader to the procedure which will be employed silently through the rest of the history, forming the basis for his analysis of how humans control and are controlled by power.

Finally, continuing the tradition of Homer and Herodotus, Thucydides employs speeches to convey the actors' intellectual and emotional response to events. In a much disputed passage he insists on the accuracy of his reports despite the difficulties of memory and selection (1.22). This accuracy must be conceived not as verbatim reporting, but as a truthful presentation of the speakers' attitudes and arguments, in the light of the surrounding narrative and of Thucydides' overall interpretation of events. Thus Pericles' speech over those fallen in the first year of the war (2.35–46) accurately presents Pericles' understanding of the glory of Athenian imperial dynamism and the desirability of placing civic goals above personal ones. It indicates Thucydides' recognition of the greatness of Pericles' leadership, yet at the same time serves as a foil to a more negative view of Athens. This negative view is found first in the immediately subsequent account of Athens suffering from the plague of 430–428, which shows the Athenians despairing, amoral, and helpless (2.47–54), and later in the terrible defeat of the Athenians in Sicily and in the civil war which divides the city soon thereafter (books 7 and 8). Although Thucydides abandoned Herodotus' technique of employing frequent dialogues, a few short dialogues serve to heighten particular moments of pathos. The famous "Melian dialogue" (5.84–113) represents an extraordinary development of this technique, as Athenians and Melians debate, in brief exchanges, the obligation of an imperial power to rule, and of an independent city to resist. The Athenians insist that their immensely greater strength excludes the notion of justice, which can only be between equals; the Melians search desperately for some reason to believe they can resist successfully.

"We think that the gods (apparently) and men (certainly) always and by natural necessity rule wherever they can exercise their power," the Athenians tell the Melians (5.105). The statement for Thucydides is both true and tragic. Humans strive for what gods possess by nature. The purpose of his history is to allow his readers "to examine clearly both what has happened and what will happen again similarly in the future, as determined by what is human" (1.22.4). With these words Thucydides explicitly states what was implied by Herodotus, that his narrative is not simply a record of events in the past, but a tool for understanding how humans act, and therefore what they will do in some future time. His belief in the usefulness of history is thus based on the notion of a constant human nature which will regularly act in the same way; for instance, to rule wherever it can. His *History* is conceived as a case study in "what is human": the phrase indicates not only human nature and human behavior, but also human circumstances, the human situation. Thucydides' perspective is decidedly pessimistic, for to examine clearly does not mean to control. In describing minutely the plague at Athens, Thucydides expresses the hope that it might be recognizable if it recurs, but gives no hope for a cure: "for neither were doctors able to cure it . . . or any other human skill" (2.47). His passion for precise description matches and may have been influenced by that of the medical writers who were active at this time, but description is not cure. War, like the plague, reveals the weakness of human nature: "Many atrocities afflicted the cities during the internal conflicts, things that continue to happen and will keep happening as long as human beings have the same nature, though more intense or more tranquil or different in their manifestations as individual circumstances impose themselves. In peace and in good times both cities and individuals have better dispositions, since they are not afflicted by pressures over which they have no control. But war, by taking away the prosperity of everyday life, becomes a violent teacher and assimilates most men's impulses to their circumstances" (3.82). The rational analysis of history reveals the irrational bases of human nature, thereby revealing also the universal truths of the human condition. Since all are subject to the human condition, historical knowledge for Thucydides is useful for understanding, but cannot offer control of events.

The contrast between intelligent understanding and human action is often expressed in terms of the antithesis judgment–emotion. Both Herodotus' and Thucydides' histories explore the ability of human intelligence to understand and prepare for the future. Herodotus uses the dual motifs of wise advisers and oracles to dramatize human blindness and contrast it with divine knowledge. Neither the advice of Solon nor an oracle from Delphi can teach Croesus his own vulnerability as a human being, even in the midst of prosperity, and Xerxes suffers the same fate. Thucydides confines his history to the human realm, but he constructs his narrative, especially by the use of the participants' speeches, as a constant effort to make decisions concerning the future. Reason regularly is shown to be weaker than emotion. Pericles' far-seeing assessment of the Athenians' reasons and resources for war, or the Spartan king Archidamus' exhortation to caution, are overwhelmed at Athens by the emotional reaction of the Athenians at the invasion of their territory or the losses from the plague, and at Sparta by rash confidence in victory. Gradually, as the war progresses, and as the reader learns more, Thucydides reveals unexpected features of human nature. Thus the arrogance of the Athenians and the foolish hopefulness of the Melians in the Melian dialogue prepare the reader for Athens' vain attempt to conquer Sicily. In Thucydides' eyes their defeat followed from their confidence and was the greatest disaster of Hellenic history. "In every way they were completely defeated. They suffered enormously, the proverbial 'absolute destruction,' both infantry and ships. There was nothing that did not perish: few out of many returned home" (7.87). Time and again Thucydides focuses on human suffering, not just the great events such as the civil war on Corcyra or the destruction of the Athenians in Sicily, but the ruthless stoning of a trapped Corinthian detachment (1.106) or the massacre of a village – men, women, children, and animals – by barbarian mercenaries (7.29). Thucydides' narrative, like Homer's, accents human suffering and loss.

Thucydides originated the type of military–political history which has dominated European historiography ever since. He also introduced the writing of contemporary history and the use of a tightly controlled chronological format. His method combined diligent comparison of eyewitness reports and intellectual analysis of underlying causes. His technique joins accurate historical report with a keen sense of the tragic. Thucydides brings together an objective, apparently distanced narrative style, moving imperturbably through the summers and winters of the war, with extremely powerful scenes, vividly described and emotionally charged. Readers are caught up in this tension, so that their emotions are engaged with the historical figures as they attempt to understand what is happening around them and plan their course. Absorbed emotionally and intellectually in the war, the reader is forced to confront what it means to be human. The apparent objectivity of Thucydides' historical writing leads via an intense emotional involvement to a tragic understanding of human glory and failure.

Xenophon: Exploring Military and Political Leadership

Xenophon (ca. 428–354) was born into an upper-class family at Athens in the early years of the Peloponnesian War. He briefly associated with Socrates, served in the Athenian cavalry, and later accompanied the Persian prince Cyrus on his fruitless attempt to wrest the throne of Persia from his brother. When Cyrus was killed, he fought his way back to Greece at the head of ten thousand Greek mercenaries, after which he joined the army of the Spartan king Agesilaus in Asia Minor. Having been exiled from Athens, he retired to live near Olympia on an estate granted him by the Spartans. Unlike the two preceding historians, his history was not his sole literary effort – he experimented with a variety of genres or modes of historical and philosophical writing, in which invention and history were mixed in varying proportions. His experience in Persia and Asia Minor moved him to make the challenges of military and political leadership the major theme of his varied writings. These include his *Anabasis*, an artful memoir of his adventures on the march from deep inside hostile Persian territory, a series of Socratic dialogues, and a philosophical novel, the *Cyropaideia*, a fictional account of the life of Cyrus the Great. Leadership, or more often the lack of it, is the focus as well of his *History of Greece* (*Hellenica*).

The *History*, which begins in late summer 411, must have been originally conceived as a sequel to the work of Thucydides. The work falls into two major segments. The first continues the narrative of the Peloponnesian War to the defeat of Athens (411–404 BC); the second treats the ineffective struggles for primacy among the Greek states from 404 to 362 and the battle of Mantinea, after which, as Xenophon writes, "Both sides claimed the victory, but neither side appeared better off for territory, or cities, or power than before the battle. There was even more uncertainty and confusion in Greece after the battle than previously" (Hell. 7.5.27). The first segment differs in style from the second and was apparently written at an earlier date. It is divided into campaigning years and references are occasionally made to summers and winters.

The second segment abandons continuous treatment of events by seasons for a series of illustrative episodes. The narrative thus has surprising omissions, such as a four-year gap (403–399) between the first two episodes. Nevertheless it singles out a number of significant events in the decades after the Peloponnesian War. In this segment Xenophon makes no effort to establish a chronological framework, preferring to make connections between events by simple succession and by repetition and variation of themes.

Xenophon did not follow the Thucydidean model of history: his love of anecdote and dialogue are closer to Herodotus. His experiences inspired a didacticism which expressed his deep convictions on the virtues required by true leaders, on pan-Hellenism, and on traditional religious and moral obligations. In the *History of Greece*, a more overtly didactic work than those of Herodotus or Thucydides, Xenophon self-consciously pointed to the lessons of history. His history demonstrated that the internecine, destructive warfare of the Greeks made them vulnerable to their enemies, especially Persia, without giving any city a secure hegemony.

The *History* offers a series of studies of different kinds of leaders, which reveal the paucity of good leadership which was the chief reason for Greece's sorry condition. Anecdotes and episodes illustrate the ability of good leaders to outwit the enemy and to win the loyalty of their troops, and the disastrous effects of vicious or ineffective leaders. Thus in the first segment of his history, Xenophon paints the contrasting styles and outcomes of the rigid traditional Spartan commander Callicratidas, who alienated his supporters and met his death with useless courage, and Lysander, the wily fox who played sycophant to the Persian prince Cyrus to win money for his fleet, tricked the Athenians, and finally starved Athens into surrender.

The history also reveals the weakness of major cities in Greece in the early fourth century BC. Xenophon shows that democratic Athens destroyed itself in excesses such as the trial at which they condemned their own generals en masse (1.7). Sparta's oligarchic, militaristic society in many ways appealed to Xenophon. Nevertheless, he presented Sparta's policies as destructive, and never more so than when it permitted a Spartan general to capture and hold the citadel of Thebes in violation of sworn treaties (5.2.25–36, cf. 5.4.1), an irreligious act which led to war and the loss of much of Sparta's territory. On the other hand he holds up the valiant behavior of the tiny city of Phlius for praise:

I shall write of this [Phlius' action] in some detail. For if one of the great powers does some fine and noble action, all the historians write about it; but it seems to me that if a state which is only a small one has done numbers of great and glorious things, then there is all the more reason for letting people know about them. . . . There is no question that men who did deeds like this must be called noble men and great warriors. (7.2.1, 16)

Unlike his predecessors, Xenophon does not present himself as a diligent investigator. Nowhere in the *Hellenica* does he refer to his sources, indicate that he had compared different accounts, or suggest that the history required great effort. He does not try to win his reader by referring to his own presence at events, or to his close ties with Spartan leaders: he even refers to his own *Anabasis* under a pseudonym (3.1). Since he lived among Spartans and knew many of them well, he is by far our best source for internal events and customs at Sparta. His history has generally a Spartan point of view, though Xenophon is often critical of Spartan policy and individual Spartans. After his return from Asia in 395, however, he could also have entertained on his estate visitors from all over Greece who attended the Olympic games. If he wished, he could have heard stories from several points of view, but it is not clear that he used them for his narrative, or sought to integrate different perspectives into his historical writings.

Xenophon's *Hellenica* is a selective account, which chooses between incidents worthy of treatment and those which can or should be passed over. Xenophon often is silent about matters he knows well. He does not mention, for example, that Sparta was deprived of two-fifths of its territory after its defeat by Thebes in 371 BC, nor does he note that his son was one of the Athenian cavalrymen who died in the battle of Mantinea. The principles of selection are much disputed. Once ascribed solely to the author's Spartan bias, limited sources, or incompetence, it is now apparent that they represent a conscious decision on how he wanted to write his history.

Xenophon was a sophisticated author who redefined historiography in his own terms, borrowing themes and techniques from his predecessors, but creating his own kind of episodic narrative in which selected political actions were evaluated in terms of the leadership qualities and moral values they displayed. More optimistic than Thucydides, he wished that his historical narrative could train contemporaries to lead their cities well.

Polybius

Xenophon created a new style of history as a response to the needs of his own times, filtered through his interest in the relation between ethics and government and his experiences in Athens, Persia, and Sparta. Two other major historians of the fourth century, Ephorus and Theopompus, attempted a larger view. Ephorus' thirty-volume history expanded his coverage in time and space, treating the major areas of the known world from soon after the Trojan War to his own day, inventing what we might call today the first universal history. His contemporary Theopompus resembled Xenophon in composing a continuation of Thucydides, entitled *Hellenica*, but he also composed a vast (fifty-eight books) history of his own times, his *Philippica*, centered on the career of Philip II of Macedon. Often read and quoted in antiquity, only fragments of these works are now preserved.

Two centuries later Polybius of Megalopolis (ca. 200–118) continued Ephorus' effort to cover the whole Mediterranean world, undertaking in his *Histories* to describe and explain the marvelous rise of Rome in the period 220–167. In this period Rome defeated Carthage, Macedonia, and the Seleucid kings and brought all the Mediterranean basin under its power. Polybius himself, a leader of the defeated Achaean Confederation in Greece, was taken as hostage to Rome and kept there until 150. He became friends with leading Romans, including Scipio Africanus the younger, and while there wrote most of his massive historical work. First projected as a series of 30 books that would describe Roman history to the year 167, he expanded it to 40 books after new wars with the conquered states convinced him that he should explore the effects of the Roman conquest down to 146, the year Rome destroyed both Carthage and Corinth. Polybius' history thus began some 20 years before he was born (his prolegomena started 21 years before that, in 241), but about a quarter of his book was contemporary history. Books 1–5 survive intact, together with many long fragments, from which we can make some statements about his achievement.

Although he has many vivid narrative passages, Polybius stands out as an exceptionally didactic historian, pedantically explaining his intentions and methods at every step. These statements represent our most thorough account of the theory of ancient historiography as seen by a practitioner. Polybius says that he writes "pragmatic" history, that is narrative focused on political actions, like Thucydides. Building upon Thucydides, he formulates (3.6–7) a theory of historical causes which contrasts the apparent beginnings of historical events with the deeper causes that lay behind. A historian must explain the decision processes which start a war, as well as the wider historical process behind each event. Polybius thus narrates at length how decisions were made and castigates historians (the so-called "tragic historians") who prefer melodramatic scenes of a battle or the capture of a city over thorough exploration of the institutions of a city, the speeches of ambassadors, or the topography of a battle.

His book-length digressions on the Roman constitution (Bk. 6), a polemic against previous historians (Bk. 12), and a discussion of geography (Bk. 34) represent a major innovation. These digressions provide in-depth treatment of fundamental factors underlying the history of his period. Thus, Book 6 of his *Histories* examines Rome's government (offering in the process the fullest ancient account of the theory of the mixed constitution), using Greek political theory to clarify Roman realities and thereby explain Rome's success. Rome's stable, constitutional combination of monarchical, oligarchic, and democratic elements, its military practices (such as army units and the construction of the Roman camp), and its religion gave it an ability to overcome all obstacles and laid the basis for its empire. The book analyzes the underlying causes of Rome's rebound to preeminence after Hannibal's apparently decisive victory over Rome at Cannae, just as Polybius insisted that a history should. In this way, his historical analysis was able to focus not just on the immediate event, but on multiple levels of historical process. An index volume (Bk. 40) facilitated reader reference.

Polybius employs a chronological structure based on the numbered series of Olympiads, which could express the unity that Rome achieved. Using one system, he could coordinate events in Italy, Greece, and Africa, although he has to adjust the years slightly so that they ended with the end of the summer campaigning season. The first two books lay out the background events of 241–220 in different parts of the world. The next three books begin the Olympiad sequence (220–216) but treat the events of all four years in each theater separately. Finally, in Books 7 and following, when events become more intermingled, all events of each year are narrated, rotating through the theaters, before moving to the next year. The structure of Olympiad years gave his work a chronological order, while multiple references to simultaneous events unite the actions scattered in different theaters.

Polybius' privileged access to the Roman upper-class meant that he could gather much information directly from conversations, but he was also an active researcher, studying inscriptions and topography (autopsy of the terrain was essential, he felt), quoting the texts of early treaties between Carthage and Rome, interrogating eyewitnesses, and comparing and criticizing his written sources, Roman, Greek, and Carthaginian.

Polybius' pragmatic approach still leaves room to evaluate political action in moral terms. The basic outlook is the traditional Greek aristocratic morality which honored courage in battle and condemned ignoble acquisition of wealth and betrayal of friends and fellow citizens. Roman self-discipline and perseverance he considered simultaneously political, military, and moral virtues, which led to their present eminence. Nevertheless, evaluation did not stop with success. In the last ten books, Polybius' history moved from a celebration of Rome's rise to a critique of her rule. His *Histories* were not meant to be an encomium of Rome: like all other ancient Greek historians, Polybius wanted his readers to draw useful moral and political lessons from his work.

His contributions as a historian were first, to engage a major theme over the whole area of the Mediterranean world, second, to employ a chronological scheme linked to an external objective sequence, and third to extend the analysis of causes to underlying factors such as political institutions and geography. Finally, he showed unusual diligence in research and investigation of oral, written, and documentary evidence. His study of the Achaean league and of Rome's mixed constitution significantly influenced eighteenth-century political theory and the American constitution.

Arrian

Finally, it is useful to glance at two Greek authors writing in the second century AD, under the Roman empire, when the Roman peace and the revived prosperity of Greece permitted a new flourishing of Greek literature. Arrian of Nicomedia (ca. 85–160 AD), after studying with the philosopher Epictetus, rose to the rank of Roman consul and provincial governor, but still found time to become a prolific writer. His most famous extant work is his *Anabasis* or *History of Alexander the Great*, though he also composed several major histories that are now lost. In addition, he is responsible for writing the *Discourses* and *Manual* of the Stoic philosopher Epictetus. His Alexander history, like several works by previous authors on the same theme, combined biography and the history of the conquest of the Persian empire. The tone is expressly laudatory, but also offers criticism of Alexander's violence and barbaric behavior, which Arrian, like many other writers, thought became especially apparent after Alexander had become king of Persia. Self-mastery is a theme which underlies the more obvious interest in the tactics of sieges and battles. Alexander could conquer the world, but could he conquer himself? The history thus responds to the contemporary interest in the virtues of the emperor, and may have been inspired especially by the emperor Trajan's ambition to conquer Parthia, the successor of the Persian empire.

Arrian affirms that he will use two contemporary sources, Ptolemy (a close associate of Alexander, later king of Egypt) and Aristobulus, both of whom accompanied the campaign. Where these two disagree, he will select "what appears more believable and most worthy of narration" (preface, 1). To these he adds stories from other authors, sometimes identified as "what is said." The effect of this choice is that his account has much less of romance and imagination than our other extent accounts of Alexander (all of the imperial period), a fact that led earlier scholars to treat him as our most valuable source. It is significant that he chose to search out and follow sources contemporary to Alexander, rather than the multitude of more recent accounts available in his own day. However, Arrian's reasons for choosing these two sources are not especially rigorous: he argues that both of them had accompanied Alexander, and had written after his death, when there would be no reason to distort the truth, and besides Ptolemy was a king, for whom "it would be more shameful to lie." The accounts identified as "what is said" can usually be traced to the more romantic accounts in circulation in his day.

Arrian's history, recounting events which occurred over four hundred years before, depends completely on written sources: his contribution lay in the choice of relatively reliable sources, effective selection and narration of incident, and the imposition of an overall interpretation of the man. He is remarkably successful, although it should be noted that a smooth and plausible narrative does not necessarily produce an accurate historical reconstruction. We may therefore challenge his right to be considered on all occasions superior to more romanticized accounts, despite his careful choice of written sources and his literary ability in narrating the events of Alexander's life.

Plutarch

Arrian had philosophic interests and combined history with biography in the *Anabasis*. Plutarch of Chaeronea (ca. 45–125 AD), a philosopher, never attempted narrative history, but deserves a place here because of his series of *Parallel Lives* of Greek and Roman statesmen, an ambitious reinterpretation of history in terms of the lives of great men from the conquered Greeks and the conquering Romans, set side by side. The forty-six *Lives* in twenty-two books include the earliest legendary founders, Theseus and Romulus, and come down to the deaths of Antony and Cleopatra in 30 BC. The Greek lives include a heavy proportion of Athenian statesmen of the fifth century, but also five Spartans, Alexander the Great, and two Hellenistic kings; the latest is that of Philopoemen, who died in 182 (young Polybius carried the urn in his funeral procession). The Roman lives span all of Roman republican history, but special emphasis is given to the last tumultuous years of the republic, with *Lives* of Caesar, Cicero, Pompey, Brutus, Cato the Younger, Crassus, and Mark Antony. Each Greek is paired with a Roman of similar character and situation to form a separate book. For most pairs, a short comparison between the protagonists appears at the end. The order of publication of the books is disputed (it is not chronological), except for the three pairs which Plutarch identifies as the fifth, tenth, and twelfth books. Six late republican lives, which are also much longer than the others, belong toward the end of the series.

Whereas Arrian was one of the first persons of Greek culture to pursue high office in the imperial administration, Plutarch chose to practice philosophy, living quietly in his native town of Chaeronea, in Delphi, where he was a priest of Apollo for many years, and in Athens, the cultural center of Greece. The *Lives* represent only a fraction of his writings, many of which are lost; his surviving essays, collectively called *Moralia*, equal in volume the extant lives. He visited Rome at least twice, made a number of friends and acquaintances among Romans of the highest level, and was granted Roman citizenship. Romans of the upper-class prided themselves on their knowledge of Greek literature and philosophy, and the *Lives* are dedicated to a prominent senator and military commander closely associated with the emperor Trajan. Plutarch's readership would have consisted of the ruling elite of both cultures.

Like Arrian, Plutarch writes of events long past, and depends on earlier historians, although wherever possible he supplements them with his own observation of monuments or stories from his friends or local informants. Biography of the Plutarchan type did not exist before him, and earlier biographies were not an important source. An omnivorous reader in the historians and antiquarians of Greece, time and again he quotes authors and incidents known from no other source. He came to Latin late and his reading of Roman literature is correspondingly restricted, but he cites major authors such as Livy and Cicero, the biographer Nepos, and some lesser figures. For both Greek and Latin biographies, he privileges sources contemporary with the hero, especially those written by the protagonist himself: Solon's laws and poems, Pericles' decrees, Demosthenes' speeches, Sulla's memoirs. Although he famously stated that he "wrote biographies, not history" (*Alexander* 1), it is more accurate to say that he reshaped historical narrative into biography. This reshaping necessitated a new interpretation of the protagonist and often an imaginative reconstruction of the circumstances behind an event. From a comparison of six of the late Roman republican lives that treated many of the same events and that were composed more or less during the same period, we can ascertain valuable clues as to his method, which are confirmed by other lives. Even when treating the same events, Plutarch refocused the action to make each protagonist the center of the life devoted to him. Historical information not relevant to the biography was condensed or stripped away, thus creating a style of biography that remains important even in our own era. Judgments too changed from life to life, as the new protagonist's point of view was favored. In creating his narrative, Plutarch occasionally compressed, simplified, or displaced material. Usually chronological sequence furnished the major organizing scheme, but it coexisted with and often yielded to thematic and rhetorical structures. Incidents and anecdotes were frequently gathered under a thematic head, or introduced by association, rather than in chronological order.

The impulse to biography was certainly encouraged by contemporary circumstances, when the whole empire depended on the actions and thus the character of one man, but it also grew from Plutarch's own philosophical interests, especially in practical ethics. Moral teaching and writing had long employed short anecdotes of ethical behavior by rulers or great men to make a point, though usually anecdotes of philosophers were favored for the purpose. Plutarch's genius was to treat a man's life as material for study, placing individual anecdotes into a historical framework, so that the reader could see the circumstances in which the statesman acted and evaluate his whole life rather than a brief moment of courage or wit. Plutarch expected readers to draw both practical and ethical conclusions from the lives he narrated.

Historians frequently employed explicit or implicit comparisons – for example, Herodotus and Thucydides compare Athenian and Spartan values and actions. Plutarch, by setting Roman and Greek lives side by side, stimulates the reader to think more profoundly and with more precision about the protagonists' virtues and weaknesses and how they are strengthened or attenuated in different circumstances. Often the comparison suggests tensions between conflicting goods, or between moral good and practical success. Most of Plutarch's statesmen have major flaws, so that the reader must admire and criticize the same person, and sometimes the same traits. Written as Greek speakers were beginning to enter into the upper levels of imperial government, the *Parallel Lives* also assert the value of the Greek heritage, while recognizing that Romans often more successfully embodied Greek virtues than the Greeks themselves. The biographies are aimed at elite readers of both nations.

Very much a document of their times, yet filled with vivid reconstructions of statesmen's lives over a period of centuries, the *Lives* are perhaps the most important single source for our understanding of the world of Greece and Rome. Equally important, they established a biographical approach to historical understanding and knowledge that exercised major influence in the Renaissance and the eighteenth century, and has remained influential in the subsequent evolution of historical thought and writing. Plutarch's use of anecdotes and contemporary sources became a mainstay of biography; his comparative method was seldom imitated.

The Legacy of the Ancient Greek Historians

The ancient Greek historians lie at the foundation of the European tradition of historiography. Herodotus and Thucydides established the genre. What did these historians contribute to the development of historical thought? In imitation of and in competition with Homeric epic, they originated a large-scale narrative focused on a major conflict, selecting incidents and speeches to reveal both the thinking and emotions of individuals and cities and underlying themes and patterns of action. They established the use of chronological systems: Herodotus organized by the reigns of the Persian kings; Thucydides by campaign years. Faced with extremely complex narratives, they devised compositional structures to accommodate diverse types of information. Most importantly, they sought out and compared different accounts of events, confirming them from visible monuments, testing them against each other and the known outcome, and expressing their own judgment. Thus in their histories historical knowledge depended on evidence and required an attempt to establish a true account despite the limits and biases of their sources. Herodotus established the notion of history as including culture and geography; Thucydides the more restricted focus on politics, war, and great men.

Thucydides states explicitly what seems implied by Herodotus, that his history is meant to provide useful knowledge for his contemporaries and for future generations. Historical narrative makes clear the lessons of events, which may guide future action, or at least offer understanding of future events. Later Greek historians interpreted this notion of usefulness in different ways, but it remained a constant of historical writing, with profound influence on modern historians.

After the classical period, Greek historical writing continued to make significant contributions to historical thought. Polybius extended the concept of causation to include analysis of institutions and other deep causes, and thus helped shape the constitution of the United States. Arrian and Plutarch consciously selected contemporary sources when composing history of the distant past. Plutarch invented historical biography. His combination of historical summary and anecdotes revealing character had significant influence in the early modern period, when men thought they could consciously shape their character. Greek historical writing forged links between political lessons, biographical information, and philosophical insights into the human condition. It established itself between literature, philosophy, and rhetoric as a serious genre.

The ancient Greek historians offer exceptional models against which to measure modern historical writing. The methods of history have become more refined, but the fundamental questions remain: why is understanding the past important, and to whom? Why must we constantly strive for the most accurate past possible, and not settle for facile generalizations or popular myths? The founders set high standards for all later authors. The study of the past is our most powerful tool for understanding who we are as human beings, what constraints we live under, what possibilities for greatness and folly we contain within ourselves. For them, knowledge of the past was not for a few mandarins but was necessary to all persons who wish to know themselves and the world in which they live. Especially, they presumed that an understanding of the past was essential to everyone who wishes to shape the present and influence the future. The leading Greek historians did not write to push a partisan agenda, nor to seek refuge from their present, but to express the reality of the human condition as they saw it, and attempt to draw what lessons they could for human action. They used the most powerful tools they knew to establish the truth of what had happened, and their finest literary skills to present it to their public. Several were pessimistic: they saw only too well how folly often prevailed over judgment. Human ignorance is vast, and wisdom hard to find and quick to flee. But they attempted to see clearly, to express what they saw succinctly and forcefully, to persuade their contemporaries to act not blindly but with understanding. They hoped their histories would change men, and change the world. The modern historian has no less a vocation.

REFERENCES AND FURTHER READING

Ancient historians have been cited by book and chapter numbers. The book divisions of Herodotus, Thucydides, and perhaps Xenophon are not original, but made by scholars in antiquity. Excellent commentaries to individual historians are available for Thucydides (Gomme, Hornblower), Xenophon (Krentz), Polybius (Walbank), and Arrian (Bosworth); Herodotus is served in English by How and Wells, good but now out of date, and in Italian by Asheri et al. This list includes English translations with brief but useful commentaries for Herodotus, Thucydides, Xenophon, and Arrian, and selections from Plutarch.

General

Fornara, C. W., *The Nature of History in Ancient Greece and Rome*, Berkeley, Los Angeles, and London, 1983.
Hornblower, S. (ed.), *Greek Historiography*, Oxford, 1994.
Luce, T. J., *The Greek Historians*, London, 1997.
Marincola, J., *Authority and Tradition in Ancient Historiography*, Cambridge, 1997.
Shrimpton, G. S., *History and Memory in Ancient Greece*, Montreal, 1997.
Woodman, A. J., *Rhetoric in Classical Historiography*, London, 1988.

Herodotus

Herodotus, *The Histories*, trans. R. Waterfield, with introduction and notes by C. Dewald, Oxford, 1998.
Boedeker, D. (ed.), *Herodotus and the Invention of History*, Arethusa, 20 (1987).
Gould, J., *Herodotus*, London and New York, 1989.
Hartog, F., *The Mirror of Herodotus*, Berkeley, Los Angeles and London, 1988.
Immerwahr, H. R., *Form and Thought in Herodotus*, Cleveland, 1966.
Lateiner, D., *The Historical Method of Herodotus*, Toronto, 1989.

Thucydides

Thucydides, *The Peloponnesian War*, trans. with introduction and notes by S. Lattimore, Indianapolis, 1998.
Connor, W. R., *Thucydides*, Princeton, 1984.
Hornblower, S., *Thucydides*, London, 1987.
Rood, T., *Thucydides: a Narratological Approach*, Oxford, 1998.

Xenophon

Xenophon, *A History of My Times*, trans. R. Warner, introduction and notes by G. Cawkwell. Harmondsworth, 1979.

Dillery, J. D., *Xenophon and the History of his Times*, London and New York, 1995.
Gray, V. J., *The Character of Xenophon's Hellenica*, Baltimore, 1989.
Tuplin, C., *The Failings of Empire: A Reading of Xenophon Hellenica 2.3.11–7.5.27*, Stuttgart, 1993.

Polybius

Eckstein, A. M., *Moral Vision in the Histories of Polybius*, Los Angeles and Berkeley, 1995.
Sacks, K., *Polybius on the Writing of History*, Berkeley, Los Angeles and London, 1981.
Walbank, F. W., *Polybius*, Berkeley, Los Angeles and London, 1972.

Arrian

Arrian, *History of Alexander and Indica*, 2 vols, trans., with introduction and notes by P. A. Brunt, Cambridge, MA, 1976 and 1983.
Bosworth, A. B., *From Arrian to Alexander. Studies in Historical Interpretation*, Oxford, 1988.
Stadter, P. A., *Arrian of Nicomedia*, Chapel Hill, 1980.

Plutarch

Plutarch, *Greek Lives* and *Roman Lives*, trans. R. Waterfield, introduction and notes by P. A. Stadter. Oxford, 1998, 1999.
Duff, T., *Plutarch's Lives. Exploring Virtue and Vice*, Oxford, 1999.
Scardigli, B. (ed.), *Essays on Plutarch's Lives*, Oxford, 1995.

CHAPTER THREE

Historical Thought in Ancient Rome

J. E. LENDON

The Roman Historical Tradition

Italy's master, and Carthage's bane, Rome was five hundred years founded, before Romans began to write the history of their nation. Quintus Fabius Pictor, the first of the craft at Rome, came from a line with an old taint of Greek folly, and inherited the jeering name Pictor, "the painter," from an ancestor mocked for his soft Hellenic joys. Admirable Romans of the historian's generation – that of the Second Punic War (218–201 BC) – had nicknames like Africanus, won by subduing Hannibal's Carthage, or Marcellus, "the little Mars." Then the Romans were a martial folk, and grim: they knew little of literature and the Greek arts; what they knew most mistrusted. Although Fabius Pictor wrote of the Roman past, both his models and his prose were Greek. The writing of history at Rome was no native bloom, but flowered from an old Hellenic tree.

Fabius Pictor's work is lost, except for wretched scraps. The writings of his first successors, in Greek and then in Latin, are lost as well, bar shards: these authors we call the Annalists, because some of them borrowed for their works the year-by-year structure of the *Annales Maximi*, the annual reports of the chief state priest on events important or curious, which later Romans mined for knowledge of early times. The Annalists' works were plain, to later taste unpolished. Modern scholars' diligence surmises how these lost authors used each others' lost writings, and pursues with passion the fleeting ghosts of ghosts in surviving works. Quarrels ensue, and conclusions command the assent of none but conclude them.

Latin historical works that survive *in extenso* were written no earlier than the second half of the first century BC, in generations when the stern old Roman scorn of Greek letters had yielded to their embrace. The three major surviving Latin historians, participants in a self-conscious tradition, are Sallust, writing in the forties and thirties BC, Livy, around the turn of the millennium, and Tacitus, around AD 100. All wrote about wars and high politics, and all sought moral lessons in the achievements or failures of great men. Their works all bear the imprint of the standing of their authors and the troubles of their times. Julius Caesar's (100–44 BC) accounts of his Gallic and Civil Wars, which tormented schoolboys in the days before subjects like Driver's Education drove Latin from the schools, are technically not history but commentaries (*commentarii*), a Roman official's account of his achievements. But Caesar borrowed many literary techniques from Greek historians, especially from the sober Xenophon.

Gaius Sallustius Crispus (ca. 86–34 BC) – whom we call Sallust – was creature of Caesar's in the civil wars against Pompey, and was rewarded with the lucrative governorship of Roman North Africa. This was high elevation for a "new man," the term at Rome for a politician without prominent ancestors and so obliged to rise by his own merits. The corruption of Sallust's administration attracted the notice even of his contemporaries, a generation grown old in barratry. Returned to Rome, Sallust avoided punishment – by Caesar's influence, no doubt – but was expelled from public life. When Caesar died, so too did any hope of political rebirth, and Sallust turned to the writing of history to achieve in letters the *éclat* he had been denied in politics. In so doing he joined a shadowy tradition of frustrated late Republican politicians who, unwilling to subsist in cushioned obscurity, kept themselves in the public eye by the display of unusual excellences. His history writing made Sallust a fellow-sojourner at once of Lucullus, who sought fame through the luxury of his life and table, and of Cato the Younger, who schooled himself harshly to austerity and philosophy, and became famous by castigating sybarites like Lucullus.

Sallust's historical interests focused, unsurprisingly, on the fortunes of the excluded and self-made. His annalistic *Histories*, beginning at the death of Sulla (78 BC) had probably only reached 67 BC at their author's death; they are lost, except for fragments. What survive are two short topical essays he wrote earlier, in the late forties, soon after the assassination of Caesar. The *War against Catiline* tells the story of a failed conspiracy against the Republic set afoot in 63 BC by Lucius Sergius Catilina. Catiline was an evil patrician – a scion of one of Rome's proudest families – ruined by his vices and denied, in his own eyes unjustly, the political success that his high birth merited. The *War against Jugurtha* tells of the bastard nephew of the king of Numidia, who seized the kingdom by his own talents and made war upon the Romans (111–105 BC). Because the Romans were commanded by the corrupt and craven sons of high families he was for a long time successful. The Jugurthine war was finally brought to a victorious end by Gaius Marius, a virtuous "new man," who rose by his excellence as a soldier, prevailing against the bitter forces of inherited privilege.

Sallust's choice of subjects, and his treatment of them, owes much to his own experience in politics and civil war. His yearning for careers open to talent and his contempt for the aristocracy of birth is highly unusual in what survives of Roman writing, which is by and large plumply conservative. But liberal opinions were unknown at Rome: what appears liberal in Sallust is in fact reaction in the tradition of Cato the Elder and the Gracchi, a wistful longing for an imagined, yeoman past when the reputations of the great families – upon which their degraded descendants so leaned – were yet being forged by great deeds.

Titus Livius (59 BC–AD 17) – whom we call Livy – had no anguish of ship-wrecked ambition to exorcise in his writing; from what little we know of him he seems to have had no political career at all. Years of propertied leisure, and the benevolent interest of Augustus, Rome's first emperor, gave him time for his gigantic history of Rome from its founding – hence its title, *ab Urbe Condita, From the founding of the City* – down to 9 BC. Over forty years, from the mid-twenties BC until after the death of Augustus in AD 14, and in one hundred and forty-two book rolls – what would be more than eight thousand modern pages – Livy unrolled more than seven hundred years of Roman history; the logistics of shelving such a work in a world of scrolls would itself have been formidable. From the beginning of the Republic in 509 BC, when his material became rich enough, he employed an annalistic – year-by-year – structure. But within a book a theme may be carried on through a number of years, and sets of five and ten books form elegant unities.

From his vast work there survive thirty-five books, in two blocks, covering the periods from Rome's mythical origins to 292 BC, and from the Second Punic War against Carthage to Rome's slow throttling of Greek independence (218–167 BC). In contrast to Sallust's steaming resentment, Livy's milder prejudices are the conventional ones of the Roman aristocracy: patriotism, hatred of demagogues, fearful suspicion of the poor, and reverence for the trinity of dignity, birth, and bravery. In lost books dealing with recent events he praised Julius Caesar's enemy Pompey, who was also the choice of the Roman aristocracy when the realm was sundered between them in civil war. Augustus, Caesar's heir, genially chaffed Livy as "the Pompeian." But Livy was no revolutionary; antiquity credited him with unusual even-handedness. While to Sallust the writing of history was a means of carrying on a political career from the sidelines, Livy was a pure scholar, concerned with his place in the tradition of writers rather than statesmen. An imperial prince whose awkwardness seemed to deny him a public career, the historian encouraged in the writing of history: discovered behind a curtain after Caligula's murder, Livy's protégé became the emperor Claudius.

Cornelius Tacitus (ca. AD 56 – after 118) had a shining political career in darkening times. He was a creature of the Flavian emperors; as he baldly tells us, "my political distinction was begun by Vespasian, advanced by Titus, and much augmented by Domitian" (*Histories* 1.1).* But Vespasian was harsh, and Domitian a brooding despot: from his reign Tacitus emerged a ferocious censor of autocracy and its minions. Guilt, too, contributed, so thorough was his own complicity in Domitian's crimes: "our hands bore Helvidius to the dungeon . . . it was us Senecio drenched with his innocent blood" (*Agricola* 45). In AD 98, two years after Domitian's murder, Tacitus published his *Agricola*, a short biography of his father-in-law who had governed, and campaigned, in wild Britannia. In it Tacitus examined the compromises necessary to be a traditional Roman great man – glorious in war and politics – under Domitian's jealous and iniquitous monarchy. Soon after, he published his *Germania*, an ethnographical treatise on the Germans, but also a mirror to show the Romans the putrefaction of their morals: his depiction of the Germans would recall to any ancient reader the stark virtues of the free Romans of old. Several years later Tacitus published a *Dialogue on Orators*, another meditation on how men could be great under tyranny; now his conclusions were even more somber than in the *Agricola*. Around AD 109 Tacitus completed the first of his masterworks, a chronicle of his own times from the reign of Galba to the death of Domitian (AD 69–96); we, following sixteenth-century editors, call the surviving four-and-a-fraction books the *Histories*. The extant chapters treat the civil wars of AD 69–70, that "year of the four emperors" after the death of Nero in which the severe Galba was murdered and replaced by Otho, Vitellius ousted Otho, and finally the stern Vespasian supplanted Vitellius. Perhaps a decade later Tacitus put the finishing touches to his *Annals* (also a modern title). This laid bare the background of the *Histories*, from the death of Augustus in AD 14 to the death of Nero in 68. The first books cover the increasingly cruel reign of the saturnine Tiberius; those relating the lunatic sway of Caligula and the early days of Claudius are lost. Another surviving portion deals with the declining years of Claudius, the accession of Nero, and the latter's descent into madness; but Tacitus' account of Nero's death too has perished.

The psychology of tyrant and subject, of lick-spittle and rebel, is Tacitus' broadest theme; the *Histories* and *Annals* are the most compelling and damning portrait of autocratic government in the Western tradition. Although in the *Agricola* Tacitus praises his father-in-law for his tactful accommodation to the regime, and sneers at the futility of overt dissent (*Agricola* 42), his paragons in his mature works are the doomed intellectual opponents of the emperors, men like the historian Cremutius Cordus (*Annals* 4.34–5) and the

---

* With a small number of exceptions, all modern editions of a given work by a classical author use consistent book and section numbers and are therefore cited in that fashion rather than by page number. For translations of the authors discussed and cited in this chapter, see the discussion of accessible English editions that follows the chapter.

philosopher Thrasea Paetus, "virtue itself" (16.21), to whose defiance of Nero Tacitus consecrates the last surviving pages of the *Annals*. Men possessed of the courage in the face of tyranny that Tacitus himself lacked, they were Tacitus' heroes. And such men were rare: to Tacitus, as to Livy and Sallust, the lower orders were bad by nature; but to Tacitus the members of his own stratum rarely lived up to their potential to be good. Here was the verdict of a senior statesman, revolted not by failure but by the bitter taste of his success.

More than two centuries after the death of Tacitus, Ammianus Marcellinus (ca. AD 330–395) took up the story where Tacitus had left it in AD 96, but his only surviving books are those covering AD 353–378, from the reign of the bleak Constantius to the disastrous battle of Adrianople, the passing bell of the Roman empire in the West. Of the fourth century AD – the indian summer of the Roman world – Ammianus is our best informant. With Ammianus closes the high Latin tradition of the writing of Roman history.

Chance has also preserved a variety of minor Latin historical works, among them continuations of Julius Caesar by bluff anonymous authors, and potted histories of Rome by the Blimpish Florus (through the reign of Augustus) and the toadying Velleius Paterculus (to AD 29). A history of the world by the Augustan Pompeius Trogus, ranked high along with Sallust, Livy, and Tacitus by the ancients, survives to us only in Justin's sad summary. Related to history in goals and method was Suetonius' *Lives of the Caesars*, which draws upon the Greek tradition of lives, *bioi*, moralizing biographies of great men of the sort penned by Plutarch. From the time of Julius Caesar to the reign of Domitian Suetonius provides a gossipy supplement to Tacitus where Tacitus survives, and sometimes our major witness where he does not.

The curious *Historia Augusta* takes up soon after Suetonius leaves off, beginning with a life of the emperor Hadrian (AD 117–138) and profiling the acts and oddities of emperors and pretenders through the late third century. It purports to be the work of six different authors in the late third or early fourth centuries; in fact it is a colossal hoax, the work of a single author in the last years of the fourth century. For the second- and early third-century emperors the hoaxer did his homework, and the *Historia Augusta* is, *faute de mieux*, a major source for the history of the second century. But when his own information dried up, he invented, and invented too fictional sources to quote: from the life of Alexander Severus (AD 222–235) onward the author sweeps joyfully away on a flood-tide of lies.

The Greek Legacy

The Roman historical tradition grew out of the Greek: more than a century before Sallust, the acute Polybius (ca. 200 – after 118 BC) was already writing

Roman history to explain to his fellow Greeks the rise of Rome to world power. The Latin historical tradition clings like a vine to a thriving Greek tradition which in every succeeding generation continued to blossom with far more historical writing than the Latin, even on Roman subjects. Who wants to know Roman legends of their earliest days must apply not only to Livy, but to the Greek account by Dionysius of Halicarnassus; for the wars of the Republic one turns to Greek works by the second-century-AD Appian; for the politics of late Republic and empire the Greek *Roman History* of the biting early third-century senator Cassius Dio is indispensable; and for the period from the death of Marcus Aurelius to the reign of Gordian (AD 180–238) Dio's credulous Greek contemporary Herodian is a major source. Greek was the *lingua franca* of the Mediterranean, and so Josephus, a Jew, naturally chose Greek for his account of the rebellion of his people against Rome in AD 66–70.

The works of the major Latin historians are products of the profoundly Hellenized aristocratic culture of the late Republic and empire. To the Romans – as to the Greeks – history was a branch of *belles lettres*, and *belles lettres* occupied a great place in upper-class life. Roman aristocratic education by then was occupied almost exclusively with words, with the grinding and polishing of orators. Roman aristocratic society expected every one of its sons not only to be a competent public speaker, but preferably also to seek distinction with words in some other realm, as a poet, a philosopher, an antiquarian, or a historian. Even iron-bound marshals wrote poetry, even the cruel, ironic Sulla, even Julius Caesar, even the batrachian Tiberius. Literary accomplishment was a badge of rank, like the half-moon on the sandal that denoted a senator of Rome.

So to the Romans the writing of history was not, as to contemporary historians, a job; it was a form of cultivated amusement in an aristocratic milieu where it was unthinkable to work for a living, but where purposive amusement was nearly compulsory. History came under the rubric of *otium*, leisure, rather than *negotium*, tiresome public affairs. Like poetry or show rhetoric the writing of history was essayed by rich men to earn the applause of other rich men; in spirit the effort that produced such writing was far more like serving on the board of a great opera company than like grinding the sausage machine of modern academic history.

The Greek literary tradition that the Romans inherited was fiercely competitive, and this ethos found an easy reception among the competitive Roman aristocracy. "Emulation of glory" drove Roman historians (Justin, preface 1; cf. Pliny *Epistles* 5.8.1–2). The loss of the works of their many rivals leaves Sallust, Livy, and Tacitus as towers standing gaunt in their generations. But once other bastions stood, and all regarded one another with jealousy and suspicion. Publication was in most cases a matter of public recitation, either to a small party of élite friends, or to all comers; a bench shattered by the vast buttocks of an audience member could quite ruin the occasion, especially if the historian could not control his own hooting (Suetonius, *Claudius* 41.1).

In a world where the cultivation of words was so refined, the first concern of any Roman writing history – and often the only concern of any Roman reading it – was the excellence of its literary style, and the pleasure this gave. Sallust modelled his prose on the Greek historian Thucydides and upon the fierce second-century-BC politician and polymath Cato the Elder. "Cut-short epigrams, words coming before expected, and obscure brevity" is how Seneca described Sallust's writing (*Epistles* 114.17); we notice too his speed, his taste for archaic words, and for artfully awkward structures that arrest the reader's attention. Epigrams sparkle amidst the narrative's hard coal, Jugurtha describing Rome as "a city for sale and doomed betimes, if it can find a buyer" (*Jugurtha* 35.10).

Livy rejected this bristly tradition, preferring to follow Cicero's advice that history ought to be written in a style "flowing and fluent, coursing gently and evenly, avoiding the sharpness and stinging epigrams of the courtroom" (*de Oratore* 2.64). Livy imitated the silky prose of Cicero, itself rooted in Greek antecedents. "Milky abundance," Quintilian called Livy's style (*Institutes* 10.1.32). Rolling phrases balance each other to a nicety; loving attention is paid to the poetical rhythms of words. The effect is that of retiring in the senescence of the year to a quaint and superior sea-side inn, and drowsing in an over-stuffed red chair – a brandy to hand, and one's feet on a somnolent dog – to listen to the crash of the Atlantic, and muse upon other men's peril. Tacitus in turn rejected Livy's smooth (or soporific) style and went back to Sallust's, glorying in the rocks and flumes of the "rough water" tradition (Cicero, *Orator* 39). If Sallust flogged two words to do the work of three, Tacitus was Simon Legree over a single set of sweating syllables. His fiery epigrams are perhaps the highest achievements of Latin prose: of the Romans, "they make a desert, and they call it peace" (*Agricola* 30); of the chaos after the death of Nero, "those who had not an enemy in the world were destroyed by their friends" (*Histories* 1.2). To read Tacitus is to drink something tart and astringent and cleansing, an acrid vermifuge.

A Roman reader's expectations for the style of narrative passages were high; for the style of introductions and speeches, higher. Roman historians had inherited from the Greeks the custom of placing brief speeches in the mouths of historical personages, speeches which the reader understood were largely the historian's free composition. Subject and tenor might be appropriate to the historical mouthpiece, but more than a nod to the actual style of the historical speaker (some of whose real speeches might well survive) was unusual: the competitive goal was to do better than any previous historian who had written a similar speech.

The felicitous convention of composing speeches for his characters gave the historian a counterpoint to accompany the melody of his narrative. The plans of generals, and the motivations of actors – as the historian deduced them – might be expressed in speeches; paired orations might rehearse the arguments for and against a course of action. In speeches manifestos could be expounded and questions of political philosophy revolved without shattering the proscenium with a editorial intervention. In the hands of Tacitus, the master ironist, the high hopes and ideals speakers express reveal them as blind naïfs or hypocritical grotesques.

The historian at Rome composed his work – we should imagine – by accumulating the literary efforts of his predecessors, by listening to those accounts being read aloud by slaves (perhaps choosing one to follow most closely), and then composing mentally, and finally dictating to an amanuensis, his own, purportedly better, version. The relationship of the Roman historian to previous literary histories is that of *aemulatio*, imitation combined with one-upmanship, the same drive that links the Roman poet to his predecessors when he struggles to recast Homer's "like generations of leaves are men" (*Iliad* 6.146) to better the previous versions of Mimnermus, Simonides, Bacchylides, Apollonius, Virgil, and Horace. *Éclat* follows from doing the same thing better, not from doing something wholly new or different. Roman history, as a consequence, remained forever close to its Greek roots.

The cult of literary *aemulatio* – and the extremely stern rules of public deportment that bound a Roman aristocrat – ensured that the Roman historian did not make a regular practice of leaving his luxurious seat to seek documentary evidence, to consult dusty tablets in archives, to clamber up walls to examine bronze inscriptions of laws and treaties, or to ferret out volumes of old rituals. How much Roman historians used non-literary evidence is controversial, but the controversy swings between "hardly at all" and "far less than we would." When a historian does consult an original document he will often pat himself on the back until his elbow cracks; the impulse to seek such material often itself arises from the yearning to vaunt over a predecessor proved wrong.

So *aemulatio* served finally as a guardian of veracity. The rules of the game of history, as inherited from the Greeks, demanded that it be true as well as elegant. "This is the particular quality of history: who undertakes to write history must sacrifice to the goddess Truth alone" (Lucian, *How to Write History* 40; cf. Cicero, *de Oratore* 2.62). The Roman historian was vividly aware that his was a fiercely competitive tradition, that he was one of "a mob of writers," as Livy put it, "who always believe that they can introduce truer facts or overcome rough antiquity in their style" (preface 2–3). While he strove to establish his superiority by biting his predecessors he knew that his juniors had teeth just as sharp: Roman historians told the truth because truth was an object of rivalry. But did the shabby struggle for truth take second place to the colorful tournament of style? That was the leading subject of scholarly controversy in the 1980s and 1990s: the champions of style have, perhaps, the more vigorous arguments, but the champions of veracity are invisibly ballasted by the need of today's historians of Rome for material they can use, and so may win in the end.

History written by the Romans was the history of great men and events, of grand affairs, wars and politics. The blindness of Roman historians to the countless toilers who supported on their aching backs the high deeds of high men is surely related to their lofty social standing. But the reasons behind the Roman focus on grand narrative are also more deeply grounded in ancient habits of mind. Herodotus, founder of the historical tradition of which the Romans were the eventual heirs, announced that he undertook his investigations "that time might not draw the color from human achievements, and that those great and wondrous deeds, both of Greeks and barbarians, not become unrenowned" (1.1). When Livy (preface 3) speaks of the magnitude of Roman history, he is expressing the same idea: that great deeds and men have of themselves a moral right to be celebrated, recorded for posterity, and protected from human forgetfulness, all in proportion to their greatness (cf. Cicero, *de Oratore* 2.63; Pliny, *Epistles* 5.8.1). To Tacitus as well, great men have a right to a memorial in his work (*Annals* 16.16), but he characteristically exploits the convention, spreading suspicion and gloom with a dark parade of doomed grandees, each introduced at the moment of his death. The duty of the Roman historian, then, was not just to his audience and himself; it was also to his material. Ironically today's radical historian, seething with moral earnestness to give voice to the oppressed and the voiceless, feels a very similar ethical duty to his subject.

The Roman historian's sense of obligation to great events and persons constrains his choice of what to include in his work. Especially if he is writing a chronological survey, a mass of important men and doings foreign to his main story press themselves upon his conscience. Works of Roman history thus have a rag-bag, stop-and-go quality to them. Stories that stretch over some years in Livy, concerning perhaps the origins and conduct of a war, are suspended again and again that the author might list each new year's magistrates, prodigies, political trivia, and religious observances. In this the historian reflects the structure of his sources, so often annalistic lists of disconnected happenings. But the Roman historian's tolerance of this clumsy structure, like his ancient reader's, is rooted in the author's sense of duty to his material. Some stories have a right to be told, even if they ruin the telling of others.

The Roman Contribution

Without reference to its Greek origins, the Roman historical tradition is incomprehensible. But at Rome the stakes were higher. Somewhere the Romans had misplaced their native body of divine myths and legends of superhuman heroes

– the material that became epic and tragedy among the Greeks. When the Romans noticed the lack of that important suitcase, they desperately made up the loss by stealing Greek luggage, by adopting Greek theology, and by striving to insinuate themselves (with ardent Greek encouragement) into the Greek heroic tradition. Rome, it conveniently developed, had been founded by a refugee from Troy. With no mythic past of their own, the Romans found that their historical past was all the past they had. And so their historical past was obliged to perform the functions of norm-setting and education for which the Greeks relied upon Homer and their heroic legends.

By Sallust's day, this solemn office of Roman history was attended by a sense of foreboding alarm. The Republic of the Romans had been visibly cracking for nearly a century: there had been tyrants and demagogues, proscriptions, seditions, and civil wars. No Roman by then could think his world unshaken. To the intellectual classes the questions of the age were, How did we come to this pass? and, What is to be done? Progressive schemes, abstract formulations, and economic theorizing were alike foreign to the Roman mind. If things were bad, it was because men were wicked. So the questions Romans asked themselves were, How did we become so evil? and, How can men be made virtuous again? Those questions, urgent from a fear of general catastrophe, are the questions that drive the classical Latin historical tradition. None of the historians knew that Rome would survive them by centuries, or that the epoch of their tottering fatherland's greatest power was yet to come. They felt the rush of air in a falling world; the abyss was real to them; vertigo drove their pens.

Wondering why men were bad or good, a Greek – like Polybius – might look first to the constitution that had formed them. To the Roman mind men molded states, rather than states men. Human character was shaped – or mis-shaped – by the presence of human examples of good or bad conduct. Such *exempla* were not inert, not just bashfully present to be imitated; they exerted, rather, a gravitational force on those around them. Good examples would, willy-nilly, make men good. A very few bad examples could be useful as a warning, if men were strictly warned against them; but too many bad examples would in themselves corrupt men, and so the body politic.

Like most pre-modern peoples, the Romans did not have a sense that their distant past was different in kind from the present. They did not even draw the firm black line that many Greeks did between the historical past and the heroic age of Homer and tragedy, when gods walked the earth and the laws of nature were apt to be suspended. The extreme past of the Romans might be obscure and reported only by unreliable legend, but the men who had lived then were not seen as alien in purposes and motives, merely as broadly better than the men of the present. The past, then, could be ransacked for *exempla* in the service of the present. The search for powerful *exempla*, magnets to draw contemporaries to good behavior and to repel bad, is the single greatest driver of the Latin historical tradition.

Sallust's analysis of the decline of Roman morals in the *Catiline* (5.9–13.5) was celebrated in antiquity; St. Augustine was to adopt it wholesale in the *City of God* (1.30). Alluding to Sallust's own stained past Macrobius twitted him as "the most profound rebuker of *other men's* luxury." Sallust's Romans, once an austere, clean-living folk, avid only for glory, just and harmonious at home, brave in the field, were corrupted over time by the twin contagions of avarice and ambition. Pivotal events in this decline, according to Sallust, were the destruction of Carthage (146 BC; cf. *Jugurtha* 41.2–3), fear of which had kept the Romans pure, and Sulla's reign: Sulla's seizure of power (82 BC) bade all men to pillage, and his eastern campaign rotted in luxury the spirit of the army. By Sallust's day the Republic, once "the fairest and best" of states, had become the "worst and most criminal" (*Catiline* 5.9), its folk "the basest of men" (12.5).

In this scheme of moral decline Sallust chose to write about a pair of incidents in the recent past when morals were sinking but not – as in Sallust's own day – wholly foundered. In that middle time Rome continued to breed a few avatars of true Roman virtue, "new men" like Marius. In Sallust's own time "even the new men, who of old were accustomed to out-do the nobility by their excellence, seek commands and offices by guile and banditry rather than upright practices" (*Jugurtha* 4.7). The prevailing vices were already then powerful corruptors: the patrician Catiline is wicked by nature but made worse by the corruption of the times (*Catiline* 5.8); the virtuous young Jugurtha (a Numidian, but symbolizing Roman youth), making his way by his own merits, is demoralized by Roman company (*Jugurtha* 8.1–2). But then such corruption was not inevitable. Now, says Sallust, so universal and powerful are the examples of wickedness that they defeat all resistance, and make nearly all men bad (*Catiline* 53.5).

But not quite all. "In my own memory," Sallust writes, "there have been two men of enormous excellence, although of different character: Marcus Cato and Gaius Caesar" (*Catiline* 53.6). Cato the Younger and Julius Caesar appear as players in the *Catiline*, arguing over the fate of the conspirators, the one urging severity (52), the other mercy (51). But Sallust presents Cato and Caesar not only as paladins of the falling past, but as rare heroes in the fallen present: when he wrote they were less than a decade dead. Sallust's famous juxtaposition of their characters, of the equal glory they derived from their different excellences, is, in fact, a prescription for the regeneration of the Republic, revealing the mix of moral qualities required:

> Caesar was deemed great because of the favors he did and his generosity, Cato because of the moral stringency of his life. The former became brilliant through his kindness and clemency; his austerity gave the other dignity. Caesar gained glory by giving, assisting, and pardoning, Cato by never giving a bribe. The one was a refuge for the wretched, the other a bane to the wicked. The one was praised for his adaptability, the other for his firmness. (*Catiline* 54.2–3)

So despite Sallust's black pessimism, there is still hope. Even amidst moral free-fall good men are still born to Rome, and she is not, as he fears, "a mother exhausted by childbearing" (*Catiline* 53.5). Yes, Caesar and Cato are only two men, and mortal enemies, the reader is expected to know. But after long consideration Sallust had concluded that all the excellence of old Rome depended on "the exceptional virtue of a few citizens" (53.4). The moral decline of Rome is not irreversible by nature, or long continuance, or degree. A handful of good men might serve as exemplars to reform the rest. Certainly there are enough striking examples of bad behavior to avoid: painting those in heavy outline is a large part of Sallust's purpose.

It is in Livy, beginning his work in the twenties BC, after another round of civil war, that we meet with the possibility that the moral decline of Rome cannot be reversed. In the preface to his work he laments how "with the gradual decline of discipline, morals slid, and then more and more collapsed, and finally began to plunge, which has brought us to our present pass when we can endure neither our vices nor their cures" (preface 9). To Livy the contemplation of the past and its virtues provides as much a refuge from, as a medicine for, the vices of the present (5). The loss of the books of the history dealing with the years after 167 BC makes it impossible to trace in detail Livy's aetiology of Roman moral decline: he seems to have blamed the introduction of luxury on the return of Manlius Vulso's army from the East in 187 BC (39.6.7–9) rather than on Sulla's campaign a century later, but evidently he concords with Sallust in looking to imported goods and vices as a cause of moral slippage.

Yet despite his gloom Livy has a profound faith in the power of historical examples to uplift morals and the state:

> what is especially health-giving and fruitful about the knowledge of history is that you behold evidences of every kind of example set forth on a splendid monument; from this you can choose what to imitate, for yourself and for your state; from this you can choose what to avoid, wicked results having wicked beginnings. (preface 10)

The sweet well of historical examples, in Livy's view, has the power to heal men and the state in proportion to its depth and purity. And Rome's is uniquely deep and clean, for "no state was ever greater nor more scrupulous in religion, nor richer in good examples; never was there a state into which avarice and luxury came later, nor where poverty and frugality were held as much in honor" (11). The task Livy sets himself is to communicate these *exempla*, both good and bad, and so he does, book after book. Beginning his account in an uncorrupt age allows him many more examples of good conduct than Sallust. If his reader models himself on the good *exempla*, and shuns the bad, he will himself become good, and with more good men the state may, perhaps, recover.

The search for *exempla* shaped the way that Livy and the authors he drew upon wrote about Rome's distant past. By Livy's day the Romans had a very long history, and had very little reliable information about its first four hundred and fifty years. To satisfy the appetite for early *exempla*, stories were elaborated from a tiny kernel of fact, or worked up from legend, or simply invented. A yearning to use the past to nurse the present, combined with a deficient sense of the differentness of former days, tended to create a vision of early times that was a mirror of the present. When Rome's historians wrote about Rome's first centuries, contemporary need created a great deal of improving fiction, and the pressing issues of the late Republic – political violence, the factional politics of optimate versus *popularis* – were projected back into the Republic's very first days. Livy inherited, continued, and elaborated, a late Republican tradition about Rome's early history that was often more useful than true.

If in Livy's early books the search for *exempla* attracted the author to hallowed fiction, the quest for *exempla* also structured Livy's treatment of better attested times. The survival of many of the books of the Greek Polybius, upon whom Livy often drew, makes it possible to witness the process of Livy's hewing *exempla* from less than ideal historical stone. Both Polybius and Livy, for example, describe a peace conference in November of 198 BC between King Philip V of Macedon and the Roman general Flamininus and his Greek allies; this was during the Second Macedonian War, before the battle of Cynoscephalae (197 BC) when the Romans broke the power of Macedon. King Philip V was a cynic and a wit, "more satirical by nature than became a king," as Livy frowns (32.34.3). Since Philip's cruel jokes confirm the wickedness of an enemy of Rome, they make their way faithfully from Polybius' account into Livy's. To an observation by an envoy with poor eyesight, the king rejoined "even a blind man can see that" (Polyb. 18.4.4 = Livy 32.34.3). But Polybius alone reports Flamininus' chortling enjoyment of Philip's witticisms (Polyb. 18.6.1, 5, 18.7.5), and a sally of the Roman's own. Philip wanted the Greek terms in writing: he had, he complained, no one to consult. Flamininus retorted that this was hardly surprising, since he'd killed all his friends. The king smiled sardonically; he had met his match (Polyb. 18.7.6). Livy does not describe Flamininus' reactions. Exchanging droll abuse with an enemy of Rome is wholly unsuitable behavior for an exemplary Roman marshal – a mold that Flamininus' opportunism and dishonesty had already strained – and so Livy airbrushes it away. What is "not necessary for the *exemplum*" (Justin, preface 4) is discarded, and with it goes Polybius' exquisite portrayal of the growth of mutual respect between two world-weary statesmen.

To Tacitus, writing under emperors a century later, there is no question of healing the Republic. His puzzle is how an individual can live a virtuous life beneath imperial tyranny, ruled and surrounded by monsters, of how "great men can exist even under bad princes" (*Agricola* 42). Writing of the empire Tacitus reverses the logic of Sallust and Livy: he agrees with Sallust and Livy that under the Republic moral decline created political decay (cf. *Histories* 2.38; *Annals* 3.26–28), but when that decay culminated in the imperial regime, and "there was nothing left of the old and honest ways" (*Annals* 1.4), it was then the logic of that regime that kept men bad – the emperor, his minions, and subjects alike. The corruption of the regime destroys even private ethics. The reign of emperors is the reign of envy: in the face of the autocrat's suspicion of good and great men, those around him must be wicked or dead.

Tacitus' belief that politics form morals under the empire – rather than the other way round – would seem to call for a political program. But to Tacitus a program would be futile: morals are too thoroughly depraved for political reform to rescue. The imperial regime is merely the way the inescapable hell of moral collapse is organized; it is still hell under any constitution. Sometimes it seems that the only freedom left is to die well, and Tacitus is fascinated by how his characters die. In such a world all that remains is hope for better emperors, like Nerva and Trajan under whom Tacitus wrote (*Agricola* 3; *Histories* 1.1). There is hope also – as in Sallust – that there may occasionally arise a man of "great and noble virtue" who "conquers and overcomes the vices common to states great and small, envy and misprision of rectitude" (*Agricola* 1). The historian plays a role. Like Sallust and Livy, he offers *exempla* of good and bad behavior (*Histories* 1.2–3; *Annals* 4.33). But Tacitus does more. "The special duty of history" is not only to ensure that "virtues are not passed over in silence" but to "subject vicious words and deeds to the terror of the infamy of posterity" (*Annals* 3.65). Tacitus' hope is that his work will make bad men in the future think twice of their infamies, lest they too conjure up a Tacitus to scourge them.

The force of Tacitus' moral terrorism upon the miscreants of later days depends on the persuasiveness of his depiction of evil, of "savage commands, accusations without cease, false friendships, the destruction of innocents" (*Annals* 4.33). Tacitus is not much given to lying, but ingenious rhetorical devices are used to apply black paint. When Tiberius succeeds to the purple the reader is immediately prejudiced by being told of "the first crime of the new reign" (*Annals* 1.6). Anonymous speeches purporting to represent public opinion or gossip breed suspicion (e.g. 1.9–10, 1.46). Most effectively, the reader is continually offered a seemingly free choice between two interpretations of events, one innocent and one malign: "Untimely fate – or the craft of their stepmother Livia – cut off Lucius and Gaius Caesar" (1.3). Tacitus reflects the impossibility of certainty about political events beneath a secretive autocracy, but feigned perplexity serves also as a tool of innuendo.

The moral tenor of Roman thinking, manifested in the search for *exempla* and Tacitus' ambition to deter future evil, accounts for the Roman historians' turning away from some of the aims and mechanics of their Greek teachers. Comparison to Polybius is illuminating. Polybius shares with Herodotus, and the Romans, a sense of duty to the magnitude of his material (1.1.5, 1.2.1–7). But to Polybius, as to Thucydides, history is also a practical guide to affairs, a teacher of pragmatic techniques in politics and war, a handbook of amoral effectiveness (1.1.2). This function of history, to make men skillful as well as good, is not prominent in the Latin tradition. To stress the strictly practical value of history was to sunder competence from principle in a way that made Romans uncomfortable. Their concept of excellence, of *virtus*, was supposed to comprehend both. A bad man but effective, like Sallust's Catiline or Tacitus' Sejanus, demanded to be presented as an *exemplum* of evil.

Like his Greek predecessors, Polybius had a self-conscious intellectual interest in the working of historical causation (3.6–7). Thucydides' famous formulation of the origins of the Peloponnesian War – "the real cause I consider to be the one which was formally most kept out of sight; the growth of the power of Athens, and the alarm this inspired in Lacedaemon, made war inevitable" (1.23.6) – reveals a subtle understanding of cause and pretext, of the independent volition of groups, and of the operation of impersonal forces. Polybius' own contribution to this thinking was an emphasis on the role of chance in human affairs. Greek notions of historical causation often echo in Latin authors, but the Roman passion for harvesting *exempla* ensures that the Romans tend to rely on a more limited set of causes than the Greeks. They prefer personal to impersonal causes: things happen because men make them happen; the actions of men, in turn, grow out of their characters more than their circumstances. In Sallust's Catiline the modern reader sees a man embittered by his inability to reach the goals imposed upon him by his family and his class. But Sallust sees an "evil and depraved nature" made worse by the wickedness of the times (*Catiline* 5.1–8).

Finally, like other Greeks before him Polybius was vitally interested in how we know what we know about the past, in the process of deciding which reports to credit and which not (e.g. 3.9). Livy echoes Herodotus and Thucydides in drawing a line across time and expressing skepticism about the reliability of information from beyond that line, embodied in poetry and myth (preface 6–8): his caution was amply justified; even more caution would have been. But Latin history's moral purpose reduced – never eliminated – anxiety about method. If an *exemplum* was strictly pointed, it was less important that it be strictly true.

Conclusion

The contemporary practice of history carries on an unbroken tradition extending back through the Romans to the Greeks. Since the fall of Rome, that tradition has been driven by two engines, historians looking to their coevals – or imitating or rebelling from their teachers – and historians reaching back over the centuries to classical models, especially – since Latin authors were long more accessible than Greek – to the historians of ancient Rome.

In the Middle Ages Sallust was especially revered. A school text – manuscripts come down with "very fine" jotted in their margins by medieval pedagogues – Sallust was armored against neglect by the endorsement of St. Augustine. Many a chronicler shows the imprint of Sallust, and mostly for good. But respect could over-ripen into idolatry, and long passages might simply be cribbed from the master. The fourteenth century rediscovered Livy, the fifteenth Tacitus. Both were recruited into politics, Livy inspiring republicans like Machiavelli and Tacitus valued first as a counselor of guile to princes and of stoic submission or cunning flattery to subjects. Livy and Tacitus struggled long for primacy as stimulus and model for historians; first Livy had the better of it, but the late sixteenth century saw Tacitus finally triumphant amidst the pan-European intellectual vogue of Tacitism. Over time the eye shifted from Tacitus as counselor of tyrants to Tacitus as their foe: so Tacitus became the darling of eighteenth-century republicans, and under that mask found his way over the Atlantic. "The first writer in the world without a single exception," Thomas Jefferson called Tacitus, for he spoke to men rebelling against tyranny and longing for a just republic.

The decline of classical education in the twentieth century has deprived contemporary historians of the familiarity with the Romans that previous generations took for granted. Now one of Clio's eyes is blinded. Now many historians' sense of the tradition in which they work – oddly, for students of the past – extends no further back than the writings of those who taught them. Today to know the Romans a conscious effort is required. And contemporary conditions and fashions direct effort elsewhere. The Romans do not appeal to the main strains of today's historical thinking.

The passionate Romans are an embarrassment to contemporary historians who champion dispassion: history written to make men better makes them cringe; history written to prop up a falling world makes them blush. They find the Roman caress of literary style frivolous or mendacious; they find the Roman scowl of moral censure boring. The example of virtue that attracted the Romans repels them; the historian's quest for such examples revolts them.

More cruelly, the Romans are ignored by their legitimate children. For if the Greeks are the progenitors of the ideals of impartial history, the *engagé* tradition descends from the Romans. But today's radical historians fancy that they – or their teachers – were the first to tear down old heroes and set up new, the first to right old wrongs, the first to beat from uncried good the rats of time. They are heirs-at-law to a proud and ancient house – passed down from Rome over two millennia – but they blush to own a patrician patrimony: Roman history written to champion the few against the many makes them spit.

Past days found the Roman historians congenial, because past ages found them necessary. It was to Tacitus that men returned, those men who had to understand Hitler and Stalin to fight them. But we do not face such foes: ours is a complacent and a voluptuary age; like Elagabalus we riot in rose petals. Happy are the men who have no need of Tacitus. Yet it is not the Romans who change, only those who read them. The bad times will come again, no doubt, and men will turn again to the historians of Rome. With an ancient cold patience they wait long their call: when called they will come, like Drake to his drum, or Arthur, who sleeps beneath Camelot.

ACCESSIBLE ENGLISH EDITIONS OF LATIN HISTORIANS

In its *Penguin Classics* series Viking Penguin publishes economical paperback English translations of the surviving books of Livy (*The Early History of Rome* [books 1–5], trans. A. de Sélincourt; *Rome and Italy* [books 6–10], trans. B. Radice; *The War with Hannibal* [books 21–30], trans. A. de Sélincourt; and *Rome and the Mediterranean* [books 31–45], trans. H. Bettenson); Sallust (*The Jugurthine War and The Conspiracy of Catiline*, trans. S. A. Handford); Tacitus (*The Agricola and Germania*, trans. H. Mattingly; *The Annals of Imperial Rome*, trans. M. Grant; and *The Histories*, trans. K. Wellesley); and Ammianus Marcellinus (*The Later Roman Empire*, trans. A. Wallace-Hadrill).

The chief paperback competition to the *Penguin Classics* is the growing Oxford University Press *Oxford World Classics* series which at the time of writing offers translations of parts of Livy (*The Rise of Rome* [Books 1–5], trans. T. J. Luce; and *The Dawn of the Roman Empire* [Books 31–40], trans. J. C. Yardley) and Tacitus (*Agricola and Germania*, trans. A. Birley; and *The Histories*, trans. W. H. Fyfe).

The works of all the Latin historians, major and minor, and writers in related genres, along with those of the other classical authors discussed or cited in this chapter, are also available in facing Latin (or Greek) and English hardback editions from the comprehensive Loeb Classical Library (Harvard University Press and Heinemann).

REFERENCES AND FURTHER READING

Brunt, P. A., "Ciecero and Historiography," in *Philias charin: Miscellanea di studi classici in onore di Eugenio Manni*, vol. 1 (Rome, 1980) pp. 311–40; reprinted in id., *Studies in Greek History and Thought* (Oxford, 1993) pp. 181–209.

Dorey, T. A. (ed.), *Latin Historians* (New York, 1966).

Forneara, C. W., *The Nature of History in Ancient Greece and Rome* (Berkeley and Los Angeles, 1983).

Kraus, C. S. and A. J. Woodman, *Latin Historians* (*Greece and Rome* New Surveys in the Classics 27; Oxford, 1997).

Laistner, M. L. W., *The Greater Roman Historians* (Berkeley and Los Angeles, 1947).

Luce, T. J., "Tacitus on 'History's Highest Function': *praecipuum munus annalium* (Ann. 3.65)," *Aufstieg und Niedergang der römischen Welt* 2.33.4 (1991) pp. 2904–27.

Marincola, J., *Authority and Tradition in Ancient Historiography* (Cambridge, 1997).

Mellor, R., *The Roman Historians* (London, 1999).

Wiseman, T. P., *Clio's Cosmetics* (Leicester, 1979).

——, "Practice and Theory in Roman Historiography," in *History* 66 (1981) pp. 375–93; reprinted in id., *Roman Studies: Literary and Historical* (Liverpool, 1987) pp. 244–62.

Woodman, A. J. *Rhetoric in Classical Historiography* (London, 1988).

Chapter Four

Historical Thought in Medieval Europe

Gabrielle M. Spiegel

Historical writing in the Middle Ages defies easy definition. It was largely practiced by authors with little or no training and driven by concerns very far from the modern preoccupation with an accurate recovery of the past "as it really happened." The study of medieval historiography thus long suffered at the hands of modern scholars, who tended to devote their efforts to identifying what could be accepted as historically "true" in medieval accounts of the past and to expurgating everything that could not. Indeed, the litany of errors of which the practice of historiography in the Middle Ages stands accused offers little encouragement to scholars drawn to its study: its philosophical alliance with theology, which evacuated from history its human purpose and meaning; its literary alliance with rhetoric, which made it inimical to the pursuit of truth; its exemplarist and stereotypical use of historical events and persons for moral teaching, denying them what a modern historian would consider their historicity, their relationship to a historical context; its concern with experience, custom, and repetition, rather than reason, individuality, and process; even its absence from the curriculum of medieval pedagogy, which meant, as V. H. Galbraith once remarked, that the serious study of history in the Middle Ages was "nobody's business." To the above failings one normally adds its low level of literary achievement, approaching at times narrative unintelligibility; weak notion of historical evidence; lack of sense of anachronism; propagandistic intentions; substitution of symbolic interpretation for causal analysis; and vulnerability to invasion by fiction, forgery, myth, legend and miracles. In short, medieval historiography, from a modern perspective, is inauthentic, unscientific, unreliable, ahistorical, occasionally irrational, often illiterate, and wholly unprofessional.

A short essay on historical thought and writing in Medieval Europe cannot possibly hope entirely to dispel this host of criticisms. The problem is complicated by the extreme diversity of historiographical forms and practices in the Middle Ages, ranging from universal chronicles to highly local monastic histories, from simple annalistic entries to works informed by complex theological schemes, all for the most part initially written in Latin but, by the High Middle Ages, increasingly employing a wide variety of vernacular languages, themselves influenced by emerging national literatures. In this chapter I would like to offer some general observations on the way in which the medieval historian approached his task and his text and, as a consequence, on how we might profitably consider medieval histories as both literary forms dedicated to encoding a body of "facts" deemed important to various segments of medieval society, and as purveyors of the medieval sense of the past. One of the interesting characteristics of the writing of history in the Middle Ages is its combination of a widely shared set of assumptions about the nature of historical reality and "truth," and the absence of any set protocol for its writing, leading to the extreme diversity of forms noted above. I will conclude with a brief overview of its evolution from the period of late antiquity through the High Middle Ages.

Characteristics of Medieval Historical Thought

The diverse nature of medieval thought about history is reflected in the terms used to designate works that treated the past. Although in general history was defined as the pursuit of "true things about the past," there was no uniform terminology used to describe it. Medieval writers generally borrowed their definitions of history from classical Roman rhetoricians such as Cicero and Quintilian, for whom the past functioned as a school of moral instruction, a storehouse of examples of good and evil conduct that illuminated principles of behavior and taught men how to live. Quoting Cicero's famous definition of history as " the witness of the past, the light shed on truth, the life-giving force to memory, the guide to life" (*De oratore*, II, IX, 36), they considered history to be a form of moral exhortation. This exemplarist function of history linked it to rhetoric, for it was the orator's duty to guide the historian's expression in order to achieve moral persuasiveness. No matter how attenuated the literary form of the medieval chronicle, it takes as its point of departure the essentially rhetorical conception of history as a means to persuade men to imitate good and avoid evil. The basic purpose of historical writing, then, is edification; at least in theory it is more concerned with the propagation of moral idealism than with a concrete analysis of reality. By their very adherence to the exemplar theory of history, medieval historians expressed the belief that history had a moral and political utility beyond mere description of the deeds of the past.

It is probably fair to say, however, that the medieval historian honored rhetorical rules of composition more in the breach than in practice. The typical complaint of rude speech and lack of literary learning with which each writer began his work betrayed not only the inculcated habit of monastic humility (and until the twelfth century, those who wrote history were largely monks), but also a true sense of literary limitations that could not be overcome. Although such complaints were themselves part of rhetorical convention, the poignant warning with which the monastic historian Rigord prefaces his *Short Chronicle of the Kings of France* has the ring of truth: "Do not expect in my small narrative the eloquence of Tully [that is, Cicero], since I will have done well if, from the confusion of facts, an orderly arrangement emerges which will escape the bite of censure."[1]

This humble sense of literary accomplishment was accompanied by modest terminology to describe the historian. As Bernard Guenée has demonstrated, medieval authors employed a wide variety of terms to designate their activity as historians. Through much of the early Middle Ages, the nomenclature used was *chronicus* or *historicus*, titles which by the thirteenth century had evolved into *chronographus* and *historiographus*, though the former set, in both eras, was the more common, expressing the medieval belief that the historian was distinguished as a writer concerned with the *series temporum*, the unfolding of events in time. In fact, the medieval historian rarely thought of himself as an author at all and more frequently described his activity as *compilare, colligere, excerpere, breviare*, or *redigere* – compiling, gathering, excerpting, abbreviating, or redacting – rather than as composing. *Scriptores* ("writers") was a designation reserved for copyists and calligraphers, while *auctores* ("authors") generally meant those ancient or authoritative Christian writers whose texts were being "borrowed" as the basis of the historian's own compilation.

The task of history, as well, directed itself to a less ambitious goal than that articulated by Cicero, and, in the words of the sixth-century Spanish bishop, Isidore of Seville, sought simply to produce a *narratio rei gestae*, a narrative of "things done." To be sure, Isidore added that the historian's narrative must be achieved *sine mendacio proferuntur* – without lying – but what the historian aimed at was not so much "truth" in a philosophical or epistemological sense, as an account of "true things," those *res gestae* known to the historian either through experience or antecedent texts. Not surprisingly, therefore, the classical distinction between "history", "chronicle", "annals" and the like tended to yield to a new genre of history that arose in the Carolingian period called the *gesta*, an account of "deeds" made memorable by virtue of those who performed them, whether kings, bishops, saints, or sinners, rather than by their chronological scope or intrinsic importance. By the High Middle Ages, "chronicle" and "deeds" were the terms most frequently used to indicate historical texts. Accompanying this terminological reduction was a tendency to ignore generic distinctions that had been important to the ancients and had held on through the early Middle Ages. In fact, medieval Europe was able to sustain an enormous variety of historiographical genres, including universal chronicles, monastic histories, biographies, hagiographies, imperial, royal and dynastic chronicles, as well as aristocratic, urban and scholastic texts, but it cared little for the formal distinctions that might be thought important to their definition. Genre as such mattered little to medieval writers of history.

If medieval historians borrowed heavily from the rhetorical traditions of Romans like Cicero to articulate the goals of their work, these formulae were there to establish a sense of continuity in historiographical practice. But their underlying anxiety about such continuity stemmed from the fact that beginning with the Christian era, there was a fundamental transformation in the ways that people viewed the nature of time, historical reality, and Creation itself.

To the Greeks and the Romans, history was an operation against time, an attempt to save human deeds from the futility of oblivion. Time was seen as cyclical, an order embodied in Nature to which men must submit the rhythm of their lives. To defeat time and gain the permanence of the natural universe would mean to enter into the everlasting, to insert the mortal into the realm of cosmic immortality. For Christians, on the other hand, time is linear, beginning with Creation and closing with Christ's Second Coming and the day of Last Judgement, and bifurcated in the middle by the central event in the Christian scheme of the world, the Incarnation – the appearance of Christ – which gives meaning to the time which preceded and the time which succeeds His Coming. Man is no longer trapped in the treadmill of a meaningless revolution of events, but locates himself within the human economy of salvation represented by the progress of human history.

The implications of this new view of time were enormous and critical for a Christian understanding of history. In developing these implications, early churchmen drew upon the Jewish heritage, with its sense of the Jews as the elect of God, a Chosen People, selected by God to fulfill His work on Earth, to enact a role in history and to give evidence to His being as witnesses to the power of God on Earth. Thus behind the notion of the "elect Nation" is the belief that God has not given up on His creation; that despite the Fall and its manifold consequences, God has not forsaken the world and man, but chooses still to work out the providence of His people. Thus part of the prophetic insight of Judaism is a belief in the presence of God in history, imparting to the course of events a providential scheme and significance. This in turn means that the natural order is not a finished one, not completed and autonomous, but one through which God still works and into which He intervenes with both miracles and punishments. History, therefore, testifies to the enduring concern of God with His creation. It is through God's operation within history – within time itself – that His intentions for man are realized. In this way, Christianity envisions the admixture of the natural and the supernatural in history, which in turn becomes the stage upon which the drama of mankind is played out, for it was only by acting within history Himself – as the Incarnate Christ – that God gave man the means for personal salvation.

A paradoxical result of this new understanding of history as the stage upon which God acts was that it became both immeasurably more, and at the same time immeasurably less, important than it had been for the ancients. More important, because history was a mirror through which to read God's intentions. As the twelfth-century theologian John of Salisbury put it, the purpose of writing history for Christians was to show how "the invisible things of God may be clearly seen by the things that are done."[2] But also less important, for ultimately what mattered was not what "was done" – what really happened – but what could be learned about God from it. No one better expressed the consequences of the Christian tendency to substitute symbolic interpretation for close analysis of events than Marc Bloch when he wrote that "in the eyes of all who were capable of reflection, the material world was scarcely more than a mask, behind which took place all the really important things; it seemed . . . also a language, intended to express by signs a more profound reality. Since a tissue of appearances can offer but little interest in itself, the result of this view was that observation was generally neglected in favor of interpretation."[3]

Another result of the providential scheme underlying the Christian view of time was that history was, by implication, universal, since God reigned over the world at large and offered redemption to all of mankind. Early Christian historians such as Eusebius devised a method, known as canon tables, for integrating the multiple systems of reckoning time used by ancient peoples, which worked by listing in parallel columns the rulers, dynasties and deeds of the Assyrians, Sicyonians, Egyptians as well as Romans, Christians, and Jews. Eusebius's *Chronicle*, in which the canon tables appeared, was translated into Latin in the fourth century by St. Jerome. In the view of Walter Goffart, the *Chronicle* of Eusebius-Jerome stands as "the common ancestor of Latin chronicles."[4] By the eighth century, Bede had created a universal system of dating by counting time before and after Christ (BC and AD), a system still in use, reaffirming the centrality of the Incarnation to the Christian idea of history. Similarly, Eusebius's *Ecclesiastical History* (ca. 325) demonstrated the confluence of Roman and Christian history after Constantine's conversion, while reformulating the basic understanding of events, which now centered on the sacred.

A historical work of comparable universal scope, though rather different philosophical orientation, was written in the fifth century by St. Augustine, who in *The City of God* (AD 413–426) sought to demonstrate the inevitable mixing of the sacred and profane in human history as a legacy of Original Sin. As a result of the Fall of Adam and Eve, as a consequence of and a punishment for their "original sin" of rebellion against God, human life in this world became penal. Mortality, death, misery, suffering, crimes, the conflict among men – all those evils which had no place in human nature as it was created – are the characteristics of fallen man. However, even after the Fall, God did not entirely abandon His creature man. He sent Christ to redeem man and bestowed upon a select few the ability to receive the gift of grace. By the operation of unmerited grace, those predestined to salvation are released from the penalties inflicted upon the mass of fallen mankind and are promised a life of eternal blessedness with God after the Last Judgment, making up the invisible city of God, while those destined for damnation constitute the city of man. But before the end of time, the history of the two cities are intermixed. To Augustine, history is not a cycle of destruction and recreation, but a form of restoration through which man regains the grace he lost in the Fall. Man's individual destiny is not, as with the ancients, bound up with the natural course of history itself, but with the operation of Grace within the natural, created order.

The reason for studying history is, for Augustine as well, to discern God's hidden purposes for man. Along with Orosius's *Seven Books against the Pagans*, composed as a continuation to Augustine's *City of God*, and other patristic works, Augustine was to influence the fundamental outlook of Christian historiography down to the twelfth century, strengthening its symbolic thrust while providing a model for integrating the histories of various peoples into a single, comprehensive narrative of universal history. At the same time, the *City of God* enhanced the Christian sensitivity to the disparity between religious ideals and human sinfulness and mutability, paving the way for the fusion of hagiography – the biography of saints' lives – and historiography, a combination found frequently in early medieval historians like Bede and Gregory of Tours.

Once history became universal, a means of periodizing it beyond the central division supplied by the Incarnation became necessary. Medieval historians tended to draw upon the Bible for chronological schemes, using, for example, the dreams and prophecies found in the Old Testament Book of Daniel concerning the succession of World Empires or that of the six ages of the world, based on the days of Creation in Genesis in one version, or the six periods between the opening of the first and the seventh seal mentioned in the Book of Revelation (5:1). A tripartite scheme, favored because of its numerological similarity to the Trinity, could be found in the Babylonian Talmud. Referred to as the *vaticinium Eliae* (the prophecy of Elijah), it envisaged three main periods of world history: one before the law (the giving of the Torah), under the law, and following the law (the period of the Messiah). Adapted to Christianity, in which the central period was that of Christ's advent, this tripartite or trinitarian scheme was taken up in the twelfth century by Joachim of Fiore, who used it to predict the end of the world in the mid-thirteenth century. For the most part, however, such schemes generated by universal history were set aside when history became national rather than universal, and remained in the province of philosophical and mystical speculations on history, rather than of chronicles.

Although biblical schemes of periodization failed to capture the medieval historian's imagination, the influence of biblical modes of thought on medieval historiography was nonetheless profound, in particular by creating a way of establishing connections between events which derived from the application of biblical typological exegesis to secular history. The typological interpretation of the Bible by medieval exegetes sought to overcome the separation of the two Testaments by establishing a relationship of "fulfillment" between events in the Old Testament and those in the New. In typological or what Erich Auerbach calls "figural" interpretation,[5] the earlier event, analogous to the later, becomes a foreshadowing, a "type" of it. As Richardson has explained:

> The typological interpretation of the Bible differs from the allegorical in that it detects a real and necessary correspondence in the structure and meaning of the original or "typical" event or complex of events to the new application or fulfillment of it. Accordingly, the idea of the fulfillment of Scriptures will mean . . . the fulfillment of history, the making explicit of what was implicit in the pattern of earlier historical events by the movements of the later events, the deepening of the meaning of history itself as this meaning is revealed to the prophetic insight.[6]

By means of typological interpretation, the significance of the past is reaffirmed for the present; the old becomes a prophecy of the new and its predeterminant in the sense that its very existence determines the shape and interpretation of what comes later. In this way, the past becomes an explanatory principle, a way of ordering and making intelligible a relationship between events separated by vast distances of time.

It seems obvious how monastic chroniclers, trained on the daily reading of the Bible, could easily have transferred this way of reading Scripture to the interpretation of history. What is involved is the secularization of typology, its application to the material supplied by history rather than sacred events. As early as the second century, Christian writers began to view occurrences in their own lives as the fulfillment of Old Testament prophecies. It is not hard to imagine, once this step was taken, how the present came to be viewed as a fulfillment not only of sacred prophecies but of other events themselves. Thus, when the chroniclers drew analogies between their rulers and David, Alexander the Great, Constantine, or Charlemagne, they were not merely ascribing a particular list of attributes to their subject. They were affirming a positive, virtually causal relationship between what a David or Constantine had done and the deeds of the "new David." The record of the past was seen as having a relation to the present that was more than morally prescriptive, if less than what we would consider as scientifically causal. In this way, the past not only explains the present, it exercises an indirect influence over contemporary events. It was the sense of an implicit relationship to what had happened before that made it unnecessary for medieval historians to investigate the immediate causes of occurrences.

The typological nature of medieval historical thought also helps to explain its weak sense of chronology. To date an event precisely in the past means fixing its significance as a distinct object, separated from the present. But typology wishes to break down the barriers between past and present, to draw events out of the past and make them live in present experience. It operates with what Tom Driver calls the "principle of contemporaneity," in which "time and historical occurrence refuse to take their place in a chronology of the past. The event which *was* meaningfully enters the *now*."[7] Because history is a mode of experience, and not merely ascertainable fact, it refuses to die, to remain chronologically fixed in the past. Rather, history is construed as tradition, assuming a certain identity between what happens "then" and "now." Hence, like the Balinese studied by Clifford Gertz, medieval people searched "the past not so much for causes of the present as for the standard by which to judge it, for the unchanging pattern upon which the present ought properly to be modeled but which, through accident, ignorance, indisicipline or neglect, it so often fails to follow."[8] To the very degree that people in the Middle Ages sensed the reality of the past, they were incapable of perceiving with equal acuteness its distance, leading to the weak sense of anachronism so often noted. On the other hand, such an attitude endowed the past with great utility for understanding and legitimating the politics of the present.

The political utility of history in the Middle Ages derived from medieval society's traditionalist orientation to the past. Indeed, few complex societies have so clearly regulated their life in accordance with their vision of history. Medieval social life was governed by custom, that is, historical precedent, so much so that even innovations in social and legal practices were given the force of custom. As custom, social practice was both legitimized and made prescriptive: because it was customary it was *ipso facto* good, and because good, to be followed. Politically, the situation was more complex. In theory, medieval government originated in the divine will of God, functioned at His behest, and strove to do His bidding. This conception of the extra-temporal dimension of medieval politics was summed up in the lapidary formula *rex Dei gratia* (king by the grace of God) and symbolized in the consecration ceremony of the king. The theological basis of medieval government was, in this sense, consciously unhistorical, for consecration asserted a right to rule *de novo*, irrespective of the past. Nevertheless, consecration established only the legitimacy of rulership; it provided medieval kings and rulers with few guides to action and little in the way of explicit programs of political policy. These were drawn, instead, from the record of the past. Along with divine right, medieval governments justified their dominion on the grounds of what Max Weber called the "authority of the eternal yesterday."[9]

It is only by appreciating how deeply this attitude of piety toward the past ran in medieval society that we can begin to understand the use made of history. In such as society, as Joseph R. Strayer remarked, "every deliberate modification of an existing type of activity must be based on a study of individual precedents. Every plan for the future is dependent on a pattern which has been found in the past."[10] The eternal relevance of the past for the present made it a mode of experiencing the reality of contemporary political life, and the examples the past offered had explanatory force in articulating the true and correct nature of present forms of political action. In this way, the past itself constituted an ideological structure of argument, one that sought legitimacy from the borrowed authority of history understood as a putatively real, though highly permeable and fragile, tradition. Thus, what made historical writing important in the Middle Ages, was precisely its ability to address contemporary political life via a displacement of current concerns to the past, and to embed both prescription and polemic in an apparently "factual" account of the historical legacy that the past had bequeathed.

In part, this explains the enormously rich use made of forgeries, historical legends, and myths in medieval political life, for they could be shaped to present needs. Precisely because it was so little known in any critical sense, the past could become a vehicle of change. All that was needed was to recreate it in the image of the present, and then claim its authority for the legitimation of contemporary practices. Perhaps the most egregious example of this process is the fabrication of a crusading past for Charlemagne by the monks of Saint-Denis at precisely the time when French kings took up the cross. But this is only one among many illustrations of what is, in the end, a fundamental posture toward history. It meant that the medieval chronicler utilized a very fluid perspective with regard to past and present. The search for the past was guided by present necessities; but so, too, the historical understanding of the past determined the presentation of contemporary events, shaping a vision of the past that could be manipulated to supply legitimacy to the present. Virtually all histories written in the service of the developing monarchies or princely fiefs in the High Middle Ages share this view of the political utility of history. This political use of history promoted its polemical and propagandistic tendencies, a characteristic that grew stronger as traditions of "national" historiography developed, seeking to root loyalty and devotion to newly powerful rulers in the past.

Needless to say, such a view of the underlying nature of historical reality affected the ways in which medieval historians constructed their narratives, leading them to favor, in the words of Nancy Partner, "intelligible sequence, firmly linked to 'meaning' in history,"[11] that *series temporarum* or sequence of morally meaningful events that made up the *res gestae* constituting the historian's object of study. Narrative structure in most medieval historical texts, as in medieval literature more generally, consisted of a series of episodes or tableaux serially ordered in paratactic juxtaposition along a temporal axis not of fixed dates (i.e. chronology) but of sequences. Because the connection between these juxtaposed scenes is serial rather than causal – parataxis being the grammatical term for hard narrative juxtaposition without causal or temporal links or syntactical subordination – the overall effect of such organization is to produce a non-developmental, episodic narrative informed by a theme that is continually reexpressed in separate events. This is the pattern found in early medieval historical texts like Gregory of Tours' *History of the Franks*, which is notable also for the vividness of its portrayal of events and persons. Indeed, what mattered most to medieval readers was not logical explication but acute observations of human behavior whose Christian and moral meaning could, thereby, be the more easily discerned. Both Latin and vernacular historians created narratives formed of a series of episodic units that aimed at presenting sharply defined, visualized scenes and exemplary heroes in action-oriented, rather than logically analyzed, sequences, preferring what Auerbach termed "visual plasticity"[12] to historiographical explanation. The result was a narrative made up of chronologically strung-out but causally unrelated series of events which developed along a more or less clearly defined temporal axis, which alone functioned as the ordering principle of presentation. So pervasive is this style of historical narration that one is forced to conclude that it represented a clear aesthetic choice on the part of both writers and audiences in the Middle Ages.

To modern eyes, the medieval historian's purely serial, seemingly plotless mode of writing history seems chaotic, if not altogether senseless. But the surface barrenness of many texts simply requires us to learn to read them with different eyes. Beneath the digressive veneer of their discourse, most medieval historians firmly emplotted their texts to produce structures of moral meaning and ideological arguments, for few historical texts in the Middle Ages were written out of disinterested curiosity about the past. In some texts, devices such as the symmetrical balancing of good and evil *exempla*, the creation of bipartite narratives, repetition, and the thematic interlacing of event-clusters served as cohesive forces in otherwise dispersed narratives, testifying to the historian's intentions and controlling sense of design. Once we learn to understand a medieval chronicle's structural characteristics and narrative economy as the submerged vehicle of its meaning, the richness of the historian's enterprise becomes suddenly much more apparent.

Evolution of Historical Writing

Most of the characteristics of medieval historical thought sketched in the first part of this essay are evident in the writings of chroniclers and historians from the earliest periods and remain common ways of thinking about and writing history throughout the Middle Ages. To say this, however, is not to imply that medieval historiography did not undergo substantial changes during the thousand or more years that the period includes. Innovations on both the formal level and in the chroniclers' content and language were constant, responding to changes in the nature of medieval society itself. Perhaps the best example of this after the patristic period is the creation of the first "barbarian histories," the work primarily of four authors: Jordanes (AD 500–554), who treated the early history of the Goths in a text commonly known as the *Getica*; Gregory of Tours (AD 538–94), who wrote a *Historia Francorum* (*History of the Franks*) the most important early work on the Franks, that group of Germanic peoples whose deeds so powerfully shaped European history; Bede (AD 672–735), whose *Ecclesiastical History of the English People*, recounting the fall of the Britons and the rise of the Anglo-Saxons to preeminence in England, can be considered one of the most outstanding works of history written in the Middle Ages; and finally, Paul the Deacon (AD 720–99), a Benedictine monk at Monte Cassino, whose *History of the Lombards* chronicled their succession to the Romans in the Italian peninsula. A closer look at these works, foundational in many ways for Western European historiography, not least because they were continuously employed and copied, can serve as a useful introduction to the specific form that historical thought took in medieval Europe.

Patristic historians such as Eusebius, Jerome, Augustine and Orosius, who were responsible for first articulating the underlying scheme of Christian historiography and its rhetorical and theological orientation, were concerned primarily to indicate the continuity between and relations among Romans and the newly created body of Christians. Their histories were universal both because Christianity as a world religion demanded it, and because they remained at heart Romans as well, and one of the meanings of *Romanitas* in the late Imperial/early Christian period was the universality of Roman rule and culture. Indeed, Eusebius, in his *Ecclesiastical History*, had explicitly given the universal spread of Roman rule a function in the Christian economy of salvation. According to Eusebius, the imperial expansion of Rome had served as a preparation for the advent of Christianity and facilitated its spread after the conversion of Constantine the Great and the eventual adoption of Christianity as the official religion of Rome.

In the post-patristic period, however, with the break-up of the Roman Empire into two distinct halves – a Greek-speaking Eastern Empire whose successor state was Byzantium and a Latin-speaking Western Empire that eventually collapsed, due to the combined effects of weak administration, economic devolution, social disruption, and the barbarian invasions – the principal concern for historians was not how to unite Romans and Christians, but rather how to account for and ultimately integrate into a Christian world the barbarian peoples who came to inhabit what had formerly been a Roman world. In taking up this problem, the "narrators of barbarian history," as Goffart calls them, became the first true historians of Europe. At the same time, they laid the seeds for the emergence, in the post-Carolingian period, of national historiographies, since their focus on the new "peoples" or *gens* of Europe inscribed the pre-history of the national groupings that were to take shape by the end of the Middle Ages.

Perhaps it is not surprising that of the four historians concerned the earliest – Jordanes – should also be the most faithful to older traditions of Roman historiography, writing the history of the newly arrived Goths on the pattern of Roman/Byzantine history in a work called *De Origine actisbusque Getarum*, (*On the Origin and deeds of the Getae*), "Getae" being the name that Jordanes employs for the Goths. Himself of Gothic origin, Jordanes traces the origin of the Goths to what he calls "Scandza," thereby bestowing on them a Scandinavian genealogy. He recounts their subsequent migration into the sphere of the Roman Empire where they settled, becoming a part of Roman history. Walter Goffart has argued that the *Getica* (the title usually used for Jordanes's text) was not written in isolation, but formed part three of a multi-volume work, whose first two parts constituted a text known as the *Romana*, dedicated to Roman history down through the reign of Justinian. Taken together, the *Romana* and the *Getica* ultimately describe the fusion of the Romans and Goths, recounted in the *Getica* in the narrative of the birth of a child of mixed blood named Germanus – half Roman, half Goth – whom Jordanes employs to figure the successful melding of the once separate stocks and thereby to offer a romantic, "happy ending" to his chronicle.[13] The question of how to narrate the appearance of new, non-Roman peoples into spaces formerly part of the Roman Empire remained a central one for post-patristic historians, although it does not appear that Gregory of Tours or Bede were aware of Jordanes's *Getica* when they began to write. In these authors, moreover, the outlook is decidedly more Christian.

Gregory of Tour's *History of the Franks* – a title given in later manuscripts; Gregory simply called it the *Ten books of History* (*decem libri historiarum*) – is a work that has struck modern-day scholars as profoundly "medieval" in a way that Jordanes is not. Gregory was Bishop of Tours, a metropolitan see of the Frankish realm, and heir to its founder, St. Martin of Tours, one of the principal confessors in the early Christianization of Gaul, and later, along with St. Denis, one of France's most important "national" saints. Gregory came from a family that had long supplied bishops of the Church in Langres, Lyons, and Clermont and was himself elevated to bishop at the age of thirty-four. His sense of the past is conditioned by his ecclesiastical training and affiliation, even though he is best remembered today for his narration of secular history, in particular that of Merovingian France.

Gregory's *History* is filled with harrowing tales of the doings of Merovingian kings and queens and written in a Latin that has significantly fallen off from the standards of late antiquity. Chaotic in organization and sometimes in grammar, Gregory's historiography seems to function as a mirror of the bar-

barous times in which he lived. In addressing a contemporary audience, Gregory meant to appeal to them in a vivid, sensuous language which forgoes the niceties of classical rhetoric in favor of that "visual plasticity," which Auerbach defined as "medieval" precisely in relation to Gregory's work. His *History* is unusual in being concerned primarily with contemporary events; of the "ten books of histories," fully six are devoted to his own day. His goal is to preserve the memory of the barbarian past while at the same time offering strongly sketched *exempla* of good and bad behavior, defined in terms of conventional Christian morality.

Heir to the Augustinian view of history as composed equally of sacred and profane events, Gregory also filled his pages with miracles and wonders, saints and martyrs constituting as legitimate subjects of historical discourse as secular rulers and their errant offspring. To Gregory, all alike form part of historical experience: the miraculous and the quotidian, the good and the evil, saints and sinners, whose deeds are recounted as bare facts, unaccompanied by rhetorical embellishment. The "truth" of his narrative lay in its relation to lived experience, rather than abstract intellection, and that truth was embodied in stories of *res gestae*, past and present stories which turned *facta* into *dicta* (deeds into words), as Sallust, the Roman historian most widely read in the Middle Ages, and Isidore of Seville, recommended. In his bare accounting of events without an encompassing design beyond his moral preoccupations, Gregory offers a model of much that passed for historiography in medieval Europe. Vivid, exemplary individual events are set down in a chronological sequence that resembles annalistic reporting. The goal of his narrative is moral instruction and enlightenment, and it is achieved by scrutinizing the events of contemporary history for the lessons they can convey.

If Gregory of Tours illustrates to perfection the digressive, seemingly plot-less character of medieval historiography, the same cannot be said of Bede. Although Bede shares with Gregory many common traits, notably a strong tendency to combine history and hagiography, political narrative and miraculous events, oral testimony and textual learning, his *Ecclesiastical History of the English Peoples* blends all these elements so seamlessly, with such a strong narrative drive and purpose, beauty of language and skill in depiction, that he has won near unanimous acclaim for his historiography, praise bestowed only grudgingly, if at all, on Gregory. A key to Bede's overall design is provided by the title of his work, which is borrowed from Eusebius's *Ecclesiastical History*, indicating the theological and providential scheme that frames his narrative of the "English people," offering in the microcosm of English history an instance of the broad providential scheme that Eusebius had first laid out. Just as Eusebius saw in Roman history the hidden hand of God guiding events to create the conditions necessary for the introduction and spread of Christianity, so Bede presents the passing of dominion in England from the Britons to the Anglo-Saxons as a result of God's providential action, which condemned the Britons to fall before the conquering invaders because they had refused to preach the word of God. As Robert Hanning remarked, Bede's *Historia Ecclesiastica* "is the unique chronicle of an empire built on educational principles."[14]

Bede was a monk in the Northumbrian abbey of Jarrow, which he had entered as a child of seven and where he spent his entire life. The *Ecclesiastical History* was written in 731, toward the end of Bede's life (d. 735), after he had composed a large number of works dealing with history: two universal histories on the model of Eusebius; a series of saints' lives, including a prose version of the *Life of Saint Cuthbert* that would figure importantly in the *Ecclesiastical History*; a monastic account of the founding of his abbey, the *History of the Abbots of Wearmouth-Jarrow*, as well as the treatise on chronology, the *De temporum ratione* (ca. 725) that generated the new system of Christian dating noted above.

In narrating the fall of the Britons, Bede drew upon earlier English historical texts, in particular Nennius's *Historia Britonum* (*History of the Britons*) and the *De Excidio Britonum* (*On the Ruin and Conquest of Britain*) of Gildas, who supplied Bede with his main theme of God's punishment of the Britons for their sins. In Bede, these sins are specified as the refusal to preach the word of God to the other peoples inhabiting the isle of Britain, above all the English. The central chapters of the *Ecclesiastical History* narrate the expansion of Christianity throughout Britain, greatly aided by the preaching of Ionian monks. Bede then recounts the ultimate conversion to and cultivation of Christianity by the victorious Anglo-Saxons. They become the newly "chosen people" of Britain who usher in a golden age, against which, Bede intimates, the falling standards of his own time will be judged.

Throughout, Bede interweaves hagiographical accounts of saints' lives, narrates miracles and dreams, and foregrounds theological issues as central to his story, all the while pursuing the political history of England, above all in Northumbria. His melding of historiography and hagiography; his use of cultic figures as exemplary heroes; his concern with ecclesiastical liturgy and cultic life and with their significance for a political history governed by providential forces, would reappear in the conversion tales of later peoples like the Normans. Bede's skill in combining the various strands of his narrative, along with the strong plot of his story and underlying structure, has made him the premier example of medieval historiography from the eighth century down to the modern age.

The reputation of Paul the Deacon (AD 720–99), the last of the "narrators" of the new barbarian peoples of Europe, has not fared so well. Much read in the nineteenth century by folklorists such as the Brothers Grimm as a source for what they believed were oral testimonies of early Germanic legends that had made their way into Paul's *History of the Lombards*, Paul nonetheless has failed to impress modern scholars, despite his clear popularity in the Middle

Ages, which preserved over one hundred manuscripts of his text. Paul is perhaps best known today as a member of the circle of court scholars gathered at Aachen by Charlemagne, where he wrote poetry and composed a history of the Bishops of Metz (*Gesta episcoporum Mettensium*), commissioned by Agilram, the presiding bishop. While a monk at Monte Cassino, the famous abbey founded by St. Benedict, he wrote a *Life of Gregory the Great*, and it was after his return to Monte Cassino from Charlemagne's court in 785 that he undertook to write the *History of the Lombards*.

Monte Cassino lay in Italy in the province of Benevento, whose prince at the time was Grimoald III (788–806). The *History of the Lombards* was written after the conquest of Lombardy by Charlemagne – a fate which the southern province of Benevento had escaped and which Paul stops short of narrating in his history. On the simplest level, Paul's Lombard *History* functions as an early "mirror of princes," a book of edification and moral instruction for Grimoald III, whose ancestor, Grimoald I (d. 671), figures as its exemplary hero. Running to six books, the *History of the Lombards* opens with an ethnic prologue and, in the manner of Bede, presents the Lombards as a new "chosen people," who initially prosper but subsequently lapse into sin, are deprived of their rule, but are raised up once again by the favor of Providence which smiles upon King Grimoald I, the hero who repulses the Byzantine invaders and restores Lombard rule. The work is incomplete and ends with the death of Luitprand in 744, in all likelihood because Paul died before finishing it, thus leaving out the subsequent fall of the Lombard kingdom to the Franks and their incorporation into the Carolingian empire. The theological framework is much less pronounced in Paul's *History of the Lombards* than in Bede's *Ecclesiastical History* and perhaps for this reason the work has failed to win the acclaim awarded his English predecessor. It remains true, however, that all four "narrators of barbarian history" are resolutely Christian in orientation, interpreting barbarian history from the point of view of Christian values and a more or less consciously applied theological scheme of history. Nonetheless, in highlighting the advent of new peoples and recounting their settlement, conversion to Christianity, and ultimate rise to political leadership of the West, all four – but most especialy Gregory and Bede – provided foundational narratives for the further evolution of national historiographies, and thus merit the extended treatment provided them here.

Properly "national" history, in the sense that the term is understood today, is the product of the break-up of the Carolingian Empire, which had seen itself as a successor to Rome and had, if briefly, attempted to revive imperial dreams of glory, projecting Charlemagne as a "new Constantine" in whom the dual universality of Rome and Christianity was alive once more. The collapse of Charlemagne's Empire, marked by the Treaty of Verdun (843) after the rule of his grandson, Louis the Pious, and the subsequent emergence of France and Germany as successor realms, fundamentally changed the context in which medieval historiography developed. At once more local and more politically orientated, the writing of history became much more closely tied to the aspirations and ambitions of kings and princes, around whom medieval society was in the process of reorganizing itself. In doing so, it achieved a political utility foreign to its earlier practice.

The two most developed national historiographies in the Middle Ages were those of England and France, no doubt because both developed free of the imperial and Roman traditions that continued to haunt the German Empire and its dependent Italian city-states. An especially rich stream of historical works developed in England, particularly in the Anglo-Norman and Angevin periods (1066–1399). Built on the foundations supplied by Nennius, Gildas and Bede, it also borrowed from the *Anglo-Saxon Chronicle* which, for the years after the Norman conquest was written in Latin and continued through to the succession of Henry II in 1154. One effect of the influence of the *Anglo-Saxon Chronicle* was to impart to English history a more secular, annalistic, and dynastic framework than had been the case in Bede's history. A magnificent tradition of English historiography emerged, beginning with Dudo of Saint-Quentin, and developing, in the twelfth century in both Latin and in the vernacular, a tradition that on the Latin side included works by Eadmer, Orderic of Vitalis, William of Poitiers, William of Jumièges, William of Malmesbury and Geoffrey of Monmouth, Henry of Huntington, William of Newburgh, Robert of Torigni, Gervase of Canterbury, Ralph Diceto, and Gerald of Wales – to mention only the most famous – and on the vernacular side Gaimar, Jordan of Fantosmes, Benoît of Saint-Maur, Wace and their successors.[15] In the thirteenth century, the abbey of St. Albans emerged as a center of historiographical production, providing the institutional home for huge works such as those of Matthew of Paris's *Chronica Majora*.

In France, after the break-up of the Carolingian Empire, the production of history was widely dispersed in the ninth and tenth centuries among monastic houses, whose chroniclers proved fairly indifferent to the royal framework that had been important under the Merovingians and early Carolingians. But by the eleventh century, with the *Historia Francorum* of Aimoin of Fleury, based in part on Gregory of Tours, the writing of royal history revived, to have an uninterrupted career until the end of the Middle Ages. Royal history reappears first at Fleury and Saint-Germain-des-Près and then, most powerfully, at the abbey of Saint-Denis. By the end of the thirteenth century, the monks of Saint-Denis had become the quasi-official chroniclers of the kings of France, creating a huge body of materials in both Latin and, with the first installment of the *Grandes Chroniques de France* by Primat in 1274, in the vernacular as well.[16] The chronicle tradition of Saint-Denis constituted a vast corpus that included regnal histories in Latin by Suger, Rigord, Guillaume le Breton and Guillaume de Nangis, among others. Translating this corpus into French, the *Grandes Chroniques* condensed the genealogical and dynastic memory of France into a simple edifice that portrayed French history as the story of the *trois races* of kings – Merovingians, Carolingians, and Capetians – and narrated French medieval history as a dynastic chronicle of successive kings from the legendary Pharamond forward. To an extraordinary degree, the structure of dynastic history created at the abbey of Saint-Denis persisted well through the seventeenth century, and left traces even upon the ways in which French medieval history has been taught in French schools to the present day.

Comparable, though less rich and uniform traditions of historiography emerged in Germany to chronicle the ruling Saxon, Salian, Hohenstaufen and other dynasties that rose to the imperial throne. In Italy, the absence of monarchy meant that the revival of Italian historiography took place primarily with the revival of the city-states, from the twelfth century forward, reaching their height of power in the Renaissance.

Medieval historical thought responded to transformations in social as well as political life. Altough it is impossible in an essay of this scope to illustrate the multiplicity of ways in which social as well as political contexts shaped and reshaped historiographical narrative, one example of this phenomenon can be seen in the emergence of genealogically patterned chronicles, which responded to changes in medieval social organization, in particular among aristocratic families of northern France. As a specifically historiographical phenomenon, genealogy intrudes into historical narrative at precisely the time when noble families in France were beginning to organize themselves into vertical structures of patrilineal *lignages* that transmitted the family name, title, and patrimony from father to son.[17] As property came to be passed exclusively from father to oldest son, the representation of lineage became primarily a representation of the transmission of lands, ignoring other members of the biological family who were not included in the patrimonial inheritance.

Written above all to exalt a line and legitimize its power, a medieval genealogical history displays a family's consciousness of itself and its importance, and signals the family's intention to affirm and extend its place in political life. Even here, however, in narratives that were closely linked to the social realities of the family, medieval genealogies passed easily into ideological statements about a family's real or imagined claim to political authority and prestige. Thus, the twelfth-century aristocratic family, once geographically settled and in possession of land, castle, and family name, began to temporalize itself in terms of an uninterrupted lineal ascent stretching from a heroic foundation in a mythical past, down through successive generations of male inheritors of the family patrimony, to the present representative of the line. Like medieval kings, aristocratic families asserted their identity through the fictionalization of their past, validating their claims to authority by means of genealogical descent from an heroic founder.

In the thirteenth century, the development of medieval social life and institutions generated an enormous proliferation of historiographical forms, from urban chronicles to huge scholastic compendia such as Vincent of Beauvais's *Speculum Historiale*. The rise of the medicant orders similarly stimulated new strands of historical writings devoted to the lives of the founders St. Dominic and St. Francis, as well as histories of these and other new monastic orders originating in the twelfth century. Indeed, so diverse and rich was the production of history in the final centuries of the Middle Ages that no brief survey can hope to touch upon all its aspects. In general, these later chronicles continued to describe history as a moral tale of good and evil and as evidence of God's participation in human affairs.

Suffice it to say in closing that in both Latin and the vernacular, the writing of history in the Middle Ages was a complex, diverse and multiform practice, which helped to shape, as much as it was shaped by, the evolving structures of medieval life. Respect for the past and reliance upon it for political or social legitimacy gave history a more central place in medieval life than in modern times, and it was the very centrality of history to medieval society that made it so responsive to changing needs and ideologies, hence so easily manipulated. From earliest Christian times to the last centuries of the Middle Ages, writers of history proved sensitive to the most pressing problems of their society and imprinted the past with their needs and preoccupations. If this meant a vision of history considerably less "scientific" than we are used to today, the loss of accuracy was more than compensated for by the compelling relevance that the past seemed to possess for contemporary society. Nor should one underestimate the degree to which our present understanding of the Middle Ages remains dependent on the information supplied by medieval historiographical texts, for in the course of producing their texts medieval chroniclers and historians preserved and conveyed to later ages an enormous fund of information for which no other sources of the period exist.

Despite enormous differences from the modern practice of history as shaped by nineteenth-century positivism, medieval historiography nonetheless bequeathed to later ages significant features that persist down to our own age. The focus of medieval "national" historiographies on royal dynasties, the shaping of history around religious and moral values, the exemplarist and rhetorical cast to historical writing, and the prominence awarded political figures and events remained characteristics of Western historiography well through the seventeenth century and beyond. As the embodiment of a form of historical consciousness in which the past looms large as the ultimate source of social tradition, political practice, moral value and ideological legitimacy, medieval historiography helped to shape that respect for and reliance upon the past which was a marked characteristic of Western Europe for so many centuries. Moreover, among a variety of continuities between medieval and modern patterns of historical thought, not least is a comparable linear conception of time, marked by a periodization imbued, if only implicitly, with a notion of human progress toward a better end. Initially, that end – salvation – lay outside of time itself, but ultimately was secularized and incorporated into the modern notion of the idea of progress.

Finally, it might even be said that the medieval historian's sense of humility before history, his awareness of the partial, fragmented, and ultimately unknowable nature of historical reality, though derived from a religious viewpoint, nonetheless shares many characteristics with a postmodern sensibility emphasizing the partial, fragmented, and mediated character historical knowledge. From this perspective, medieval historiography sometimes strikes a curiously postmodern note and seems to anticipate historiographical themes that fully emerge only in the mid-twentieth century.

NOTES

1   Nec in narriuncula mea Tullianam eloquentiam aut flores recthoricos expectetis, quia mecum bene agitur si ex veteri confusione tracta et succinte facta digeries morsus reprehensionis evaserit. Bibliothèque Municipale, Soissons, MS 129, fol. 130r.

2   *The Historia Pontificalis of John of Salisbury*, ed. Marjorie Chibnall (London, 1965), p. 3.

3   Marc Bloch, *Feudal Society*, vol. 1, trans. L. A. Manyon (Chicago, 1961), p. 83.

4   Walter Goffart, *The Narrators of Barbarian History Jordanes, Gregory of Tours, Bede and Paul the Deacon (AD 550–800)*, (Princeton, 1988), p. 48.

5   See Erich Auerbach, *Mimesis The Representation of Reality in Western Literature*, trans. Willard Trask (Princeton, 1953).

6   Quoted in Tom F. Driver, *The Sense of History in Greek and Shakespearean Drama* (New York, 1960), p. 60.

7   Driver, *The Sense of History*, p. 53.

8   Clifford Gertz, "Politics Past, Politics Present: Some Notes on the Uses of Anthropology in Understanding the New States," in *The Interpretation of Cultures* (New York, 1973), p. 334.

9   *From Max Weber*, ed. Hans H. Gerth and C. Wright Mills (New York, 1958), p. 78.

10 Strayer, in Jacques Barzun, ed., *The Interpretation of History* (Princeton, 1943), p. 10.

11 Nancy Partner, *Serious Entertainments: The Writing of History in Twelfth-Century England* (Chicago, 1977), p. 59.

12 Auerbach, *Mimesis*, p. 116.

13 For this interpretation, see the chapter on Jordanes in Goffart, *The Narrators of Barbarian History*.

14 Robert Hanning, *The Vision of History in Early Britain* (New York, 1966), p. 83.

15 For a comprehensive survey of English historiography in the Middle Ages see Antonia Gransden, *Historical Writing in England c.559–c.1307*, (Ithaca, New York, 1974) and for the vernacular tradition in particular, M. D. Legge, *Anglo-Norman Literature and its Background* (Oxford, 1963).

16 See Spiegel, *The Chronicle Tradition of Saint-Denis* (Leiden and Boston, 1978), Gabrielle M. Spiegel, *Romancing the Past: The Rise of Vernacular Prose Historiography in Thirteenth-Century France* (Berkeley and Los Angeles, 1993); and Gabrielle M. Spiegel, *The Past as Text: The Theory and Practice of Medieval Historiography* (Baltimore, 1997).

17 See Georges Duby, "Remarques sur la littérature généalogique en France aux XIe et XIIe siècles," and "Structures de parenté et noblesse dans la France du nord aux XI et XIIe siècles," both in *Hommes et Structures du Moyen Age* (Paris, 1973). Also, R. Howard Bloch, "Etymologies and Genealogies: Théories de la Langue, Liens de parenté et genre littéraire au XIIIe siècle," *Annales, E.S.C.* 36 (1981): 946–62; Gabrielle M. Spiegel, "Genealogy: Form and Function in Medieval Historical Narrative," *History and Theory*, 22 (1983): 43–53; and Léopold Genicot, *Les Généalogies* [Typologie des Sources du Moyen Age] (Turnout, 1975).

REFERENCES AND FURTHER READING

Ariès, Philippe, *Le Temps de l'Histoire*, Monaco, 1954.

Auerbach, Erich, *Mimesis The Representation of Reality in Western Literature*, trans. Willard Trask, Princeton, 1953.

Beer, Jeannette M. A., *Narrative Conventions of Truth in the Middle Ages*, Geneva, 1981.

Brandt, William J., *The Shape of Medieval History Studies in Modes of Perception*, New Haven and London, 1966.

Breisach, Ernest, *Historiography: Ancient, Medieval and Modern*, Chicago and London, 1983.

Galbraith, V. H. *Historical Research in Medieval England*, London, 1951.

Goffart, Walter, *The Narrators of Barbarian History Jordanes, Gregory of Tours, Bede and Paul the Deacon (AD 550–800)*, Princeton, 1988.

Gransden, Antonia, *Historical Writing in England c.559–c.1307*, Ithaca, New York, 1974.

Guenée, Bernard, "L'historien par les mots," in Bernard Guenée ed., *Le Métier d'Historien au Moyen Age: Etudes sur l'historiographie médiévale*, Paris, 1977.

——, *Histoire et Culture Historique dans l'Occident Médiéval*, Paris, 1980.

Hanning, Robert, *The Vision of History in Early Britain*, New York, 1966.

Hay, Denys, *Annalists and Historians: Western Historiography from the VIIIth to the XVIIIth Century*, London, 1977.

Kelly, Donald R., *Faces of History Historical Inquiry from Herodotus to Herder*, New Haven and London, 1998.

Partner, Nancy, *Serious Entertainments: The Writing of History in Twelfth-Century England*, Chicago, 1977.

Spiegel, Gabrielle M., *The Chronicle Tradition of Saint-Denis A Survey*, Leiden and Boston, 1978.

——, *Romancing the Past: The Rise of Vernacular Prose Historiography in Thirteenth Century France*, Berkeley and Los Angeles, 1993.

——, *The Past as Text: The Theory and Practice of Medieval Historiography*, Baltimore, 1997.

Vaughn, Richard, *Matthew Paris*, Cambridge, 1958.

CHAPTER FIVE

Historical Thought
in the Renaissance

PAULA FINDLEN

In the middle of the fourteenth century, the Italian humanist Francesco Petrarch (1304–74) composed a letter to posterity in which he explained his fascination with the past. "In order to forget my own time," he wrote, "I have constantly striven to place myself in spirit in other ages, and consequently I delighted in history."[1] History, for Petrarch, was a means of transporting oneself to a better world. Immersed in the past, Petrarch found solace in the companionship of beloved Roman writers such as Cicero, Livy, Quintillian, and Varro. His contact with their words, freshly revealed in manuscripts scattered throughout the monastic libraries of Italy and France, produced a highly subjective response. More than anything, he wanted to speak to the dead. In a series of passionate letters, Petrarch posed questions to his literary heroes that they could no longer answer in their own voice. As his knowledge of their lives expanded, often complicating his initial assumptions about the past, Petrarch found himself asking different questions. History presented itself to him in the form of a dialogue, whether with Cicero or his favorite Christian writer Augustine. It was the basis for a dynamic relationship with those "other ages" that were indeed difficult to know.

Words alone did not conjure up the past, but helped to shape how Renaissance scholars understood historical artifacts – not only manuscripts but a wide variety of objects that represented the past. Petrarch belonged to a society that had begun to see the material world as a repository of ancient memories. His trips to Rome in 1337 and 1341 strongly shaped his vision of history. Traveling through the Eternal City, he observed a landscape of ruins – fragments of the past containing whispers of ancient conversations that he resurrected in his imagination. Almost a century later, in December 1424, the antiquarian Ciriaco d'Ancona (1391–ca. 1457) would take Petrarch's Roman epiphany a little further when he argued that only the stones could speak reliably of the dead. "It appeared to him . . . that the stones themselves afforded to modern spectators much more trustworthy information about their splendid history than was to be found in books."[2] Every ancient manuscript, coin, statue, and building fragment conjured up traces of an ancient society that Renaissance humanists believed to be the height of civilization. Petrarch's dissatisfaction with his own time, which he polemically called the "Dark Ages," emanated from a deep-rooted fascination with the splendors of a vanished world.[3] This fascination with ancient Rome gave Renaissance historiography much of its distinctive, creative intellectual identity. At the same time, however, a new vernacular history of recent times helped to shape a new historical consciousness that would have an enduring influence on the subsequent historical study of modern persons and events. Renaissance historians launched debates about the historical accomplishments of women and about the proper methods for historical research, raising questions that remain important in historical thought today.

Sensing the Past: Similarities and Differences

Valuing the past for its *pastness*, its utter difference from one's own time, is a fundamental insight of the Renaissance. "[O]ur own age has always repelled me," confessed Petrarch.[4] In the hands of an eloquent humanist, the past became a location from which to alter one's relationship to the present. Petrarch did not see the society of the fourteenth century as naturally evolving from all that had preceded it. He traced its less salutary features to a rupture in civilization – the decline of the Roman empire. Notwithstanding the fact that Christianity had flourished primarily after this period, Petrarch saw the political and cultural life of Rome as infinitely superior to the world of medieval Christendom. Attempting to find traces of the virtues of ancient Rome in the mid-fourteenth century, he poetically described the possibilities for cultural rebirth and renewal.

Petrarch's allegorical vision of a future reinvigorated by its relationship with the past provided some of the crucial ingredients for nineteenth-century historians retrospectively to call the period beginning with Petrarch and ending with figures such as Niccolò Machiavelli (1469–1527) and Giorgio Vasari (1511–74) the "Renaissance."[5] If Petrarch did not invent the "Renaissance" – a word most famously associated with the Swiss historian Jacob Burckhardt's *The Civilization of the Renaissance in Italy* (1860) – he certainly sketched its salient features more eloquently than any other scholar of his time. By the time Vasari used the term *rinascita* to describe the first stage of the "rebirth of the arts" in his *Lives of Eminent Artists* (1550), Italian Renaissance society had fully absorbed the idea of cultural renewal that Petrarch formulated. Indeed, Vasari wrote that he had been inspired by "the methods of the greatest historians" to divide the history of artists into three distinct periods that began with the age of Giotto and Cimabue and culminated with the era of Leonardo and Michelangelo.[6]

The age of the Renaissance has often been considered synonymous with the birth of a kind of modern historical consciousness.[7] Awareness of the past is an important precondition to its preservation and interpretation. Had Petrarch not valued a particular moment in history, he would never have looked for its material and textual remains. "What is all history but praise of Rome?" he remarked, summarizing the singularity of his vision of the past.[8] The raw ingredients of the past were subsumed within this particular narrative. There was no other past worth considering, save to examine its deficiencies in relation to this golden moment. Other histories did not matter because they did not praise Rome.

Modern history – with its emphasis on documentation and its complex assessment of the relationship among evidence, methodology, interpretation, and narrative – belongs to a later age. But such things do not emerge *ex nihilo*. The methods of history, and critical reflection on their uses, are much older than the modern era of professional history writing. The great intellectual historian Paul Oskar Kristeller described Renaissance humanists as "the predecessors of modern historians." Despite Petrarch's pronouncements, no one who reads the works of Renaissance historians can doubt that they did more than simply praise Rome. At times, they fully rejected this idea by exploring other historical moments – the Middle Ages and the Renaissance itself – that Petrarch would not have valued. The study of Renaissance historiography invites us to examine the craft of history in a highly experimental stage. Between the mid-fourteenth and the mid-sixteenth centuries some of the first people to describe themselves as historians debated what Peter Burke has called the "sense of the past." [9] The result was a lively and variegated body of historical thought and writing, whose themes were often more "modern" than the classical images of Renaissance culture may suggest.

Many of our tacit assumptions about modern historical thought emerged piecemeal in the scholarly debates of the Renaissance. The exponential growth of historical writing in the fifteenth and sixteenth centuries was a direct outcome of the position of history in humanistic conceptions of knowledge.[10] Many Renaissance scholars considered history to be the first of the seven liberal arts that an educated person should cultivate, a foundation for all other disciplines. Humanists argued vociferously against the view, offered by the Greek philosopher Aristotle in his *Poetics*, that history was inferior to poetry and less closely tied to philosophy because it dealt more with concrete facts than with general truths.[11] They found validation for their elevated conception of history in the writings of other ancients. No respectable Renaissance humanist could write history without thinking of the guidelines that Cicero had set down in *De oratore* regarding the importance of chronology, geography, and above all style in historical writing.[12] Livy, Caesar, Sallust, and Tacitus among the

Romans, Herodotus and Thucydides among the Greeks, and Eusebius among the early chroniclers of Christianity were but a few of the many ancient models that Renaissance historians sought to emulate. By the early fifteenth century it was widely recognized that history was a discipline of ancient origins with modern applications.

History became a public kind of knowledge, particularly in the city-states of Renaissance Italy where humanistic studies flourished and claims of *roman-itas* (a Roman legacy) allowed fifteenth-century Italians to feel that they participated in a living heritage. Writing history was a highly political act which is surely why so many of the great Renaissance historians were also great statesmen, or at least humanist secretaries employed in the service of the state. When the Florentine chancellor Leonardo Bruni (1369–1444), who was buried by his fellow citizens in 1444 holding a copy of his *Histories of the Florentine People*, advised Battista di Montefeltro, wife of Galeazzo Malatesta, that she should study the past to understand "the origins and progress of one's own nation," he reflected the transformation of Petrarch's highly personal experience of the past into a broad-scale program for cultural renewal.[13] It was Bruni, after all, who demolished the medieval mythology of Florence, as a city reconstructed by Charlemagne after its sack by Totila, to argue that its true origins lay in republican Rome.

Bruni's Florence was a gloriously indigenous creation – a living embodiment of the virtues of the distant past that supplanted any claims of foreign rulers to have remade Italy in their image. He helped to establish a distinguished tradition of Florentine historical writing that culminated in Machiavelli's popular *Florentine Histories* (1520–5). Cities such as Venice, lacking the Roman antiquity on which Florence's claim to greatness rested, had to import the past in order to create a genealogy that rivaled that of Rome, or conquer it through their acquisition of mainland cities such as Verona that boasted some of the most famous Roman ruins. The Venetians thought more acutely about the importance of writing their own history after the terrible defeat at Agnadello in 1509. At the very moment that the Venetian Republic seemed threatened by foreign aggression, its Great Council established the position of state historiographer, appointing Pietro Bembo (1470–1547) because he was known for his eloquence. By the sixteenth century many rulers saw the virtue of having an official historian on the payroll, not only in Venice but in most of the major Italian states and many of the northern European monarchies and principalities. A century after Petrarch, the search for origins was no longer simply a personal preoccupation of individual humanists but a lavish civic project.

Historical writing in the late fourteenth and fifteenth centuries took several distinctive forms. The first, represented well by Bruni and the distinguished tradition of Florentine chancellors who wrote the history of their city while in office, drew directly upon ancient models of historical writing. Bruni, for example, believed from his reading of Livy that it was a noble thing to record the history of a city from its origins. He was perhaps the first Renaissance humanist to cite Tacitus as validation for his praise of the republican tradition of governance against the tyranny of empire. And he composed his *Histories* in an elegant, classically informed Latin that demonstrated the importance of imitating the ancients, even in the language in which one wrote about the past.

In papal Rome, curial humanists took this idea to new heights, outdoing each other to prove their skills as grammarians, philologists, and geographers. The growing strength of the Renaissance papacy in the fifteenth century and the emphasis placed upon cultural pursuits by popes such as Nicholas V provided scholars with numerous opportunities to demonstrate the depth of their engagement with the past. The papal secretary Flavio Biondo (1392–1463), for instance, wrote a series of books on Rome and Italy in the 1440s and '50s that combined careful descriptions of Italy's topography with its history. His *History from the Decline of the Roman Empire*, spanning the period from AD 410 to 1441, countered Petrarch's preference for pre-Christian Rome by chronicling the Middle Ages.[14] It also employed many of the techniques used by Ciriaco d'Ancona, who had traveled throughout the Eastern Mediterranean in order to uncover the remains of ancient Greece. While few Renaissance historians followed Biondo's lead, it is not surprising that a scholar employed by the papacy would see the significance of revising Petrarch's view of the medieval "Dark Ages."

A deeper engagement with sources produced a different kind of history – one more reflective of the process by which the past was reconstructed. In the midst of the vast editorial project that made the newly built Vatican Library a repository for some of the best examples of ancient Greek and Roman writing, scholars found that their philological talents could also be put to work on religious documents, often with quite subversive results. Where else but in Renaissance Rome ought one to know how the Romans wrote? Increased knowledge of the differences between classical and medieval Latin made it possible to spot forgeries. In 1439, Lorenzo Valla (1407–57) famously exposed the *Donation of Constantine*, a document that allegedly transferred temporal authority over Rome from the emperor to the pope in the fourth century AD, as an eighth-century forgery. Building on Petrarch's fundamental insight into the specificity of the past, Valla articulated better than any of his contemporaries the idea of historical anachronism. Language, he argued, was a product of history and culture. Eighth-century ways of writing, for example, differed from fourth-century Latin in such obvious things as the names of cities and such subtleties as the kinds of words used for many ordinary human activities. The art of history could now rest on a new kind of linguistic science that examined the historical conditions under which documents were produced.

Little wonder that in the early sixteenth century Erasmus would find Valla's *Annotations on the New Testament* so interesting that he decided to publish it.

It was Valla who remarked, "The truer history is, the more powerful it is."[15] Disciples such as Angelo Poliziano (1454–94), who rigorously adopted Valla's methodology, gradually transformed how humanists looked at sources, insisting that the earliest version of a manuscript should always be the most authoritative. *Ad fontes* (to the sources) became a much more meaningful battle cry once scholars understood the difference between a source written at the time and documents purporting to describe events decades or even centuries after they occurred. By the middle of the sixteenth century, the idea of the "original source" was well established, thanks in no small part to the work of fifteenth-century humanists who privileged the antiquarian tasks of examining manuscripts and coins as cultural artifacts over the more grandiose writing of history that occupied colleagues such as Bruni. The collection of reliable primary sources and artifacts became one of the era's most enduring contributions to modern historical scholarship.

Bruni, Valla, and the traditions they fostered represented two different dimensions of humanist historiography – one designed actively to shape contemporary political narratives about the past (and hence affect contemporary political life) and the other emerging from the growth of new kinds of scholarship that carefully examined artifacts from the past. By the sixteenth century, it was commonplace to consider history an essential public activity that demanded special skills to execute well. Scholars had greater access to the full range of ancient histories, which provided a wide array of models to imitate, and they understood well that there was no single way to approach the past. At the same time knowing the past seemed more urgent in the face of all the problems – war, politics, and ultimately faith – that had begun to tear their world apart yet again, much as the Roman world had fallen apart in late antiquity.

History for Whom?

The classical model of Renaissance historiography had a limited readership at best. Bruni's *Histories*, for example, was not published until 1476. The fact that it appeared in Italian rather than Latin, part of a state-commissioned project to make his work more accessible, suggests that even those who created history in imitation of the ancients understood the value of accessibility. As modern historians such as Hans Baron and others have argued, Bruni's *Histories* fused ancient models of history with the vernacular tradition of medieval chronicles to provide a new history of Florence. From the start, he relied on sources in his own language while admiring the way the Romans wrote history. The hybrid quality of Bruni's work poses a fundamental question: how did classically inspired and vernacular traditions of historiography work together to create history?

History was thus not an exclusively learned enterprise that led inevitably to ancient Rome. Local chroniclers, who composed histories in the margins of their account books and family diaries, populated late medieval and early Renaissance cities, especially in places such as Florence where literacy was relatively high and merchants understood the value of writing things down. Writing about one's family and writing about the events through which they had lived were inextricably intertwined. Giovanni Villani's famous chronicle of Florentine life, begun in the 1320s and interrupted by his death during the 1348 plague, offers an interesting counterpart to Petrarch's letters to the dead. Villani recorded the events of his day not because of his dissatisfaction with the present but precisely because he believed that he lived in interesting and important times. He had no need to search for a distant past because he felt that contemporary events justified the writing of a chronicle.

A chronicle, of course, is history from a singular perspective. It offers one person's story, or at best a family's vision of the world they inhabit, which is why such materials have been of great interest to later historians attempting to reconstruct Renaissance society.[16] Chroniclers who wrote about their own times and the cities of their birth had no need to consult sources other than their own experience and knowledge. Their models for historical writing emerged from their account books – pragmatic records of life's daily occurrences – and from periodic reflection on what life offered them. They sifted through the events of their time in search of what was memorable. The more eloquent obviously drew upon tales of chivalric romance and popular stories moved from an oral to written tradition in the manner of Boccaccio's *Decameron*, making the people in their historical narratives resemble the fictional characters who pleased them. Still others aspired to write "world chronicles" that did indeed move beyond the personal to a universal account of history, but this was the exception more than the norm.

The silk merchant Goro Dati (1362–1435), one of the most interesting Florentine diarists of the early fifteenth century, also composed a *History of Florence* which he began around 1409. Unlike Bruni's *Histories* which began in ancient Rome, it started in 1380. The fact that Dati could not imagine writing about a past that preceded his own adulthood suggests an important distinction between the classical and vernacular traditions. Poggio Bracciolini (1380–1459), the humanist chancellor whose *Florentine History* (written in Italian between 1455 and 1459) focused largely on recent events, began his history by recording the events that had occurred in 1350. Bartolomeo della Scala's (1430–97) ambitious twenty-volume Latin history of the same city grew so lengthy that by the time he completed the fourth book in 1497, he had only reached the year 1267. To write history in Latin was to think of a more distant past. To write in one's own language was to think of the present.

The more immediate sense of the past recorded in chronicles played an important role in the development of Renaissance historiography, offering an alternative to the genealogical impulse of humanist historiography. Chronicle writing strengthened the connections between history and memory, emphasizing the importance of one's own experience in establishing the significance of the past. When Florence's greatest historian Francesco Guicciardini (1483–1540) presented his *History of Italy* (1540) as a record of "those events which have occurred in Italy within our memory," he invoked a tradition of historical writing that owed a great debt to the merchant chroniclers of the fourteenth and fifteenth centuries, including his decision to write in Italian.[17] Guicciardini's style of historical writing reflected the lessons of Renaissance humanism. But his sense of what mattered drew strength from the idea that historians should interpret their own times.

Guicciardini's search for meaning in the events of his lifetime led him, along with many of his contemporaries, to create a chronology of recent history that subsequently influenced nineteenth- and twentieth-century accounts of the Renaissance.[18] Just as Florentine chroniclers singled out 1434 – the year of Cosimo de' Medici's return from exile – as a crucial date in the history of Florence, Guicciardini identified 1494 as the moment from which Italy's fortune had been supplanted by a series of misfortunes. But it was also a moment when the world in general had changed. Chronology was very much on the mind of Renaissance chroniclers, for the establishment of key turning points in history gave shape to the narrative of the past. Guicciardini belonged to a generation that celebrated watershed events such as the birth of the printing press, the greatness of Florence under the Medici, and Columbus' discovery and conquest of the Americas as signs of the importance of the modern world in relation to antiquity. "Most people believe that our age, from 1400 onward, is the most fortunate period in Florence's history," wrote the Florentine merchant Giovanni Rucellai (1403–81) in the private chronicle he composed in the late fifteenth century.[19] By the 1530s, Guicciardini could only lament the wasted opportunities that had squandered this prosperity.

Guicciardini's history was a tragedy – a genre of historical writing that suited well the Renaissance fascination with the loss of an earlier culture, a pristine faith, and a large empire. It was also a celebration of a contemporary golden age – no longer remote like Petrarch's Rome but fresh in the memory of those who wrote – that had ended brutally and unnecessarily, not simply with the death of Lorenzo de' Medici in 1494, but through a whole series of calamities that culminated in the French and Spanish invasions of Italy after 1494. We might say that Guicciardini shared Petrarch's alienation from his own times. But he did not long for a distant past. Recent events haunted him – even more than they did his Florentine compatriot Machiavelli, who advised his ideal ruler in *The Prince* to read history in order to learn from the past.

Guicciardini's magisterial history, woven from many separate narratives and sensitive to the contingency of the past, represented the evolution of vernacular historiography into a powerful form of historical writing that equaled, if not surpassed the best work in the classical Latin tradition. Still, this was not the only approach to writing the history of one's own time. In Venice, Marin Sanudo (1466–1535) obsessively gathered materials for the history of his age. The modern edition of his diary is a hefty fifty-eight volumes. Filled with the news and rumor of the day and supplemented by popular printed broadsheets, the precursors of the modern newspaper, Sanudo's diary was an entirely different kind of historical record. A messy, inchoate work, Sanudo's chronicle attempted to survey the length and breadth of the Venetian Republic and followed the late medieval tradition of writing down the memorable events of one's own lifetime. To his disappointment, it did not win him an appointment as Venice's state historiographer – a position requiring eloquence in Latin and good political connections. But it is even today a fundamental source for the history of Venice, precisely because it was never transformed into a finished history.

The once novel forms of vernacular historiography became familiar by the end of the sixteenth century. In northern European countries such as France and England, writing in the vernacular signified a cultural distance from the Roman heritage in which the Italians took such great pride. Estienne Pasquier (1529–1615), for example, composed his *Researches on France* (1560) entirely in French. While drawing upon Latin sources such as Julius Caesar's description of Gaul, Pasquier made a point of translating all his material into French in order to make it more accessible. By the time Nicolas Vignier (1530–96) created his *Historical Library* (1575–88) in his capacity as royal historiographer, it seemed obvious that such a work should be in French. The language of history had political consequences and it was never a neutral choice. Historians who argued for the distinctiveness of a French nation and its culture could not make their point persuasively in a universal language that had conquered Gaul. Conversely a region such as the Holy Roman Empire, composed of numerous states with different languages and eventually different religions, could not simply settle on German as the language of the state. Although historians might speak of an ancient Germania, it was far safer to write in Latin, a language removed in time and place from the thorny politics of the present.

The English more closely approximated the French in their preference for vernacular history as an expression of national identity. They enthusiastically translated most of the major works by Italian historians in the late sixteenth century in order to absorb Italy's historical lessons in their own language.[20] But English historians also pushed their work far beyond the boundaries of Italian history and culture. Imprisoned in the Tower of London, the disgraced Walter Raleigh (ca. 1552–1618) ambitiously re-wrote *The History of the World* (1614). In that same decade, the antiquarian schoolmaster William Camden (1551–1623), best known for his *Britannia* (1586), a history and geography that emphasized Britain's Anglo-Saxon origins, published his *Annals; or the*

History of the Most Renowned and Victorious Princess Elizabeth, late Queen of England (1615). Camden understood how important it was to make history an indigenous tradition. He subsequently founded the first chair in history at Oxford in 1622, naming it after himself.[21]

Challenging the Narrative: The Emergence of Women's History

If critiquing the Roman version of the past, or appropriating it for one's own ends, represented an important development in Renaissance historiography, questioning the lineage of illustrious men (*viri illustres*) offered an equally important challenge to the traditions that Renaissance historians inherited and developed. Biography played an important role in Renaissance historiography. From the age of Petrarch onwards, retelling the lives of individuals noteworthy for their valor in war, politics, philosophy, and faith became a dynamic part of the growth of historical writing. By the fifteenth century learned rulers and scholars filled their studies with portraits of illustrious predecessors in order to inhabit their world. The Florentine bookseller Vespasiano da Bisticci's (1421–98) *Lives of Illustrious Men*, composed in the late fifteenth century, reflected the more popular aspects of this genre by providing long entries on recently deceased contemporaries such as Cosimo de' Medici and the humanist Niccolò Niccoli, who was so obsessed about the past that he reputedly dined on ancient Roman plates. Bisticci also composed his *Book in Praise of Women* in the 1470s and '80s to complement his more well-known project on famous men. He thus added another dimension to biographical writing, but, like many Renaissance humanists, Bisticci understood the writing of women's history as a distinct genre from the histories of states and the men who made them famous.

Women's history had an important place in Renaissance historiography. Around the same time that Petrarch reveled in the glory of Rome, Giovanni Boccaccio (1313–75) decided to make women the subject of two works that would become some of his most widely read books. A decade after composing the *Corbaccio* (1355), now viewed as a controversial work of medieval misogyny, Boccaccio published *Concerning Famous Women* (1365). Praising 106 women, the majority of whom were described in Greek and Roman sources, Boccaccio created the first history of women's accomplishments and launched an influential genre; Bisticci's biographies, for example, were loosely based on the model that Boccaccio had created. While we might see Boccaccio's work as responding to renewed interest in the lives of illustrious men – which, in part, it surely did – it also offered an account of women's lives that would become a focal point for almost three centuries of debate about the place of women in the historical record. Boccaccio primarily praised women for traditional feminine virtues – chastity, silence, and obedience. Subsequent histories argued, however, that female accomplishments ought to be measured by the standards of male biography. They pointed to many examples of women whose accomplishments equaled or surpassed those of men and took Boccaccio to task for misrepresenting the place of women in the historical record.

The most famous response to Boccaccio came from the daughter of an Italian physician who earned a living from her pen in French court society. Christine de Pizan (1365–1431) wrote *The Book of the City of Ladies* (1405) in response to repeated statements by male scholars that women lacked virtue and accomplishments. While we might not conceive of Pizan's work as a traditional history, in fact, it made the historical record an important part of the argument about women's abilities and achievements. Pizan populated her imaginary city with "ladies from the past as well as from the present and future," but overwhelmingly the inhabitants came from the first category. History revealed that women had done many things that men claimed they could not do. The study of the past, in short, validated a new image of women. Pizan claimed that her city was so well populated that it – and the memory of the women within it – would survive "from one generation to another."[22]

Two decades after Pizan finished her powerful retort to medieval misogyny, the Florentine chancellor Bruni was in the process of composing a letter to Battista Malatesta about what she ought to study. He singled out history as especially suited to a woman's intellectual abilities, having denied her the right to study rhetoric because it was a public art. Facts were well-suited to a female mind. "These, then, the woman of high promise will go on to acquire, the more so as they make pleasant reading," wrote Bruni. "For there are no subtleties to be unravelled, no knotty *quaestiones* to be untied; only narrations of facts that are easy to grasp, and, once grasped . . . will never be forgotten."[23] One can only wonder what the learned Battista thought of such an ambiguous endorsement for the genre of writing that would subsequently give Bruni literary fame.

Yet if history was deemed uncomplicated enough that even women might read it, this gave it an important place in the education of women learned in the humanist tradition. The fact that educated women had access to historical writing, ancient and modern, made it possible for them to transform the historical narrative to suit their own ends. From Christine de Pizan in the early fifteenth century to Mary Astell in the late seventeenth century, women writers repeatedly argued for their own version of the past. Pizan wrote of her own experience, "I betook myself to history – to the history of former times, from the beginning of the world."[24] History offered a consolation for the troubles of supporting her family as a young widow; she did not write only of women but also composed a chivalric *Book of the Deeds and Good Manners of the Learned King Charles V.* In many respects, she would have understood Petrarch's entry into the past as a form of alienation from the present. Pizan's "city of ladies" echoed many of the same themes as Petrarch's letters to the dead. She sought to create a world, based primarily on a reading of the past, populated with women who contradicted the limits Boccaccio and other male authors had placed upon them – and who could join Pizan in her own private conversations with the dead.

In the fifteenth and sixteenth centuries, the debate engendered by Pizan's response to Boccaccio made history a contentious terrain for male and female writers who involved themselves in the *querelle des femmes*. One of the most influential works in this genre of late Renaissance literature was the German scholar Henricus Cornelius Agrippa's *Declamation on the Nobility and Pre-eminence of the Female Sex* (1526). First delivered as a Latin oration at the University of Dôle in 1509, its publication earned Agrippa (ca. 1486–1535) the position of imperial archivist and historiographer at the court of Margaret of Austria. When it was translated into most European vernacular languages, it became an excellent example of the power of the printing press to disseminate new ideas.

Agrippa's *Declamation* exemplified the uses of the past to subvert common opinion. Examining the ancient opinions of jurists and theologists, he found little in the historical record to justify the limits imposed upon women. "Let us read trustworthy historians from antiquity," he wrote, thus suggesting that the task of the historian was to look beyond the prejudices of his – or her – own age. With great subtlety, Agrippa indicated that history itself was the antidote to the present. "From the histories of Greeks, Latins, and barbarians, ancient as well as modern, I could still recount innumerable exceptional women, but in order not to extend this work beyond measure, I have striven to remain silent"[25] Three years later, Agrippa published his controversial *On the Uncertainty and Vanity of the Sciences* (1530), which attacked historians for their errors of incompetence, incredulity, and prejudice. He so infuriated his patron Margaret that she demanded that the faculty of theology at Louvain examine it for impiety. Undoubtedly Agrippa's own experiences in writing the history of women had led him to his highly negative assessments of other historians.

By the time the Venetian scholar Lucrezia Marinella (1571–1653) published *The Nobility and Excellence of Women* (1600), she could state with supreme confidence that men who denied the existence of learned and accomplished women possessed "little knowledge of history." The history to which she referred, of course, belonged to the tradition initiated in the writings of Pizan and Agrippa, who resuscitated a different part of the past in order to make women's accomplishments more visible. At the same time, Marinella recognized that this kind of history was not yet universal. She chastised many historians who "have not recounted women's most worthy actions but have remained silent about them," and she explicitly mentioned Boccaccio's *Corbaccio* as a text that denied women their rightful place in history.[26] We can well imagine that many of the political histories composed by Bruni, Machiavelli, Guicciardini, and the like exemplified Marinella's contention that silence was even worse than criticism.

While Renaissance historiography generally made a point of not rewriting or revising narratives from the past – believing that ancient history had been written best by the ancients, and that the history of Florence was best told in successive narratives by members of subsequent generations – the history of women was one of the most important exceptions to this rule. Only by altering the vision of the past, searching for those "trustworthy historians" that Agrippa praised, could history become meaningful in this context. Very few women wrote history. Even Queen Elizabeth I, learned in her own right, never thought that the history of her reign should be written by a woman. Yet women had an important role in Renaissance historiography. They occupied a tenuous place on the margins of most narratives, but their controversial story needed constant retelling as long as the general historical record offered little scope for women's accomplishments.

An Art in Search of a Science: Historical Methodology

Renaissance historians realized that studying the past was no simple affair. Choosing one's subject, finding the right sources, and developing a good methodology were already pressing questions by the sixteenth century. Despite the privileged place of history in the humanist curriculum, Renaissance historians occasionally found themselves the butt of jokes. "What would you call the writer who told you about effects without looking for any causes?" wrote Francesco Patrizi (1529–97) in his *Ten Dialogues on History* (1560). The answer of course was a historian.[27] Then as now, philosophers chastised historians for their obsession with facts at the expense of more general conclusions.

Many Renaissance historians would have disagreed with Patrizi about the shallowness of their enterprise. Bruni famously described history as "a long continuous narrative, causal explanation of each particular event, and appropriately placed judgments on certain issues." Guicciardini, responding perhaps to the critics, specifically denied that the historian's task was "to know effects, because these are known to all." Yet the question remained as to whether historians could convince critical readers that they had moved beyond an iteration of facts, or found a method for ascertaining the reliability of their evidence. "[I]f anything in history delights or teaches, it is what is presented in full detail," wrote Machiavelli in his popular *Florentine Histories.*[28] For every historian who argued for the analytical qualities of his discipline, there were others who insisted on and defended the empirical beauty of description.

Assembling facts was no simple matter. Guicciardini never loved facts for their own sake, but he chastised fellow historians for omitting "facts well known to their contemporaries, simply because they presupposed everyone knew them." Stressing that future readers would not know the information that his own generation took for granted, he reminded historians that if they did not try to imagine how the well-known facts of their own era could easily disappear, they ran the risk of writing only for the present. "[T]he sole purpose of writing history," Guicciardini explained, "is to preserve memories forever." As contemporary history grew in popularity during the first half of the sixteenth century, scholars had a growing collection of often conflicting sources, all of which raised questions about how the past ought to be remembered. The French jurist Jean Bodin (1530–96), for example, expressed enormous frustration over the fact that bishop Paolo Giovio's *Histories of His Own Times* (1550–2) seemed to contradict Guicciardini's account of the same period, not only in matters of interpretation, but also in its substance. "[T]hey do not resemble each other more than a circle a square."[29] Bodin harshly criticized Giovio (1483–1552) for inventing speeches and falsifying documents, but he praised Guicciardini for his higher standards of evidence, thereby showing how the new standards for historical scholarship were spreading across Europe.

Appropriately enough, Guicciardini had commented on this very problem. "Documents are rarely falsified at the start," he observed. "It is usually done later as occasion or necessity dictates".[30] As a statesman who had worked in Florence and then as the papal governor of Romagna, Guicciardini had many opportunities to observe the uses of documentation. He understood well the kind of history written by Giovanni Simonetta (d. 1491), secretary to the Sforzas in Milan and the author of the *Commentaries on the Deeds of Francesco Sforza*. Simonetta wrote his history from the very documents that he helped to organize in the ducal chancery archive – documents that he frequently retrieved as part of on-going diplomatic negotiations between the Sforza regime and other rulers. Guicciardini also profited from access to the archives. He availed himself of his own family's papers in writing the history of Florence, and he used his political connections to consult the entire archive of the Ten, the Florentine committee that dealt with foreign affairs, incorporating this material in his *History of Italy*. Guicciardini actually was able to do what many historians still dream of – take the archive home to consult at his leisure.

Giovio presents an interesting point of contrast, though he also wrote his history from a position of unusual access. In Rome, where he began his *Histories* in the 1510s, he enjoyed conversations with every well-informed visitor who passed through the papal city and access to a wealth of documents in the Vatican Library. Rome was perhaps one of the few places in Europe from which one could see the entire world, which is exactly what Giovio aspired to do. His *Histories* were not limited to Italy but discussed European-wide events in relation to the Americas, the Far and Near East, and Russia; he was one of the first European historians to chart the growth and power of the Ottoman empire because he was able to interview travelers and merchants who had spent time there. Giovio spent other parts of his life in Florence, under the patronage of Cosimo I, and in his native city of Como, but it was Rome's cosmopolitan atmosphere that gave Giovio his best material and his global view of human history. In short, he demonstrated that one could derive different visions of the past than the one Petrarch had formulated in the papal city.

Bodin may have found Giovio's history less reliable than Guicciardini's because Giovio relied more heavily on oral testimony. Both historians used oral and written accounts of recent events to write the history of the present, but Guicciardini drew more of his information from archival documents. Both were aware of the difficulties of ascertaining the truth, no matter what method or source historians might use. Giovio presented himself as an impartial narrator who focused only on "the purity of the historical truth" when he wrote as a historian. Yet he acknowledged that no historian could escape the accusation that he wrote from his own prejudices, as he discovered when readers of his *Histories* criticized the book for being too sympathetic to either the Holy Roman Empire or to the French monarchy – two positions that could not be more opposite from each other. Giovio felt that he had found a reliable method by reviving the Greek tradition of eyewitness history. He would not have agreed with the German humanist Markus Welser, who responded to the French statesman Jacques-August de Thou's (1553–1617) efforts to write a history of Europe with the pessimistic conclusion that the French and the Germans would always write history from their own perspective. "Truth lies at the bottom of a well," Welser wrote in 1604. "[But] we drink water from the surface . . . especially when relying on the testimony of others to scoop it up."[31]

Truth was a slippery terrain upon which historians debated the art and science of their discipline. Renaissance historical writing was a literary art in search of a new kind of science. Although debates about the "art" and "science" of history are often portrayed as a distinctive feature of modern historiography, Renaissance scholars were already actively discussing which approach to history was preferable, and how the two approaches might fruitfully be combined. Prior to the sixteenth century history primarily belonged to the realm of art – problems of style, narrative, and subject occupied historians more than questions of methods and sources. Yet Guicciardini invoked the "laws of history" as he began his *History of Italy* in 1538. What did he mean by this phrase? From Cicero, Guicciardini had derived a concept of "true history," but this dealt only tangentially with issues that historians today consider to be the foundation of a good methodology (though, as noted earlier, Guicciardini emphasized the importance of written documents). Among other things, the idea of "true" history reaffirmed the centrality of political narrative to historical thought, reinforcing the belief in history as a form of knowledge that served the public good. In his *Method for the Easy Comprehension of*

History (1566), Bodin distilled this concept of history into a maxim when he wrote: "[H]istory for the most part deals with the state and with changes taking place within it."[32] History's laws, in this traditional sense, therefore referred to political and moral lessons rather than to universal patterns of historical development. They had very little to do with the evidence by which one accounted for the past. But the practical interest in the lessons of history helps to explain why eloquence was prized as highly as good historical judgment, and why political history prevailed over histories of culture and religious faith at least until the Reformation.

Despite the general agreement on the value of eloquence and political writing, some historians began to raise methodological questions about why history, among all the disciplines, lacked any distinctive set of rules. The problem with history was that it seemed to be filled with utterly contradictory statements about what historians ought to do with the past. Scholars trained in the antiquarian tradition paid great attention to questions of evidence, as Valla famously demonstrated in his account of the forged "Donation of Constantine," but they were less prescriptive in their pronouncements about the kind of history that truly mattered. By our standards, they made greater contributions to a rigorous historical method, though their histories were (and are) far less read than those of Guicciardini and Machiavelli. Writing primarily for other scholars steeped in ancient sources, they debated highly technical problems, much like modern professors of history. They not only insisted on the critical examination of documents, but also argued that history could not be properly understood without a good grasp of chronology. Bodin, whose *Method* reflected an early attempt to lay the groundwork for a philosophy and science of history, underscored the importance of properly dating events when he wrote: "Those who think they can understand histories without chronology are as much in error as those who wish to escape the windings of a labyrinth without a guide" – a methodological claim that would still resonate in a twenty-first century graduate seminar.[33]

The English statesman Francis Bacon (1561–1626), who called the study of antiquities "imperfect history," could have learned a few things from contemporaries such as the formidable chronologist Joseph Justus Scaliger (1540–1609). It was Bacon, after all, who famously misdated the year of Henry VII's death in his *History of the Reign of King Henry the Seventh* (1622). As long as history was an art more than a science, this kind of error did not call into question Bacon's skills as a good historian. Bacon wanted to write a political narrative – the first part of the history of Tudor–Stuart England, an ambitious project for which Machiavelli, not the philologist Valla, provided the most importance source of inspiration.

Generally speaking, allied fields such as antiquarianism, chronology, and law developed the more scientific aspects of history. Both antiquarianism and chronology favored intense examination of specific evidence over a broad, sweeping vision of the past. In each of those specialized disciplines, we can point to specific methods by which Renaissance scholars came to a consensual understanding of the status of a historical artifact, or the most reliable date for a particular event. Such work may not have been as exciting or provocative as the historical commentaries of Machiavelli, and yet it laid the foundation for what we understand to be reliable historical knowledge.

Law offered a similar promise of creating a secure foundation for historical knowledge. By the middle of the sixteenth century, especially in France where a strong tradition of legal studies existed, scholars began to consider the possibility of using principles derived from law to create a science of history. In many respects, the rules that legal scholars such as François Baudouin (1520–73) developed were not dissimilar from the guidelines for good antiquarian scholarship, though they dealt more explicitly with the concept of the reliable witness. Legal historians affirmed that primary sources (*primi auctores*) were preferable over derivative accounts. Eyewitness narratives needed to be distinguished from written documents, because oral and written evidence were two different forms of truth with different procedures of cross-examination. Originals took precedence over copies – a principle that anyone who had ever signed a notarial contract or made a will would have understood. The legal tradition insisted more strongly than the literary tradition of historiography that the reliability and authenticity of sources was the best guarantor of truth.

Whereas antiquarians directed their efforts towards new kinds of sources – inscriptions, coins, and buildings – jurists preferred written materials with which they were already familiar. Legal documents became the mainstay of the kind of careful research Baudouin pioneered. Such documents generated a history that differed from the political narratives of chronicles; the new interest in such documents made the archive a fundamental location from which to write history. Charters, the essential source for modern medieval studies, attracted the early attention of the new French school of historical thought. Reconstructing the history of rights, privileges, and institutions, French Renaissance historians not only helped to give birth to medieval studies but began to construct a history of France that rejected the Italian humanist account of a universal history written from a Roman perspective.

By the seventeenth century, antiquarian and legal methods of historical scholarship combined in the work of a court historiographer such as Emanuele Tesauro (1592–1675), who proudly described himself as digging through "all the archives of Savoy and of the provincial cities . . . [in search of] the most ancient and certain records" to write his *History of the August City of Turin*.[34] There were many other historians, however, who continued to shun such practices, and to envision history as a literary tradition. When Estienne Pasquier decided to quote extensively from primary sources, he was criticized by readers who found the idea of the quotation puzzling – aesthetically displeasing at best and outright plagiarism at worst. The footnote, that most distinctive claim to authority in modern scholarship, was nowhere in evidence, though the idea that historians should credit their sources – indeed have a few sources – could be found in many Renaissance histories.[35]

Virtually all of the techniques of modern historical scholarship thus appear in Renaissance historians' random, often piecemeal efforts to collect, organize, and use evidence. The importance of history to Renaissance society is apparent in the diversity of its historical writing, in the willingness of leading scholars to debate the methods by which good history must be written, and in the general belief that history provided both an essential form of cultural literacy and a reliable foundation for many other disciplines. The new print culture of the era stimulated the production of historical works and spread new historical debates to a broader reading public. In most instances, such debates occurred at crucial moments in the political history of a particular region – the rise and decline of republican and Medicean Florence, the foreign invasions of Italy, the wars of religion in France and Germany, and the inauguration of the Stuart regime in England. Complex, disturbing events seemed to stimulate the search for historical understanding and perspective. In retrospect, we can see quite vividly the crucial role of historical thought in the public life of the Renaissance.

The Renaissance sense of the past helped to sharpen definitions of historical periodization. By the end of the seventeenth century, historians generally imagined the world to be divided into three eras: ancient, medieval, and modern. Each of these categories of historical time was a product of Renaissance historical thought. Although we have carved up the "modern era" into smaller, more discrete entities, and also denied the Renaissance much of what nineteenth-century historians saw as its cultural modernity, we have continued to use and struggle with a historical narrative first written in the Renaissance. The fact that Petrarch's vision of Rome, and the pleasures of inhabiting the past, still captures our imagination is one sign that the Renaissance is alive, even when we reject the specific vision of history he held so dear. But there are other aspects of Renaissance historical thought that have acquired new meanings and significance in our own time: the debates about written and oral sources of historical information, about the political implications of historical examples, about the role of women in historical events and historical writing, and about the literary and scientific components of historical knowledge. The continuing vitality and passion in these debates should remind us of how Renaissance historiographers described their own struggles to interpret the past. "For history, as you know, is a very ticklish business," observed Estienne Pasquier after completing his *Researches on France*.[36] The inability of Renaissance scholars to settle on a single method, or a unified set of guiding principles by which to write history, resulted in a kind of productive anarchy. Fortunately historians are still living and working within this creative legacy of

Renaissane cutlure, because the past is far too variable and subtle a landscape for any single method or approach to prevail.

NOTES

1   Donald R. Kelley, *Versions of History from Antiquity to the Enlightenment* (New Haven: Yale University Press, 1991), p. 221.

2   Francesco Scalamonti, *Vita Vita viri clarissimi et famosissimi Kyriaci Anconitani*. Ed. and trans. Charles Mitchell and Edward W. Bodnar (Philadelphia: American Philosophical Society). *Transactions of the American Philosophical Society*, Vol. 86, Pt. 4, p. 117.

3   The classic study of this subject remains Theodor Mommsen, "Petrarch's Conception of the 'Dark Ages,'" *Speculum* 17 (1942): 226–42; see also Carol Quillen, *Rereading the Renaissance: Petrarch, Augustine, and the Language of Humanism* (Ann Arbor: University of Michigan Press, 1998).

4   Kelley, *Versions*, p. 221.

5   See Walter Ferguson, *The Renaissance in Historical Thought* (Boston: Houghton Mifflin, 1948), for a full discussion of the historical emergence of the idea of the Renaissance; and Paula Findlen, *A Fragmentary Past: The Making of Museums in Renaissance Italy* (forthcoming).

6   Peter Burke, *The Renaissance Sense of the Past* (New York: St. Martin's Press, 1969), p. 42.

7   Depending on which historian one reads, the Renaissance either is presented as the birth of modern historiography – e.g. Ferguson, *Renaissance* – or as an important precursor – e.g. Anthony Grafton, *The Footnote: A Curious History* (Cambridge, MA: Harvard University Press, 1997). The latter view represents the more nuanced results of recent scholarship, but many themes of modern historical thought can be found in the works of Renaissance historians.

8   Mommsen, "Petrarch's Conception," p. 237. I have modified Mommsen's translation to conform with the one found in Donald R. Kelley, *Faces of History: Historical Inquiry from Herodotus to Herder* (New Haven: Yale University Press, 1998), p. 130.

9   Paul Oskar Kristeller, *Renaissance Thought: The Classic, Scholastic, and Humanist Strains* (New York: Harper Torchbooks, 1961), pp. 105–6; and Burke, *Renaissance Sense*.

10 History did not have a formal place in the education curriculum until the growth of the Jesuit college system in the late sixteenth and seventeenth centuries. Eric Cochrane, "The Profession of Historian in the Italian Renaissance," *Journal of Social History* 15 (1981): 56; and idem, *Historians and Historiography in the Italian Renaissance* (Chicago: University of Chicago Press, 1981).

11 Aristotle, *Poetics* 1451 b 5–11. This passage is discussed in Anthony Grafton, *Commerce with the Classics: Ancient Books and Renaissance Readers* (Ann Arbor: University of Michigan Press, 1997), p. 13.

12 Cicero, *De oratore* II.15. Roberto Weiss, *The Renaissance Discovery of Classical*

Antiquity (Oxford: Blackwell, 1988), 2nd edn.; and Arnaldo Momigliano, *The Classical Foundations of Modern Historiography* (Berkeley: University of California Press, 1990) provide an excellent starting point for readers interested in the relationship between antiquity and Renaissance history.

13 The above quotation appears in Leonardo Bruni, "On the Study of Literature (1424)," in *The Humanism of Leonardo Bruni: Selected Texts*, ed. and trans. Gordon Griffiths, James Hankins, and David Thompson (Binghamton, NY: Medieval and Renaissance Texts and Studies, 1987), p. 245.

14 This was also true of Biondo's other works: *Roma instaurata* (1440–6) and *Roma triumphans* (1456–60). Most notably, Biondo's *Italia illustrata* (1448–53) became a model for other national histories such as Conrad Celtis' *Germania illustrata*.

15 Grafton, *Commerce*, p. 18.

16 For good examples of this kind of writing, see Gene Brucker, ed., *Two Memoirs of Renaissance Florence: The Diaries of Buonaccorso Pitti and Gregorio Dati* (New York: Harper and Row, 1967); and Vittore Branca, *Merchant Writers in the Italian Renaissance*, trans. Murtha Baca (New York: Marsilio Publishers, 1999).

17 Francesco Guicciardini, *The History of Italy*, trans. Sydney Alexander (New York: Collier Books, 1969), p. 3.

18 Mark Phillips aptly describes Guicciardini's *History* as "a post-mortem on the Italian Renaissance." Phillips, *Francesco Guicciardini: The Historian's Craft* (Toronto: University of Toronto Press, 1977), p. 135.

19 Giovanni Rucellai, "A Merchant's Praise of Florence," in *Images of Quattrocento Florence: Selected Writings in Literature, History and Art*, ed. and trans. Stefano Ugo Baldassarri and Arielle Saiber (New Haven: Yale University Press, 2000), p. 73.

20 In addition to the works of Machiavelli and Guicciardini, see, for example, Thomas Blundeville, *The True Order and Methode of Wryting and Reading Hystories* (1574), a translation of treatises by Francesco Patrizi and Giacomo Aconcio. David R. Woolf, *The Idea of History in Stuart England* (Toronto: University of Toronto Press, 1990), pp. 3–4.

21 Alain Schnapp, *The Discovery of the Past*, trans. Ian Kinnes and Gillian Varndell (New York: Abrams, 1997), pp. 139–41; and Richard Helgerson, *Forms of Nationhood: The Elizabethan Writing of England* (Chicago: University of Chicago Press, 1992), p. 129. Camden's *Britannia*, much like Bruni's *Histories*, first appeared in Latin and was subsequently translated into English in 1610.

22 Christine de Pizan, *The Book of the City of Ladies*, trans. Earl Jeffrey Richards (New York: Persea Books, 1982), pp. 254, 117.

23 Griffiths, Hankins, and Thompson, *Humanism of Leonardo Bruni*, p. 246.

24 Natalie Zemon Davis, "Gender and Genre: Women as Historical Writers, 1400–1820," in *Beyond Their Sex: Learned Women of the European Past*, ed. Patricia A. Labalme (New York: New York University Press, 1980), p. 158.

25 Henricus Cornelius Agrippa, *Declamation on the Nobility and Preeminence of the Female Sex*, ed. and trans. Albert Rabil, Jr. (Chicago: University of Chicago Press, 1996), pp. 95, 89.

26 Lucrezia Marinella, *The Nobility and Excellence of Women and the Defects and Vices*

of Men, ed. and trans. Anne Dunhill, introduced by Letizia Panizza (Chicago: University of Chicago Press, 1999), pp. 83, 81. Listing the accomplishments of women, past and present, in the late fifteenth century, the Brescian humanist Laura Cereta (1469–99) wrote, "All history is full of such examples." Laura Cereta, *Collected Letters of a Renaissance Feminist*, ed. and trans. Diana Robin (Chicago: University of Chicago Press, 1997), p. 78.

27 Burke, *Renaissance Sense*, p. 84. I have modified Burke's translation slightly.

28 Kelley, *Versions*, p. 240; Phillips, *Francesco Guicciardini*, p. 97, n20; and Niccolò Machiavelli, *History of Florence*, in *Machiavelli: The Chief Works and Others*, trans. Allan Gilbert (Durham: Duke University Press, 1989), vol. 3, p. 1031.

29 Francesco Guicciardini, *Maxims and Reflections of a Renaissance Statesman*, trans. Mario Domandi (New York: Harper Torchbooks, 1965), p. 77; and Jean Bodin, *Method for the Easy Comprehension of History*, trans. Beatrice Reynold (New York: Octagon Books, 1966), p. 61.

30 Guicciardini, *Maxims*, p. 71.

31 T. C. Price Zimmerman, *Paolo Giovio: The Historian and the Crisis of Sixteenth-Century Italy* (Princeton: Princeton University Press, 1995), p. 236; and Grafton, *Footnote*, p. 139.

32 Bodin's admiration for Guicciardini ran so deep that he called Guicciardini the "father of history." Bodin, *Method*, pp. 153, 61.

33 Bodin, *Method*, p. 303.

34 Cochrane, "Transition," p. 36.

35 Huppert, *Idea*, p. 33; and Grafton, *Footnote*, p. 229.

36 Huppert, *Idea*, p. 62.

REFERENCES AND FURTHER READING

Brown, Patricia Fortini, *Venice and Antiquity: The Venetian Sense of the Past*, New Haven: Yale University Press, 1996.

Burke, Peter, *The Renaissance Sense of the Past*, New York: St. Martin's Press, 1969.

Cochrane, Eric, *Historians and Historiography in the Italian Renaissance*, Chicago: University of Chicago Press, 1981.

Davis, Natalie Zemon, "Gender and Genre: Women as Historical Writers, 1400–1820," in *Beyond Their Sex: Learned Women of the European Past*, ed. Patricia A. Labalme, New York: New York University Press, 1980, pp. 153–82.

Ferguson, Walter, *The Renaissance in Historical Thought*, Boston: Houghton Mifflin, 1948.

Findlen, Paula, *A Fragmentary Past: The Making of Museums in Renaissance Italy*, forthcoming.

Gilbert, Felix, *Machiavelli and Guicciardini: Politics and History in Sixteenth-Century Florence*, 2nd edn. New York: Norton, 1984.

Grafton, Anthony, *The Footnote: A Curious History*, Cambridge, MA: Harvard University Press, 1997.

Green, Louis, *Chronicle into History: An Essay on the Interpretation of History in*

Florentine Fourteenth-Century Chronicles, Cambridge: Cambridge University Press, 1972.

Huppert, George, *The Idea of Perfect History: Historical Erudition and Historical Philosophy in Renaissance France*, Urbana: University of Illinois Press, 1970.

Ianziti, Gary, *Humanist Historiography under the Sforzas: Politics and Propaganda in Fifteenth-Century Milan*, Oxford: Clarendon Press, 1988.

Kelley, Donald R., *Foundations of Modern Historical Scholarship: Language, Law, and History in the French Renaissance*, New York: Columbia University Press, 1970.

——, "Humanism and History." In *Renaissance Humanism: Foundations, Forms, and Legacy*, Vol. 3. *Humanism and the Disciplines*, ed. Albert Rabil, Jr. Philadelphia: University of Pennsylvania Press, 1988, pp. 236–70.

——, "Renaissance Retrospection." In his *Faces of History: Historical Inquiry from Herodotus to Herder*, New Haven: Yale University Press, 1998, pp. 130–61.

Mommsen, Theodor, "Petrarch's Conception of the 'Dark Ages,'" *Speculum* 17 (1942): 226–42.

Phillips, Mark, *Francesco Guicciardini: The Historian's Craft*, Toronto: University of Toronto Press, 1977.

Streuver, Nancy S., *The Language of History in the Renaissance: Rhetoric and Historical Consciousness in Florentine Humanism*, Princeton: Princeton University Press, 1970.

Weiss, Roberto, *The Renaissance Discovery of Classical Antiquity*, 2nd edn., Oxford: Blackwell, 1988.

Wilcox, Donald J., *The Development of Florentine Humanist Historiography in the Fifteenth Century*, Cambridge, MA: Harvard University Press, 1969.

Woolf, David R, *The Idea of History in Early Stuart England*, Toronto: University of Toronto Press, 1990.

PART II

The Shaping of Modern Western Historical Thought

Historical Thought in the Era of the Enlightenment

JOHNSON KENT WRIGHT

Serious scholarly discussion of the historical thought of the Enlightenment began with Ernst Cassirer's *The Philosophy of the Enlightenment*, published in 1932. Setting out to overturn what he called the "Romantic myth" of the "unhistorical Enlightenment," Cassirer insisted that, far from neglecting history, it was the eighteenth century that had established the "conditions of possibility" for all of modern historiography. Thirty years later, the efforts of Cassirer and others to rehabilitate Enlightenment historical thought had produced a remarkable turn-around. In a famous essay of the mid-1960s, Hugh Trevor-Roper could declare that history as a "continuous science" began not with Ranke or Niebhur, but with the "philosophical historians" of the eighteenth century – Voltaire, David Hume, William Robertson, and Edward Gibbon. Their achievement was made possible, above all, by the definitive secularization of European thought in the Enlightenment. Freed from devotional distortions, the "philosophical historians" were the first to abandon the descriptive or didactic aims of traditional history, in order to pursue the ambition that has defined historical science ever since – to provide rational *explanations* of historical change and development. Indeed, Trevor-Roper suggested, the capacious philosophical outlook of these historians compared favorably with the narrower, more conservative optic of the Rankean professional historiography that succeeded it.

Today, another thirty years later, the historiography of the Enlightenment is enjoying a significant renewal of scholarly attention. If the substance of Trevor-Roper's assessment remains unchallenged, preoccupations have nevertheless shifted somewhat in the interim. The change can be seen above all in the two most important works of recent years in English, both major surveys of the field – Karen O'Brien's *Narratives of Enlightenment: Cosmopolitan History from Voltaire to Gibbon*, and J. G. A. Pocock's multi-volume study of Gibbon and his contemporaries, *Barbarism and Religion*. It is no accident that

the primary focus of both studies should be less on the "philosophical" content
of eighteenth-century historiography than on its narrative *form* – for, very
much in tune with the times, the problem of *narrative* is now at the center
of all discussion of the historical thought of the Enlightenment. At the same
time, the work of O'Brien and Pocock also makes it clear that a contemporary survey of this terrain cannot confine its attention to Voltaire, Hume,
Robertson, and Gibbon alone. For it turns out that the emergence of "philosophical history" depended crucially on the existence of a body of writing that,
if it exceeded the boundaries of historiography proper, certainly belonged to
"historical thought" in a wider sense of the term. Trevor-Roper in fact called
attention to the indispensable catalytic role played by Montesquieu's *On the
Spirit of the Laws* – without question the major work of social thought of the
Enlightenment. But Montesquieu was not alone. For the eighteenth century
was of course the great age of "conjectural" history – sweeping speculative
reconstructions, typically narrative in form, of the totality of human history.
This was perhaps the most characteristic literature of the French and Scottish
Enlightenments alike, describing the major works of such figures as Turgot,
Rousseau, and Condorcet, and Adam Ferguson, John Millar, and Adam Smith.
One of the great merits of Pocock's work in particular is to restore the writing
of Gibbon and his peers to this larger intellectual context.

This essay, then, will look at historical thought in the epoch of the Enlightenment through a slightly more wide-angled lens than that of Trevor-Roper
– though, like the latter, it excludes German thought of the later eighteenth
century, which is surveyed in the next chapter of this volume. The essay begins
by considering older traditions of historiography that persisted in the eighteenth century, and then turns to the emergence of novel theories of
socio-political development, chiefly from within the framework of natural
jurisprudence – the background for such figures as Vico and Montesquieu. A
closer look at both "conjectural" and "philosophical" history follows, together
with consideration of how these forms of writing were extended beyond
Europe itself, as European historical vision began for the first time to encompass the globe. Having looked at some of the advances of Enlightenment historical thought, the essay concludes with reflections on its transitional status
in the wider development of modern historiography.

Pre-Enlightenment Traditions

The first major works of the European Enlightenment – Montesquieu's
Persian Letters, Voltaire's *Letters Concerning the English Nation* – date from
the 1720s and 1730s. The origin of the outlook expressed in them, however,
is conventionally traced to the last quarter of the seventeenth century, to the

episode of intellectual turmoil that the French historian Paul Hazard once described as "the crisis of European consciousness." This was the period of creative ferment that loosened the grip of both Christian and classical authority over European thought, thus paving the way for the intellectual revolution of the Enlightenment. It was no accident that one major tradition of pre-modern narrative historiography came to an end at precisely this point. The last great work of Christian "universal history," Bossuet's *Discourse on Universal History* of 1681, was soon rendered obsolete by the irreversible de-Christianization of Europe's cultural elites. A little over a decade later, the title of Cellarius's compendium announced the secular periodization that would henceforth dominate European historiography: *Universal History Divided into an Ancient, Medieval, and New Period.*

Two other traditions of early-modern historiography proved more resilient in this period, however. One was the entire range of "antiquarian" or "erudite" history, whose roots lay in Renaissance source-criticism and Reformation sectarianism, and whose chief aim was the collection and preservation of every kind of record of the past – philological, documentary, archeological, numismatic, artistic, architectural. The watershed for antiquarian historiography came with an episode vividly described by Hazard: the onslaught of a skeptical "Pyrrhonism," which aimed at undermining all secure knowledge of the past, on epistemological grounds above all. The results were not merely destructive, however. The one enduring masterpiece of Pyrrhonism, Pierre Bayle's *Historical and Critical Dictionary* (1697), was hailed by Cassirer for having performed a "Copernican revolution" in historical methodology, by demonstrating once and for all the role of "subjectivity" in establishing all historical "facts." As it happened, erudite historiography not only survived the assault of Pyrrhonism, but went on to enjoy a final flowering in the eighteenth century. This was owing, on the one hand, to the resources and continuity offered by monastic patronage, and, on the other, to the stimulus and audience supplied by an emergent world of academies and learned societies. In France, for example, the Benedictine Maurist Order not only presided over the publication of a remarkable series of source collections for both ecclesiastical and secular history, but it also sponsored the major studies of documentation and chronology of the period, Jean Mabillon's *On Diplomacy* (1681), and *The Art of Verifying Dates* (1750). The Maurists also helped to inspire what was perhaps the most distinguished individual contribution to erudite history, that of Ludovico Muratori (1672–1750), Ducal Librarian at Modena, whose work as collector and editor laid the documentary foundations for the modern study of medieval Italy. Muratori was just one of dozens of industrious antiquarians, who prolonged the routines of this style of historiography to the end of the Old Regime and beyond. If it was always possible for "erudition" to attract Enlightened scorn – the attacks of D'Alembert and Voltaire are notorious instances – antiquarian historiography nevertheless provided one of the indispensable starting points for the achievements of "philosophical history" proper.

The same is true for the equally resilient early-modern traditions of political historiography. Starting with the Renaissance, nearly every political unit in Europe, from the smallest city-state to the greatest territorial monarchy, generated a lively narrative literature on its own past. The original model for this kind of writing, established by Machiavelli and Guicciardini, was thoroughly neo-classical in its aims and methods, seeking to explain the cyclical rotation of forms of government in terms of the interplay of institutional form and moral content – the virtues or "corruption" of the one, the few, and many. Designed to capture the evolution of the classical *polis* and Renaissance city-state, the model naturally had to be adapted for the different environment of the northern kingdoms, where the central object of historical dispute typically proved to be the "ancient constitution" of absolutist or proto-absolutist monarchies. One unexpected result, to which the resources of erudition contributed a good deal, was a gradual "sociologization" of political historiography, shown above all in the emergence of the concept of "feudalism" as a socio-economic category. J. G. A. Pocock's reconstruction of these transformations in seventeenth-century English historical thought, *The Ancient Constitution and the Feudal Law*, is a classic in modern intellectual history.

The "crisis" in European thought, as Hazard described it, challenged neo-classicism of any kind, most notably in the form of the famous debate between the "Ancients and the Moderns" – the "Battle of the Books" in Britain – which is conventionally thought to have produced a decisive victory for the advocates of cultural and aesthetic "modernity." Yet as Pocock himself went on to show in *The Machiavellian Moment*, what is impressive is the persistent vitality of neo-classical political historiography, which continued to describe rotations or "revolutions" in forms of government in the manner of Polybius, Tacitus, and Machiavelli, right through the eighteenth century. No episode in its history is more striking than the debate over the "ancient constitution" of the French monarchy in the epoch of the Enlightenment, which was dominated by historians committed to civic humanism of one kind or another – aristocratic, in the case of the comte de Boulainvilliers, democratic in that of the abbé de Mably. As we shall see, "philosophical history" itself owed a central debt to the neo-classical historiography of the early-modern period.

From the Laws of Nature to *The Spirit of the Laws*

Nevertheless, the specific novelty of Enlightenment historical thought depended on a decisive break with the norms of neo-classical historiography, at one key point above all. The object of neo-classical history remained the political *state*, whose vicissitudes continued to be explained chiefly in terms of the *cyclical* rotation of forms of government. The Enlightenment, on the other hand, has always been associated with the emergence of the earliest conceptions of long-term unilinear development, focused not on political forms but on social structures – theories of *socio-economic progress*, in other words. Where should the origins of these be sought? A certain conventional wisdom holds that Enlightenment theories of development and progress can be regarded as "secularizations" of Christian conceptions of temporal salvation and redemption. This was the burden of Carl Becker's famous set of lectures, *The Heavenly City of the Eighteenth-Century Philosophers*, contemporary with Cassirer; an updated version of the same claim lies behind Jean-François Lyotard's notorious references to the "grand narratives" of the Enlightenment in *The Postmodern Condition* (1979) and subsequent works.

Whatever the validity of these claims in general – they are, of course, a standard device for challenging the legitimacy of the Enlightenment – it happens that the later seventeenth century did see the emergence of a novel conceptual vocabulary for understanding long-range historical development. Surprisingly enough, the vocabluary was supplied by a tradition of thought not typically associated with theories of historical change, that of early-modern "natural jurisprudence" or "natural rights" theory. Indeed, from the standpoint of the Romantic historiography that Cassirer saw as an obstacle to a true appreciation of the Enlightenment, the Enlightenment was "unhistorical" precisely because it subscribed to the venerable Western traditions of natural law – that is, to belief in a set of timeless norms, established by God or inscribed in "nature," and reflected in a fixed set of human dispositions and traits. If these beliefs gave rise to the revolutionary concepts that established modern political thought – the notion of a "state of nature" in which individuals possessed equal "natural rights," and of the "social contract" that founded "civil society" – their very universalism and abstraction could also act as obstacles to a fully *historical* understanding of human change and diversity. The emergence of modern historical sensibility, on this view, was born of a frontal rejection of the concepts of natural law, chiefly by the thinkers of the German Counter-Enlightenment.

Today, however, such claims can no longer be sustained. The result of several decades of intensive study of the actual record of early-modern natural jurisprudence has been virtually to reverse the older view: far from being seen as obstacles to the emergence of theories of historical change and development, seventeenth- and eighteenth-century traditions of natural law are today commonly regarded as their seedbeds. The crucial figures here were the founders of what, for the Enlightenment, was the "modern" school of natural law – Hugo Grotius, Thomas Hobbes, and Samuel Pufendorf. The decisive innovation belonged to Pufendorf (1632–94), who developed a historicized account of the transition from "nature" to "civil society" by suggesting that it had proceeded by stages, essentially defined in terms of property regimes and modes of subsistence. Here was the analytic kernel for most of the great stadial explanations of history of Enlightenment, the famous "four-stages" theory above all, to which we will return below.[1] An arcane teaching in the seventeenth century, still often theological in purpose, the work of the "modern" school of natural law underwent a vast process of popularization and diffusion in the first half of the eighteenth, from which it emerged thoroughly secularized and shorn of much of its archaic legalism. In this form, it provided not just a conceptual vocabulary but something closer to a set of "absolute presuppositions" for all social and historical thought in the eighteenth century.

The most striking results of this process in the first half of the century, prior to the full harvest of stadial history proper, were to be found in idiosyncratic individual performances, at a creative distance from the mainstream of natural jurisprudence. Two such enterprises, whose receptions in the eighteenth century form a striking contrast, stand out. One lay outside the Enlightenment altogether. Working in life-long obscurity in Naples, Giambattista Vico (1668–1744) devoted an intellectual career to forging a "new science" of society, chiefly by way of systematic criticism of contemporary thinkers. Vico's methodological starting point was a theological critique of Cartesian epistemology, which yielded a famous principle, that "the true and the made are convertible" – in effect, a claim that our knowledge of the historical world, owing to the essential identity of the knower and the known, was not only different from our knowledge of nature, but was in certain ways superior to it. At the same time, Vico's critical engagement with the "modern" natural lawyers led to recurrent experimentation with alternate, even retrograde forms of historical periodization. *Universal Law* (1720–2) restored the distinction between sacred and profane history, subdividing the latter into five stages whose evolution was governed by a kind of dialectic between laws and arms. In the successive editions of Vico's major work, *The New Science* (1725, 1730, 1744), this was refined into a three-stage "ideal universal history," a stylized recapitulation of ancient Roman history, which distinguished between theocratic, aristocratic, and democratic ages – plus a fourth, anarchic stage, which returned the cycle to its starting point. Vico was, of course, a thinker notoriously out of step with his own time. Almost entirely ignored in the eighteenth century, even in Italy, his work awaited its rediscovery by Michelet in the nineteenth, which almost immediately raised it to the cult-like status it has enjoyed ever since.

Four years after the last edition of *The New Science*, a French thinker published his own attempt at a "new science" of politics and history. The themes addressed in *On the Spirit of the Laws* (1748) are, in fact, not far from those of Vico – but expressed in a vastly different idiom, unmistakably that of the Enlightenment. For Montesquieu (1689–1755) was already the major figure of the early Enlightenment in France. He made his literary debut with a brilliant epistolary novel, *Persian Letters* (1721), which used the device of alien observation – visitors from Safavid Persia – to hold up a critical mirror to European civilization. Looking back to classical civilization, Montesquieu then attempted a rational explanation of its greatest enigma, the rise and fall of the Roman Empire: *Considerations on the Causes of the Grandeur of the Romans and of their Decadence* (1731–2) was one of the last masterpieces of Machiavellian historiography, on the verge of its transformation. These works paved the way for *On the Spirit of the Laws* – but its achievement was on another scale entirely. Immediately recognized as the greatest work of social thought of the age, its stature has only grown over time. The structure of *On the Spirit of the Laws* is notoriously miscellaneous, at least in appearance. An opening book proclaimed a kind of Cartesian natural jurisprudence, defining all law – divine, natural, political and civil – as "the necessary relations deriving from the nature of things." Montesquieu then devoted twelve books to the presentation of a universal taxonomy of three "forms of government," republican, monarchical, and despotic, each governed by a different subjective "principle" – virtue, honor, and fear, respectively. Apparently switching gears, he turned, in the next twelve books, to the multiple causal determinants – geography and climate, manners and morals, commerce and finance, demography and religion – that together formed not the "principle" but the "spirit" of the laws, for which Montesquieu claimed a kind of causal primacy. *On the Spirit of the Laws* then closed with a series of historical investigations, focused above all on the earliest history of the French Monarchy, and ending with the stabilization of the "feudal government" of the Middle Ages.

At first glance, this looks like a recipe for an indeterminate pluralism – and indeed, much of the impact of *On the Spirit of the Laws* depended on the way it served as an encyclopedia illustrating every conceivable form of social and historical explanation, from the most bluntly material to the most ethereally ideal. Nevertheless, the profusion conceals a convergence of Montesquieu's concerns on a tantalizing historical question, never articulated as such in the text, but obvious to every reader – the explanation of the unique *dynamism* of European historical development, in a global perspective. The enduring achievement of *On the Spirit of the Laws* lay in the combination of the two avenues of explanation he pursued in this regard. Globally, and all too crudely, of course, Montesquieu's theory of geographical and climactic determinism consigned the world outside of Europe to the largely static or cyclical routines of "despotism." The historical development specific to the West was then explained in terms of the long transition from the classical world of virtuous agrarian republics to the modern world of commercial monarchies. It was no accident that Montesquieu ended his book – "where most writers begin," he noted – with the emergence of feudal society, for here alone, in his view, was an explanation of European exceptionalism to be sought.

Stadial and "Conjectural" History

No work had a greater impact on the development of social and historical thought in the eighteenth century. Indeed, the appearance of *On the Spirit of the Laws* unleashed a flood of equally ambitious totalizations of the social field – though with a crucial difference. Political taxonomy, of the kind that still dominated Montesquieu's analysis, was now left firmly behind in favor of theories of stadial social development, explicitly presented as such. Of these, far and away the most important was the "four-stages" theory, which now emerged definitively from the legal cocoon in which it had developed. The major survey of the topic remains Ronald Meek's *Social Science and the Ignoble Savage* (1976), whose account of its origins stresses not so much its natural jurisprudential framework as the catalytic role played by ethnographic reports on "savage" societies, particularly those of North America.[2] The first statements of the theory followed immediately on the heels of *On the Spirit of the Laws*, in both France and Scotland, in writings of the fifties by Turgot, Quesnay, Helvétius, and Gouget, and Dalrymple and Kames. Its most spectacular presentations then came in the great masterworks of the Scottish Enlightenment – Adam Ferguson's *An Essay on the History of Civil Society* (1767), John Millar's *The Origin of the Distinction of Ranks* (1771), and, in more fragmentary form, Adam Smith's *An Inquiry into the Nature and Causes of the Wealth of Nations* (1776).

For all the different aims of these works, they shared two fundamental claims. It was the Scottish historian William Robertson who gave the most famous expression to the first, an assertion of causal primacy: "In every inquiry concerning the operations of men when united together in society, the first object of attention should be their mode of subsistence. Accordingly as that varies, their laws and policy must be different."[3] Secondly, there was a general tendency for these "modes" to advance through progressive stages – from hunter-gatherer, to pastoral, agricultural, and "commerical," or, more simply still, from "savagery" to "barbarism" to "civilization," the last coming in two different forms. This was no more than a "tendency," however. The four-stages theory was not a doctrine of historical inevitability, much less one of necessary evolutionary "progress" toward some pre-determined goal. Ferguson, Millar, and Smith were perfectly aware of the difference between this simple heuristic model and the actual record of human history, involving the fate of scores of separate nations, in vastly different geographic zones. In particular, their Scottish perch tended to make the stadial theorists acutely sensitive to the transitive impact of societies, at different levels of development, upon one another. Nor were any of these writers simple champions of the "commercial" civilization of modern Europe. Even Smith, the most sanguine about its prospects, expressed numerous anxieties about the effect of the modern "division of labor" on human well-being. At the other end of the spectrum, Ferguson's distinction in the Scottish Enlightenment was to bring the political values of civic humanism to bear on its key themes. The last parts of the *Essay on the History of Civil Society* mounted a withering attack on "commercial" civilization for its relentless destruction of political community, the supreme model for which remained the martial citizenry of ancient Rome. Ferguson's own image for capturing the notion of "unintended consequences" in history was thus rather different from Smith's "invisible hand": "Like the winds, that come we know not whence, and blow withersoever they list, the forms of society are derived from an obscure and distant origin . . . and nations stumble upon establishments, which are indeed the result of human action, but not the execution of any human design."[4]

It was Ferguson's younger associate Dugald Stewart who coined the term "conjectural history" to describe at least some of the writing of his compatriots. Meek objected to the phrase as a general description of the major stadial theorists of the Scottish Enlightenment, on the grounds that their works never substituted "conjecture" for empirical demonstration, as the phrase implied: Ferguson, in particular, deployed a rich array of up-to-date evidence for his analysis of the "savages" of North America and "barbarians" of Siberia. But the term is accurate enough as a description of much of the stadial meta-history written in the second half of the century. The French Enlightenment was particularly prolific in producing this kind of writing, some of it very far indeed from the sober analysis of Scottish four-stages theory. Perhaps the most stunning work of "conjectural history" of them all was Jean-Jacques Rousseau's *Discourse on the Origin and Foundations of Inequality Among Men* (1754), which opened with the author's resolve to "set aside the facts." The first part of the *Discourse*, an extended description of the "natural state" of mankind (sustained by ethnographic evidence as well), in fact aimed at a complete demolition of the concept of natural "sociability" as it had descended from Pufendorf. Having dispatched the "modern" natural lawyers, Rousseau then set out in the second part to sketch his own, alternate theory of development, which in effect superimposed a classical conception of political rotation on a simple stadial model: a first "revolution" established formal families and incipient forms of property; a second, driven by the invention of metallurgy and agriculture, created private property in land and the division of labor; and a third revolution led to the invention of the political state – which then evolved, roughly speaking, from an original democracy, to aristocracy, and finally to "despotism," the standard form of all present-day states.

Rousseau's presentation was completely detached from conventional historiographic periodization, but the connections were easy enough to trace. Among other things, Rousseau's second *Discourse* is a vivid reminder that stadial theories could as easily be ones of historical *regress* as of progress – of *maldevelopment* rather than development.[5] At the same time, of course, France also produced what is, by common consensus, the supreme expression of historical *optimism* of the Enlightenment. Condorcet's *Sketch for a Historical Picture of the Progress of the Human Mind* (1793), the introduction to an unfinished larger work, projected no fewer than ten stages in the development of human society: the first three corresponded roughly to the eras of "savagery," "barbarism," and "civilization" familiar from four-stages theory; the next six were essentially epochs in *intellectual* history, with the discovery of ideas serving as the motor-force for change, from ancient Greece to modern Europe; while the tenth, inaugurated by the French Revolution itself, pointed toward an imminent end-state of development, defined by three conditions: "the abolition of inequality between nations, the progress of equality within each nation, and the true perfection of mankind."[6] Written under the shadow of the guillotine, Condorcet's *Sketch* itself marked the end of an intellectual age.

Philosophical History

By the time Condorcet wrote, the great flowering of "philosophical history" proper had run its course as well. It can be said to have begun with the publication of the first version of Voltaire's *Essay on Manners* and the first volume of Hume's *History of England* in 1754 and ended with the last volumes of *The History of the Decline and Fall of the Roman Empire* in 1788. In between had come Robertson's *History of the Reign of the Emperor Charles V* (1769) and *The History of America* (1777), as well as Raynal's and Diderot's *History of the Two Indies* (1770–80). As we noted at the outset, what has most attracted the attention of recent historians is the *narrative* structure of these works. In particular, what was common to all the "philosophical historians" was an "Enlightened" or "cosmopolitan" narrative of European development, which brought the philosophical and analytic insights of Montesquieu or the stadial theorists down to the firm earth of detailed historical reconstruction and explanation.

The first to produce a version of this "Enlightened narrative" was Voltaire (1694–1778), who was a full generation older than his nearest contemporary among the "philosophical historians." This meant that his intellectual formation took place in precisely those years in which the prestige of historiography in France had sunk to its lowest levels, owing in part to the kinds of doubts raised in the skeptical literature of Pyrrhonism. Voltaire absorbed not a little of this outlook himself: always capable of posing the sharpest questions about the reliability of historical knowledge, his own insouciance toward evidence and citation later earned him the rebuke of Robertson and Gibbon. Nevertheless, no one in the eighteenth century did more to restore the fortunes of history, indeed to re-invent it as a form of popular literature.

Voltaire's starting point as a historian was in a conventional genre of neo-classical historiography, one that took not the state but its leading actor as its object. His first major work was a *History of Charles XII* (1731), in which Voltaire's royalism found expression in the moral contrast between the two great northern kings who collided in battle at Poltava (1709) – Charles XII's vain hunt for "glory" versus Peter I's sober resolve to "civilize" the domains of Russia. Voltaire next turned to the greatest of all absolute monarchs, starting to write *The Age of Louis XIV* as early as 1735. In the long course of its composition, however – a full version was not published until 1751, and then revised and expanded in 1753 – the *mirror-of-princes* mold of Voltaire's earliest work was left behind. Everything here points to the impact of *On the Spirit of the Laws*, both as inspiration and as foil. For as Voltaire announced on its first page, *The Age of Louis XIV* was in effect a charter for a new kind of history, whose object was an entire "age," viewed as a political, social, and cultural totality – close to the sense of Montesquieu's "spirit." On the other hand, the actual age chosen for scrutiny betrayed a political outlook distant from that of Montesquieu. For Voltaire, the reign of the Sun King was the latest and greatest of the four ages in history in which Enlightened "monarchs" had presided over an effervescence of the arts and sciences – the other three being Athens under Pericles, Rome under Augustus, and Florence under the Medici.

From here it was a short step to Voltaire's major work, the *Essay on Manners and the Spirit of Nations* (1754), which apparently began life as a response to Emilie du Châtelet's queries about the shape of world history. The *Essay* in fact began outside of Europe, with brief profiles of the civilizations of China, India, Persia, and the Arab world. Here there was explicit disagreement with Montesquieu: Voltaire objected vigorously to the latter's claims that "despotism" was "natural" to these lands. But Voltaire's chief purpose in appealing to extra-European civilizations was tactical, intended to strip Judaism and Christianity of any central role in world history. That done, the main narrative of the *Essay on Manners* was primarily a European one: the story, stretching from the depths of the Dark Ages to the threshold of the "enlightened" epoch of Louis XIV, of the slow emancipation of a common European intellectual and artistic culture from the pall of "barbarism" and "religion." Not surprisingly, Voltaire was unable to keep the full international promise of the *Essay*, whose central narrative in fact tends to dissolve into discrete national histories. He revised the text extensively over the next fifteen years, eventually adding an opening essay on ancient religion, entitled "The Philosophy of History," thus coining the term. But what these revisions principally reveal is a gradual subordination of the project to the polemical demands of the great campaign against religious "fanaticism" that absorbed Voltaire's energies in those years. As O'Brien suggests, in the course of revision, "the satirist steadily gets the better of the historian." Nevertheless, the historical "narrative of

Enlightenment" silhouetted in *The Age of Louis XIV* and the *Essay on Manners* was a pivotal achievement, the secular, philosophical model for those that followed.

If Voltaire moved, in a sense, from history to philosophy, the direction was reversed in the career of the second major "philosophical historian." It was the failure, as he saw it, of his *Treatise of Human Nature* that prompted David Hume's (1711–76) shift, first, to the social and political terrain of his *Essays* and then to the *History of England* itself. This six-volume work was written and published, famously, in reverse order: two volumes on the Stuarts appeared in 1754, as *The History of Great Britain*; two on the Tudor period followed in 1759, and two on medieval Britain in 1761, by which point the whole had become the *History of England*. Where Voltaire's "narrative of Enlightenment" had emerged from a partisan attachment to French Absolutism, whose virtues were then projected onto the cultural history of the continent as a whole, Hume's narrative developed out of a focus on the political history of the major European nation to have overthrown Absolutism – an achievement that the Scottish historian scrutinized from a unique vantage point, at once intimate and alien. Indeed, Hume's own major claim for the *History of England* was that he had risen above partisanship, in analyzing the most bitterly factious political culture in all of Europe.

His point of departure was to demolish the central shibboleth of conventional English historiography, the notion of an unvarying "ancient constitution" of the realm: the first achievement of the *History of England*, from the Stuart volumes onward, was to re-write English political history in terms of the *evolution* of political structures. If this made it possible for twentieth-century commentators to declare Hume a "scientific Whig" in the end, the Stuart volumes also revealed his skill at making concessions to Tory sentiment along the way – his delicate portrait of the finale of Charles I being the major case in point. As he moved back in time, Hume's optic both deepened and widened, as he began to establish the *differentia specifica* of English history by reference to wider European contexts. The background to the Tudor volumes was thus the Reformation as a whole, which set in stark relief the central irony of English history for Hume, the umbilical connection between religious fanaticism and political libertarianism: "So absolute was the authority of the crown, that the precious spark of liberty had been kindled, and was preserved, by the puritans alone; and it was to this sect, whose principles appear so frivolous and habits so ridiculous, that the English owe the whole freedom of their constitution."[7] Thus was the great Scottish theme of "unintended consequences" transferred to the realm of ideology.

It was left to the concluding volumes on medieval and pre-medieval Britain to place both politics and ideology in a still wider "sociological" context. In them, Hume charted the rise and fall of the "feudal system" in England, a variant on a general European pattern, whose history he sketched in a famous appendix. It is not surprising that Hume had been the earliest theorist of the notion of "national character" in the Enlightenment. For the *History of England* was nothing less than an attempt to reconstruct the emergence of a distinctive English national identity, explaining its peculiarities against the background of a larger pattern of European development. As it happened, the most striking English rejoinder to it came from one of the rare female historians of the epoch. Although the eighteenth century saw, for the first time, the emergence of a considerable feminine audience for historiography, there remained very few women among its major producers. One of the most notable exceptions, however, was Catharine Macaulay (1731–91), whose own *History of England* (1763–81) could hardly have been more partisan – an intransigently republican account of the century of revolution in England, thoroughly neo-classical in method and outlook. Hume treated Macaulay with respect, even while referring to her political milieu as "those insolent rascals in London and Middlesex."[8]

Meanwhile, Scotland's second great "philosophical historian" had launched his career with a patriotic narrative of his own, the *History of Scotland* (1759). William Robertson (1721–93) stands somewhat apart in this company. Not only did he enjoy a long and successful academic career, as Principal of the University of Edinburgh, but he managed an exalted ecclesiastical one as well, serving as Moderator of the General Assembly of the Church of Scotland from 1763 to 1780. A moderate Presbyterian belief in divine providence proved not to be incompatible with the writing of "narratives of Enlightenment," however – such belief was perhaps even a condition of it, in Robertson's case. This can already be seen in a striking sermon of 1755, "The Situation of the World at the Time of Christ's Appearance," which sketched a sociologically sophisticated account of the rise and triumph of early Christianity. A sociology of religion was central to the *History of Scotland* as well, at the climax of its larger political narrative, when post-feudal Scotland fell prey to the more powerful and mature monarchy to its south. For Robertson, a patriot whose writings echo the civic humanist themes characteristic of the Scottish Enlightenment, the Union of Crowns was a catastrophe, bringing to a tragic end the history of Scotland as a free nation. The Union of 1707 pointed toward an ulterior redemption, however, with Scotland entering as junior partner in a fully modernized "united kingdom."

A decade after publishing the *History of Scotland*, Robertson returned to the sixteenth century, as the crux not just of British, but of all modern European history, expanding his vision to take in the entire continent. *The History of the Reign of Charles V* (1769) was Robertson's version of *The Age of Louis XIV*. He prefaced the main part of the book with "A View of the Progress of Society in Europe," a brilliant synoptic survey of the rise and decline of feudal civilization. This set the stage for Robertson's own "narrative of Enlightenment": an account of the emergence of the first international state system out

of the collapse of feudal society, in and through the creative ordeals of imperial contention and religious reformation in the sixteenth century. The former
explained the attempt to see this process through the prism of the reign of the
greatest imperial contender. But the real center of gravity of *The History of
Charles V* lay in Robertson's account of the Reformation, the unique moment
of spiritual renewal and intellectual emancipation that set the course of modern
European history. Even before a stable "balance of powers" had been achieved,
of course, the long career of European colonial expansion had been launched.
This was to be the subject of the last phase of Robertson's career as historian.
A vast narrative account of the European conquest and settlement of the
Americas was planned, but, partly owing to the interruption of the American
War for Independence, was never completed. The hallmark of the portion
published in 1777 as *History of America*, recounting the Iberian conquest of
South America, was the self-conscious deployment of Scottish stadial theory:
here the four-stages theory served to explain the sheer scale of the catastrophe resulting from the collision of such vastly differing civilizations. Going one
step further afield, Robertson then closed his historiographical career with an
essay written during the Hastings trial. *An Historical Disquisition concerning
the Knowledge which the Ancients had of India* (1791) was an impressively
broad-minded plea for the reform of British rule in India, on the grounds of
the antiquity and sophistication of Indian culture, equal in dignity to that of
the ancient Mediterranean.

The historiographical development of Voltaire and Robertson thus followed
similar paths, as both moved from national starting points – continental-
Catholic or provincial-Protestant – to general interpretations of European
development as a whole. Voltaire gestured at a global narrative as well, and
Robertson undertook to write the history of what he regarded as the most
significant episode in recent world history. By the time Robertson's *History
of America* was published, however, a work of global history of even grander
ambition had already reached a second edition. No consideration of "philosophical history" in the Enlightenment could overlook the *Philosophical
and Political History of the Establishments and Commerce of the Europeans
in the Two Indies* – first published in 1770 and revised in 1774 and again in
1780 – a work that has also attracted increasing scholarly attention in recent
years. Part of the reason for this lies in its singular genesis and form. The brain-
child of the Abbé Guillaume-Thomas Raynal (1713–96), the *History of
the Two Indies* was rivaled only by the great *Encyclopedia* of Diderot and
D'Alembert as a truly *collective* enterprise. Leaning heavily on editorial assistance – Denis Diderot (1713–84) himself probably wrote as many as a third
of its pages – Raynal wove together, often with substantial re-writing, a fabu-
lous range of sources, supplied by an intelligence network that spanned the
globe. The scope of the work was equally unprecedented. The aim of *The
History of the Two Indies* was nothing less than a narrative account of the Euro-

pean colonization of Asia, Africa, and the Americas, from the fifteenth century to the present – the largest promise made in the "philosophical history" of the Enlightenment, and one largely made good, if in the form of a "polygraphic" potpourri. Finally, the work of Raynal and Diderot was also one of strenuous moral and political advocacy. The contributions of Diderot, in particular, constitute the major critiques of European slavery, colonialism, and imperialism of the epoch – another reason for the respect the *History of the Two Indies* commands today.

For our purposes, though, the interest of the work lies in the historical analysis that sustained Raynal's and Diderot's political program. Despite the central emphasis placed on *commerce* as a motor-force of European expansion, four-stages theory of the Scottish kind made only fleeting appearances in the text. Instead, the chief analytic categories in the *History of the Two Indies* were "feudalism" and "despotism" – terms which, lying on the frontier between the social and the political, had already been the occasion for dispute between Montesquieu and Voltaire. For the former, these named virtually antithetical types of society, the first unique to the European past, the second the most "natural" social form in the rest of the world. Voltaire, by contrast, not only tended to efface the distinction between the two, seeing them as micro and macro variations on a single pattern, but also denied geographical specificity to them: "feudalism" and "despotism" were at home around the globe, within and outside Europe. For their part, Raynal and Diderot occupied a middle ground between these extremes, amalgamating the two positions: the distinction between "feudalism" and "despotism" was maintained, yet examples of both could be found around the world. The result was that the *History of the Two Indies* tends to see an oscillation *between* "feudalism" and "despotism" as perhaps the central pattern of change in history – except in Europe, which had managed at some point to escape both, with enormous, and paradoxical, consequences for the rest of the world. On the one hand, the dynamism of European "liberty" had unleashed an unprecedented cycle of destruction and suffering around the globe; on the other, this very process held out the promise, in the long run, of a world beyond "feudalism" and "despotism" alike.[9]

If Raynal and Diderot brought "philosophical history" down to the present, in a sweeping vision of the world as a whole, the last of the great philosophical historians turned resolutely to the distant past, and a single episode within it – or so it seems, at first glance. In fact, Edward Gibbon (1737–94) was perfectly placed to effect a kind of grand synthesis of every historiographic tradition we have considered thus far. An Englishman with a thoroughly Continental intellectual formation, he made his literary debut in French. The *Essay on the Study of Literature* (1761) was a late intervention in the methodological dispute that had divided *philosophes* from *érudits* in France. In it, Gibbon argued that history would only become a "science of causes and effects" if it managed to reconcile philosophical analysis and erudite evidence. This program was no mere velleity: Gibbon came closer than any other historian of the epoch to meeting its double demands.[10] On the one hand, the achievement of the *Decline and Fall of the Roman Empire* famously depended on an incomparable command of ancient sources and modern erudition, meticulously laid out in the footnotes that are one of the greatest pleasures of this text. On the other, Gibbon was in some ways the most "philosophical" of the great narrative historians of the Enlightenment. Uncommitted to any single explanatory system, his writing shows a profound awareness of the full range of theory made available by his predecessors; Montesquieu, Voltaire, Robertson, and the luminaries of the Scottish Enlightenment are constant presences in his pages.

In fact, everything suggests that Gibbon's initial inclination as a historian was to follow the path indicated by the "narratives of Enlightenment" of Voltaire, Hume, and Robertson, with their focus on the emergence of a modern European civilization out of the decay of feudalism. A *History of the Liberty of the Swiss* was started and then set aside. But the momentous decision to study the end of classical antiquity – which Gibbon later described as having been taken in Rome in 1764 – by no means signaled a turning away from the problem of the beginning of European modernity. His "General Observations on the Decline of the Empire in the West," an early text inserted at the end of the third volume of the *Decline and Fall*, makes it clear that Gibbon saw his long excursion through Roman antiquity, and then the Latin and Greek Middle Ages, as the necessary preamble to the history of the "one great republic" of modern Europe. Moreover, it is also clear that he intended from the start to take his story down to 1453 – that is, to the threshold of Robertson's sixteenth century. The first volume of *The History of the Decline and Fall of the Roman Empire* was published in 1776. Despite the famous lines about the happiness and prosperity of the "human race" under the Antonines, Gibbon wasted little sentiment on the Empire, nor betrayed much nostalgia for the Republic behind it. His account of its fall in the first volume began with internal decay – demotion of the Senate and rise of "Oriental" ostentation – and ended with the suicidal poison of the embrace of Christianity, described in such acidic tones in the notorious Chapters XV and XVI that Gibbon felt obliged to dilute them in later editions. The end of the first volume left the most enduring image of the historian – second only to Voltaire as a mocking scourge of "superstition." But five more volumes of *The Decline and Fall* followed. The next two, which appeared in 1781, start with the shift of the center of gravity of the decaying empire to the Greek East and end with the barbarian dismemberment of the West. The final three volumes, published in 1788, then surveyed another thousand years of history, contrasting the fates of the two great historic zones into which the Empire had broken – the gradual emergence, in the West, of a new civilization out of the catastrophic collision of Romans and "Gothic" barbarians; and the paralytic persistence of the Byzantine successor state in the East, until it succumbed to the attacks of different kinds of barbarians – Arabic, Turkic, Persian.

Not surprisingly, it is the Gibbon of the last three volumes of the *Decline and Fall* who has attracted so much attention from the recent scholars of the "Enlightened narrative." For Karen O'Brien, Gibbon's achievement was to have provided a rich new *cultural* account of the origins of European civilization, based on a distinction between the mere "imitation" of Roman forms that characterized the Greek East and the more volatile and creative "emulation" of them in the Latin and Germanic West. J. G. A. Pocock highlights the extraordinary delicacy of Gibbon's handling of both the entire range of "barbarian" societies across Eurasia, and the infinite, fertile complexity of both Latin and Greek theology. Most surprisingly of all, he suggests that Gibbon's distinction among the "philosophical historians" derived from a devotional stance of his own, a sober, disenchanted Anglicanism – which would bear comparison with Robertson's more explicit Presbyterianism.

Conclusion

Probably no formula for capturing the Enlightenment in our time has had a wider circulation than Jean-François Lyotard's claim, in *The Postmodern Condition* and later works, that it was the first source of those "grand narratives" of scientific advance and political emancipation that came to define the modern social imaginary – and which could now be discarded in the face of postmodern incredulity. This was plainly an update of earlier caricatures of the Enlightenment as an epoch of mindless and overweening confidence in historical "progress." But like all caricature, Lyotard's claim contains an element of truth, at least in regard to eighteenth-century historical thought. For what was common to both the "conjectural" and the "philosophical" history of the Enlightenment was indeed *narrative* writing of unprecedented grandeur and ambition. Armed with novel explanatory devices such as the four-stages theory, the great conjectural historians of the Scottish and French Enlightenments provided the first general accounts of human historical development of the modern world: their successors would be Marx and Weber. As for "philosophical" history proper, what could be grander than the subjects tackled in the major works of Voltaire, Hume, Robertson, Diderot and Raynal, and Gibbon – a sweeping survey of Europe's cultural emancipation from "barbarism and religion," a narrative of national development of unparalleled sociological and psychological sophistication, an attempt at a totalization of the pivotal epoch of modern European development, an effort to capture the entire record of European imperialism in the Americas and Asia, and, finally, a massive reconstruction of the long transition from the classical to the modern world? What distinguished these works from preceding forms of historiography was not only the sudden expansion of scope beyond the fates of princes and political states, but above all their unprecedented explanatory ambition – story-telling deployed not merely to chronicle, but to *explain.*

It takes nothing away from the achievements of conjectural or philosophical history, in assessing their legacy, to point out that both were very much "unfinished" enterprises – much like that of the Enlightenment "project" as a whole. Despite Trevor-Roper's claims for the modernity of the historiography of Voltaire or Gibbon, it remains the case that the decisive advances that created the "normal science" of historiography as we know it still lay in the future at the end of the eighteenth century. These included the development of a historicist ideology, claiming a special privilege for historical interpretation among the social sciences – the work in the first instance of German thinkers at the end of the century; the durable professionalization of the discipline, whose institutional hallmarks were the university chair and specialized journal – still novelties in most countries at mid-nineteenth century; and finally, the opening of state archives and enormous expansion in the publication and circulation of sources that created the evidentiary basis for modern historiography – work still only just underway, even in the advanced West, at the end of the nineteenth century. Legends about Enlightenment faith in historical "progress" persist against all evidence. But in fact, no dominant ideology remotely comparable to nineteenth-century historicism was available in the eighteenth, whose notions of historical development remained partial and tentative: for all of the traffic between them, a large gulf continued to separate the speculative totalizations of conjectural history from the more local enquiries of the philosophical historians. Lacking institutional support and definition, the careers of Voltaire, Hume, Robertson, and Gibbon remained the unreproducible performances of virtuosic amateurs, Gibbon's appeals to the "vocation" of the historian notwithstanding. Finally, the innovations of eighteenth-century historical thought were essentially theoretical and conceptual ones, ultimately dependent on stocks of empirical evidence supplied not by the historian, but by various ancillary figures – annalists, antiquarians, and voyagers.

The limits to historical vision in the era of the Enlightenment were not, however, merely a matter of "external" impediments, but were imposed by the vantage point of the eighteenth century itself. In retrospect, the work of the conjectural and the philosophical historians alike can be seen as converging on a single historical problem, one that could only have come into view for the first time in that epoch – how to account for the specific dynamism of European development in the medieval and early-modern period, which already seemed to mark out Europe for a unique fate among the earth's nations, most of whom had begun to feel its impact. All that was possible in the eighteenth century, before the "age of revolutions" – democratic, industrial – transformed the problem in imponderable ways, was a set of preliminary attempts at explanation, necessarily unfinished. For the conjectural historians, this was a matter of establishing the procession of "modes of subsistence" that seemed to underlie European development, together with suggestive accounts of the actual mechanisms of change between them – anticipations of the far more specific theories of a Marx or a Weber. The major works of the philosophical historians look like so many attempts to define the central issues and episodes in what a later generation would call a debate over the "transition" – cultural effervescence, political ferment, state-system and religious revolution, colonial expansion, the enduring legacy of antiquity.

The limits of this historiography, as a collective explanation of Europe's transition to modernity, are obvious enough. Its undiminished vitality, two centuries later, however, is equally clear. There is no better sign of the actuality of the historical thought of the Enlightenment today than the complete discomfiture of Lyotard's call for an end to "grand narratives" in the social sciences. For far from an abandonment of the field, the last quarter-century has of course seen an extraordinary flowering of the largest-scale narrative historiography, suggested by names as various as those of Fernand Braudel and William McNeill, Perry Anderson and Immanuel Wallerstein, Michael Mann and Ernest Gellner. The immediate theoretical inspiration for this recent historical sociology is typically some combination of Marx and Weber, of course. But it also remains impressively close in spirit to the great conjectural and philosophical historians of the European Enlightenment, the completion of whose original project of *explanation* of the largest and most difficult problems in history remains very much on the agenda today.

NOTES

1 See Istvan Hont, "The Language of Sociability and Commerce: Samuel Pufendorf and the Theoretical Foundations of the 'Four-Stages Theory,'" in Anthony Pagden, ed., *The Languages of Political Theory in Early-Modern Europe* (Cambridge: Cambridge University Press, 1987), pp. 253–76.
2 For an alternate account of the development of the "four-stages" theory, see Stein's *Legal Evolution*.
3 Cited in Meek, *Social Science and the Ignoble Savage*, p. 2; the formula is from Robertson's *History of America*.
4 Ferguson, *An Essay on the History of Civil Society*, p. 119.
5 That they often were in France was established some time ago in a small classic on the topic, Henry Vyverberg's *Historical Pessimism in the French Enlightenment*.
6 Condorcet, *Selected Writings*, p. 158.
7 Cited in O'Brien, *Narratives of Enlightenment*, p. 83.
8 See Pocock, *Narratives of Civil Government*, pp. 175, 256–7.

9 For a more extended analysis, see Girolamo Imbruglia, "Despotisme et féodalité dans l'*Histoire des deux Indes*," in *L'Histoire des deux Indes: réecriture et polygraphie*, ed. Hans-Jürgen Lüsebrink and Anthony Strugnell, *Studies on Voltaire and the Eighteenth Century* 333 (1995), pp. 105–17.

10 See the classic essay by Momigliano, "Gibbon's Contribution to Historical Method," in *Studies in Historiography* (London: Weidenfeld and Nicolson, 1966), pp. 40–55.

REFERENCES AND FURTHER READING

Becker, Carl, *The Heavenly City of the Eighteenth-Century Philosophers*, New Haven: Yale University Press, 1932.

Cassirer, Ernst, *The Philosophy of the Enlightenment*, trans. Koelln and Pettegrove, Princeton: Princeton University Press, 1932.

Condorcet, *Selected Writings*, edited by Keith Michael Baker, Indianapolis, Bobbs-Merrill, 1976.

Ferguson, Adam, *An Essay on the History of Civil Society*, edited by Fania Oz-Salzburger, Cambridge: Cambridge University Press, 1995.

Forbes, Duncan, *Hume's Philosophical Politics*, Cambridge: Cambridge University Press, 1975.

Hazard, Paul, *The European Mind: the Critical Years, 1680–1715*, trans. by J. Lewis May, New Haven: Yale University Press, 1953.

Meek, Ronald, *Social Science and the Ignoble Savage*, Cambridge: Cambridge University Press, 1976.

O'Brien, Karen, *Narratives of Enlightenment: Cosmopolitan History from Voltaire to Gibbon*, Cambridge: Cambridge University Press, 1997.

Pocock, J. G. A., *Barbarism and Religion. Vol. I: the Enlightenments of Edward Gibbon, 1737–1764*, Cambridge: Cambridge University Press, 1999.

——, *Barbarism and Religion. Vol. II: Narratives of Civil Government*, Cambridge: Cambridge University Press, 1999.

Stein, Peter, *Legal Evolution: the Story of an Idea*, Cambridge: Cambridge University Press, 1980.

Trevor-Roper, Hugh, "The Historical Philosophy of the Enlightenment," in *Studies on Voltaire and the Eighteenth Century*, 24 (1963): 1667–88.

Vyverberg, Henry, *Historical Pessimism in the French Enlightenment*, Cambridge, MA.: Harvard University Press, 1958.

CHAPTER SEVEN

German Historical Thought in the Age of Herder, Kant, and Hegel

HAROLD MAH

The late eighteenth and early nineteenth centuries was a particularly fertile period in Germany for the development of new ideas of history, ideas that proved to be enormously influential in modern historical thought. The German rethinking of historical writing began as a reaction to what Germans saw as the inadequacies of the "universal" or "philosophical" histories of the Enlightenment. On the basis of the assumption of a common human nature, Enlightenment historical writing subsumed all cultures into a single historical typology or a single continuous historical development. Certain French Enlightenment historians further concluded that contemporary France embodied the most advanced developments of civilization and that other nations would do well to imitate France. Against Enlightenment universalism and French arrogance, Germans in the late eighteenth century, such as Johann Gottfried Herder, drew from new intellectual movements that advocated the primacy of intense subjective experience and feeling, particularly in connection to one's immediate culture and surroundings. Other Germans, such as Justus Möser, wanted to write history that addressed Germany's specific religious and legal traditions, its decentralized, less urban society, and its diversity of small states or principalities. These different currents, all directed against Enlightenment universalism, issued in the first crucial formulations of what has come to be known as "historicism" – the notion that historical subjects should be studied, not in relation to transhistorical standards, but according to their own social and cultural terms.

The emergence of historicism fundamentally reoriented the study of history, especially as it found adherents in German universities. But while becoming a powerful movement in German intellectual life in the late eighteenth century, it by no means went unchallenged. In the 1780s and 1790s Immanuel Kant inaugurated a philosophical revolution in Germany that while criticizing some conventional Enlightenment ideas also rehabilitated others, including the

Enlightenment conception of history. Against the historicism of Herder, Kant offered his own rewriting of Enlightenment universal history, one that was now recast in terms of Kant's immensely influential ethical thought.

Kantian philosophy, particularly his ethics, defined the philosophical issues and affected the historical writings of the younger generation of intellectuals of the 1790s. To deal with the challenges issued by Kantian philosophy some of the philosophers of this younger generation revived the large-scale construction of metaphysical systems, which sought to understand the development of many different kinds of phenomena, from the natural world to human society, by incorporating them into a single, all-encompassing philosophical explanation. The concern with the problems of Kantian philosophy and the new interest in comprehensive metaphysical explanation are particularly evident in historical thought in the far-reaching philosophy of history of Georg Wilhelm Friedrich Hegel in the 1820s.

For some Germans, such as Justus Möser, the desire to focus on German traditions in new forms of historical writing testified to their sense of satisfaction and certainty about the value of their society, but for others – for Herder in the 1760s, for the generation of the 1790s and beyond – rethinking history in general and German history in particular pointed to a deep sense of cultural and philosophical alienation. This sense of alienation was exacerbated by the epic events of the French Revolution, especially as it slipped into regicide, the Terror, and international war. For German historical thought, the Revolution signalled a quickening of historical change, a sense that historical events had suddenly accelerated, so that Europe now seemed on the throes of a breakthrough into an entirely new stage of human history. For some writers of German history, such as Möser, this feeling of impending epochal historical change filled them with fear and dread. With the notable exception of Herder, German historicists generally and quickly enlisted into the service of political reaction. The incipient cultural nationalism implied in historicism's elevation of German customs and traditions passed into a political nationalism after Napoleon's conquest of Germany in 1806.

For other Germans, such as Herder, Kant, and Hegel, the French Revolution was an event full of a cultural and political promise, that they believed was relevant to German conditions. Although their enthusiasm for the Revolution diminished as it fell into increased violence and war, they nonetheless hoped that it was a harbinger of significant political reform in Germany. In the course of the first decades of the nineteenth century, as Prussia and other German states attempted to make fundamental social and political changes in response to the Revolution and Napoleon, Hegel in particular came to associate the final outcome of the long, metaphysical course of history with what appeared to him to be the new political system emerging in Germany. The remarkable developments of the Revolution and the way that Germany was adapting pointed, in Hegel's historical thought, to an imminent "end of history," when all the major conflicts of history would be at last resolved. As the Prussian and other German states failed to live up to Hegelian expectations in the 1830s and 1840s, the philosophical universal history of Hegel would give way to a new kind of universal history – the social and economic history of Karl Marx – and the expectation of an end of history would be deferred into a future communist society.[1]

Historicism Before 1800

In 1774 Johann Gottfried Herder (1744–1803), the well-known writer, linguist, and collector of folk poetry, published an essay "Also a Philosophy of History for the Cultivation of Humanity" ("Auch eine Philosophie der Geschichte zur Bildung der Menschheit"). As the title's "Also" self-consciously indicates, Herder believed his essay offered a different view of history, an alternative to what he considered the dominant form of the Enlightenment's so-called "philosophical" or "universal" history. Built on classical, medieval, and humanist natural law traditions, Enlightenment history regarded human nature as generally unchanging, and human behavior in diverse periods as therefore susceptible to evaluation according to transhistorical, rational principles. Historical study was aimed at drawing pragmatic lessons from the past for the present or it sought to derive universally applicable rules of human behavior.

This generalizing impulse in Enlightenment history was strongly evident in the event that had motivated Herder's angry, mocking essay. The Prussian Academy of Sciences had set as the topic of one of its essay contests the question: "Which were the happiest people in history?" – a question that assumed that there was one, uniform understanding and measure of "happiness" for all cultures.[2] For Herder, the arrogance that he identified in this question was compounded by the nature of the organization asking it. Remodeled by the Prussian King Frederick II to conform to his Francophile tastes, the Prussian Academy officially operated in the French language (although German and Latin could also be used) and every pronouncement of the Academy seemed to Herder to be infected with not just Enlightenment dogma but with French arrogance.

The French philosopher Voltaire, whom Frederick had brought for a short time to Berlin (unhappily for both, as it turned out), had given his own, particularly French gloss to Enlightenment history. In the course of writing his famous histories – notably, *Essai sur les moeurs et l'esprit des nations* (*Essay on the Manners and the Spirit of Nations*, 1745–50) and *Le Siècle de Louis XIV* (*The Age of Louis XIV*, 1751) – Voltaire coined the term "philosophical history" by which he meant history writing that would provide "useful truths." For Voltaire, one of the most useful and indubitable truths was the recognition of France's unparalleled material and cultural accomplishments since Louis XIV. At no other time, according to Voltaire, had a society produced such social and cultural refinement. Paris had even come to surpass Athens and Rome in "the art of living."[3] The exquisite taste and gracious sociability of the French court and the aristocratic salons of the seventeenth century had yielded the greatest achievements of culture in the form of French classical tragedy and art. France's long climb from barbarism to the perfected culture of France under Louis XIV and his successors had set a standard for civilization that Voltaire wanted other cultures to follow.

The German princes and writers who adopted French standards and the universalizing impulses of the French Enlightenment incited Herder to write his tract, which offered over and against "philosophical history" another view that was "also" a philosophy of history. Herder ridiculed the claims of Germany's Francophile cosmopolitans, such as Frederick II, and their belief that a debased, parochial German culture has been thankfully superseded. Who needs "a father-land or any kinship relations," he asks mockingly, when we can all be "philanthropic citizens of the world? . . . The princes speak French, and soon everybody will follow their example, and then, behold, perfect bliss" ("Yet," p. 209). A cosmopolitan, intellectual culture, proffered as the "Enlightenment" of the age, produces historical writing that subsumes diverse societies – "nations," as Herder calls them here – under the same set of principles and operations. For Herder, this history written according to universal standards is merely a pretext for imposing one's own contemporary views on everyone else: "the general, philosophical, philanthropical time of our century," he writes, "wishes to extend 'our own ideal' of virtue and happiness to each distant nation, to even the remotest age in history" ("Yet," p. 187).

For Herder the most intolerable of universalizing histories are the self-serving works of French writers, such as Voltaire, but he also criticizes Enlightenment histories that seem more appreciative of historical differences – such as Montesquieu's typology of different forms of political organization or the Scottish historian Adam Ferguson's identification of different stages of economic life. All these writings, according to Herder, are still variants of a questionable universalism. Montesquieu applies his typology to all political regimes and Ferguson offers the same fixed progression of stages to all societies.

For Herder a culture, society, or nation possesses the same individuality as a person; both persons and groups display particular combinations of changing qualities that resist facile generalization: "What depth there is," Herder writes, "in the character of a single nation which, even after repeated and probing observation, manages to evade the word [i.e. generalization] that would capture it and render it recognizable for general comprehension . . ." ("Yet," p. 181). To understand a nation or a culture requires an approach that fully recognizes its unique character and development; this emphasis on the individuality and genetic nature of cultures calls for sympathetic identification, an "*Einfühlung,*" or empathy, not the mechanical or formulaic application of abstract generalizations. This is Herder's historical imperative: "You must enter into the spirit of the nation before you can share even one of its thoughts and deeds" ("Yet," p. 181). Against the Enlightenment notion that all cultures are susceptible to analysis from the same measure of rational standards, typology, or set of historical stages, Herder asserts the irreducible individuality of cultures, which must therefore be understood according to their own values and principles. To the question of the Berlin Academy – "Which was the happiest society in history?" – he thus responds: "each nation has its center of happiness within itself, just as every sphere has its own center of gravity" ("Yet," p. 186). For Herder, there can be no judgment about a culture, society, or nation that goes beyond the terms set by the entity itself. The notion of the unique, genetic, and incommensurable character of societies in history is often called "historicism," a designation that should not be confused with the more recent turn of phrase "New Historicism."[4]

What Herder was asserting in general terms in his brilliant, polemical tract was already being practiced in specific historical studies by Justus Möser (1720–94), a secretary to the noble estate (*Ritterschaft*) in the bishopric of Osnabrück in northwestern Germany. As the author of the widely-read and well-received multi-volume *History of Osnabrück* (1762–71), Möser sought to comprehend Osnabrück's institutions, laws, and customs solely according to their own principles and particular development. His main concern was to show how the carefully balanced constitutional and religious arrangements of eighteenth-century Osnabrück, which Möser believed yielded peace and prosperity, had issued from long centuries of successful opposition by the estates of Osnabrück to the centralizing Holy Roman Empire. The message of Möser's history was thus the direct opposite of Voltaire's: that provincial resistance and not submission to imperial authority had issued in this particular society's "happiness." Osnabrück, in Herder's terms, had found its own "center of gravity."

With their injunction to study a society's history according to its particular character and evolution, Herder's views and Möser's practices strongly influenced subsequent German historical work including the writings of two important professors at the new University of Berlin during the 1820s. The legal philosopher and historian Carl Friedrich von Savigny (1796–1861) advocated a historical as opposed to rationalistic (identified as Napoleonic) jurisprudence, while Leopold von Ranke (1795–1886), Germany's foremost historian, assimilated historicist principles into his professionalization of the discipline. Through Ranke, his students, and his students' students (who included many Americans in the late nineteenth century) historicism exerted an influence that has reached widely into contemporary academic history, which routinely reiterates the original historicist imperative of understanding historical subjects internally or on their own terms.

Given historicism's broad influence and the often-noted similarities between Herder's philosophy of history and Möser's writing of history, it is important to recognize that Herder and Möser also had some significant differences in their views. Herder's thought was a product of the German *Sturm und Drang* (Storm and Stress), a movement of young German writers and poets, including the young Johann Wolfgang von Goethe (1749–1832), who opposed a rationalistic and mainly French Enlightenment with an emphasis on natural and emotional expression. Möser, by contrast, wrote as a supporter of the nobility and the system of estates in the small principality of Osnabrück. His writing lacks Herder's *Sturm-und-Drang* fervor and emotionalism, and he has been called a representative of Germany's "corporatist Enlightenment," that is, a defender of established social hierarchies who also accepted the need for some gradual reform.[5]

A historicist approach to history is one that ostensibly provides a more accurate, specific representation of the past since it addresses the concrete particularities of its subject. But what should be noted is that historicist histories were guilty in their own ways of historical myth-making. Both Herder and Möser required a mythical, idealized past to authorize their rejection of a cosmopolitan past and present. Strongly influenced by Rousseau, Herder's history is constructed along the lines of nostalgic Rousseauist history, according to which an original social condition of simplicity, truthfulness, and self-reliance was ruined by corrupting luxury and the emergence of a refined, international culture of false appearances and uncertain morality. Where Rousseau in various writings identified a superior original condition of society in antiquity, particularly in ancient Sparta and the Roman Republic, Herder found it in what he calls "the North," in the German tribes that preceded and followed the Roman Empire. The influx of those tribes into the collapsed Empire created the feudal social system which, as Herder describes it, breathed new life into a stagnant countryside. Original German society, notwithstanding its roughness or coercive practices, was for Herder a place of clear moral purpose and social harmony: "In the patriarch's hut, the humble homestead, or the local community," he explained, "people knew and clearly perceived what they talked about, since the way they looked at things, and acted, was through the human heart" ("Yet," p. 204).

Möser also created a mythological origin for Osnabrück – what one commentator has called an agrarian version of civic republicanism, or what we might say is a Germanized version of ancient republicanism that Rousseau identified as his golden age. According to Möser, the well-functioning constitution of eighteenth-century Osnabrück also derived from Germany's tribal past, in this case a pre-feudal "Saxon" commune of independent freeholders who came together during crises to defend themselves in an armed militia. Eighteenth-century Osnabrück's strong estate system and the privileges of its aristocracy were rooted in those original principles of propertied autonomy and shared self-defense against external domination. Together, aristocratic privilege and the durable estate system had acted as a check to the authority of the Holy Roman Empire. The differences between Herder's amorphous sentimental allusions to an archaic German past and Möser's focus on specific institutions to legitimate their existence resulted in quite distinct reactions to the French Revolution. Like other members of the *Sturm und Drang* (including the young Goethe and Friedrich Schiller (1759–1805)), Herder chafed under the authority of the existing German aristocracy – which suggests one reason why he preferred an idealized past. When the French Revolution broke out, he vigorously welcomed it and supported it well into the Terror, long after most other initial German supporters had abandoned it. Möser, however, as a supporter of Germany's corporatist structures and Osnabrück nobility, joined a strong, conservative opposition to the Revolution, shedding the initial sympathy he had for some social reform and arguing in the most reactionary way for the preservation of social hierarchy.[6]

Although Herder's favorable response to the French Revolution suggests that historicists responded to the changing political events in varied and complex ways, historicism's principle of the incommensurable individuality of cultures and nations was most easily enlisted into the cause of political conservatism. The historicist and conservative legal philosopher Savigny, for example, viewed the Revolution and its successor Napoleon as the logical and nightmarish result of the Enlightenment's universalizing mission. One could not and should not, these historicists argued, seek to impose French standards on Germany, which rightfully followed its own traditions, customs, and values. The political uses of historicism by German conservatives in the era of the Revolution and Napoleonic conquest underscore one of historicism's important implications, namely, that it has always suggested a moral and epistemological relativism. It suggests a moral relativism in that its principle of the incommensurable individuality of nations means that one country cannot legitimately judge another. German conservatives thus insisted that French Enlightenment and Revolutionary ideas of social reform were entirely irrelevant to German conditions. In addition to its moral relativism, historicism also suggests an epistemological relativism, because its emphasis on the distinctiveness of each culture's ideas and identity implies that people from one culture can never truly understand the cultures of other peoples. In the absence of transhistorical or transcultural standards of human behavior that allow one to evaluate another culture's actions or institutions, how can one hope to comprehend fully or definitively another culture? Historicism, in short, excludes the possibility of a comparative knowledge of other cultures and suggests that each culture is ultimately isolated from all others.

Herder occasionally raised the possibility that historicism undercut cross-cultural moral judgment but for the most part it did not particularly trouble him, nor the great German historians of the nineteenth century, such as Ranke.

Much later the issue of moral relativism came to haunt one of Herder's and historicism's greatest heirs and interpreters, the twentieth-century German historian Friedrich Meinecke (1862–1953). In the midst of the wars and social tumult of the early twentieth century, Meinecke looked back on more than a century and a half of German history and historical thought with the concern that German historicism and its relativist implications had helped to bring about what he identified as the fateful erosion of moral clarity and resolution in German history.[7]

The other consequence of historicism – its implicit epistemological relativism which separates individual cultures from each other – did bother Herder, as we can recognize in a significant revision in his thought. In "Also a Philosophy of History" of 1774, Herder argued for the radical incommensurablity of nations, a characteristic that makes it impossible to find in history a general underlying order or to attribute to it a single purpose or *telos*. As he says in a mocking dismissal of universal history, only God is capable of such overarching vision, and he refuses to have anything to do with the common Enlightenment (and early-modern European) reference to the attained "maturity" of the human race, a metaphor or trope that implies a single course and teleological development for all cultures.[8] But in the 1780s, in one of his last works, *Ideas For a Philosophy of History* (*Ideen zur Philosophie der Geschichte*), Herder has significantly changed his views.[9] In *Ideas*, he returns to a universal history of the human race; indeed, the work is so far-reaching that it begins before the human race with a discussion of the solar system and the natural history of the earth. From there it proceeds to a series of portraits of different peoples, moving, in the conventional form of universal history, from Asia, the Middle East, ancient Greece and Rome, to the German tribes in Western Europe, and the emergence and development of European states in the early-modern period.

The *Ideas* seems to return to Enlightenment history in its scope and its assertion that all these periods and cultures are connected according to an overarching plan or purpose. What links past and present cultures together is that they all develop, to use Herder's term, "*Humanität*," the creative powers and potentialities of human beings. The development is progressive; hence Herder now says that human abilities have developed to a greater extent than before, and he now adopts the same teleological language that he had repudiated in "Also a Philosophy of History." He describes a continuous development of the human race from infancy (in *Ideas*, the early Hebrews) to full maturity (the Romans and subsequent societies). This revived universal history, which links together many disparate cultures, hearkens back to Enlightenment models of comprehensiveness, linearity, and progressiveness, but it does so in a way that preserves some of the historicist principle of respecting the individual character of each society. Each age and culture strives to realize *Humanität*, but each does so in a way appropriate to its own stage of development.

This means that one should not measure earlier cultures by later ones, since each is appropriate to the particular age of the race. Whatever one thinks of Herder's attempt to fuse universal history and particularist historicism, its reconciling strategy influenced German intellectuals in subsequent generations. A more rigorous synthesis of universal history and historicism was especially evident in Hegel's philosophy of history.

Kantian Universalism

One of the most critical reviews of Herder's *Ideas* was written by his former teacher and mentor, Immanuel Kant, who also published his own outline of a philosophy of history in the same year that Herder's work appeared.[10] Both Kant's "Idea for a Universal History With a Cosmopolitan Purpose" of 1784 and his review of Herder's *Ideas* in 1785 indicate new directions in German philosophy and historical thought that would have far-reaching significance for German intellectuals in subsequent decades. In the mid-1780s Kant's reputation as an important philosopher was on the rise. Word was spreading of his pathbreaking work in epistemology, his *Critique of Pure Reason* (1781), which seemed to sum up the accomplishments and limitations of Enlightenment sensationalism or sensationalist psychology, a theory of knowledge based on the centrality of sense perception. The publication of his second critique, on ethical theory, *The Critique of Practical Reason* (1788), pointed to ways of going beyond the Enlightenment, as it emphasized how human beings can transcend the constraints of sensationalist psychology. In Germany, Kantian ethical philosophy and its assertion of a transcending rational human autonomy would serve as the unavoidable points of departure of much of the philosophy and historical thought that would arise in the 1790s.

Kant's essay on history and his review of Herder appeared between the publication of the first two *Critiques* and show the influence of both, of the first Critique's analysis of Enlightenment sensationalist epistemology and the second's construction of a new ethics. In his review, Kant praises Herder's imagination and his fluid, poetic style, but on the whole he is extremely critical of Herder's views. Expressing his concerns with the limitations of Enlightenment epistemology, Kant points out how Herder draws from a version of sensationalist psychology to reach conclusions that are entirely speculative. He is particularly critical of Herder's induction that there is a natural "genetic force" at work in all individuals and cultures that drives them to develop unique and harmoniously formed personalities. Against this postulate of a natural internal force that produces singular and integrated identities, Kant cautiously makes what he thinks is the only empirical observation about history that is legitimate: "all that nature reveals to us is that it abandons individuals to total destruction and preserves only the species."[11] Where a sentimental

Herder finds in each individual and collectivity a beneficent individualizing that constitutes a great chain of developing *Humanität*, Kant's more rigorous empiricism concludes that no such linkage and purpose naturally exist. On the contrary, history shows that individuals and societies, following their own self-interested natures, end up destroying each other.

This unavoidable "empirical fact," as Kant says, may seem to be an obstacle to writing universal history – a history that connects all societies – and one might ask why Kant is even concerned with writing a universal history. "Idea for a Universal History With a Cosmopolitan Purpose" in fact begins with a recognition of the apparent irrationality or purposelessness that seems to undercut universal history: "we can scarcely help feeling a certain distaste on observing [people's] activities as enacted in the great world-drama, for we find that, despite the apparent wisdom of individual actions here and there, everything as a whole is made up of folly and childish vanity, and often of childish malice and destructiveness."[12]

Kant's epistemological work on the limits of human sense perception puts into question the writing of universal history, particularly in the optimistic, forgiving form of Herder's *Ideas*. But Kant's ethical thought of the 1780s, which will result in the *Critique of Practical Reason*, offers quite different conclusions about human powers and purpose. In the second *Critique*, Kant takes issue with the Enlightenment conclusion that its sensationalist psychology mandated a naturalistic or utilitarian ethics. For the Enlightenment, the primacy of the sensory nature of human beings meant that they were ultimately motivated by the pursuit of pleasure and the avoidance of pain. Given this fundamental natural condition, morality, for many Enlightenment thinkers, should operate in accordance with an individual's natural desires, instincts, and self-interests, with the pursuit of pleasure and the avoidance of pain. In the second *Critique*, Kant reverses this common naturalistic and utilitarian view of Enlightenment ethical thought. He concludes that a human being's compelling sensuous impulses do not naturally lead to moral behaviour, but, in fact, undercut it. Human beings act as moral agents not when they seek to realize their natural impulses, but when they rationally control or even suppress them. The ability to exercise such rational control over natural desires and interests is in fact what defines for Kant human autonomy, the exercise of mastery over oneself.

Kant's "Idea for a Universal History" combines the cynical view of human failings found in his criticism of Herder and his critique of Enlightenment sensationalism with the affirmation of rational and moral autonomy found in his ethical philosophy. His essay seeks to show how moral and rational autonomy ultimately wins out over the compelling force of natural, individualistic self-interest and desire. Notwithstanding the apparent demoralizing lessons that history offers about human nature, Kant's purpose is to recuperate Enlightenment universal history by reformulating it in the more rigorous terms of his ethical theory.

The "Idea for a Universal History" begins by pointing to a paradox that follows from Kant's initial observation of the destructive, irrational self-interested individualism of human beings. He notes that individuals who pursue their own interests and desires in society tend to isolate themselves because of the resistance they encounter from others. Individual behavior naturally tends to reinforce a narrowing individualism at the expense of social coherence. But at the same time, Kant adds, people cannot abandon society, since only there can they develop the "natural capacities" to fulfill their desires and interests. The consequence, according to Kant, is an "unsocial sociability" – a constant pushing and pulling of people in society. This ambivalent experience of individuals in society reshapes their individual desires and interests, so that they, for example, come to be driven by new motivations, such as "the desire for honor, power, or property." These socially mediated desires lead human beings to develop their talents, cultivate taste, undergo a "process of enlightenment," and thus travel the long road "from barbarism to culture." Through these small, arduous steps of development, Kant writes, "a *pathologically* enforced social union is transformed into a *moral* whole" ("Idea," pp. 44, 48).

Humanity as a whole is thus taught to affirm its moral, rational autonomy. The many selfish acts of individuals push and pull against each other in their many societies, until people ultimately learn to submit to a rational authority. This growing adherence to rationality is for Kant the essential characteristic of historical progress. Individuals and societies come and go, but the race as a whole is advanced, until it reaches the point where it might imagine what a fully moral and rational society would be like. Kant postulates that such a society of fully rational persons would seek to develop all human powers without constraint. And in another work, he imagines that this society would be republican in political form. Sounding like Rousseau in *The Social Contract*, he believes that a republic is the only political system suitable for a society of morally and rationally autonomous individuals. The problem for Kant was how to reach this ideal society from a present historical condition in which the power of immoral instinct and self-interest still dominated.

Like many other Germans, Kant welcomed the French Revolution. And even after its darkest period of violence and the Terror, when other German supporters completely repudiated the Revolution, he held fast to the idea that the Revolution's occurrence still offered proof of the progress of the human race. For one real, concrete moment, it transformed, he believed, the abstract principle of rational autonomy into a political reality.[13] But although the Revolution was a harbinger, Kant hoped, of a future republic, it also showed that people were not yet ready to live up to the demands of rational and political self-mastery. In the mid-1790s, the pressing political issue for Kant was how human beings were to be governed to prepare them to become their own masters in a republic. The French Revolution had shown the dangers of creating a republic before people were prepared to be republicans, but how could the proper skills of republicanism be acquired? Here Kant falls back on a favored default solution of the Enlightenment to the question of how to establish a legitimate rational form of government in the midst of still authoritarian governments and undereducated populations. Kant counsels obedience to existing monarchs, and, in a formulation that sums up the wishful political thinking of the Enlightenment, he says that it is the duty of these monarchs to govern *as if* they were republicans.[14] The delusion in this proposal is especially striking if we remember that Kant offered it in the mid-1790s, precisely when the Prussian government under Frederick William II had imposed a new regime of censorship that had suppressed Kant's own writings on religion.

For Kant, the ideal political constitution for free autonomous citizens is a republic, and the question remains of how that ideal republic could emerge out of the existing state system. At the end of his essay on universal history, Kant suggests further that a perfect "republic" would in fact go beyond states altogether. He concludes the "Idea for a Universal History" by reaffirming another utopian Enlightenment principle and hope: that an ideal moral and rational society must result in an "universal cosmopolitan existence." This can be considered, he says, the "hidden plan of nature," what an earlier Christian view of the world regarded as the work of divine providence in history ("Idea," pp. 50–3).

Metaphysics and History

Kantian philosophy exerted an enormous influence on German intellectual life. The 1790s witnessed an outpouring of commentaries on his writings, especially on the second *Critique*. A variety of prominent writers of this period, from Schiller and Goethe to Johann Gottlieb Fichte (1762–1814) and Georg Wilhelm Friedrich Hegel (1770–1831), bore witness to the significance of the second *Critique*. One reason that *The Critique of Practical Reason* was so influential was that it provided a particularly rigorous idiom for expressing the intellectual mood of the 1790s. Writers of the *Sturm und Drang*, such as Herder, had been dissatisfied with both Enlightenment ideas of society and German institutions, and they sought alternative ideas and institutions that would provide a sense of cultural unity and fulfillment. German *Zerissenheit*, as Germans nicely call this sense of alienation, was a motivating impulse behind Herder's formulation of historicism and his idealization of an older German culture. The sense of alienation on the part of young intellectuals intensified in the 1790s, manifesting itself in works of early German Romanticism and

German idealist philosophy, including, in the latter, the theories of Fichte and Hegel.[15]

Kantian philosophy offered a new way of formulating the social and cultural discontent of the intellectuals of the 1790s and of suggesting the terms that would be required in a resolution. Many intellectuals were in particular inspired by the second *Critique* and its affirmation of the rational autonomy of human beings. But they also saw in the second *Critique* that this promise of human freedom seemed to require an inevitable self-division or self-alienation, as Kant opposed rational autonomy to natural self-interest, desire, and instinct. The second *Critique* suggested, in other words, a fundamental opposition between people's pursuit of rational freedom and their surrender to the narrow and animalistic demands of human nature. That opposition between the call of reason and the compulsions of a lower human nature served as the broad terms in which intellectuals conceptualized their own alienation. To overcome all resistance to human freedom, without experiencing self-division or alienation, was the defining issue of a generation.

The events of the French Revolution emphasized the difficulties of fulfilling the Kantian aims of German intellectuals. Broadly elated at the fall of the Bastille and then generally horrified at the execution of Louis XVI, the Terror, and the European wars, German intellectuals struggled to make sense of the same contradiction that bothered Kant, namely, how the Revolution seemed both to confirm and refute the promise of rational autonomy. To deal with their own sense of *Zerissenheit* and the apparent political contradictions of the day, some young intellectuals, including Fichte, Friedrich Schelling (1775–1854), and Hegel, sought to subsume and resolve them in philosophies of far-reaching comprehensiveness. Thus the 1790s witnessed a return to metaphysical system-building of the sort not seen since the seventeenth century but now reconceived according to the concerns of the period and the influence of Kantian philosophy. These elaborate philosophical systems assimilated natural science, mathematical thought, ethics, and, in the case of Hegel, the developments of human history.

Hegel's injection of metaphysics into history is immediately evident in how he refers to the typical actors or agents of historical writing. No longer are individuals, nations, and the human race the ultimate actors of history. Rather a force or a will, what Hegel calls "spirit" (*Geist*), operates through them.[16] Comparing his notion of spirit to the Christian notion of providence, Hegel seems to use the word as his special term for God, as some commentators have also argued. What should be noted, however, is how Hegel's spirit differs significantly from mainstream Christian notions of God. Unlike the always complete and perfect God of mainstream Christianity, Hegel's spirit evolves through different forms, including historical forms, into a state of completion. Spirit manifests itself in and passes through different kinds of thinking and corresponding institutions. As it passes through these forms of thought or consciousness and their associated institutions, spirit develops in increasingly rational and complex ways, until it attains a consciousness and a set of institutions in which contradiction and alienation are rationally overcome. The emphasis on an increasingly explicit consciousness or awareness of reason and its presence in institutions is important because the development of spirit is in fact the development of reason itself. Hegel's system describes how spirit comes to recognize that it is itself essentially rational and that its arduous, multi-faceted development was all along a plan of reason to realize or embody itself in the world. Hegel's philosophy of history describes the process through which reason comes to know itself and to make itself real: "The insight then to which . . . philosophy is to lead us is that the truly good – the universal divine reason – is not a mere abstraction, but a rational principle capable of realizing itself" (*Philosophy*, p. 36). In his assertion that spirit's highest state is its rational self-recognition and its embodiment in reality, Hegel, in his own highly metaphysical fashion, echoes Kant's celebration of rational autonomy and its mastery over natural impulses. Indeed, thinking in a Kantian vein, Hegel calls spirit's rational self-consciousness and its embodiment the realization of freedom.

The way in which Hegel shows how spirit develops in history into a condition of rationality and freedom also shares some similarities with Kant's "Idea for a Universal History." Hegel opens his *Lectures on the Philosophy of History*, given in the 1820s, with the same preliminary gesture that Kant made in the "Idea." Hegel concedes that empirical facts apparently refute his belief that reason operates throughout history; he recognizes that human beings are for the most part driven by their sensuous and natural impulses, passions, and self-interests. The result, Hegel says, in a memorable turn of phrase, is to make history appear as a "slaughter-bench" on which individuals and societies are sacrificed to human folly and selfishness (*Philosophy*, p. 21). Notwithstanding the appearance in history of gross irrationality and immorality, Hegel's intention in the *Lectures* is to show how spirit's metaphysical unfolding into full rationality is also at work in history. To redeem human history as a movement of rational spirit, he argues like Kant that the many ostensibly selfish or egoistic acts of individuals in history have yielded consequences that greatly exceeded those specific acts. The drive to power of such figures as Julius Caesar, Alexander the Great, and Napoleon Bonaparte produced new forms of political organization far superior, Hegel argues, to those that preceded them, and the legacy of those new organizations extended far beyond the lives of the "great men." The "cunning of reason," as Hegel famously calls this paradox, lets selfish interests and passions work for it, suffering the destruction and deaths they cause in order to create progressively more rational forms of political organization (*Philosophy*, p. 33).

The history of political organization or the state is thus the proper subject of what Hegel calls philosophical history – "[i]n the history of the World only

those people can come under notice which form a state" (*Philosophy*, p. 39) –
a focus that in itself is not necessarily ethnocentric depending on what Hegel
means by a "state." He nevertheless shows a distinctly Western bias, which is
completely conventional for his period, when he rehearses the usual chronology of universal history. In world history, according to Hegel, spirit ascends
from East to West, from ancient China, India, and Persia, through the ancient
Greek and Roman empires, to what he calls the "German world," which covers
Western Europe from the Middle Ages to the Enlightenment and the French
Revolution.

In focusing on the development of states, Hegel is not giving in to an
authoritarian state-worship, as some commentators have wrongly concluded,
but he is again making a Kantian-derived argument about freedom. His point
is that spirit's movement from one of his states to the next entails a progressive articulation of the supremacy of law (ultimately in its most rational form
as a set of universal principles) over narrow self-interest and caprice. Hegel is
particularly concerned with demonstrating that the rule of rational law is
increasingly established as the principle of advancing states; he is less interested in the specific content of laws. He tends in other words to see laws as
general, philosophical abstractions rather than as products of a specific
culture's unique customs and development. This is one reason Hegelian philosophy and history were so disliked by his colleagues at the University of
Berlin, the historicists Savigny and Ranke.

Hegelian history tries to find a rational, abstract principle in a historical phenomenon and then attempts to show how that principle is further developed
in subsequent historical awareness and social and political institutions – a procedure that historicists regarded as an ahistorical imputation of rational abstraction and teleology to the historical record. The philosophical method of
Hegelian history is particularly evident in the last sub-section of the *Lectures*
on the "German World," entitled "the modern age." Hegel defines the
modern age as the one in which spirit finally enters into rational self-
consciousness, and the first period of the modern age and of rational self-
consciousness is the German Reformation. Alluding to Luther's doctrine of
justification by faith alone and his rejection of Papal authority, Hegel inter-
prets the Reformation as spirit's new awareness that it should think and act
independently of the dictates of external authority or according to what it
recognizes as flowing internally from its own essential spirituality. In the Reformation, in other words, spirit recognizes its own proper form as free
spirituality; it affirms its own spiritual nature as the source of moral and intellectual authority. This is the historical breakthrough of individual freedom in
history, which defines the modern self. (Catholic countries, including Catholic
Germany, by implication sink "behind the spirit of the age.")

This new self-reliant, self-conscious spirit then continues to develop in different ways, through the Enlightenment, until it comes to another momen-

tous self-recognition in the French Revolution. In the form of Revolutionary consciousness, spirit has now come to recognize that not only its own inner essence is spiritual but also that its spiritual essence is so powerful and expressive that it can rebuild the world according to its own principles of reason. Hegel writes about the meaning of the Revolution: "Never since the sun had stood still in the firmaments and the planets revolved around him had it been perceived that man's existence centers in his head, i.e. in thought, inspired by which he builds up the world of reality" (*Philosophy*, p. 447; trans. modified). In the Revolution a modern rational spirit recognizes that it can project its own interior, subjective sense of freedom into the external, objective world of social and political institutions, rebuilding them according to rational principles. Here Hegel, like Kant, celebrates the Revolution for accomplishing precisely what conservatives and historicists (although not of course Herder) condemned: the displacement of the authority of established custom, tradition, and religion by a belief in the possibility of fashioning society according to abstract, universal principles of right.

The Revolution for Hegel announced the decisive historical arrival of the idea that human beings could use their own reason to redesign society and government. But conferring this significance on the Revolution does not mean that he thought that the Revolution had fully accomplished or objectively realized that idea. When he first learned of the Revolution, while a student in university, he joined other Germans, including Herder and Kant, in welcoming it as a great progressive development in politics. But as he grew older, and as the Revolution slipped into regicide and Terror, he came to see the Revolution as a kind of excess, or madness, of pure rationality, of a reason that had become too abstract. Like Herder and Kant, as his *Lectures on the Philosophy of History* of the 1820s indicate, Hegel continued to affirm the Revolution's initial project of introducing into the objective world of social and political institutions a new sense of rational autonomy and law, but he turned elsewhere for what he thought would be the final objective social and political order that would fully realize rational freedom. And one lesson of the Revolution was that the objective fulfillment of spirit, while realizing its principles of rational freedom rigorously, should not fully break with some established institutions or the concrete particularities given by the past.

Hegel's mature political and historical thought thus appears to synthesize the Kantian emphasis on the development of abstract and universal rationality and the historicist appreciation of tradition and continuity. In another work of the 1820s, *The Philosophy of Right*, Hegel outlines an ideal social and political order that fully manifests spirit's achieved rationality in its institutions. This ideal order unites both features conventionally called "modern" (e.g., a "civil society" of unfettered individualistic pursuit of self-interest, government by rational bureaucracy) and those called "traditional" (e.g., political representation according to estates, including the nobility; the preservation of guilds;

the recognized authority – if not the conventional power – of inherited monarchy). The ideal order of *The Philosophy of Right* did not exactly correspond to any actually existing society, but there are strong reasons to think that the state Hegel looked to in the 1820s was Prussia, which had enacted some reforms in response to Napoleonic conquest. Prussian reformers had brought Hegel to the newly established University of Berlin and from there he became known as the most important philosopher in Germany. He was a friend of high-ranking Prussian civil servants and received the support of the state, even as he fell into conflict with the historicist Savigny who was at the same university.

The issue of whether Prussia actually lived up to the terms of Hegel's ideal state was a pressing one for his philosophy. The Hegelian system aimed for a full resolution of contradictions and alienation, and that meant that the system should not only exist in abstract thought or philosophy, but also be realized in objective social and political institutions. Without an objective realization of spirit, there would always be a gap – a space of alienation – between what was ideal and what actually existed. For this reason, we should take Hegel at his words, albeit with many tensions and ambiguities, when he says in *The Philosophy of Right* that "what is rational is actual and what is actual is rational."[17] His systematic formulation of philosophy, he believes, places him at the so-called "end of history," when all the struggles of the past have culminated in an achieved rational unity of individual and society. If actually existing society refused to live up to the imputed reconciliation, if Prussia turned out to be far less "rational" than Hegel wanted to believe, then that discrepancy raised questions about the validity of Prussia as the appropriate fulfillment of spirit or the validity of the philosophy itself. The progressively widening gap between the requirements of Hegelian philosophy and the reality of an increasingly conservative Prussia after Hegel's death precipitated a series of reconsiderations of Hegelian philosophy, that, among other developments, contributed to the emergence of the so-called Young Hegelians in the late 1830s and 1840s. The critical reappraisal of Hegelian philsophy by Hegel's younger followers had enormous implications for historical thought. The young Karl Marx, proceeding from controversies in the Hegelian school, evolved from a Hegelian "idealist" philosopher who believed in the evolution of spirit into the "historical materialist" of 1845. For Marx the materialist, the Hegelian idea of spirit was now no more than a phantasy that concealed the real, concrete evolution of economic and social structures.[18]

Before and Beyond History

In 1874 Friedrich Nietzsche published the second of his self-styled "untimely" meditations, "On the Advantage and Disadvantage of History for Life." This work was untimely, Nietzsche thought, because it went against one of the dominant currents of nineteenth-century thought, namely, the "surfeit," as he put it, of German historical thought and writing. The writers discussed in this essay inaugurated a century of German devotion to historical thinking, whether in the historicism of Herder and Möser, which was carried on and professionalized in the work of Ranke and his students, or in the philosophical universal history that culminated in Hegel's *Lectures* and that, in turn, gave way to Marx's materialist version of universal history. At the end of the century Nietzsche put into question all writing about history by asking a meta-question: for what general purpose does one think historically? What is the relationship between multifarious, intensive, and extensive German historical thought and "life"? In answering this question Nietzsche was criticizing the practices and institutions of German historical writing as he pointed out how different forms of historical thought served not to comprehend the challenges of life but to evade them. One might reach a similar conclusion about some of the writers discussed in this essay.

From one perspective, the historicists Herder and Möser sought to provide histories that would account for the concrete particularities of German development, and in Herder's case, this use of history would also help to remedy the sense of alienation he felt in German and European culture. But while their focus on the uniqueness of Germany and Osnabrück led to more accurate and more appreciative particularist histories, it also implied a set of distortions. Both Herder's and Möser's historicist histories required the assumption of a mythical past. A mythical event or development functioned for them as a privileged origin establishing a standard whose continuous influence was then perceived to be disseminated throughout the rest of history, so that subsequent events or developments could be measured against it or legitimated by it. That originating event or development thus overshadowed what came after it; it reduced or even canceled out the historical significance of subsequent events. German tribalism thus defined the truly German, while the French culture that many of Germany's rulers had adopted in the eighteenth century was rejected as alien or anti-German. This desire to root a German past in a mythic origin produced considerable and rich historical writing, but its denial of the significance of subsequent events and cultural changes also amounted to a denial of certain historical developments. Historicism, in other words, can paradoxically be seen as the expression of a desire to overcome history, whether it was the cosmopolitan influence of French culture or other undesirable developments in social and political life.

This odd paradoxical desire to escape history by writing history is even more evident from a reversed point of view – from the point of view of endings rather than of beginnings. When Hegel wrote that history came to an end he was drawing on an ancient, classical way of thinking about time and culture, one that had recently been revived by the famous art historian Johann Winckelmann (1717–68) in the mid-1760s. Hugely influential, Winckelmann's writings were read and admired by many German writers and intellectuals of the late eighteenth century, including the educational reformer Wilhelm von Humboldt (1767–1835) who carried Winckelmann's classical ideals into the reconstruction of the German Gymnasium or high school. One of the key notions of this classical revival was the idea that cultural developments reached a state of completion in the fullness of time. On this view, when a proper formula, technique, or style has been perfected in art, it should then be established as a permanent norm, which can be reproduced or refined but not changed. The realized ideal form or technique steps, as it were, out of time, and in that position it presents itself for appreciation or contemplation.

This notion of transcending time in a state of completion is found in many different writings of the late eighteenth and early nineteenth centuries. It is strongly evident in Hegel's philosophy of history. As we have seen, his system of philosophy requires that the critical contradictions and deepest alienations of history are overcome in the present, and that a new era of the recognition and contemplation of this accomplishment is to follow. The importance of this ahistorical classical thinking in a deeply historicizing philosophy is a paradox that suggests the same motive that is suggested in historicist myths of origin – namely, that one attends to historical development in the most elaborate way in order to overcome history, to transcend its contradictions, transience, and mortality. A similar notion of historical transcendence concludes Marx's theory of historical development. History, for Marx, develops to the point where human beings have overcome the major problems that generated significant historical change. But as a disillusioned Hegelian, as a theorist of social and economic history, Marx projected the final resolution of those problems into the future and imagined that resolution to have an economic form, as communism.

The Legacy of German Historical Thought

From German historicism and the new German philosophy of history of the late eighteenth century, modern historical thought has inherited some of its most effective methods and concerns, but also some of its deepest, recurring problems. German historicists, such as Herder and Möser, taught later historians to study and appreciate the distinctiveness of past cultures and societies. Assimilated into Ranke's professionalization of history and disseminated by his students, historicism's imperative of understanding a historical subject on its own terms has become the first principle of much of modern academic history.

At the same time that historicism introduced particularizing tendencies in the study of history, so that historians became increasingly concerned with the specific differences between cultures and societies, German philosophers of history renewed the opposing tendency of historical thought, the universal history of the eighteenth century. Infused with Kantian ethical concerns and then with Hegelian metaphysics, philosophy of history again offered the promise of locating universal patterns and overarching purpose or meaning in history. This generalizing impulse, freely comparing and measuring different societies against each other, informed the social scientific histories of the next century and a half, from the varieties of Marxist history, through the comparative historical sociology of Max Weber, to the histories of "modernization" of the 1950s and 1960s.

Each of the main currents of German historical thought in the late eighteenth and early nineteenth centuries has thus exerted important, diverse, and enduring influence on the approaches of modern historical writing. But the importance of German historical thought lies not just in its legacy of new approaches and methods. It lies as well in the unresolved, and possibly unresolvable, problems that German historical thought has also bequeathed. Along with its assumptions and approaches, the conceptual limitations and wish fulfillment of German historical thought have entered into modern historical argument. Thus, the historicist problems of moral and epistemological relativism have recurrently appeared as controversial issues in academic debates, most recently in the concern with how a historicist emphasis on the unique identities of social groups has resulted in the fragmentation of the historical study of society. At the same time, modern universalist histories have continued to face charges of making facile overgeneralizations. In recent years, this complaint has taken the specific form of a criticism of a basic assumption of all universalist histories, namely, that it is possible for a historian to operate from a privileged, objective point of view, one that is not only putatively undistorted by the biases and limitations of his or her own society but is all-seeing in its freedom to look into other societies.[19] Even the paradoxical, wishful desire of German philosophy of history to transcend history by writing history has continued to inform historical writing. The universalist desire to reach a condition beyond disconcerting historical transformations has been evident not just in the Marxisms of the twentieth century but also in the Cold War, and now post-Cold War, historical imaginings of the West, for which Hegel's "end of history" has reappeared as the so-called "end of ideology" and the final triumph of a modern liberal capitalism.[20] We might expect that like all such previous wishes, contemporary versions of the end of history will turn out to be more illusion than reality. German historical thought from Herder to Hegel opens a modern era of historical thought; the enduring relevance of German historical thought is still strongly evident in contemporary historical writing, not just in its methods and themes but also in the continued appearance of its unresolved problematic implications and unlikely wishes, which periodically raise unsettling questions for historians.

NOTES

1 The historical thought in this period has been generally examined in Herbert Schnädelbach, "History" in *Philosophy in Germany, 1831–1933* (Cambridge, 1984), pp. 33–65; Reinhart Koselleck, *Futures Past: On the Semantics of Historical Time* (Cambridge, MA, 1985), pp. 148–50, 251–3; Friedrich Meinecke, *Historism: The Rise of A New Historical Outlook* (London, 1972) and his *Cosmopolitanism and the National State* (Princeton, 1970).

2 I have not followed the translation of the title in the accessible English translation of excerpts from the essay, which is misleadingly called "Yet Another Philosophy of History for the Enlightenment of Mankind," in F. M. Barnard, ed., *J.G. Herder on Social and Political Culture* (Cambridge, 1969), pp. 171–223. I have used the translation of the text which is henceforth cited as "Yet" in parentheses with page number(s).

3 Voltaire quoted in Meinecke, *Historism*, pp. 56–7. This important book on the emergence of historicism was originally published in German as *Historismus*, a title that was unfortunately translated into an English neologism, *Historism*, that no one currently uses. I use the term "historicism" to refer to what in German is called "Historismus."

4 A term coined by the American English professor Stephen Greenblatt, "New Historicism" seeks to coordinate a period's diverse cultural phenomena as expressions of the circulation of political power, and in this sense is principally inspired by the work of Michel Foucault. In its desire to see all historical periods as operating in this fashion, New Historicism, for Herder, would be distinctly "anti-historicist."

5 Jonathan Knudsen, *Justus Möser and the German Enlightenment* (Cambridge, 1986).

6 On Möser, ibid., 165–74; on Herder and the French Revolution, see Frederick Beiser, *Enlightenment, Revolution, and Romanticism: The Genesis of Modern German Political Thought* (Cambridge, MA, 1992), pp. 215–21.

7 Isaiah Berlin discusses Meinecke's qualms in Berlin, "Foreword," to Meinecke, *Historism*, pp. xi–xii.

8 Another prominent German writer, Gottfried Lessing (1729–81), uses this standard trope in his essay on universal history of 1780, "The Education of the Human Race," and it is implied in Kant's famous opening to his essay "An Answer to the Question 'What is Enlightenment?'" of 1789, where he wrote: "Enlightenment is man's emergence from his self-incurred tutelage." Immanuel Kant, *Political Writings* (Cambridge, 1991), p. 54.

9 An English translation of excerpts is Johann Gottfried Herder, *Reflections on the Philosophy of History* (Chicago, 1968).

10 An intriguing aspect of Herder's university education in Königsberg is that his two most influential teachers stood as direct opposites of each other in their thought: the rigorously reasoning Kant on the one side, supporting the Enlightenment, and the Pietist, mystical Johann Georg Hamann (1730–88) on the other, attacking the Enlightenment.

11   Immanuel Kant, "Review of Herder's *Ideas on the Philosophy of History of Mankind*," in *Political Writings*, p. 209 and see p. 217.

12   Immanuel Kant, "Idea for a Universal History With A Cosmopolitan Purpose," 42. Hereafter cited as "Idea" followed by page number(s).

13   Immanuel Kant, *The Contest of the Faculties* (New York, 1979), pp. 159–61.

14   Ibid., 165.

15   Mah, *Phantasies of Identity in France and Germany, Diderot to Nietzsche* (forthcoming), on Herder's social alienation; on the generation of the 1790s, see Charles Taylor, *Hegel* (Cambridge, 1975), pp. 3–46; George A. Kelly, *Idealism, Politics, and History* (Cambridge, 1975); M. H. Abrams, *Natural Supernaturalism: Tradition and Revolution in Romantic Literature* (New York, 1971); Raymond Plant, *Hegel* (Bloomington, IN, 1973), Panajotis Kondylis, *Die Entstehung der Dialektik* (Stuttgart, 1979); Beiser, *Enlightenment*.

16   G. W. F. Hegel, *Philosophy of History*, trans. J. Sibree (New York, 1956), p. 20. Hereafter cited in text as *Philosophy* followed by page number(s).

17   G. W. F. Hegel, *Philosophy of Right*, trans. T. M. Knox (Oxford, 1967), p. 10.

18   John Toews, *Hegelianism: The Path Toward Dialectical Humanism, 1805–1841* (Cambridge, 1981); Harold Mah, *The End of Philosophy, the Origin of "Ideology": Karl Marx and the Crisis of the Young Hegelians* (Berkeley, 1987).

19   On both these criticisms in contemporary historiography, see Peter Novick, *That Noble Dream: The "Objectivity Question" and the American Historical Profession* (Cambridge, 1988), pp. 415–629.

20   Ibid., p. 300 and for a similar wish turned into post-Cold War triumphalism, see Francis Fukuyama, *The End of History and the Last Man* (Toronto, 1992), which carries over Hegel's desire to stop history but mangles many of Hegel's ideas and arguments.

REFERENCES AND FURTHER READING

English editions of primary texts

Hegel, Georg Wilhelm Friedrich, *The Philosophy of History*, trans. J. Sibree, New York: Dover Books, 1956.

——, *Hegel's Philosophy of Right*, trans. T. M. Knox, Oxford: Oxford University Press, 1972.

Herder, Johann Gottfried, *J. G. Herder on Social and Political Culture*, trans. F. M. Barnard, Cambridge: Cambridge University Press, 1969.

——, *Reflections on the Philosophy of History*, trans. T. O. Churchill, Chicago: University of Chicago Press, 1968.

Kant, Immanuel, *The Contest of the Faculties*, trans. Mary J. Gregor, New York: Arabis Books, 1979.

——, *Political Writings*, trans. H. B. Nisbet, Cambridge: Cambridge University Press, 1991.

Selected secondary works

Abrams, M. H., *Natural Supernaturalism: Tradition and Revolution in Romantic Literature*, New York: W.W. Norton and Co., 1971.

Beiser, Frederick, *Enlightenment, Revolution, and Romanticism: The Genesis of Modern German Political Thought*, Cambridge, MA: Harvard University Press, 1992.

Berlin, Isaiah, *Vico and Herder: Two Studies in the History of Ideas*, London: Hogarth Press, 1976.

Kelly, George A., *Idealism, Politics, and History: Sources of Hegelian Thought*, Cambridge: Cambridge University Press, 1969.

Koselleck, Reinhart, *Futures Past: On the Semantics of Historical Time*, Cambridge, MA: MIT Press, 1985.

Knudsen, Jonathan, *Justus Möser and the German Enlightenment*, Cambridge: Cambridge University Press, 1986.

Mah, Harold, *The End of Philosophy, the Origin of "Ideology": Karl Marx and the Crisis of the Young Hegelians*, Berkeley: University of California Press, 1987.

——, *Phantasies of Identity in France and Germany, Diderot to Nietzsche*, forthcoming.

Meinecke, Friedrich, *Historism: The Rise of a New Historical Outlook*, Princeton: Princeton University Press, 1972.

Pascal, Roy, *The German Sturm und Drang*, Manchester: Manchester University Press, 1967.

Reill, Peter Hans, *The German Enlightenment and the Rise of Historicism*, Berkeley: University of California Press, 1975.

Schnädelbach, Herbert, *Philosophy in Germany, 1831–1933*, Cambridge: Cambridge University Press, 1984.

Taylor, Charles, *Hegel*, Cambridge: Cambridge University Press, 1975.

Toews, John, *Hegelianism: The Path Toward Dialectical Humanism*, Cambridge: Cambridge University Press, 1981.

CHAPTER EIGHT

German Historical Writing from Ranke to Weber: The Primacy of Politics

HARRY LIEBERSOHN

German historical writing as founded by Leopold von Ranke (1795–1886) was a response to the challenge of building a nation-state. Since the Reformation, Germany had suffered from political division and economic backwardness; at last, many believed in the early nineteenth century, the moment had come for Prussia to create a nation-state which could serve as the worthy political stage for the assertion of German culture alongside its French and English rivals. Ranke belonged to a generation of historians who were both scholars and public intellectuals. They were the heirs to a long tradition of German university learning, and they carried German scholarship's renowned exhaustive research to new heights. They were public intellectuals too, however, who played a significant role in overcoming provincial loyalties and persuading elites from all parts of Central Europe to join the task of creating a unified nation-state.

Nationalism, and nationalist historical writing, existed in many parts of nineteenth-century Europe, and we need to look more closely at the culture of Ranke and his contemporaries in order to understand their distinctive achievement and its lasting impact. Their tradition of historical writing was the creation of an exclusive elite, the Protestant educated middle class. Two features of its outlook deserve special mention. Its sensibility was profoundly Lutheran. Many of its leading spokesmen in the nineteenth century came from homes in which the faiths of the Reformation still had real meaning, either because there were pastors in the family, or because mothers or fathers created an atmosphere of religious piety.[1] Their Protestantism was not necessarily a religious faith; it was a culture, a set of attitudes and practices that pervaded many areas of life and made its members feel apart from Catholics and Jews. Even among secularized intellectuals religious identity remained important. Many, regardless of religious belief, viewed national unification with religious fervor as an event that would charge their lives with extraordinary meaning.

The politics at the center of their historical writing was not just another name for the management of power. Rather, it was the drama of collective past suffering remembered by the historian and redeemed through the making of a national community. Politics mattered above everything else because it seemed to promise a secularized redemption from the divisions of German history.

A second defining feature of this educated elite was its turn to Prussia for national leadership. After the end of the Napoleonic wars, Prussia seemed to be a youthful, modernizing state that had the *brio* to break through the existing boundaries of the European political map. Austria was Catholic, and unacceptable for that reason alone; other North German states such as Saxony or Baden were too timid and small ever to play a major role in international politics. Prussia, by contrast, had a sense of collective superiority dating back to the time of Frederick the Great. Although Napoleon's armies later dealt Prussia's troops a crushing defeat, a band of reformers had created a brilliant new center of learning, the University of Berlin, and instilled a renewed confidence in Prussia's political leadership. With Prussia in mind, Ranke and his peers thought of political history above all as the history of the *state*, the center of intelligent action that brought peace, prosperity and enlightenment to its citizens.

We shall see that this original vision of the primacy of politics became a creative irritant for Ranke's most imaginative successors. They exposed the limitations of political history and explored other dimensions of human experience that he had neglected or integrated all too smoothly into his pageant of the triumph of the modern state. Yet it was not so easy for them, even at their most critical, to dismiss the primacy of politics; though they argued with it, or tried to subvert it, subsequent generations of German intellectuals remained haunted by the promise of German nation-statehood.

Leopold von Ranke: The Primacy of Politics

Ranke was the most celebrated shaper of this north German conception of history as a story of nation-state formation. In volume after volume he chronicled French, English and central European history of the early-modern period, surveyed Prussian history, and wrote more specialized studies of Spanish, Italian, and Habsburg history and a history of the Papacy as well as forays into Ottoman history, a biography of Wallenstein, and a history of Serbia. The tone was lofty and self-assured, the writing detailed and clear. The foundation was indefatigable industry in European archives. Ranke himself had the status of an academic great power, so to speak, serving as a professor at the University of Berlin after 1825 and official historian of Prussia after 1841.

Ranke's reputation has been damaged by a phrase that may once have been singled out in admiration, but in our own day has become grounds for dismissal from serious consideration: the historian, he wrote, should write about the past "as it really was."[2] It calls up an image of him as a serene master removed from the prejudices of partisan politics. Yet it is difficult to understand how anyone – whether disciple or critic – could actually read his works and come to the conclusion that they demonstrate bloodless objectivity.

What is striking instead is Ranke's dedication to a clearly stated set of principles. In tome after tome he opposed what he called theory: "Political theories hold sway virtually everywhere. How seldom it is that people test a venture or an institution according to its inner conditions; people satisfy themselves instead with applying the measuring-stick of theory to it."[3] This statement from 1832, the opening of an important manifesto for a political journal that he was editing, was a protest against the ideologies that had inspired the French Revolution of 1789 and that had shaken Europe again in France's Revolution of 1830. Ranke countered the tyranny of theory with a call for what we today would call historical specificity, or attention, as he put it, to the inner conditions of historical phenomena.

Ranke's protest against "theory" did not imply an absence of concepts to lead him to significant historical subjects. On the contrary, he was bold and clear about his guiding concerns and how they led him to his choice of subjects.

The first of these concerns was the nation. Ranke had a Romantic belief in the existence of primeval national types – Celtic, Germanic, Latin, and Slavic – which evolved but remained the source of all later cultural developments down to his own time. In his different histories, he dramatized the development of Europe as the story of how these different groups fulfilled their potential through inner development, mixture, and conflict with one another. Hence he summarized the development of England into a world power as the triumph of "northern Germania," a phrase that makes little sense today, but had its place in his gallery of racial types.[4] The history of France provided him with a particularly rich setting for this kind of racialized historical observation, with its Celtic indigenous peoples (according to Ranke their practice of human sacrifice and belligerence made them "the most dangerous enemy of the civilized nations alongside whom they live[d]")[5] , the Roman conquest and latinization of Gaul, Germanic immigration, and the synthesis of Germanic and Latin worlds.[6] The different ethnic components did not disappear, but remained the elements of later history:

> The history of the formation of peoples is something like the history of the earth. It has, so to speak, an intrinsic geological character; one can distinguish the formation of different formative moments (*Bildungsepochen*). But in human history there is nothing lifeless; ethnic elements (*Völkerelemente*) that come into contact or share a common border affect one another continuously, conflicting or striving toward an organic union.[7]

Ranke's language leads into a world that is no longer our own. His geological and biological metaphors point to a notion of race or ethnicity that grounds human history in inborn, natural capacities. Yet it would be anachronistic to confuse his conception of ethnic or racial character with later conceptions of race. Writing long before Social Darwinism and far removed from the materialism of his own time, he had a more fluid understanding of characteristics that can change, be exchanged, and even eventuate in the formation of new national types, as, he supposed, had happened in France. Perhaps the English word "folk" best conveys today what Ranke had in mind, as when we, heirs to the Romantics, speak of folk songs or folk art to designate popular creative expressions that may become the starting-point of a national culture.

Writing in the early nineteenth century at a moment of national movements across Europe, Ranke thought of nationhood hand in hand with the formation of the modern *state*. Like many of his contemporaries, Ranke was tantalized by the dream of forming a state that could protect Germans from the existing great powers, above all France, and serve as a framework for the expression of their national culture. His work gave clear historical outline to the belief of Germany's Protestant middle class that its moment of national destiny had come. Ranke looked back to the Holy Roman Empire – that century-old, rambling confederation of states in Central Europe, ingloriously dissolved by Napoleon – as Germany's proto-state; instead of going on to mature statehood, in the fashion of France and England, it had been shattered by the religious wars of the sixteenth and seventeenth centuries.[8] He intertwined the failure of the Holy Roman Empire to evolve into a nation-state with Germany's religious history. The Reformation, starting with Luther's challenge to the dominance of Rome a moment of German historical glory, turned into a cause of political division and decline. While Ranke strove – herewith a sample of his famous impartiality – to honor Austria as the representative of German Catholic culture, he looked to Prussia as the leader of Protestant interests.

Like other advocates of Prussian leadership, Ranke came from elsewhere. Born and educated in Saxony, he admired, indeed adulated the Prussian state as the savior of Protestant Germany. His writings contributed to the idealization of Prussia which made the German historical profession an important historical actor in its own right, contributing to the national movement that eventuated in the formation of a Prussia-dominated Germany. By the standards of the historical profession in our own time, Ranke projected the notion of nationhood into a pre-national early-modern period; most historians today would agree that Prussia before the nineteenth century was a dynastic state run by and for a tiny elite with no consciousness of a "national" mission to create a united Germany. This is only to say, however, that he was a person of his own age and class. The Protestant educated elite threw itself into the task of nation-building with all the fervor of followers of a religious movement.

Ranke and his fellow historians simply could not discern the tensions between their nineteenth-century nationalism and their commitment to grasping the "inner conditions" of earlier institutions.

The religious dimension of German nationalism is essential to Ranke's historical writing. For Ranke – a descendant of generations of Lutheran ministers (although his own father was trained in law) who started his studies at the University of Leipzig in theology – religion was one of the formative powers of history, along with nation and state, and his national and political concepts cannot be understood without reference to his Lutheran outlook. Ranke's piety led him to believe that European history was the theater for the realization of religious truth over time – that is, for the triumph of Western Christianity. This belief set firm limits to his idealization of nationality and organized power; for Ranke, nation and state were the local, concrete expressions of God's will in history, but needed to be absorbed into larger Christian and human communities. Hence Ranke's conception of history was worlds apart from what Gerhard Ritter after World War II, trying to understand the pathology of recent German history, called the *Dämonie der Macht,* the demonic logic of power exercised for its own sake.[9] The nationstate for Ranke had significance only as part of a transnational, providential plan for the redemption of all humanity.

What, in retrospect, is the significance of Ranke's historical thought? One helpful point of comparison is his French contemporary, Alexis de Tocqueville. Like Ranke, Tocqueville was suspicious of the abstract ideologies inherited from the eighteenth century and the revolutionary movements that had transformed them into a new political order in France and other parts of Europe after 1789. Unlike Ranke, however, who remained deeply provincial despite his wide European travels, Tocqueville was cosmopolitan despite his French patriotism and Norman roots. Ranke viewed the world from Berlin; Tocqueville in *Democracy in America* stepped outside of Europe and viewed the movement of history from the towns and country of the New World. As for their political beliefs, Ranke was traumatized by the memories of revolution in Europe, and he could not admit that Germany had been deeply affected by the French Revolution and Napoleon. Tocqueville, by contrast, though from a conservative aristocratic milieu, strove in the 1830s to see the hand of providence in the democratic movements of the modern era and asked how the lessons of American democracy could benefit France's steady advance toward a democratic political order. Ranke embraced his era's faith in historical progress; Tocqueville was ambivalent, torn between his belief in the inevitability of progress and his insight into its dangers to freedom. Ranke comforted his contemporaries with truisms that define him as a thinker from another era; Tocqueville challenged his readers to engage in self-criticism and remains a vital thinker today.

Ranke's limitations should not make us indifferent to his enduring strengths. His historical writings are valuable not for the pseudo-objectivity wrongly attributed to them, but for their rare synthesis of political commitment and appreciation of historical diversity. His belief in Prussia's political destiny was a driving force behind his writings, but he could still write three thick volumes commemorating the victory of parliamentary government in early-modern England. Neither ideologue nor antiquarian, Ranke achieved a *balance* of political motive and historical judgment. Critical to Ranke's legacy to subsequent generations of historians was the primacy of politics in historical narrative. His chronicling of political actors and events challenged later generations to acknowledge the centrality of politics even if they turned to other dimensions of historical experience.

Jacob Burckhardt: Culture between Politics and Religion

When we turn from Ranke to Jacob Burckhardt (1818–97), a different stretch of the Central European cultural landscape comes into view. Suddenly we are no longer in brisk, modernizing Berlin, capital of an upstart state ready to challenge venerable Austria for Central European hegemony. Instead we remove ourselves to tiny Basel, a city without centralizing ambitions even within Switzerland, aloof from the great national struggles of the age. From a prominent (though financially modest) Basel family, and permitted to make long stays in Italy, France, and Germany, Burckhardt could view contemporary politics from an independent vantage-point. But not without his own commitments and passions: the social conflicts of the nineteenth century had reached his native city, and Burckhardt could not know how much longer its elite leadership would be able to contain the forces of modern democracy. He wrote with contemporary engagement as well as distance toward the great power politics of his time.[10]

It is tempting to stylize this move from Ranke and Berlin to Burckhardt and Basel as a shift from politics to culture – from the great chronicler of the formation of modern nation-states to the art historian best remembered for his history of the Italian Renaissance. This would be a misleading exaggeration, however. Burckhardt studied with Ranke and retained a lasting admiration for his former teacher. To be sure, culture takes on a new prominence in Burckhardt's writings; he is one of the founders of cultural history in the modern period. But his is not a cultural history without politics. He remained true in his own way to his master by understanding culture through its interaction with politics.

How did Burckhardt conceive the task of cultural history? He provides us with an outline in his book, originally a set of lectures, *On the Study of*

History.[11] Here Burckhardt defines three formative forces (*Potenzen*) in world history: politics, religion, and culture. Each can be analyzed apart from the others, but in historical practice they overlap, and each conditions the other two. Here one can see Burckhardt's development away from Ranke toward an original conception of history. For Ranke, politics and religion are central; while affirming their importance, Burckhardt adds culture as an irreducible third principle. Free human expression takes on a novel dignity and interest. At the same time, it would be anachronistic to read Burckhardt as a late twentieth-century student of culture *avant la lettre*; always cautious and skeptical, he avoids totalizing claims for man's autonomy as meaning-maker. Culture does not, as in the more radical forms of cultural anthropology inspired by Clifford Geertz, become the master key to interpreting human action; in his lectures and books, he always analyzes it in dynamic relationship to politics and religion.

The post-Rankean prominence of culture comes to the fore in Burckhardt's most famous book, *The Civilization of the Renaissance in Italy (Die Kultur der Renaissance in Italien)* (1860). Its scope is wide – still astonishingly so if one picks it up today. Burckhardt satisfies the reader's curiosity about "high" cultural topics such as the rediscovery of antiquity, humanism, schools, philology, historical writing, poetry, and art; but with a curiosity worthy of Montaigne he also explores the quest for celebrity, humor and wit, travel, the situation of women, household life, thievery, magic, attitudes toward the Church, astrology, and beliefs about the afterlife. The book's unity as a study of culture lies not in its subject-matter, but in its theme, the radical emancipation of the individual from communal constraints. This principle animates the life of the Renaissance era down to its smallest details.

Any study of culture is an *interpretation* of culture. This assertion, familiar to us today from the anthropological writings of Clifford Geertz, comes through in the opening lines of Burckhardt's introduction:

> This work bears the title of an essay in the strictest sense of the word. No one is more conscious than the writer with what limited means and strength he has addressed himself to a task so arduous. And even if he could look with greater confidence upon his own researches he would hardly thereby feel more assured of the approval of competent judges. To each eye, perhaps, the outlines of a given civilization present a different picture . . . In the wide ocean upon which we venture the possible ways and directions are many; and the same studies which have served for this work might easily, in other hands, not only receive a wholly different treatment and application, but lead also to essentially different conclusions.[12]

In these lines, Burckhardt is our contemporary. He announces a program for the interpretation of culture which is still remarkable for its full consciousness of the multiplicity of possible points of view and the arbitrariness of any single choice. It contains an acute methodological awareness that the historian of culture is a limited, temporal being who is shaped by the culture of his or her own time.

However aware he may have been of the many possibilities of interpretation, Burckhardt did not hesitate to put the firmest possible stamp on his own. A single theme guides his history of the Renaissance from beginning to end, the emergence of modern individualism in response to the creation of the modern state. The structure of this finely wrought work follows this theme: part one is called "The State As a Work of Art," and only thereafter follows a part on "The Development of the Individual." After his brief methodological reflection in the book's opening paragraphs, Burckhardt plunges the reader into the political conditions of late medieval Italy, which he describes as a struggle to create a political order fully autonomous from the interference of religion or tradition. The state appears as the first work of art of the cultural movement that becomes the Renaissance. In the Italian states dependent on neither kaiser nor pope, he writes,

> we detect the modern political spirit of Europe, surrendered freely to its own instincts, often displaying the worst features of an unbridled egoism, outraging every right, and killing every germ of a healthier culture But wherever this vicious tendency is overcome or in any way compensated a new fact appears in history – the State as the outcome of reflection and calculation, the State as a work of art.[13]

Next Burckhardt treats his readers to a succession of rulers who combined ruthlessness and talent in their will to create a new public order. These states, according to Burckhardt, are the most important condition for the appearance of free individuals, in his thesis the first modern men and women.[14]

It is, then, a thoroughly political book, not in the sense of propagating an ideology, but in its organization and its attention to the state. It is also a book at odds with "art appreciation" and antiquarianism: Burckhardt's aim is not contemplation of the beautiful, but insight into the ambivalence of modern culture. The emancipation of the individual contains possibilities both admirable and evil. Burckhardt asks his reader to be horrified by tyrants' exercise of power as well as impressed by the brilliance of Italy's creativity across the arts and sciences. His text shimmers with ambiguities; it sacrifices neither moral judgment nor wonder in its view of a historical epoch. Burckhardt's own standpoint is not that of an aesthete, but of a scholar who, at his father's urging, studied theology for four years before continuing his education in history. While Burkhardt later emancipated himself from formal religious faith, he retained a Lutheran insight into the potential for radical evil inherent in the exercise of power and in the purely secular culture of the modern era. His study of the Renaissance invites us to appreciate artistic achievement in its complex relationship to human moral capacities.[15]

Although most famous for his history of the Renaissance, Burckhardt was also deeply immersed in the study of the classical world. His *Greek Cultural History* (1898–1902) continues to deserve our attention today.[16] Here again Burckhardt's mastery of historical form still makes his work a suggestive model for the possibilities of writing cultural history. Its four thick volumes (posthumously published from his lecture notes) deal with politics, religion, culture, and the epochs of Greek culture from early to late antiquity. Once again the starting point is politics. Here, though, the political order is the opposite of the one described in his history of the Renaissance. The polis is a tyrannical community demanding absolute devotion from its citizens and consuming them with torture, dishonor and exile when they run afoul of it.

Religion, which is subordinated to culture in his interpretation of the Renaissance, comes into its own in this work, for the creativity of the Greeks, amid the violence and uncertainty of the polis, has as one of its chief sources their religious beliefs. The pantheon of the gods, according to Burckhardt, is a late and superficial development which never took a deep hold on individuals. Rather it is the rituals of honoring the dead and of sacrifice that serve as an impetus to creativity. From the honor due to the dead emerges the cult of the hero, and the cult of the hero feeds the Greek striving for the highest brilliance and the awe of an observing public. Sacrifices are accompanied by a chorus, which serves as the starting-point for Greek theater. The ancient Greeks, according to Burckhardt, are imbued with a deep pessimism about the value of life which they overcome through their activism and their art.[17] There is a rich ethnological turn to this work that anticipates the *fin de siècle*'s fascination with the primitive as well as the late twentieth-century alliance of cultural anthropology and history.[18]

Friedrich Nietzsche: History as Cultural Criticism

Burckhardt's elevation of culture to the status of a basic historical principle contained an implicit critique of Prussia's political success, for Prussia could grow in wealth and territory, but it could neither buy nor force its way to an authentic culture. A more radical cultural critique came from his younger colleague at the University of Basel, Friedrich Nietzsche (1844–1900). Nietzsche was not a Basel insider, even though he turned out to be a natural match for the intellectual milieu he discovered there. Like Ranke he came from small-town Saxony, from a modest family with a pastoral lineage. It was by chance that he ended up teaching in Basel, and yet the happenstance suited his style of thinking. Whereas Ranke headed north, and assimilated the traditions of Prussia, Nietzsche ended up outside the German Empire, viewing its shortcomings from Alpine heights, poised between Germany, France, and Italy, where he was free to judge Germany from the standpoint of a cosmopolitan European. From this remove he demoted politics and religion – two of Burckhardt's trio of basic historical forces – and instead asserted the primacy of culture as the measure of human history.

Nietzsche's dissertation and first book, *The Birth of Tragedy* (1872), laid out the argument for the primacy of culture, and it did so in the spirit of an exultant German nationalism. Prussia's victory over France in 1870–1 completed the creation of a German nation-state – as far as Bismarck wished to pursue it, at least – fulfilling the dreams of Ranke and most other educated Protestant Germans. Nietzsche rushed his dissertation into print in order to supply the newly formed empire with a guide for making a culture that would be a worthy match for its newly achieved greatness. Classical philologist that he was, he imagined this culture in keeping with the ancient Greek ideal of *sophrosyne* as a balance of strength and discipline, or in his mythical formulation, of Dionysian and Apollonian impulses. Already in this work, Nietzsche's anti-political prejudice is very much in evidence as he criticizes earlier, liberal political interpretations of the origins of tragedy (as an outgrowth of a democratic political will) in favor of the deeper teaching of an instinctual vitality which first found expression in the cult of Dionysus and was later given order and refinement by the cult of Apollo.[19] Nietzsche believed that the Dionysian capacity for affirming life and its intrinsic suffering had been reborn in Germany's musical tradition from Bach to Wagner and that it would serve as the starting-point for a cultural renaissance in the newly created German Empire.

Elation soon gave way to depression for sensitive observers in the early 1870s as the dream of national unity gave way to the realities of class, confessional and regional conflict. No one gave fiercer expression to this mood of disillusionment than Nietzsche. For the next half century and beyond, his work became the model of cultural criticism for his contemporaries; the ponderings of a lonely, exiled professor of philology (to be put on disability pension in 1879, plagued with headaches and stomach ailments) influenced writers, artists, musicians, thinkers, and ideologies across the political spectrum.[20] Nowhere was he more effective than in his critique of historical thinking in Germany, delivered in "On the Uses and Disadvantages of History for Life" (1874), one of the essays collected under the title *Untimely Meditations* (1873–6). The very first essay, "David Strauss, the Confessor and the Writer," turned culture against politics with its observation that "a great victory is a great danger" – and that the reaction to the war with France was "capable of turning our victory into a defeat: *into the defeat, if not the extirpation, of the German spirit for the benefit of the 'German Reich'*."[21] With this warning Nietzsche announced the break-up of the alliance of Prussia and historical progress that had inspired historical thinking for the preceding half century. The advance of Prussian arms, industry and bureaucracy masked the creative poverty of the new German society and state. In this and in his subsequent writings Nietzsche enchanted his readers with a style of cultural criticism that seemed dazzling compared to academic historians' analysis of the state as the locus of power. To be sure, power is not absent from Nietzsche's meditations: on the contrary, it is ubiquitous, and it is no accident that we associate Nietzsche's name with his unfinished collection of aphorisms on the will to power. But this was far removed from a Rankean – or Burckhardtean – grappling with the state as the organized center of power in the modern world.

Max Weber: The Sociology of Modern Politics and Culture

If the German nation-state was for the young Ranke a dream and for Nietzsche an immediate experience, for Max Weber (1864–1920) it was a *fait accompli*, the achievement of his parents' generation. Germany as a great power was not a novelty, but a given; what to do with its great power status was the question confronting its social scientists.[22]

Weber viewed the new German Empire from multiple points on the Central European landscape. He was born and raised in Berlin and taught at different times in Freiburg, Heidelberg, Munich, and Vienna. It was in provincial Heidelberg that he spent his most creative years, beginning in 1896; here is where he produced the stream of methodological essays that have shaped the behavioral sciences down to our own time, where he wrote his famous essay on the Protestant ethic, and where he conceived his encyclopedic work, *Economy and Society*; here he belonged to a milieu of creative professors, most famous among them the theologian Ernst Troeltsch; here too he influenced younger thinkers who would soon become famous names in their own right, including Karl Jaspers, Ernst Bloch, and Georg Lukács. From their Heidelberg post in the Southwestern province of Baden, Weber and his Heidelberg circle could not observe German politics up close, but this had its advantages; they were not representatives of the Prussian state, and their distance afforded a certain freedom to observe and criticize. At the same time Baden had its own liberal elite, its own confrontation with mass politics, and its own centers of industrialization; it was not at all removed from the social and political tensions resulting from political unification and rapid economic transformation. This was the setting in which Weber's historical conceptions matured after the turn of the century.[23]

Weber was by profession an economist and a jurist, not a historian; but he studied and worked at a time when economics, his primary affiliation by training and occupation, was a historical discipline. German economists thought of themselves as servants of the state, and the prominent Berlin economists Gustav Schmoller and Adolf Wagner were conspicuous for their dedication to

Prussia. In particular Schmoller (who came from Württemberg in the South-west and was one more of those immigrants who idealized their new Prussian home) traced the economic development of Prussia as the story of a providential rise to national greatness. Max Weber's first methodological essays included a critique of this kind of idealization of the state, which he attributed to a sublimated Lutheran adulation of secular authority, and called for a firmly delimited, empirical analysis of economy and society.[24] Contemporary events stimulated his insistence on political analysis free of illusions: the jejune behavior of Emperor Wilhelm II, the inability of his educated liberal friends to comprehend their own diminishing political significance, the ideological pretensions of the Social Democratic Party (caught between its revolutionary Marxist rhetoric and its reformist political practice), and anti-modern romanticism among German students goaded him to educate Germans to political realism and responsibility.[25]

By training and talent a tough-minded social scientist, Weber came late to culture as a subject of inquiry. After the turn of the century, however, his interests and circle of friends rapidly expanded, and his writings over the next decade and a half are still one of the best starting-points for the interpretation of culture. Scholars since the 1960s have pointed out that Weber was a close reader of Nietzsche. It is certainly the case that his categories of analysis refine Nietzsche's image of humanity as the meaning-making species, whose specific dignity lies not in its rationality, but in its ability to give form, whether in art, literature or politics, to a personal vision. Weber appropriated this insight for social science. Human beings, he argued, give shape and direction to an otherwise meaningless world through the application of subjective principles. From innumerable possible choices, social actors select a course of action on the basis of personal values; from the chaotic mass of materials from the past, historians select certain problems for study that they consider significant for themselves and their contemporaries. A Nietzschean insight was at work here, but so, too, was a critical delimitation. Weber asked social scientists not to worry about absolute truths, but to understand the *perceptions* of social actors – how individuals derive values from religion, politics, sexuality, science, and art as motive for actions. In contrast to Nietzsche, Weber in his scientific work was not interested in promoting values, but in understanding them. The cultural turn in Weber's social science was a methodological advance, not a philosophy of life, and it aimed at turning social scientists into better readers of actors from alien times and places.

Weber's celebrated and controversial essay on *The Protestant Ethic and the Spirit of Capitalism* (1904–5) exemplifies his understanding of historical analysis. It begins with a problem of meaning: why should early-modern capitalists have ceaselessly accumulated money (and why should early modern workers have engaged in disciplined labor) which went beyond satisfying anyone's personal needs? The answer was that the Puritans' ascetic dedication to work in the world alleviated their anxiety about salvation. Weber was not concerned with whether they were right or wrong in this religious belief. It was precisely the interpretive social scientist's task not to get stuck in preconceptions about what Puritans "should" believe, or to approve or disapprove, but to look at their everyday practice as a motor of modern history. Generations of later social scientists have disputed his account of the origins of modern capitalism, but for interpretive social scientists and, more recently, the new wave of historians of everyday life, his essay remains a stimulating demonstration of the connections between ideas, mentality, and action.

Two essays that Weber wrote near the end of his life go beyond empirical social science to offer his philosophy of the history of science and of politics in the West. Both essays demonstrate the power of sociological analysis for understanding these two preoccupations of nineteenth-century German historical thought. Weber focuses on the *means* by which human beings have tried to achieve their ends and how those means have in turn defined what human beings can possibly hope to achieve. In "Science as a Vocation" (1917), Weber analyzes how the German university is undergoing the transformation from a community of economically independent researchers (who are either independently wealthy young men awaiting a professorship, or professors who own their own means of production, the small libraries and modest stock of equipment once necessary for research) to dependent, salaried employees within a huge division of labor. Reviewing the history of learning since classical antiquity, Weber dismisses the different paths to truth envisioned by the learned of previous epochs: the Socratic search for truth through examination of concepts, the theological belief in salvation through dogmatic system, and the Renaissance quest for knowledge of unchanging nature through scientific experiment. Instead the modern researcher explains the specific means appropriate to achieving specific ends. This is one aspect of the "disenchantment of the world" that Weber insists is an indelible feature of modernity.[26]

"Politics As a Vocation" (1919) makes parallel arguments which begin, again, with a consideration of means: in contrast to earlier eras in which political elites controlled the instruments of a monopoly of legitimate violence in their societies, the modern politician, like the modern scientist, is normally a salaried employee. The metaphor of "machine politics" to describe the control of modern mass elections is, he points out, a significant one: modern politics operates with a machine-like predictability, and the average politician is not a visionary, but an insignificant part of the whole. In politics as in science, the means of production (of power and knowledge) have overwhelmed the ends, so that the modern scientific enterprise and modern state now reproduce their bureaucratized existence without serving any further end.[27] Weber's vision of history, like that of his predecessors, took shape in response to the fate of the

German nation-state. His mood of disenchantment was in stark contrast to Ranke's belief that Prussia was progressing toward fulfillment of Germany's providential destiny; instead he was gripped in the "Vocation" essays by the spectacle first of years of industrialized war between bureaucratized states, then of Germany's catastrophic defeat.[28]

Scholars have long noted that Weber's dialogue in the "Vocation" essays is not just with Nietzsche, but also with Marx. From his earliest writings on the economic history of ancient Rome, Weber was clearly schooled in a Marxian attention to means and modes of production and to the formative role of class relations; as we have seen in the "Vocation" essays, Weber writes in close parallel to Marx, with scientists and politicians in the role of workers who have lost control of the means of production and are reduced to the role of dependents in a self-sustaining, meaningless system. Yet the differences that separate Weber and Marx are no less obvious. Weber anticipates no redemption, no utopia, no movement toward a genuinely revolutionary moment; on the contrary, all attempts to undermine or overthrow the existing systems will only end in defeat or reinforcement of the very systems they are supposed to challenge. At the moment of its triumph in the newly formed Soviet Union, Marxism as political ideology is the object of an acute and prescient critique in Weber's essays. Yet the news is not all bad; as the philosopher Karl Löwith observed, for Weber these modern systems are the conditions for a distinctly modern kind of freedom.[29] Human beings have gained the painful but emancipating knowledge that a sustaining system of meaning does not come from the outside – from systems of knowledge or from social organizations; instead individuals are thrown back on their inner resources for giving a satisfying shape to the external world. The heroic personality – whether in the service of science, or politics, or art or eros – will find his or her own calling and will struggle to realize it.

There is a second crucial moment of contrast to Marx. Marx wrote and thought entirely within Enlightenment categories, confident in the legitimacy of Western science and the bankruptcy of other outlooks on the world. Weber, true to his own program of mapping perceptions and to his agnosticism about ultimate truths, did not share this confidence. Western rationality in his writings is only one possible form of rationality among many. In a series of essays on what he calls the "world religions" – of Christianity, Ancient Israel, India, China, and Islam – he outlines the psychological effects and typical forms of social action resulting from each of these religious systems. The essay on Ancient Israel, perhaps the most important of them all, reflects extensively on political defeat and the prophetic ethos, which in turn is a major source of Western rationalization. These essays are among the most remarkable historical achievements of any age, bringing penetrating insights to bear on these societies and cultures through the centuries.[30]

Extending the Meaning of Politics

Ranke's critics have enjoyed a wide readership in the English-speaking world since 1945. Isolated in their own time and skeptical toward modern mass politics, they have turned into counselors and sources of inspiration for historians writing in a democratic age.

Burckhardt's tone of civilized pessimism about the direction of history seemed borne out by the course of two world wars; it deeply appealed to historians contemplating the past with mass destruction and death camps in recent memory. His emphasis on the multi-causality of history – on the potency not just of state power, but of religion and culture as well – seemed exemplary to historians who wished to break out of the confines of political history, but were not interested in analyzing the mass phenomena of social or economic history. Looking at intellectual history in the United States since 1945, we can see that a dialogue with Burckhardt has been deep and continuous. One of the most prominent examples is Carl E. Schorske's *Fin de Siècle Vienna: Politics and Culture*. The very title suggests its Burckhardtean affinities; the interplay between politics and culture, in which art and ideas are conditioned but never wholly determined by their polity, may be read as a response to the opening pages of Burckhardt's history of the Renaissance, in which the politics of the Italian city-state become the setting for the era's creative achievements. At the same time it offers a vision of culture significantly marked off from Burckhardt's, for instead of a unified historical tableau (as in Burckhardt's *History of the Renaissance*) it re-creates Viennese high culture as disparate fragments that no longer submit to a single, unified plan. More recently, Lionel Gossman's *Basel in the Age of Burckhardt* draws on and criticizes Burckhardt's historical writing. It situates Burckhardt, Nietzsche, and other intellectuals in the city-state of Basel, but – even while renewing our appreciation for their milieu as a refined and cohesive way of life – draws subtle attention to the anti-democratic politics interwoven with their aestheticism. At the end of the twentieth century, Burckhardt remains a fruitful and a challengeable model for cultural history.

Nietzsche has had a sensational impact on post-World War II historiography through the writings of Michel Foucault. From early to late, his writings show a creative appropriation of Nietzschean insights. In an early book like *Discipline and Punish: The Birth of the Prison*, power, as in Nietzsche's writings, it is ubiquitous, an energy that exists before the state and that pervades society and state, shaping all human relations into oppositions of master and mastered. A second Nietzschean theme is the intertwining of knowledge and power; the quest for truth is only a cover for the will to power, and the systems of the social scientists are the nets that snare its victims in mental institutions (in *Birth of the Asylum*), prisons (in *Discipline and Punish*), and categories of sexual identity (in *The History of Sexuality*). Like Nietzsche, Foucault is a master of paradox who combines extraordinary erudition with a critique of all knowledge as an effect of the ever-expanding network of power relations. A third methodological idea is the "genealogy" – the path of practices that leads backwards from seemingly unproblematic present-day ideals, including our most cherished notions of humanitarianism, to hidden motives of hatred and resentment. Foucault continues Nietzsche's critique of Judaeo-Christian morality, and its successor, modern liberal humanitarianism, with an enormous *j'accuse*: according to these critics Western morality enforces conformity on human beings, defining a normal community and condemning the "abnormal" to marginalization and punishment. What begins in Nietzsche as an aristocratic doctrine of superiority to the "herd" becomes, in Foucault, a protest against the repressive norms of post-1945 European society and its historical predecessors.

Finally, there is Max Weber and his influence on historical writing: so vast since 1945 that one can hardly begin to take measure of it. His essay on *The Protestant Ethic* set off a debate on the origins of modern capitalism that can only be described as a scholarly industry in its own right. More significant than Weber's specific claims was his method of studying the psychological response of individuals to collective norms, which are best investigated in an era's therapeutic literature, whether in Sunday sermons (the material for Weber's study) or later forms of psychological guidance or manipulation. More broadly, Weber was a key intellectual model for the cultural anthropology of Clifford Geertz's *Interpretation of Cultures*, which insists that human beings are meaning-makers whose actions reveal a consistent pattern which the social scientist translates for his or her readers. Creative appropriation of this Weberian insight is visible in the essays of Natalie Z. Davis on seventeenth-century France, which apply them to new areas – notably the history of women – that Weber himself neglected or treated with deprecation. Finally, Weber's essays on the world religions take on a new interest in recent years as European history begins to think comparatively beyond European boundaries. The scholarly literature he drew on is now out of date, but not his call for an outline of different forms of rationality that have coexisted and conflicted since antiquity. One of the unifying features of Weber's writings is that they never lose sight of the centrality of power, understood in a form that would have been recognizable to Ranke. The state and its analogues are never far from his field of vision; his sensitivity to economy and society are not ways of ignoring the holders of organized power, but only deepen our appreciation of the many conditions of rational political action and its effects on every other sphere of human behavior. To this extent, Weber remains one of Ranke's legitimate heirs.

German historical writing as founded by Ranke was a response to the challenge of nation-building, and it started out by emphasizing politics as the dramatic center of human history. Politics in this tradition means *state* power, not the class struggle of the Marxian tradition or the ubiquitous diffusion of control described by Foucault. This political history became a creative starting-point to subsequent generations, who sought ways to expand beyond it. Until the end of World War I, theirs was a rather closed discussion among Protestant intellectuals, members of an elite trying to prepare itself for the trials of managing a newly formed, unstable nation-state. Outsiders to the German historical profession – Burckhardt in Basel, Nietzsche as a classical philologist, Weber as an economist – enriched this discussion and wrote philosophical reflections on the past and histories that speak directly to us as the works of Ranke do not. Yet the primacy of politics as defined by Ranke persists in Burckhardt and Weber. By continuing to read their works we acknowledge the significance of the state and of political history, which Ranke announced with an enduring authority. Like his German critics, even when attempting to leave him behind we may find ourselves acknowledging the primacy of politics in diverse societies and cultures.

NOTES

1   On Protestantism and the German middle class, see Luise Schorn-Schütte and Walter Sparn, eds., *Evangelische Pfarrer. Zur sozialen und politischen Rolle einer bürgerlichen Gruppe in der deutschen Gesellschaft des 18. bis 20. Jahrhunderts* (Stuttgart, Berlin and Cologne: Kohlhammer, 1997).

2   The famous citation is from Leopold von Ranke, *Geschichten der romanischen und germanischen Völker von 1494–1514*, in idem., *Die Meisterwerke*, vol. 1: *Fürsten und Völker*, ed. Willy Andreas (Wiesbaden: Vollmer Verlag, 1957), p. 4. It comes in his introduction to the first edition, dated 1824.

3   Leopold von Ranke, "Einleitung zur historisch-politischen Zeitschrift," (1832), *Sämmtliche Werke*, vols. 49–50: *Zur Geschichte Deutschlands und Frankreichs im 19. Jahrhunder* (Leipzig: Duncker & Humblot), 1887, 49/p. 3.

4   Leopold von Ranke, *Sämmtliche Werke*, vols. 14–15: *Englische Geschichte vornehmlich im 17. Jahrhundert* (Leipzig: Duncker & Humblot, 1877), 1/p. 4.

5   Leopold von Ranke, *Sämmtliche Werke*, vol. 8: *Französische Geschichte vornehmlich im sechzehnten und siebzehnten Jahrhundert*, Erster Band (Leipzig: Duncker & Humblot, 1876), p. 3.

6   Ibid., pp. 3–13.

7   Ibid., pp. 13–14.

8   Leopold von Ranke, *Sämmtliche Werke*, 7: *Zur Deutschen Geschichte. Vom Religionsfrieden bis zum dreissigjährigen Krieg* (Leipzig: Duncker & Humblot, 1888), p. 3.

9   Gerhard Ritter, *Die Dämonie der Macht. Betrachtungen über Geschichte und Wesen des Machtproblems im politischen Denken der Neuzeit* (Munich: Leibniz Verlag [R. Oldenbourg Verlag], 1948).

10 In addition to the works cited in the bibliographical suggestions appended to this essay, see Lionel Gossman, *Orpheus Philologus: Bachofen versus Mommsen on the Study of Antiquity*, Transactions of the American Philosophical Society 73/5 (1983).

11 Jacob Burckhardt, *Force and Freedom: Reflections on History*, ed. James H. Nichols (New York: Pantheon, 1943).

12 Jacob Burckhardt, *The Civilization of the Renaissance in Italy*, trans. S. G. C. Middlemore, 2 vols. (New York: Harper and Row, 1958), 1: 21.

13 Ibid., p. 22.

14 Ibid., p. 143.

15 Burckhardt discussed the role of religion in his own intellectual formation in the autobiographical sketch published in his complete works. He studied theology at the University of Basel for four years, from 1837 to 1839, before switching to history; in retrospect he praised his theological education as invaluable preparation for the historian. See Jacob Burckhardt, *Gesamtausgabe*, vol. 1: *Frühe Schriften* (Stuttgart, Berlin and Leipzig: Deutsche Verlags-Anstalt, 1930), ed. Hans Trog and Emil Dürr, p. vii.

16 Jacob Burckhardt, *Gesamtausgabe*, vols. 8–11: *Griechische Kulturgeschichte*, ed. Felix Stähelin and Samuel Merian (Stuttgart, Berlin and Leipzig: Deutsche Verlags-Anstalt, 1930–1).

17 On pessimism and the affirmation of life, see especially Jacob Burckhardt, *Gesamtausgabe*, vol. 9: *Griechische Kulturgeschichte*, part 2, ed. Felix Stähelin (Stuttgart, Berlin and Leipzig: Deutsche Verlags-Anstalt, 1930), pp. 355, 356–67.

18 Cf. Carl E. Schorske, *Fin de Siècle Vienna: Politics and Culture* (New York: Knopf, 1980), p. 189.

19 See Nietzsche's critique of political interpretations of the tragic chorus in *The Birth of Tragedy/The Genealogy of Morals*, trans. Francis Golffing (Garden City, New York: Doubleday, 1956), p. 47.

20 H. Hinton Thomas, *Nietzsche in German Politics and Society, 1890–1918* (Manchester: Manchester University Press, 1983).

21 Friedrich Nietzsche, *Untimely Meditations* (Cambridge: Cambridge University Press, 1983), p. 3. Italics Nietzsche's.

22 See Harry Liebersohn, *Fate and Utopia in German Sociology, 1870–1923* (Cambridge, MA and London: MIT Press, 1988).

23 On the cultural history of Heidelberg in Weber's generation see Hubert Treiber and Karol Sauer, *Heidelberg im Schnittpunkt Intellektueller Kreise. Zur Topographie der "geistigen Geselligkeit" eines "Weltdorfes": 1850–1950* (Opladen: Westdeutscher Verlag, 1995).

24 Max Weber, *Roscher and Knies: The Logical Problems of Historical Economics*, trans. and introd. Guy Oakes (New York and London: Free Press, 1975).

25 Wolfgang Mommsen, *Max Weber and German Politics*, trans. Michael & Steinberg (Chicago: University of Chicago Press, 1984).

26 Max Weber, "Science as a Vocation," in *From Max Weber: Essays in Sociology*, trans. and ed. Hans Gerth and C. Wright Mills (New York: Oxford University Press, 1946), pp. 129–56.

27 Weber, "Politics as a Vocation," in ibid., pp. 159–79.

28 On the dating and context of the "Vocation" essays, see Max Weber, *Gesamtausgabe*, Abteilung I, Band 17: *Wissenschaft als Beruf 1917/1919 – Politik als Beruf 1919*, ed. Wolfgang J. Mommsen und Wolfgang Schluchter in Zusammenarbeit mit Birgitt Morgenbrod (Tübingen: Siebeck, 1992).

29 Karl Löwith, *Max Weber and Karl Marx*, ed. Tom Bottomore and William Outhwaite, trans. Hans Fantel (London and Boston: George Allen and Unwin, 1982).

30 Max Weber, *Gesammelte Aufsätze zur Religionssoziologie*, 3 vols. (Tübingen: Mohr, 1921–47). On Weber's significance for a contemporary, comparativist approach to world cultures, see James Boon, *Other Tribes, Other Scribes: Symbolic Anthropology in the Comparative Study of Cultures, Histories, Religions, and Texts* (Cambridge and New York: Cambridge University Press, 1982).

REFERENCES AND FURTHER READING

Berding, Helmut, "Leopold von Ranke," in *Deutsche Historiker*, ed. Hans-Ulrich Wehler, vol. 1, Göttingen: Vandenhoeck und Ruprecht, 1971, pp. 7–24.

Berkowitz, Peter, *Nietzsche: The Ethics of an Immoralist*, Cambridge, MA and London: Harvard University Press, 1995.

Gilbert, Felix, *History: Politics or Culture? Reflections on Ranke and Burckhardt*, Princeton: Princeton University Press, 1990.

Gooch, George P., *History and Historians in the Nineteenth Century*, 2nd rev. edn., London and New York: Longman, Green, 1952.

Gossman, Lionel, *Basel in the Age of Burckhardt: A Study in Unseasonable Ideas*, Chicago and London: University of Chicago, 2000.

Iggers, Georg G., *The German Conception of History: The National Tradition of Historical Thought From Herder to the Present*, Middletown, CN: Wesleyan University Press, 1968.

Kelley, Donald R., *Faces of History: Historical Inquiry from Herodotus to Herder*, New Haven: Yale University Press, 1998.

Krieger, Leonard, *Ranke: The Meaning of History*, Chicago and London: The University of Chicago Press, 1977.

Mommsen, Wolfgang J., *Max Weber and German Politics*, Chicago: University of Chicago Press, 1984.

Schorske, Carl E., "History as Vocation in Burckhardt's Basel," in *Thinking with History: Explorations in the Passage to Modernism*, Princeton: Princeton University Press, 1998, ch. 4.

Weber, Marianne, *Max Weber: A Biography*, trans. Harry Zohn, introd. Guenther Roth, New Brunswick and Oxford: Transaction, 1988.

CHAPTER NINE

National History in the Age of Michelet, Macaulay, and Bancroft

THOMAS N. BAKER

"The dearest dead," said a sage, "are the best, are the nearest the resurrection."
Jules Michelet, *Histoire de France* (1833)

The historian Benedict Anderson has called it an "imagined community" – the sense of sovereign national collectivity shared by a body of people.[1] This sense of connection and common purpose that we call nationalism is *imagined* because it is a virtual community. Rather than emerging out of face-to-face personal relationships (as in local communities), it is summoned into being by the resources of imagination and constituted principally through language, myths, rituals, ballads, and the offices of print. In short, it is like all traditions an invented one, but one with a peculiar depth of resources at its advocates' disposal. In part for this very reason nationalism has become among the most pervasive and persuasive of modern ideologies. When nationalistic currents of thought and emotion emerged in the era of political revolution and reaction that stretched from 1776 to 1867, these currents, along with ideals of republicanism and liberalism, inspired a variety of struggles for national unification and liberation in both the Old and New Worlds. Since then, the related idea that the only legitimate state is an ethnic-national state has also fueled countless irredentist adventures and wars of self-determination, and such ideas have sped the breakup of more than a few empires.

Nationalism as it first developed in the nineteenth century both shaped and was shaped by the field of historical study as it was then coming to be constituted in the West. Not that all histories of the day were national in scope or outlook. The spectacular growth of popular historical writing between 1800 and 1850 in places such as France, Great Britain, and the United States likewise was marked by studies of regions, localities and religious denominations. But histories of nations – that is, histories that sought to document and thereby conjure a culturally or politically powerful nascent "national" consciousness from a welter of memories, myths, traditions, and established "facts" – were among the most characteristic works of mid-nineteenth-century historiography. Men such as Jules Michelet (1798–1874) in France, Thomas Babington Macaulay (1800–59) in Great Britain, and George Bancroft (1800–91) in the United States, whose multi-volume "people's" histories explicitly promoted the moral purpose of nation-building, emerged as some of their generation's best known and most influential historians. Since these men often simultaneously held positions of public trust as politicians, diplomats, or popular lecturers *and* spoke directly to an expansive new middle-class readership rather than to an audience of professionally trained historians alone, they shaped public opinion much more directly than did either their precursors or descendants. For these reasons, the intellectual activity of the nineteenth century's national historians was a key component in the West's invention of modern national consciousness.

This essay will sketch out some of the important philosophical and political patterns of thought that fostered these developments in national historiography, with an eye toward assessing their legacy for our own pursuit of the past. As the national histories written in this tradition were profoundly shaped by the particular political and social situations in which they were produced, we will necessarily be called to note their differences as well as to mark their commonality. Let us turn first to the latter task.

National Historians as Post-Enlightenment Thinkers

The cohort of nineteenth-century national historians that includes Michelet, Macaulay, and Bancroft has often been classed as essentially *romantic* – that is, one shaped by an ideology that historians and literary critics call romanticism. This nomenclature is problematic. To begin with, romanticism was in practice a variegated literary, cultural, and philosophical phenomenon that developed in an assortment of national contexts over a succession of generations. Even at its most unified it was often less a movement or a school of thought than an intellectual disposition. More troublesome still for our purposes, certain incarnations of romanticism sought explicitly to undercut the capacity of historical thought to say much of anything meaningful about the human condition. One philosophical goal of the self-described literary and cultural romantics in early nineteenth-century Germany and England, for instance, was to propagate the basic illusion that only the poet and his or her works could transcend the corruptions of history. When such thinkers treated historical phenomena, they tended toward a kind of idealism that began with the "philosophical idea of the thing" and proceeded to look through and beyond the historical past toward what was purported to be life's essence. This example should give us pause. Certainly it is true that some nineteenth-century national historians and their work *did* feature characteristics akin to particular varieties of literary and philosophical romanticism – an inclination to revalue the Middle Ages or a willingness to read ancient popular ballads as repositories of poetic truth, for instance. But to classify them all under the designation *romantic* would be to impose a false coherence on the historiographical traditions of the age. Doing so would also risk misleading us into overestimating the extent of the new national historians' break with their immediate past. Rather than labeling them romantics, I suggest we would do better to call our national historians *post-Enlightenment* intellectual figures. Among other advantages, this terminology has the virtue of forthrightly recognizing the manner in which these men remained heirs to significant elements of Enlightenment thought, even as they defined themselves against the historiography and philosophy of the preceding age.

As a group, the nineteenth century's national historians tended to lament most those currents in Enlightenment thought that presupposed the historical past to be a hindrance to rational social reorganization. By the 1820s, when the new national histories were beginning to be written, the so-called philosophical history of the past century was roundly criticized for being driven by an abstract theoretical bias that denied the particularity of the past, especially the national past. Faulted, too, was the ironic rationalist mode in which many late eighteenth-century thinkers had cast their surveys of the past. For Enlightenment thinkers such as Voltaire, David Hume, Edward Gibbon, and Constantin Volney, men who were dedicated to the proposition that the ground of truth and social advancement was human reason, the record of the past was preeminently a chronicle of folly, irrationality, and religious superstition. This skeptical outlook would not do for the new national historians, who as a rule aimed to restore positive meaning to the past. In contrast to the eighteenth century's intellectual sympathy for the sensationalist psychology of John Locke and Etienne Bonnot de Condillac, the new generation of historians in Great Britain, France, and the United States largely embraced the teachings of Scottish moral philosophy and, to a lesser extent, German philosophical idealism. The Scots in particular neatly sidestepped the epistemological problems that had pushed late Enlightenment thinkers toward skepticism and materialism by declaring common sense to be both an antidote to metaphysical speculation and a serviceable guide to ethical decision-making. Significantly, this new philosophical outlook meant that, in the hands of well-meaning practitioners, the past was now thought to be eminently susceptible to empirical investigation and moral judgment alike.

Yet in turning from the Enlightenment's rationalist extremes, the new national historians did not entirely repudiate their predecessors' project. Instead, they generally worked to realize what they judged to be its best aims. Certainly, both cohorts of historians viewed themselves as toiling in the cause of progress and reason. A defense of principles of human rights, for instance, figured in both traditions. Yet whereas eighteenth-century historiography drew on a belief in human nature's uniformity to teach generalizations about society, nineteenth-century historiography (often following the lead of the German philosopher Johann Gottfried Herder) usually treated social development in a manner that was more sensitive to the particularity of past epochs and the peculiar destiny of national cultures. Starting from the conviction that existing histories fatally falsified the meaning of past events – either by entombing it within dry-as-dust antiquarian tomes or by hopelessly compromising it in the service of conservative reaction – the new national historians constructed a teleology of the past that purported to uncover and revivify the heritage of what they called, by turns, *liberty*, the *people*, or the *nation*. In this respect, it is fair to classify them preeminently as genealogists who aimed to legitimate a progressive order by locating the specific, historical origins of liberty and fraternity in the more or less distant national past. In heralding their discoveries, they naturally assumed that the modern nations whose history and pre-history they set forth in their narratives were essentially indivisible collectivities. Politically, this meant that nineteenth-century national historians, with several notable exceptions, tended to espouse a liberalism that was associated with representative government, the rule of law, and the protection of private freedoms. Certainly they set themselves decisively against the forces of post-Revolutionary monarchical and clerical reaction, whose traditional claims to embody the nation they sought to supplant. Just as decisively, they recoiled from the specter of irreconcilable class divisions raised in the 1840s and 1850s by historically minded socialists such as Louis Blanc and Karl Marx.

And what of the literary style adopted by the great national historians of the mid-nineteenth century to convey their understanding of the past's meaning? For most of them it was much more than window dressing. Scholarship in this generation *was* beginning to be shaped by the existence and idea of the archive. Throughout the nineteenth century, primary sources became increasingly available as evidence for investigators wishing to draw meaning from the past. Yet the commitment of "professional" historians to the "scientific" pursuit of truth that gained favor later in the century was still mostly a kind of scientistic veneer for the generation of authors who helped invent the modern historical conception of nationhood in the years following the Napoleonic War. These historians drew inspiration from historical fiction and biographical portraiture as much as they did from the model of inductive science, and grand narrative was their preferred literary mode. The mission they undertook undoubtedly demanded nothing less, for to make the past live again and thereby awaken national consciousness to a sense of its prerogatives meant engaging readers' imaginations as well as appealing to their intellect.

In this essay, we will consider how national histories produced in France, Great Britain, and the United States during the mid-nineteenth century exemplify the general pattern sketched above.

France: Toward National History as Resurrection

Nineteenth-century French historiography unfolded in the shadow of the Revolution, haunted by the challenge of determining whether the benefits of this titanic event could be dissociated from its liabilities. For the country's national historians this question was mostly about how to locate the Revolutionary tradition's essence in the constitutional spirit of 1789 rather than in the Jacobin Terror. Such concerns were not solely academic ones. In the post-Napoleonic era, failure to establish this case meant ceding control of the past to the Ultras, the conservative Catholic monarchists who sought to reinterpret the nation's history so as to consolidate and justify their return to political power. It was this situation that provided the backdrop against which the modern French tradition of national history emerged.

The journalist and historiographer Augustin Thierry (1795–1856) offered among the first intimations of what might be accomplished by this new style of history. An habitué of the liberal intellectual circles that gathered to oppose ultraism during the Restoration and later provided administrative, polemical, and scholarly support to the July Monarchy of Louis Philippe, Thierry served the constitutional republican cause by demonstrating that the French tradition of liberty pre-dated the Revolution. "Men of freedom, we too have forebears," he proclaimed in a passage from his work that might stand for the whole.[2] This proclamation was nothing less than a call in the name of the people to reinvent the nation in the image of the bourgeoisie. To accomplish this task, Thierry's *Lettres sur l'histoire de France* (1827, revised 1829), *Dix ans d'études historiques* (1834), and *Récits des temps mérovingens précédés de considerations sur l'histoire de France* (1840) developed a national genealogy that located the cradle of France's modern liberties in the medieval Communes' assertion of municipal freedoms against arbitrary feudal and ecclesiastical power. Here was the wellspring of the universal values of reason, justice, and the rule of law that would eventually be enshrined as a national principle with the triumph of the Third Estate in 1789, then felicitously reestablished in Louis Philippe's constitutional monarchy of 1830 to 1848. For Thierry, this lineage was liberal through and through; as he observed in an early journal article, it is not the principle of popular sovereignty, but that of reason and law, embodied in the form of bourgeois political morality, that is destined to guide the nation. "The people counts for a great deal in the population, but does it count for a great deal in the nation? Is not the nation made up of those who can think, who can judge, who can feel in harmony with the public interest? The people forms a separate society as long as it remains merely popular; its voice is null as long as it speaks against reason."[3]

This characteristically liberal vision of a heroic bourgeois nation conceived in reason is what Thierry most certainly had in mind when, as a young man, he called for the displacement of the untruths of the "philosophical school" of eighteenth-century historians by truly popular histories of the French nation. If such histories were to bind the people to liberal ideals by inculcating their preservation as a holy duty, then France's historiography had also to be purged of what Thierry called "writers without imagination, who were unable to describe."[4] Here we begin to discern the influence on French historiography of Britain's Sir Walter Scott (1771–1832), the novelist and poet whom Thierry called the "greatest master of historical divination that has ever existed."[5] For after reading translations of Scott's *Waverly* novels in the late 1810s, Thierry became convinced that the power of imagination was necessary both to discover the reality of the past and to portray it adequately. As the French historian phrased his thoughts in his 1825 study of the Norman Conquest, "The task is to find a way across the distance of centuries to men, to represent them before us alive, and acting upon the country in which even the dust of their bones could not be found today. . . . These men have been dead for fully seven hundred years, their hearts stopped beating with pride or anguish seven hundred years ago; but what is that to the imagination? For the imagination there is no past, and the future itself is of the present."[6] In Thierry's art of national history, narrative and analysis were to be seamlessly woven in such a way as to enlist readers' sympathies in their own salutary political indoctrination.

Certainly this was a start toward defining a French tradition of national history grounded in imaginative narratives and dedicated to the people's interests. But it was the eccentric and prolific genius Jules Michelet who ultimately went the farthest in using French history to write the nation into being. The son of a humble republican printer, this gifted student of the past rose swiftly through the French educational system. By 1838 he held concurrently a chair in History and Moral Philosophy at the Collège de France and a position as director of the historical section of the National Archives, both in Paris. Such professional posts aptly expressed the liberals' vision of the patriotic promise of a centralized secular educational establishment. For Michelet used his standing as a dynamic public lecturer and interpreter of the past to proselytize tirelessly for a national faith centered on an egalitarian brotherhood of the French people. His intellectual output in this cause was as compelling as it was prodigious – among twenty-odd studies that range from a translation of the Italian historical philosopher Vico to treatises on nature and love, Michelet's *Histoire de France* (1833–69), *Histoire de la Révolution française* (1847–53), and the popular polemic *Le peuple* (1846) are still regarded as classics of French historiography. These works were also, in his day, readily adjudged subversive.

During the tumults of 1848, Michelet was temporarily suspended from his chair at the Collège de France; ultimately, Louis Napoleon had the outspoken populist purged from the nation's professorate as a security risk in 1851.

Michelet's greatest works about the idea of France all begin with the proposition, akin to a mystical faith, that the French people are peculiarly fitted by history and national character to transcend their social and political divisions. Grounded in the people's instinctive love of land and sovereign faculty of devotion and sacrifice, but even more elementally in the sociable character of humanity itself, this capacity for unity would be realized as a kind of great friendship that is heroic because, as the historian told his readers, it leads "us to love one another in spite of clashing interests, differences of conditions, and inequality."[7] Initially, Michelet's egalitarian faith took the form of support for the liberal constitutionalism of the July Monarchy. Yet eventually he came to believe that too many Frenchmen had gone bad under this regime and were afflicted by industrial alienation, atomistic individualism or heedless money grubbing. The bourgeoisie especially appeared to have lost its national spirit and capacity for action, withdrawing inward from the very countrymen whose embrace might yet save these lawyers, bureaucrats, and shopkeepers from themselves. "Men of property," Michelet asked in *Le peuple*, "do you know what will not move any more than the land itself? It is the people. Trust in them."[8]

Once, Michelet had been prepared to hope that the spirit of Christian sacrifice and devotion could foster the sort of disinterested love capable of overcoming such divisions. In the early volumes of his *Histoire de France*, for instance, the Christ-like suffering of the virgin saint Joan of Arc in her struggle against the English invaders is portrayed as the moral example that first inspires the French people to recognize themselves and act as a nation. A kind of epitome of the great medieval devotional guide known as the *Imitation of Christ*, her death showed Frenchmen how the true spirit of Christianity might be lived. Yet what had begun in the spirit of universal devotion and sacrifice, Michelet judged to have ended with the Middle Ages in an orgy of sectarian hatred and religious warfare that spoiled the Christian ideal. Following the eighteenth century's misguided attempt to engineer society as a kind of machine, it had remained for the French Revolution to propound a new theory of love, sacrifice, and egalitarian faith that Michelet now preached to the French people in his histories and lectures.

This ideal was profoundly bound up in the historian's own crises of self. Having found traditional religious faith wanting, Michelet had turned to his "noble country" to take the place of what, in his journal, he called "the God who is escaping us" and to "fill in us the incommensurable void which Christianity left when it died."[9] But was this new faith up to the task? Could it both console and revitalize? These were questions the historian confronted with tragic immediacy when his first wife Pauline died in 1839. So distraught was

Michelet following Pauline's death that he even caused her body to be exhumed in order to contemplate mortality in her remains, only to be faced anew with a sense of life's ineffability. After a period of spiritual despondency, the widower ultimately reclaimed meaning from history itself. This he did by adopting a new faith that denied death by a virtual resurrection of the past, one in which the historian fused his identity with that of his countrymen, both living and dead. In effect, the nation became for Michelet the only sure source of immortality. It was this conception of the individual fused in the general that ever afterward emboldened Michelet to assert that he was, quite literally, a man of the people, born in their midst and embodying the deepest currents of their being. But while the people – and by this term Michelet always meant the peasantry first and foremost – might intuitively grasp the best gifts of their patrimony, he alone, as their historian, was capable of the full realization or expression of France's Revolutionary spirit. Uniting the instinct of the simple with the reflection of the wise, Michelet's true national historian was no mere chronicler, but a procreative genius in the sense that he is described in *Le peuple*: "the harmonious and creative man who manifests his inner excellence by a superabundance of love and strength, and who proves it not only by fleeting actions but also by immortal works through which his great soul will remain united with all mankind."[10] For such a person, the telling of national history might be used to effect a kind of glorious convergence of consciousness that promised to obliterate time and make brothers of a nation's citizens, the living and the dead, by linking them in an almost preternatural bond of sympathy. Of course, this is precisely the enduring national outcome Michelet was striving to produce in his own histories.

As the people's prophet, Michelet bequeathed France a legacy of national history that discovered the salvation of the state in the promise of a revitalized revolutionary brotherhood of liberty and fraternity. These great principles figured as "the true introduction to universal love,"[11] offering salvation not merely to the French people, but, as their premier historian saw it, to the world as a whole. In thus resurrecting the past to serve humanity's future, Michelet always opposed his histories to the forces of monarcho-clerical conservatism, philosophical idealism, and international socialism alike. For him, every one of these ideologies was trumped by nationalism, which figured as both a salutary and essential structure of human consciousness, a form of collective self-possession that, at its best, overcame social divisions, reconciled adversaries, and even made war obsolete. National feeling "is ever the life of the world," Michelet declared at the height of his influence. "If it were dead, all would be dead."[12] Yet there is sufficient saber rattling and national chauvinism in Michelet's heroic vision of France's special destiny to see how a more aggressive and sinister legacy of nationalistic pride might spring from the one whose coming he had prepared. That, too, was a product of the French tradition of national history.

Britain: Making the World Safe for Whiggism

Across the Channel in the kingdom of Great Britain, the forces of popular unrest and conservative reaction unleashed in the wake of the French Revolution loomed large in the progress of that country's national historiography as well. Nineteenth-century Britons who investigated the past almost invariably searched it for answers to contemporary political and social troubles. One of the era's chief questions concerned the capacity of the Tory-dominated state, which had weathered the French Revolutionary threat, to continue to survive without granting concessions to either the commercial and professional middle class or the Victorian industrial and agricultural poor. The outbreak of a wave of nationalist and socialist revolution on the Continent in 1848 only served to underscore the seriousness of the popular agitation for political and economic redress in Britain, first in the campaign to enact electoral reform in the early 1830s, then to establish Chartism in the 1840s. All these developments provided the backdrop against which British historians fashioned narratives of their country's past and in the case of subject peoples like the Scots, fixed their place within the Union. In contrast to the quasi-mystical tradition of Revolutionary national history that triumphed in France, however, British national history developed along less populist lines, mostly as an extension of the Whig heritage.

This Whiggish tendency stemmed in part from the historical tradition against which Victorians defined themselves. Even as late as the mid-nineteenth century, David Hume's *History of England* (1754–61) remained the preeminent national history. Hume's compelling work therefore had remarkable staying power, and like much Enlightenment-era historiography, his historical study was an extension of his philosophy, what he called, in the second edition of his *Essay Concerning Human Understanding* (1752), a "record of wars, intrigues, factions and revolutions" that figured as "so many collections of experiments, by which the politician or moral philosopher fixes the principles of his science."[13] This "philosophical" approach alone had weighed against the production of a "people's" history in the style of Thierry or Michelet. But Hume (1711–76) was also an Anglo-Scottish Tory and a religious skeptic who used his history to dismiss the enthusiasts of religion and Whiggish civil freedoms in Great Britain's past as demagogic corrupters of the public good. What Whigs saw enshrined in common law as Englishmen's fundamental liberties, Hume viewed as mere "privileges," more or less dependent on the monarch's strength and will. In his own day, the Scotsman's main competitor had been the violently pro-Whig Catharine Macaulay, but her *History of England from the Ascension of James I to the Death of Anne* (1763) generally lost credit in the wake of the violent excesses of French Revolutionary republicanism. Hume, on the other hand, went from strength to strength. His

History of England was reprinted in 1778, 1789, and 1791, then eleven more times between 1808 and 1832, including several editions for "family use." As late as 1848, England's first active professor of history (1807–49), William Smyth – who used the Scottish historian exclusively for his lectures – could say with only slight exaggeration, "It is Hume who is read by everyone. Hume is the historian whose views and opinions insensibly become our own. He is respected and admired by the most enlightened reader; he is the guide and philosopher of the ordinary reader, to whose mind, on all topics connected with our history, he entirely gives the tone and law."[14]

Although the nineteenth-century Whigs sported other contenders against the Tory Hume, they found their best hope for a national historian of similar stature in Thomas Babington Macaulay. The son of an evangelical abolitionist, Macaulay made his reputation as a critic of literature and history for the *Edinburgh Review*, beginning with an essay on Milton published in 1825. On the strength of his critical productions, Macaulay was soon sponsored for a seat in Parliament, where he became celebrated for his set speeches advocating the Reform Bill. Next, he served the Empire by filling a seat on the Supreme Council of India, where he authored a new criminal code for the inhabitants of the sub-continent before returning to Britain to serve in the Whig national government. During this period in his life, Macaulay also found time to write and successfully publish poetry; his *Lays of Ancient Rome* was a bestseller in 1842. If this résumé suggests the idea that Macaulay was a bit of a jack-of-all-trades, such a conclusion would not be entirely off the mark. For it is a remarkable breadth of erudition, virtuoso fluidity of narration, and supreme confidence in critical judgment, rather than an extraordinary depth of analysis that marks Macaulay's work. This is no less true of the critical reviews than it is of his masterwork, the *History of England* (1848–55).

Macaulay's *History* is preeminently a testament to literary craftsmanship and narrative art. Like most of his contemporaries and predecessors (including Hume), Victorian Britain's greatest national historian saw the archives chiefly as places to go to corroborate his interpretive presuppositions, though he did pride himself on his innovative use of broadsheets, lampoons, and domestic account books to illuminate the "spirit" of past ages. The result of this predilection is most evident in the famous third chapter of Macaulay's *History*, a social and cultural portrait of England in 1685 that probably best realized the dictum its author developed in his 1828 essay on "History": that, to do the past justice, the "truly great historian" must, in addition to narrating battles and dynastic maneuvers, also reclaim for his readers the materials of everyday life that heretofore only "the novelist has appropriated."[15] In this respect, the essayist pointed to the wonderful effect generated by the same *Waverly* romances of Sir Walter Scott that had also inspired Augustin Thierry. No historian seemed to Macaulay capable of rendering the "whole truth," because no one could ever hope to canvas *all* transactions of the past. Instead, the most faithful historian, like the great historical novelist, was the one who could render the "character and spirit of the age . . . in miniature" by exhibiting "such parts of the truth as most nearly produce the effect of the whole."[16] That a history thus vividly written would benefit popular morals and political governance was to Macaulay an unquestionable certainty, since, being received by the "imagination as well as by the reason," its lessons would "not merely be traced on the mind" but "would be branded into it."[17]

Excavating and revivifying the past in this fashion apparently posed few methodological dilemmas for the empirically minded Macaulay, who was particularly contemptuous of the metaphysical philosophy that was driving German historiography at the time. "What trash!" he commented to his journal in the mid-1850s. "What a waste of the powers of the human mind – I declare that I would rather have written [the poet William Cowper's amusing ballad] John Gilpin than all the volumes of Fichte, Kant, Schelling and Hegel together."[18] This dismissive attitude led John Stuart Mill, the English utilitarian, to see his contemporary as parochial and anti-intellectual: "In politics, ethics, philosophy, even history, of which he knows superficially very much – he has not a single thought of either German or French origin, and that is saying enough;" Macaulay "is what all cockneys are, an intellectual dwarf – rounded off and stunted, full grown broad and short, without a germ or principle of further growth in his whole being."[19] This judgment is somewhat unfair. A man temperamentally averse to abstract thinking, Macaulay – like the Scottish Common Sense philosophers, social critics, and historians with whom he was associated at the *Edinburgh Review* – saw social and historical change as occurring gradually and generally without the kind of design that appealed to a theorist like Mill. For Macaulay, the study of history was, at its best, a kind of inductive science in the tradition of Francis Bacon (the "Prince of all philosophers"[20]) that offered to show how peculiar circumstances of time and place determine the kind of law and government best fitted to a specific people.

Given this disposition, it is not surprising that Macaulay's politics, and those of his national history, ran to moderate Whig constitutionalism, with religious liberty and adherence to the rule of law as his guiding virtues. Truth be told, the historian's temperament recoiled from anything that savored of religious or political extremism. "I hate Puseyites and Puritans impartially," he once told his journal, while he branded the embodiment of eighteenth-century revolutionary freethinking as "that stupid worthless drunken dirty beast Tom Paine."[21] Hence it was that Macaulay's vaunted reformism steered between reactionary conservatism on one hand and so-called political and religious enthusiasm on the other. In his *History of England*, the Stuart kings are roundly condemned, but then so are the Puritan religious reformers. The historian's greatest praise is reserved for the judicious moderation of the Revolution of 1688, an event which he judged to have forestalled a destructive civil

war, thereby making Great Britain safe for private property, commercial prosperity, religious liberty, and moral amelioration. Yet for all Macaulay's whiggish credentials, the social and political troubles of his own day ultimately
warranted from him little more than what one modern scholar calls "classic
trimming" – that is, advocacy of only such reforms as were absolutely necessary to stave off disaster. Certainly, nineteenth-century England's premier
national historian had little good to say about the industrial democracy proposed by Chartists. Nor was Macaulay keen to follow Continental political
thinkers such as Karl Marx and Louis Blanc into what the British historian
called a new barbarism of socialism or anarchism calculated to undo in "thirty
years" all that "thirty centuries have done for mankind."[22]

If Thomas Macaulay is rightly regarded as the greatest exemplar of whiggism's ascendancy in British nineteenth-century national historiography, that
ideology's triumph in the United Kingdom is perhaps even more pointedly
driven home by the concurrent Scottish variant of the British model. In the
early eighteenth century, historians north of the English border had located a
tradition of liberty in the Scots' heritage as a Presbyterian nation. But under
the intellectual influence of the Edinburgh Enlightenment, which understood
society to be advancing by "stages" toward a more perfect civilization, the
fiercely independent Covenanters once celebrated as freedom fighters by Presbyterian national historiography were reinterpreted in the eighteenth century
as anti-modern religious enthusiasts whose fanaticism had served as cover for
the feudal nobility's political and personal ambitions. Rather than celebrating
a national religious heritage, whiggish historians such as the Presbyterian Moderate William Robertson (1721–93) explained the growth of liberty by looking
to models of free government in the classical world and to the positive effects
of post-Union Anglicization in the commercial transformation of Scottish
society. In effect, the civil freedoms claimed by many Scots were redefined, in
accordance with their newly adopted Anglo-British identity, as an outgrowth
of modern social and commercial development within the British Union rather
than as the result of an ancient constitution or particular feudal national past.
Modern scholarship suggests that even Robertson's student Sir Walter Scott,
the historical novelist who is often held up as the epitome of romantic Scottish nationalism, saw the Borderlands and Highlands that provided the setting
of his *Waverly Novels* (1814–32) more as realms of arrested social development than as repositories of ancient liberties. Certainly that was the opinion
of his countrymen at the whiggish *Edinburgh Review*, one of whom wrote of
Scott in 1832, "It has been said that he displays a spirit hostile to the progress
of modern civilization, and labours too much to make us in love with the venerable errors of former times. Such a fault will not be felt by one who reads
his works aright; who perceives that his attachment to the manners of antiquity is to be considered merely as a poetical attachment. He is won by their
picturesqueness, and by their peculiar applicability to those purposes which lie

within the province of romance. But to suppose, that because his imagination delights in them, his judgment must approve, is an unfair deduction. We have seen nothing in the writings of Sir Walter Scott, as we have unfortunately in the writings of other men of no mean talent, which indicates that he regards with an evil eye the increasing spirit of modern improvement."[23] By and large, it was the Anglo-British heritage of civil freedoms, purveyed in Scott's novels and in the multi-volume national histories of Patrick Fraser Tytler (1791–1849) and John Hill Burton (1809–81), that characterized the mainstream of nineteenth-century Scottish historiography.[24] This development effectively short-circuited the vital link between liberty and a primordial nationhood that might have generated a politically potent nationalist tradition in the style of Thierry or Michelet.[25]

The United States: "Westward the Star of Empire Takes its Way"

With the French, as with others aspiring to republican governance, nineteenth-century national histories had shown how the people's liberties might yet be expanded or secured; with the British, national histories of the same era largely taught that these liberties needed to be preserved. Across the Atlantic Ocean in Great Britain's former North American colonies, history played an equally important role in shaping popular national consciousness. Yet unlike in Britain or France, historians in the United States keen to construct a national history confronted a peculiar circumstance associated with that country's post-colonial status: the infancy of the American state and the cultural diversity of its constituent peoples. How was one to write a national history of a (still precarious) union of states less than two or three generations old? The country's early historians generally finessed the problems associated with this question by defining the national heritage as a popular spirit of freedom that pre-dated the Revolutionary state and resided historically in the hearts and minds of a people who were, from the start, proto-Americans. In doing so, these historians downplayed, ignored, or explained away both the nation's multiethnic roots and its long-standing tradition of slaveholding and racial prejudice. They could so readily do so because, by and large, they saw themselves and their nation as the embodiment of a purified stream of English Protestant dissent that was destined to give the world a new birth of humanity. In much the same way that Jules Michelet imagined France's special destiny as *the* exemplar of universal brotherhood, the first generation of US national historians played out Puritan millennial themes of the chosen people in a post-Puritan idiom of democratic nationalism.

This result should not surprise us, as so many pre-Civil War American historians were the lineal descendants as well as the intellectual and cultural heirs of that tradition's founders. By rough count, nearly 50 percent of them hailed from New England. Of these men (and they were almost all men), many of the most eminent were gentlemen of wealth and leisure educated in the liberal religious atmosphere of Harvard College. Bostonians William Hickling Prescott (1796–1859), Francis Parkman (1823–93), John Lothrop Motley (1814–77), and Richard Hildreth (1807–65) all began publishing significant works of historical scholarship and imagination in the years preceding the Civil War. In the same era, the New England Unitarian editor Jared Sparks (1789–1866) made a career out of publishing multi-volume editions of documentary and biographical material relating to the American Revolutionary experience. Yet by far the most influential antebellum historian in the United States to work in the tradition of national history was George Bancroft. The son of a liberal Congregationalist clergyman, the younger Bancroft followed his undergraduate education at Harvard College with doctoral training in the German universities at Göttingen and Berlin. After returning to the United States, he accepted a position teaching Greek at Harvard, and then joined a colleague in 1823 to found the innovative Round Hill School at Northampton, Massachusetts. During his eleven-year tenure at Round Hill, Bancroft began contributing to the *North American Review* the articles and book reviews that would lead him to a dual career in politics and history. An 1831 article opposing the Bank of the US and a growing reputation for patriotic oratory ultimately brought Bancroft to the attention of the up-and-coming Jacksonian Democrats, in whose service he would fill a number of important bureaucratic and diplomatic posts over the years. At the same time, however, Bancroft was researching, writing, and publishing his ten-volume *History of the United States from the Discovery of the Continent* (1834–74), the magisterial work that would establish his reputation as the dean of American national historians.

Although the influence of doctoral training in Germany led Bancroft to trumpet his brand of historical inquiry as an empirical science, the nature of its governing laws suggests how, in his hands, the study of the past remained a branch of what nineteenth-century Americans called moral philosophy. Consider the fact that chief among the "laws" established by Bancroft's "science" of history was that the people's will demonstrates humankind's moral progress. "It is the uniform tendency of the popular element to elevate and bless Humanity," he proclaimed in a famous oration on "The Office of the People in Art, Government, and Religion" delivered at Williams College in August 1835. "The exact measure of the progress of civilization is the degree to which the intelligence of the popular mind has prevailed over wealth and brute force; in other words, the measure of the progress of civilization is the progress of the people."[26] What made this advance possible, indeed pre-ordained it, and simultaneously marked out the historian's true metier as the chronicler and herald of progress, was the common people's innate capacity to discern moral truth through the exercise of what Bancroft called humankind's God-given reason. Here, the historian meant not "reason" as it was conceived by eighteenth-century sensational psychology, that is, a "faculty which deduces inferences from the experience of the senses." Instead, he invoked a "higher faculty" in the tradition of Scottish Common Sense philosophy and nineteenth-century German idealism, one in "which from the infinite treasures of its own consciousness, originates truth . . . , an internal sense which places us in connexion with the world of intelligence and the decrees of God."[27] It is this intuitive dimension to Bancroft's thought that has led some modern scholars to label him a "transcendental" historian, one in league with Ralph Waldo Emerson and Henry David Thoreau. But to insist on the primacy of this particular pedigree would be to mask the theologically conservative cast of much of Bancroft's thought, which interpreted history as the unfolding of divine will. One sign that the son was less liberal in religious sensibilities than even his own Unitarian father is the enunciator's role played by the eighteenth-century New Light theologian Jonathan Edwards in Bancroft's *History*. In that work, Edwards is credited with having postulated a philosophy of progress that is "nobler than the theory of [the Italian philosopher] Vico: more grand and general than the method of [the French historian] Bossuet." According to Bancroft, "it embraced in outline the whole 'work of redemption,' – the history of the influence of all moral truth in the gradual redemption of humanity. . . . [Edwards] knew that, in every succession of revolutions, the cause of civilization and moral reform is advanced." So Bancroft continued: "Nothing appears more self-determined than the volitions of each individual; and nothing is more certain than that the providence of God will over-rule them for good. The finite will of man, free in its individuality, is, in the aggregate, subordinate to general laws. This is the reason why evil is self-destructive; why truth, when it is once generated, is sure to live forever; why freedom and justice, though resisted and restrained, renew the contest from age to age, confident that messengers from heaven fight on their side, and that the stars in their courses fight against their foes."[28]

This Neo-Edwardsean outlook led Bancroft to compose a work of history that was every bit as fervent in its nationalist ardor as those produced in France during the same era, yet far more manifestly religious in interpretive thrust and tone. Throughout Bancroft's *History of the United States* the superintending hand of Providence furnishes the frame of reference that guides his narrative to its natural conclusion in the exemplary democratic union of the onetime British colonies. This we know as much from the start, for Bancroft commences his relentlessly teleological *History* with the declaration that, true to their Anglo-Saxon and Reformation lineage, "The spirit of the colonies demanded freedom from the beginning."[29] Thereafter, the historical drama that ensues is never really a question of *whether* this spirit of freedom will actually shape the developing traditions of intellectual life, religious liberty, and self-government. The only historical question is *how* and *when* the American conception of freedom will vanquish counter-forces in colonial society such as British mercantilism, Anglican episcopism, or chattel slavery and the slave trade (which "crime"[30] the American colonists were said always to have opposed in spirit). Certainly, the materialist temper that, to Bancroft's way of thinking, damned the great democratic revolution in France had no chance in the New World; the American colonists, the *History* told its readers, "were neither skeptics or sensualists, but Christians."[31] Their revolt against superstition and ecclesiastical tyranny never led them, as it did the philosophes, to repudiate religion itself. So it is that when Bancroft remarks that "The republic was to America a godsend," he meant his assertion to be taken quite literally: "It came, though unsought, because society contained the elements of no other organization. Here, and in that century, here only, was a people, which, by its education and large and long experience, was prepared to act as the depository and carrier of all political power."[32]

This statement is critical to understanding the seemingly paradoxical mix of revolutionary sentiment and conservative temper that characterizes Bancroft's thought. Certainly, in the well-established tradition of American exceptionalism, he believed the United States to be a beacon of hope to the world: "It was the office of America to substitute for hereditary privilege the natural equality of man; for the irresponsible authority of a sovereign, a dependent government emanating from the concord of opinion; and, as she moved forward in her high career, the multitudes of every clime gazed towards her example with hopes of untold happiness, and all nations of the earth sighed to be renewed."[33] Yet the people having effected a national union ordained by Divine Wisdom, it now had to be preserved according to His word. For Bancroft, that meant squelching post-Revolutionary discontent and division, as with Daniel Shays's agrarian revolt of 1784, in favor of the new federal Union. Much like Thomas Macaulay, the American George Bancroft thus left his country a legacy of national history whose liberal rhetoric ultimately served the status quo.

National History Today

The crucial assumption shared by many early national historians of the West that the will of Providence, in the form of the people's voice, is manifested in historical developments, and that an empirical study of the "facts" of the past can be made to yield a sense of that spirit, is a supposition roundly discredited among modern academic scholars. Also discredited are the casual research and documentary techniques that were practiced by many of the first generation of national historians. Yet, in several noteworthy ways, we in the modern world remain heirs to the historiographical tradition established by Michelet, Macaulay, Bancroft, and their contemporaries. Certainly, today, the view persists, though it is regularly disputed, that the most viable sovereign entity is an ethnic-national state; popular national histories written in the "people's" name to establish this doctrine are still published in places like Serbia and the Ukraine. In the West's more established democratic societies, nationalism also continues to exert a significant influence on both the popular public interpretation of history and on historical education in particular. For all of postmodern scholars' efforts to deconstruct the myths and presuppositions that sustain nationalist modes of thinking, for instance, the shape and programs of many of today's academic departments continue to reflect the nationalist assumptions that the founders of the historical discipline took from their forebears. Graduate study programs (in many of the humanities and social sciences as well as in history departments themselves) more regularly offer "national" fields of concentration than they do ones that are international or thematically comparative in scope. History textbooks also routinely define their subject in ways that would not entirely outrage a nationalist like George Bancroft or Thomas Macaulay. Certainly, this result derives in part from the bureaucratic demands of the modern nation-state, whose functionaries often see historical study and the public invocation of history generally as instruments of patriotic discipline. Yet it also stems from the continuing capacity of national traditions to provide a meaningful context that helps to explain human behavior.

In this respect, the long-term trajectory of nationalist historical thought looks much like that of its traditional historical competitor, the other great ideological "ism" developed out of the political and social crises of the mid-nineteenth century – that is, Marxism. While Karl Marx and his intellectual descendants generated an historiographical tradition of class-based analysis that dismissed national loyalties as transient expressions of an unstable industrial capitalist system, this oppositional stance should not blind us to the similarities that characterize the two paradigms of thought. Historically, both nationalist and Marxist traditions shared an overarching teleological orientation that encouraged their respective practitioners to make grand and compelling, albeit contradictory, claims in the name of the "people" about the nature of historical reality and history's proper course. Both traditions also faced an intellectual crisis of sorts in the wake of the tragedies of World War Two and the Cold War, the experience of which served, among professional historians particularly, to weaken the truth claims of these explanatory paradigms. Yet ultimately, neither the intellectual concepts of class or nationalism could be abandoned by modern historians without substantially impoverishing the profession's analytical lexicon.

NOTES

1   Benedict R. O'G. Anderson, *Imagined Communities: Reflections on the Origin and Spread of Nationalism*, 2d edn., London and New York, 1991, esp. pp. 1–7.

2   Augustin Thierry, *Dix ans d'études historiques*, 183, quoted in Ceri Crossley, *French Historians and Romanticism: Thierry, Guizot, the Saint-Simonians, Quinet, and Michelet* (London and New York, 1993), p. 46.

3   Thierry, "Des Nations" (1817): p. 34, quoted in Lionel Gossman, "Augustin Thierry and Liberal Historiography," in *Between History and Literature* (Cambridge, MA and London, 1990), p. 107.

4   Thierry, "Autobiographical Preface," in *The Historical Essays, Published under the Title of "Dix ans d'études historiques," and Narratives of the Merovingian Era* (Philadelphia, 1845), p. xii.

5   Ibid., p. xi.

6   Thierry, *Histoire de la conquête de l'Angleterre par les Normands*, 1: 430, quoted in Gossman, "Augustin Thierry and Liberal Historiography," p. 95.

7   Jules Michelet, *The People*, trans. John P. McKay (Urbana, Chicago and London, 1973), p. 157.

8   Ibid., pp. 109, 89.

9   Michelet, *Journal*, 1: 83, quoted in Crossley, p. 198.

10 Michelet, *The People*, p. 143.

11 Ibid., p. 183.

12 Ibid., p. 182.

13 Hume quoted in John Kenyon, *The History Men: The Historical Profession in England since the Renaissance* (Pittsburgh, 1983), p. 41.

14 Hume, *Lectures on Modern History* (2 vols., 1848), 1: 126, quoted in Kenyon, *The History Men*, pp. 56–7.

15 Macaulay, "History," in *Works of Lord Macaulay* (New York, 1900), 5: 157–8.

16 Ibid., 5: 129, 157–8.

17 Ibid., 5: 160.

18 Macaulay, *Journal*, November 13, 1857, commenting on the "Metaphysics" article in the *Encyclopedia Britannica*, quoted in Joseph Hamburger, *Macaulay and the Whig Tradition* (Chicago and London, 1976), p. 171.

19 J. S. Mill quoted in Hamburger, *Macaulay and the Whig Tradition*, p. 176.

20 Macaulay quoted in Hamburger, *Macaulay and the Whig Tradition*, fn. 30, 214.

21 Macaulay quoted in ibid., pp. 15, 36.

22 Macaulay, *History of England from the Accession of James the Second* (London, 1849–1861), 2: 663.

23 [T. H. Lister], "The Waverly Novels," *Edinburgh Review* 55 (April 1832), 74, quoted in Colin Kidd, *Subverting Scotland's Past: Scottish Whig Historians and the Creation of an Anglo-British Identity, 1689–c. 1830* (Cambridge, 1993), p. 266.

24 John Fraser Tytler, *History of Scotland* (9 vols., Edinburgh, 1828–43); and John Hill Burton, *The History of Scotland* (new edn., 8 vols., Edinburgh and London, 1876).

25 Only among sectarian splinter groups associated with the Seceders (who broke with the Kirk in 1733 when it sanctioned erastian reforms) did a historiography persist that made the Scottish national past a repository of freedom and liberty, as in the ecclesiastical histories and biographies of the Rev. Thomas McCrie (1772–1835). My discussion of the Scottish historiographical tradition is indebted to Kidd, *Subverting Scotland's Past*, esp. pp. 185–280.

26   Bancroft, "The Office of the People in Art, Government, and Religion," in *Literary and Historical Miscellanies* (New York, 1855), pp. 426–7, quoted in Robert S. Canary, *George Bancroft* (New York, 1974), p. 5.

27   Bancroft quoted in Nye, *George Bancroft: Brahmin Rebel* (New York, 1972 [1944]), p. 100.

28   Bancroft, *History of the United States of America, from the Discovery of the Continent* (centenary edition, 6 vols., Boston, 1879), 2: 546–57.

29   Bancroft, *History of the Colonization of the United States* (Boston 1834), p. vii, quoted in Canary, *George Bancroft*, 5.

30   Bancroft, *History of the United States of America*, 2: 555.

31   Ibid., 2: 177.

32   Bancroft quoted in Richard C. Vitzthum, *The American Compromise: Theme and Method in the Histories of Bancroft, Parkman, and Adams* (Norman, 1974), pp. 20–1.

33   Bancroft, *History of the United States of America*, 3: 10.

REFERENCES AND FURTHER READING

Anderson, Benedict R. O'G, *Imagined Communities: Reflections on the Origin and Spread of Nationalism*, 2nd edn., London and New York: Verso, 1991.

Bancroft, George, *History of the United States of America, from the Discovery of the Continent*, six volumes, centenary edition, Boston: Little, Brown, and Company, 1879.

Canary, Robert H., *George Bancroft*, New York: Twayne Publishers, 1974.

Crossley, Ceri, *French Historians and Romanticism: Thierry, Guizot, the Saint-Simonians, Quinet, Michelet*, London and New York: Routledge, 1993.

Culler, A. Dwight, *The Victorian Mirror of History*, New Haven and London: Yale University Press, 1985.

Gossman, Lionel, *Between History and Literature*, Cambridge, MA and London: Harvard University Press, 1990.

Hamburger, Joseph, *Macaulay and the Whig Tradition*, Chicago and London: The University of Chicago Press, 1976.

Hobsbawm, E. J., *Nations and Nationalism since 1780: Programme, Myth, Reality*, Cambridge: Cambridge University Press, 1990.

Kenyon, John, *The History Men: The Historical Profession in England since the Renaissance*, Pittsburgh: University of Pittsburgh Press, 1983.

Kidd, Colin, *Subverting Scotland's Past: Scottish Whig Historians and the Creation of an Anglo-British Identity, 1689–c.1830*, Cambridge: Cambridge University Press, 1993.

Kraus, Michael, and Joyce, Davis D., *The Writing of American History*, revised edition, Norman: University of Oklahoma Press, 1985.

Macaulay, Thomas Babington, "History," in *The Works of Lord Macaulay*, 5: 122–61, New York: Longmans, Green, and Co., 1900.

——, *History of England from the Accession of James the Second*, five volumes, London: Longman, Brown, Green, and Longmans, 1849–61.

McGann, Jerome J., *The Romantic Ideology: A Critical Investigation*, Chicago and London: The University Press of Chicago, 1983.

Michelet, Jules, *History of France*, 2 vols., trans. Smith G. H., New York: D. Appleton and Company, 1857.

——, *The People*, trans. John P. McKay, Urbana, Chicago, and London: University of Illinois Press, 1973.

Nye, Russell B., *George Bancroft: Brahmin Rebel*, New York: Octagon Books of Farrar, Straus & Giroux, 1972 [1944].

Thierry, Augustin, "Autobiographical Preface," in *The Historical Essays, Published under the Title of "Dix ans d'études historiques," and Narratives of the Merovingian Era*, pp. 7–24, Philadelphia: Carey and Hart, 1845.

Vitzthum, Richard C., *The American Compromise: Theme and Method in the Histories of Bancroft, Parkman, and Adams*, Norman: University of Oklahoma Press, 1974.

White, Hayden, *Metahistory: The Historical Imagination in Nineteenth-Century Europe*, Baltimore and London: The Johns Hopkins University Press, 1973.

CHAPTER TEN

Marxism and Historical Thought

WALTER L. ADAMSON

Our conception of history is above all a guide to study, not a lever for construction after the manner of the Hegelians. All history must be studied afresh, the conditions of existence of the different formations of society must be individually examined before the attempt is made to deduce from them the political, civil-legal, aesthetic, philosophic, religious, etc., notions corresponding to them. Only a little has been done here up to now because only a few people have got down to it seriously.

Friedrich Engels (August 5, 1890)

No view of history has been more misunderstood or oversimplified than that of Karl Marx. It is commonly believed, for example, that Marx was an economic determinist who imposed a rigid evolutionary pattern on history in which an invariable sequence of modes of production – from primitive village communities through ancient kingships, feudalism, and capitalism – was inevitably leading to a communist society. Marx, it is also commonly said, approached society mechanistically, deducing the acts and beliefs of individuals from social structure, especially class position, and failing to accord culture any significant role in historical understanding and explanation. Such views are not without some foundation in Marx's writings, but, as we will shortly see, they depend on a selective reading that fails to appreciate important tensions and complexities in Marx's evolving theories. Properly understood, Marx's theories not only provide the basis for a sensitive and nuanced approach to empirical history but remain a stimulating source for historical thought and practice even after the "cultural turn" historical studies have taken in the past two decades.

Though anyone as controversial as Marx is bound to suffer many unsympathetic readings, it must be admitted that misunderstandings of his view of history have largely been the product of the many shifts in his own intellectual trajectory or, what amounts to the same thing, the fact that he never explicated his view of history in any comprehensive and definitive work. His fullest statement in *The German Ideology*, an unpublished manuscript he co-authored with Engels in 1845–6, is based on a political theory he would soon abandon. Apart from that work, we have a methodological statement referring to the study of social life generally in which new assumptions about history emerge (1857); a summation of his intellectual development in which *The German Ideology*'s view is restated but with somewhat different, even contradictory implications (1859); several detailed historical narratives dealing with recent revolutionary events in France (hence closer to historical journalism than reflective history); two prolix accounts of the genesis and nature of the capitalist mode of production, accounts that follow the methodological precepts of the 1857 essay and involve historical reflection but which are not history *per se*; and a number of letters by Marx and, especially, the late Engels, commenting on how historical writing should and should not be done. All offer helpful insight into what Marx's mature view of history might have been, but none state it unequivocally. To understand what this view is, then, we need to retrace his intellectual footsteps in order to place the various statements about history in relation to one another.

Marx's Critique of Hegel

Marx was trained as a philosopher and began as a left Hegelian. Left Hegelians believed that Hegel was right to see history as a dialectical unfolding of *Geist* (Spirit) through which the "rational" and the "real" were ultimately united, but that he was wrong to identify this final realization of history with the modern nation-state. Marx spent much of 1843 engaged in a critique of Hegel, whom he faulted both for his insufficiently revolutionary politics and for his tendency to interpret every earthly phenomenon in relation to a single overarching "Idea." Nonetheless, he did adopt Hegel's two-level view of the nature of what is – his ontology of existence and essence. Essences, according to this early Marx, are the final (perfect) states towards which existents are striving. They are separate from existents only as potentialities; they can be realized only in and through existence. Thus, even though essences cannot be located empirically in present reality, they are not simply to be deduced metaphysically. We become aware of them on the basis of our "needs," which are evidences of a lack that indicate how an existent could become a realized essence.

Reality, then, has an inherent teleology but its direction is set by "man" in accordance with his anthropological nature, which the early Marx understood in terms drawn from Ludwig Feuerbach. In Marx's rendition of this view, human beings appear, in essence, as a species of laboring animals, yet they are unique in the creativity of their labor, which allows them to reshape and, in the end, recreate their environment. Fully realized, the creative essence of humans will produce a society in which each individual's creative essence is realized – in Marx's terminology, a communist society. At the same time, this communist society is nature's essence, for man is nature's mode of completing itself by bringing itself to self-conscious awareness. Nature, like Hegel's "Idea," needs human history for its development, and human history also requires nature for human development and progress. Nature existed prior to man but it attains its essence only through man; essential nature is a humanized nature. Human and natural history, then, can be emplotted as a single story in which *the* nature of the species, originally given as a potential, unfolds toward the full normative realization of nature as a whole. And though its teleological end is evident from man's productive nature, an empirical historian might still write this universal history by locating the "needs" that humans experienced along the way and considering how they engaged in creative activity to meet those needs.

The most important innovation in this Feuerbachian revamping of Hegel is the changed status of the human knower. While for Hegel the human knower was simply an instance of a larger *Geist* (Spirit) both collectively human and divine, the early Marx already treated the pursuit of knowledge as just another creative activity of humankind, no different in ontological status than any other. For Hegel, philosophy represented the queen of the sciences in that it afforded a comprehensive picture of the whole of existence and, in that sense, lay above or outside it. For Marx, in contrast, the pursuit of knowledge was immanent in the world and lacked any privileged vantage point. Marx's early anthopology or view of human nature implied, then, not only a more material view of history (the story of human creative action) but also a purely secular, scientific approach. Although Marx continued to use a Hegelian ontology that was ultimately metaphysical, his new anthropology opened the way to a new importance for empirical history and social science.

Late in 1844, Marx began an intellectual collaboration with Engels whose bent of mind and preferred style of investigation were much more empirical and scientific than were Marx's. Under his influence, Marx came to see that his anthropology of human creative action was still too abstract when the goal of that activity was conceived in the Feuerbachian terms of realizing a "human" or "species essence." In the "Theses on Feuerbach" (1845), Marx resolved the "human essence" into "the ensemble of social relations."[1] There are no fixed, human essences; all we have are what *The German Ideology* will call "living human individuals" (MER, p. 149). The problem of alienation, which presumes an essence that we are alienated from, was replaced in his mind by the problem of exploitation, which could only be overcome by the political action of the proletariat, not by the working out of logical operations in human life. "Social life is essentially practical," Marx now averred. "All mysteries which mislead theory into mysticism find their rational solution in human practice and in the comprehension of this practice" (MER, p. 145).

Confident that he finally had both feet on the ground, Marx sought to articulate in *The German Ideology* the "premises" of history, premises that can be "verified in a purely empirical way" (MER, p. 149). There are, first, "living human individuals" whose creative life-activity aims to produce the means to satisfy materially felt needs. These means, together with the social relations or "mode of life" that surround them, represent a "mode of production" (MER, p. 150). Yet, secondly, the satisfaction of needs leads to new needs, and thus to the development of new technologies to satisfy them, which in turn become the basis for new modes of production. While Marx's brief summation of these modes of production suggested increasing complexity, he did not here imply any determinism of economic or technological development. He simply offered a concrete explanation for such development based on human nature, needs, and the social relations in which they are embedded. History emerges in this text as a succession of generations, each of which exploits and seeks to develop the productive forces taken over from its predecessors. It is an open-ended process, a string of contingent outcomes forged by human actors satisfying needs they themselves produce. Metaphysical language about hidden essences coming to realization is now wholly absent, and what Marx called "real, positive science" takes its place. "When reality is depicted [scientifically], philosophy as an independent branch of knowledge loses its medium of existence," he declared, and "its place can only be taken by a summing-up of the most general results, abstractions which arise from the observation of the historical development of men" (MER, p. 155).

Despite such declarations, however, philosophy does not so much disappear in Marx's writings after 1845 as become transformed into social theory, one based entirely on empirical events and yet far more than a mere "summing-up" of their "general results." Theoretical abstractions from the historical process came to serve Marx as a guiding orientation for empirical research more or less in the way that "historical ideal types" would later serve Max Weber. Marx was never satisfied with empirical description. He wanted to grasp each era theoretically in terms of the logic of its mode of production and then to use that theoretical construct as the basis for empirical histories that would ultimately correct the theory. Because of the importance he attached to this mutual interaction of theory and history, Marx certainly took empirical history very seriously, even if his own preoccupation lay mainly in the domain of theory. Yet Marx cannot be said to have consistently maintained the same view of history after 1845 because the theoretical status he attributed to history changed, largely in relation to changes in his political outlook. To understand the source of the variations in his post-1845 view of history, we must look briefly at how theoretical shifts as well as political events affected his political theory.

Marx's Conceptions of History and Theory

In 1844, Marx believed that "philosophical criticism" and the "proletariat" as the universal class were two expressions of the same historical realization of the essence of nature and humanity. But the proletariat was accorded only a "passive" role as the "material basis" of the transformation; it was philosophical criticism that first realized essence and that could therefore stimulate the people to carry out their destiny. The primacy of philosophy is unmistakable in the gendering of Marx's explanatory metaphor: emancipation occurs when the "lightning of thought has penetrated deeply into this virgin soil of the people" (MER, p. 65). Once Marx had made his empirical turn of 1845, however, he repudiated any notion of philosophy's leading role and gave primacy to the proletariat, which schools the philosopher rather than the reverse. In the third "Thesis on Feuerbach," he turned against the doctrine "dividing society into two parts, one of which is superior to society" and argued that the "changing of circumstances . . . can be comprehended and rationally understood only as revolutionary practice" (MER, p. 144). "Thought" now *is* "material reality" in terms of its ontological status, and both thought and reality are actively led by the proletariat. Revolts like that of the Silesian weavers, coupled with emerging labor militancy of the "hungry '40s," led Marx and Engels to the robust confidence of *The Communist Manifesto* where they argued that "for exploitation, veiled by religious and political illusion, it [the bourgeoisie] has substituted naked, shameless, direct, brutal exploitation . . . and man is at last compelled to face with sober senses, his real conditions of life, and his relations with his kind" (MER, pp. 475–6).

But the revolutions of 1848 failed, and it was Marx who, "with sober senses," concluded in 1851 that bourgeois society was not stripping itself of false appearances, that the bourgeoisie was not history's great demystifier but had, on the contrary, found the means, symbolized by Louis Napoleon, to reestablish the old mystifications of "the sabre and the cowl" (MER, p. 597). The bourgeoisie did not demystify because it retained a political and ideological capacity to cover over what its relentless economic exploitation unearthed. Not surprisingly, then, Marx returned in the 1850s to a sharp distinction between surfaces and depths. Appearances *were* deceptive. The proletariat was not self-schooled by the labor process. Theory was necessary, and perhaps crises too, to awaken it out of its slumber. While *The German Ideology* assumed a social reality that was self-clarifying, and could therefore dismiss philosophical talk of underlying "essences" in favor of a self-sufficient empirical analysis of social appearances, the *Grundrisse* and *Capital* reintroduced the appearance –essence dichotomy in order to distinguish two levels of social reality, the one representing society for ordinary (fetishized) consciousness, the other representing society as Marx's science of political economy reconstructed it. Grasping this second, deeper level of social reality became the task of historical understanding and the key to future political transformation.

Likewise, contemporary political developments also prompted Marx to reassess the theoretical status of history. In *The German Ideology*, he assumed that empirical history was largely self-sufficient for the task of social analysis, and he went so far as to prefigure his future intellectual work essentially in terms of the activity of the historian. Theoretical "difficulties," he argued there, could be removed "only [by] the study of the actual life-process and the activity of the individuals of each epoch" (MER, p. 155). But beginning in 1857 with the *Grundrisse*, a social theory occupying the deep level of analysis that philosophy had assumed in 1844 became the key to resolving the difficulties presented by the welter of empirical histories. The *Grundrisse* and *Capital* offered theoretical analyses of the unfolding of capitalism and theoretical models of its inner workings. They revealed a broad and intimate familiarity with capitalism's complex history but made no effort to present that complex history. Marx did not pursue these analyses because of any inherent interest in the variety of case histories upon which they drew, nor indeed in their problems or material components (he had little interest in economics for its own sake). Instead, he believed that a social theory of capitalism carried fundamental significance for modern politics and that modern politics could be properly redirected only by means of an understanding of how capitalism has developed, how it works, and how it might be overcome.

Marx set out the methodological premises of this theoretical enterprise most fully in the 1857 preface to the *Grundrisse*. Here he first separated himself from Hegel through a distinction between the "concrete" and the "concrete in the mind." Hegel, he wrote, succumbed to the illusion that "concrete" life or "the real," being the product of the human spirit, developed from the abstract to the concrete in precisely the same pattern as did "thought" or the "concrete-in-the-mind." In other words, Hegel's dialectic was both a description of "the process by which the concrete itself comes into being" (MER, pp. 237–8) and an intellectual method. But such a formulation, Marx argued, confused the movement from abstract to concrete that is "abstract" (in the sense of being a "concrete in the mind" or thought reconstruction "in the head") with the movement from abstract to concrete that is "concrete" (that is, the unfolding of empirical history). The distinction is crucial. For though the logical development of a thought-whole always proceeds from the abstract to concrete (i.e. from simple to complex and mediated), the development of the actual concrete sometimes follows this pattern but sometimes does not.

Thus, to recall Marx's examples, the historical movements from possession to property, and from money to capital, have exhibited the simple-to-complex pattern in all historical cases up to now. However, as Inca civilization demonstrates, complex economic forms such as "cooperation" or a "developed division of labor" have sometimes existed before simpler forms such as money, thus producing the reverse pattern.

Yet the historical implications of this critique were much more far-reaching than any catalog of errors about historical causation or progression would suggest. Because for Hegel the concrete-in-the-mind and the actual concrete were one and the same, he could assume that a conceptual presentation of historical logic was necessarily the same as the events themselves. Hegel's historical works, therefore, read as relentless unfoldings of tripartite, dialectical patternings in which the role of actual historical events became merely illustrative of a higher philosophical meaning. Marx, in contrast, could never assume that historical events would fit the pattern of his theoretical construction. The latter was certainly based on historical understanding, but its status was that of an abstract, conceptual facsimile of historical reality, one useful for investigating, interpreting, and explaining it, and therefore for gaining critical leverage on it, but never to be mistaken for an empirical history. Therefore, for Marx, empirical histories were crucial not only for correcting potential flaws in the general model but also for understanding specific cases, which, as concrete particulars, were always expected to depart from generic patterns. Theory, as the epigraph from Engels asserts, should guide the study of history but could never replace it.

Because the developmental logic of concrete cases so often differs both from theoretical models and from one another, Marx also rejected Hegel's notion of historical teleology. This was the second major premise of the preface to the *Grundrisse*. History could not be reconstructed in forward motion, as the early Marx himself had done even as late as *The German Ideology*, but must proceed, in effect, backwards. "Human anatomy contains a key to the anatomy of the ape," Marx wrote in an oft-quoted line, yet one could not reliably move from ape to man (MER, p. 241). Evolutionary histories, Marx argued in the *Grundrisse*, invariably mislead. Such histories assume that theoretical categories can be treated as historical constants, yet these categories always in fact bear an important relation to the mode of production in which they originate. And since categories are always internally related to other categories within a mode of production, it is uncritical to assume that they can be treated as being identical to their apparent counterparts in later modes of production where the elements to which they are internally related may be very different. The category of labor, for example, means one thing in feudal society, quite another in capitalist society. Historical analyses which fail to recognize such critical distinctions are likely to fall into the whiggish trap in which "the latest form [of society] regards the previous ones as steps leading up to itself, and since it is only rarely . . . able to criticize itself . . . always conceives them one-sidedly" (MER, p. 242).

In the *Grundrisse*, then, Marx's goal was not a universal history and certainly not a Hegelian history that read the long progression of past events as producing the present as a "result." Rather his goal was a theoretical presentation of the genealogy and anatomy of capitalism as a mode of production. And this presentation reflected a third and final premise of the 1857 preface: that the "method of presentation" represents a retracing (in reverse order) of the steps encountered during investigative research. Research sets out to understand complex entities like the capitalist mode of production by examining the elements of which it is composed (like social classes), and then, in turn, by examining the ever simpler elements of which they are composed (like wage labor and capital) until we finally arrive at the simplest elements (like exchange value, prices, needs) which reveal the innermost connections of the object under investigation. Presentation then turns in the reverse direction and, by beginning with those inner connections of simple elements, progressively unfolds the concrete whole not as "the chaotic conception" with which research began but as a "rich totality of many determinations and relations" (MER, p. 237). If all of this movement, forward and back, is successfully negotiated, we will have not a history but a theoretical model which, as Marx conceded, "may appear as if we had before us a mere a priori construction" (MER, p. 301). Yet, so long as it is properly understood as a provisional map rather than the actual territory, this "material world . . . translated into a form of thought" will offer a powerful investigative tool for subsequent historical inquiry. Neither the *Grundrisse* nor *Capital* offered a substitute for history; rather they aimed to open it to a rigorous examination that would be fruitful both analytically and politically. In short, for Marx, social theory must precede the empirical study of history, but historical realities must also be permitted to challenge and revise theory.

Such are the methodological premises that guided these two theoretical works. In *Capital*, the care with which Marx pursued his logic of presentation was especially evident. He began with a close analysis of the nature of the commodity form precisely because he regarded it as modern capitalism's simplest category in which its innermost connections became visible. From the commodity form, he then reconstructed the capitalist mode of production moving from the more abstract categories of the "money form" to the increasingly complex, concrete workings of capital at the level of the individual enterprise and the national and international economy. With this reconstruction, Marx believed he had exposed the exploitation hidden in the apparent contractual equality of the capitalist relations of production, and while his reconstruction certainly applied to the histories of all capitalist societies and depended upon historical insights gleaned from studying bourgeois societies, he did not regard it as anything like a history of those societies. His analysis ignored, for example, the ways in which elements of precapitalist modes of production lingered on under capitalism. Yet, he believed that his theoretical analysis would help historians interested in the concrete workings of actual capitalist societies to appreciate their historical mix of capitalist and precapitalist elements.

Of more immediate concern to Marx, however, were the political ramifications of his analysis in *Capital*. He believed that his account offered workers an analytical and developmental but non-teleological understanding of the mode of production that governs their individual lives. Grasping its inner connections, they would come to recognize themselves in it and, thereby, break through fetishized consciousness to an historical understanding of the sources and nature of their exploitation and, finally, to the political engagement through which they would produce a socialist alternative and, ultimately, a communist society. Yet the late Marx did not consistently adhere to this approach to politics. While his letters to Engels after 1848 often implied that the workers would undertake political action, they also sometimes suggested a skepticism about the educability of the working class. And while this skepticism was never explicitly linked to an economic and technological determinist position, his later statements do suggest that Marx sometimes planted his hopes in an automatic working out of historical processes as much as or more than in an emerging theoretical consciousness in the proletariat.

This determinist or nomological conception of history is suggested by allusions Marx made, usually in prefaces and afterwords, to "laws . . . working with iron necessity toward inevitable results" (MER, p. 296) and the like. Its fullest articulation came in the 1859 preface to the *Critique of Political Economy*, a text that has assumed canonical status especially among so-called "orthodox" Marxists, which probably explains why its view of history is so commonly associated with Marx's name. According to this view, history involves the progressive development of the "forces of production" (raw materials, technology, labor, and related knowledge). As those forces become more and more efficient, people are progressively freed from the need to rely on unwanted labor to satisfy their needs. In the earliest modes of production, this "realm of necessity" remains large and people must work all the time just to meet their physical needs. Gradually, as new technologies develop, small surpluses are produced and at least some people can enter a "realm of freedom." This emergence of class division implies new "relations of production" (structures of ownership and authority). In the capitalist mode of production, industrial technologies permit mass production and a rather large surplus, but its relations of production continue to limit the realm of freedom to the few. Nonetheless, these relations prove stable in the short run because they are reinforced by "legal and political superstructures" as well as by ideological forms of consciousness corresponding to them. In the long run, however, the inherent contradiction between inegalitarian productive relations and powerful (potentially egalitarian) productive forces will produce an "epoch of social revolution" in which workers (those who sell their "labor power" for a wage) transform the "entire immense superstructure" and produce a general solution to the class antagonisms that have hitherto governed all societies. Private ownership of the means of production will be abolished and the productive forces will be unleashed for the benefit of all humankind rather than only for a small class of capitalists. While a small realm of necessity will always persist, everyone will now become freed from it to the same degree.

In this account, then, history threatens to return to the Hegelian assumption that historical events merely illustrate the unfolding of a higher philosophical logic. The most basic historical forces are large-scale institutional ones that are "independent of their [men's] will" (MER, p. 4). While historical investigation is not precluded, its basic contours seem determined in advance. Those who read *Capital* with this view of history in mind therefore see its theoretical account as revisable only in terms of how and when it reaches its appointed end, not whether it will do so. And, for that reason, according to this account workers need not read and understand *Capital*; they must merely play out the historical role it assigns them, whether they do it consciously or unconsciously.

There seems to be little doubt that Marx held two differing sets of expectations about the political overcoming of capitalism, one predicated on an activist proletariat consciously making its history, the other on the more impersonal working out of preordained historical tendencies. Each corresponded to certain beliefs Marx held, and he never openly confronted and decisively made the suppressed political choice they implied. Because of this equivocation, there are also two plausible interpretative extremes regarding what Marx meant when he asserted his famous claim for the primacy of economic forces in history, that is, the claim that "the mode of production of material life conditions the social, political and intellectual life process in general" (MER, p. 4). At the strong end of the interpretative continuum, economic primacy implies that history is fundamentally the progressive development of the forces of production which, quite independently of human intentional activity, determine all historical outcomes "in the last analysis" and by a wholly objective process. At the weak end, economic primacy implies only that history, being human history, is made in accordance with human anthropology. As we have seen, in this anthropology man is in essence a producing animal, where production refers to creative life activity in general and not merely the sphere of labor for exchange. In this view, then, human experience is primarily creative activity in which thought and other aspects of culture emerge, much in the way that for Sigmund Freud the symbolic imagination that produces dream content is ultimately bound up with available experience. What is not first produced cannot be thought just as what is not first experienced cannot be dreamt.

In a famous letter of 1890 to Joseph Bloch, Engels tried to clarify what it meant to call a conception of history "materialist" by saying that "the *ulti-*

mately determining element in history is the production and reproduction of real life" (MER, p. 760). In so doing, he meant to make room for historical explanations based on a wide variety of factors other than "economic" ones. The study of social life, he implied, involves recognizing a complex interplay of structural forces, meanings produced by cultural experience, and individual thought and action. Yet, like Marx, he did not make clear whether this interplay was ultimately governed by economic primacy in the strong or weak sense, and we will probably do best simply to recognize that Marx and Engels were equivocal here. Likewise, it would seem to make little sense to try to determine which one among the various styles of Marxist history writing that have prevailed among historians is the most faithful to Marx. The early Marx viewed history in a metaphysical light; after 1845 his approach was invariably empirical. But his later views of history still varied widely in terms of how economic-determinist they were, how human-centered or impersonal-institutional they were, and whether they regarded history in an evolutionary way or were restricted to a theoretical appraisal of capitalist society in which the key to the anatomy of the ape lay in man and not the other way around.

Only this much can be said with certainty: despite the diversity in his approaches to understanding history and its significance, Marx himself always wrote theoretically informed history with a sharply empirical bent. Moreover, these histories were scrupulously non-reductive and the strong sense of economic primacy nowhere governed them. In *The Eighteenth Brumaire of Louis Napoleon*, his most widely quoted historical pamphlet, Marx brilliantly deployed a famous vignette about history repeating itself "the first time as tragedy, the second as farce" in order to prefigure his thesis about the fears experienced by "late" generations of revolutionary actors who, "just when they seem engaged in revolutionizing themselves and things . . . anxiously conjure up the spirits of the past . . . to present the new scene of world history in this time-honored disguise and this borrowed language" (MER, pp. 594–5). Yet the thesis itself was established through a rigorous, empirical analysis of events in France, 1848–52. Likewise, in his two other historical narratives on revolutionary events in France – *The Class Struggles in France, 1848–1850* and *The Civil War in France*, which takes up the Paris Commune of 1871 – Marx consistently worked through the empirical record with great care to arrive at a larger theoretical argument, which he then presented as an opening thesis. In this way, his histories treated the method of presentation as the reverse of the logic of investigation just as he advised in the *Grundrisse*. Standing behind these local histories lie broad historical expectations about revolutionary outcomes and presuppositions about their historical causes, all of which reflect Marx's theoretical understanding of the dynamics of the capitalist mode of production. Yet, while these factors surely guided his view of the deepest meanings in contemporary events, they were never used to explain obscure empirical connections or otherwise imposed upon events. In his actual histories, then, Marx remained truer to his critique of Hegel than in some of his more rhetorical pronouncements.

Marx and Later Marxist Historians

The same can be said for most if not all of the professional historians who trace their central commitments to Marx's influence. While economic determinist views of history have been popular among some Marxist theorists and academic philosophers, they have only rarely been used in the actual writing of Marxist history (and then with disastrous results). Marxist history is necessarily informed by Marxist theory; indeed it is from this theory that it derives its unique strengths. Theory provides a rational, orienting structure to the Marxist historian's presuppositions and expectations, but, as prominent modern students of hermeneutics like Hans Georg Gadamer remind us, some such set of presuppositions and expectations is always present at the outset of interpretation. Moreover, Marxist historians have been no less rigorous than other historians in recognizing that theory must always be revisable on the basis of historical inquiry. Any historical investigation must stand on its own in the sense of being governed entirely by available documentary evidence. Where conclusions are reached that show the inadequacy of received theoretical categories, it is the latter that must be revised. Theory and history, then, represent mutually reinforcing exercises whose logics and practices are nonetheless distinct.

If the strong sense of economic primacy is generally absent from Marxist history, it is also true that the twentieth-century Marxist theorists regarded today as the most imaginative developers of Marxist theory – most of whom wrote at least some history – have moved it in non-reductive directions respectful of the importance of culture as well as social structure for the comprehension of human thought and action. Foremost among these in the early twentieth-century was the Italian Marxist, Antonio Gramsci. Writing in the aftermath of the Russian Revolution of 1917, Gramsci was impressed by the relative absence in Russia of the complex civil societies that characterized western European nations. In Russia the state could be seized in an act of force because it was not supported by, and interconnected with, the vast array of cultural organizations, ideologies, beliefs, and social and political rituals that provided Western states with their legitimacy. Underdeveloped states like czarist Russia simply "dominated" their populations; the more advanced states of the West ruled primarily by "consent" grounded in "civil society."

Likewise, Gramsci saw the class structures of Western societies as much more complex than in Russia, yet such societies were no less hierarchical and class-divided. Governance by consent was possible because of what Gramsci termed the cultural "hegemony" of the state in civil society. It followed that if revolutionary parties were to gain power in the West, they would have to pursue a long-term strategy of building an alternative hegemony, that is, a cultural fabric of values, practices, institutions, and symbols with which the popular masses were identified. In this sense, what the Marx of the 1859 preface had called the "superstructures" became the key locus of analysis in Gramsci's Marxism. And when, imprisoned by Mussolini, Gramsci wrote about the history of the Italian struggle for political independence, it was precisely the failure of the radical parties to forge the cultural allegiances of rural peasants and urban popular classes into a genuine mass movement that most preoccupied him.

Marx believed that the working class had a latent oppositional consciousness to capitalism, but he had never developed a cultural understanding either of the basis of that consciousness in life or of what would be required to make it fully manifest. Gramsci's contribution to Marxist historical thought lay precisely here. While Marx could therefore sometimes fall into an understanding of social life that reduced it to large-scale impersonal forces on the one hand and individual thought and behavior on the other, Gramsci moved the cultural ground that lay between these two domains into the center of his social and historical analysis.

Marxist historians who came to prominence in the years of the Cold War, such as Eric Hobsbawm and E. P. Thompson, continued to focus on the cultural ground that Gramsci had opened to view. In particular, Thompson's *The Making of the English Working Class* (1963) was an enormously influential example of how to study emerging class consciousness in relation to its basis in a cultural community rather than as any sort of simple reflection of economic circumstances. In his view, the English working class grew out of eighteenth-century traditions of artisanship, a cultural milieu based on values of decency and mutual aid and connected with languages of religious solidarity and social idealism. In this milieu, loyalties were sustained primarily because of a common identification with a way of life rather than out of any utilitarian calculations of class interest. The triumph of Thompson's book was the magnificent historical detail it amassed to show how a class emerges – not from ideologies imposed from above or from economic crises but out of a matrix of lived cultural experience, that is, out of the routines, rituals, rules of conduct, and celebrations that make up a way of life. It was this way of life that provided fertile soil for new socialist organizations like trade unions and not the other way round.

Both Gramsci and Thompson, however, broadened the cultural dimensions of Marxist history before the full impact of semiotics, structuralism, and other movements in cultural anthropology was registered on the practice of historical writing. If their efforts helped to sustain interest in the Marxist tradition through much of the twentieth century, it is the sociological and historical work of Pierre Bourdieu that has done most to insure that Marx-inspired historical thinking continues to have a place in the two decades since what is commonly known as the "cultural turn."

Though Gramsci and Thompson were attentive to the ways in which cultural codes, values, and practices had a reality independent of social forces and structures, they did not always insist on recognizing the way the latter were themselves initially constituted by cultural patterns. Gramsci, for example, sometimes spoke of intellectual groups or political parties as if they were entirely the products of the forces of hegemony in the state and ruling classes. In contrast, Bourdieu explicitly insists that the comprehension of material reality, whether by individuals or groups, is always initially structured by a priori and generally unconscious cultural codes. Modes of perceiving social reality are therefore never immediate and unproblematic, nor are they ever simply imposed from without. Instead, they always begin with an interpretation based on the symbols, values, and meanings that constitute and are constituted by a particular way of life. In modern, capitalist societies, these particular ways of life and their underlying interpretive codes involve different amounts and combinations of what Bourdieu calls "cultural capital" (e.g. education and prestige) and "economic capital" (e.g. wealth and income). Collections of people with similar amounts and combinations of capital, according to Bourdieu, may well coalesce into a self-conscious class, but he takes care not to leap (as he thinks traditional Marxism did) from the "class-on-paper" to the "real" class. Unlike Marx, Bourdieu thinks that classes are generally in the process of realization and almost never get realized.

In Bourdieu's view, then, class is not a thing-like element of social structure but a cultural code underlying a particular mode of life, which must be understood in relation to cultural codes underlying other modes of life in the same society. As such, his attitude towards class illustrates his effort to build a more symbolically sensitive, Marxist historical theory, one that focuses on what he calls "fields" (as against objective structures) and that accords primacy to the "relations" among the constituent elements of the field rather than on those elements treated objectively and in isolation from one another. As such, it would seem to be a form of Marx-inspired historical theory well suited to the current intellectual climate.

Marxist History Today

Still, when one looks back on the corpus of work done by Marxist historians of the several generations who followed Engels's call for more Marxist history, one is also likely to be impressed that many of the problems this tradition so vigorously attacked are no longer alive in the way they once were. Revolutions still exist, and certainly much work remains to be done so that we can more fully understand the revolutions of the past. Yet the Marxist expectation that revolutions would prove emancipatory has been so soured by the experience of the twentieth century that the problem threatens to become "merely historical" rather than theoretically resonant, at least in any positive sense. The point is, of course, compounded by the abject failure of the Soviet Union as a carrier of Marxist hopes. Similarly, industrial proletariats still exist, yet as postindustrial societies come into being, no one is likely to regard them as history's "final" class in the way Marx did. The same could be said for the historical implications of many other concepts of Marx's theory. Empirical and material realities, in other words, have increasingly challenged and discredited the theory.

Thus the question inevitably arises: will Marxist theory continue to inform and inspire historians in the way that it has in the past? The answer, I would suggest, depends upon how one defines "Marxist theory." If one means by it Marx's own theory in *Capital* and elsewhere, then the answer is surely no. This theory is itself an historical artefact, one that may still be read with profit for insight into Marx's own era and its immediate aftermath but not as a general guide to contemporary historical inquiry. Yet, as we have seen, Marx himself believed that history – both in the sense of lived events and the written account of them – must be treated as a corrective to theory, and that theory must therefore be continually revised. Thus, if one means by Marxist theory the theoretical efforts of those inspired by Marx to produce a critical theory of modern society, one that is attentive to the advances made in historical theory more generally, then the answer is just as surely yes.

Bourdieu, I have suggested, offers a particularly supple example of current Marx-inspired historical theorizing. Yet there are certainly other theorists concerned to understand the cultural dynamics of the modern capitalist mode of production and the emancipatory potentials they may or may not open up who continue to be very influential upon historians. First-generation theorists of the Frankfurt School, such as Max Horkheimer and, especially, Theodor Adorno and Walter Benjamin, have inspired countless histories, particularly of the origins and dynamics of modern "mass culture." Equally influential has been the work of the second-generation Frankfurt School theorist, Jürgen Habermas, especially his *Structural Transformation of the Public Sphere* (1962), which has transformed the field of Enlightenment history and produced a rich historiographical literature in addition to inspiring many monographs.[2] In each of these cases, Marxist history has come to mean the project of writing history informed by a critical theory of modern society that remains informed by Marx's intellectual dispositions and values but that largely abandons Marx's own theoretical writings as a direct guide to historical inquiry.

In making this move, historians working in the Marxist tradition pursue a trajectory begun by Marx himself. Marx's earliest conception of history was teleological. Metaphysically based, it was also subject to empirical investigation. This combination of religio-metaphysical and scientific-secular assumptions exploded in 1845 when Marx accepted a purely secular, immanent view of history. History now became "real, positive science," and metaphysical language about emerging essences disappeared. Yet, while Marx may have imagined the end of philosophy in 1845, philosophy returned to his work in a purely secular guise as "theory" after the disappointments of 1848. Derived from a mix of historical investigation and critical analysis of the categories that such investigations expose, theory for the mature Marx became the essential guide to the infinite manifold of human experience. Historical events, in Engels's later words, were always to be "studied afresh," but based on presuppositions and expectations drawn from theory. Historical study, which informed theory in the first place, became a continuous correction upon it. While, as we have seen, Marx's politics led him into some equivocation about how fundamentally theory would ever be corrected by historical events, even in his most nomological moments Marx would not have denied in principle the correctability of theory by history. And although Marx almost certainly never imagined that the fundamental contours of a theory of the capitalist mode of production might change, he left open the possibility that they might. Thus the theory that initially replaced philosophy in the role of a relatively fixed knowledge becomes as revisable as the histories it seeks to guide.

It should come as no surprise, then, that the long history of Marxist historical inquiry since Marx's death has made necessary the continuous revamping of theory as much as it has provoked the writing and rewriting of history itself. That is as it should be. One does not expect empirical histories simply to replicate theory. Indeed, such histories are vital and necessary precisely because they reveal elements of reality that theory does not discuss. So long as history appears to "flesh out" or complicate reality as understood by theory, no necessary revision of the latter is suggested. Even when a particular history shows theory to be misleading or counterproductive for the understanding of that case, theory is not necessarily in need of revision. For it may be that what is anomalous in a particular case comes to light only because of the theory's existence; this is the sense in which, as we say in everyday life, "the exception proves the rule." It is when the exceptions show that we have the wrong rules – when historical cases cast doubt on the fundamental categories of the theory and their relationship to one another – that history demands the revision of theory.[3]

Yet anyone surveying the horrendous misery and hitherto unimaginable carnage that twentieth-century actors have produced in Marx's name will likely recognize that the relation of history and theory in Marxism has only rarely been saved from distortion by politics. Indeed, it is through tracing the connections among theory, history, and politics in Marx's own writings that one can locate their tragic connection to the misery and carnage that came in their wake. While it would be unreasonable to hold Marx fully responsible for the sins of his later followers, there is also little doubt that his conception of theory contained a tragically fateful duality. As a successor to philosophy, one in which philosophy is faulted for having "only interpreted the world in various ways" rather than changing it (MER, p. 145), theory was conceived by Marx as an orientation both for political action and for historical investigation. As we have seen, these two purposes can lead to equivocation and obscurity. Should Marx's late work be read fundamentally in light of the open-ended, historical premises set out in the 1857 preface to the *Grundrisse* or those of the more rigid, determinist 1859 preface to the *Critique of Political Economy*? The premises themselves are mutually contradictory, deriving as they do from different political understandings of the nature and usefulness of theory. Yet this equivocation and obscurity have proven to be far from a merely "theoretical" matter. Marx's belief that theory could offer a comprehensive orientation for practice was grandiose, illusory, and partly responsible for the subsequent, political catastrophes that have befallen humankind. Clearly, this belief must be jettisoned. Marx's notion of the mutual interaction of theory and history for the benefit of understanding human life is of great value – but only when purged of any faith that an abstract theory can provide a comprehensive guide to political action. That theoretically, informed history may prevent us from repeating this or that mistake of the past, and help clarify an approach to this or that problem in the future is certainly to be hoped. But the idea that historical theory can and ought to lead to a totalistic revamping of human life was the twentieth century's foremost recipe for disaster.

NOTES

1 Karl Marx and Friedrich Engels, *The Marx–Engels Reader*, ed. R. C. Tucker (New York: Norton, 1978), p. 145; hereafter cited in the text as MER.
2 On Habermas's work and historians, see especially Craig Calhoun, ed., *Habermas and the Public Sphere* (Cambridge, MA: The MIT Press, 1992).
3 For an exemplary case in which historical investigation, albeit by a sociologist, demanded the revision of theory, albeit theory as held by a Marxist historian, see Craig Calhoun, *The Question of Class Struggle: Social Foundations of Popular Radicalism during the Industrial Revolution* (Chicago: University of Chicago Press, 1982).

REFERENCES AND FURTHER READING

Adamson, Walter L., *Marx and the Disillusionment of Marxism*, Berkeley, Los Angeles, and London: University of California Press, 1985.

Berlin, Isaiah, *Karl Marx: His Life and Environment*, 3rd edn., New York: Oxford University Press, 1963.

Bourdieu, Pierre. *Practical Reason: On the Theory of Action*, Stanford: Stanford University Press, 1998.

——, *Distinction: A Social Critique of the Judgement of Taste*, trans. R. Nice, Cambridge, MA: Harvard University Press, 1984.

Cohen, G. A., *Karl Marx's Theory of History: A Defence*, Princeton: Princeton University Press, 1978.

Elster, Jan, *Making Sense of Marx*, Cambridge and New York: Cambridge University Press, 1985.

Gramsci, Antonio, *Selections from the Prison Notebooks*, ed. and trans. Q. Hoare and G. Nowell Smith, New York: International Publishers, 1971.

Kolakowski, Leszek, *Main Currents of Marxism*, 3 vols., trans. P. S. Falla, Oxford: Clarendon Press, 1978.

Lichtheim, George, *Marxism: An Historical and Critical Study*, 2nd edn., New York: Praeger, 1965.

Rader, Melvin, *Marx's Interpretation of History*, New York: Oxford University Press, 1979.

Seigel, Jerrold, *Marx's Fate: The Shape of a Life*, Princeton: Princeton University Press, 1978.

Thompson, E. P., *The Making of the English Working Class*, London: Gollancz, 1963.

PART III

Patterns in Twentieth-Century Western Historical Thought

CHAPTER ELEVEN

The Professionalization of Historical Studies and the Guiding Assumptions of Modern Historical Thought

GEORG G. IGGERS

John Higham in his book on the American historical profession, *History* (1965), noted: "The historical movement of the nineteenth century was perhaps second only to the scientific revolution of the seventeenth century in transforming Western thought and shaping our modern mentality." The key to this transformation in Higham's words was the "extensive organization and professionalization of research."[1] This is in many ways a correct observation although the role which professionalization played in shaping modern historical thought may not have been quite as significant as the above statement suggests.

We must start out with a definition of professionalization as it applies to the study and writing of history. On one level it meant that history was now written by persons whose profession it was to write history and who replaced historians who had written history as supposed "amateurs." At least in the Western tradition the great narrative historians prior to the nineteenth century had been men – women such as Catharine Macaulay in the eighteenth century had been the exception – who like Thucydides, Tacitus, or Machiavelli wrote from their experiences in public life or gentlemen of leisure such as Edward Gibbon. The Chinese tradition had been different, reflecting a political society very different from that of the West. Here as early as the Tang Dynasty (seventh century CE) an imperial History Office was set up, followed by provincial and local history offices in which the historians were civil servants and through which many government officials passed on their way to higher offices. There were no parallels in the West at the time where historical studies were pursued primarily by individuals, not by state employees working collectively as in East Asia where the Chinese model was followed in Japan, Korea, and Vietnam. The first attempts in the West at institutionalizing historical

studies occurred in the second half of the seventeenth century with the founding of the *Académie des Inscriptions et des Belles Lettres* in Paris and of smaller
academies throughout Europe which encouraged and promoted research. It
was, however, primarily done by persons, many of them nobles and clergy,
whose prime occupation was not scholarship.

Professionalization and the Critical Study of Documents

Yet professionalization in the modern sense did not involve mere occupational
status but also a well formulated ethos which Peter Novick in his book on the
American historical profession characterized as the ideal of objectivity. Leopold
Ranke in 1824 in the famous preface to his earliest book expressed the credo
of later professional historians when he rejected the function assigned to
history writing previously "of judging the past, of instructing men for the
profit of future years" and insisted that the task of the historian was "merely
to show how it actually occurred" (*wie es eigentlich gewesen*). He himself
believed that this could only be done by relying exclusively on primary sources,
on "memoirs, diaries, letters, reports from embassies, and original narratives
of eyewitnesses."[2] The professionalization of history from this perspective
coincided with its transformation into a science in the German sense of a
Wissenschaft. The concept *Wissenschaft* defined science more broadly than the
Anglo-American term which considered the natural sciences, with their quest
for abstract formulations and laws, the norm for scientific study. History, as
understood by Ranke and professional historians after him, was clearly not such
a science. Ranke differentiated between "two ways of acquiring knowledge
about human affairs – through the perception of the particular and through
abstraction. . . . These two sources of knowledge are therefore to be kept
clearly distinguished."[3] Later theorists (e.g. J. G. Droysen, Wilhelm Dilthey,
Max Weber) thus distinguished between the natural sciences and cultural
sciences (*Geisteswissenschaften* or *Kulturwissenschaften*). These sciences, which
included history, required methods of inquiry which took into account the
elements of meaning and intention in human affairs, which were lacking in the
hard sciences.

Nevertheless what gave history and other cultural sciences their scientific
character was the rigorous way in which they conducted research. In this sense
musicology, the study of art and of literature, linguistics, and religion could
all be identified as sciences. Yet Ranke insisted that history – and this applies
to the other cultural sciences as well – must not be viewed as "an immense
aggregate of facts," but that "historical science at its best is both called upon
and able to rise in its own way from the investigation and contemplation of
the particular to a general view of events and to the recognition of their objectively existing relatedness."[4]

But what defined history as a science and as a professional discipline was not only its methods, that is the manner in which it pursued knowledge, but the place it occupied in institutions of higher learning, primarily universities but also research academies. What distinguished the professional historian from the amateur was the rigorous training he underwent in such an institution. In contrast to France and England, history had been taught in Germany since the Protestant Reformation at universities. However, these universities were mostly training institutions for medicine, law, and theology. Only in the course of the eighteenth century, primarily at the University of Göttingen, founded in 1737, did research play an important role in the recruitment of faculty and were appointments made specifically for history. The emergence of history as a discipline went parallel with the development of philology as a scholarly field. Philology involved the critical analysis and the understanding of texts on which scholarly history depended. This first involved the analysis of both classical and Biblical texts. Important contributions to the critical analysis of texts had been made in the seventeenth century by French and Belgian clerics, the Maurists and Bollandist fathers, and by the secular academies in the eighteenth century, but it was at the German universities in the eighteenth century that the analysis of classical and Biblical texts was systematized. J. G. Gatterer at Göttingen in the 1770s first established a seminar in which aspiring historians were trained with the help of the so-called auxiliary sciences such as paleography, diplomatics, and heraldics to examine the authenticity and credibility of documentary sources. In addition philology, as practiced by classical scholars such as F. A. Wolf in his *Prolegomena to Homer* (1795) and already earlier by Biblical scholars, pursued hermeneutical approaches which sought not merely to establish the authenticity of sources but to understand them within the historical framework of their time and culture. History thus increasingly became a craft, as Marc Bloch called it, not merely the occupation of antiquarians or of interested persons of leisure.

Professionalization is generally seen as part of a process of modernization. However, the fact that this process took place with greater speed at the German universities than elsewhere may have been connected with an uneven process of modernization and reflected both the greater modernity and at the same time the relatively greater backwardness of Germany in many aspects of life in comparison with France and Great Britain. Civil society with its broadly educated aristocratic and upper middle class, particularly in Great Britain, already possessed many of the characteristics of a market economy, but this market system was less fully developed in Germany, where a larger portion of the social and political elites consisted of civil servants. Higher education played a different role in Germany than in England and France. Since the Protestant Reformation the universities in Germany trained civil servants in the various autocratic states. The development of a comparable bureaucracy came much later in Great Britain and in the United States where the schools of higher education, primarily the undergraduate colleges, aimed at training not specialists but gentlemen with a broad humanistic education who would be able to assume leading positions in society and in politics. The latter function of transmitting a humanistic education was assumed in France by the secondary schools, the *lycées*, while the universities, which had been regarded as relics of a premodern age, were neglected after the Revolution. In their place a small number of select institutions of higher learning such as the *Ecole normale supérieure* were established to train the future intellectual elite of the nation.

It was only in the wake of the French Revolution and the Napoleonic invasions that a modern university system was established in Germany and that the professionalization of historical studies took place. The founding of the University of Berlin in 1810 occupied a central role in this transformation. It was part of a broad reform of education initiated by Wilhelm von Humboldt. The reform strengthened the role of the Greek and Roman classics in the humanistic *Gymnasien*, the secondary schools, which served to prepare a highly select student body for the universities. At the core of the reform of the secondary schools was Humboldt's ideal of cultivation or *Bildung*, intended to provide the upper middle class or *Bürgertum* with a solid liberal education founded on the Western tradition of classical culture as a preparation for its role in public life. Instead of making wealth the criterion of status, as was increasingly the case in Western European societies where a market economy was already more firmly established in public consciousness than in Prussia, Humboldt wanted status to be linked to culture and education. The new University of Berlin represented a radical break with older universities. It was no longer perceived primarily as a professional school, preparing physicians, lawyers, and pastors for a relatively static traditional society, but an institution in step with the conditions of the modern world. Instruction was to be joined with research, which was assigned a key place in the new university. This new stress on the centrality of research was embodied in the teaching of Barthold Georg Niebuhr who came to the university in 1810. Building on the philological studies of the eighteenth century, particularly on the pioneer work of F. A. Wolf for Homeric Greece, Niebuhr began to question the entire transmitted history of Rome, specifically Livy's histories, and began to write a history based on hard evidence such as law codes and physical relics, e.g. coins and architectural remains, which reflected the structure of Roman society. Similarly just as Wolf had contended that the Homeric poems had been composed orally by many authors and combined only later, Niebuhr postulated the oral transmission of early Roman history through poems. The critical examination of the remnants left by the past was the starting point of professional historical studies. It was the task of the historian to reconstruct the lost world from this fragmented evidence.

Niebuhr was only briefly at the University of Berlin before joining the diplomatic service in 1816 and going to the University of Bonn in 1823.

Ranke's impact on the professionalization of historical studies was much more significant. Not only the critical approach to the sources was crucial to professionalization but a whole infrastructure and culture of scholarship which accompanied it. Ranke was trained in the methods of classical philology at the University of Leipzig. He began his career in 1818 as a teacher of classics and history at a *Gymnasium* in the small Prussian provincial town of Frankfurt on the Oder. He was deeply influenced by Niebuhr's *Roman History* and by Thucydides on whom he wrote his dissertation. In a methodological appendix to his first book, *The Histories of the Latin and Germanic Peoples from 1494 to 1514*, in which he dealt with the emergence of the modern European state system in the period of the Italian wars, he judged the previous literature on the subject, particularly the classical treatments of the period by Francesco Guicciardini and Paolo Giovio, negatively because in his opinion they practiced the critical examination of primary sources inadequately. Since then his judgment of these historians has been considered too severe. He himself used the reports of the Venetian ambassadors, which he found in manuscript form in Berlin, as the foundation of his narrative. The book resulted in his appointment to the University of Berlin where he taught until his retirement in 1871. In contrast to the traditional lectures which conveyed information, the seminar which he organized gathered a small select group of students in a working group, who, generally at his home, devoted themselves under his direction to the critical examination of sources. Beginning in 1837 his students began to publish the *Annals of the German Empire under the House of Saxony*. These seminar sessions according to the British historian George P. Gooch inaugurated the critical study of the Middle Ages.

Critical history required the critical reconstruction of sources. An important beginning had been made in the seventeenth century by Belgian Jesuit and French Benedictine monks, the so-called Bollandists and Maurists, mentioned above, who had critically examined the lives of the Saints, gathering at times the ire of Church authorities when they proved cherished beliefs to be mistaken. Ludovico Muratori in the eighteenth century began to publish documents of medieval Italian history; this was followed in the first half of the nineteenth century by the *Monumenta Germaniae historica* launched in 1819, the *Collection des documents inédits sur l'histoire de France* initiated by Guizot in 1833, the *Rolls Series* in England begun in the 1860s, and similar collections elsewhere. For work in modern history the opening of public archives which began in the nineteenth century was important. Thus Ranke's subsequent works depended on his use of archives in Vienna, Italy, Prussia, Paris, and London.

Ranke should not be given undue credit for the establishment of history as a professional discipline. The seminar method had already been well established in classical philology before Ranke came to Berlin. Nevertheless, by the middle of the century virtually all universities, first in the Protestant but then also in the Catholic parts of the German-speaking world, had adopted the pattern of instruction introduced in Berlin. A part of the process of professionalization was also the transformation of the doctorate into a research degree and the expectation in the Germanies that in addition to a doctoral dissertation a second more extensive dissertation, the *Habilitation*, was required to qualify for university teaching. A community of scholars came into being still divided along national or linguistic lines. One of the first scholarly journals preceding German journals was the Danish *Historisk Tidskrift* (1840). In 1859 the *Historische Zeitschrift* was founded by Ranke's student, Heinrich von Sybel. There were, of course, many other journals and reviews which dealt with historical topics, the *Edinburgh Review* in Great Britain, the *Revue des Deux Mondes* in France, the *Nation* in the United States, but none of these considered themselves scholarly journals addressing a professional public; they rather sought to address a general, educated public. In the course of the last third of the nineteenth century new historical journals sprang up in almost all Western countries and in Japan, such as the the French *Revue Historique* in 1876, the Italian *Rivista storica* in 1884, the *English Historical Review* in 1886, the *American Historical Review* in 1895, and similar journals elsewhere. These were akin to journals in other scientific disciplines. They were to present the results of research to scholars working on similar themes. The extensive review sections which all of them contained were intended to provide the basis for critical exchanges within a scholarly community. Associations of historians were formed, such as the American Historical Association in 1884. Annual meetings were held in America beginning in 1884. German historians followed suit in the 1890s, and beginning in 1898 international congresses of historians began to meet.

By the time these journals and associations were founded the process of professionalization had already proceeded to a high degree. Considerable credit has been given to Ranke as the initiator of this process. Thus the American Historical Association in 1885 elected him as its first honorary member, hailing him "the father of historical science." The process, however, was not even. Ranke indeed had considerable influence on the shaping of history instruction and research in the areas of medieval and modern history in Germany through influential historians such as Georg Waitz, Wilhelm von Giesebrecht, and Heinrich von Sybel who had been his students. Historians in France and in the United States followed suit. Yet in neither country was the new discipline a carbon copy of the German model.

The institutional character was different in the three countries. In France the institutions of higher learning were state controlled but much more centralized than in Germany; in the United States higher education was highly decentralized with many universities and colleges operating as private corporations. Paradoxically the French defeat in the war with Prussia in 1870–1 led in France to a positive view of the German university system with its research imperative. The *Ecole des Chartes*, founded in 1821, had, as its name suggested, been dedicated to the critical examination of documents and was concerned primarily with the training of librarians and archivists, not historians. The *Ecole Pratique des Hautes Etudes* was founded in 1868 with a focus on research. While lectures predominated in the universities, the seminar method was introduced at the *Ecole Pratique*. The 1870s also saw the revitalization of the universities. While most of the universities, other than the Sorbonne, had stopped to function after the French Revolution as teaching institutions and mainly retained the function of administering examinations, they were now reorganized as centers which combined teaching with research. In the United States Johns Hopkins University, which opened its doors in 1876, offered graduate work in history, including the Ph.D. degree patterned on the German doctorate. While undergraduate education had been patterned on the English universities as schools intended to provide a general liberal arts education, the American graduate schools patterned themselves on the German university. The German influence was enhanced by French historians such as Gabriel Monod and Ernest Lavisse and an even larger number of Americans who had studied in Germany and then played an important role in the shaping of the discipline of history. The Japanese invited Ludwig Riess, a disciple of Ranke, to organize the historical seminar at the newly established Tokyo Imperial University which followed German patterns.

Throughout Europe, including Eastern Europe and Russia, a similar process took place, more slowly in some countries such as Great Britain, the Netherlands, and Italy, as well as in Spain and in Latin America. But even there the process was completed in the course of the first half of the twentieth century. In Britain with a few exceptions, such as John Robert Seeley, who was committed to German *Quellenkritik*, the critical study of documents, the great Victorian historians did not hold university posts. Lord Acton, who did, had in fact studied in Germany and dedicated the opening article of the first issue of the *English Historical Review* to "German Historical Schools," but he remained more of an essayist than a research scholar. Doctoral degrees were introduced at Oxford only in 1917 and in Cambridge in 1920 but became mandatory for university teaching only relatively late. In China, later than in Japan, the process of professionalization followed Western patterns – although American intellectual influences were stronger than German ones. By the end of the nineteenth century, the confrontation with the imperial powers had demonstrated the inadequacy of traditional world views and patterns of scholarship. But in the case of China as well as those of Japan and Korea modernization must not be identified totally with Westernization; China had a long tradition of textual criticism and its own kind of philology. Long before similar works appeared in the modern West, Liu Zhiji (661–721) had written a classical work on historical criticism. Although a major impact for the professionalization of historical studies came from nineteenth-century Germany, it everywhere took on forms rooted in national cultural and intellectual traditions. By the second half of the twentieth century the professionalization of historical studies at institutions of higher learning and research centers had become the norm world wide. During the 1950s in Nigeria and after decolonialization elsewhere in Africa universities were established with departments of history following the Western pattern.

Professional History's Relation with Literature

Professionalization, as we already suggested, was intimately connected with an ethos governing historical studies and writing. This ethos demanded strict objectivity from the historian. History was to become a science. This meant a break with the rhetorical tradition which had governed Western, but also Far Eastern, historiography, since classical antiquity. Until then, it was argued by various historians of modern historiography, history had had the function of studying the past to instruct the present; in Cicero's words it was to be the *magister vitae*. The historian is thus obliged in Ranke's words to strict "impartiality" (*Unparteilichkeit*). But the liberation from the rhetorical function of history also required an end to the expectation that the historian aim at literary perfection. For Ranke, "strict presentation of facts, no matter how conditional and unattractive they might be, is undoubtedly the supreme law."[5] History should thus no longer be viewed primarily as a literary genre.

This posited a sharp distinction between history as a science practiced by professionally trained scholars and history as a literary activity pursued by amateurs. Yet the separation between the two was by no means as clear as it has often been presented. The nineteenth century experienced a heightened interest and fascination with history which expressed itself both in scholarly and literary works. As Daniel Woolf has observed recently: "History continued to rival the novel as the most popular of genres, but this was a rivalry of mutual benefit – at no other time have the relations of fiction and nonfiction been so close and so symbiotic."[6] Particularly outside of Germany, but even there, historians who had no academic affiliations played a very important role. We think of François Guizot, Alexis de Tocqueville, Louis Blanc, and Jean Jaurès in France, of Thomas Carlyle, Henry Thomas Buckle, John Richard Green, and W. E. H. Lecky in Great Britain, of William Prescott, John Motley, George Bancroft and Henry Adams (the last two had very brief academic connections) in the United States, of Gustav Freytag and Franz Mehring in Germany, and of Benedetto Croce (who was a philosopher) in Italy, to name only a few. And this continued into the twentieth century: John and Barbara Hammonds, Sidney and Beatrice Webb, Mary Beard (the wife of Charles Beard), H. G. Wells, Emil Ludwig, Oswald Spengler, Arnold Toynbee, Barbara Tuchman, Winston Churchill, and Philippe Ariès (who only late in life received an academic appointment) come to mind.

History increasingly replaced philosophy in the nineteenth century as the area of knowledge which could offer enlightenment to important aspects of human existence. The writings emanating from the new critical historiography of the nineteenth century were perceived by a broad public not only as works of scholarship but also as literature. These two aspects were inseparably intertwined. The great works which came from the new scholarly orientation, including all of Ranke's major histories and Theodor Mommsen's *Roman History*, for which he received the Nobel Prize for literature in 1902, were works of synthesis which appealed to a broad literate public. Moreover, the language of history, unlike that of other disciplines, was remarkably free of jargon and technical expressions. Yet in the course of the twentieth century, professionalization led to increasing specialization which in turn led to an increasing isolation from the general public.

Professionalization meant the transformation of history into a science. But the opposition of J. G. Droysen to Buckle in the 1860s reflected the very different ways in which science could be understood. Thomas Buckle, a gentleman historian, in his *History of Civilization in England* (1857–61) had argued that history, if it was to be scientific, needed to interpret historical development according to natural law. Droysen, a German university professor, in his famous critique of Buckle, "On Raising History to the Level of a Science," argued for the special character of historical science as a discipline which resisted the reduction of its findings to abstract generalizations. Among practicing historians Buckle's brand of positivism had little appeal, even among advocates of social history such as Karl Lamprecht in Germany, Henri Berr in Belgium, or Frederick Jackson Turner in the US at the turn of the twentieth century. Only after 1945 did the idea that history needed to become a social science and that such a science could not operate without theoretical models involving a degree of quantification win broad support among economic and social historians. Geoffrey Barraclough in an account of the status of historical studies prepared for UNESCO in the 1970s wrote that the "search for quantity is beyond doubt the most powerful of the new trends in history."[7] The American economic historian Robert Fogel went a step further in an exchange with the British historian Geoffrey Elton. Fogel argued that history if it were to be scientific must follow the logic of inquiry and explanations of other sciences and thereby would become the domain of highly trained specialists. As a consequence it would no longer be accessible to the general public. Yet few historians have followed this path. The twentieth century has by no means seen a radical break between historical scholarship and literature. Many of the great historical works have combined scholarly techniques with literary elegance which made them attractive and accessible to a broad general public. This has been particularly true of some of the historians of the French *Annales* school such as Emmanuel Le Roy Ladurie, Georges Duby, and Jacques Le Goff, of Italian microhistorians such as Carlo Ginzburg and

Giovanni Levi, and of American gender historians such as Natalie Davis. Thus the separation between history and literature implied in the professional ethos was by no means complete. The great works by professional historians since the early nineteenth century have fused scholarship with literature.

Ranke already recognized that history was both science and art and that as art it must reproduce its subject matter with "poetic power which does not think up new things but mirrors its true character."[8] But he insisted that the border between scholarly or scientific history and value judgments must be rigidly maintained. The historian must be impartial, i.e. withhold judgment and observe the past as it was. Yet he was convinced that there are objective forces, of a "spiritual" and "moral" character, at work in history. He thus shared with Edmund Burke the belief that the political and social order as it evolved was essentially sound and that radical reform went against the nature of history. Objectivity consisted in recognizing this order. Ranke rejected the idea that there is chaos in history. The forces which manifest themselves in history, he noted, "cannot be defined or put in abstract terms, but one can behold them and observe them." Above the manifoldness of history there is the "hand of God."[9]

Professionalization and Politics

It is striking that in the course of professionalization in the nineteenth century, historical studies everywhere became increasingly political and ideological. The rise of professional scholarship and of the new "scientific" history it generated were closely related to the strong currents of nationalism. Ranke saw nationalism as the driving force of nineteenth-century Europe but fitted it into a European system of great powers the emergence of which was the central concern of his histories. Unlike the historians of the Prussian School who followed him, he was too good a European to be a German nationalist. His "impartial" view of history justified the conservative monarchical order in Restoration Europe and his conviction of the special place of Protestantism in Europe since the Reformation. Nevertheless the great interest throughout Europe and North America in the national past contributed massively to the establishment of modern scholarship such as the initiation of the great collections of medieval sources, foremost the *Monumenta Germaniae historica*, the explosion of archival studies in the newly opened archives, and the extensive production of national histories. This movement was not restricted to Germany but as the century progressed became world wide. The career of Jules Michelet offers a French example of how archival research and the construction of national myths merged. Archival studies everywhere went hand in hand with a political agenda which combined nationalistic aims with a defense of a bourgeois social order.

It appears that the historians went into the archives by no means open to what the sources would tell them but to find confirmation for their preconceptions. Professionalization by no means displaced political commitment. Droysen thus on the one hand set out guidelines for honest historical studies and on the other hand used archival evidence to produce a legend of the national mission which the Prussian Hohenzollern monarchs allegedly had followed since the early modern period. To an extent historians such as Ranke's disciple Heinrich von Sybel openly admitted that all history was colored by the political outlook of the historians who studied and wrote it. "Every historian who has had any significance in our literature has had his colors. There have been believers and atheists, Protestants and Catholics, liberals and conservatives, historians of all parties, but no longer any objective, impartial historians.[10] The so-called Prussian School of historians to which Sybel, but also Droysen and the notoriously chauvinistic Heinrich von Treitschke belonged, identified themselves as professional historians, yet at the same time openly proclaimed that their scholarship served a political purpose, the pursuit of a powerful German national state which combined economic liberalism and the guarantee of certain civic rights with a semiautocratic monarchy guaranteeing the privileged position of the aristocracy and the solid middle classes. In the United States somewhat later the so-called Dunning School invoked a Rankean commitment to objectivity to pursue a racist interpretation of the Reconstruction following the American Civil War in order to give scholarly justification to the practice of racial segregation.

In the case of the German historians as well as of historians in most of continental Europe, many of them civil servants, there existed a close relationship between their scholarship and the aims of the state. Their scholarship, for example on the causes of and the responsibility for the outbreak of the First World War, were often closely coordinated with the government, especially the Foreign Office, not only in wartime, as was the case in the United States during World War I, but also in peacetimes. This did not mean direct control by the state over research and writing; in fact academic freedom, while sometimes violated, was more firmly established in Germany than in the Unites States where universities were governed by boards of trustees which at times interfered with instruction and in personnel matters. But the social, denominational, and political criteria which governed the recruitment of faculty created a consensus which guaranteed identification with the established political order, whether monarchical in Germany or republican in France. After Germany's defeat in the First World War, a majority of the professional historians in Germany rallied against the Weimar Republic. The pattern of professionalization as it occurred in Germany, France, the United States, and Japan was repeated with some delays elsewhere with modifications reflecting national cultures and intellectual traditions. Effi Gazi in a recent study of the establishment of the historical profession in Greece compared the Greek development with that in Germany and France on the one hand and with other South Eastern European states – Romania, Bulgaria, and Serbia – on the other. Her study demonstrates how in all these countries the formation of professional historical disciplines, with all the institutions, associations, and publications this entailed, coincided with the use of scholarship to promote aggressively nationalistic agendas.

The recruitment practices of the profession guaranteed that its members came from a relatively limited, homogeneous segment of the population. It also guaranteed the exclusion of women and for a long time also of Jews and often of Catholics and of political dissenters as Peter Novick has shown for the American historical profession. Well into the twentieth century the university was a male preserve. Women had been better represented among historians prior to the nineteenth century as long as history was primarily a literary genre. Women had always been active in literature, even if fewer in numbers than men. Only late in the twentieth century did discrimination in the profession against women diminish.[11]

Critiques of Professionalization

The critique of professionalism and its ideal of objectivity came from several sources. Here Friedrich Nietzsche's early attack on the professional ethos in his famous essay on "The Advantage and Disadvantage of History for Life" (1873) is noteworthy. But Nietzsche failed to appreciate the contradictory character of the professionalization of history. He saw its self-proclaimed value neutrality and objectivity without understanding the contradictions between its professed program and its actual practice. He considered the academic historians as "a host of thinkers who merely watched life," whose aim was the "increase of knowledge" for its own sake, and who burdened living human beings with the masses of facts from the past. "Has not the constellation of life and history changed (in our time) with a mighty malevolent barrier stepping between them . . . through *the demand that history become a science?*"[12] (Nietzsche's italics). Yet Nietzsche did not understand the extent to which this call for history to become a detached science was ignored, and that history rather was used for very practical aims which lacked a scientific basis. Another critique came from Marx and the Marxists who did not object to history becoming a science but were much more cognizant of the ideological character of academic historiography than Nietzsche.

By the turn of the century the conception of history and historical inquiry which dominated in the historical profession was challenged from within the profession. Unlike Nietzsche, these critics such as the "New Historians" in the United States and the circle around the French philosopher Henri Berr and the sociologist Emile Durkheim did not object to the profession's commitment to science but criticized it for not being sufficiently scientific as did the founders of the influential French journal, *Annales*, Lucien Febvre and Marc Bloch in the interwar period. They argued that the sharp distinctions which historians had made since Ranke between the natural and the humanistic sciences could not be maintained. Science, they held, requires generalizations; it also requires empirical methods. Historiography as it had developed since Ranke had stressed that historians must concentrate on the particular as it manifests itself in the sources but erred in assuming that the past revealed itself directly through the documents. Like any other science or field of study, historiography, they suggested, must approach the subject of its study with clearly formulated questions and must test its conclusions against the evidence. A great number of historians such as Charles Beard in the United States, Henri Berr in Belgium, and Lucien Febvre and Marc Bloch in France now criticized the concentration on politics and statesmen which they considered to be narrow and called for an expansion of history to encompass broader sections of the population. This posited a closer relationship between history and the social science disciplines, such as economics and sociology. A new social history was to examine the function of social structures and processes within history. The older historiography with its primary concern with events and great personalities was thus considered outdated and elitist, that is both unscientific and undemocratic.

In Germany Karl Lamprecht had made these charges when he sought in the 1890s to rewrite German history taking into account the social and cultural context within which national history took place. Few historians accepted his belief in the laws which governed the histories of the individual nations but many favored a closer cooperation between history and the empirical social sciences, especially sociology and economics and in France also anthropology and geography. While for the older historiography, history was to take the form of narrative, the newer history, with its greater concern for social factors, introduced a stronger analytical note. Max Weber represented this trend with his conviction that all societies constitute webs of meaning which must be understood, not merely explained. He also occupied a middle road between the historicism of the older school, with its stress on intuition, and the functionalism of social science approaches for which the intentions and volitions of historical agents were of secondary importance. Yet all these various historical strategies shared in the conviction that historians should be professionals who are committed to a research ethos which requires detachment and objectivity.

It is important to stress that there never existed a paradigm which governed historical studies and guaranteed consensus among all historians. In the period during which historical studies were professionalized throughout the world, such a paradigm was approximated. But the German model on which this paradigm rested was accepted nowhere without important modifications, not even in Germany. This quasi-paradigm broke down over the course of the twentieth century, however, and it was replaced by a greater variety of historical outlooks and research strategies. The social science approaches, as we mentioned above, gained momentum in the three decades immediately following World War II. The demand for quantification and the construction of explanatory models not only in economic history but also in historical demography, electoral behavior, and even the history of mentalities required specialists with increasing training and qualifications in quantitative methods. Often a narrative acount, free of jargon and comprehensible to a broad audience (for example, the first volumes of Emmanuel Le Roy Ladurie's *The Peasants of Languedoc* [1966] and Robert Fogel's and Stanley Engerman's study of American slavery, *Time on the Cross* [1974]), was followed by a separate methodological second volume containing the empirical evidence intelligible only to specialists trained in quantitative and computer methods. These approaches, as Fogel willingly conceded, were to increase the gulf between the professional historian and the educated public.

Yet at this very point, the pendulum swung back. At a time in the 1970s when the computer became freely available to historians, a reaction took place against an overly professionalized and specialized historiography. Greater stress was placed on cultural factors which required methodological approaches quite different from those of the social historians. Thus the cultural anthropologist Clifford Geertz wrote that "believing with Max Weber that man is an animal suspended in webs of significance he himself has spun, I take culture to be those webs, and the analysis of it to be therefore not an experimental science in search of law but an interpretive one in search of meaning."[13] On the surface the new cultural history since the 1970s appeared to have returned to positions shared by the older historiography of the nineteenth century – the stress on narrative, the commitment to "understanding" the volitions and intentions of concrete human beings, the concern for the particular. But the political concern of this history was radically different; its focus was the life of the many who had been neglected before, rather than the high and mighty. It thus accorded women a place in history. An inherent critique of professional historiography and of the professional ethos accompanied this turn in historical writing. Postmodern theorists, who generally were not historians but literary critics and philosophers, questioned the assumptions upon which both the major part of nineteenth-century historiography and also the social history of the twentieth century had rested. One set of assumptions rested on the belief in the coherence and direction of history. From the post-modern perspective coherent history as such did not exist; the historian created histories. But the critique went further. It questioned the idea which was dear to both the older historians and the social historians, namely the idea that there was ever a "real" past which could be approached objectively. Not only did history have no coherence other than the one which the historian bestowed on it, but the world itself had none. We perceived the world only through the medium of language; but language, it was claimed by new "linguistic" post-Saussurian thinkers, was a self contained system which did not reflect reality but created it. If this is the case, the borderline between history and literature and history and fiction dissolves. Hayden White thus argued that "historical narratives are verbal fictions, the contents of which are as much *invented* as *found* and the forms of which have more in common with their counterparts in literature than they have with those in the sciences."[14] This means that history is essentially a literary enterprise, much as many pre-professional historians had assumed. What the historian writes is not determined by the research he does, but by the story he intends to construct. Giving precedence to the shaping power of narratives rather than to research, however, would mean the destruction of the professional ethos of the historian.

Yet few historians have followed White toward such a radical critique of the modern professional ethos. Historians have learned from the postmodern critique of their craft. They have become increasingly critical of older notions of a "grand narrative" governing Western history. They have taken into account many more aspects of social and cultural life and many more segments of the population. But there has been no radical break between social and cultural history; social historians have been increasingly open to cultural factors and cultural historians continue to base their work on solid research. There were calls after the cultural turmoils of the late 1960s for a deprofessionalization of historical studies. The history workshop movement, which had its origins with the founding of the *History Workshop* in Great Britain in 1976 and was imitated in Sweden and Germany, wanted to bring about cooperation between professional historians and common people who were to dig for their roots. But the pressures for professionalization have been too strong for these efforts to be very successful. Universities continue to be the main centers of historical research and writing. A majority of historians continue to aim at careers in these institutions. And not withstanding the critique of the professional ethos in recent years, this ethos with its research imperative continues to govern decisions of recruitment and promotion.

The Limits and Importance of Professionalization

A few concluding observations. The professionalization of historical studies must be seen in its historical context. Professionalization did not lead to the objectivity which was the aim of its ethos. We must remain aware of the profound tension which has always existed between the ethos of professionalism and the actual practice of professional historians. The ethos demanded absolute objectivity of the historian. Ranke had wished to "extinguish his self" and let history speak through him. Fustel de Coulanges had expressed a very similar sentiment. Professionalization was to guarantee this objectivity, and yet the professionalization of historical studies was part of national awakenings and was instrumentalized to serve political agendas. This led the African-American historian and sociologist W. E. B. Du Bois in his critique of the racism of the Dunning School to suggest that historical scholarship which claims recognition as a science in fact turns out often to be propaganda dressed as scholarship.[15] There is a good deal of validity to Du Bois' critique, but he himself maintained sufficient confidence in scholarly procedures to attempt to set straight the record of the role of Blacks in the Reconstruction of the South.

Professionalization led to greater methodological sophistication in establishing the past as it occurred. We fully recognize that the past does not reveal itself directly "as it actually occurred" but is always constructed by the observer. In this sense all history is interpretation. The past as such is elusive, as is Kant's "thing in itself." But the interpretations of the past are not fully arbitrary; they depend on a real past. In this sense the past is not "invented" in the way Hayden White suggested, although it is also not merely "found." Professionalization has contributed immensely to the understanding of the past. It has also often taken the form of a certain arrogance when historians claim to speak with the authority of a scientist. The fact that the professional ethos has so often been instrumentalized or politicized does not mean that it is wrong. The historians who used scholarship in the service of ideological agendas violated the very ethos of professionalism. While pure objectivity is an unattainable aim, it remains an ethical imperative which demands intellectual honesty and serious efforts to become aware of one's own biases and preconceptions. Historians obviously do not require professional status to write honest history, and professional status does not guarantee scientific objectivity. Historians can arrive at definitive views of reality even less than scientists in other fields. There clearly exist different perspectives on what constitutes the past. In this sense history like other disciplines involves a continuous dialogue in which interpretations of historical realities are examined, revised, and extended. It is seldom possible to establish the past "as it actually occurred," but it is often possible to dismantle historical myths, and this is an important function of honest scholarship. The fault of much professional scholarship is that it has not done this but has used a scholarly habitus to buttress its own distortions of history.

NOTES

1 John Higham, Felix Gilbert, Leonard Krieger, *History* (Englewood Cliffs, NJ, 1965), pp. ix–x.

2 Leopold von Ranke, *The Theory and Practice of History*, Georg G. Iggers and Konrad von Moltke, eds. (Indianapolis, 1973), p. 137.
3 Ibid., p. 30.
4 Ibid.
5 Ibid., p. 137.
6 D. R. Woolf, "English Historiography – Modern (since 1700)" in D. R. Woolf, ed., *A Global Encyclopedia of Historical Writing* (New York, 1998), vol. 1, p. 277.
7 Geoffrey Barraclough, *Main Trends in History* (New York, 1979), p. 89.
8 Ranke, *Theory and Practice of History*, p. 44.
9 Ibid., p. 138.
10 Cited in Georg G. Iggers, *The German Conception of History*, p. 117.
11 See Bonnie Smith, *The Gender of History. Men, Women, and Historical Practice* (Cambridge, MA, 1998).
12 Friedrich Nietzsche, *On the Advantage and Disadvantage of History for Life* (Indianapolis, 1980), p. 23; translation slightly revised.
13 Clifford Geertz, "Thick Description: Toward an Interpretative Theory of Culture" in his *The Interpretation of Cultures* (New York, 1983), p. 5.
14 Hayden White, "Historical Texts as Literary Artifacts" in *Tropics of Discourse* (Baltimore, 1982), p. 82.
15 See W. E. B. Du Bois, "The Propaganda of History," the final chapter in his *The Reconstruction in America 1860–1880* (New York, 1935).

REFERENCES AND FURTHER READING

Barnes, Harry Elmer, *A History of Historical Writing*, 2nd. edn., New York, 1962.
Breisach, Ernst, *Historiography: Ancient, Medieval, and Modern*, Chicago, 1983.
Burke, Peter, *The French Historical Revolution. The Annales School 1929–1989*, London, 1990.
Butterfield, Herbert, *Man on His Past. The Study of the History of Historical Scholarship*, Cambridge, 1955.
Den Boer, Pim, *History as a Profession. The Study of History in France, 1818–1914*, Princeton, 1998.
Elman, Benjamin A., *From Philosophy to Philology. Intellectual and Social Aspects of Change in Late Imperial China*, Cambridge, MA, 1984.
Gazi, Effi, *"Scientific" History. The Greek Case of Comparative Perspective (1860–1920)*, New York, 2000.
Gooch, George P., *History and Historians in the Nineteenth Century*, London, 1914.
Higham, John, Felix Gilbert, Leonard Krieger, *History*, Englewood Cliffs, NJ, 1965.
Iggers, Georg G., *The German Conception of History. The National Tradition of Historical Thought from Herder to the Present*, 2nd. edn., Middletown, CT, 1983.
Keylor, William, *Academy and Community. The Foundation of the French Historical Profession*, Cambridge, MA, 1975.

Novick, Peter, *That Noble Dream. The "Objectivity Question" and the American Historical Profession*, Cambridge, MA, 1988.

Ranke, Leopold von, *The Theory and Practice of History*, ed. Georg G. Iggers and Konrad von Moltke, Indianapolis, 1973.

Ringer, Fritz, *The Decline of the German Mandarins: The German Academic Community 1890–1933*, Cambrige, MA, 1969.

Stern, Fritz, ed., *The Varieties of History from Voltaire to the Present*, New York, 1973.

Twitchett, Denis, *The Writing of Official History under the T'ang*, Cambridge, 1992.

Wang, Q. Edward, *Inventing China Through History: The May Fourth Approach to Historiography*, Albany, 2001.

Woolf, D. R., *A Global Encyclopedia of Historical Writing*, 2 vols., New York, 1998.

CHAPTER TWELVE

The History of Armed Power

PETER PARET

In recent decades the historical study of armed power and its military and political uses has taken a new turn, which once again raises questions about the nature of the field and its place in the discipline of history in general. The changes that have occurred and are continuing are not absolute, but a matter of degree. They consist in an expansion of the subject and of the methodologies used in studying it – in particular, a more frequent and deliberate adaptation of concepts and techniques of the social sciences and humanities. Some historians of war have always recognized the political sources and ramifications of their subject. Interest in the social, economic, administrative, and cultural sources and effects of military organization and of warfare was never absent, but it has become more general and sustained in the past two centuries. It might seem sufficient to discuss these changes without referring to what has gone before. But an exclusive concentration on the present would be misleading.

The historiography of war and of its military and civil institutions has, of course, experienced earlier innovations and shifts in scholarly emphasis. More recently, especially since World War I, some of these changes have come, faded, and reappeared in slightly different form, and it may be that this particular area of historical specialization more than most reflects methodological issues that were addressed in the past but continue to pose problems for the contemporary historian. Their persistence says something about the field: the difficulty of defining and interpreting a subject that is markedly different from its context and yet deeply embedded in it; the variety of expertise needed to analyze a subject that ranges from weapons technology and bureaucratic politics to behavior in conditions of extreme danger; the psychological and ethical challenges posed to the historian by a subject in which the threat and reality of killing are central elements.

The first two sections of this essay, therefore, take note of some earlier histories that define the field and that continue to bear on issues of importance to contemporary scholarship, either as historiographical turning points or as examples of larger trends. The essay's third and fourth sections discuss the recent past and the condition of the historical study of armed power and its uses today.

Some Historians of War from Antiquity to the Enlightenment

It requires no special insight to realize that combat is not the whole of war, and that war is only one of the functions of armed force and of the civil and military institutions that together make it possible. From antiquity on, some historians of war took an expansive view of their subject, which went beyond the incidence of armed conflict. Others did not, and over long periods in western historiography narratives and interpretations of war narrowed into accounts of combat. Reasons varied for emphasizing this particular aspect, or for widening the narrative focus and analytic scope; but they were always affected by the concepts of history prevailing at any given time – by the historian's purpose and by the listener's or reader's expectations.

Thucydides took note of the political conditions and psychological factors that in 431 BC led to the Peloponnesian War. It was self-evident to him that the structure of society shaped military organization and even determined ways of fighting, and his words make plain that he thought of tactics not only as resulting from social structure and cultural values, but also as their indicator: how Athenians fought tells us something about their community. Polybius's history of the Punic Wars in the third and second century BC is integrated political–military history. He gives serious attention to political debates and to the psychology of leaders and social groups as well as to battle. That these writers had themselves been administrators, politicians, and soldiers contributed to their recognition of the complex rather than unitary character of the conflicts they wrote about.

With the decline of Rome, their works faded in the awareness of later writers on war and of their public. Medieval accounts of war were heavily marked by the symbolic and mythic qualities of combat, though these reflected social and political considerations, until under changing conditions the works of antiquity entered a second life. From the Renaissance to the end of the Enlightenment editions of Polybius, Vegetius, Caesar, and other classical authors, with commentary pointing to the contemporary relevance of their ideas, exerted a powerful influence not only on the historical study of war, but also on men's thinking about present and future wars and how to fight them.

Nevertheless the earlier models of an integrated history of war were not easily adapted to the sixteenth and seventeenth centuries. Exhortations of leaders, the agonistic theater of battle, noble deaths were topoi better suited to the exemplary, moral purposes of much of historical writing of the time and to its rhetorical character than the nuts and bolts of warfare. For the historian's patrons and readers, dramatic narrative held greater attraction than the analysis of means and ends. If the slowly developing specialization of scholarship created new methods of studying the past and of presenting the results of research, it also – at least for the time being – worked against the comprehensive approach of the most sophisticated historians of antiquity. It was difficult for the historian – and remains difficult today – to develop comparable degrees of interest and knowledge in the various interdependent areas that together make up war, and that in the military–civil aggregate hold the key to its understanding.

The historical study of war, whether in general histories or in works devoted to a particular conflict, again became divided between histories that emphasized battle and histories that followed a broader approach – a division that has lasted to this day. Often it has been the general historian, moving back and forth between society, culture, politics, diplomacy, and war, who has given an ultimately more accurate account of war than writers who did not look beyond the battlefield.

Machiavelli began his *Florentine Histories*, the first eight books of which were completed by 1525, by pointing out that his principal predecessors, Bruni and Poggio, described the foreign policy and wars of Florence but had little or nothing to say about the city's internal politics and social conflicts, and their impact on its wars. His account, he promised, would bring internal and external events together.[1] Machiavelli's decided opinions on the character of contemporary war in Italy, his hatred of the mercenaries on which the Papacy and the city-states largely relied, his faith in a militia as cheaper, more effective, and perhaps conducive to a healthier, more just society – all are reflected in his *History*, but more fully developed in his *Art of War* and *The Prince*. His treatment of politics and personalities is more searching than that of military events, which he outlined rather than analyzed. But even this degree of integration was unusual. The work's influence – a much debated topic – was at any rate not immediate.

The difficulties historians faced in dealing with war is suggested by how few, in the second half of the seventeenth century, even attempted to write a history of the Thirty Years War, or of one of its major phases, that combined an account of the more important events with an analysis – from whatever perspective – of the political, economic, and military issues. Instead the literature consists of editions of diplomatic documents, partisan chronicles, memoirs, and lurid accounts of the sacking of towns, the devastation of the countryside, rape and pillage without end. The sensational, unreflective narrative of organized mass violence became a distinct literary genre, which has retained its popular appeal to this day, and which – whether historians of war recognize it or not – serves as a backdrop to their work and helps to characterize their field. Throughout the seventeenth century this literature grew in volume, most of it more useful as raw material for the later scholar than as historical interpretation. The historian's ability to address a subject that every year gave new proof of its power to affect all phases of European life grew only slowly, in stages.

Voltaire took an important step forward. His histories, based on a close if willful reading of the more readily available literary sources, embedded war in the political culture of Europe. He discussed campaigns as extensions of diplomacy – although he was more informative on the specifics of negotiations than on the specifics of battle – and as an expression of the personality of princes and the ethos of social elites, for whom war was a stage on which the values by which one lived were made manifest. It was not his intention, he declared in the *Siècle de Louis XIV*, to "write a simple account of campaigns, but rather a history of manners and customs." He continued, "more than enough books are filled with the minutiae of war and its details of human fury and misery. The aim of the present study is to draw the principal characteristics of these upheavals, to clear away the mass of minor facts so that the truly important ones become visible, and, if possible, also the attitudes and the spirit that motivates them."[2] But in his text he at least summarized such matters as innovations in weapons and tactics, changes in the command structure and administration of the French forces, and the creation of a militia – a combination of military and non-military topics by no means frequent even today.

On the other hand, his treatment of war and of military institutions is limited by his failure to say much about the common soldier, and by his schematic treatment of battles, even when he writes about them at length. Not only are his accounts of the course of combat superficial, the place a particular battle occupies in the strategic scheme, and even its consequences, often remain obscure. He treats battle as a clash of princely wills and existential challenges to officers, to reveal their courage, manners, and largeness of spirit in victory or defeat. Not infrequently he even omits the numerical strength of one or the other antagonist – an indispensable factor in the tactical equation, which, as Clausewitz later noted, was often passed over in the military literature of the ancien régime.

Typical of Voltaire's treatment of combat is his account of the Battle of Steenkerke in 1692, in the sixteenth chapter of the *Siècle de Louis XIV*. It opens with an anecdote about a spy, who may or may not have brought about the tactical surprise of the French forces, and then outlines the French movements as the battle gradually turns against them, until two royal princes restore the situation and change imminent defeat to victory. The account ends with the observation that the battle gave rise to a new fashion for wearing lace jabots with pretended casualness, which mimicked the French caught unprepared by the enemy.[3] The author writes as a gentleman, well-informed on matters of state, family connections, and tables of precedence, personally acquainted with some of the princes and marshals who appear in his pages, who discusses calmly and clearly – with an occasional philosophic aside – the actions of other gentlemen.

Two historians, very different from one another, supplied some of the most important matter missing in Voltaire's account of war: Frederick the Great and Johannes von Müller. Frederick's *History of the Seven Years War*, written immediately after the fighting ended, and not intended for publication in the author's lifetime, is a work by a contemporary and the leading figure of the conflict.[4] He freely notes his mistakes and those of his generals but writes from a Prussian perspective and bias. He must often guess at his opponents' intentions; on the other hand, he can be very reserved on matters on which he is well informed. An episode such as his dismissal for incompetence of his brother and designated successor, Prince August Wilhelm, is passed over with a few noncommittal words. Frederick has been criticized for insufficiently marking the changes in the political and strategic situation during the war. But although he organized his manuscript by years rather than in analytic phases, he clearly traces Prussia's gradual encirclement, gives detailed if subjective evaluations of the opposing strategies, describes the course of the fighting, and weighs its political and economic consequences.

Perhaps never before had a historical work traced the links between the details of military action, foreign policy, and domestic economic and political conditions with such clarity. In part this was the consequence of Frederick not writing for immediate publication, and of the unusual situation in which he and his state found themselves. Not only formally, but in effect, he was head of government, commander-in-chief, and commander of the main field army in one; and whereas France, Russia, or Austria could suffer any number of defeats without experiencing more than slight tremors, Prussia's resources were so limited that every strategic move or battle carried political risks. Possibly the depth of Clausewitz's later recognition of the relationship between war and politics owes something to the fact that in the Frederician and Napoleonic eras Prussia was still the weakest of the major powers.

In the *History of the Seven Years War* and in his other historical writings, Frederick distinguishes between seasoned and inexperienced soldiers, discusses levels of training, morale, fatigue, and loyalty to the commander and the unit but says little about the general attitude and motives of the common soldier – and not much more about those of the officer. He takes an authoritarian, occasionally paternalistic view of military manpower, which remains an inert instrument in his hands. In Johannes von Müller's Swiss histories, which began to appear in 1780, the Swiss fighting man, individually and as a member of his community, becomes a leading actor. Müller started to write at a time when the rights of groups of the population were under attack in some cantons, and when shifts in the European system threatened the independence of the confederation. His purpose was to stimulate the country's political regeneration by recalling to his readers how the medieval Swiss overcame local rivalries and jointly expelled the foreign intruder. Even after the confederation became a French satellite in the 1790s, the basic tenor of Müller's work did not change. He idealized the Swiss past. No doubt he exaggerated the extent to which the will to be free acted as a universal motive. He did not sufficiently analyze the social elements and pressures that stimulated the people's readiness to fight, but he did not invent it either. He based himself on intensive archival research and on an exceptionally broad array of printed documents (though he seems to have attributed similar degrees of authority to all), and by emphasizing the interdependence of civil and military factors rather than their difference, he drew an unusually inclusive picture of Swiss history.

Müller did not associate freedom with a particular form of government. He differentiated oligarchic, aristocratic, and democratic cantons, and within each community distinguished between nobles, burghers, subjects, and serfs. But he interpreted the will to use force against outsiders as a motive acting on all social groups. His first book, *Histories of the Swiss*, concludes: "Our far from adequate account of these many victories shows a united people overcoming ignorant knights and their undisciplined followers by means of growing military skill. We see the people exploiting the country's mountains and passes, but never forgetting its own values. It fights for freedom, and the more it fights the freer it becomes. Again and again the people demonstrate that military virtue makes up for anything else, and that without it statecraft means nothing."[5]

War is central to Müller's histories, and central to his conception of war is the ordinary fighting man, whether Müller depicts him choosing his commander in an assembly of the community, sacrificing himself for the common good, or bringing down the feudal host. At the Battle of Sempach, Müller takes care to note, Duke Leopold of Austria fell victim to "a common man from Schwyz." At the time of the American and French Revolutions and the Napoleonic empire, Müller linked the individual with large events and placed the ordinary soldier on the stage of world history. His books were an early assertion in the scholarly literature of the importance of the man in the ranks, whatever the cause for which he fought and whatever the ideology of his leaders.

Early Stages in the Modern History of Armed Power

In the course of the nineteenth century, as history acquired the character of a scientific academic discipline, the study of armed power in the past was transformed by new methodologies and new questions – or, more accurately, should have been transformed: with the growth of the middle class and the expansion of the reading public, the literature on war also increased, but much of it continued to follow conventional paths of narrative and biography.

Among the innovations, two stand out. One was campaign history based on the vast amount of documentation accumulated in the military archives, particularly since the seventeenth century, and written by officers serving in a new type of institution: the historical sections attached to a general staff. The second major development was the increasingly sophisticated integration of the study of war and its institutions with other elements in the history of a period or country. The links that earlier historians might have mentioned occasionally now became a continuing concern. These new works might emphasize the military but indicate its links with the non-military context. Or they aimed at a balanced treatment of the interaction of war and of such other elements of their subject as dynastic motives, religious beliefs, and social change – a now classic example is Leopold von Ranke's *History of France, primarily in the 16th and 17th Century* (1852–61).

Early forms of this development are found in many works of the Revolutionary and Napoleonic periods. Especially interesting in their methodology and interpretations are the writings of Carl von Clausewitz. History fascinated him in its specifics as much as in its grand sweep, and he valued the study of the past as an end in itself. But he also used history as a way of achieving a generalized theoretical understanding of war. His many analytic narratives of campaigns were based on a still limited but critically sifted body of documents, memoirs, and secondary sources. They were case studies, several many hundreds of pages in length, which allowed Clausewitz to see war over centuries in a comparative perspective that led to the identification of unique phenomena on the one hand, and confirmed the existence of universals on the other. Speculative thought, combined with historical interpretation, enabled Clausewitz to develop a theory of war as such. Wars, he argued, always consist of the same elements, which interact dynamically – for instance, the tendency of opposing sides to escalate their military effort reciprocally, a process that may or may not be modified and limited by non-military, political, financial, or ethical considerations. An example, drawn from World War I, would be the German declaration of unlimited submarine warfare, an escalation carried out regardless of its likely political consequences. These general elements and their relationships – which may be thought of as building blocks of theory – are affected by the specific conditions under which they function at any particular time, which make each war unique. Historical analysis makes theory possible. Theory, in turn, adds depth to historical interpretation.

Clausewitz attached no utilitarian purpose to history, aside from its role in developing theory. Both in itself and in its contribution to theory, history was a means of achieving understanding, and consequently had to be as objective as possible. To write history for an ulterior purpose, as Johannes von Müller had glorified the Swiss wars to inspire his contemporaries, was to interfere with the *Erkenntnis* of the past and to compromise any theoretical insights that could result from it. As a young soldier Clausewitz had served against the

French Revolution, and later considered opposition to Napoleon a moral as well as a political imperative. But in his histories and in the historical passages of his principal theoretical work, *On War*, he interpreted the Revolution's destruction of the ancien régime, which "made war the business of the people as a whole," as an achievement of world-historical significance, and he analyzed Napoleon with the same scientific engagement with which he discussed Frederick the Great. His history of the War of 1806, in which Napoleon overran Prussia in a matter of weeks, is centered on an exploration of the failures of Prussian society, institutions, and leadership, so unforgiving that his Berlin publisher could not include the manuscript in Clausewitz's collected works, and it remained unpublished until 1888, nearly six decades after his death.[6]

This degree of ideological detachment did not usually characterize official campaign history, but as this branch of the literature matured in the last decades of the nineteenth century, it became possible to follow the growth of military institutions and the course of military operations from the inside – on the basis of the documents generated in the process of raising, equipping, training, and employing very large numbers of men.

Representative of these works are the first official historical series on a war fought by the United States, *The Medical and Surgical History of the War of the Rebellion*, – i.e., the Civil War – published in six volumes between 1870 and 1889 by the Office of the Surgeon General; the superb fourth volume of *La Campagne de 1800 en Allemagne* by Charles Alombert and Jean Colin of the *Section Historique* of the French General Staff (1900); and the three-volume institutional and organizational history, *Das Preussische Heer der Befreiungskriege*, edited by Bernhard Schwertfeger of the German General Staff (1912–14[20]). Accounts by the rank-and-file of campaign and garrison life, some published in the seventeenth and eighteenth centuries, others discovered in the archives, were mined for larger studies or published in modern editions. Many more official works and documentary publications followed on world wars I and II and the conflicts since 1945. It is important to note that by 1900 this vast literature consisted only in part of campaign and unit history. Much of it now addressed organizational and technical subjects; social issues, such as manpower policies; and the economy, especially supply, transport, and the production and distribution of uniforms and equipment. In the course of the twentieth century, national economic policy and political and ideological issues also became major themes – for instance in the multi-volume West German history of World War II, *Das Deutsche Reich und der zweite Weltkrieg* (1979–1990).

Their broad range of subject matter is an obvious strength of these publications, as is the authors' and editors' continuous, long-term access to masses of documents, which as early as the 1880s stimulated comparative and statistical analyses. Against these advantages must be weighed the possibility of selective and biased treatment, present in all historical writing, but here perhaps exacerbated by institutional and political pressures. That some French and German histories before 1914 emphasized the power of the offensive undoubtedly reflected doctrinal concerns of the time; debate over the possible falsification of casualty figures in the official British history of World War I continued well beyond World War II; Schwertfeger's rejection of the liberal claim that middle-class volunteers played a decisive role in Prussia's final campaigns against Napoleon expressed the class bias of the army's leadership on the eve of World War I – even if his criticism was largely correct. That some official histories were written to advance the training of officers, or to celebrate traditions of the service or provide other spurs to patriotism, was a further ambiguity that cast a shadow even over works of rigorous scholarship.

Authors of official histories also wrote books that were not part of official programs. A notable example is Jean Colin, whose book *The Transformations of War* (1912) converted a mass of highly technical research into a brilliant synthesis for the nonspecialist. Others were civilian scholars with close links to the services, for instance the Oxford historian Charles Oman, author of numerous studies of medieval and Napoleonic warfare, and John Fortescue, librarian to Edward VII and George V, who over the span of some thirty years published his multi-volume *History of the British Army* (1899–1930).

The detailed reconstruction of military policy and of operations in the field, whether by official historians or scholars with access to service archives, nourished the second major development of the time: high-level integrative history. Oman and Fortescue could not have written their inside accounts a century earlier. But far more innovative methodologically were two German scholars, Hans Delbrück and Otto Hintze. Delbrück's major work, *History of the Art of War within the Framework of Political History* (1900–20), was not a history of wars, but a history of how wars were fought – not *Kriegsgeschichte* but *Geschichte der Kriegskunst.* Particular battles and campaigns revealed the resources and attitudes of the societies that waged them. Together, the military components and the non-military factors that created or affected them formed "a single thread among the interlacing threads of universal history."[7] At most, historians had treated these military–civil links impressionistically; Delbrück now subjected them to systematic, comparative analysis. He began with historical accounts and documentary sources, which he measured against the remaining evidence of the events themselves – the nature of the battlefield, the technological characteristics of the time – and their social and institutional context. He also drew on evidence from the present. If in the 1890s Prussian infantry with rifles and packs could not run more than 150 yards in formation before losing the ability to engage the enemy in hand-to-hand combat, then Herodotus's statement that in the Battle of Marathon the heavily armed Athenian phalanx assaulted the Persian line after running 1640 yards could not be accurate. Nor was it possible in the limited space between the mountains and the sea in which the Persian army was drawn up to maneuver and feed a force of the size Herodotus claimed. With pragmatic arguments of this kind, backed by close reading of the texts, Delbrück radically changed the picture of war from antiquity to the early-modern period. His adaptation of Clausewitz's concept of two basic types of grand strategy – to destroy the enemy or to exhaust him – led to a much debated reinterpretation of eighteenth- and early nineteenth-century warfare.

Social factors were an important part of his analysis, but Delbrück still identified his focus as the interaction of war with politics and policy. He paid much attention to economic conditions, but as a factor that shaped the character and magnitude of the military effort rather than as a basic political and social force. Although he was very sensitive to the role of ideas and culture, they occupy a subsidiary place in his interpretations. Nevertheless his fundamental concepts have retained their validity, and have proved sufficiently elastic to accommodate later additions.

Hintze disagreed with some of Delbrück's interpretations of Frederick the Great and Napoleon but was at one with him in recognizing the explanatory potential of the interaction of civil and military elements in history. His most significant observations on these links occur in his essays on comparative history, particularly in "Military Organization and the Organization of the State" (1906). In this study, written in Delbrück's expansive spirit, Hintze outlined a typology of civil–military considerations in government from antiquity to the present. He drew on Herbert Spencer's distinction in his *Principles of Sociology* between "two basic types of state and social organization" – the "military" and the "industrial" – to develop a comparative perspective on political formation throughout history, in which, he pointed out, the military always played a major and often a decisive role. Hintze's view of history was the opposite of formalistic. He did not conceive of " 'the organization of the state' in the narrow, constitutional, and juridical sense that deals only with the distribution of the state's functions and powers among its various executive agents. If we want to find out about relations between military organization and the organization of the state, we must direct our attention particularly to two phenomena . . . first, the structure of social classes, and second, the external ordering of the states – their position relative to each other, and their over-all position in the world."[8]

One result of Hintze's work was to clarify the role of military institutions in building the state. Their defensive and offensive function was self-evident; equally important was their internal role. The upkeep of troops required administrative agencies; bureaucrats and soldiers jointly extended the real rather than symbolic power of the central authority. Hintze developed this theme in other studies, for instance in the 1919 essay "The Commissary and his Significance in General," in which he traces the military origins of the Prussian civil bureaucracy and compares it to the early French army intendants as developing "a new type of public servant [free of local ties], corresponding to the spirit of the absolutist reason of state."[9] As Felix Gilbert writes in his edition of Hintze's essays, he "combined the scholarly traditions in which he had grown up – the ideas of the Prussian historical school and Ranke's 'primacy of foreign policy' – with notions developed in the younger science of sociology." In his employment of methods of research and interpretation beyond those of his own discipline, Hintze stands for the most significant development in the modern history of armed power and war: its interdisciplinary expansion.

The magnitude of the changes that occurred in the next two generations may be indicated by the following titles: French sociological studies, which unlike Hintze's essays are occupied less with the state than with such topics as the army's place in society, the professionalization of the officer corps, and the effects of conscription and military service on rural society, culminating in such works as Raoul Girardet, *La Société militaire dans la France contemporaine (1815–1939)* (1953), and Emile G. Léonard, *L'Armée et ses problèmes au XVIIIᵉ siècle* (1958); textual analyses and the history of ideas combined with political and military history, such as Hans Rothfels, *Carl von Clausewitz: Politik und Krieg* (1920); and such pioneering explorations of the economic causes and consequences of war as Richard Pares, *War and Trade in the West Indies* (1936). New themes and new methodological conceptions continued to emerge; but the interaction of history with other disciplines and the transformation of history itself had become the basis for much of the most significant work in the field.

The Recent Past

World War II, the advent of the nuclear age, and the end of colonialism affected the historical study of war and of its institutions in ways that are not yet fully understood. The magnitude and pervasiveness of armed conflict from the 1930s on certainly confirmed the subject's significance. One response was the publication of extensive series of official accounts throughout the world, together with thousands of memoirs, biographies, and histories, which ranged from serious scholarship to the derivative pandering of a seemingly inexhaustible fascination with modern conflict in all its forms. Two generations after Germany and Japan surrendered, *The World at War* – to appropriate the title of a still frequently shown television program – remains a focus of attention in every medium.

By the 1950s, however, a reaction against the study of World War II, and even against the history of war in general, became evident in colleges and universities. The intensity of this reaction varied from country to country; it was more pronounced in the United States than in England and Scotland, where universities continued their long tradition of teaching and supporting research in military and naval history, and by the 1960s they even expanded their programs. In the United States, war in the American past remained an important part of the curriculum in American history; but the history of war as a field of specialization – never prominent in American academia – was largely eliminated from course offerings and was rarely drawn on for dissertation topics.[10]

Long-held attitudes combined with pressures of the day to bring about this change. The widespread if deeply mistaken belief that the nuclear age was eliminating war (UN peacekeepers have now served on more than fifty missions throughout the world), caused some scholars to fear that to study and teach the history of war meant lending it a spurious authenticity and slowing its disappearance. The conflict over American policy in Southeast Asia gave moral and political urgency to this belief. Military history of every kind was associated with ROTC texts and other official publications. That some of the most intelligent analysts of nineteenth- and twentieth-century war and diplomacy were on the staff of research institutions that worked for the Department of Defense – Bernard Brodie and Paul Keczkemeti of RAND are two examples – reinforced this view. Sponsored research was declared as incompatible with academic independence and objectivity.

The political concerns that helped drive this reaction came largely from the left, and especially from mainstream liberalism. Communists might denounce a book on war as an expression of American imperialism; but military history had played a role in communist thought from Marx and Engels on, and was not rejected as such (Albert Soboul's *Les Soldats de l'an deux* (1959) is a noteworthy example of Marxist military history in the ultimate phase of communism). The liberal position was more ambivalent. Liberal historians of war are not rare – George Macaulay Trevelyan, for instance, whose works on Garibaldi and early eighteenth-century England have been called "preeminently military histories."[11] Other liberal historians dismissed even wars fought for the liberal ideal of national self-determination as a sorry subject for the historian – the mid-Victorian Henry Thomas Buckle is an early example. They and their modern descendants could never quite renounce the conviction that wars were an aberration imposed by self-centered interests on innately peace-loving peoples. Their view of past and present reality also influenced their judgment of the nature of history – the discipline's purpose and methods, and its "appropriate" subject matter. Social history, which gave non-elites a new powerful voice in our understanding of the past, became the academic hero of the period, not only because of the importance of the subject, the study of which continued a long historiographical development, but also for ideological and cultural reasons. The history of armed power was relegated to the role of a disagreeable intruder in the world of scholarship. Because it encompassed many social themes – the power of the state to induce and force men, and increasingly women, to fight, for instance – one might have expected that the history of war would also benefit from the historian's new interest in the common people; but that change was slow in coming.

More recently the reaction against war as a subject to study and teach has again weakened. This newest turn coincides with, and may be part of, the larger process of fragmentation that is affecting history as a discipline. More than in the past, history today is divided into intellectual and professional camps that hold differing views on the discipline's basic concepts and standards. The dividing lines between these centers of ideas and academic influence are not firmly drawn; their concerns and approaches overlap. The multiplicity of standards may pose problems for the historian; but it also creates a less dogmatic academic environment in which all themes and varieties of history find a place.

The New History of Armed Power

In some respects the historical study of armed power today has not changed greatly from its condition fifty or a hundred years ago. In other ways it is very different. The age-old division between a narrow and a broader approach to the subject has persisted, the one continuing to be as valid as the other. The specifics of a battle or campaign not only illuminate the society and culture of the people engaged in it, as events of vital importance to their participants, and often of larger military, political, or cultural significance, they are worth interpreting for their own sake. But even concentrated operational studies may benefit from some attention to the context, just as treatments of broader themes may be strengthened if the realities of combat are not ignored.

In the abstract, the value of an integrative approach is now widely acknowledged. Even textbooks declare that "the study of military history has all too often been undertaken as if war existed in a vacuum."[12] But the implementation of this insight remains difficult, and works that strike a convincing balance between the military and non-military elements of their subject – which need not mean parity – are still the exception. Official history continues to be the major historiographical influence it has been since the nineteenth century. It feeds a vast amount of information to the literature, but is more than a provider of material. Together with conventional studies, official programs sponsor projects of reinterpretation and – like the French Centre d'études d'histoire de la Défense – make space for experimentation and debates on methodology. Contacts with universities and research institutions are common.

Popular history is another constant. It accords with the mass-orientation of our culture, and today more than ever provides a broad backdrop of information and entertainment to specialized scholarship. In the nineteenth century, Michelet, Droysen, and Macauley – to name three political and cultural historians who took war seriously as a social and nation-building force – addressed the educated public, as did less demanding authors, who found many additional readers in the upwardly mobile products of compulsory education. Since then the consumption of scholarly history has shrunk, and that of popular history – which emphasizes combat and leadership far more than the context of war – has grown. Apart of some works of serious scholarship expressed in broadly accessible form, popular history consists of derivatives, which range from honest adaptations to oversimplifications and knockoffs of other peoples' research. On the one hand, this literature makes some readers receptive to more demanding studies; on the other it corrupts standards of judgment and lends a spurious authority to writers who catch the passing moods of the media culture. However scholars feel about popular history, it has become a force in their professional lives. Directly or indirectly it affects the dissemination and reception of their work, and sometimes also its intellectual content and style.[13]

Narrowly focused operational history and what I have called integrative history, official and popular history, are certainly no longer what they were in the first half of the twentieth century. The old forms are filled with some new content. The expansion of themes and methods, which has marked the field at least since the Enlightenment, is continuing. Disciplines ranging from psychology and anthropology to linguistics have either entered the field or now play a much larger part in it. Operational and strategic history have not disappeared, but have lost their former centrality. In recent decades other subjects have been emphasized: the social history of armed forces, the latest stage in the emergence, over the past two centuries, of the common soldier as a major theme, combined with the history of elites and of voluntary and compulsory service; the role of armed forces and of their military and civil institutions in politics and the structure of the state; and the interaction of war with technology and popular and elite culture.

A further step of integrative history are studies that blend military and non-military elements so thoroughly as to defy categorization. An example is William Caferro's *Mercenary Companies and the Decline of Siena* (1998), which demonstrates a disjuncture of Sienese political and military institutions in the later Trecento that resulted in the city's loss of independence – the reverse of military administration leading to the expansion of political power in the history of the major European nation-states. Caferro's monograph is neither economic, political, nor military history, but an amalgam that reflects the historical reality far better than do the customary fields of academic specialization.

The deployment of other disciplines for the purposes of interpreting the past has increasingly involved the use of new theories and terminology. Two recent conferences exemplify some of the options: a meeting on military change at the end of the Enlightenment, held at the *Akademie der*

Wissenschaften in Berlin; and a colloquium on the "new history of battle," sponsored by the French Centre d'études d'histoire de la Défense.[14] Most of the papers of the Berlin conference keep theory in the background, but many have a strong comparative and interdisciplinary orientation. Their subjects encompass themes from strategy to the social and cultural impact of war. The smaller French colloquium refers more often to theory in its effort to apply the findings of the – rather vaguely defined – "new history" and of the social sciences to the historical study of battle. The extent to which battle pertains to "l'histoire évènementelle" or to "l'histoire de la longue durée" is a major theme. Historians who are currently doing innovative work – that is, who ask and respond to new questions in ways that range from analytic narrative to highly theoretical methodologies – will judge these efforts differently. Some will find that conceptual and technological discussions lead to new insights; for others they restate and possibly distort the self-evident. But it must be remembered that innovation takes many forms: one of the most original works on war in recent decades, John Hale's *Artists and Warfare in the Renaissance* (1990), owes little to theoretical experimentation.

"La nouvelle histoire bataille" of the *Centre d'études d'histoire de la Défense*, and such related terms as "the new history of the soldier," or simply "the new military history," carry no precise meaning. They refer to expanded methodologies, and perhaps also to at least a partial thematic shift away from battle toward the interaction of armed power with other elements, although "the new history of battle" seems to return the focus to the subject of violence. To some the term suggests if not absolute change then a breakthrough; but a more widely accepted meaning appears to be an accumulation of separate innovations – drawn principally from social history, anthropology, and linguistics – which in the aggregate tip the balance from old to new. Some historians may find it useful to categorize their work as a way of setting it apart; but they and their readers should keep two points in mind: the history of armed power from which the new military history separates itself consists not merely of conventional battle narrative but of much else besides – comparative and interdisciplinary studies, and ways of dealing with their subject that go far beyond the traditional combination of operational history with the history of politics and diplomacy, to borrowings from sociology, social history, the history of ideas, even the history of the common soldier. In short, it is difficult to draw a line between the "old" and the "new." A second reservation is the necessarily time-bound character of the "new history." A new method soon becomes, if not old, then at least familiar and a point of departure for the next innovation.[15] Or does the "new military history" refer only to a given socio-cultural direction, which remains worthwhile even if it is no longer the newest? "The historical study of armies and war as keys to social history is now a well-travelled road," a reviewer noted several years ago of a monograph on medieval warfare published in 1994.[16] He could have made the same comment a decade or two earlier. In the end, the "new military history," like all terms of self-identification, conveys its full meaning only to the initiate.

In the history of armed power today, however it is labeled and however it combines with other disciplines, the subject of violence occupies an ambiguous place. Research on such topics as the relations of armed forces and society or the interaction of economics and war may actually lead away from it. Nevertheless, violence is central to every aspect of the historical study of war, even if it is only potentially present, as an institutional function that may never be implemented or as the intended or inadvertent consequence of policy.

Considered in this way, the subject of violence and its historical study may assume a number of different forms. To greater or lesser extent combat consists of violence, but descriptions and analyses of battle can turn violence into an antiseptic abstraction. Individual experiences are easily lost in the outline of the larger event, to say nothing of the notorious difficulty of reconstructing combat episodes, even when they are contemporary. The methodology developed by S.L.A. Marshall and others in World War II and Korea, of sending teams of observers and interviewers into action, has not yet fulfilled its early expectations. Put differently, violence, the defining element of war, remains in many respects something vague and poorly understood, which is not offset by knowledge of the outcome.

In another form, violence – whether innate in the human being or culturally and socially induced – may act as a cause or precondition of war. The issue obviously demands interdisciplinary exploration. Probably the most useful contribution the historian can make is to decipher what may be called the functional motives of particular conflicts. Biological and psychological factors and their manipulation may also be present in these motives, which nevertheless possess a distinctive defensive or aggressive existence of their own: the concern to maintain a measure of autonomy in the international system, the preservation of internal peace, the release of economic and social energies, and so forth. Michael Howard has given a clear summary of the matter from a historian's perspective in the title-essay of his collection, *The Causes of Wars*, revised edition (1973).

The protagonists in these conflicts are larger socio-political entities, ranging from tribes to nation-states, alliances, and international leagues. But it is the individual who has to bear and use arms. Even wars that are widely regarded as justified and that evoke public support, including the readiness to serve, can never wholly eliminate disparities between private and public interest. Evidence from the recent and more remote past tells us that some individuals, if given a choice, would rather accept the consequences of aggression or the destruction of a cherished political system than fight. Nor does the obligation to fight always fall evenly on every part of society. Throughout history, every conceivable type of society and political system has protected or excluded groups of the population from military service, and has employed official coercion and social pressure to compel other groups to serve – which is a particularly embracing form of violence, since it forces people not only to become potential victims but also potential agents of violence.

At times scholarship has minimized the disparities between the interests of the individual and of political and social authority, or – appealing to one or the other ideology – has folded the individual's interest into the larger cause of the community or the nation. At other times historians have attributed major significance to the separation. In either case, the fact that for the individual war may be a matter of life or death, and that it justifies behavior that in another context would be illegal and immoral, gives the historical interpretation of war its special character.

Every field of history has its own complexities. The history of armed power is burdened and charged with the intellectual and moral challenges of violence. Moral considerations may sharpen or blur the historian's vision, in any case they further complicate it. The fact that violence is a timeless and universal phenomenon, which extends from war to all areas of the human experience, makes the subject still more difficult to interpret within the confines of an academic sub-discipline. But the difficulties also suggest the field's significance. Historians who study violence in the many forms it has assumed in the institutions and uses of armed power explore an endlessly tragic but crucial element in history. If they penetrate to its core, to the psychological and social motives and implications of violence, their interpretations will not only add greatly to our knowledge and understanding of the past, they will also possess a relevance that goes far beyond it.

NOTES

1   Niccolo Machiavelli, *Istorie fiorentine*, Milan, 1962, pp. 68–9.
2   Francois Marie Arouet de Voltaire, *Siècle de Louis XIV, Oeuvres complètes*, 19, Deux-Ponts, 1791, pp. 59–60.
3   Ibid., pp. 145–8.
4   Frederick the Great, *Histoire de la guerre de sept ans, Oeuvres*, ed. J. D. E. Preuss, 4, Berlin, 1847.
5   Johannes von Müller, *Die Geschichten der Schweitzer*, Boston [i.e. Bern], 1780, p. 444.
6   The first three chapters of *Observations on Prussia in her Great Catastrophe* are included in Carl von Clausewitz, *Historical and Political Writings*, ed. Peter Paret and Daniel Moran, Princeton, 1992, pp. 30–84.
7   Hans Delbrück, *Geschichte der Kriegskunst im Rahmen der politischen Geschichte*, Berlin, 1962, 1, p. 1. The slightly confusing syntax of Delbrück's statement is usually misinterpreted, and I have retranslated it. Walter J. Renfree has published an English version of the work, *History of the Art of War within the Framework of Political History*, Westport, CT, 1975– .

8   Otto Hintze, "Military Organization and the Organization of the State," in *The Historical Essays of Otto Hintze*, ed. Felix Gilbert, New York, 1975, p. 183.

9   Ibid., p. 300. The quotation from Felix Gilbert that follows is from his introductory note, ibid., p. 179.

10 In 1954 a survey of 493 colleges and universities showed that no more than 37 offered or intended to offer one – or in a few cases more than one – course in military history. Louis Morton, "The Historian and the Study of War," *Mississippi Valley Historical Review* 48/4 (March 1952), p. 601. Another study, eight years later, arrived at a comparable result, Dexter Perkins and John L. Snell, *The Education of Historians in the United States*, New York, 1962, p. 76.

11 Michael Howard, *War and the Liberal Conscience*, New Brunswick, 1978, p. 10.

12 Richard A. Preston and Sydney F. Wise, *Men in Arms: A History of Warfare and its Interrelationships with Western Society*, New York, 1970, p. 1. The work, which went through several revisions, is a knowledgeable and clearly organized survey, but despite its introduction retains a conventionally military focus.

13. In a recent article, "Four-Star Generalists," in *The Atlantic Monthly* (October 1999), Robert D. Kaplan argues that "at a time when the humanities are perceived as a domain of lackluster academics," the great popular interest in war makes popular military history particularly important as a mediator between scholarship and society. The author has little to say about content but stresses the need for "clear, nonacademic prose," which is to ignore the explanatory potential that linguistic and other social science theories may possess, and rightly or wrongly equates popular and narrative history.

14 *Die Wiedererweckung des Krieges*, ed. Joachim Kunisch and Herfried Münkler, Berlin, 1999; *Nouvelle Histoire Bataille*, No. 9 of the Cahiers du Centre d'études d'histoire de la Défense, Paris, 1999.

15 For a discussion of the new military history in the early 1990s, see my essay "The History of War and the New Military History," in Peter Paret, *Understanding War: Essays on Clausewitz and the History of Military Power*, Princeton, 1992.

16 Olivier Guyotjeannin, review of Andrew Ayton, *Knights and Warhorses. Military Service and the English Aristocracy under Edward III*, Bury St. Edmunds, 1994, in *Mediavistik*, 11 (1998).

REFERENCES AND FURTHER READING

Best, Geoffrey, *War and Law since 1945*, Oxford, 1994.

Browning, Christopher, *Ordinary Men: Reserve Police Battalion 101 and the Final Solution in Poland*, New York, 1993. A profound study of the rank-and-file in ideological war.

Coddington, Edwin B., *The Gettysburgh Campaign: A Study in Command*, New York, 1968. Exemplary, unusually comprehensive campaign history.

Coffman, Edward M., *The Old Army: A Portrait of the American Army in Peacetime, 1784–1898*, New York, 1988. Non-theoretical, intensely specific social history.

Doughty, Robert A., The *Breaking Point: Sedan and the Fall of France, 1940*, Hamden, CT, 1990. One of the best analytic narratives of a segment of the Second World War.

The Harmon Memorial Lectures in Military History, 1959–1987, ed. Harry Borowski, Washington, DC, 1988. Thirty lectures sponsored by the US Air Force Academy, beginning with a talk, "Why Military History," by W. Frank Craven.

Howard, Michael, *The Franco-Prussian War*, New York, 1961. A model history of a war from its origins to its aftereffects.

Makers of Modern Strategy from Machiavelli to the Nuclear Age, ed. Peter Paret, Princeton, 1986. Twenty-eight essays on theorists and practitioners of war.

Mallett, Michael, *Mercenaries and the Masters: Warfare in Renaissance Italy*, London, 1974. A masterly knitting together of the essential military and non-military issues.

Paret, Peter, *Imagined Battles: Reflections of War in European Art*, Chapel Hill, 1997. An interdisciplinary essay in the history of war, art, and culture.

Parker, Geoffrey, *The Army of Flanders and the Spanish Road, 1567–1659*, New York, 1972. The administrative and logistic mechanics of warfare in early modern Europe.

Redlich, Fritz, *The German Military Enterpriser and his Work Force: A Study in European Social and Economic History*, 2 vols., Wiesbaden, 1964–5.

Shy, John W., *A People Numerous and Armed: Reflections on the Military Struggle for American Independence*, New York, 1976. Military history that expands into the history of society and of mentalities.

CHAPTER THIRTEEN

Total History and Microhistory: The French and Italian Paradigms

DAVID A. BELL

In 1963, physicists Murray Gell-Mann and George Zweig postulated the existence of the sub-atomic particles called quarks – the ultimate smallest building blocks of matter. Just two years later, researchers at Bell Laboratories in
New Jersey, working with a new generation of radio telescopes, found a faint
signal emanating from literally the entire sky – wherever they chose to look.
At first they attributed the phenomenon to human interference or equipment
defects, but astrophysicists soon came to realize that they had detected nothing
less than the distant echoes of the primordial Big Bang. They were seeing
nearly to the beginning of time and the limits of the universe.

In a century marked by such a huge expansion in the human sense of scale,
it is perhaps no surprise that historians, in their own way, also undertook radical
experiments with the scale on which they observed their subject matter. In the
years after World War II, French historians linked to the famous historical
journal *Annales: Economies, sociétés, civilisations* took the lead in advocating a
"total history" that would bring geographical, demographic, economic, social,
political and cultural approaches to the past into a single capacious embrace.
More recently, historians in both France and Italy have taken the lead in advocating something of the reverse: microhistory, or the use of particularly rich
documentary sources to put individuals, events or social networks under the
historical equivalent of the electron microscope.

Both total history and microhistory emerged out of history's complex relationship with the social sciences, yet paradoxically, both also embodied a desire
to move away from social science and to recapture something of history's initial
vocation as an expressive art form. Total history admittedly enjoyed its great
vogue at the moment of the profession's most intense engagement with quantification in the 1960s and 1970s. Yet the breathtaking ambition of leaping
from the scattered traces found in archives and libraries to the "totality" of
past human existence demanded impressive efforts of the imagination as well

as of the calculator. Works like Fernand Braudel's *The Mediterranean* derived their power not only from the statistics their authors marshaled, but from poetic evocations of the living landscape – "the half-wild mountains, where man has taken root like a hardy plant," the desert's "devouring landscape, like the 'unharvested sea' of Homer . . . Immensity and emptiness: poverty and destitution."[1]

Microhistory, meanwhile, has explicitly rejected large-scale social scientific models, so as to focus in minute detail on particular individuals, dense tissues of inter-personal relationships, and the operation of human free will. Many of the most successful microhistories have evoked illustrative episodes in the past with cinematic intensity: early eighteenth-century New Englanders kidnapped from their homes to Canada by Iroquois in the depths of winter, the weak and wounded left to die in the snow or finished by a quick hatchet blow; Parisian apprentices gleefully slaughtering cats in a symbolic strike at their master; a young widow in Renaissance Florence angrily turning on her lover after he denied their secret marriage and married another woman; a sixteenth-century French adventurer posing as a long-lost soldier, accepted even by his purported wife, until his discovery, trial and execution (this last episode actually made it to the screen, in *The Return of Martin Guerre*).[2] Certain microhistories have much the same relation to film that the great nineteenth-century works of narrative history did to the novel.

"Total History" and Levels of Historical Experience

Unlike microhistory, "total history" never became a distinct genre, with a recognizable canon of works and an accompanying theoretical literature.[3] To begin with, the idea was hardly an invention of the twentieth century. Varieties of total history had appeared at many stages of the profession's development, notably in the Enlightenment turn towards the "history of society," and in the early twentieth-century American "New History." James Harvey Robinson wrote in 1912: "History includes every trace and vestige of everything that man has done or thought since first he appeared on earth." Recent French practitioners of "total history" have themselves differed as to the meaning of the term. Fernand Braudel (1902–86), the leader of the *Annales* school of social history, used the phrase to describe his masterpiece *The Mediterranean*.[4] Yet subsequent French "total history" took shape as much in reaction against Braudel as in emulation of him.

A certain idea of totality – of capturing the organic whole of a society through scientific description and analysis – can be traced back through the *Annales* school to the work of the sociologist Emile Durkheim and his follower François Simiand, at the turn of the twentieth century. Durkheim paid close attention to the religious and cultural bonds that unite societies. Simiand, however, tended to exclude matters of culture and belief, and also singular events, from the field of social scientific research. In writings that would have enormous influence on French historians, he argued that properly scientific analysis demanded quantifiable subject material available in consistent form over extended periods of time, such as wheat or land prices, the size of land-holdings, or numbers of births and deaths. He therefore urged historians to concentrate rigorously on these "serial" sources, while shunning both cultural matters and singular or accidental occurrences, which he scornfully labeled "*histoire événementielle*."[5] Braudel shared this point of view, dismissing events as mere foam on the surface of history that distracted attention from the more significant deep currents of geological, social, and economic change.

In *The Mediterranean*, Braudel did seek to master an unprecedentedly broad span of human experience, ranging from the geological *longue durée* through the medium-term ebb and flow of economic cycles down to the political *courte durée* of political history in the reign of Spain's Philip II. In the process, he marvellously captured the relationship between human beings, their physical environment, and the movement of money and goods. His work helped usher in a golden age of historical geography (a subject in which he, and many of his students, had received formal training), and also of quantitative economic history. But in keeping with Simiand's creed, he downplayed the importance of events, and almost entirely ignored the worlds of culture and ideas. The great wave of *Annales* social history of the 1940s and 1950s followed his example. Typical of the spirit of the time was the great economic historian Ernest Labrousse, who showed how the price of grain in Paris reached a record high immediately before the fall of the Bastille in 1789, and triumphantly declared of the French economy: "tout dérive de la courbe" (everything follows from the curve of prices).[6]

But of course not *everything* follows from the curve, and no truly "total" history can limit itself to the geographical, social, and economic. It was out of this recognition that the next generation of the *Annales* proposed adding a fourth level of historical experience to Braudel's tripartite scheme of geo-logical, economic and short-term political change. They labeled this fourth level "*mentalités*," a broad and imprecise term which covered everything from religious beliefs to popular entertainment to the traditional forms of high culture, giving little consideration to distinctions of class or gender. Yet despite this imprecision, "mentalities history" enjoyed a great vogue in the 1950s and 1960s, and at its most successful offered an innovative perspective on the history of shared cultural assumptions. Robert Mandrou offered one stimulat-ing example in a general history of early modern France to which he gave the subtitle "An Essay in Historical Psychology." Philippe Ariès, an independent historian working in tandem with the *Annales*, brilliantly illuminated chang-ing attitudes towards children, arguing that only in the modern period did childhood come to be seen as a distinct, and uniquely innocent, phase of life. And yet another successful deployment came in a work which explicitly proclaimed itself an "adventure in total history": Emmanuel Le Roy Ladurie's 1966 *The Peasants of Languedoc*.[7]

Le Roy Ladurie's research began with exactly the sort of "serial" sources advocated by Simiand, notably records of the tithe and landholdings in the large sourthern French province of Languedoc from the fifteenth to the eighteenth centuries. With their help, he traced out what he called a "great agrarian cycle," as the population rose from its "low water-mark" after the Black Death, to crest and swell and dash itself against the inflexible growth limits imposed by the prevailing agricultural technology, plunging the peasantry into misery, despair, and revolt. Like Braudel, Le Roy Ladurie firmly located this history in geography, evoking in lyrical accents the flow of men and animals over mountains and through valleys. Like Braudel, he carefully delineated patterns of change in trade and industry, and paid due attention to politics as well. But unlike Braudel, he also extended his grasp to the great religious and cultural phenomena of his period, especially the spread of literacy and the penetration of the Reformation into southern France. While eschewing the rigid determinism of much Marxist analysis, he nonetheless showed how Protestantism appealed most strongly to particular social classes (especially artisans), and had its greatest success precisely at a moment of maximum economic misery.

The Peasants of Languedoc represented a clear conceptual advance beyond *The Mediterranean*. Yet it came at a price, for Le Roy Ladurie only achieved his fuller version of "total history" by drastically reducing the scale of observation: from a great sea, its myriad coasts and their hinterlands, to a single, relatively homogeneous province. Nor was Le Roy Ladurie an exception in this regard. Rather than imitating Braudel, Le Roy Ladurie's generation of *Annalistes* hewed to the map of France, carving it up to study one province after another, or even smaller regions such as the Beauvaisis, the subject of Pierre Goubert's majestic doctoral thesis. Others tightened the focus even further in the 1960s and 1970s, limiting their research to single cities.[8] True "totality," it was coming to appear, simply could not be captured on the large canvas envisioned by Braudel. To the contrary, it required studying human society in microcosm, taking inspiration as much from William Blake as from Durkheim: "to see a world in a grain of sand." "Total history" was eliding into microhistory.

Once again, Le Roy Ladurie led the way. Even while recounting the epic of his great agrarian cycle, he had not been able to resist pausing at length to savor a particularly colorful and evocative event: the bloody strife in the town of Romans in 1580, when the starving lower classes, reduced to eating grass, used the symbolic forms of the annual Carnival to challenge the position of their masters, and in response were massacred.[9] Still, these pages of *The Peasants of Languedoc* remained faithful to the *Annales*' social scientific perspective, for they used the Carnival principally to illustrate the working out of "deeper," more fundamental social and economic forces. Le Roy Ladurie did not portray the people of Romans as independent actors, and did not present the event as a significant example of historical change in its own right. In the classic *Annales* fashion, the true motors of change remained the slow, long-term cycles of geography, demography, and economics. Microhistory as a genre of its own would only take shape when historians, in addition to changing the scale of their observations, also revolted against the idea that the microcosm did little but passively reflect the macrocosm.

Disillusionment and the Turn to Microhistory

This revolt against the social scientific paradigms that had engendered "total history" began in the 1970s, and it followed from a process of triple disillusionment. In the first case, there was a methodological disillusionment with quantitative social science. Were historians justified in taking categories initially designed for studying contemporary industrial societies subject to ceaseless statistical measurement and polling – categories such as income, wealth, profession, class, political allegiance – and imposing them on the very imperfect records of the very different societies of the past? Was not something lost in aggregating thousands or millions of persons, who had not even thought in such terms, into a "proletariat" or "bourgeoisie"? And did not the mechanical procedures used by computers in large-scale quantification only compound the problem? In an intellectual climate increasingly shaped by French post-structuralist philosophy, the great, overarching abstractions used by the social scientists seemed increasingly unsatisfactory, and increasingly vulnerable to the pinpricks of close reading. Skeptics found a champion in the English social historian E. P. Thompson, who railed in memorably sharp and witty phrases about the distortions of the past entailed by a blind devotion to social scientific models, not to mention "the gross reiterative impressionism of a computer, which repeats one conformity *ad nauseam* while obliterating all evidence for which it has not been programmed."[10] It is no accident that, although Thompson was not himself a microhistorian, the leading Italian practitioners of the genre frequently cite him as an authority. In his emphasis on the autonomous agency of even the poorest and weakest members of society, on the shifting, malleable nature of social categories and group identities, and on the importance of reconstructing the living texture of past experience, Thompson had a critical influence.

The second disillusionment was political. Before 1970 much of the historical profession in Europe had belonged to the militant left, often communist, and had paid at least lip service to one or another variety of "scientific" Marxism. But, as Giovanni Levi has written, after 1970 there began "years of crisis for the prevailing optimistic belief that the world would be rapidly and radically transformed along revolutionary lines."[11] Socialist regimes fought each other, while the triumph of communism in Southeast Asia led to genocide in Cambodia. The nascent environmental movement radically challenged the Left's confidence in technological progress. Thanks to the burgeoning feminist movement, women's liberation came to seem a more pressing and feasible matter than the triumph of the proletariat. In this changed atmosphere, a Marxist ideology rigidly focused on a reified "working class," and on the inevitable working out of vast historical forces, seemed increasingly irrelevant. Far more attractive was a Thompsonian vision of "history from below" in which the common people, rather than acting in lockstep obedience to historical "laws" and the dictates of "vanguard" parties, acted to shape their own identities and destinies.

Finally, there took place what might best be called a professional disillusionment. During the 1950s and 1960s, throughout the Western world, the historical profession, along with universities in general, had undergone enormous expansion and professionalization. Systems of higher education once largely restricted to social elites, and marked by a distinctly aristocratic sensibility, mutated into vast bureaucratic organizations welcoming half or more of successive age cohorts. To establish credentials, and justify promotion, historians in this new system found themselves under greater pressure than ever before to publish, while at the same time competing with a swelling number of colleagues to say significant things about the historical source material. The result, inevitably, was hyper-specialization, with an ever-narrower focus on ever-narrower topics, and the establishment of myriad subfields, each with their own journals, book series, conferences and organizations. The idea of history as a uniquely accessible subject, of interest to a general educated public, seemed increasingly remote to most of its professional practitioners. The triumph of rigorous social science methodologies, and the social scientific emphasis on history as a series of problems and narrow case studies, rather than a series of stories, only heightened these tendencies.

To be sure, these three disillusionments were not felt equally across international borders. Professional disillusionment was felt far more strongly in Britain and America than in France, where leaders of the profession like Braudel and Le Roy Ladurie maintained significant public visibility. In Italy, the commitment to a "scientific" history remained strong, while concern for readability and engaging with the general public had relatively little importance. Political disillusionment played out differently in Italy, where left-wing militancy had been widespread among dynamic younger historians, than in France, where many *Annalistes* had remained aloof from it (or, as in Le Roy Ladurie's case, had left activism behind after brief, youthful flings with the Communist Party). Nonetheless, the three disillusionments created an overall framework in which microhistory could emerge and flourish.

In the middle of the 1970s, there appeared two works which together would establish the genre. While both were devoted to what previous generations of historians would have considered mere footnotes to history, their broad implications, impressive literary qualities, and refusal to emulate the model of social scientific case studies made them anything but hyperspecialized or inaccessible. In 1975, the indefatigable Le Roy Ladurie published *Montaillou*, the study of a southern French village in the high middle ages.[12] The Albigensian heresy had flourished in this small, remote location, and in the early fourtheenth century a rigid and domineering Inquisitor, Jacques Fournier, had taken the extraordinary step of arresting virtually the entire population and subjecting them to detailed interrogations. The resulting, lengthy records were well known, but Le Roy Laduire read them in a new, ingenious way. Instead of focusing yet again on the heresy and its repression, he carefully picked out the small, banal details of daily life that emerged in the course of the prisoners' responses, and used them to reconstruct a picture of the village as a whole. As he himself put it, he treated the interrogatories as anthropological reports from the field. Women exchanging gossip while delousing each other, a priest preying sexually on his parishioners, a shepherd leading his flock on long, patient treks through the Pyrenees: with great skill, Le Roy Ladurie wove such vignettes into a brilliant tapestry, centered on the mundane image of the *ostal*, or household, which dominated the villagers' economic and social lives, and also their thoughts of heaven. It is true that, except in its choice of scale, the book did not offer a particularly sharp challenge to the *Annales* paradigm. As in the earlier treatment of the Carnival at Romans, Le Roy Ladurie presented his subjects as evocative, but still somewhat passive illustrations of much larger general patterns. Yet the extraordinarily vivid portrayals of forgotten individuals went beyond the analysis of social structures, won *Montaillou* a large audience, and opened up new vistas for the profession as a whole.

Just one year later, Carlo Ginzburg published a work of even greater import: *The Cheese and the Worms*. Like Le Roy Ladurie, Ginzburg had plunged into the wonderfully rich records of the Catholic Inquisition, and found a heresy case of irresistible color and interest. Unlike Le Roy Ladurie, however, he did not treat the heresy as incidental, but made it the breathing center of his story. The case involved an obscure Friulian miller, known as Menocchio, first arrested in 1584 and finally put to death in the last year of the sixteenth century. Under interrogation, he expounded a bizarre, idiosyncratic series of beliefs: "I have said that, in my opinion, all was chaos, that is earth, air, water and fire were mixed together; and out of that bulk a mass formed – just as cheese is made out of milk – and worms appeared in it, and these were the angels." Menocchio's "cosmos" appeared both relativistic and materialist, and on occasion he even invoked the Koran. In an impressive piece of historical detection, Ginzburg determined which books Menocchio had read, how he had read them, and how, in the dynamic context of the Reformation and the invention of printing, the miller had come to express his conclusions openly. Ginzburg also argued, provocatively, that in the final analysis, Menocchio had made use of confused fragments of advanced philosophy and theology "to express the elemental, instinctive material of generation after generation of peasants" – that his trial transcript provided a blurred look into nothing less than an essentially autonomous, ancient, unwritten peasant culture.[13] Unlike Le Roy Ladurie, Ginzburg gave a strong sense of his subjects as active agents in history, helping to shape cultural patterns rather than simply reflecting them.

Microhistory of the Extraordinary, Microhistory of the Ordinary

In the quarter-century since these books appeared, and in large part following from their example, microhistory has emerged as a significant historical genre. It has also increasingly split into two distinct currents, which might be labelled "the microhistory of the extraordinary" and the "microhistory of the ordinary."[14] The first and better-known of these takes as its principal subject either an extraordinary set of sources, or an extraordinary event, or both. Often drawing explicit inspiration from the cultural anthropology of Clifford Geertz, historians have used these materials as privileged texts offering points of entry into unfamiliar cultures.[15] In many cases, the historians' own posture as intrepid explorers has reinforced this anthropological analogy: the silt of time having formed a thick coat over many of the cases, they came to light only thanks to the historians' own forays deep into the alien cultures buried under the dust and clutter of the archives. Thus Gene Brucker, exploring the rich notarial and judicial sources of early modern Florence, uncovered the bitter quarrel between Lusanna di Girolamo and her alleged secret husband Giovanni di Ser Lodovico della Casa. In the same sources, Judith Brown found a dossier pertaining to the life of a lesbian nun, Benedetta Carlini of Vellano, who was first investigated for her unusual mystical experiences, including the appearance of stigmata on her body. David Sabean's long-term social historical research in the archives of Württemberg turned up a number of fascinating episodes – including the murder of a village pastor and the live burial of a village bull – which he used to explore the relations between peasant communities and the state in early modern Germany.[16]

Other microhistories have returned to events that generated extensive commentary at the time, yet even here the historians could generally claim to have rescued extraordinary material from undeserved obscurity. This was the case, most strikingly, with the "return of Martin Guerre," the story mentioned above of the sixteenth-century Frenchman who took on another's identity, lived for a time with his wife, was discovered, tried and executed, and then largely forgotten until Natalie Zemon Davis retold the story in the 1980s. Similarly, Arlette Farge and Jacques Revel's *Logiques de la foule* reexamined a famous set of riots in mid-eighteenth-century Paris, subjecting the police dossiers to close readings so as to tease out the radical political implications of what appeared, on the surface, a panic over the alleged kidnapping of children by the police. Richard Kagan revisited the fascinating case of Lucrecia de Léon, controversially put on trial by the Inquisition in Toledo in the 1590s, after transcripts of her visionary dreams began to circulate widely in manuscript. John Demos sought a new perspective on the famous case of New Englanders taken as prisoners to Canada, highlighting not the famous preacher who returned to Massachusetts, but his daughter who remained "unredeemed," eventually converting to Catholicism, marrying a Mohawk Indian, and refusing to return to her family.[17]

In a 1979 article, Carlo Ginzburg and Carlo Poni presented "microstoria" as a newly successful Italian export that had managed to upset a pattern of French–Italian intellectual trade long weighted in favor of France. Indeed, in the late 1970s and early 1980s the Italian journal *Quaderni storici* led the way in publishing examples of the new genre, drawing on the richness of the Italian archives.[18] Yet as the material cited above suggests, the use of microhistory in pursuit of the "extraordinary" has perhaps had the greatest influence among American historians eager to engage with a broader reading public, and to reinvent history as a narrative form. Historians such as John Demos, Jonathan Spence, James Goodman and Simon Schama, investigating subjects that range from Qing China to 1930s Alabama, have all treated their works as experiments, not only in historical form, but in narrative style.[19] Goodman told the story of Alabama's "Scottsboro Boys," black youths whose trial for raping two white women became an American *cause célèbre*, from multiple perspectives, in an approach that owed something to Akira Kurosawa's film *Rashomon* as well as to more conventional historical narratives.

This fascination with narrative, often with cinematic accents, has not only led American microhistorians far from the engagements with social science described above, it has also generated two important critiques of the genre. First, it has been charged, microhistorians have let their desire to tell a good story trump serious engagement with the problematic nature of their source material. In most cases, this material was compiled by legal authorities – both secular and religious – who followed particular, formulaic textual conventions, recorded evidence in accordance with rigid rules of procedure, and even altered the original language of testimony (for instance, the Inquisition translated Montaillou villagers' Occitan into Latin, which Le Roy Ladurie then rendered into French). In a critique of Brucker's *Giovanni and Lusanna*, Thomas Kuehn suggested that microhistorians, eager to see themselves as anthropologists working with native informants, "have . . . broadly assumed the transparency of their narrative representations." Yet Brucker's trial records, Kuehn pointed out, contained not one, single, transparent story, but two conflicting ones, recounted by the competing parties in the formulaic language of the law. They offered no certain way of piercing through the narrative veil to grasp a true, underlying reality. Robert Darnton's mesmerizing account of the "Great Cat Massacre of the Rue Saint-Séverin," which he based on a fictionalized, formulaic memoir written years after the fact, has received similar criticism.[20]

Further problems are posed by narrative styles that treat historical subjects like the characters of a novel or film: can such works avoid anachronistically imposing a present-day sense of motivation onto figures in an alien past? In *Martin Guerre*, for instance, Natalie Davis highlighted not only the extraordinary imposter, Armand du Tilh, but also Bertrande de Rols, the woman who accepted Armand as her long-lost husband Martin Guerre. Davis depicted de Rols as a spirited, independent agent, a woman struggling to carve out the best possible destiny for herself in a patriarchal world. Did the evidence justify this interpretation, or was the book projecting a modern feminist sensibility onto the sixteenth century?[21] Similarly, in the most controversial pages of *The Unredeemed Captive*, John Demos speculated as to how the young Eunice Williams might have reacted to seeing her father after many years of separation, imputing to her a sense of resentment and anger that may have reflected twentieth-century notions of parent–child relations as much as or more than the eighteenth-century sources.

The second path taken by microhistory has largely skirted these potential pitfalls of presentist projections onto the past, and attracted a different set of critiques. Here the focus has been not on the extraordinary, but precisely on the ordinary and mundane, or at most on what Edoardo Grendi has called the "normal exception" – actions that violate certain norms, thereby leaving traces in the archives, but that do so routinely. Alain Corbin has gone to particular lengths to ensure that his choice of subject did not correspond to any extraordinary or retroactive criteria, quite literally blindfolding himself in the archives, choosing a dossier at random, and using it as the starting point for the biography of an "unknown man."[22] This second form of microhistory, like the first, also operates on the smallest possible scale, and also requires rich, dense archival material. But rather than privileging certain especially colorful materials as points of entry into a foreign culture, it seeks to pick apart the tangled tissue of ordinary, banal, interpersonal relations, so as to reveal what Giovanni Levi, its most influential practitioner, calls "an individual's constant negotiation, manipulation, choices and decisions in the face of a normative reality which, though pervasive, nevertheless offers many possibilities for personal interpretations and freedoms."[23]

To the extent that this microhistory of the ordinary takes inspiration from anthropology, it does not look to Durkheim, or even Geertz, who share important assumptions about the uniformity of cultures and the social scientist's ability to find a single key to those cultures. It relies much more heavily on

Erving Goffman's work on social interactions, and the Norwegian Fredrik Barth's stress on the incoherences, heterogeneities and conflicts within cultures, best grasped on a "micro" level. This microhistory claims not to read a culture as a static text, but rather to investigate processes of change and conflict in as detailed a manner as possible. In this sense, as Jacques Revel has noted, it remains close to "the old dream of a total history, but this time reconstructed from the bottom up."[24] It also tends to pay very close attention to the ordinary conventions and formulae employed in its sources, because to a large extent its purpose is precisely to track and understand changes in the conventions and categories through which individuals understand the social world.

This variety of social history has remained very much an Italian specialty, although thanks to the influence of Jacques Revel, leader of what remains of the *Annales* school, it has also had a considerable impact in France, extending even to the history of the French Revolution. Its best-known work is Giovanni Levi's 1985 *Inheriting Power: The Story of an Exorcist*.[25] Despite the title, which hinted at a flashy, Ginzburgian tale of heresy, readers instead found a dense, meticulous, "total history" of the small seventeenth-century Piedmontese village of Santena over a fifty-year period. Levi paid particular attention to the strategies employed by individuals, families, and groups to maintain and advance their social position and landholdings, focusing on the judge Giulio Cesare Chiesa and his son, a vicar and exorcist. In the book, as throughout his work, Levi emphasized the slow, uncertain, constantly negotiated manner by which a traditional feudal economy changed, rejecting theories of sharp, sudden, large-scale transitions carried out by forces beyond the control of the participants. It is vintage "history from below," but deliberately confined to the smallest possible space, teasing all possible meaning out of the often-mundane source material.

Like the Anglo-American "New Cultural History," Levi's style of microhistory has proven particularly effective in tracing out the processes by which terms such as "class," "profession," and "gender" acquired new and potent meanings. Yet where the Anglo-American historians have mostly seen these processes as impersonal, and studied them by applying linguistic analysis to political and literary texts, the Italian microhistorians have used small-scale archival analysis and stressed individual agency, showing how meaning slowly changes in response to a succession of individual decisions. It is an approach which requires painstaking, enormously detailed analysis and frequently makes for exceptionally difficult reading – quite different from "extraordinary" microhistory. Works of "ordinary" microhistory often lack a clear thesis and make uncertain contributions to larger historical dialogues. But where successful, as in Simona Cerutti's study of the rise of professional corporate bodies in early-modern Turin, they illuminate the complexity of historical change in such a manner as to defeat any attempt blithely to project sweeping, present-day social scientific assumptions back onto the past.[26]

Microhistory and the Problem of Generalization

It is precisely in the problem of integrating the microscopic scale of observation with other, larger ones that microhistory of both varieties has remained most unsatisfying. Of what, if anything, was the seventeenth-century village of Santena typical? Giovanni Levi does not say. Once historians have highlighted the individual agency of landowners or artisans in a single community at a single moment in time, how do they then proceed to understand the aggregate history of thousands or millions of landowners or artisans over a time-span of centuries? Few microhistorians have matched Carlo Ginzburg's daring in generalizing from the experience of a single individual to that of an entire peasant culture across the centuries. Gareth Stedman-Jones has scathingly criticized microhistorians, particularly Levi and his French followers, arguing that their emphasis on individual agency prevents them from even considering the wide range of historical phenomena which require analysis at a broad, general level. For Brad Gregory, the attention to individuals, and the abandonment of any attempt to elucidate long-term historical forces and laws, "exaggerates both the fragility of large institutions and the contingency of their development."[27]

It is in facing such questions about the relation between the particular and the general that the analogy with the physical sciences, so frequently employed in discussions of microhistory and total history, finally breaks down. In studying the physical world, scientists can count on a uniformity of physical laws across all their scales of observation, whether they are looking at quarks or quasars. But nothing of the sort can be assumed about social interactions. In discussing individual decisions, historians and other social scientists look to a host of situation-specific psychological, cultural, social, and political factors which can be related only with great approximation and difficulty to the impersonal social, political, and economic factors which govern the behavior of humans in the aggregate. Drawing connections between these two disparate scales has of course been one of the great challenges of the social sciences since their birth in the eighteenth century. Microhistory has clarified the problem by drawing renewed atttention to the problem of scale itself, but it cannot be said to have yet offered many new and persuasive answers.

In short, microhistory, like "total history" before it, has a mixed balance sheet. Particularly in its Anglo-American manifestations, it has provided a new, vivid genre of historical writing that has helped revive history as a narrative art, and has thereby aided the historical education of a general reading public outside the walls of academia. Both varieties of microhistory have highlighted the agency and autonomy of individuals throughout history, including especially women and members of the lower classes. In this way, microhistory has returned real men and women to the center of the historical enterprise, and helped call many arrogantly overarching generalizations about social processes into question. Finally, perhaps most importantly, microhistory has put the problem of scale itself at the heart of the historical enterprise, making historians aware that they cannot take their organizing frameworks for granted but need to adjust their scale of observation to the problem at hand.

Yet these accomplishments are offset by significant problems. The vividness of "extraordinary" microhistory has often come at the expense of satisfactory engagement with stubbornly problematic source material. The meticulous engagement with the sources on the part of "ordinary" microhistory has often come at the expense not only of vividness, but of clarity and coherence. And the genre as a whole has as yet proven frustratingly incapable of integrating its microscopic scale of analysis with the larger ones through which we organize our overall sense of the past. In short, the microhistorical lens has shown us many grains of sand in all their strange and often wonderful detail and complexity, but it has not yet found the world in them.

NOTES

1   Fernand Braudel, *The Mediterranean and the Mediterranean World in the Age of Philip II*, Siân Reynolds, trans., two vols. (New York, 1972), vol. I, pp. 29, 173.

2   John Demos, *The Unredeemed Captive: A Family Story from Early America* (New York, 1994); Robert Darnton, *The Great Cat Massacre and Other Episodes in French Cultural History* (New York, 1984); Gene Brucker, *Giovanni and Lusanna: Love and Marriage in Renaissance Florence* (Berkeley, 1986); Natalie Zemon Davis, *The Return of Martin Guerre* (Cambridge, MA, 1983).

3   It would be an exaggeration to speak of a united "school" of microhistory, but it has certainly emerged as a distinct genre, to judge by the anthologies and the-oretical literature that has accumulated around it. See especially Edward Muir and Guido Ruggiero, eds., *Microhistory and the Lost Peoples of Europe*, trans. Eren Branch (Baltimore, 1991); Florike Egmond and Peter Mason, *The Mammoth and the Mouse: Microhistory and Morphology* (Baltimore, 1997); Jacques Revel, ed., *Jeux d'échelles: La micro-analyse à l'expérience* (Paris, 1996).

4   Quoted in Peter Burke, *The French Historical Revolution: The Annales School, 1929–89* (London, 1990), p. 9; Braudel, vol. II, p. 1238.

5   Quoted in Fernand Braudel, "History and the Social Sciences: The *Longue Durée*," in Jacques Revel and Lynn Hunt, eds., *Histories: French Constructions of the Past* (New York, 1995), pp. 115–45, quote from p. 118.

6   C.-E. Labrousse, *La crise de l'économie française à la fin de l'ancien régime et au début de la Révolution* (Paris, 1944), p. xxix.

7   Robert Mandrou, *Introduction à la France moderne (1500–1640): Essai de psychologie historique* (Paris, 1961); Philippe Ariès, *L'enfant et la vie familiale sous l'ancien régime* (Paris, 1960); Emmanuel Le Roy Ladurie, *The Peasants of Languedoc*, trans. John Day (Urbana, 1974, orig. Paris, 1966).

8   Pierre Goubert, *Beauvais et le Beauvaisis de 1600 à 1730* (Paris, 1960); Maurice Garden, *Lyon et le Lyonnais au XVIIIe siècle* (Paris, 1975); Jean-Claude Perrot, *Genèse d'une ville moderne: Caen au XVIIIe siècle* (Paris, 1975).

9   Le Roy Ladurie, *The Peasants of Languedoc*, pp. 192–7.

10 Quoted in Carlo Ginzburg, *The Cheese and the Worms: The Cosmos of a Sixteenth-Century Miller*, trans. John and Anne Tedeschi (London, 1980 [orig. 1976]), p. xxi.

11 Giovanni Levi, "On Microhistory," in Peter Burke, ed., *New Perspectives on Historical Writing* (University Park, Pennsylvania, 1992), pp. 93–113, quote from p. 93.

12 Emmanuel Le Roy Ladurie, *Montaillou, village occitan de 1294 à 1324* (Paris, 1975).

13 Ginzburg, *The Cheese and the Worms*, quotes from pp. 5–6, 61.

14 The following discussion is endebted to Brad Gregory, "*Is* Small Beautiful? Microhistory and the History of Everyday Life," *History and Theory* 38/1 (1999): 100–10. Gregory prefers a distinction between "episodic" and "systematic" microhistory. I find this somewhat unsatisfying, because certain of the "episodic" works rely more on the extraordinary nature of the documentation than on the unusual nature of the "episode" itself.

15 See esp. Clifford Geertz, *The Interpretation of Cultures: Selected Essays* (New York, 1973).

16 Brucker, *Giovanni and Lusanna*; Judith C. Brown, *Immodest Acts: The Life of a Lesbian Nun in Renaissance Italy* (Oxford, 1986); David Warren Sabean, *Power in the Blood: Popular Culture and Village Discourse in Early Modern Germany* (Cambridge, 1984).

17 Arlette Farge and Jacques Revel, *Logiques de la foule: l'affaire des enlèvements d'enfants*, Paris 1750 (Paris, 1988); Richard L. Kagan, *Lucrecia's Dreams: Politics and Prophecy in Sixteenth-Century Spain* (Berkeley, 1990); Demos, *The Unredeemed Captive*. Another remarkable American micro-history is Laurel Thatcher Ulrich's *A Midwife's Tale: The Life of Martha Ballard, Based on Her Diary* (New York, 1990).

18 Carlo Ginzburg and Carlo Poni, "Il nome e il come: scambio ineguale e mercato storiografico," *Quaderni storici*, no. 40 (1979), pp. 181–90. For a representative sample of this work see the articles collected in Muir and Ruggiero.

19 See, in addition to Demos, Jonathan Spence, *The Death of Woman Wang* (New York, 1976); James Goodman, *Stories of Scottsboro* (New York, 1994); Simon Schama, *Dead Certainties: Unwarranted Speculations* (New York, 1991).

20 Thomas Kuehn, "Reading Microhistory: The Example of *Giovanni and Lusanna*," *Journal of Modern History*, 61 (1989): 512–34, quote from p. 517; Robert Darnton, "The Great Cat Massacre of the Rue Saint-Séverin," in idem,

The Great Cat Massacre, pp. 73–101; Roger Chartier "Texts, Symbols and Frenchness," in idem, *Cultural History: Between Practices and Representations*, trans. Lydia Cochrane (Ithaca, 1988), pp. 95–111.

21 Robert Finlay, "The Refashioning of Martin Guerre," *American Historical Review* 93/3 (1988): 553–71. See also Natalie Zemon Davis's spirited response, "On the Lame," in ibid., pp. 572–603.

22 Quoted in Muir and Ruggiero, p. xv; Alain Corbin, *Le monde retrouvé de Louis-François Pinagot: sur les traces d'un inconnu, 1798–1876* (Paris, 1998).

23 Giovanni Levi, "On Microhistory," p. 94

24 Jacques Revel, "Microanalysis and the Construction of the Social," in Hunt and Revel, *Histories*, p. 497.

25 On the French Revolution, see Jean Boutier, "Les Courtiers locaux de la politique," *Annales historiques de la Révolution française*, vol. LXVI (1994), pp. 401–11; Giovanni Levi, *Inheriting Power: The Story of an Exorcist*, trans. Lydia Cochrane (Chicago, 1988, orig. 1985).

26 Simona Cerutti, *La ville et les métiers: Naissance d'un langage corporatif (Turin, 17e-18e siècles)* (Paris, 1990).

27 Gareth Stedman Jones, "Une autre histoire sociale? (note critique)," *Annales: Histoire, Sciences Sociales*, vol. LIII, no. 2, 1998, pp. 383–94; Gregory, "*Is* Small Beautiful?" p. 109.

REFERENCES AND FURTHER READING

Burke, Peter, *The French Historical Revolution: The Annales School, 1929–1989*, Cambridge: Polity Press, 1990.

Davis, Natalie Zemon, *The Return of Martin Guerre*, Cambridge, MA: Harvard University Press, 1983.

Ginzburg, Carlo, *The Cheese and the Worms: The Cosmos of a Sixteenth-Century Miller*, trans. Anne and John Tedeschi, Baltimore: Johns Hopkins University Press, 1980 [orig. 1976].

Le Roy Ladurie, Emmanuel, *Montaillou: The Promised Land of Error*, trans. Barbara Bray, New York: G. Braziller, 1978 [orig. 1975].

Levi, Giovanni, *Inheriting Power: The Story of an Exorcist*, trans. Lydia G. Cochrane, Chicago: University of Chicago Press, 1988 [orig. 1985].

Muir, Edward and Guido Ruggiero, eds., *Microhistory and the Lost Peoples of Europe*, trans. Eren Branch, Baltimore: Johns Hopkins University Press, 1991.

Revel, Jacques, "Microanalysis and the Construction of the Social," in Jacques Revel and Lynn Hunt, eds., *Histories: French Constructions of the Past*, trans. Arthur Goldhammer et al., New York: The New Press, 1995, pp. 492–502.

CHAPTER FOURTEEN

Anthropology and the History of Culture

WILLIAM M. REDDY

Anthropologists and historians began borrowing both theoretical ideas and research methods from each other with particular intensity about 1970. Soon the two disciplines came to share a number of concerns and buzzwords: "power" and "hegemony"; "identity" and "performance"; "diversity," "resistance," and "change"; "moral economy" and "political economy"; and of course newly minted conceptions of both "culture" and "history." But were they ever really speaking the same language? On the one side, historians talked about a trend called "the new cultural history"; on the other, anthropologists extolled the virtues of "historical ethnography." This terminological difference was but the tip of a larger iceberg of as yet unborrowed methods and unshared problems that were seldom noticed. Like star-crossed lovers, the two disciplines saw beautiful things when they looked in each other's eyes; but privately each wondered: "What does she see in me?" Both deplored the "old way" of doing things – although they associated this old way with quite different practices, often the very thing the other discipline was most anxious to borrow.

Anthropology is a field that is theoretical first and substantive second; like other social sciences it owes its existence to a theory (or, perhaps, a family of related theories). History is, by contrast, a constitutive feature of modernity itself. The modern consciousness of history dates back to the era of the French Revolution. It was only after the Revolution, as Leora Auslander and Susan Crane have shown, that Europeans began to become conscious of different historical periods as ineffably separate, distinctive, yet bound to each other by the incontrovertible logic of time's arrow.[1] Before 1789, current fashion consisted of whatever the king preferred. If he changed his taste in furniture, so did everyone else. Out with the old, in with the new. The Revolution only continued the same game, at first, legislating new fashions in clothing, in etiquette, in calendars. But after 1815, in the disillusioned afterglow of Waterloo, suddenly observers discovered the infinite charm of ruins and antiques: gothic, renaissance, baroque, rococo; battered cathedrals and bare ruined choirs lifted the spirits of poets to sublime heights. In addition, the schools of new nation-states needed stories to justify their existence. From that day to this, history's place in the curriculum has been as solid as marble. This helps to explain historians' relaxed attitude toward theoretical issues, their insouciant disdain for the details of epistemology. So long as one has the dust of archives on one's fingertips, the smell of decaying ink in one's nostrils, the faraway look of someone imaginatively engaged with reconstructing something dead and gone, one's work may be counted as useful. Anthropologists, by contrast, agonize over the politics of field work, and make embarrassed remarks about this outmoded "rite de passage" that still seems to define them better than anything else. From the time of Frazer and Durkheim to the present, they have had to scramble for new justifications of their discipline in tune with the West's most recent reconceptualization of its tumultuous relationship with the non-West. They have brought back travelers' tales from such far-flung venues that, to drum up interest and justify the effort, they have sought to link these tales with issues of universal concern: human nature, kinship, religion. But in the days of the jumbo jet and containers ships, they have lost their monopoly on travel. Contemporary theory has challenged their capacity to talk about the universal, as well. Thus, in the last twenty years, anthropologists have had to scramble more than usual.

This sharp contrast in foundations and the peculiarities of the current conjuncture help to explain why the relationship between the two disciplines has waxed and waned. In the 1970s, there was a sense of freshness and excitement about first contact on both sides of the disciplinary fence. But then in the early 1980s a rising generation of anthropologists discovered literary criticism, and the joys of deconstructing texts, and set out to "write culture." Historians were left to borrow without lending. Shortly thereafter, two-way exchange was overshadowed by the rise of postmodernism, as all work became, it seems, interdisciplinary. More recently, amid postmortems and debriefings – a general academic stock-taking that we seem to be unable to complete – the sense of a special relationship between the two disciplines, based on shared concerns, has grown dim.

The Sovereignty of Culture (1950–1970)

At the core of our mutual concerns and our mutual misunderstandings is the idea of "culture." Since 1980 or so, anthropologists have lost faith in this word; many interpreted this trend as a crisis, even a catastrophe for the discipline, since culture was its raison d'être. Others celebrated the end of the "imperialist nostalgia" implicit in the way the word was used before.[2] All anthropologists continue to use it today, however – sometimes in quotes only, sometimes only in its adjectival form: the "cultural context," "cultural capital," "cultural practices," or just simply "the cultural." Attempts to replace it with terms such as "discourse" and "poetics" appear to have dissipated. But historians, who had only just discovered its charms, never understood all the mea culpas, all the sackcloth and ashes that the concept of culture inspired in the ethnographic community.

The anthropological generation of the 1950s and '60s – including such figures as Clifford Geertz, Victor Turner, Edmund Leach, Claude Lévi-Strauss, David Schneider – developed a particularly powerful way of thinking about culture, quite distinct from their predecessors'.[3] It was this powerful new concept of culture that first attracted the interest of a number of historians, who set out, with a missionary zeal, to awaken their colleagues to its virtues. But no sooner had they done so than anthropologists seemed to develop an allergy to their great achievement; on their side, initial interest in history was sparked by a search for intellectual ointments that could cure the itching. From this initial miscue, others followed.

What was so powerful about the new concept of culture anthropologists had perfected by the 1960s? Reopen Lévi-Strauss's 1962 essay *Totemism*.[4] Most of the book is taken up with a critique of previous efforts to define, categorize, and explain certain peculiar naming practices found in a wide variety of ethnographic settings. (The term *totemism* refers to the use of "totems" – usually the names of animals or plants – to categorize individuals.) The similarities that seem to unite these naming systems are just an illusion, Lévi-Strauss insists. The attempts that have been made to explain them, he argues, have all been misconceived. So-called "totemic" names for tribal subgroups, moieties, clans, and so on, had been explained variously as serving functions – social functions, emotional functions, psychological functions. Durkheim, Malinowski, Firth, Elkins and others had all attempted to account for totemic naming practices as socially or psychically instrumental. But Lévi-Strauss would have nothing of it. "Impulses and emotions explain nothing," he asserts (p. 71). The "formal properties" of intellectual activities "cannot be a reflection of the concrete organization of the society" (p. 96). Behind the peculiar diversity of practices and ideas that anthropologists had previously attempted to categorize as "totemism" – and therefore as a special, perhaps salient, characteristic of primitive man – Lévi-Strauss finds only a more general, and purely intellectual, fact. Plants and animals are "good to think" (p. 89). They permit "the embodiment of ideas and relations conceived by speculative thought." "Every human mind," he triumphantly concludes, "is a locus of virtual experience where what goes on in the minds of men, however remote they may be, can be investigated" (p. 103). "Objective mind," then, not only accounts for the categorizing and naming activities, the myths and cosmologies of primitive communities; it is also the shared ground that allows the ethnographer's imagination to penetrate those alien systems and come to appreciate them.

These assertions bear a remarkable resemblance to the claims of Clifford Geertz, in a seminal essay published in the same year, "Person, Time, and Conduct in Bali."[5] Geertz admitted only one universal human need to account for the Balinese cultural structures he analyzed. "[C]ertain sorts of patterns and certain sorts of relationships among patterns recur from society to society, for the simple reason that the *orientational requirements* they serve are generically human. The problems, being existential, are universal; the solutions, being human, are diverse" (p. 363). The need for orientation – a purely cognitive, or symbolic, need – recurs from society to society, in Geertz's view, but very little else. Gregory Bateson, Margaret Mead, even Ruth Benedict had been willing to go further than Geertz in the direction of endowing cultural patterns with functions, usually psychological. For Benedict, emotions such as frustration, rivalry, or grief were given in individual temperament, establishing tendencies and needs that a culture addressed either well or poorly.[6] Geertz, in "Person, Time, and Conduct," turned the tables on this approach by identifying a Balinese emotion, *lek*, that was entirely the product of culture. Resulting from the profound Balinese emphasis on exterior calm, bland cordiality, commitment to ceremony, and individual effacement, *lek*, which Geertz translated as "stage fright," was "a diffuse, usually mild, though in certain situations virtually paralyzing, nervousness before the prospect (and the fact) of social interaction, a chronic, mostly low-grade worry that one will not be able to bring it off with the required finesse" (p. 402). Thus, a series of cultural structures – a calendrical system, a naming system for persons, and a corresponding code of etiquette: structures developed in response to the bare human need, the purely cognitive or intellectual need, for orientation – determine, in the end, the individual's most intimate anxieties. Nor was this interpretation isolated within Geertz's analyses of culture. Repeatedly he asserted the capacity of religious systems, cosmologies, customary practices, to establish moods, to create a tone, to shape affect. Culture, in short, created the individual's feelings and identity.

In the same years, Victor Turner added his influential voice to the rising chorus of strong claims about culture. In 1969, for example, he criticized Lévi-Strauss for his narrowly intellectual focus, which neglected both ritual practice and emotion.

> Although Lévi-Strauss devotes some attention to the role of ritual and mythical symbols as instigators of feeling and desire, he does not develop this line of thought as fully as he does his work on symbols as factors in cognition. . . . The symbols and their relations as found in *Isoma* [an Ndembu ritual] are not only a set of cognitive classifications for ordering the Ndembu universe. They are also, and perhaps as importantly, a set of evocative devices for rousing, channeling,

and domesticating powerful emotions, such as hate, fear, affection, and grief. They are also informed with purposiveness and have a 'conative' aspect. In brief, the whole person, not just the Ndembu 'mind,' is existentially involved in the life or death issues with which *Isoma* is concerned.[7]

Lévi-Strauss excluded subjectivity and feeling from consideration because they were inchoate. "As affectivity is the most obscure side of man," he wrote, "there has been the constant temptation to resort to it, forgetting that what is refractory to explanation is *ipso facto* unsuitable for use in explanation. A datum is not primary because it is incomprehensible: this characteristic indicates solely that an explanation, if it exists, must be sought on another level."[8] Geertz, by contrast, argued that, just because of its formless dynamism, feeling, too, was a realm that culture could, must shape. Cultural patterns, he insisted, impose "upon the continual shifts in sentience to which we are inherently subject a recognizable, meaningful order, so that we may not only feel but know what we feel and act accordingly."[9] Turner seemed closer to Geertz, although his claim that rituals could be devices for "rousing, channeling, and domesticating powerful emotions" suggested that emotions retained a certain independent importance. All three anthropologists announced a new autonomy for culture, a new purity and power; none felt the need for help from psychology to understand how culture was grounded at the individual level – such grounding was intellectual or existential in character – none treated culture as subsidiary to, or derivative from, social structure. Culture made its own grounds. No longer could culture be seen as just another level or layer of system, as it had in the past. It simply was the system.

Simultaneously, primitive cultures acquired a new dignity; the very idea that some cultures were "primitive" in the sense of inferior or less rational, was cast into doubt. So long as social structure and psychology were primary, differences between modern Western and nonwestern "primitive" societies had seemed great. But the new emphasis on the power of culture implied an insistence on a strictly relativist stance *vis-à-vis* cultural difference. The genius of human speculative reason and poetic comprehension was at work everywhere in the world, and everywhere produced equally delicate flowers.

Historians Discover Culture (1970–1980)

The leveling implications of this new conception of culture were particularly appealing to social historians. In the 1960s, new social historians had found that methods borrowed from sociology were congenial tools in the rewriting of history "from the bottom up." But they also quickly found the results less than satisfactory. Surely it was not enough, to save the poor of the past from the "enormous condescension of posterity,"[10] merely to count their households, gauge fertility rates and geographic mobility, tabulate strikes and tote up union membership figures. At the end of all the tables and graphs, the down-trodden still looked very much like inferior versions of their aristocratic and middle-class superiors – shaped by market forces and political realities, they appeared simply to be less savvy at exploiting them.

This helps to explain the excitement with which many historians received the 1971 article by E. P. Thompson, "The Moral Economy of the English Crowd in the Eighteenth Century."[11] Thompson castigated economic historians for dismissing eighteenth-century incidents of crowd action as mere "rebellions of the belly" and for explaining their occurrence in terms of crude "social tension" charts (p. 77). To understand popular behavior, he asserted, we must come to see how it contributes to a "more complex, culturally mediated function, which cannot be reduced – however long it is stewed over the fires of statistical analysis – back to stimulus once again" (p. 78). Thompson praised the comparative richness of interpretation available in "a social anthropology which derives from Durkheim, Weber, or Malinowski." "We know all about the delicate tissue of social norms and reciprocities," he continued,

> which regulates the life of Trobriand islanders, and the psychic energies involved in the cargo cults of Melanesia; but at some point this infinitely-complex social creature, Melanesian man, becomes (in our histories) the eighteenth-century English collier who claps his hand spasmodically upon his stomach, and responds to elementary economic stimuli. (p. 78)

In a sharp rebuff to such reductionism, Thompson contended that the English poor grounded their collective protests "upon a consistent traditional view of social norms and obligations, of the proper economic functions of several parties within the community, which, taken together, can be said to constitute the moral economy of the poor" (p. 79).

Equally riveting to historians were the early essays of Natalie Z. Davis, especially "The Reasons of Misrule," first published in 1971, and "The Rites of Violence," first published in 1973.[12] In the latter essay, Davis made a move precisely parallel to Thompson's in her attempt to make sense of sixteenth-century French religious riots. Like him, she attacked an older historiography that ascribed violent outbreaks of crowd action to economic factors: high prices and dearth. Like him, she found cultural order where others had catalogued only spasms: complex improvised rituals of theological justification, purification, argument, and punishment were perpetrated on the churches, homes, and bodies of religious opponents.

In such early works of the "new cultural history," a rosy picture of the culture concept – stripped of its ambiguities, its development, its current problems – enabled historians to challenge a rising fashion for quantitative and sociological explanation. In the context of Cold War polemics, social historians had been sucked into endless debates involving pro-capitalist, social-democratic, and Leninist standpoints – debates over such issues as whether working-class living standards had risen or fallen during the Industrial Revolution, whether the wage laborers of revolutionary Paris or the labor aristocracy of Victorian London really constituted a "class" or not, whether Chartism or the AFL were expressions of false consciousness. The culture concept allowed a handful of historians to step forward and cry "a plague on all your houses" – while wrapping themselves in a cloak of moral superiority, embroidered with ethnographic visions of the sensitivity and humanity of the oppressed. The new, expansive culture concept of Geertz, Lévi-Strauss, and their peers – but especially that of Geertz – was perfectly suited to this task, a fact which helps to explain why Lynn Hunt would remark in 1989 that "At the moment, the anthropological model reigns supreme in cultural approaches" among historians.[13]

To be sure, historians were not discriminating in their borrowings of ideas about culture, not at first. To them, it mattered little whether Evans-Pritchard had been too abstract when drawing his diagrams of segmented tribal structures; his Nuer were nonetheless infinitely more vivid, more three-dimensional than, say, the Lancashire workers enumerated in the endless tables of Michael Anderson's 1971 kinship study, or the strikers who marched up and down the hundreds of graphs in Edward Shorter and Charles Tilly's massive 1974 review of labor activism in France.[14] Nonetheless, it was only the more powerful notion of culture as autonomous system, free of entanglements with psychology and social structure, that could do the political work cultural historians wished to accomplish.

Historicizing Culture (1980–1990)

But the distilled, omnipotent concept of culture perfected by Geertz, Turner, Lévi-Strauss and others soon began to inspire widespread disquiet among their fellow anthropologists. In fact, given the importance and clarity of the new concept – given its position at the endpoint of a long development – it is remarkable how quickly it came under attack. It is also remarkable that anthropologists now consider this concept of culture to be the "classic" version of the concept, and equally remarkable that they continue to mull over its weaknesses and to define themselves by means of the precise character of their opposition to it.[15]

Disquiet among anthropologists focused on three aspects of the new culture concept: (1) its synchronic character, (2) its inability to deal with diversity and conflict, and (3) the relation between the ethnographer and his or her subjects that this concept implied. Of these three areas of concern, only the first two engaged the interest of historians. In addition, as feminists began to insist on greater attention to women and to gender in both disciplines, the problems posed by their demands were much simpler for historians to resolve than for anthropologists.

One major source of disquiet over the new concept of culture concerned its "synchronic" character – that is, its utter inability to take change into account. On this score, historians and anthropologists easily came to agreement; something had to be done. An early proposal came from William Sewell, whose 1980 cultural history of labor in France found a "dialectical logic" driving cultural change forward from one era to the next. The French Revolution founded its justification of private property on the transforming effects of men's labor on nature, Sewell argued. In the post-revolutionary era, however, real wage laborers found their ability to acquire or accumulate property curtailed; even their most immediate needs went sometimes unmet. In effect, the new principle of property, when put into practice, gave rise to a contradiction whose cultural force lay behind the emergence of a labor movement and a new "class consciousness" after 1830. This approach anticipated Bourdieu's elaboration of a theory of practice; and Sewell subsequently became a champion of practice theory as a means of understanding how cultural structures were realized or altered through their contingent, circumstantial enactments by specific persons in specific times and places.[16] Here, culture's autonomy (*vis-à-vis* social structure or psychology) was retained; but it was now brought into dialectical relation with "practice." The concept of practice was elevated to equal status, as an independent, extralinguistic, and dynamic element that shaped meaning as much as culture, and constantly reshaped them with the passage of time. This move constituted an effort to enrich substantially the contribution of what Geertz or Turner regarded as relatively empty "existential" features of life. Besides requiring "orientation," agents were engaged in a constant shuttling between cultural models and contingent, dynamic practices, where unintended consequences could create contradiction and force change.

Similar proposals on the anthropology side were not long in coming. For example, Renato Rosaldo, in 1980, attempted to gauge the flexibility actors derived from their sense of history and their legitimating narratives about the past. The Philippine hill people he studied used a highly elastic sense of clan membership to interpret insults, define enemies, and rally support for head-hunting raids.[17] They made up narratives about the past that were not untrue, but which, through a selective process, focused oppositions and alliances to warrant violence in the present. Marshall Sahlins, in two collections of essays that focused on contact situations in the Pacific, published in 1981 and 1985, treated cultural structures as scripts for performances, and performances as moments that put the structures at risk.[18] Performance – a rite, the choice of a sexual partner, a battle, a claim to land – opened to the possibility of failure, innovation, redefinition. Thus, cultural structures, in the very moment they were realized were, and were supposed to be, vulnerable to transformation.

When Hawaiians greeted the first British sea captain to arrive on the island as an embodiment of their god Lono, they applied a powerful structure to a highly contingent, new, and unpredictable situation. It was this very application of structure that drove events out of control, when Captain Cook failed to leave the island on schedule and was murdered by a priest. The temporal sequence of performances, Sahlins argued further, could help sort out the otherwise vague or contradictory assimilations and oppositions of cultural structures such as Fijian notions of kingship. Time allowed elements to turn into their opposites smoothly and without confusion. Building on these accomplishments, Sherry Ortner's study of the history of Sherpa Buddhism published in 1989 offered a sophisticated application of practice theory to the understanding of cultural change. Social life, as culturally constructed, confronted individuals with often painful contradictions; but it also offered them compelling schemas of action (in the form of myths, stories, ritual transformations) for resolving those contradictions. How such schemas would be applied in the practical elaboration of individual lives was very much up to the "loosely structured" individuals themselves, and their responses represented a kind of improvisation which, over time, accumulated into cultural and social history.[19]

But while progress was quickly made on the adaptation of the culture concept to historical change, a number of developments induced many anthropologists and historians to turn their immediate attention elsewhere. Some anthropologists sought to remedy the ahistorical and apolitical flatness of the culture concept by an aggressive turn to political economy, usually Marxist in character, drawing on dependency theory and world-systems theory. In some instances, culture was reduced to a decidedly secondary and contingent status, as anthropologists such as Eric Wolf and Sidney Mintz turned their attention to the economic and political history of European empires.[20] For them, meaning and ritual were dependent registers of very raw and very real power configurations. Other anthropologists who recognized the importance of global political and economic forces, nonetheless sought to fashion an adequate Marxist theory of culture to account for the impact of these forces on lived experience. For this diverse and brilliant group, Marx provided the historical framework they needed; and many of them embraced the works of E. P. Thompson – especially his notion of "moral economy" – as a model for their historical understanding of culture. In the work of such anthropologists as Maurice Bloch, Jack Goody, William Roseberry, James C. Scott, Richard Fox, and Michael Taussig, modes of production, world trade in tropical commodities, labor discipline, and subsistence needs were found to interact with hegemonic cultural orders through a delicate and reversible field of force.[21] Closely related to this impulse was the elaboration of so-called "subaltern studies" by a group of Indian historians under the leadership of Ranajit Guha.[22]

A second major development of the late 1970s and early 1980s was the rise in importance of post-structuralism, which tended to influence the two disciplines strongly, but independently. Its impact was felt quite differently in each field, and therefore tended to blunt specific cross-disciplinary collaboration. Within the discipline of anthropology, post-structuralism represented a challenge to traditional approaches to fieldwork, and undermined accepted notions about the relation between ethnographer and informant. The autonomous and all-powerful culture trumpeted by the likes of Geertz, Turner, and Lévi-Strauss now came to be seen as an artifact of the ethnographer's method. But, insofar as informants and their communities constructed discourses of their own about the social world, they were engaging in precisely the same kind of creative work as the ethnographer. Thus ethnographers and the communities they studied were reduced to the same level. Researchers therefore began to focus on the contingent and transient relationship with informants as the only solid point of reference, in a world of diverse, often conflictual discursive structures. Likewise, they focused on the act of writing and the relationship of ethnographer to reader established by the ethnographic text. Ethnographers, they insisted, were telling stories, elaborating a kind of poetic rhetoric around the idea of culture, whose own troubled epistemological status was its first and most important lesson about social life in general.[23]

Historians' response to post-structuralism was initially quite different. Foucault, in particular, denied historical continuity and saw history as proceeding by a series of ruptures separating each successive age, ruptures that reordered fundamental epistemological conceptions of language and therefore rendered the past incomprehensible to the present. Such a conception of change encouraged historicist approaches – approaches, that is, that emphasized the difference of each period from the next, and the internal coherence of each period as a separate, articulated moment in its own right. But cultural approaches such as those of E. P. Thompson or Natalie Davis were already encouraging an historicist outlook and, initially, poststructuralism did little to disturb this trend. An early response, which continues to pay dividends, was to examine the types of subject matter that Foucault's work had opened up: prisons, asylums, clinics, the epistemology of nineteenth-century social science, the body and sexuality, the history of psychiatry.[24]

More challenging to the accepted canons of historical explanation was the suggestion that discourse itself had a determining or shaping role in the outcome of the great episodes of European nation-building. In the late 1970s, both Gareth Stedman Jones (in England) and François Furet (in France) intervened in troubled debates about the precise class composition of central national political movements (Chartism and Jacobinism); both insisted that class composition was irrelevant to understanding the historical significance of these movements. They were, instead, shaped by particular discourses or "languages" – sets of related terms such as "rights," the "nation," the "people," "aristocrats." These languages determined what it was possible to think and what forms of legitimacy it was possible to claim. The special status of political language during the French Revolution, according to Furet, followed from the collapse of royal authority and filled the institutional vacuum left by this collapse with abstract notions that were the instruments of power for whomever could seize them and wield them effectively. Stedman Jones argued that the language of Chartism inherited from eighteenth-century English radicalism a schematism of legitimacy that made it impossible to conceive of a specifically class-based political movement. More generally, he argued that social movements and social consciousness were expressions of, subordinate to, language. This reversal of the usual Marxist lines of causation (from "superstructure" down to "base"), he insisted, helped one understand the failure of class consciousness to emerge in nineteenth-century Britain – classic home of the industrial revolution. Each of these bold interventions (and others not mentioned here) have given rise to fruitful, ongoing debates.

The Wider Influence of Post-Structuralism

While it would be beyond the scope of this essay to trace through all the ramifications of the debate over post-structuralism in both disciplines, it is necessary to make at least three more remarks.

First, post-structuralism derived in part from a critique of Lévi-Strauss's structural anthropology by a number of French philosophers in the late 1960s. Post-structuralists denied the unity, coherence, and political innocence of cultural structures; seeing both diversity and power at play in these structures, they preferred to call them "discourses." They offered one important kind of challenge to the sovereign conception of culture proclaimed by Lévi-Strauss, Geertz, Turner, and others around 1960, discussed earlier in this essay. It was this conception of culture that gave initial impetus to collaboration between the two disciplines. As a result the integration of post-structuralist ideas into both disciplines tended to move practitioners in similar directions, even if they were, for a time, drawing less on each others' work. Thus works of history that have been heavily influenced by the debate over post-structuralism often have a decidedly ethnographic flavor. In works such as Patrick Joyce's *Democratic Subjects* (1994), or Mary Poovey's *History of the Modern Fact* (1998), attention is focused on the orienting concepts, epistemological structures, and social categories of the communities under examination.[25] What makes these examinations differ from, say, Geertzian ethnography, is a greater appreciation of the political stakes of language as well as of the diversity of types of language in play at any given moment. A political field of force shapes, and is shaped by, discourses, in an unfolding that constitutes a history of the unspoken, a narrative of change in the implicit, in the taken-for-granted. Such works represent a type of study that goes beyond the older genres of social history, intellectual history, or ethnography. Likewise, works of anthropology heavily influenced by post-structuralist thinking show a heightened attention to diversity, conflict, and change – they are works of history.[26]

Second, the impact of post-structuralism has been closely associated in both disciplines with feminist theory and the effort to give gender its proper role in the understanding of social life. It is easy enough to see why feminist ethnographers felt uneasy with the classic conception of culture that had developed in their discipline since the 1930s. It was not simply that most ethnographers had focused on men and their doings. It was not simply that the very idea of culture implied a fixity that accepted female subordination as a common, uninteresting fact in most cultural contexts. When women went into the field, they were treated differently; denied entry to certain male venues and practices, they were often given privileged access to the times and places of female togetherness: domestic intimacy, child care, menstruation ritual. When they compared the communities they studied with accounts of them penned by male colleagues, they often saw two different, co-existing worlds. Awareness of a diversity of discourses was forced on them, as was awareness of the crucial character of the enthographer–informant interaction. The influential work of Lila Abu-Lughod shows how useful and powerful post-structuralist insights were under such circumstances.[27]

By now it is happily possible to list numerous studies of gender, by both anthropologists and historians, which are so similar in conception they might as well belong to the same discipline. Here are some salient examples. Irene Silverblatt, author of *Moon, Sun, and Witches: Gender Ideologies and Class in Inca and Colonial Peru*,[28] reconstructs the conception of gender prevalent in the precolonial Inca empire, showing that this vast state relied on a parallel hierarchy of male and female religious institutions and ceremonies, drawing the elite of its subject communities into collaboration through marriage exchange and high-prestige rituals of human sacrifice. Here, then, was a far-flung government that defied Engels' famous theory that gender inequality originated with the founding of states. Edna G. Bay, author of *Wives of the Leopard: Gender, Politics, and Culture in the Kingdom of Dahomey*[29] uses precisely the same approach, and very similar documents (a mixture of travel accounts, colonial administrative records, and latter-day indigenous testimony), to examine the development of Dahomey's extraordinary palace aristocracy in the days of the eighteenth- and nineteenth-century slave trade. Women occupied high positions, exercised great influence, and staffed a formidable elite palace guard of "amazon" warriors. Bay explores the intricate articulation of palace social structure, strategies of rule by the leading families, and the evolving demands of the slave trade over the years. Reading these studies, one would not be able to say which scholar was trained as an anthropologist (Irene Silverblatt), which as a historian (Edna Bay). Anthropologist Jane Fishburne Collier's recent work, *From Duty to Desire: Remaking Fami-*

lies in a Spanish Village,[30] traces dramatic shifts in conceptions of courtship and marriage in a Spanish village where she has engaged in fieldwork over a period of decades. She examines how individual choice has come to overrule calculations based on family honor and wealth in marriage decisions since World War II, and how this process has accompanied a modernist reconception of family and tradition as a (gendered) haven from modernity. Ann Farnsworth-Alvear, trained as a historian, recently published *Dulcinea in the Factory: Myths, Morals, Men, and Women in Colombia's Industrial Experiment, 1905–1960*.[31] Drawing on extensive oral interviews and examination of private company archives, Farnsworth-Alvear proposes that the relation between gender and class (and race could easily be added to this matrix) is easier to sort out if gender differences are seen not as dichotomous but as defined by normative codes that identify a number of possible males and females. She shows how, in Medellín, such a code was deployed by factory owners to create an attractive image of women's wage labor that muted its danger to women's reputations for chastity and submissiveness. And she shows how women workers responded to this normative image in a variety of ways, sheltering under its umbrella, exploiting its contradictions, making space for themselves in its silences. The authors of both these works show a lively awareness of the complexities and ambiguities individuals face in fashioning life patterns for themselves. Both authors go beyond simple conceptions of oppression and resistance to probe the delicate compromises and personal innovations that make up the tissue of life in any social order.

Third, the best recent work, while drawing on the post-structuralist concept of discourse, does not fully embrace this concept. Studies appearing over the last decade (including studies such as those on gender mentioned in the last paragraph) have established a powerful new model for the practice of ethnographic history. This model accepts the reality of a social or practical dimension that lies, in the last instance, beyond the reach of discursive structures. Even if great caution must be exercised in characterizing this social pole of historical reality, it cannot be neglected. Its analysis is carried out tentatively; if sociological terms such as *class, clan, kinship, institution*, or *community* are used, it is only for their heuristic value. The danger of reification is never forgotten. The ideas of "power" and "hegemony" provide a bridge between the social and the discursive poles of analysis, because discourse, in Foucault's conception, creates power, on the one hand, and because, on the other, social practice is the place where power and hegemony are registered, and their effects become visible.

Looking Forward from the Present

Two recent, magisterial, multi-volume works – one by the anthropologists John Comaroff and Jean Comaroff, the other by historian David Sabean –

illustrate the strengths of the new state of play, and the pay-off of the last three decades of interdisciplinary collaboration.

The Comaroffs' on-going project is an account of the interaction between the Tswana of South Africa and English missionaries, from first contact in the early nineteenth century down to the struggle against apartheid of the recent past.[32] They examine the social orders and hegemonic discourses on both sides of the interaction with equal thoroughness. To do this, they have had to remake themselves as historians of nineteenth-century British culture, even as they deployed remarkable anthropological virtuosity in reconstructing pre-contact Tswana culture from the misleading scraps of documents provided by European observers. Like omniscient observers, the Comaroffs recover initial misunderstandings on both sides, and the calculated exchanges Tswana and English entered into – prompted by Tswana fears of raiding by their fellow Africans on one side, and by a dawning comprehension among the missionaries that conversion could only go forward hand-in-hand with a process of "civilizing." The Comaroffs show that, just as the choice to be a missionary was inseparable from an experience of a certain dissatisfaction and marginalization within England, so the appeal of the missionaries was felt most strongly among marginal strata of Tswana society: the destitute, junior royals, women of all ranks. The work of translation was never complete, and as a result the Tswana and the English found each other "banal, incapable of richly textured understanding or poetic subtlety."[33]

Doing history in an ethnographic framework is essential for the Comaroffs because they regard social knowledge and experience as situated "along a *chain of consciousness* . . . a continuum whose two extremes are the unseen and the seen, the submerged and the apprehended."[34] The most critical domain to understand, they insist, is in the middle of the chain, "the realm of partial recognition." Here is where new movements and ideological challenges may arise. Here is where resistance can live an only partially recognized existence, giving murky form to preliminary responses to hegemony.

David Sabean's massive analysis of the history of a single Würtemberg village across almost two centuries of its existence (roughly 1700 to 1870) is another ethnographic tour de force.[35] By carefully coordinating hundreds of records of village court disputes, land sales, shifts in crop rotation, in outmigration, and in wage labor, Sabean is able to track two enduring changes. First, the coming of the new crops and stall feeding techniques of the agricultural revolution placed a new burden of intensive field labor on the shoulders of women, and this change brought in its turn a crisis of marriage. Second, as population expanded, and economic inequality increased, the elite stratum of the village became increasingly endogamous, until, Sabean argues, it becomes reasonable to think of this elite as a class. One of the strong points of the second volume of Sabean's study is an extended examination of the relationship between class and marriage. Is it possible, Sabean asks, that a German bourgeoisie gradually came to define itself in the nineteenth century by means of characteristic patterns of endogamous alliance? Fascinating case studies illustrate the argument. Here is a new approach to the concept of social class in European history that could only have come from work based on an immersion in both the disciplines of history and anthropology. Like the Comaroffs, Sabean understands that no social condition, pattern of action, or institution can be understood except through an interpretive method that is first and foremost ethnographic. At the same time, he, like they, goes beyond the moment of interpretation, to examine relationships through the political prism of discourse.

These impressive studies testify to the value of a now long collaboration between practitioners of both disciplines. However, there are also disconcerting signs that this collaboration remains circumscribed and sporadic. One important trend in recent historical work by anthropologists, for example, has no analogy among historians. This is work on the impact of the very idea of culture on the self-understanding of colonial and postcolonial societies. In a now classic study, Nicholas Dirks showed how the British carefully preserved the institutional forms of Hindu ritual kingship in a small South Indian state, while they systematically robbed these forms of all significance through the encroachments of colonial administration and tax collecting.[36] In this case, the colonial subjects collaborated – at least for a time – in the British project of preservation, transforming their very ethnic authenticity into a product of British domination, an offering, a show for others. More recently, John Pemberton has shown how a complex ceremony of Javanese kingship, and elaborate notions of what counted as authentically Javanese, were developed through collaboration between indigenous elites and Dutch colonial administrators in the nineteenth and early twentieth centuries.[37] The outcome in both cases is a kind of social practice and way of talking that cannot properly be considered "non-Western" culture, precisely because it derives from innovative attempts to respond to Westerners' expectations – using indigenous material, to be sure, but in ways that detach them from their formative contexts. This is a kind of study that historians have yet to attempt. Among historians, significant effort has been devoted to elaborating a method associated with the term "microhistory" that asserts the quasi-independence of the particular and the general, and likewise of the great events and trends of history and the preoccupations of individuals living real, local lives.[38] These efforts respond to concerns very close to those driving anthropologists to reexamine the culture concept; but there seems to be little contact between these largely Continental historians and North American anthropologists.

Many historians work entirely within the cultural contexts in which they grew up, or in very similar contexts. They do not have to confront the daunting prospect of human difference that is anthropology's special concern; they do not have to justify their interests on theoretical grounds, because they address national publics already curious about their own pasts. Even when examining a subject that is inherently cultural and of great interdisciplinary interest – such as, for example, national memory – historians easily slip into parochial commemoration. Cultural historians too readily accept the compartmentalization of their research along conventional lines; they examine the family, theater, religion, consumerism, or crime. Inadvertently they accept the validity of such subdivisions, losing sight of the larger picture. But the holism of ethnographic method remains one of its great strengths. Even the most skeptical anthropologists offer their readers ways of apprehending whole communities, whole symbolic orders, however qualified these apprehensions must be, however fragmented the larger pictures. They are obliged to do this by the yawning differences that separate the publics they address from the contexts they work in. Historians must constantly refresh their sense of such difference; for the compartmentalizations they accept may reflect the very cultural order they most ardently wish to question and to understand.

Anthropologists likewise still depend on field work for most of their evidence and they, just as easily, slip into the illusion that the present is self-explanatory. Anthropologists have strong links with several disciplines; but often it appears as if these links are forged only one at a time. Anthropologists who draw on psychology or linguistics continue, for the most part, to write in the ethnographic present. There has been a remarkable flowering of new research on emotions, for example, since the days when Turner and Geertz declared emotions to be the province of culture. "Psychocultural" anthropologists such as Douglas Hollan and Jane Wellenkamp, working with models derived from clinical psychology, have insisted with eloquence that culture has limits, and that the psychic unity of the human species makes all communities and all individuals available to our empathy. Others, such as Catherine Lutz and Lila Abu-Lughod, applying post-structuralist theory to emotional discourse, have defended the power of cultural practices to make emotions. Perhaps the majority working in this vibrant new field have fallen somewhere in between these two positions. The political implications of a wide variety of emotional cultures have been carefully explored. But none of these researchers has attempted to come to terms with historical change, or even to coordinate their models with those developed by historical ethnographers.[39] Anthropologists who draw on literary theory often seem to withdraw into intimate, tropological spaces where they interact with one or two informants. It is sufficiently challenging, in their view, to find a modicum of order in the details of one life; and the idiosyncratic lives they have examined represent so many cautionary tales, vivid reminders of the pitfalls of hasty cultural generalizations.

Indeed, in anthropology, there is concern that the discipline is fragmenting along the lines of these interdisciplinary links and is losing any sense of unifying mission. Has cross-disciplinary contact gone too far? Still not far enough,

I think. Anthropology will survive because of the urgency of its questions; historians will continue to benefit from listening to these questions, recognizing how many of them we ought also to be asking, and drawing on the expertise anthropologists display in answering them. Despite the remarkable accomplishments of interdisciplinary collaboration, anthropologists and historians have different ways of traveling, doing research, and struggling to comprehend both alterity and change. These differences of style ensure that there are always fresh lessons to be learned from attempting that radical merger of perspectives that allows us to discern the "realm of partial recognition" and to write its history.

NOTES

1   Leora Auslander, *Taste and Power: Furnishing Modern France* (Berkeley: University of California Press, 1996); Susan A. Crane, *Collecting and Historical Consciousness: New Forms for Collective Memory in Early Nineteenth-Century* (Ithaca, NY: Cornell University Press, 2000).

2   Renato Rosaldo, *Culture and Truth: The Remaking of Social Analysis* (Boston: Beacon, 1989).

3   To appreciate just how new this idea of culture was in the context of anthropology, see the highly critical discussion in Melford E. Spiro, "Cultural Relativism and the Future of Anthropology," in *Rereading Cultural Anthropology*, edited by George E. Marcus (Durham, NC: Duke University Press, 1992), pp. 124–51.

4   Translated by Rodney Needham (Boston: Beacon, 1963).

5   Reprinted in Clifford Geertz, *The Interpretation of Cultures* (New York: Basic Books, 1973), pp. 360–411.

6   Ruth Benedict, *Patterns of Culture* (Boston: Houghton & Mifflin, 1934), pp. 251–78.

7   Victor W. Turner, *The Ritual Process: Structure and Antistructure* (Chicago: Aldine, 1969), pp. 42–3.

8   Lévi-Strauss, *Totemism*, p. 69.

9   *The Interpretation of Cultures*, p. 80; quoted by William H. Sewell, Jr., "Geertz, Cultural Systems, and History: From Synchrony to Transformation," in *The Fate of "Culture": Geertz and Beyond*, edited by Sherry B. Ortner (Berkeley: University of California Press, 1999), pp. 35–55, quote on p. 45.

10 E. P. Thompson, *The Making of the English Working Class* (New York: Vintage, 1963), p. 12.

11 *Past and Present* 50 (1971): 76–136.

12 Both articles reprinted in Natalie Zemon Davis, *Society and Culture in Early Modern France* (Stanford: Stanford University Press, 1975).

13 Lynn Hunt, "Introduction," in *The New Cultural History*, edited by Lynn Hunt (Berkeley: University of California Press, 1989), pp. 1–22, quote on p. 11.

14 Michael Anderson, *Family structure in nineteenth century Lancashire* (Cambridge: Cambridge University Press, 1971); Edward Shorter and Charles Tilly, *Strikes in France, 1830–1968* (Cambridge: Cambridge University Press, 1974).

15   See, for example, the essays in two recent anthologies, Nicholas B. Dirks, ed., *In Near Ruins: Cultural Theory at the End of the Century* (Minneapolis: University of Minnesota Press, 1998); Sherry B. Ortner, ed., *The Fate of "Culture": Geertz and Beyond* (Berkeley: University of California Press, 1999).

16   See, for example, William H. Sewell, Jr., "A Theory of Structure: Duality, Agency, and Transformation," *American Journal of Sociology* 98 (1992): 1–29.

17   Renato Rosaldo, *Ilongot Headhunting, 1883–1974: A Study in Society and History* (Stanford: Stanford University Press, 1980).

18   Marshall Sahlins, *Historical Metaphors and Mythical Realities: Structure in the Early History of the Sandwich Islands Kingdom* (Ann Arbor: University of Michigan Press, 1981), and *Islands of History* (Chicago: University of Chicago Press, 1985).

19   Sherry B. Ortner, *High Religion: A Cultural and Political History of Sherpa Buddhism* (Princeton, NJ: Princeton University Press, 1989).

20   Eric R. Wolf, *Europe and the People Without History* (Berkeley: University of California Press, 1982); Sidney W. Mintz, *Sweetness and Power: The Place of Sugar in Modern History* (New York: Viking Penguin, 1985).

21   Representative works by these authors: Maurice Bloch, *Ritual, History, and Power: Selected Essays in Anthropology* (London: The Athlone Press, 1989); Jack Goody, *Cooking, Cuisine, and Class: A Study in Comparative Sociology* (Cambridge: Cambridge University Press, 1982); William Roseberry, *Coffee and Capitalism in the Venezuelan Andes* (Austin: University of Texas Press, 1983); James C. Scott, *The Moral Economy of the Peasant: Rebellion and Subsistence in Southeast Asia* (New Haven: Yale University Press, 1976); Richard G. Fox, *Ghandian Utopia: Experiments with Culture* (Boston: Beacon, 1989); Michael T. Taussig, *The Devil and Commodity Fetishism in South America* (Chapel Hill: University of North Carolina Press, 1980).

22   See, for example, Ranajit Guha, ed., *A Subaltern Studies Reader, 1986–1995* (Minneapolis: University of Minnesota Press, 1997).

23   See Vincent Crapanzano, *Tuhami: Portrait of a Moroccan* (Chicago: University of Chicago Press, 1980); Paul Rabinow, *Reflections on Fieldwork in Morocco* (Berkeley: University of California Press, 1977); James Clifford and George E. Marcus, eds., *Writing Culture: The Poetics and Politics of Ethnography* (Berkeley: University of California Press, 1986); James Clifford, *The Predicament of Culture: Twentieth-Century Ethnography, Literature, and Art* (Cambridge, MA: Harvard University Press, 1988).

24   Representative titles from French historiography include: Patricia O'Brien, *The Promise of Punishment: Prisons in Nineteenth-Century France* (Princeton, NJ: Princeton University Press, 1982); Jan Goldstein, *Console and Classify: The French Psychiatric Profession in the Nineteenth Century* (Cambridge: Cambridge University Press, 1987); Robert A Nye, *Crime, Madness, and Politics in Modern France: The Medical Concept of National Decline* (Princeton, NJ: Princeton University Press, 1984); Dorinda Outram, *The Body and the French Revolution: Sex, Class, and Political Culture* (New Haven: Yale University Press, 1989); Carolyn J. Dean, *Sexuality and Modern Western Culture* (Twayne Publishers, 1996). See also, in general, Jan Goldstein, ed., *Foucault and the Writing of History* (Oxford: Blackwell, 1994).

25 Patrick Joyce, *Democratic Subjects: The Self and the Social in Nineteenth-Century England* (Cambridge: Cambridge University Press, 1994); Mary Poovey, *A History of the Modern Fact: Problems of Knowledge in the Sciences of Wealth and Society* (Chicago: University of Chicago Press, 1998).

26 See, for example, Geoffrey M. White, *Identity Through History: Living Stories in a Solomon Islands Society* (Cambridge: Cambridge University Press, 1991); Ted Swedenburg, "Occupational Hazards: Palestine Ethnography," in *Rereading Cultural Anthropology*, edited by George E. Marcus (Durham, NC: Duke University Press, 1992), pp. 69–76; Debbora Battaglia, "On Practical Nostalgia: Self-Prospecting among Urban Trobrianders," in *Rhetorics of Self-Making*, edited by Debbora Battaglia (Berkeley: University of California Press, 1995), pp. 77–96; Louisa Schein, "Performing Modernity," *Cultural Anthropology* 14 (1999): 361–95; E. Valentine Daniel, "The Limits of Culture," in *In Near Ruins: Cultural Theory at the End of the Century*, edited by Nicholas Dirks (Minneapolis: University of Minnesota Press, 1998), pp. 67–91.

27 Lila Abu-Lughod, *Veiled Sentiments: Honor and Poetry in a Bedouin Society* (Berkeley: University of California Press, 1986); "Writing Against Culture," in Richard G. Fox, ed., *Recapturing Anthropology: Working in the Present* (Santa Fe, NM: School of American Research, 1991), pp. 137–62.

28 Irene Silverblatt, *Moon, Sun, and Witches: Gender Ideologies and Class in Inca and Colonial Peru* (Princeton, NJ: Princeton University Press, 1988).

29 Edna G. Bay, *Wives of the Leopard: Gender, Politics, and Culture in the Kingdom of Dahomey* (Charlottesville: University of Virginia Press, 1998).

30 Jane Fishburne Collier, *From Duty to Desire: Remaking Families in a Spanish Village* (Princeton: Princeton University Press, 1997).

31 Ann Farnsworth-Alvear, *Dulcinea in the Factory: Myths, Morals, Men, and Women in Colombia's Industrial Experiment, 1905–1960* (Durham, NC: Duke University Press, 2000).

32 Jean Comaroff and John L. Comaroff, *Of Revelation and Revolution: Christianity, Colonialism, and Consciousness in South Africa* (Chicago: University of Chicago Press, 1991); a second volume (of three) appeared under the title *Of Revelation and Revolution: The Dialectics of Modernity on a South African Frontier* (Chicago: University of Chicago Press, 1997).

33 Comaroff and Comaroff, *Christianity, Colonialism*, p. 240.

34 Ibid., p. 29.

35 David Warren Sabean, *Property, Production, and Family in Neckarhausen, 1700–1870* (Cambridge: Cambridge University Press, 1990); *Kinship in Neckarhausen, 1700–1870* (Cambridge: Cambridge University Press, 1998).

36 Nicholas B. Dirks, *The Hollow Crown: Ethnohistory of an Indian Kingdom* (Cambridge: Cambridge University Press, 1987).

37 John Pemberton, *On the Subject of "Java"* (Ithaca, NY: Cornell University Press, 1994).

38 For an introduction, see Jacques Revel, ed., *Jeux d'échelles: La micro-analyse à l'expérience* (Paris: Gallimard, 1996).

39 Douglas W. Hollan, and Jane C. Wellenkamp, *Contentment and Suffering: Culture and Experience in Toraja* (New York: Columbia University Press, 1994); see also Arthur Kleinman, and Joan Kleinman, "Suffering and Its Professional

Transformation: Toward an Ethnography of Experience," *Culture, Medicine and Psychiatry* 15 (1991): 275–302; Lila Abu-Lughod and Catherine Lutz, "Introduction," in *Language and the politics of emotion*, edited by Catherine Lutz and Lila Abu-Lughod (Cambridge: Cambridge University Press, 1990), pp. 1–23; Niko Besnier, "Language and Affect," *Annual Review of Anthropology* 19 (1990): 419–51; John Leavitt, "Meaning and Feeling in the Anthropology of Emotion," *American Ethnologist* 23 (1996): 514–35.

REFERENCES AND FURTHER READING

Comaroff, Jean and John L. Comaroff, *Of Revelation and Revolution: Christianity, Colonialism, and Consciousness in South Africa*, Chicago: University of Chicago Press, 1991.

——, *Of Revelation and Revolution: The Dialectics of Modernity on a South African Frontier*, Chicago: University of Chicago Press, 1997.

Dirks, Nicholas B. ed., *In Near Ruins: Cultural Theory at the End of the Century*, Minneapolis: University of Minnesota Press, 1998.

——, *The Hollow Crown: Ethnohistory of an Indian Kingdom*. Cambridge: Cambridge University Press, 1987.

Guha, Ranajit ed., *A Subaltern Studies Reader, 1986–1995*, Minneapolis: University of Minnesota Press, 1997.

Hunt, Lynn ed., *The New Cultural History*, Berkeley: University of California Press, 1989.

——, *Politics, Culture, and Class in the French Revolution*, Berkeley: University of California Press, 1984.

Ortner, Sherry B. ed., *The Fate of "Culture": Geertz and Beyond*, Berkeley: University of California Press, 1999.

——, *High Religion: A Cultural and Political History of Sherpa Buddhism*, Princeton, NJ: Princeton University Press, 1989.

Pemberton, John, *On the Subject of "Java,"* Ithaca, NY: Cornell University Press, 1994.

Revel, Jacques ed., *Jeux d'échelles: La micro-analyse à l'expérience*, Paris: Gallimard, 1996.

Sabean, David Warren, *Property, Production, and Family in Neckarhausen, 1700–1870*, Cambridge: Cambridge University Press, 1990.

——, *Kinship in Neckarhausen, 1700–1870*, Cambridge: Cambridge University Press, 1998.

Sahlins, Marshall, *Historical Metaphors and Mythical Realities: Structure in the Early History of the Sandwich Islands Kingdom*, Ann Arbor: University of Michigan Press, 1981.

——, *Islands of History*, Chicago: University of Chicago Press, 1985.

CHAPTER FIFTEEN

The History of Science, Or, an Oxymoronic Theory of Relativistic Objectivity

KEN ALDER

As a phrase, "the history of science" has the ring of an oxymoron. At first glance the two terms cancel each other out; and only on closer examination (and this is what a good oxymoron should accomplish) do the juxtaposed terms suggest a larger unexpected meaning: like "deafening silence," "clever fool," or "relativistic objectivity." This essay will review some of the larger unexpected meanings attributed to the term "history of science" over the past two centuries, though it concentrates on the period since the 1960s, when a recognizable sub-discipline called the "history of science" came into being. The central contention of this essay, however, is that despite the existence of this thriving sub-discipline, with its own professional societies, academic departments, journals, and problematics, the history of any given scientific subject need not *in principle* be treated differently than the history of any non-scientific subject: avant-garde art, peasant abortifacients, the Rosicrucians, or American meritocracy – all of which, in fact, have been treated with aplomb by historians of science.

That said, science's preeminent status in the self-understanding of the modern West, and the role of technology in producing the West's material and political preeminence, plus a set of well-worn assumptions about the relationship between the former and the latter, have greatly accentuated some of the distinct *practical* problems posed by the history of scientific and technological topics. In particular, these entwined assumptions have, since World War II, made the field a contentious site for debates over the legitimacy of narratives of progress and over claims about the objectivity with which investigators study the natural world – and human affairs as well. For this reason, the history of the history of science is an excellent point of access to more general debates over the "objectivity" of historical study. Indeed, in the past decade, the history of science has served as an intensifier for many of the epistemological quarrels which have exercised general historians and other scholars in the academy. For that reason, the essay will close with a review of the "Science Wars" of the mid-1990s, which seemed to pit defenders of scientific objectivity against a motley crew of cultural relativists.

Science versus History?

What does it mean to say that the two terms "history" and "science" cancel each other out? Consider first the way that a contemporary practicing scientist typically treats the history of his or her own discipline. The view of such a practitioner is hardly irrelevant. Until World War II, scientists were the principal authorities on the history of their respective fields, and they still produce the histories that define their disciplines for their colleagues, as well as popular accounts that inform the lay public.

To judge them by their footnotes, the vast majority of today's practicing scientists seem to regard the origin of their own particular sub-(sub)-discipline as lying perhaps three, five, or at most ten years in the past. In this, they are assuming that any results worth preserving from previous times have been either explicitly or implicitly incorporated within the scientific literature of recent date. To ensure that their own research article will be well received (which means that they have preemptively fortified it against a slew of anticipated objections), they seek to make their text engage the relevant knowledge within its domain and exclude everything that is erroneous or irrelevant. On this view, the history of a scientific discipline is entirely subsumed within the current state of the art. Science is an on-going present which swallows its own past. As for the sort of history which dares to place the development of a scientific discipline within concurrent social and political developments, it can, at best, be understood as a history of error: a history of how the intellectual and material circumstances of the past "distorted" the findings of the scientists of a particular historical period, much as a working scientist might explain how a rival laboratory failed to understand a phenomenon because they lacked the proper apparatus, technique, or interpretive framework.

This is not, of course, what practicing scientists typically *say* about the history of their sub-(sub)-disciplines. Rather, it is the role that history serves within their scientific practice. When queried explicitly about the history of their field, scientists usually trot out the names of a few illustrious "founder-heroes" whose eponymous theories have set the terms for the larger discipline to which they belong. Thus, they cite "Newton's" theory of gravity, "Darwin's" theory of natural selection, or "Einstein's" theory of relativity. The actual beliefs, arguments, and methods of these illustrious forebears are here taken to be roughly identical to the way these materials (the theories of gravity, evolution, and relativity) are presented in the textbooks and lectures which the scientists have assimilated in the early years of their training.

But scientists who have taken the plunge and actually read the texts of these eminent forebears have usually found the experience disconcerting. Newton's calculus takes the form of a geometric analysis inaccessible to the researcher trained in modern mathematics; his religious writings were willfully heretical by the standards of the deists who claimed him as their inspiration; and his obsession with alchemy and biblical chronology are hard to square with his status as the founder of rational mechanics. For his part, Darwin wrote six editions of *On the Origin of Species* in which his phrasing subtly altered with regard to whether evolution is purposeful or not, and with regard to the validity of the inheritance of acquired characteristics; moreover, his tens of thousands of notebook pages show that in the crucial discovery years of the 1830s he wrestled with Malthusian population theory, the Laplacian nebular hypothesis, and never did manage to properly organize the finches he brought back from the Galapagos. As for Einstein's 1905 paper on special relativity, it opens with a discussion of Maxwell's electro-magnetism and never mentions the Michelson–Morley experiment (usually said to have inspired Einstein to prove that the ether does not exist). How have scientifically trained historians treated these incongruities? To the extent that they paid any attention to such texts, they rescued their heroes from the partial understandings of the period in which they labored. They set aside Newton's alchemy and demonstrated the equivalence of his geometric methods with modern algebraic notation. They credited the Darwin of the 1830s with a eureka experience in the Galapagos, and an "intuitive" understanding of the logic of population genetics which would only emerge formally in the evolutionary synthesis of the 1930s. And they stripped the electro-magnetism from Einstein's history and cited the Michelson–Morley experiment as justifying his repudiation of the ether. In short, any aspect of a scientist's work that did not fit into the progressive development of scientific knowledge was either ignored, or viewed as an incidental mistake that was later corrected. Such was the state of history of science until the 1960s.

If this description reads like a caricature, it is not meant to be dismissive. Why should scientists monopolize the writing of the history of their own chosen domain any more than artists, aristocrats, or Anabaptists do their histories? To be sure, practitioners bring valuable insider knowledge to bear on the telling of their own past, but they would hardly be insiders if they didn't have axes to grind. (Professional historians also have axes to grind, of course, though they do so mostly on the heads of other historians.) For most scientists – like most historically minded artists, aristocrats, or Anabaptists – the past is a resource to tap for current gain, part of their on-going argument with contemporaries. Thus, the founders of the science of genetics in the first decade of the twentieth century reached back to "discover" Gregor Mendel as a precursor, extracting from his obscure forty-year-old papers his discovery of the genetic ratios, while jettisoning the context within which Mendel derived the production of what he called "characteristics." Mendel was a plant-breeder interested in making hybrids, not a biologist interested in finding a mechanism for heredity. By contrast, these early twentieth-century geneticists were asserting that inheritance was discontinuous and drove evolution in sharp leaps, while engaged in a debate with their rival biometricians who asserted that genetic variation was gradual. Hence they were hardly keen to emphasize Mendel's interest in hydridization.

What about the other side of the history-of-science oxymoron? For most general historians, science has been less an explicit subject of study than a form of knowledge either to envy and emulate, or to resent and repudiate. It is worth noting that many historians have hoped that the scientific method would help them conduct a more rigorous investigation of the past. For instance, the rise of erudite history and the "science of diplomatics" in the late seventeenth century was associated with the concurrent search among natural philosophers for scientific particularities. These important tools for distinguishing authentic from forged documents, and for establishing basic historical chronologies, were touted as having validity independent of the person, place, and context of their discovery, much like the "empirical facts" found by natural philosophers. And the advent of "professional" history at the end of the nineteenth century – usually associated with a critical analysis of texts and the injection of social science into historical study – drew inspiration, in the minds of many historians, from the success of the scientific physiology and the medical sciences, as well as on the success of fields such as social statistics.

More generally, the rise of science as a model of positive knowledge whose sum was ever-increasing through the action of disinterested investigators has, since the Enlightenment, provided the intellectual backbone for self-confident historical narratives of progress that pervaded histories of Western civilization, European nationalism, material prowess, and intellectual achievement. This convergence of scientific and historical study around a common story of progress went hand-in-hand with a social convergence. Today, the career path of an academic scientist and an academic historian do not differ dramatically; both are trained in intensive graduate-school apprenticeships, publish articles in specialized peer-reviewed journals and monographs with university presses, and are vetted for tenure by informed communities of senior colleague-peers before being given final approval by college deans and university presidents.

To be sure, other historians have explicitly positioned their field against science, emphasizing the representational aspects of historical writing, the way narrative mimetically reproduces the past for readers. But however much they have emulated or rejected scientific *methods* of historical study, or portrayed science and technology as prime *movers* of historical development, general historians have usually ignored science and technology as a *subject* with its own historical unfolding. Major synthetic works on early modern European history, such as Fernand Braudel's supposedly comprehensive history of the material conditions of Europe between 1400 and 1800 completely ignore the radical changes in attitudes toward nature in this period. College textbooks in American history pay lip-service to famous inventors, business leaders, and war-time researchers, but overlook the century-long transformation in how scientific and technical work has been conducted. That is, when general historians do treat science, they have tended to regard it as an unmoved mover which radiates intellectual influence and inspires powerful "applications" (technologies) which themselves drive historical change. As we will see, this view of science itself has a history. In sum, the history of science – as composed by both ex-scientists and general historians – has largely consisted of Whig history, in which the scientific winners write the account in such a way as to make their triumph an inevitable outcome of the righteous logic of their cause.

Against these views, the disciplinary practitioners of the history of science have for the past forty years asked that the history of scientific winners and losers be treated with a degree of symmetry, such that those retrospectively judged to have gotten the "right" answer are accorded the same *form* of historical explanation as those retrospectively judged to have gotten the "wrong" answer. By this they mean to suggest that the true science of an age is as much a product of its social and political context as is its erroneous science, and hence that science is a mover that is also moved. In the view of the partisans of the "strong programme in the social construction of knowledge," who first pushed this demand for symmetry in the 1970s, the content of scientific theories directly reflects the interests of its sponsors. Throughout that decade, these "externalists" engaged in a running battle with "internalists," who responded that the reality of nature so sharply constrained scientific results that science could only be understood by following its own unfolding logic. At the same time, the social constructionists were also denounced as insufficiently reflexive by cultural critics of a linguistic bent who asked how social scientists could be so certain that they themselves had correctly identified the factors which shaped scientific inquiry, while denying that natural scientists had any certain insight into their own objects of study.

Amidst all these epistemological positionings, there has been, of course, considerable room for the blurry compromises which typically constitute the practice of history – and the history of science. Indeed, history of science today seems content to strive for a kind of historicism which proceeds with an acknowledged "double-vision." Undeniably, historians of science (like general historians) select their subject matter with an eye on those views which have proved triumphant, if only because they wish to engage contemporaries in their research. And this presentism inevitably colors their accounts. However, historicists attempt to disregard as much as possible the distinctions between truth and error not available to contemporaries. It would be churlish (they say) to sort such assertions into bins of "right" and "wrong" by our retrospective lights. Historians ought to identify with scientific actors who do not know the outcome of their disputations, without necessarily blinding themselves to the ironies the historian knows loom ahead. In sum, these historians of science have asked to be allowed to treat their subject in the same way that historians of other subjects treat theirs, whether they study art, aristocrats, or Anabaptists. But, as we will see, their efforts to draw nearer to historical practice have been continually bewitched by the special status of science in the self-understanding of the West.

Phase 1: Scientists as Historians

The earliest histories of science were composed by practicing natural philosophers, especially those who played a leading role in the scientific institutions of early-modern Europe. They thereby sought to establish the then novel proposition that science was a product of the detached mind. The preferred format was biographical, on the model of the eulogies pronounced upon the death of academic colleagues. In France, Bernard de Fontenelle raised this form to a high art in his 40-year tenure as Permanent Secretary to the Parisian Academy of Sciences from 1699 to 1739.[1] These *éloges* did more than recap the technical achievements of the departed savant, they served as secular sermons on the moral qualities of the honest investigator of nature. The life of a natural philosopher, like his work, was permeated with the virtues of self-sacrifice, disinterestedness, and stoic calm. The qualities of concision, candor, and service to country elevated the natural philosopher to a par with other heroes of the realm (statesmen, generals, men of letters) and implied that his selfless contribution to the accumulation of true knowledge had likewise bestowed on him a measure of immortality. These *éloges* were preached in order to reassure gathered colleagues, console a bereaved family, and inspire young practitioners to join their august company. They connected life and work, but in such a way as to deny that wider social influences shaped scientific knowledge: these rigorous philosophers, vigorous experimenters, and solitary thinkers were, of all men, those who were the least distracted by their surroundings. They were held to be especially indifferent to the lure of money. Indeed, the fact that these academies admitted only men emphasized their disengagement from the world of social and personal entanglements said to be the special province of women. Yet the *éloges* also had to contend with knotty problems of historicism because the orator did not necessarily concur with the honored dead. For instance, Fontenelle, the Cartesian, disagreed with the views of the Newtonians he buried. In other cases, the subject's early interpretations had been superceded by the time of his death. By and large, the candor of the orator required him to acknowledge these differences, while exhibiting the larger harmony of the scientific community. To do so, this community of self-selected savants invoked the personal qualities of early-modern elites who predominated in their particular culture. In England, members of the Royal Society invoked the gentleman's credibility. In France, members of the Academy of Science invoked the aristocrat's honorable service to country, even when the practitioners themselves were born of humbler station.

By the early nineteenth century, however, investigators of nature aspired less to membership in this corporate community of immortals than to partnership in professional societies that vetted and published their work, and which were organized around disciplines like physics, biology, chemistry, etc. A crucial element in legitimating knowledge as objective in this period was the way that investigators (scientists, engineers, etc.) increasingly passed judgment on one another using the same impersonal criteria they used to judge their objects of study. That is, they connected the "two faces" of objectivity – the independent status of the material object and the disinterested stance of the evaluator of that object – via a disinterested evaluation of evaluators. The spread of examinations and quasi-public criteria of admission to institutes of higher learning signaled the emergence of that peculiar panopticon known as meritocracy, thereby creating the social conditions for a community of "self-distancing" inquirers. The character of this community still differed in subtle ways in different contexts. In France, it was validated and coordinated by service to the state. In England, the sociability remained more closely tied to that of the voluntary society or gentleman's club. Yet where scientific credibility had once rested in part on the personal characteristics of the natural philosopher as honest gentleman or honorable aristocrat, it increasingly resided in the mechanisms which bound the community together, and the allegiance of the practitioner to its collective codes.

That said, the *éloge's* tone of self-sacrifice and disengagement from the social world was still being struck in the stand-alone life-and-work biographies of scientists that began to appear in the early nineteenth century. Some offer superb accounts of their subject's scientific achievements, and draw on private letters and notebooks. An exemplary text is the biography of Isaac Newton by the Scottish physicist, David Brewster.[2] A superbly documented history based on manuscripts as well as published science, it places Newton as "near the gods" as it is possible for a man to come. The story of Newton's life, Brewster notes, was "unmarked with dramatic events," leaving his scientific achievement as the book's sole narrative. Yet Brewster proved reluctant to assimilate Newton's extensive dealings with alchemy, saying that alchemy was a youthful indiscretion which Newton abandoned for "more noble pursuits," despite admitting that Newton continued to work on alchemy all his life. Nor did Brewster reconcile Newton's celestial mechanics with his heterodox religious views regarding an interventionist God, long out of favor in Britain. This heroic account of science as the work of individual genius befit the age's wider emphasis on individual achievement in commerce, empire, and learning.

Alongside these biographical approaches of the early nineteenth century there appeared a set of disciplinary histories composed by practitioners usually in their period of retirement. These works nicely reinforced the form of professional organization that had come to define the scientists' career. Among the first and finest of these was the six-volume, 4000-page history of astronomy published in the 1820s by Jean-Baptiste-Joseph Delambre, a leading French astronomer and one of the co-founders of the metric system.[3] This monument to erudition is rarely read today, but it is unusual only in its extraordinary thoroughness and its author's mastery of ancient languages and texts. Nonetheless this history remained closely tied to the biographical approach of the *éloges*; the volumes are structured as a chronological sequence of biographies of great astronomers, and this is no accident. As Permanent Secretary for the Physical Science in the Academy of Sciences of the early nineteenth century, Delambre composed several dozen of these *éloges*, as well as biographical sketches of illustrious natural philosophers – from Ptolemy to Kepler to Lagrange – published in the monumental compendium of French biography, the *Dictionnaire biographique*.

In his astronomical history, Delambre provided some brief facts about the savant's personal background, a few sentences regarding his training, then concentrated almost exclusively on a critical appraisal of his methods and accomplishments. Delambre assessed the astronomer's results in light of current knowledge, and the implicit narrative is one which we might call a "relay-race of knowledge," in which there is heroism in having run one's lap as well as one can. Astronomers were among the first investigators of nature to be drawn to the history of their science because the past was an important source of empirical data. To track celestial phenomena over a long period of time, astronomers often have recourse to the data of long-dead observers, including those as far back as Babylon and Egypt. For this reason, they had to disentangle observational data from the models which had guided their predecessors, and restate old assumptions in up-to-date formalism. Delambre's mining of the past respected the limits of bygone knowledge, but did so to an instrumentalist end.

A third form of scientist-composed history of science to emerge in the nineteenth century was the "total history," marshaled to validate a particular philosophy of science, and to paint a rosy picture of science's future. William Whewell, the natural philosopher who coined the term "scientist" in his 1837 *History of the Inductive Sciences* – thereby naming the new-style professional practitioners – understood science to be comprised of a set of disciplines, themselves continually fractioning, while always making coherent progress toward positive knowledge.[4] For Whewell, progress was a progress of understanding. Hence, rather than map out a simple chronology of geniuses and their dis-

coveries, his account offered a rational reconstruction of the necessary intellectual conditions which had prompted such major scientific innovations as
Newton's discovery of the law of universal gravitation. This focus on ideas as
preconditions for scientific progress gave science a historicist cast. More generally, Whewell subscribed to the Enlightenment view that "science" had first
been broached by the Greeks, left to stagnate during the Middle Ages, and
only revived in its modern robust form in the seventeenth century.

The general explosion of the technology-driven economy in the later nineteenth century also led scientific practitioners to claim a certain degree of credit
for these innovations, without thereby implying that they were personally
motivated by material gain. To claim a connection between science and technology was hardly new, of course; the utility of science had been trumpeted
since the days of Francis Bacon, and even before. But leading scientists like
William Thompson now buttressed their assertion that they had got their
science "right" by the material fecundity – and profitability – of the "applications" their knowledge had produced: chlorine bleaches and chemical dyes,
the trans-continental and trans-Atlantic cables, or the accuracy of ballistics fire.
William Thompson became Lord Kelvin in the process. In turning to the world
of commerce for validation, scientists continued to maintain a distinction
between applied (technological) knowledge which was understandably
guarded with some secrecy by its corporate sponsors *versus* pure (scientific)
knowledge which was openly published and shared among practitioners. This
division was given institutional form in two sites of research: (1) the new
corporate research labs founded at Bell Telephone, General Electric, Du Pont,
Siemens, and the other giants of the Second Industrial Revolution, and (2)
the new research university, based on the German model, where "pure" scientific research was pursued into the properties of nature, albeit with an eye
on important technical spin-offs.

Phase 2: Science as Intellectual History

The history of science as the history of "ideas on the march" was offered to
the general public by various popularizers in the latter nineteenth century –
particularly as controversy swirled around the theological implications of evolutionary natural history. The historian Andrew Dickson White's 1897 *History
of the Warfare of Science with Theology in Christendom* capped a trend toward
using historical accounts to celebrate the triumph of science over traditional
thought.[5] The battle for the Western mind was here portrayed as a zero-sum
game in which scientific truth was gradually crowding out religious superstition and dogma. White was a co-founder of Cornell University, who believed
that "science, pure and applied" should have equal status with humanist and
ministerial training at American universities. He deployed scientific philologi-

cal criticism to debunk scriptural literalism and to paint a heroic tale of scientific progress against the prevailing orthodoxies of the past and present. In doing so, he drew clean lines between science, religion, and magic, and stripped the founding giants of seventeenth-century science of their religious fervor (while acknowledging the contradictions, as he saw it, in some of the earliest of the breed, like Francis Bacon). Histories of Galileo were particularly popular during the nineteenth-century *Kulturkampf*, as science sought to recruit young practitioners with tales of martyrs who had refused to serve the powers that be. Again, science was being presented as the antithesis of party politics and factional religion. And the place where science was being done was increasingly the research university – based on the German model – where specialists in the disciplinary departments replicated their ranks by training large numbers of doctoral students in laboratories organized around research projects. For instance, Justus Liebig's laboratory in Giessen had already begun in the 1830s to conduct both foundational research in organic chemistry and contribute to advances in artificial fertilizer and infant formula.

But if science consisted of the march of ideas, surely ideas were themselves human creations. Ernst Mach was a late nineteenth-century Viennese polymath who marshaled the history of science to support his view that scientific laws were nothing more than economical descriptions of sensations. His positivism laid out a scheme of progress in which synthesis was a purely human project of efficient explanation. A contemporary, the accomplished French Catholic physicist, Pierre Duhem, employed a somewhat similar philosophy, albeit one more skeptical of the comprehensiveness of scientific theories, and of the ability of crucial experiments to distinguish among them. Duhem, however, marshaled his philosophy in the service of a more explicitly historical program, an attempt to give a more positive evaluation to the role of medieval scholastic thought in the history of science. Indeed, Duhem argued that Galileo could have been reconciled with the Catholic Church had he not stubbornly insisted on the material reality of the Copernican theory. Mach and Duhem were both scientists and philosophers, yet their work suggested that the development of new science was in some important sense historically bounded.

The dominant philosophy of science of the early twentieth century was logical positivism, which drew upon these earlier philosophical strands to portray science as built upon an accumulation of empirical findings subsumed into ever-broader covering laws. In the variant proposed by Karl Popper, these laws were themselves falsifiable, and hence provisionally true. This view of the history of science was given a logical form by the members of the "Vienna Circle" on the model of the sciences themselves.

The rise of the Nazis disrupted the intellectual life of Europe and offered a painful example of how political ideology could distort scientific research in the heart of one of Europe's proudest self-policing research communities. The

Nazi eugenics policies were henceforth to be cited as an example of the horrors that could occur when politicians interfere with science (though the policies were in fact modeled to some degree on inter-war American sterilization programs). A similar perversion of the autonomy of science was the Nazi's repudiation of Einstein's relativity theory in favor of "Aryan" physics. The advent of World War II further disturbed scientific research on the Continent, while of course, teaching the world that scientists (even in Germany, as well as in the United States) could contribute to the development of powerful new technologies from rockets to atomic bombs. One scholar who had already fled to America was the Belgian liberal, George Sarton, who had founded the journal *Isis* in 1912 and helped establish the History of Science Society in the 1920s. Through his writings and professional organizing, he sought to demonstrate that scientific progress was the single universal project to which people of all traditions might contribute. Another émigré was Alexandre Koyré, a Russian who had been teaching in France, and who became the most influential historian of science at mid-century. Koyré worked within a tradition of intellectual history, using textual exegesis to distill a history of pure thought out of the controversies of seventeenth-century science. Koyré understood that the science of that age had been bound up in a passionate theological debate, even if the unintended consequence was to make God unnecessary.[6] For many general historians who came of age in the immediate wake of World War II, this sort of work still exemplifies the history of science at its best.

Such an idealist view of science might seem odd, however, in an age when scientists had so forcefully demonstrated their capacity to manage large technical projects and deliver terrifying powers of destruction. Indeed, this image of the scientist as an investigator insulated from social pressures was deliberately cultivated by the same scientists who had directed these projects and who now wanted the US government heavily involved in funding research. Moreover, a particular style of history of science served their image-making in this regard.

The two scientists who did more than anyone else to organize America's scientific war effort during World War II – and the Manhattan Project in particular – were the chemist, James B. Conant, and the computer scientist, Vannevar Bush, also known as the university presidents of Harvard and MIT respectively. Shortly after the start of the Cold War, Bush became the principal founder of the National Science Foundation, an organization created to permit an enormous expansion in the funding of "pure" science by the federal government. Bush justified this project on the grounds that pure science would ultimately bear practical fruits. But he insisted that for this to occur, scientists had to retain control over the direction of research themselves. Indeed, it was in this period that double-blind reviews became the norm for conducting scientific medical research, as well as the means by which peers evaluated scholarship, both in science and in history. Meanwhile, Conant, back at Harvard, belonged to a group of scientists who believed that for lay citizens to partic-ipate in decisions regarding nuclear weapons, the American elite needed to be educated about science. To that end, he initiated a general studies curriculum that would teach non-science undergraduates about the rigors of scientific knowledge-making via the history of science. This included reading through a series of case-studies of famous experiments in the history of science. This book series transformed the logical positivists' view of the history of science into a pedagogical program.

Thomas Kuhn became interested in the history of science when he took time off from his doctoral research in physics to teach for Conant's history of science course. Kuhn is still the person most often associated with the study of the history of science today, and for good reason. His suggestion that the science of any given period is governed by a "paradigm" that defines the con-cepts, problems, and methods which constitute the discipline, itself spawned something like a paradigm shift in the history of the history of science. As is the case in many a revolution, the results often horrified their inaugurator, taking twists he never anticipated. Kuhn's 1962 book, *The Structure of Scien-tific Revolutions*, argued that science could not be understood as a gradual accumulation of empirical knowledge (as the logical positivists had claimed), but had been marked by radical shifts in perspective which themselves set the terms for which empirical facts mattered and how they were to be understood.[7] The ur-shift was the scientific revolution of the seventeenth century, but Darwin's evolutionary theory or quantum mechanics also marked radical dis-ruptions within the conceptual development of the life and physical sciences respectively, setting the terms for a period of what Kuhn called "normal science," during which the discipline wrestled with a coherent set of problems and used well-honed problem-solving tools.

Kuhn's focus was on scientific change, but his view undermined any sim-plistic notion of scientific progress. His central unit of analysis was not the individual scientific genius, but the community which accepted science and solved the problems of normal science. This scientific community was a lan-guage community, largely self-regulating, and isolated from the social world. Indeed, according to Kuhn, the high degree of consensus commanded by a paradigm is what marked a community as engaged in science (as opposed to the social sciences or humanities, where such a consensus rarely prevailed). At the same time, however, Kuhn inadvertently opened a vast space for the social causation of scientific change because his explanation of what sparked a sci-entific revolution was so impoverished alongside his persuasive account of the discontinuities themselves. Kuhn suggested that revolutions occurred when researchers unearthed scientific anomalies that seemed incompatible with received notions. But to the extent that Kuhn argued that scientific facts – anomalies included – took on importance only in the context of some partic-ular paradigm, he never clarified what suddenly transformed these anomalies into pressing problems for the scientific community. Moreover, Kuhn's use of psychological analogies for the shifts in perspective that accompanied new paradigms seemed to imply that scientific theory choice might have a non-rational component.

Yet even as he trumpeted discontinuity in scientific thinking, Kuhn remained wedded to a history of science whose governing epistemic blocks were structured around coherent theories. Such a position was itself now susceptible to criticism, and in the 1970s Paul Feyerabend launched an attack on the very notion that science possessed a coherent conceptual structure.[8] This was a time of wider discontent with science and scientific technology as being complicit in the terrors of the Cold War, the devastation of Vietnam, and the despoliation of environment. Such accusations were an understandable extension of the scientists' own claim that their theories had been validated by the technological fruits they had produced. Science, having been sold as an instrument of power, was now condemned as beholden to the powerful.

It was in this period that a number of programs in the history of science took shape, several of them located in their own degree-granting departments, as had already been the case at Harvard. Some were structured as autonomous history of science programs, such as Wisconsin, Johns Hopkins, and Penn. Others were constituted as history and philosophy of science departments, such as Indiana. Still others remained within the history departments, such as Princeton, Berkeley, and UCLA. In more recent decades, a number of programs have been structured as "science, technology and science" departments, such as UC San Diego, Virginia Tech, Cornell, and MIT. These differences reflect the diversity of approaches to science studies in the past few decades.[9]

Phase 3: Science as Social History

Materialist explanations for scientific innovation were not new in the 1960s. In the 1930s, Boris Hessen, a Soviet scholar, had shocked British historians with his claim that Newton's mechanics were the expression of British imperial and commercial interests, as exemplified by the aid that Newton's celestial mechanics offered in the calculation of longitude at sea. The postulate that modern science had first emerged as an expression of the class interests of a revolutionary bourgeoisie was taken up with considerable sophistication after the war by Marxist historians such as Christopher Hill, who connected the seventeenth-century scientific revolution with the broader English revolutions of the period.

One of the most important social accounts of the origins of science was the work of the sociologist Robert K. Merton, who drew on the infamous Weber thesis on the origins of capitalism to suggest that religion – or at least a particular brand of Protestantism – rather than going to war with science in the seventeenth century, had in fact promoted a scientific attitude.[10] First published in 1938, the text was reissued to a more appreciative audience in 1970. This was a deeply historicist project to explain the motives for scientific study in the language of the historical actors, and provide a macro-historical account of enduring scientific norms, such as priority of discovery, universalism of results, visible evidence, and the practical utility of knowledge. The specifics of Merton's thesis – positing an Anglo-centric scientific revolution driven by radical Puritans – has been contested, but his larger message that science is embedded in its social and political matrix has remained. That said, Merton always stopped short of asserting that the specific *content* of scientific theories had been dictated by the religious or political context.

The sociologists of the 1960s and 1970s who extended Merton's program in just this direction called their project the "strong programme in the social construction of science." These sociologists of knowledge adopted from Kuhn the notion that scientific change was driven by extra-scientific forces and the assertion that new theories could not in any simple way be called superior to the old. This school of thought – also known as the Edinburgh school – claimed that science is social through-and-through, and that its self-aggrandizing claim to have found a method to produce transcendent truth should be given no more credence than the comparable self-flattery of revealed religion or primitive cults.[11] Thus, they investigated "pseudo-sciences" like phrenology and "almost-sciences" like gravity waves with the same attention they devoted to "hard" sciences like quantum physics. They made visible the political views and social status of scientists, as well as the institutional loyalties which guided their research, thereby opening up room for a history of women and sexism in science. These historians and sociologists also sought to explain the widespread acquiescence among the laity to the scientists' view that they alone had a purchase on the truth, and how this had been used to make contentious social policies palatable. Hence, they focused on institutions like the Mechanics Institutes of early nineteenth-century England, where popular science had been preached to the lower orders in such a way as to suggest that the rise of industrial production, and the inequalities of wealth that accompanied it, were an outcome of scientific advance, and hence uncontestable. Finally, they criticized ideological movements which had claimed scientific standing by showing how these foundational scientific accomplishments had themselves been predicated on social and political assumptions. Thus, historians of science noted that the derivation of Social Darwinism from Darwinism was hardly surprising given the degree to which Darwin had himself been influenced by his reading of Malthusian social theory during the years he discovered the mechanism of natural selection. Linked to this approach were comparative studies contrasting the distinct reception that scientific innovations, like Darwinism, had received in America, England, France, Russia, Japan, and other cultures.

Perhaps a minority of the studies produced by historians of science in the 1970s took fully to heart this social constructionist epistemology, yet as a heuristic, this relativistic stance liberated the history of science from Whiggism. In looking at science as more than the history of ideas, historians also began to pay more attention to the practice of science in the laboratory and to treat science as a form of work. This directed their attention to the unpublished notebooks that were the record of non-public science. And this in turn revealed that many of the most famous scientific experiments – such as the Nobel-prize-winning oil-drop experiment of Robert Millikan – had not followed standard protocol, but had been jerry-rigged to confirm a pre-supposed answer, albeit one confirmed myriad times since. These laboratory studies brought into relief the many people who contributed to science without ever appearing on the author page – "invisible technicians" in the phrase of Steven Shapin. It also suggested a degree of autonomy for experimentalists, who had their own research traditions and did not necessarily take their cue from paradigm-setting theorists.

This scholarship also brought into question the relationship of science to technology. An autonomous Society for the History of Technology had been founded in 1958, and many of its members have shown that the development of technology depends on much more than the simple application of scientific knowledge to practical affairs. Instead, they argue that technological innovations proceed by their own rule-of-thumb practices based on everything from engineering knowledge to artisanal know-how, and take their cue from the corporate or state-military context in which they emerge. Even such supreme examples of science's contribution to technology as the Manhattan project have been reconsidered in this light. The making of the atomic bomb depended on a vast array of experts in chemical engineering, industrial planning, and a host of "lesser" technological sciences, all wielded into a coherent project by "system managers." And although the Los Alamos physicists possessed powerful insights into the regularities of nuclear phenomena (without which the bomb would have been unthinkable), their model of the nucleus and their explanations for fission were hardly "correct" by today's standards. A similar story can be told about the history of medicine.

Given this diversification of topics, actors, and sites of investigation – and the increasing propensity of historians to delve into case studies rather than stitch together synthetic histories – one might well begin to wonder whether "science" itself constituted a coherent subject. An often underestimated prop of this proliferation of research was the massive effort undertaken to publish the manuscripts of the most famous scientists and technologists. Whole industries of historians were engaged to publish the complete works of Charles Darwin, Albert Einstein, Thomas Edison, Isaac Newton, James Clerk Maxwell, and a host of secondary figures. Like the magisterial *Dictionary of Scientific*

Biography (edited by Charles C. Gillispie and published by Scribner in 16 volumes between 1970 and 1980), these biographical projects owed their backing to the lingering assumption that science was best understood as the achievement of creative individuals. Yet the thoroughness of these publications inevitably demonstrated the inconsistencies, multiple influences, and shifting contexts within which scientists worked, as well as the enormous numbers of men and women who had contributed to science in diverse ways.

Phase 4: Science as Cultural History

Throughout the 1960s and '70s externalist studies had been denounced by defenders of the sanctity of the scientific method as somehow implying that science was "relativist." Since the 1980s, the externalists have also been criticized as insufficiently reflexive about their own scientistic methods by humanists of a linguistic bent. These humanists chide social scientists for hypocrisy. How, they ask, can social scientists deny that natural scientists can identify causes in the natural world, while arguing that they can confidently identify the social factors that shape science? Are sociologists better scientists than, say, biologists or physicists? Indeed, many sociologists have since backed away from their claims.

Under the influence of post-structuralists of various denominations, cultural historians of science have since shifted their attention to the history of how the boundaries between various disciplines of knowledge-making have been constructed, as well as the creation of the all-pervasive boundary between nature and society. Bruno Latour, for instance, has denied that such boundaries – however powerful they may be as fictions – can explain techno-scientific practice. Instead, he has emphasized the blurring of society and science, humans and non-humans, in "hybrids" linked via networks. For instance, Latour shows how the Pasteurians of nineteenth-century France were able to invoke their new-found laboratory microbes to mobilize sweeping hygienic reforms in the world outside the laboratory. Indeed, the Pasteurians succeeded to the extent that they transformed the outside world into a kind of laboratory they could dominate with the same ease they dominated the glassware in their experiments. In a sense, society is made in the laboratory as much as science is made in society.[12]

A exemplary study in the new cultural history of science is *Leviathan and the Air-Pump* by Steven Shapin and Simon Schaffer. This study focuses on the controversies surrounding Robert Boyle's attempt to use an early air-pump to validate his experiments with gases. Boyle tightly controlled access to his often-faulty pump, while engaging in a prolix literary strategy to persuade others that his results were credible. His rhetorical techniques were a crucial component of his success. He disarmed critics by admitting to false starts, advanced his opinion with modesty, and devalued "theory" to avoid dogmatic disputes. These tropes became a model of proper sociability for members of the Royal Society, the London academy for natural philosophy which Boyle helped found. His opponent in this controversy was the notorious materialist political philosopher, Thomas Hobbes. Hobbes' model for producing natural knowledge was predicated on the universal assent achieved by geometric demonstration. He despised the gentlemanly consensus of the Royal Society, which he denounced as a dangerous dilution of the authority of the absolutist monarch. Shapin and Schaffer's study connects the microcosm of the air-pump, the micro-politics of the Royal Society, and the macro-polity of the Restoration compromise to suggest how the solution to the problem of knowledge was the solution to the problem of the social order.[13]

An allied line of inquiry is the study of gender and science pursued by diverse historians, among them: Donna Haraway, Ruth Hubbard, Evelyn Fox Keller, Thomas Laqueur, Elizabeth Lloyd, and Londa Schiebinger.[14] The post-Enlightenment identification of women with their reproductive and sexual functions has made the history of science a valuable way to expose the way that gender (a set of cultural assumptions about social roles) has been linked to sex (a set of biological attributes and functions, variously described). This work suggests how both sex *and* gender are historical categories, shaped by presuppositions brought to their research by scientists who are usually male.

Among the most promising recent projects in the history of science has been the call for a history of objectivity itself, pursued by scholars such as Lorraine Daston, Peter Galison, Theodore Porter, and others.[15] These studies recognize the term's polyvalent meaning, distinguishing, for instance, between objectivity as impartiality, and objectivity as an asymptotic approach to the truth-of-the-matter. This scholarship has suggested a new periodization of science, preserving the seventeenth century as a crucial moment when certain particularities (both natural and historical) came to be understood as "facts" that could be detached from the context of their discovery, while also recognizing changes in the conception of science that took place in the nineteenth century, when objectivity came increasingly to be guaranteed by the "mechanical" way empirical results were generated and represented without (apparent) human intervention. In each period, investigators of nature were expected to subscribe to social codes, for instance, of self-abnegation, which guided their practice. Such an analysis would also apply to the work of historians, and runs in parallel to the debates over historical objectivity described in Peter Novick's *That Noble Dream*.

One could cite many other fine works in this field, yet they have not escaped the knotty problems that come with the study of science in a culture where

science is touted as its unique contribution to world civilization, widely understood as the high road to truth, and considered the sole domain where genuine
progress is possible.

Conclusion: Beyond the Science Wars?

The so-called "science wars" of the mid-1990s erupted when a physicist named
Alan Sokal ridiculed the constructionist view of science. Sokal's Voltairean
coup was to slip a parodic gobbledygook deconstructionist account of contemporary physics into the pages of *Social Text*, a scholarly journal of literary
theory whose editors (Andrew Ross and Stanley Aronowitz) had been eagerly
pulling science down to the same truth-status as the humanities. Sokal simultaneously published an exposé of his deed in *Lingua Franca*, and the prank
received front-page attention from *The New York Times*, which had recently
been campaigning against boondoggle "big science," and in particular, against
the $10 billion Superconducting Supercollider, supposed to be the crowning
achievement of twentieth-century American physics.[16]

Sokal's hoax had precedents within the world of scientific research: from
the Piltdown Man prank to more recent instances of scientific fraud. But the
more salient point is that Sokal's hoax fell on well-prepared ground. In 1994,
Paul R. Gross and Norman Levitt had published *Higher Superstition*, an attack
on the glib repudiation of natural science which they said had permeated the
"academic left." By the "left" here, Gross and Levitt meant to finger a motley
crew of post-modern humanists who identified science as the source of an
oppressive, essentializing absolutist knowledge. Sokal himself was a leftist of
the old school, who believed science offered the best hope of universal equality and improvement in the human material conditions. Yet his coup quickly
became ammunition in the on-going culture wars which pitted right-wing
canon-huggers against multi-cultural political correctors. Somewhat per-
versely, Sokal's allies on the political right also accused the post-modern left
of having given sustenance to anti-science forces like the Creationists – as if
Creationists needed support from academics when they had the Christian
Coalition behind them.

Many historians of science reacted as though they had been tarred with
the same brush and retreated. At the 1996 annual conference of the History
of Science Society, the plenary session was devoted to the Sokal Affair. Three
of the four prominent speakers had begun their career as scientists. All had
done important work in history of science, yet all suggested that historians
of science must mend fences with science and separate themselves from the
relativistic excesses of some of their brethren. Only the history-trained scholar
suggested that, as a group, historians of science had nothing to apologize for,

that scholarship in science studies had been instructive, and that historians had evidentiary standards appropriate to their domain of knowledge.

Even a few years later, the "science wars" of the 1990s appear to have been little more than a superficial rehash of a stale debate between realists and relativists, and seem only to have distracted attention from far more important structural changes. Current transformations in the university and the dissemination of information are drawing both scientists and humanists more deeply into the marketplace for knowledge, and it is these changes which seem likely to set the future terms for the study of the history of science, and history more generally. The end of the Cold War has partially shifted the funding of science from disciplines like physics to disciplines like biology, and partially back from government laboratories to private entities. At the same time, Americans in particular have experienced an era of tremendous prosperity that has been widely and plausibly attributed to knowledge-based information industries. In the process, scientific research has become more closely interwoven with commerce. This has occurred not just in corporate laboratories, where large firms have sponsored science-based research since the end of the nineteenth century. It has also occurred in the civilian and military laboratories of the government, and in the university as well. In part, this is because both private and public universities have begun to welcome corporate financing of research centers (from pharmaceutical companies, for instance), and because science faculty have placed their know-how in the service of profit-making enterprises without giving up their university positions (as when Nobel-prize winners launch biotech or electronics firms that acquire stock valuations in the millions). Large numbers of physicists also went to work on Wall Street in the 1990s, helping assemble algorithms to predict stock prices – though they seem not to have performed any better than old-fashioned prognosticators. And many academics in the natural and social sciences now work regularly as paid consultants. Currently, government agencies, universities, and private firms are quarreling over who gets to claim patent rights to the results of their scientific staff, who themselves move with increasing ease among these institutions. This mobility is part of a more general trend throughout the knowledge-based economy, in which the hierarchical firms which once offered secure employment to professionals – and in return demanded loyalty and property-rights in their accomplishments – are being replaced with more horizontal enterprises in which individuals with know-how act as quasi-autonomous agents, selling their services and moving on.

As a result, the late nineteenth-century German model of the research university as a domain insulated from the immediate demands of the commercial world – even as its denizens promise their work will ultimately serve practical ends – seems to be giving way to a hybrid knowledge-making beast. Recent scandals have seen the results of drug trials performed by university clinicians suppressed by the sponsoring pharmaceutical company. National research laboratories race against for-profit firms to sequence the human genome (and perhaps assert some property-claim in the data). The authority of the double-blind peer-review process is threatened by pre-publication of results, including postings on the internet. Silicon Valley and Stanford University are locked in a mutual embrace. Under these circumstances, the kind of scientific objectivity founded on disinterestedness and vetted by a community of informed but disinterested peers seems likely to alter.

What do these changes in the practice of science and the structure of the university portend for history, and for the history of science in particular? For starters, attention to the history of intellectual property is sure to quicken. Also, after years of isolated case studies emphasizing the local production of knowledge, there has emerged a need for synthetic and comparative work to show how local knowledge is transmitted and coordinated. At a broader level still, emerging patterns of global exchange (both techno-scientific and cultural) will bring into relief the similarities and differences which demarcate Western knowledge-making from analogous processes in China, the Arab world, India, and the rest of the non-European globe. Important foundations for this work were laid with Joseph Needham's massive project to resuscitate the history of Chinese science.[17] More is needed. The result should be a wider appreciation of the persistence and transmutation of knowledge as it moves between cultural contexts.

But however vexed and heated these epistemological debates may be, they are but a partial instance of a problem that afflicts all historical study. Whether the subject is eugenics or slavery, the investigation of the past inevitably involves the historian in judgments which are, at some inescapable level, moral or political. Does the historian's self-imposed obligation to understand involve him or her in a degree of complicity, even apologetics? *Tout comprendre, c'est tout pardonner?* Or is the (self-imposed) obligation to criticize supposed to overpower the detachment of the analyst? In this, the history of physics is no different than the history of imperialism; and the epistemological debates surrounding the history of science but a subset of the perspectival problems that beset all historical study today.

The history of science remains an oxymoron with a larger meaning. Artists, aristocrats, and Anabaptists have also told their own histories as tales of progress, triumph, and revealed truth, and in return historians have offered these insiders a more critical appraisal of their own past. Scientists should be able to cope with a similar kind of critical history. The study of the history of science requires an immersion in – and hence a sympathy for – the concepts, methods, language, and aspirations of its actors. It also demands a degree of detachment from their interests. This is the same admonition that applies to the study of artists, aristocrats, or Anabaptists. It also certainly applies to those writing the history of the history of science.

NOTES

1   Charles Paul, *Science and Immortality: The Eloges of the Paris Academy of Science (1699–1791)*, (Berkeley: University of California Press, 1980).

2   David Brewster, *Memoirs of the Life, Writings, and Discoveries of Sir Isaac Newton* (Edinburgh: Constable and Co., 1855, first edition 1831). On alchemy, see pp. 34–35. For comments on uneventful life, see pp. 1–2 of *Life*, pub. 1831.

3   Jean-Baptiste-Joseph Delambre, *Histoire de l'astronomie*, 6 volumes (Paris: Bachelier, 1817–27).

4   William Whewell, *History of the Inductive Sciences from the Earliest to the Present Time* (New York: Appleton, 1863; first edition 1837).

5   Andrew Dickson White, *History of the Warfare of Science with Theology in Christendom* (New York: Appleton, 1899, first edition 1897).

6   Alexandre Koyré, *From the Closed World to the Infinite Universe* (Baltimore: The Johns Hopkins University Press, 1957).

7   Thomas S. Kuhn, *The Structure of Scientific Revolutions* (second edition, revised; Chicago: University of Chicago Press, 1970; first edition 1962).

8   Paul Feyerabend, *Against Method: Outline of an Anarchistic Theory of Knowledge* (London: Verso, 1975).

9   Margaret W. Rossiter, ed., *Catching Up with the Vision: Essays on the Occasion of the 75th Anniversary of the Founding of the History of Science Society, A Supplement to Isis* 90 (1999): S1–S359.

10 Robert K Merton, *Technology and Society in Seventeenth-Century England* (New York: Fertig, 1970; first edition 1938).

11 Barry Barnes, David Bloor, and John Henry, *Scientific Knowledge: A Sociological Analysis* (Chicago: Chicago University Press, 1996). Harry Collins and Trevor Pinch, *The Golem: What Everyone Should Know about Science* (Cambridge: Cambridge University Press, 1993).

12 Bruno Latour, *The Pasteurization of France* (Cambridge, MA: Harvard University Press, 1988).

13 Shapin and Schaffer, *Leviathan and the Air Pump: Hobbes, Boyle and the Experimental Life* (Princeton: Princeton University Press, 1985).

14 Donna Haraway, *Simians, Cyborgs and Women: The Reinvention of Nature* (New York: Routledge, 1991). Ruth Hubbard, Mary Sue Henifin, and Barbara Fried, eds., *Women Look at Biology Looking at Women: A Collection of Feminist Critiques* (Boston: Hall, 1979). Evelyn Fox Keller, *Reflections on Gender and Science* (New Haven: Yale University Press, 1985). Thomas Laqueur, *Making Sex: The Body and Gender from the Greeks to Freud* (Cambridge, MA: Harvard University Press, 1990). Londa Schiebinger, *The Mind Has No Sex?: Women in the Origins of Modern Science* (Cambridge, MA: Harvard University Press, 1989).

15 Lorraine Daston and Peter Galison, "The Image of Objectivity," *Representations* 40 (1992): 81–128. Theodore Porter, *Trust in Numbers: Objectivity in Science and Public Life* (Princeton: Princeton University Press, 1995).

16 For a later version of Sokal's argument, see Alan Sokal and John Bricmont, *Intellectual Impostures: Postmodern Philosophers' Abuse of Science* (London: Profile, 1998).

17 Joseph Needham, *Science and Civilization in China* (Cambridge: Cambridge University Press, 1954–).

REFERENCES AND FURTHER READING

Biagioli, Mario, ed., *The Science Studies Reader*, New York: Routledge, 1999.

Colby, R., G. N. Cantor, J. R. R. Christy, and M. J. S. Hodge, *Companion to the History of Modern Science*, London: Routledge, 1990.

Keller, Evelyn Fox, *Reflections on Gender and Science*, New Haven: Yale University Press, 1985.

Latour, Bruno, *Science in Action: How to Follow Scientists and Engineers through Society*, Cambridge, MA: Harvard University Press, 1987.

Pickering, Andrew, ed., *Science as Practice and Culture*, Chicago: University of Chicago Press, 1992.

Porter, Theodore, *Trust in Numbers: The Pursuit of Objectivity in Science and Public Life*, Princeton: Princeton University Press, 1995.

Shapin, Seven, *A Social History of Truth: Civility and Science in Seventeenth-Century England*, Chicago: Chicago University Press, 1994.

Shapin, Steven and Simon Schaffer, *Leviathan and the Air Pump: Hobbes, Boyle, and the Experimental Life*, Princeton: Princeton University Press, 1985.

Chapter Sixteen

Language, Literary Studies, and Historical Thought

Susan A. Crane

Historians write. Historians write about the past. Truisms aside (for almost nobody cares about the past because they care about historians), the fact that historians write history rather than history producing itself ought to give us pause. The past was, it "happened." But the past that was and the past that historians write are two distinct entities. The past happens in time; history "happens" when it is written and read and remembered. If we start our inquiry into the writing of history with this supposition clearly in mind, then it will surprise no reader that the very act of doing what you are doing now, reading, requires investigation. Historical understanding transpires, in large part, through reading. We historians and readers cannot assume that we know what we are doing, or what we are learning, until we understand the nature of that process. This is why literary studies and linguistic analysis have been enormously important for historians in the modern era. These modes of cultural analysis can offer insights into the nature of the historical process, the making of history and the learning of history. Theory enables inquiry into praxis. Anyone who separates the theory from the practice of historical writing is in danger of naively reproducing essentialized notions about "the way things really were."

Application of linguistic and literary theories to historical understanding has not been limited to the twentieth century, although their utility became more contentious as that century wore on. The emergence of modern historical consciousness, according to Hayden White among others, can be identified most clearly in distinctive new forms of historical writing in the late eighteenth and early nineteenth centuries. Modern Western historical thought has shown increasing concern with the complexity of language in two ways: in the study of past linguistic usages, with particular attention to uncovering the meanings of terms and texts in their specific historical contexts; and in the study of how historians write, how they produce narratives of the past, and how they deploy the languages of their own cultures. I will discuss an array of nineteenth- and twentieth-century developments in historical thought in western Europe and North America, where interest in the nature of texts and in the writing of history has figured prominently in historical investigations.

Historical Knowledge and the Study of Texts

The definition of what constitutes a "text" poses a problem for modern historical thought. How do historians define "text"? Or as a student asked her professor at Johns Hopkins University in 1979, "is there a text in this class?" The professor replied, yes, the *Norton Anthology of Literature*. The student, however, was not asking whether a textbook was going to be used in her course. She wanted to know "in this class, do we believe in poems and things, or is it just us?" A previous experience in literary critic Stanley Fish's class had taught her that "just us" constituted an interpretive community, a group whose readings of a poem or other literature comprised a system complete unto itself. The poem enabled many readings, but the ones of greatest concern to professor and student were those they achieved in the context of their mutual reading. The poem itself held no claim to authoritative interpretations or to meanings unattainable by a community of readers.[1] Similar debates about the nature of "texts" written in the past, the authority of the author, the intended meanings conveyed through writing, and the role of those who interpret texts, continue to flourish in academic settings and engender hostility and skepticism particularly within the historical profession.

Such debates, however, are not unique to the late twentieth century. Nineteenth-century historical thinkers argued, for instance, about whether material artifacts of the past carried the same kinds of historical information as written documents. Could an antique object reveal the sorts of historically useful and valid information about the past that appeared in a written document? Did myth and folklore transmit cultural memory and codes? What were the most useful and accurate sources of information? The need to define terms such as "text" for practical use and reliable research was expressed in the establishment of the modern historical discipline's own distinct methodology. The nineteenth century witnessed the formation of a historical profession, one which held chairs at established universities and propounded methodologies and modes of conduct, standardizing historical inquiry along the lines familiar to us today. Professionalization was accompanied by specialization; other academic disciplines such as art history, anthropology, archaeology, philology, linguistics and the history of religion developed alongside, and in contention with, history. We should bear in mind that the history of historical thought, in its professionalized modern mode, has occurred simultaneously with the creation of other social sciences and their definitions of texts. Thus historical practitioners defined their concept of a historical "text" or document in part to distinguish their object of study from that of other disciplines.

Specialized historical inquiry devoted a great deal of energy to determining the status of its sources. For instance, biblical criticism in the early part of the nineteenth century focused on two key issues: the historical credibility of biblical sources and the possibility of their meanings being fully understood. Methods of source criticism, thoroughly developed for the historical profession by Leopold von Ranke and his students, relied on work done by theologians and philologists in establishing the historical validity of biblical texts. Hermeneutics was developed as a mode of reading biblical texts to understand their fullness beyond what a specific author wrote in another time, such that a reader might intuitively reach beyond the "author's intention" to communicate meaning and achieve an understanding of the "horizons" of that author's world. This intuition then enabled both successful communication and the reader's own linguistic comprehension of another historical epoch.

The hermeneutic intuition of a shared horizon constituted a major breakthrough in biblical criticism. Protestant theologian Friedrich Schleiermacher (1768–1834) described this hermeneutic connection between reader and text as a conversation between past and present.[2] His biographer, Wilhelm Dilthey (1833–1911), built on Schleiermacher's notion of a textual conversation to argue that the past was not alien to the present, but accessible through traditions and customs that effectively bridged temporal distance. The philosopher Hans-Georg Gadamer (b. 1900) summarized the significance of these trends in German thought in his massive *Truth and Method* (1960), which characterized history as "the conversation which we are."[3] His fundamentally optimistic belief that each new generation could understand the past was rooted in a conception of language: "the hermeneutical problem is not one of the correct mastery of language, but of the proper understanding of that which takes place through the medium of language."[4] The medium of language enables the conversation that produces historical understanding, Gadamer explained, because language gives continuity to custom and tradition. The continuity of linguistic transmission does not ensure exact understanding, but it allows the present and the past to be in dialogue. The Old and New Testaments, for example, provided the first and best sources for understanding the Christian tradition, and they were accessible because they were transmitted linguistically, as texts, for readers.

The theory of hermeneutics optimistically offers the possibility of historical understanding without significant breaks in transmission and without interruptions and distortions. From a hermeneutical perspective, the adept reader can understand the author's meaning even better than the author himself could have. Other theorists have countered that any kind of "dialogic" understanding of the past must take into account silences, missed understandings, willful corruptions of meaning and ideological constraints. In particular, the controversial Russian theorist Mikhail Bahktin (1895–1975) argued that all language use encompasses contested meanings. Bahktin's studies of the form of the novel, particularly *Problems of Dostoyevsky's Poetics* (1929; revised 1963 and translated into English in 1983) and *Rabelais and His World* (1945; revised 1965 and translated 1968), introduced a method of discourse analysis in which words themselves were considered as sites of multiple meanings, rather than as stable representations of other thoughts or objects.[5] Bahktin described narrative structures as the result of "heteroglossia," or multiple languages interacting with each other to produce communication and diverse meanings rather than singular or constrained meanings. Languages interacted through dialogue; none could exist in isolation. In the book on Rabelais, for instance, peasants' laughter was seen not as a natural or innately human form of sharing humor. Instead, Bahktin proposed, their laughter was a specific instance of subversive communication, actively contesting social and cultural elites' intended meanings. Bahktin offered a model which historians might employ to understand social interactions through his analysis of Rabelais' depiction of the world turned topsy-turvy in the carnival mode of early-modern festivals, when power hierarchies were inverted for a day of revelry. These "carnivalesque" challenges to institutional authority, as Bahktin described them, offered insights into the power structures and modes of resistance of early-modern Europe. The study of linguistic usages in the works of Rabelais thus added a new dimension to the kind of social history that was also shifting attention to the hitherto suppressed meanings of ostensibly happy peasantry at play.

Bahktin's work must be seen in the context of modern linguistic theory. Silences and repressed discourse were not recognized as subjects of historical inquiry until the advent of structuralism and semiotics.[6] According to Roland Barthes (1915–80), "Structuralism is neither a school, a movement, nor a vocabulary, but an activity that reaches beyond philosophy, that consists of a succession of mental operations which attempt to reconstruct an object in order to manifest the rules of its functioning." The "reconstruction of the object" referred to universal human experiences and cultural processes which could be studied and understood through language as recurring, rule-governed phenomena. Structuralism was inherently comparative, seeking ubiquitous patterns and formal similarities among the diversity of cultural and temporal differences. This practice of comparative analysis was most clearly influential among the social sciences of anthropology (most notably the work of Claude Levi-Strauss), psychology (particularly Jacques Lacan), and literary criticism.

The roots of structuralism lie in semiotics (also called "semiology" or the study of signs) as developed at the turn of the century by American philosopher Charles Sanders Peirce and Swiss linguistics pioneer Ferdinand de Saussure (1857–1913). Saussure developed a notion of language as built upon a system of "signs." Saussure himself published little, but his lectures were collected and published as *The Course in General Linguistics* (1916). He divided the study of language into two components, *langue* (language) and *parole* (everyday speech), and suggested that linguists should properly study *langue* – the rules or structures that govern and make possible meaningful speech. Stressing the organizing structures of linguistic communication, Saussure argued that "language is a form and not a substance."[7] Formal study of languages, he proposed, revealed that all alike combine signs to form concepts. Thus letters, words, texts, images, indeed all forms of representation have been created using symbolic signifiers to represent specific signified concepts. Most crucially, Saussure posited that the relationship between the signified object and the word that represented it (signifier) was arbitrary: no prior existing concept or transcendent meaning determined a necessary combination of signified and signifier. Languages both create enduring meanings and provide opportunities for instantaneous linguistic applications. Saussure emphasized that the study of language must focus on the synchronic moment of a linguistic system's useful existence, rather than the diachronic study of a language's evolution. Saussure's structural linguistics insisted on building a foundation for the study of language through a holistic approach to an entire system. While he considered both the synchronic and the evolving diachronic aspects of language to be significant, he focused more on the deep structural, synchronic instance of linguistic practice. This emphasis underlies all structuralism.[8]

Structuralism, Post-Structuralism and Historical Thought

Structuralism later took the study of signs beyond linguistic analysis, opening semiotics to the entire world of human meaning-making and giving more attention to everyday uses of language.[9] Roland Barthes provided a model for this kind of analysis in his witty collection of essays, *Mythologies* (1957; translated 1972). A laundry list, a myth, a wrestling match or an advertisement for margarine became subjects for Barthes' meditations on the inter-relationships between "depoliticized speech" and the signification process. A discussion of the role of the military in modern society concludes with a slogan from a margarine advertisement: "What does it matter, *after all*, if margarine is just fat, when it goes further than butter, and costs less? What does it matter, *after all*, if Order is a little brutal or a little blind, when it allows us to live cheaply?"[10] Seeing similar patterns in signification and in lack of resistance to the power of ideological discourse in the public sphere, Barthes' "mythological" analysis vivifies the inter-relationships of meaning-making and power. In his 1973 work, *The Pleasure of the Text*, Barthes characterized these inter-relationships as "the free play of language" and the "endless play of signifiers" brought into arbitrary proximity through the continuous usage and mediation of speakers. Some critics assumed that he was sanctioning a hedonistic, relativistic understanding of meaning-making. "Arbitrarily" appropriated meanings, while both playful and meaningful in the world of advertising, seemed to undermine intentional communication. The implications for historical study seemed clear, and to many, clearly irrelevant: synchronic analysis eschewed the diachronic realm of historical meaning, presenting ahistorical systems only in the temporary present of their arbitrary (here taken to mean "meaningless and random," rather than the structuralist sense of "not necessary"), playful existence.

Many critics in the 1960s and 1970s, particularly Marxists, questioned the political implications of a theory that turned social reality into an "endless play" of linguistic signifiers. As Terry Eagleton sourly noted, "Writing [and] reading-as-writing, is the last uncolonized enclave in which the intellectual can play, savouring the sumptuousness of the signifier in heady disregard of whatever might be going on in the Elysée palace or the Renault factories."[11] By pointing to the historical failures of 1968 radicalism in France and elsewhere to explain the roots of post-structural esotericism and political disassociation, politically committed theorists such as Eagleton disdained what they perceived as a flight from political engagement into a rarified atmosphere of abstract "texts" dissociated from social relevance. The formalist limits of structuralism had already begun to provoke their own responses, however, even among practitioners such as Barthes, and a range of new "post-structuralist" ideas and methods began to permeate literary and linguistic studies during the last decades of the twentieth century.

From 1960–75, Barthes taught in Paris at the Ecole Pratique des Hautes Etudes, then received a chair in literature and semiology at the Collège de France. He wrote prolifically, analyzing both past cultures and the cultural symbols of his own time. Barthes' study of nineteenth-century French Symbolist poets in *Writing Degree Zero* (1953; translated 1968) emphasized the "intransitive act" of writing for writing's sake. As historical actors, Barthes argued, these poets perceived themselves to be broken off from historicity, mired in contingency, and struggling with feelings of guilt about their social and political irrelevance even as they aestheticized the act of writing. Barthes, acting as a critic rather than a historian, nevertheless chose to write about a specific historical moment in which historical consciousness was at risk, through a sense of cultural or social estrangement, and about a group of writers who, like Eagleton, worried about political irrelevance. The study of texts gave Barthes a certain historical sensibility even though he did not share the hermeneuticists' confidence in the direct link between historical documents and historical realities.

Post-structuralism, including its postmodern aspects, need not be perceived as fundamentally ahistorical or apolitical. The term indicates a relationship to structuralism and its *Aufhebung* or self-overcoming.[12] One of the best-known concepts of post-structuralist theory, "deconstruction," propounded a method of reading literature that appeared to shelve permanently any appeal to transcendent historical meanings in favor of an arid "textuality" and hopelessly self-contradictory interpretations. The term "deconstruction," coined by Algerian-born French philosopher Jacques Derrida (1930–), is often misconstrued as meaning "to take apart," rather in the manner of a small child opening a package. Deconstruction instead refers to a method of paying attention to the inherent instability within written texts, an instability that becomes visible through a "close reading" which pays particular attention to the "traces of difference." These traces may be obscure, but they reveal contradiction and contestation, or places in which an author attempts to control a discursive field that is already cracked along its own fault lines. Texts are never entirely coherent and thus they deconstruct themselves, as a close reading can reveal. They present the appearance of totality, completion and closure, and yet contain within themselves the traces of their own illusoriness, their own construction.

Close readings of texts from either the past or the present will reveal instability and the multiple meanings of language in use. These instabilities of meaning and linguistic uses are no more "made up" than the themes that emerge in any other kind of reading, and yet many historians and critics have responded to deconstruction with great hostility particularly because of its challenge to the idea that fixed and certain meanings are inherent in written texts, and because of its apparent disregard of any serious consideration of authorial intention or historical context. As the eminent literary critic M. H. Abrams complained, Derrida's method of interpretation produced "ghostly non-presences emanating from no voice, intended by no one, referring to nothing, bombinating in a void."[13]

Historians are perhaps more familiar with the voids and multiple voices from which historical evidence arises, whereas literary critics have been more used to the stable presence of the completed work of literature before them. The attention to multivocity within texts, reminiscent of Bahktin's "heteroglossia," makes the deconstructive method of reading particularly fruitful for intellectual historians. Derrida's manner of explication, however, has proven less than imicable. His writing style is notoriously dense, and while his style reflects the themes of his theory – refusing, for example, to make direct assertions or definitive claims for truth – many readers find him unusually difficult to understand. Playfully suggesting a myriad of meanings and metaphors within writing (his term, "*écriture*" emphasizes the written word deliberately, in opposition to Saussure's *langue* and *parole*), Derrida uses puns and etymologies less to "bombinate" than to suggest the "always already" existing mutliplicity of meanings within as well as "against the grain" of the text. Critics may dismiss such work as self-referential or self-indulgent in its reliance on the intellect of the deconstructive reader, but Barthes' "pleasure" and Derrida's "play" draw attention to the richness of language as well as to the range of the reader's responses to the text. The result of deconstructive readings, according to some, is relativistic anarchy; for others, deconstructive readings offer a liberating insight into what has been unsaid as well as said, the "traces" and silences of a discursive universe.

Another crucial issue which has arisen through poststructuralism is the (in)famous "death of the author." The deconstructive emphasis on unintended meanings renders authorship and the author's individual responsibility for the meanings inherent in the written or read text highly problematic. If texts encoded their own terms of understanding and difference, then it did not make sense to study what the author had "intended," as most twentieth-century literary criticism had quite literally intended to find out. Perhaps, in a structuralist mode, authorship could be seen as simply a "function" within a system of discourse, as Michel Foucault suggested:

> The "author-function" is tied to the legal and institutional systems that circumscribe, determine and articulate the realm of discourses; it does not operate in a uniform manner in all discourses, at all times, and in any given culture; it is not defined by the spontaneous attribution of a text to its creator, but through a series of precise and complex procedures; it does not refer, purely and simply to an actual individual insofar as it simultaneously gives rise to a variety of egos and to a series of subjective positions that individuals of any class may come to occupy.[14]

The author is here deprived of his/her role as originator and placed within a discursive field; the author is her/himself a subject of discourse, a proper name associated with a text, performing the function of authorship. Accordingly, Foucault concluded, "what matter who is speaking?" Critical readers should ask instead, "what are the modes of existence of this discourse? Where does it come from; how is it circulated; who controls it? . . . Who can fulfill the diverse functions of the subject?"[15] Literary works and other texts thus take on historical significance as expressions of cultural systems rather than as the works of individual authors. Much as social historians might see goods and services as a product of economic systems instead of the work of the individual producers, so the post-structuralist reader sees texts as a product of discursive systems instead of individual genius. The author is not thereby neglected or considered unnecessary any more than is the worker, but the meanings embedded and contested within the text may range beyond his/her control, and appear as much through reading, as through writing.

The Historical Study of Discourse

Of all post-structural thought, perhaps the greatest influence on historians has come from the work of French thinker Michel Foucault (1926–84). Like

Derrida, he was trained in philosophy rather than literature, but his work reflected a constant attention to not only the creation and transmission of meaning, but also in the social and discursive systems that enable this cultural process.[16] Foucault's early career included positions in several European institutions and also at an African university. In the course of his travels he rummaged through a variety of libraries and archives, developing a thorough and thoroughly idiosyncratic historical expertise, as well as spending time in psychiatric and medical hospitals, observing treatment. His work drew on all these experiences, but it has been roundly criticized for historical inaccuracies. From 1970 he held the chair of Professor of the History of Systems of Thought at the Collège de France and also lectured widely in other countries. His historical studies (though he always resisted the title of historian) included works on the transformation of natural history and economics (*The Order of Things*, 1966; translated 1970) and of the medical profession (*The Birth of the Clinic*, 1963; translated 1973); an analysis of the transformation of prisons in the eighteenth and nineteenth centuries (*Discipline and Punish*, 1975; translated 1977); and an ambitious history of sexuality (multiple volumes, 1976–84). Foucault developed a distinctive form of discourse analysis and a controversial notion of radical "epistemic" breaks at certain transitional moments in history – moments in which new discursive formations enabled new expressions of knowledge or belief. These apparently "agentless" breaks, in accordance with his relegation of the author to a function, seemed to remove autonomous, individual actors from the historical field; yet, as critics noted, Foucault himself relied on authorial actors, great thinkers as well as obscure ones, for the texts he excavated in his "archaeologies" of the past. In *The Archaeology of Knowledge* (1969; translated 1972), Foucault articulated a theory and praxis of poststructural historical inquiry, stressing that knowledge is a construction of culture and language rather than an objective, transparent reflection of stable realities.

One of Foucault's earliest works focused on the history of mental illness in modernity (*Madness and Civilization*, 1961; translated 1965). He argued, in language reminiscent of Derrida's critique of logocentrism, that "the language of psychiatry, which is a monologue of reason about madness, has been established only on the basis of . . . a silence. I have not tried to write the history of that language but rather the archaeology of that silence."[17] The lack of a common language between Reason and Madness had created an inarticulate, but always already present, silence (the silence of the repressed patients in asylums). The task of the historian then was to realize and articulate the terms of this silence and the discursive formation that instituted it. Knowledge itself was a particular kind of discourse situated within structures of power and desire. The essential relationship between power and knowledge became a fundamental principle for Foucault and indeed for many historians.

Discourse analysis has continued to develop since the 1960s. The idea that multiple discourses coexisted in time, and that historians might usefully consider what gave these "languages" their meanings, their expression or social enactment, was only slowly accepted. For many historians, such questions seemed to distract historical inquiry from its "real" (empirical) task of uncovering the past and to carry historical research away from social reality and toward an obsession with the mere form of historical representation. Foucault appealed to many historians, however, because he suggested possible links between discourse and specific social institutions. The work of other critics such as Derrida or Barthes, by contrast, seemed to focus much more on the internal problems of texts and writing.

Barthes' important essay "Historical Discourse" (1967), for example, raised a fundamental issue regarding the status of historical writing: "is there in fact any specific difference between factual and imaginary narrative, any linguistic feature by which we may distinguish on the one hand the mode appropriate to the relation of historical events . . . and on the other hand the mode appropriate to the epic, novel or drama?"[18] By questioning the factual status of historical narrative, Barthes opened up the floodgates of discussion about the relevance of literary and linguistic theory for historical practice. Taking as his examples French Romantic historians such as Jules Michelet, Barthes analyzed their mode of presenting the historical past, according to tropes (figures of speech, i.e. metaphor or metonymy) and "shifters" (markers of the transition from a self-referential to an ostensibly more "objective" mode of representation). The whole structure of historical knowledge, as Barthes described it, depended on the system of literary representation rather than facts gleaned from archival documents.

Prior to Barthes' essay, few practicing historians had written about the literary character of historical writing. By placing the status of history as a literary genre or narrative at the forefront of discussion, historians and critics began to acknowledge that history and historical knowledge existed in the form of written objects, as texts. The knowledge in these texts was seen to be decisively shaped by the author, but even more so by the cultural context or discursive system in which the author worked. Hayden White's *Metahistory* (1973; discussed below) made a more detailed analysis along much the same lines as Barthes, and his work came to represent what more empirically minded historians saw as a misguided fascination with the form, rather than the content, of history. Barthes and White were themselves reluctant to discuss the subjectivity of historians, but in formal ways they laid the groundwork for a consideration of historians as authors.[19]

The Linguistic Turn in Contemporary Historiography

The cumulative result of structural and post-structural theory and its impact on the historical profession came to be known as "the linguistic turn." The term was borrowed from philosopher Richard Rorty's 1967 attempt to characterize tensions between newer linguistic and more traditional analytical philosophy. Philosophers accused linguistic analysts of "a self-deceptive attempt ... to procure by theft what one has failed to gain by honest toil."[20] In other words, some philosophers, like some historians, saw linguistic and literary theory as the easy way out of hard, empirical work (as if to say: those who can, practice history; those who can't, practice theory). Others, and intellectual historians in particular, saw the new historical concern with language and symbols as a harbinger of rejuvenation in a field which already took language seriously.[21] Dominick LaCapra, an early advocate and practitioner of the new approach (with a particular interest in Derrida and in the psychoanalytic implications of literary theory), called for historians to be more open-minded about the so-called "easy work" of textual analysis. LaCapra noted that many practicing historians believed "any sustained interaction between history and critical theory [should be] condemned as 'unhistorical.'"[22] In his own work, LaCapra demonstrated the advantages of sustained textual analysis in modern French historical topics. Perhaps due to post-structuralism's French roots, its influence has been evident among French historians who incorporated a sensitivity for discourse analysis with cultural historical research, such as Lynn Hunt's work on the French Revolution.

Intellectual historians' proclivity for linguistic analysis had been evident in contemporary work outside the realm of post-structuralism. The work of two British historians of political thought, John Pocock and Quentin Skinner, has been emblematic of a deliberate effort to conduct sustained critical analysis of linguistic history, particularly the language of politics.[23] While focusing on the coherence of texts and the intentions of authors instead of the free play of signifiers, Pocock and Skinner drew on a different tradition within linguistics, namely the "speech act" theory of John Austin. Speech act theory suggested that speech was comprised of two aspects: the "locutionary force" of speaking or writing something, and the "illocutionary force" of intending to communicate. A classic example of this theory in action in Skinner's work involves Machiavelli's "advice to princes." Skinner suggests that Machiavelli's advice deliberately foiled expectations available from conventional advice literature of the time, which advocated "acting virtuously." In order to see the historical impact of this unconventional advice, Skinner argued, the historian must read not only "The Prince" but also the contemporary advice literature to which it was a response. In other words, the context of advice literature and humanist ideology in the Renaissance provides an essential foundation for understanding a "classic" text of political thought. The text cannot be fully understood in or on its own terms, since those terms are themselves drawn from the social context in which Machiavelli lived. These "conventions," as Skinner referred to them, provide normative constraints on the author's intentional communication. A status quo is thus necessary for any political innovation. Critics of Skinner's and Pocock's "contextualist" and "conventionalist" approaches find their conception of the author's role as badly limited as that of the post-structuralists. Mark Bevir saw linguistic historians as allowing authors "to creep back on the historical stage, only to restrict them to bit parts as the mouthpieces of script-writing paradigms which constitute their conceptual frameworks."[24] While they would insist on their differences, both Skinner and Pocock have pursued a history of linguistic and conceptual change through textual analysis.

The linguistic turn continued to be felt in other areas of the profession besides intellectual history. Feminist, Marxist, labor, and postcolonial (particularly Subaltern Studies) historians have also considered the implications of narrative theory and literary analysis for their fields of study.[25] In these fields, the question of agency (the intentionality and actuality of historical actors' individual and collective actions) and a desire to let suppressed and repressed historical voices enter into mainstream historical knowledge has fostered an interest in the nature of historical experience. As a historian of gender relations, Joan W. Scott writes, "we need to attend to the historical processes that, through discourse, position subjects and produce their experiences. It is not individuals who have experience, but subjects who are constituted through experience." Contrary to the Pocock-Skinner schools of thought, context does not constitute causality. Any apparent homogeneity of cultural context, social structure and linguistic convention is trumped by the actual differences that characterize individuals and their inter-relationships. Scott advocates "changing the focus and the philosophy of our history, from one bent on 'naturalizing' experience through a belief in the unmediated relationship between words and things, to one that takes all categories of analysis as contextual, contested, and contingent."[26] The situational elements of power, desire, individuality and collective action are also historically contingent. Discourse analysis allows historians to see how the complexities of multiple layers of social interaction are expressed through language, silence, cooperation and contestation.

. . . Or What's a Meta For?

If there is one text most closely associated with the "linguistic turn," it is Hayden White's *Metahistory*. White's work has become the touchstone for all inquiries into the form and meaning of historical representation. As an American professor of modern European intellectual history, Hayden White (1928–) began to study nineteenth-century historiography and liberalism in the 1950s. He was particularly influenced by literary critic Northrop Frye, whose *Anatomy of Criticism* (1957) presented a new formalist analysis of narrative fiction. White also became one of the most consistently vocal advocates of Foucault. *Metahistory* presented a highly detailed and complicated mapping

of tropes in nineteenth-century historiography in order to show how historical writing created complex narrative structures. White observed that a "metanarrative" (his own term) preceded historical research: it was an overarching
and predetermined cultural field that shaped historical narratives. Historians,
in selecting their sources and organizing their accounts in narrative form, had
always already made choices that shaped the story they told, choices that
reflected an author's poetic sensibilities. A reader's attention to the historical
plot, then, could reveal how historians had worked within the metanarrative,
what choices they had made and what they hoped to convey – as well as the
deeper assumptions they never attempted to make explicit. White portrayed
the historian as reader, and his book was a monumental exercise in reading.
Many readers, overwhelmed by the formal structuralism of White's account,
mistook this exercise for a prescriptive model for all historical work, and they
simply rejected it. White's influence, indeed, appeared to be much greater
among literary critics.[27] British literary critic Peter de Bolla emphasized the
importance of White's narrative theory as "[enabling] a 'dialogue' between
the historically determined rhetoric taken as an object of study, and the rhetorically determined point of analysis from which history writing necessarily
departs."[28]

In essence, White's work lies at a crossroads between the linguistic histories of Pocock or Skinner, and post-structuralist discursive analysis. But critics
of White's approach feared that he was urging too much attention to the historian as writer and the text as a created object, rather than the production of
historical knowledge that resulted from well-researched, well-written history.
By paying too much attention to form and not enough to content, White
appeared to bring historical work into the realm of mere narrative, like fiction.
Responsible historical writing can of course focus on form without thus
becoming fictionalized. White's next two books, *Tropics of Discourse* (1978)
and *The Content of the Form* (1987) were collections of essays in which he
responded to his critics and furthered his consideration of the narrative qualities of history. If critics were concerned that a literary approach to historical
studies reduced historians to mere literary analysts with no authority to speak
about the past, White countered that the apparent threat of relativism was productive, and that the friction between factual and fictional accounts was inherent in all narratives.

The history of the Holocaust provided a crucial test case, for White as well
as for literary and linguistic analysis in historical thought more generally.[29]
How, critics contended, could histories of an event such as the Holocaust be
described as a system of literary tropes and narrative structures? The Holocaust's place in twentieth-century history would appear to be firm: an unmit-
igated devastation, an incomprehensible horror whose very comprehensible,
very real details continue to be illuminated by historians. Yet many have argued
that the Holocaust cannot be represented adequately in any medium. As the

linguist and theorist of translation George Steiner wrote, "the world of Auschwitz lies outside speech as it lies outside reason."[30] This despairing attitude characterized much of cold-war era ethical and historical thought about the Holocaust. The philosopher Berel Lang and literary critic James Young, among others, have suggested more recently that the Holocaust has been and will continue to be successfully represented, if not in its horrific and perhaps ultimately ineluctable totality, then in the myriad of personal and historical responses to it, whether in memorials, autobiographies, "commix," or histories.[31] The event cannot resist "textualization" in some comprehensible form. Discourse of and on the Holocaust creates a historical context that includes both the literal facts of what happened and the figural representation of it. Lang insists that the specific nature of the Holocaust precludes any but the most literal accounting of its events. Such a literal account requires the most uninvolved of narrative voices, that of the "intransitive writer," who attempts neither subjectivity nor objectivity but something in the middle, a voice that allows the horror of the event to bespeak itself.

White points out that Lang's preference for the intransitive voice should refer to Barthes' discussion of the term. Barthes argued that the employment of the middle voice, or intransitive writing, developed in the tension between modernist literature and classical realism in the first half of the twentieth century. Modernist writers attempted to break down classical realist oppositions between fact and fiction, objectivity and agency. Arguing that the Holocaust is a modern and modernist event *par excellence*, White suggests that narrative written in the middle voice may be the only appropriate form of historical discourse about the Holocaust. Intransitive writing neither pretends a realism which is impossible and insulting to memory, nor an objectivity which detaches author and/or reader from the ethical and historical implications of knowledge of atrocity; nor does it sanction relativistic fictionalization of the past and its meaning.

The history of the Holocaust is a test case, not of the limits of representation, but of historical discourse's abilities to adapt appropriate forms of representation without sacrificing scholarly or moral integrity. Contrary to George Steiner, no historical event lies outside of language, literary representation or human reason; no historical event lies outside of memory and the discourses through which memory becomes meaningful. Dialogic responses to remembered events occur within discursive frameworks. Whether historians study the specific history of a linguistic usage, or the forms of representation used in historiography, we learn and we remember what we know or think we know, through language. To insist that meaning is always created through words, symbols and narratives is not to understand history in a manner which is confused, anarchic or relativistic. Language, or speech, is the tool we use to understand ourselves in relation to our pasts. History is a written form of communication about the manifest sum of many collectives' discrete knowledges about and from the past. Modern linguistic and literary studies offer historians the tools with which to articulate this self-awareness and to conduct critical inquiries about the past. A wide interest in the historical power and influence of language is one of the distinctive features of much historical thought at the beginning of the twenty-first century.

NOTES

1 Stanley Fish, *Is There a Text in this Class?* (Cambridge, MA: Harvard University Press, 1980), pp. 304–5.

2 For a more thorough discussion of Schleiermacher from the perspective of a philosopher heavily invested in post-structural thought, see Manfred Frank, *The Subject and the Text* (Cambridge: Cambridge University Press, 1997).

3 Terry Eagleton, *Literary Theory* (Minneapolis: University of Minnesota Press, 1983), p. 73.

4 Hans-Georg Gadamer, *Truth and Method* (New York: Continuum, 1988), p. 346.

5 See also Bahktin, *The Dialogic Imagination: Four Essays*, translated by Caryl Emerson and Michael Holquist (Austin: University of Texas Press, 1981) and Tzvetan Todorov, *Mikhail Bahktin: The Dialogical Principle*, translated by Wlad Godzich (Minneapolis: University of Minnesota Press, 1984).

6 On modern trends in linguistic and literary theory, see Michael Groden and Martin Kreiswirth, eds., *The Johns Hopkins Guide to Literary Theory and Criticism* (Baltimore: Johns Hopkins University Press, 1994) and the useful online edition at http://www.press.jhu.edu/books/hopkins_guide_to_literary_theory/. See also Eagleton, *Literary Theory*, pp. 91–126.

7 Quoted in John Sturrock, ed., *Structuralism and Since: From Levi-Strauss to Derrida* (Oxford: Oxford University Press, 1979), p. 10.

8 On Saussure and structural linguistics, see Sturrock, pp. 6–12; Jonathon Culler, *The Pursuit of Signs: Semiotics, Literature and Deconstruction* (Ithaca: Cornell University Press, 1981), pp. 22–4; Hans Aarsleff, *From Locke to Saussure: Essays on the Study of Language and Intellectual History* (Minneapolis: University of Minnesota Press, 1982).

9 See Richard Macksey and Eugenio Donato, eds., *The Structuralist Controversy: The Languages of Criticism and the Sciences of Man* (Baltimore: Johns Hopkins University Press, 1974); Frederic Jameson, *The Prison House of Language: A Critical Account of Structuralism and Russian Formalism* (Princeton: Princeton University Press, 1972).

10 Roland Barthes, *Mythologies* (New York: Hill and Wang, 1985), p. 42.

11 Eagleton, *Literary Theory*, p. 141.

12 For an overview of Euro-American post-structuralism as a contemporary movement, see Josué Harari, ed., *Textual Strategies: Perspectives in Post-Structuralist Criticism* (Ithaca: Cornell University Press, 1979), which has useful author and

topic bibliographies. See also Derek Attridge et al., eds., *Post-structuralism and the Question of History* (Cambridge: Cambridge University Press, 1987).

13 See the debate about deconstruction that transpired at a 1976 Modern Language Association conference between literary critics M. H. Abrams, J. Hillis Miller, and Wayne Booth. Papers reprinted in *Critical Inquiry* 3 (1977) and David Lodge and Michael Wood, eds., *Modern Criticism and Theory: A Reader* (Harlow: Longman, 1999); quoted here in Lodge, p. 246.

14 Michel Foucault, "What is an Author?" in *Language, Counter-Memory, Practice* (Ithaca: Cornell University Press, 1977), pp. 130–1.

15 Ibid., p. 138.

16 See Allan Megill, "The Reception of Foucault by Historians" *Journal of the History of Ideas* 48/1 (1987): 117–41 and *Prophets of Extremity: Nietzsche, Heidegger, Foucault, Derrida* (Berkeley: University of California Press, 1985); David Carroll, *Paraesthetics: Foucault, Lyotard, Derrida* (New York: Methuen, 1987); Hayden White, "Foucault" in Sturrock, *Structuralism*; Jan Goldstein, ed., *Foucault and the Writing of History* (Cambridge, MA: Blackwell, 1994).

17 Foucault, *Madness and Civilization*, p. xi.

18 Reprinted in Michael Lane, ed., *Structuralism: A Reader* (London: Cape, 1970), pp. 145–55; p. 145.

19 Phillipe Carrard's study of the use of first person voice by Annales school historians represents an important move towards a study of historians' subjectivity; Carrard, *Poetics of the New History: French Historical Discourse from Braudel to Chartier* (Baltimore: Johns Hopkins University Press, 1992). See also Linda Orr, *Headless History: Nineteenth Century Historiography of the Revolution* (Ithaca: Cornell University Press, 1990) and the articles by Orr and Carrard in Frank Ankersmit and Hans Kellner, eds., *A New Philosophy of History* (London: Reaktion Books, 1995). See also Susan A. Crane, "(Not) Writing History: Rethinking the Intersections of Personal History and Collective Memory with Hans von Aufsess" *History and Memory* 9 (1997): 5–29.

20 Richard Rorty, *The Linguistic Turn: Recent Essays in Philosophical Method* (Chicago: University of Chicago Press, 1967), p. 3. Compare with Rorty's later advocacy of a historicization of philosophy in Rorty Richmal, J. B. Schneewind, and Quentin Skinner, eds., *Philosophy in History* (Cambridge: Cambridge University Press, 1984).

21 See John Toews, "Intellectual History after the Linguistic Turn: The Autonomy of Meaning and the Irreducibility of Experience," *American Historical Review* 92 (1987): 879–907, and Martin Jay, "Should Intellectual History Take a Linguistic Turn? Reflections on the Habermas-Gadamer Debate" in Dominick LaCapra and Steven L. Kaplan, eds., *Modern European Intellectual History: Reappraisals and New Perspectives* (Ithaca: Cornell University Press, 1982), pp. 86–110. Among American historians, David Hollinger and David Harlan have debated this issue actively; see Harlan, "Intellectual History and the Return of Literature," and Hollinger, "The Return of the Prodigal: The Persistence of Historical Knowledge," *American Historical Review* 94 (1989): 581–609 and 610–21.

22 Dominick LaCapra, *History and Criticism* (Ithaca: Cornell University Press, 1985), p. 19. See also Lloyd Kramer, "Literature, Criticism and Historical Imag-

ination: The Literary Challenge of Hayden White and Dominick LaCapra," in Lynn Hunt, ed., *The New Cultural History* (Berkeley: University of California Press, 1989), pp. 97–130.

23 See, for example, J. G. A. Pocock, *Politics, Language and Time* (New York: Atheneum, 1971); Quentin Skinner, "Meaning and Understanding in the History of Ideas," *History and Theory* 8 (1969): 3–52, and *The Return of Grand Theory in the Human Sciences* (Cambridge: Cambridge University Press, 1985). See also James Tully and Quentin Skinner, eds., *Meaning and Context: Quentin Skinner and His Critics* (Cambridge: Polity Press, 1988).

24 Mark Bevir, *The Logic of the History of Ideas* (Cambridge: Cambridge University Press, 1999), pp. 34–5.

25 See Kathleen Canning, "Feminist History after the Linguistic Turn: Historicizing Discourse and Experience," *Signs* 19:2 (Winter 1994): 368–404; Gareth Stedman Jones, "The Determinist Fix: Some Obstacles to the Further Development of the Linguistic Approach to History in the 1990s," *History Workshop Journal* 42 (1996): 19–35; Laura Frader, "Dissent Over Discourse: Labor History, Gender and the Linguistic Turn," *History and Theory* 34/3 (1995): 213–30.

26 Joan W. Scott, "The Evidence of Experience," *Critical Inquiry* 17 (Summer 1991): 773–97; 779 and 796.

27 See H. Aram Veeser, ed., *The New Historicism* (New York: Routledge, 1989); John Zammito, "Are We Being Theoretical Yet? The New Historicism, the New Philosophy of History and 'Practicing Historians'" *Journal of Modern History* 65 (December 1993): 783–814.

28 Peter de Bolla, "Disfiguring History" *Diacritics* 16 (Winter 1986): 49–60; 57.

29 White, "Historical Emplotment and the Problem of Truth," in Saul Friedlander, ed., *Probing the Limits of Representation: Nazism and the "Final Solution"* (Cambridge, MA: Harvard University Press, 1992), pp. 37–53.

30 White quotes Steiner, ibid., p. 43.

31 Berel Lang, *Act and Idea in the Nazi Genocide* (Chicago: University of Chicago Press, 1990); James Young, *Writing and Rewriting the Holocaust* (Bloomington: Indiana University Press, 1988) and *The Texture of Memory* (New Haven: Yale University Press, 1993). White discusses Lang in "Historical Emplotment." "Commix" refers to the genre invented by Art Spiegelman to tell the story of his father's Holocaust experience in *Maus: A Survivor's Tale* (New York: Pantheon Books, 1986).

REFERENCES AND FURTHER READING

Bann, Stephen, *The Clothing of Clio: A Study of the Representation of History in Nineteenth-Century Britain and France*, Cambridge, 1984.

Certeau, Michel de, *The Writing of History*, New York, 1988.

Davis, Natalie Zemon, *Fiction in the Archives: Pardon Tales and Their Tellers in Sixteenth-Century France*, Stanford, 1987.

Eagleton, Terry, *Literary Theory: An Introduction*, Minneapolis, 1996; 2nd edn.

Gossman, Lionel, *Between History and Literature*, Cambridge, MA, 1990.

Megill, Allan, *Prophets of Extremity: Nietzsche, Heidegger, Foucault, Derrida*, Berkeley, 1985.

Spiegel, Gabrielle, *The Past as Text: The Theory and Practice of Medieval Historiography*, Baltimore, 1997.

Taylor, Mark C., *Deconstruction in Context: Literature and Philosophy*, Chicago, 1986.

White, Hayden, *Metahistory: The Historical Imagination in Nineteenth Century Europe*, Baltimore, 1973.

CHAPTER SEVENTEEN

Psychology, Psychoanalysis, and Historical Thought

LYNN HUNT

Since history's foundation as a university discipline in the last half of the nineteenth century, professional historians have often looked to other fields for new perspectives. Branching out from their discipline's original focus on political history, historians of the twentieth century studied the methods and findings of economics, sociology, and anthropology and developed economic history, social history, and cultural history, all of them powerful models for historical research and writing. One social science never quite made the list: psychology. Despite the cultural prestige of Sigmund Freud, psychological history or psychohistory failed to establish a comparable beachhead on the disciplinary front. When many historians turned, as they did between the 1970s and the 1990s, away from the social sciences toward the more humanistic branches of learning – literature and languages, art history, rhetoric and semiotics – psychology still attracted little notice. This essay is devoted to explaining why historians largely ignored psychology in their search for new approaches and how this neglect is a problem for historical thought. The essay concludes with a consideration of recent hopeful signs of new interest in incorporating psychology into historical research and writing.

What difference would it make if historians used something other than a common-sense or folk psychology in their research and writing? It would be foolish to argue that historical scholarship has suffered some irreparable harm because most historians have overlooked the problem of the psyche or the self. Rich and illuminating research has been carried out without an explicit model of the self and without an agenda for studying historical transformations in personhood. Moreover, some historians have tried to pinpoint important changes in the ideas and practices of selfhood. In recent years, cultural historians have investigated attitudes toward gender, private life, sexuality and death, all of them critical components of individual identity and personal experience. Yet this research still leaves many fundamental questions unanswered.

Can human motivation be entirely explained in social and cultural terms? Is the individual self just the name for a place where social and cultural changes work themselves out on the level of individual bodies? What do we imagine is happening inside that entity we call the self? Is individualism – the belief in the virtue of an autonomous self – a modern, Western notion and if so, how did it develop? And how can historians interested in these issues avoid falling into the trap of characterizing earlier periods and non-Western cultures as emotionally infantile? Historians can hardly be expected to provide answers to these questions if they do not pose the questions in the first place. In short, a more psychologically attuned historical discipline would pay more heed to changes over time in personhood and thereby give analytical depth to one of the most frequently invoked but rarely examined categories in historical scholarship.

The Misfortunes of Psychohistory

The attempt to establish the field of psychohistory can be traced back to Freud himself. In various works, he tried to show the relevance of psychoanalysis for understanding both general historical problems (e.g. *Totem and Taboo*, 1913 and *Civilization and its Discontents*, 1930) and individual figures in history (*Leonardo da Vinci and a Memory of His Childhood*, 1910). Although a few scholars tried to follow Freud's lead in the 1910s and 1920s by writing psychobiographies of famous historical figures, historians remained largely immune to psychoanalytic influence until after World War II. The rise of Hitler and National Socialism made explanations that emphasized irrational forces seem more compelling, and the author of a psychobiographical study of Hitler, William L. Langer, devoted his presidential address at the meeting of the American Historical Association in 1957 to urging historians to use the insights of depth psychology. The next year Erik H. Erikson published his widely reviewed psychoanalytic biography of Martin Luther (*Young Man Luther: A Study in Psychoanalysis and History*, 1958). Books, articles and dissertations in the field multiplied in the 1960s and 1970s. By the early 1970s, the *Journal of Psychohistory* had been founded, and a few history departments began to offer psychohistory as a field for doctoral study.

Yet even its most ardent defenders could not ignore the volleys of hostile criticism that soon erupted from all quarters. "Psycho-history is Bunk," proclaimed the title of one typical attack. The author of a book devoted to arguing the defects of psychohistory proclaimed that "little, if any, psychohistory is good history."[1] Initially closely tied to Freud's version of psychoanalysis, psychohistorians too often shared Freud's dogmatic belief in the objective and scientific status of his claims. Lloyd deMause, founder of both the Institute for Psychohistory in New York and the *Journal of Psychohistory*, insisted, for example, that psychohistory is "specifically concerned with establishing laws and discovering causes in precisely the Hempelian manner [Hempel believed that history should aspire to be scientific]. The relationship between history and psychohistory is parallel to the relationship between astrology and astronomy." Psychohistory is like astronomy, the real science. But when DeMause recounted how he gathered material from various epochs of history on the motivations that led to war and used his own self-analysis to penetrate the meaning of the material, he only seemed to be inflating his own subjective perceptions with scientific pretensions. And when he proclaimed that in this fashion he had discovered that psychohistory "*is a process of finding out what we all already know and act upon*," he committed history's cardinal sin of anachronism.[2] He assumed that what explained his motives in twentieth-century America was timeless and could explain motivation at any other time and place.

Perhaps most damaging, however, was the problem of evidence. Freud's conception of individual development emphasized infantile sexual feelings as the source of life-long psychological conflicts, but almost nothing is known about the infantile sexual feelings of any historical figure. As a result, critics frequently denounced psychohistorians' inferences from scanty evidence as unsupported speculation. In his study of Leonardo da Vinci, for example, Freud derived his entire analysis from one childhood memory reported by the Italian artist. Leonardo wrote in one of his scientific notebooks that he remembered "that while I was in my cradle a vulture came down to me, and opened my mouth with its tail, and struck me many times with its tail against my lips."[3] From this Freud inferred Leonardo's supposed homosexual feelings, his artistic interest in the figure of the Virgin Mary, embarrassment about his illegitimacy, his lifelong scientific curiosity, and even the smile on the Mona Lisa. In this and many other works of psychohistory, the conclusions seemed fantastic given the meager evidence available.

The derision and incredulity that had first greeted Freud spilled over onto psychohistory and only intensified with the renewed attacks on Freud's character and career in the 1970s and 1980s. By the 1990s both psychohistory and Freud had fallen into a kind of grand canyon of intellectual disrepute. In a defense of Freud published in 1993, Paul Robinson referred to the "avalanche of anti-Freudian writings." Some predicted that psychoanalysis would go the way of mesmerism and phrenology, discredited as bogus pseudo-science.[4] The scholars associated with the *Journal of Psychohistory* soon found themselves buried under the criticism. One defender tried to save the field by disassociating it from the journal. According to William McKinley Runyan, the *Journal of Psychohistory* contained so many deeply flawed articles that "it has been a public relations embarrassment for the wider field."[5]

The most adamant defenses of psychohistory inadvertently played into the hands of the critics. In a 1987 article on "The Perilous Purview of Psychohistory" in the *Journal of Psychohistory*, for example, Casper G. Schmidt glossed over the difficulty of finding evidence about infantile sexual feelings and reduced all intellectual criticisms of the field to psychological motives. He insisted that resistance to psychohistory came from fears of getting in touch with "the deepest madness of the human mind," anxieties about "facing unbearable despair" caused by the dreadful record of human history, guilt about the human potential for primitive and destructive behavior, and intense shame about human imperfections. As if to substantiate charges that psychohistorians tended to present an ahistorical view of the past, he rashly proclaimed that good parents were "so pitifully scarce" in history "as not to be found often in most centuries before the present one."[6] Schmidt's defense only succeeded in making the defects of psychohistory more glaring.

Even the most subtle and sophisticated historians working in the vein uncovered by Freud and psychoanalysis found themselves forced to take a defensive posture. Peter Gay, for example, who undertook psychoanalytic training, wrote extensively about Freud, and used Freudian insights in his work, insisted that his "continuing sensitivity to the impact of social, political, [and] economic realities on the mind" made him "hesitate to call myself a psychohistorian; rather I like to think of myself as a historian informed by psychoanalysis."[7] Gay tried to pick his way carefully around the question of culture (the historically changing) vs. nature (the timeless in human motivation). "The argument proclaiming man's cultural nature enshrines an important truth," he admits, "but, as Freud asserted over and over, not the whole truth. Psychoanalysts have never withdrawn their attention from the individual's uniqueness."[8] In this way, Gay too linked psychoanalysis with those traits in the individual that resist culture and by implication with what resists historical change. He had not resolved the central dilemma of psychohistory: how could historians, who by definition studied the changes in human life, use an approach that emphasized the timeless?

In all fairness, it must be granted that the deck was stacked against psychohistory from the start. Historians viewed psychological theories with distrust, but psychologists usually ignored history altogether in their eagerness to establish their scientific credentials. Psychology traces its origins as a science to Wilhelm Wundt, who opened an experimental laboratory for psychology at the University of Leipzig in 1879. Although Wundt himself expressed an interest in the cultural influences on psychological processes (*Völkerpsychologie*), his followers opted instead for Wundt's experimental physiological model of psychological research. Psychologists emphasized the biological foundations of psychology, relied on studies of behavior carried out in the laboratory setting, preferred quantitative methods of investigation, neglected biographical tools, and ignored most forms of social and cultural, not to mention historical, explanation. Psychoanalysis, with its emphasis on early childhood sexual feelings and clinical study of individual cases in a therapeutic setting, never fitted comfortably into this vision of psychology as a discipline. Although Freud believed that psychoanalysis could give psychiatry "its missing psychological foundation" and urged its inclusion in the curriculum of medical schools, psychoanalysis never established an enduring institutional base in universities or mental hospitals.[9] Disputes among Freudians themselves over the proper interpretation of Freud's work and the rapid multiplication of alternative psychological forms of clinical analysis also threatened the legitimacy of psychoanalysis, even within the clinically oriented community of psychologists.

Recent trends in psychology and psychiatry have in some ways pulled these fields even further away from history. The rising prominence of drug therapies as treatments for psychiatric disorders and the burgeoning of cognitive and neuroscience studies have resulted in a de-emphasis on personal subjectivity in favor of the objective factors of brain chemistry. Jeffrey Prager, a sociologist and practicing psychoanalyst, calls this de-emphasis "the death of the mind."[10] Both the natural and social sciences have come to view individual subjectivity as a red herring, a kind of mirage with no real substance. The self, according to Michael S. Gazzaniga, one proponent of this position, is an illusion or a fiction, the illusion that we are in charge of our lives. Mind, which Gazzaniga equates with consciousness, plays a very small role because ninety-eight percent of brain activity takes place outside of conscious awareness. As a consequence, for Gazzaniga "psychology itself is dead." It has been replaced by neuroscience, cognitive science, and evolutionary biology.[11]

How History Became Anti-Psychological

If psychology has generally ignored history, history has returned the favor. Although psychohistory gave psychological history a bad name among historians, its missteps did not bring on the anti-psychological bent that already characterized much of the historical profession before psychohistory made its bid as a new tool for historical research. Before 1945 a few hardy souls had hoped to systematically incorporate psychological – though not necessarily psychoanalytic – insights into historical research. The story of their failure to attract followers is instructive. One of the most influential proponents of collaboration between historians and psychologists was the French historian Lucien Febvre, who with Marc Bloch founded in 1929 the French historical journal *Annales d'histoire économique et sociale* (from 1946, *Annales: économies, sociétés, civilisations* and after 1994, *Annales: histoire, sciences sociales*). The Annales school shaped the practice of historians all over the world. Febvre called for a truly historical psychology, one that avoided the anachronism of projecting contemporary psychological notions onto the past but which also recognized the need to understand "the mental equipment" of people in history. He urged historians and psychologists to collaborate in sustained fashion. In particular, Febvre advocated the study of sensibility, that is, of the emotions and their expression, which he considered to be both individual and social in nature. Febvre described the many pitfalls awaiting historians of sensibility but also insisted that without it *"there will be no real history possible."*[12] He advised his fellow historians to investigate the history of love, the history of death, and the history of cruelty.

Febvre barely hinted at one of the major issues that would face any historical psychology when he suggested that history revealed a "long-drawn-out drama": "the gradual suppression of emotional activity through intellectual activity."[13] Did historical psychology have to subscribe to a developmental narrative (in this case the suppression of emotion in favor of intellectual life)? Febvre did not elaborate on his claim that feelings and behavior followed a discernible arc throughout human history, and at times he even seemed to contest the very idea. When he wrote his essay in the early years of World War II, after the defeat of France by Germany, he referred cryptically to the return of primitive feelings and the revival of primitive cults, implying that intellectual activities did not always succeed in holding emotional expressions in check.

Just a decade before Febvre published his essay on "Sensibility and History" (1941), Freud had argued in *Civilization and its Discontents* that civilization had progressed through the repression of the instincts by heightening the individual's sense of guilt. Freud thus explicitly linked individual human development with the advance of civilization as a whole; just as the individual learned within the family to repress aggressive instincts and unrestrained sexual impulses, so too civilization endeavored to tame the violence inherent in human relations and deflect the baser instincts into intellectual, scientific, and artistic achievements. Unfortunately, despite some surface similarities between his and Freud's arguments, Febvre said nothing at all about Freud in his essay. Febvre took a consistently hostile stance toward psychoanalysis throughout his career.[14]

Norbert Elias, a German sociologist writing in exile in the 1930s, made the first serious effort to combine Freud's insights with those of a sociological and historical perspective. In *The Civilizing Process* (1939) Elias aspired to fill out the psychological and sociological significance of the development of Western civilization. He traced the history of manners in order to show that the self itself had a history. Elias maintained that the notion of a self-contained individual – a self with invisible walls separating it from others – had only gradually developed since the fourteenth century. Over time, self-control increased as the threshold of shame lowered. People began to use handkerchiefs rather than blowing their noses into their hands; spitting, eating out of a common bowl, and sleeping in a bed with a stranger became disgusting or at least unpleasant. Violent outbursts of emotion and aggressive behavior became socially unacceptable. These changes in manners were the surface indications of an underlying transformation in the self. They all signaled the advent of the self-enclosed individual, whose boundaries had to be respected in social inter-action. In a new preface appended in 1968, Elias confirmed that he intended to show the long-term connection between control over affect in individuals and the increasing differentiation and integration of social structures (some-times called modernization). In terms not unlike those articulated by Febvre, he maintained that emotional self-control led to an increased capacity for self-detachment in thought and therefore to the possibility of scientific knowledge and mastery of nature.[15]

Elias's developmental narrative took the Middle Ages as its point of depar-ture and depicted that time period as virtually infantile in its emotional expres-sions. He described the medieval code of behavior as simple and naïve. People at the time vented their emotions more violently and directly and had there-fore fewer psychological nuances and complexities in their ideas about conduct. The strong and mighty exulted in rapine, battle, and hunting. War-riors took pleasure in mutilating prisoners. Intense piety, violent feelings of guilt, sudden outbursts of joy and hilarity, boastful belligerence, and a liking for cruelty went hand in hand in what Elias explicitly terms "childish" expres-sions and forms of behavior.[16] As might be expected, not all historians of the Middle Ages agree with these negative characterizations. Elias's pejorative depiction revealed the downside of a developmental historical psychology: the attempt to elaborate on the parallel between individual and broader cultural or social development encouraged scholars to classify earlier times as infantile, childish, or immature.

Few historians heeded the challenges laid down by Febvre, Freud, or Elias. Febvre himself did not embark on the kind of psychological history he rec-ommended, and the *Annales* school which he inspired turned instead to the "history of mentalities," which employed no particular psychological theory or approach and remained largely confined to the study of conscious beliefs and prejudices. French historians did follow Febvre's lead by examining the history of death, for example, but they focused for the most part on death as a social experience. Elias's work produced few echoes before it was translated into French in 1973 and English in 1978, and even then historians only assim-ilated it piecemeal; French historians followed Elias's lead in studying civility and court society in the seventeenth century but focused largely on the social dimension of his analysis, and psychohistorians ignored Elias altogether. Most scholars overlooked the issues raised by Elias's long-term narrative of the civilizing process as a whole.

Historians' antagonism to psychological approaches did not arise solely from their justifiable concerns about anachronism. It also derived from their political objections to the conclusions of the field known as crowd psychol-ogy, an important precursor of present-day social psychology. Although not an academic social science, crowd psychology exercised great influence on literature, the social sciences, and history at the end of the nineteenth century and continued to enjoy considerable prestige well into the twentieth. The best known practitioner of the genre was Gustave Le Bon, an independent scholar with many connections to the political elite in France. His book *The Crowd* (first published in French in 1895) drew on the work of several French and Italian investigators of mass behavior. Le Bon argued that the individual in a crowd suffers a kind of hypnosis in which his brain is paralyzed and he loses willpower. The member of a crowd "descends several rungs on the ladder of civilization" and becomes like "beings belonging to inferior forms of evolution," which he defined as women, savages, and children.[17] Le Bon believed that crowd psychology explained the "pathologies" of modern society such as workers' strikes and riots and especially socialism.

Le Bon had drawn in particular on the histories of Hippolyte Taine, an influential writer who described the crowds in the French Revolution of 1789 as savage and primitive, drunken, enraged, lustful, and bloodthirsty. Women marched at the front, Taine recounted, while criminals and vagrants whipped the crowd to a frenzy of alcoholic debauchery, culminating at times in cannibalism: "in every city [after July 14, 1789], magistrates are at the mercy of a band of savages, often a band of cannibals."[18] Taine objected to the democratizing and equalizing tendencies that had developed in France first in the Revolution of 1789 and then again after 1870 because he believed that even the most law-abiding citizen turned into a "grinning, bloodthirsty, lustful baboon" when he joined a crowd. In other words, Taine believed that democracy led to degeneration. The writings of Taine, Le Bon, and the other crowd psychologists established a link between historical psychology and right-wing politics. Although Le Bon enjoyed influence beyond right-wing circles – Freud relied on Le Bon's work when writing his *Group Psychology and the Analysis of the Ego* (1921) – the crowd psychologists' support for racist, anti-feminist, and anti-socialist positions made them especially attractive to the extreme right. Mussolini claimed to have read Le Bon's book several times, for instance, and Hitler may well have used it as a source for *Mein Kampf*.

Social historians therefore attacked the premises of crowd psychology when they set about dismantling this picture of crowds. One of the pioneers of this new "history from below," George Rudé, explicitly contradicted Taine and Le Bon in his studies of crowd actions [for example, *The Crowd in History: A Study of Popular Disturbances in France and England, 1730–1848* (1964)]. The Parisian crowds of the French Revolution were composed, he maintained, of small workshop masters and their journeymen, shopkeepers, and craftsmen, ordinary family men of the neighborhood who wanted cheap and plentiful food above all else. In short, they acted out of conscious, rational motives, not out of irrational mob psychology. Rudé insisted that crowd behavior was best explained in sociological, not psychological, terms.

Even when practitioners of history from below later turned their gaze toward the ritual and theatrical aspects of crowd violence, they insisted on this rational and social dimension. Natalie Z. Davis, for example, rejected a class analysis of religious attitudes and offered a more subtle cultural reading of crowd violence during the French religious wars, but she still avoided any systematic psychological inference. When Catholics taunted their Protestant neighbors and then mutilated their bodies after murdering them, they were acting to defend their community against the pollution of heresy. Even at their most horrifically cruel and ferocious, the rioters made a kind of rational sense; they reenacted religious rituals and took inspiration from folk justice. Like Davis, E. P. Thompson traced the crowd's belief in the legitimacy of its actions, however brutal, to its sense of community. Thompson maintained that English food rioters, for instance, believed that they were reaffirming an age-old moral economy against market-driven profiteers. Psychology never explicitly entered into his account.[19]

The rise of social history thus went hand in hand with the rejection of psychological forms of analysis. Social explanation seemed to validate the motives of ordinary people, whereas psychological interpretations effectively censured them. Even though the founding fathers of social theory and even of social history showed great interest in psycho-social linkages, the more their followers emphasized social, and therefore rational and conscious, factors, the less psychological explanation seemed to figure. As a consequence, the promise of research at the intersection between psychology and history – a prospect embraced by social theorists such as Emile Durkheim and Max Weber and early social historians such as Lucien Febvre and James Harvey Robinson – remained largely unrealized. The reaction against "psychologizing" could be brutal. Historical sociologist Charles Tilly, for example, found the psychological implications of Durkheim's theory so disturbing that he advocated throwing the theory out altogether. Durkheim had argued that the rapid social change associated with modernization created individual *anomie*, a state of individual disorientation and conflict. The result was rising suicide rates, crime, and social unrest. Tilly disputed this characterization, maintaining instead that there was no correlation between individual signs of disorientation and collective behaviors. Only "solid organizational and political variables" such as unionization, national organization, and state repression could explain fluctuations in collective conflicts.[20] The psychological dimension consequently dropped out of his analysis altogether.

Historians' recent engagements with gender and race relations, cultural history, and post-structuralist writings have done surprisingly little to increase interest in psychological explanations. Although a few historians of gender have tried to incorporate psychoanalysis into their research, feminism as a whole has taken a very critical stance toward Freud and psychoanalysis. Moreover, feminism got much of its critical edge from the belief that individual behaviors and identities are shaped by social and cultural factors. This perspective, often called "social constructionism," is shared by those interested in race relations, cultural history, and post-structuralism. All of these recent developments in historical research emphasize the role of culture and society in determining individual feelings and identities. The feminist historian Joan Scott, for example, once argued that psychoanalysis could be an important tool in analyzing the workings of gender relations, but later insisted that "It is not individuals who have experience, but subjects who are constituted through experience." Emphasizing the cultural and linguistic determinants of individual behavior, she concluded, "Subjects are constituted discursively and experience is a linguistic event."[21] The very use of the word "subject" instead of "individual" makes her position clear: experience of language, culture, and society literally subjects – subjugates – the individual.

Historians concerned with the history of culture and those interested by post-structuralist theories both argued against reductive social explanation and asserted that culture and language shape knowledge and even conceptions of reality. In their views, culture or language do not reflect prior social interests or positions; culture and language configure the expression of social meaning and therefore frame social reality rather than just mirroring it. In practice, however, such views, radical as they seemed at the time in their implications for social history, only shifted attention from one set of social practices to another. Rather than investigating, for instance, as social historians did, the social composition of crowds and their demands, cultural historians looked at the language and symbols they used. Similarly, post-structuralists examined the ways in which language itself shaped every kind of experience. As a consequence, neither cultural history nor post-structuralism included an explicit psychological dimension. This outcome should not be surprising since the original inspiration for much language or discourse analysis, the Swiss linguist Ferdinand de Saussure, had explained the fundamentally social nature of all signs in his foundational work of 1915, *Cours de linguistique générale* [Course on General Linguistics]. Although linguistic signs are psychic in that they are located in the individual's brain according to Saussure, language itself is "a social institution" and the essential meaning of the sign "is social by nature." It therefore must be studied in social terms.[22]

The rejection of psychology is especially clear in the case of Michel Foucault, the post-structuralist who exercised the most influence on historians. In volume one of *The History of Sexuality*, Foucault argued that psychoanalysis could never truly function as a theoretical discourse because it "always unfolded within the deployment of sexuality, and not outside or against it."[23] Psychoanalysis played a prime role in turning sexuality into a medical concern; it did not criticize this development. It was part of the problem in Foucault's view, not part of the solution. Foucault viewed the individual as the unwitting by-product of discourses about sexuality, an object with very little room for maneuvering on its own. The deployment of new technologies of sex, according to Foucault, precipitated a new kind of individual, one defined by his capacity for self-surveillance and by his sexual identity. "It is through sex . . . that each individual has to pass in order to have access to his own intelligibility."[24]

Foucault's self is only a nodal point in a network of discourses; it brings nothing of its own to the network and finds its interior meaning only from the intersection of network forces. Although Foucault gave subjectivity an historical dimension – perhaps his greatest contribution and the reason so many feminists have followed his lead – he, like many social and cultural historians, always construed historical meaning in cultural and linguistic, that is, collective terms. He portrayed subjectivity as the virtually automatic outgrowth of culture and discourse. He left virtually no space for a willing, desiring individual to shape his or her own destiny, in short, little space for the self as active agent. It is not surprising, therefore, that the many historians inspired by Foucault have fastened on the body, not on the self, even though Foucault himself argued that the body became the subject of regulation because it provided access to the self. For Foucault, the self was like "man," a recent invention within European culture that is now perhaps "nearing its end." It might soon "be erased, like a face drawn in sand at the edge of the sea."[25]

Since one of the few unifying tenets of post-structuralist theory has been its contesting of any unitary, stable or coherent notion of selfhood, it inevitably calls into question the very notion of self as a meaningful category. Post-structuralism effaced the self as a possible topic of interest when it argued, following Nietzsche, that to believe individuals were independent entities was simply to be trapped by grammar which posits an independent subject and object in any sentence. The self or subject is, according to Roland Barthes, for example, "only an effect of language." Any "me" is "flighty, divided, and dispersed . . . it won't hold still." Subjectivity can only be described, therefore, as "deconstructed, disunited, deported, unchained; why should I no longer speak of 'myself' when 'my' self is no longer 'one's' self?"[26] Thus development of the historical discipline and even the most challenging new movements within and around it seemed to conspire to render the historical study of selfhood nearly impossible.

The Black Box of the Psyche

By now it should not surprise the reader to learn that the psyche or self of the individual remains one of the least examined categories of historical analysis, a kind of black box with nothing visible inside. Is selfhood a universal category with no variation throughout history and therefore something like a mathematical constant? Most historians would probably agree that cultural and social, and therefore historical, differences have some kind of impact on the experience of selfhood, but there is no consensus about how best to discern or measure that impact. Scholars have traced the emergence of individual*ism* as a political and social doctrine, often finding it more prevalent in Western cultures than non-Western ones, more characteristic of modern times than earlier ones, and accepted in Protestant countries before Catholic ones – though each of these conclusions has aroused considerable controversy and charges of Eurocentrism. In one of the most ambitious attempts to uncover the historical meaning of selfhood, the philosopher Charles Taylor endeavored to untangle the "making of modern identity" (the subtitle of his book) in *Sources of the Self* (1989). He defined modern Western selfhood as a belief in a human agent with a sense of inwardness, freedom, individuality and embeddedness in nature. Taylor's analysis, which ranges from Plato to post-structuralism, definitely puts some content into the box of the self and offers a fascinating account of how the self came to be viewed in this fashion. Yet even Taylor, for all his philosophical and historical acumen, fails to define the self itself. He seems to equate it with personal identity and individual agency but says much more about the moral qualities various thinkers associated with selfhood than about the thing itself. His focus is moral rather than psychological.

Taylor's book still counts as one of many encouraging signs, however, that historically-minded scholars are no longer satisfied with treating the psyche or the self as a black box. In an article published in Febvre's *Annales* the same year as Taylor's book, Gérard Noiriel urges the development of a "subjectivist" paradigm to counter the long predominance of the "objectivist" paradigm in history. A subjectivist paradigm could be based, he argues, on "lived experience," which derives from both "objectification" and "internalization." He defines objectification as the sedimentation or crystallization of past lived experience into material forms, rules, words, and mental structures and internalization as their incorporation into individual personalities.[27] Noiriel wants to return to the approaches first suggested by the founders of social theory and social history and then elaborated further by the French sociologist Pierre Bourdieu. He thus supplements the cultural historians' and post-structuralists' emphasis on the social, cultural, and linguistic determinants of experience with a revived concept of individual subjectivity which incorporates those determinants but also presumably acts upon them.

With similar intentions but propelled in the first instance by their dissatisfaction with the results of gender history, some feminists advocate a re-evaluation of psychoanalysis. Lyndal Roper argues that gender has failed to realize its full potential as a category of historical analysis because it has been understood too exclusively as a social or discursive construction; as a result, gender historians lack an account of the connections between the social world and psychic experience and thus cannot adequately explain change. Too often gender historians assume that psychic experience follows automatically from social factors, as if the psyche or self were just a miniature version of the social world. Roper calls on psychoanalysis for help in analyzing the processes of individualization and gender differentiation.[28]

Discontent with the predominance of social explanations or "social constructionism" has helped fuel a revival of interest in the emotions, a topic first urged by Febvre and Elias sixty years ago. Much of the research undertaken in the 1980s on "emotionology" remained within the social and cultural history approach, but more recently, advocates such as William Reddy have aligned their work with new trends in anthropology and psychology. Reddy vigorously criticizes "emotional constructionism," that is, the idea that the individual is absolutely plastic, that sexuality, ethnicity, and identity are *entirely* determined by culture or society.[29] Reddy uses recent research in psychology to claim that there are universals in emotional life, whose expressions are shaped by culture and history through what he calls "emotives." From this point of departure, Reddy aspires to redefine power as control over the expression of emotions rather than control over the means of violence. This emphasis on the emotions resembles in some, but certainly not all, respects the analysis proposed by Elias.

Taken together, these new approaches and others like them adumbrate an ambitious agenda for recovering the self as an object of historical investigation. Following Noiriel's suggestion, historians could rekindle the keen interest shown by the founders of social theory and social history in psycho-social linkages, in what Febvre termed "the mental equipment" of people in the past, and seek new ways of understanding the individual's negotiation with the social and cultural world. Following Roper's example, they might reread Freud in the same spirit, not as the founder of a therapeutic school with scientific pretensions, but as a pathbreaking, yet often tentative thinker about the individual's insertion into society. And finally, responding to Reddy's cue, they can use the recent research of cognitive psychologists, neuroscientists, and evolutionary anthropologists to help fill in the outlines of a new heuristic model of the self.

Neuroscience and the Meaning of Selfhood

Historians have barely scratched the surface of this promising terrain of research, and psychology as a discipline offers no easy recipes for success in the endeavor. In the two decades between 1974 and 1993 some 31,550 articles were published in psychology in which the self figured as a topic in some fashion. Yet a psychologist reviewing the recent literature concluded that "the thousands of journal articles dealing with the self have seemed to make the answer to that fundamental question [what is the self?] more elusive rather than clearer."[30] Nevertheless, the question of the self is clearly on the agenda for a wide variety of fields, and history has an important contribution to make to this ongoing intellectual fermentation. The *Handbook of Social Psychology* (1998) concludes its consideration of the literature on the self with a section on the "Historical Evolution of Self," arguing that research on the self has flourished in the West because selfhood is seen as both precarious and extremely important in Western countries. Some psychologists are beginning to appreciate the historical dimensions of their discipline.

Ironically, in seeking new approaches to the self, psychology has inadvertently found its way back to many of the positions first advocated by Freud a century ago. Just as Freud tried to base his theories on the most up-to-date neurology and physiology of his time, so too psychologists are now avidly reformulating their discipline based on neuroscientific findings. Freud emphasized the role of the unconscious; though present-day brain researchers do not share Freud's conviction that the unconscious is filled primarily with sexual content, they give the unconscious activities of the brain even more prominence than he did, they tie those unconscious activities to emotions experienced in the body, and they often slip sex ("reproductive success") back in as the ultimate evolutionary goal of the brain. Moreover, the most recent definitions of the self in the psychological literature have a surprisingly Freudian reverberation. Although few use the terms id, ego, and superego – latinate designations introduced by the English translator of Freud's German – many cite similar functions. The *Handbook of Social Psychology* (1998) proposes, for example, that selfhood has three main "roots": the experience of reflexive consciousness, the interpersonal aspect of selfhood, and the executive function or agent.[31] The first and third fit Freud's discussion of the ego and the second is clearly related to Freud's notion of the superego. Even the most resolute neuroscience efforts to reduce all concepts of mind to brain activity end up by smuggling in some kind of concept of the self as active agent or ego. Gazzaniga, for example, claims that "a special system" which he calls "the interpreter" and locates in the left hemisphere of the brain "ties the vast output of our thousands upon thousands of automatic systems into our subjectivity."[32]

Many critics of Freud have complained that he takes the ego as a given rather than providing an account of its development, yet recent research in neuroscience underlines precisely the biological givenness of selfhood. Neuroscience studies suggest two different kinds of self: a "minimal" self dependent on brain processes and bodily sensations and a "narrative" self that provides a more or less coherent self-image tying the individual to a sense of past and future.[33] The minimal self includes a sense of ownership of one's body and agency in cognition and can be demonstrated from studies of newborns and schizophrenic patients. Newborns less than an hour old can imitate facial gestures, thus suggesting that even before the acquisition of language they can already distinguish between self and non-self, locate parts of their body, and recognize the face as human, since newborns will not imitate non-human objects. Auditory hallucinations, delusions of control, and "thought insertion" ("the CIA put a chip in my brain which told me to kill him . . .") are disorders of the sense of agency and in some cases of the sense of ownership. Patients suffering from them do not as it were recognize themselves as the agents of their own actions. Such disorders show that at its minimum the experience of self depends on a sense of ownership of one's body and an ability to recognize oneself as the agent of one own's actions in the world. They demonstrate in effect that the minimal self is located in the brain and also embedded in the body. To return to Freud's terms, these studies show that a minimal ego must be present for development of the self to take place.

The narrative self that develops out of the minimal self also depends on brain activities that process information from the body; countless studies have shown the impact of brain lesions on narrative comprehension, for example. But the narrative self is very difficult to pin down because like consciousness it has no obvious location in the brain. Neuroscience has located specific brain regions that support elements of consciousness such as wakefulness and attention, but consciousness is more than wakefulness and attention. Moreover, like language, to which it is intimately related, consciousness has both an individual biological and intersubjective or social dimension. Is it therefore in the "mind," defined as originating in individual brain activity but including some kind of belonging to a social collective? The narrative self, which is essential to consciousness but also includes unconscious feelings and memories, has been defined by some as a kind of center of narrative gravity, though others emphasize its decentered, equivocal, contradictory, and conflicted nature, again resonating with Freud's account.

Paradoxically, as psychology has merged with neuroscience its distance from history may actually be decreasing. Antonio R. Damasio has developed an influential model of the neural basis of the self that is at once biological and historical. The self, he claims, is a perspective "rooted in a relatively stable, endlessly repeated biological state" that gets its core from the structure and operation of the organism and then develops through slowly evolving autobiographical data. The self therefore depends on continuous reactivation of memories of the past and memories of plans and projects for the possible future.[34] The self is both stable because biologically rooted in the body and brain and open to history because this biological state must be continually reactivated and updated with new autobiographical information. There can be no "extended" consciousness, in Damasio's terms, no consciousness of self, without a sense of history, of memories as objects, and of time as a scale that transcends immediate experience. Moreover, the emotions play a crucial role in this notion of selfhood. Studies of neurological damage demonstrate that the emotions are essential elements in reasoning and decision making; people who lose some kinds of emotion as a result of strokes, head injuries, or tumors, also lose their ability to make certain kinds of rational decisions. Thus reason or rationality is not the categorical opposite of emotion or feeling. They actually go together. The virtue of this model of the self is that it circumvents many predictable but increasingly unproductive dichotomies. We do not have to choose between biology and history, nature and culture, reason and emotion, a stable self and a decentered one, timeless psychology and chronologically-rooted history, or individual agency and social construction. We can have our cake and eat it too.

A New History of Selfhood

Just what this cake will taste like may still be unknown, but it does seem possible that the study of the self or psyche, that is, psychology, can once again be fruitfully brought back into history. This is happening from both directions at once: neuroscientific studies demonstrate the importance of narrative, memory, and time to the sense of self; and historical studies show that the sense of personhood varies over time. The border between psychology and cognitive neuroscience is one of the most exciting domains of interdisciplinary research in the new century and that research is already having an impact on the other social sciences and on literary studies. Since memory and time play such important roles in the development of new models of self and mind–body interaction, there is no reason that history should not be involved in these developments. Memory not only constitutes and continually reconfigures the narrative self but also provides the link between the minimal and narrative self. Memory and narrative processing also connect the individual self to society, culture, and history. While biology may not provide an infinite array of possible ways to fashion the relations between emotion, reason, body, and self, it is certainly true that we have only begun to explore the ways in which culture and society channel their various expressions.

Although neuroscience has shown that the self is not a linguistic illusion and not an arbitrary product of cultural learning, it cannot by itself explain how the self gets its specific cultural and historical content. It can show, for example, that certain brain functions are necessary to the individual's insertion in society, but it cannot account for the ways individuality varies in different times and cultures. Neuroscience can try to locate the specific brain abnormalities that cause autism, for example, and it can show that autism entails an inability to understand subjectivity as well as to produce narratives. But it does not explain why subjectivity or narrative is understood differently in different times and places or for that matter why autism was only identified as a specific syndrome in the 1940s.

Anthropologists and cross-cultural psychologists have been actively investigating the ways that cultures differ in their attribution and development of personhood. In an essay that reviews much of the current work in this domain in anthropology, Andrew Strathern and Pamela J. Stewart argue that their colleagues should resist applying terms such as person, self, and individual as if they were valid universally and instead examine indigenous categories. Their study of *noman* in Papua New Guinea, a term which can mean mind, intention, will, agency, social conscience, desire or personality, demonstrates the power of this approach. *Noman* is not exactly translatable as self because it comes out of a local worldview that gives great weight to social interactions not only with other persons but also with the environment and with ancestors and ghosts. Understanding its cultural use, rather than just trying to fit it into Western notions of selfhood, has the effect of expanding the notion of personhood in new directions.[35]

A similar kind of ethnographic attitude has developed in historical studies of personhood. In his study of the "Production of the Self during the Age of Confessionalism," for instance, David Sabean insists that sixteenth-century German notions of selfhood differed in fundamental ways from those familiar in the modern period. "Neither the peasants in Württemberg in the 1580s nor Luther," he maintains, "thought of the self as a consistent center of awareness with memory as the instrument for organizing that sense of personal unity."[36] Memory was embedded in social relations, and the self was viewed as nonconsistent and decentered. Rather than presuming that people in the past had less developed or "immature" practices and concepts of personhood compared to those of the present, historians now increasingly treat past societies as indigenous cultures with their own logics of personhood. Caroline Bynum, for example, argues that medieval writing about body and self is not so undeveloped in comparison to our own. Careful reading of medieval theologians reveals that the current notions of an embodied self have more in common with medieval views than with those of seventeenth- and eighteenth-century philosophers. Moreover, medieval renditions of the mind/body problem can actually help modern thinkers move away from their preoccupation with gender and sexuality and their consequent neglect of such issues as death and work.[37]

Cognitive neuroscience has revealed how inadequate our own folk psychology is for explaining personhood, but it too is still caught up in many "folk" assumptions of the present day, including the deeply misleading assumption that the individual brain is like Robinson Crusoe, isolated and asocial.[38] A historical perspective, like an anthropological one, can help illuminate the working of those "folk" assumptions, both in the past, and by implication, in the present. By refocusing on the self, a topic that has once again popped up from under the surface of our everyday preconceptions, historians can not only reinvigorate their own scholarship but also help reshape an important interdisciplinary conversation. They can help make self, mind, and consciousness a more explicit part of historical understanding.

NOTES

1 Geoffrey Barraclough, "Psycho-history Is Bunk," *Guardian* (Manchester and London), March 3, 1973. David E. Stannard, *Shrinking History: On Freud and the Failure of Psychohistory* (Oxford: Oxford University Press, 1973), p. xiii.

2 Lloyd deMause, "The Independence of Psychohistory," in Geoffrey Cocks and Travis L. Crosby, eds., *Psycho/history: Readings in the Method of Psychology, Psychoanalysis, and History* (New Haven and London: Yale University Press, 1987), pp. 50–67, quotes pp. 50, 66. Emphasis his.

3 Sigmund Freud, *Leonardo da Vinci and a Memory of His Childhood*, tr. Alan Tyson (New York: W. W. Norton, 1989), p. 32.

4 Paul Robinson, *Freud and his Critics* (Berkeley: University of California Press, 1993), quote p. 2.

5 William McKinley Runyan, ed., *Psychology and Historical Interpretation* (New York: Oxford University Press, 1988), quote p. 17.

6 Casper G. Schmidt, "The Perilous Purview of Pyschohistory," *The Journal of Psychohistory* 14 (1987): 315–325, quotes pp. 316–17.

7 Peter Gay, *Pleasure Wars*, vol. 5 of *The Bourgeois Experience: Victoria to Freud* (New York: W. W. Norton, 1998), p. 236.

8 Peter Gay, *Freud for Historians* (New York, 1985), p. 171.

9 Freud's quotation from *Introductory Lectures on Psychoanalysis* is given in Sarah Winter, *Freud and the Institution of Psychoanalytic Knowledge* (Stanford: Stanford University Press, 1999), p. 157.

10 Jeffrey Prager, *Presenting the Past: Psychoanalysis and the Sociology of Misremembering* (Cambridge, MA: Harvard University Press, 1998), p. 212.

11 Michael S. Gazzaniga, *The Mind's Past* (Berkeley: University of California Press, 1998), p. xi.

12 Lucien Febvre, "History and Psychology [1938]," and "Sensibility and History: How to Reconstitute the Emotional Life of the Past [1941]," in Peter Burke, ed., *A New Kind of History and Other Essays*, trans. K. Folca (New York: Harper, 1973), quote from "Sensibility and History," p. 24 (emphasis in the passage is Febvre's own).

13 Febvre, "Sensibility and History," pp. 15–16.

14 Jean Maurice Bizière, "Psychohistory and Histoire des Mentalités," *Journal of Psychohistory* 11 (1983): 89–109.

15 Norbert Elias, *The Civilizing Process: The Development of Manners*, tr. Edmund Jephcott (original German edition, 1939; New York, 1978).

16 See esp. p. 201.

17 As quoted in Susanna Barrows, *Distorting Mirrors: Visions of the Crowd in Late Nineteenth-Century France* (New Haven: Yale University Press, 1981), p. 169.

18 Ibid., p. 88.

19 Suzanne Desan, "Crowds, Community, and Ritual in the Work of E. P. Thompson and Natalie Davis," in Lynn Hunt, ed., *The New Cultural History* (Berkeley: University of California Press, 1989), pp. 47–71.

20 Charles Tilly, *As Sociology Meets History* (New York: Academic Press, 1981), esp. "Useless Durkheim," pp. 95–108, quote p. 107.

21 Joan Scott, "The Evidence of Experience," *Critical Inquiry* 17 (1991): quotes pp. 778, 779.

22 Ferdinand de Saussure, *Cours de linguistique générale*, Tullio de Mauro, ed. (Paris: Payot, 1984), quotes pp. 33–4. I am grateful to Malina Stefanovska for providing me with this citation.

23 Michel Foucault, *The History of Sexuality*, Vol. 1: *An Introduction*, tr. Robert Hurley (New York, 1980), quote p. 131.

24 Foucault, *The History of Sexuality*, vol. 1: 155.

25 Michel Foucault, *The Order of Things: An Archaeology of the Human Sciences* (New York, 1970), p. 386.

26 As quoted in Paul Smith, *Discerning the Subject* (Minneapolis: University of Minnesota Press, 1988), pp. 104, 106, and 108.

27 "Pour une approche subjectiviste du social," *Annales: Economies, Sociétés, Civilisations* 44 (1989): 1435–59. The article is excerpted and commented upon in Jacques Revel and Lynn Hunt, eds., *Histories: French Constructions of the Past* (New York, 1996), pp. 579–87.

28 Lyndal Roper, *Oedipus and the Devil: Witchcraft, Sexuality and Religion in Early Modern Europe* (London: Routledge, 1994). For a similar critique of "social constructionism," see Nancy Partner, "No Sex, No Gender," *Speculum* 68 (1993): 419–43.

29 William M. Reddy, "Against Constructionism: The Historical Ethnography of Emotions," *Current Anthropology* 38 (June 1997): 326–51.

30 Roy F. Baumeister, "The Self," in Daniel T. Gilbert, Susan T. Fiske et al., eds., *The Handbook of Social Psychology*, Vol. 1, 4th edn. (Boston, MA: McGraw-Hill, 1998), pp. 680–740, quote p. 680.

31 Ibid., p. 680.

32 Gazzaniga, *The Mind's Past*, p. 24.

33 Shaun Gallagher, "Philosophical Conceptions of the Self: Implications for Cognitive Science," *Trends in Cognitive Sciences* 4 (2000): 14–21.

34 *Descartes' Error: Emotion, Reason, and the Human Brain* (New York: G. P. Putnam's Sons, 1994), pp. 238–9. See also his *The Feeling of What Happens: Body and Emotion in the Making of Consciousness* (San Diego and New York: Harcourt, 1999).

35 Andrew Strathern and Pamela J. Stewart, "Seeking Personhood: Anthropological Accounts and Local Concepts in Mount Hagen, Papua New Guinea," *Oceania* 68 (1998): 170–88.

36 David Warren Sabean, "Production of the Self during the Age of Confessionalism," *Central European History* 29 (1996): 1–18, quote pp. 4–5. Sabean develops his important notions within a Foucaultian framework that emphasizes the effort of church and state to create unified and discrete individual selves.

37 Caroline Bynum, "Why All the Fuss about the Body? A Medievalist's Perspective," in Victoria E. Bonnell and Lynn Hunt, *Beyond the Cultural Turn* (Berkeley: University of California Press, 1999), pp. 241–80.

38 Most persuasive on this subject is Leslie Brothers, *Friday's Footprint: How Society Shapes the Human Mind* (New York: Oxford University Press, 1997).

REFERENCES AND FURTHER READING

Brothers, Leslie, *Friday's Footprint: How Society Shapes the Human Mind*, New York: Oxford University Press, 1997.
  A persuasive attempt to link the findings of neuroscience to an appreciation of the social transactions that shape the mind.
Elias, Norbert, *The Civilizing Process: The Development of Manners*, tr. Edmund Jephcott, original German edition, 1939; New York, 1978.
  The most ambitious effort to uncover the historical origins of psychic processes.
Febvre, Lucien, "History and Psychology [1938]," and "Sensibility and History: How to Reconstitute the Emotional Life of the Past [1941]," in Peter Burke, ed., *A New Kind of History and Other Essays*, trans. K. Folca, New York: Harper, 1973.
  Essays by one of the founders of social history with a strong interest in connecting history and psychology.
Reddy, William M., "Against Constructionism: The Historical Ethnography of Emotions," *Current Anthropology* 38 (June 1997): 326–51.
  A sophisticated blending of cognitive science, anthropology, and history.
Roper, Lyndal, *Oedipus and the Devil: Witchcraft, Sexuality and Religion in Early Modern Europe*, London: Routledge, 1994.
  Telling critique of the limitations of gender history and vigorous argument for reviving psychoanalysis for historical investigation.

CHAPTER EIGHTEEN

Redefining Historical Identities: Sexuality, Gender, and the Self

CAROLYN J. DEAN

The history of sexuality touches on many areas of inquiry – on the history of the family, the history of women and gender, the history of science, of populations – and traverses as well a vast array of methodological approaches. Family historians, for example, measure illegitimacy rates in order to assess the impact of social developments like industrialization on family structures. Historians of women necessarily addressed sex by analyzing how and why states regulate female sexuality by limiting or outlawing access to contraception. But in what follows, I limit my inquiry to works whose primary focus is sexual behavior, sexual opinion, and sexual attitudes. In so doing, I want to ask exactly what historians of *sexuality* investigate, for they render central questions that remain relatively peripheral in works on family or women's history. How does sex become an object of historical inquiry when it is clearly about the human body's desires? What is the cultural significance of debates and discussions about sex – what does sexuality represent? And in what terms did sexuality become discussable – how was it linked to selfhood and gender identity, and how was it invested with historical meaning?[1]

The history of sexuality is a relatively recent area of inquiry in historical thought. Until the 1960s, so-called histories of sex appealed primarily to a male audience who sought erotic stimulation. Such works masqueraded as serious anthropological studies of other cultures, or as medical tracts aimed ostensibly at educating sexually naïve male readers about how to avoid the perils of venereal disease. To be sure, medical literature on sex gained legitimacy as sexual science became increasingly respectable in the interwar period (1918–39), and interwar artists, political radicals, and liberal reformers often insisted on sexual freedom. But it was not until the sixties that works calling themselves "history" about sex and unrelated to matters medical or "hygienic" – as reformers and writers euphemistically referred to the effects of proper and moderate sex – gained currency and respectability.

Numerous histories of erotica published in those years aimed less at titil-
lating readers than at liberating sex from the constraints imposed on its expression by moralists. They – Montgomery Hyde's 1964 *History of Pornography*,
for example – recount an epic struggle between sexual liberation and repression in which increasing numbers of enlightened readers recognize the centrality of sex to human creative expression. Hyde said that "Obscenity and
pornography are ugly phantoms which will disappear in the morning light
when we rehabilitate sex and eroticism," meaning that repression was a dark
force obstructing the development of natural, healthy sexuality.[2] Repression
led not only to the proliferation of pornography, of which the healthy individual would have no need, but to a world in which men and women would
confuse their so-called natural roles and seek to imitate each other. When they
spoke of "history," then, critics who scorned censorship meant a clash between
the joyous triumph of human self-understanding and the sinister forces of
repression, between those who would leave nature unfettered and those who
would shackle her, between those who would liberate the human soul and
those who would deform it. Now, attitudes to sex in a given culture measured
the progress of humankind.

Such critics, as well as doctors and moralists, all believed that sexuality, like
masculinity and femininity, was outside of history: sex was a natural force to
be repressed, regulated, liberated, or channeled by social institutions but not
in any conceivable way the *product* of human history. Still, to the extent they
equated sexual "liberation" with the progress of culture and civilization, they
suggested that sex reflects shifts in historical development. Indeed, the first
work to relate sexuality critically and precisely to specific historical formations
was published in 1964: in the path-breaking *The Other Victorians: A Study of
Pornography and Sexuality in Mid-Nineteenth Century England*, the literary
critic Steven Marcus claimed that his study was born by melding his interest
in the history of culture and ideas about the self with those of social and behavioral scientists fascinated by the empirical study of sexuality.[3]

The Other Victorians assumes that the Victorians relentlessly repressed sexuality but links prohibitions on sexual expression to the historical experience
of modernity: "as an urban, capitalist, industrial middle-class world was being
created . . . the whole style of sexual life was considerably modified. By a variety
of social means which correspond to the psychological processes of isolation,
distancing, denial, and even repression, a separate and insulated sphere in
which sexuality was to be confined was brought into existence."[4] That is, sexual
repression was necessary and particularly acute at a historical moment (the late
eighteenth and nineteenth centuries) when social advancement required the
reconstruction and disciplining of the human body and mind. Though Marcus
does not elaborate, we presume he refers to new concepts of time introduced
by work discipline and industrial capitalism, as well as new spatial divisions
between the world of work and of the home first articulated at the end of the

eighteenth century. In this context, sex, as he puts it, was not just a problem but "problematical," because its power to compel and distract posed a great threat to the demands of social discipline.[5]

Marcus thus does not judge sexual repression to be necessarily good or bad but conceives it as symptomatic of different stages of historical and social development. For example, in his view, pornography is a symptom of repression, the "price we pay for social advancement."[6] Medical men in the Victorian period disseminated fantastical treatises meant to instill fear of sexual pleasure and thereby ensure social discipline. In so doing, they generated an equally fantastical world of pornography as its antithesis – an anxiety-free world of sexual plenty rather than scarcity. Similarly, Marcus argues, the more upper-class society demands restraint in outward appearance, the more a Victorian gentleman (whose memoirs Marcus analyzes) lives an unrestrained "secret life" – a "pornographic" world of easy, frequent, and exploitative sex split off from the world of Victorian propriety. Doctors, pornographers, and gentlemen alike describe sex either in a moral vocabulary of condemnation or in a pornographic language in which sex is always good and gratifying to all, in which women (doctors said) are either "not troubled by sexual feeling" or (pornographers insisted) sexually prolific. According to Marcus, this vocabulary represents but one stage in intellectual and social development that will eventually be surpassed by more open and rational attitudes to sexuality, marked particularly by the work of Sigmund Freud.

The Other Victorians thus offered a sophisticated, historicized analysis of sexuality. Methodologically speaking, Marcus asked that we focus on how properly to characterize attitudes toward sex and seek to reconstruct the sexual organization of society and sexual experiences among persons in the past. He asked how the meanings and expressions of sex are constructed by culture, and also suggested implicitly that sex was a proper object of historical inquiry by demonstrating that sexuality intersects private and public experience – that sexual fantasies exist not only in a realm split off from public discussion but mark "official" medical discourse about sex as well. He asks how pornography, medical treatises, popular works about sex, diaries, journals, and erotic literature more generally, constitute cultural expressions of sexuality, male or female – though he insists there is little to be said about female sexuality and uses male sexuality as his only model. In this important book, Marcus defined the questions and analytical parameters of much of the history of sexuality as it was to be written – in improved and modified form – for the next twenty years.

In particular, Marcus's work articulated self-consciously the ideology of historical progress as well as the centrality of male sexuality that underlay the histories of sexuality published in the sixties and seventies. For modern sexual history recounts the birth and development of the middle-class male self: "Every man who grows up," he wrote, "must pass through such a phase in his existence, and I can see no reason for supposing that our society, in the history of its own life, should not have to pass through such a phase as well."[7] Modern sexual history unfolds away from the distorting lens of repression toward a more enlightened era, and thus toward clarity about matters sexual. Marcus, like most liberal writers and scholars of those decades, believed that sexual attitudes measure human progress, and thus believed that sexuality expresses something essential and essentially spiritual about human beings – that it was a gauge of human freedom.

Marcus's work was thus the most distinguished instance of an ideology that tied sexual freedom to historical progress. In this vision, the Victorian period emblematizes the effects of sexual repression, including the proliferation of pornography and "secret" lives, shame, and guilt that writers and scholars since the beginning of the twentieth century sought to reverse. But, as historian Peter Gay wrote in 1984, Marcus's study has "immortalized smug twentieth-century condescension" about the Victorians' ostensibly prudish attitudes to sex and, in particular, immortalized "respectable women's sexual anesthesia."[8] He argued that Marcus mistakenly took the so-called "official discourse" of Victorian sexuality at its word, particularly in reference to female sexuality, and consequently overemphasized the modern rupture with a repressive Victorian past. Gay thus adds Marcus's name to the pantheon of "anti-Victorians" – sexologists Havelock Ellis and later, William Masters and Virginia Johnson – who saw themselves rebelling against the so-called strictures of Victorian moral imperatives past and present.

This argument against Marcus forms the basis for two very different repudiations of his generation's portrait of Victorian sexuality. One group of historians, represented by Peter Gay and numerous others, including Carl Degler, Martha Vicinus, and Carroll Smith-Rosenberg, seek to revise the popular image of the Victorian past touted by Marcus and others, insisting that official views of sexuality were not necessarily reflected in private life. Moreover, though their analyses differ, these historians generally argue that even official Victorian views were not as monolithic or as homogenous as Marcus made them out to be.

This challenge to Marcus focused on female sexuality, which, we recall, Marcus had all but ignored. It was heavily influenced by the emerging field of women's history, which addressed not only women's experience, but also the regulation of and debates about female sexuality (about prostitution, birth control, and abortion, to name only a few). Historians began to trace the lives of women who rebelled against Victorian propriety and those who happily carved themselves out niches within it – *pace* Marcus, who ignored women's voices entirely and with little evidence, claimed that most women simply accepted men's stereotypes of female sexuality. But more dramatically, as Gay argues, "To define the nature of female sexuality was to do nothing less than to define the nature of marriage itself and to supply instructive clues to the quality of bourgeois communions."[9] Marcus argued that sexuality became "problematical" in the nineteenth-century; Gay and others argue more precisely that women symbolized the problematic of sex. Whether women were fundamentally maternal or sexually passionate determined not only their fitness for different social roles, but also shaped ideas about their marital obligations. The drama and importance of this debate about women's "nature" suggests that Victorians were far more ambivalent than repressive concerning matters sexual, and even, they argue, downright enthusiastic.

Drawing on surveys, correspondence, diaries, and literary sources, revisionist historians paint a generally positive picture of middle-class Victorian sexuality in which sex is not necessarily repressed but an expression of human joy and intimacy, particularly in married life. Victorian men and women understood sex, Gay and Degler argue, to be the cornerstone of married relationships, affording mutual pleasure and enhancing intimacy. They use new sources to demonstrate that Victorian women enjoyed sex, repudiating the Victorian stereotype of the sexually passive, unresponsive women for whom sexual desire was inspired by the thought of childbearing. Gay and Degler do not deny the existence of sexual ignorance, pornography, and other reminders of the bleaker world that Marcus paints. But in this revisionist interpretation, the Victorians rather than the "moderns" – meaning those doctors, writers, and thinkers who insisted on the virtues of sex and sex education – are the real paragons of enlightenment and progress: they recognized the centrality of sex and sought to integrate eroticism and love into their lives such that binding, equal, loving relationships flourished.

This revision of standard concepts of Victorian sexuality simply moves the idea that sex sustains the soul and is essential to self-fulfillment back in time. It thus challenges that teleological ascent of sexual attitudes from darkness toward light, and repression toward liberation, that characterized dominant modes of historical thinking about sexuality. In the revisionist view, the history of sexuality thus does not represent the unfolding of a pre-established script and it is not a phase in society's "life." Instead, that history is born of a struggle waged between middle-class culture and the sexual desires that threatened to undermine its moral imperatives and ideals, one that Victorian men and women engaged constantly and in varied ways. How, revisionists ask, did new attitudes toward the self – the necessity of disciplining mind and body in the interests of progress – shape and give meaning to middle-class men's and women's experiences of their bodies and their sexual unions? For if Victorians, and Victorian women in particular, enjoyed sex, then they did so ideally within the parameters of spiritual unions they believed legitimated their sexual pleasure and marked them as constrained, "civilized" people.

Many other historians nuance this unabashedly positive reinterpretation of the Victorian period: they insist that it is difficult to know whether medical treatises and other educational texts were prescriptive or descriptive, and note also that evidence about women's sexual passion is in large part anecdotal, gleaned from sources that may not be representative. Some too have argued that conclusions about female sexuality must be tempered by the reality of women's subordinate political and social position, and that Gay's celebration of women's pleasure gives other realities short shrift. Many revisionists presume, for example, that sexual intimacy and sexual secrets defined the essence of private life, a human need for intimacy, comfort, and discretion that appear to be part of the natural order of things. And yet the very categories of the public and private are historical fictions (if lived realities) first developed in the late eighteenth and the early nineteenth centuries, and they cemented women's subordination by naturalizing their place in the private realm, away from the nasty world of politics and commerce reserved for men. What, we might ask, is the relationship between this subordination and women's private sexual fulfillment? What is the relation between women's exclusion from political and social power and their ostensible private happiness?

In 1976 the French philosopher-historian Michel Foucault published a path-breaking book entitled *The History of Sexuality: An Introduction*, that dramatically departed from all extant histories of sexuality.[10] In a direct reference to Marcus, Foucault titled the first part "We 'Other Victorians'" and sought to debunk Marcus's characterization of Victorian sexuality. Foucault claims that the Victorians did not repress their sexual desires in the interests of human progress, but spoke incessantly about sex: during the Victorian period, he wrote, there was "an institutional incitement to speak about [sex]."[11]

Like the revisionists, then, Foucault repudiates the idea that the Victorians were sexually repressed. Yet any similarity is superficial, for Foucault takes issue with two interrelated presumptions that inform all prior strains of thought about the history of sexuality, in spite of their differences: that sexuality is a gauge of human freedom, and that sex is a biological force shaped by culture. Foucault argues that by the end of the eighteenth century, sex became central to the life and death of nation-states dependent on the regulation and maintenance of healthy populations. Population experts, legislators, and doctors, among others, began to develop statistical norms meant to define ideally hygienic, restrained sexual behavior best suited to capitalist demands for productive workers. The newly powerful middle-class all over Europe sought to create a symbolic "sexual body" in its own image, no longer defined genealogically after the "bloodlines" that determined status in feudal societies, but fashioned after an efficient, productive, and measurable body mapped out by experts.

Like Marcus, Foucault conceives modern sexual opinion as formed within the experience of modernity – of the time and space of factories, cities, of economically and militarily competitive nations, of a rising middle-class. But unlike Marcus, Foucault repudiates the idea that the Victorian middle-class repressed sex. Instead, he argued that demography, medicine, law, and pedagogy – disciplines he termed "technologies of sex" – *produced* sex in the interests of the powers whose aims they served. In Foucault's paradoxical view, all talk of sex had the effect of regulating sexual expression, and all provocations of erotic desire (whether the fantastical imaginings of Victorian doctors, pornographic literature, or the quiet intimacy of bourgeois unions) regulated and controlled it. Culture does not thus constrain sexual desire "unnaturally," and hence deform or distort it, nor does it provide an ideal forum, as Gay insists does bourgeois marriage, for its expression. Foucault claims instead that sexuality is not an instinct imposed upon, shaped, or channeled by culture; it has no biological life apart from its political and cultural life but is an idea constituted by and within power relations. He puts it this way: "Now, it is precisely this idea of sex *in itself* that we cannot accept without examination. Is sex really the anchorage point that supports the manifestations of sexuality, or is it not rather a complex idea that was formed inside the deployment of sexuality?"[12]

Thus repudiating any distinction between desire and culture, Foucault claims famously that "we must not think that by saying yes to sex, one says no to power; on the contrary. . . ."[13] This force Foucault calls "power" is not unitary: it does not reside in the State and it is not something possessed by anyone. It is the omnipresent and intangible condition of all social relations. Sex is a "discourse of power": it is no longer a force to be harnessed or repressed by culture – it is not a natural instinct – but is itself the effect of these technologies of sex that have no clear origin or cause though they are related to the interests of ruling elites. Those technologies produce normal and abnormal individuals, and the new science of sexology as well as psychoanalysis simply represent the increasing differentiation of human beings along this continuum: the "science" of sexuality is itself one more technology that rationalizes and regulates populations.

Foucault reinterprets the history of sexual science or "sexology" in this vein. At the end of the nineteenth century in Europe and the United States, doctors developed elaborate taxonomies of different kinds of sexual desire. The Austrian Dr. Richard von Krafft-Ebing, the most famous taxonomist of all, published a large book entitled *Psychopathia sexualis* in 1886 that introduced the terms "sadist" and "masochist" into the medical lexicon, and disseminated others, such as "homosexual." Foucault argues that these terms were not objective, scientific categories, but ones aimed at defining and regulating new kinds of people now deemed "normal" or "deviant." Krafft-Ebing's classifications thus not only identified specific sorts of desire more precisely, but also redefined self-identity in new terms. Now sexual desire was no longer only a bodily drive that one might resist or indulge, but defined a person's identity, so that, for example, the man who derived pleasure from sexual violence was not simply subject to particularly strong and particular impulses but a creature with a diagnosable psychological condition. Krafft-Ebing's sadists were certain kinds of people with specific histories: they demonstrated their affliction usually at an early age, perhaps by harming animals, and as they grew older they derived sexual pleasure from harming people. Such creatures, according to the doctor, were almost always men whose "natural" instinct to dominate went awry. Doctors thus no longer conceived sexuality as sexual practices but as defining a psychic identity whose contours they could map and whose inner life might be analyzed and controlled through the scientific investigation of sexual fantasies and behaviors. Hence sadists, masochists, homosexuals, fetishists, necrophiliacs and finally, "heterosexuals" appeared in the course of the late nineteenth and early twentieth centuries, objects now of a new science dubbed "sexology" in 1904 (*sexualwissenschaft*) by the German Iwan Bloch and transformed by Sigmund Freud into psychoanalysis – a school of thought Foucault claimed represented a particularly sinister mode of social regulation.

In this vision, sexuality marks the self in crucial ways – indeed it is the very crux of identity – but it no longer marks human freedom. Instead, it exemplifies the discipline of bodies and minds rather than a force that disrupts social order. If sex is now worth dying for, as Foucault claims, it is not because of something intrinsic to the experience of sexual pleasure, but because power relations have constituted sex in order to discipline us; they have rendered sex the "mirage," he says, in which we see ourselves reflected. "Sex," then, "is historically subordinate to sexuality. We must not place sex on the side of reality, and sexuality on that of confused ideas and illusions; sexuality is a very real historical formation; it is what gave rise to the notion of sex, as a speculative element necessary to its operation."[14] That is, all this time we have been speaking as if the pleasures of the flesh were the "real" experience with which we invest a cultural meaning – illusory, dreamy, "confused" – we call "sexuality." But it turns out that sex is just another expression of the way in which the body, seemingly beyond culture and history, is invested with power, with "sexuality."

Foucault's work thus repudiated the basic presumptions of the history of sexuality as it had been written (and was to be, since the revisionists wrote before and after Foucault's work was published), and laid out a provocative new narrative about the meaning of modern sexuality, particularly its disciplinary function. Though his work is highly controversial, it remains perhaps the single most important contribution to the field and a crucial point of reference. Most scholars in the history of sexuality address his work implicitly or explicitly and take as their own point of departure many of Foucault's insights. To summarize these insights: that the experience of sexuality is utterly mutable and never fixed, never explicable in terms of normative criteria that presume what, say, sexual fulfillment means, what "healthy" sex is, and so on; that so-called perverse identities and perversions (and normalcy) were invented at the end of the nineteenth century; that talk about sex proliferated rather than waned in the course of that century because sex was not a repressed drive but constituted as one more power relation; that sexuality was a means of regulating and disciplining populations.

We might summarize the work that Foucault's ideas generated by saying that studies now more than ever focus on how sexuality symbolizes social relations of power, say between men and women, between doctors and patients, between the State and society. Foucault's greatest influence was arguably not methodological, but lay in his substantive shift of focus away from self-liberation to social discipline, from sexual repression to sexual regulation. In other words, though historians generally accept his contention that sexual desire involves serious questions of power relations and discipline, they generally reject or ignore his insistence that sex is not intrinsic in the flesh, and seek ways to historicize Foucault's insights by reference to precise social formations. James Grantham Turner writes that Foucault "abolished all existing methods of combining sex and history," but that he "did not solve the problem of how to put these insights into practice."[15] Thomas Laqueur notes in a recent work that "I have no interest in denying the reality of sex. . . . But I want to show on the basis of historical evidence that almost everything one wants to *say* about sex – however sex is understood – already has in it a claim about gender. Sex . . . is explicable only within the context of battles over gender and power."[16]

Laqueur, one among a prolific group of historians, thus defines the field of the history of sexuality as it has unfolded since Foucault: it is now arguably the history of the regulation of the body's pleasures, understood as inseparable from "claims about gender" and often also from claims about race and class ideology. This emphasis on gender derived in part from broader developments within the historical discipline itself, as historians moved away from a focus on women's experience to another emphasis on how masculinity and femininity signified usually unequal power relations. In 1986, historian Joan Scott published a pathbreaking article in the *American Historical Review* entitled "Gender: A Useful Category of Historical Analysis" that built upon but challenged the premises of over a decade of scholarship on women's experience. Scott argued that while women's history was primarily descriptive, gender history addresses "dominant disciplinary concepts," thus challenging the very premises of historical analysis. In other words, using gender, the historian not only includes women in the history of events, but challenges the understanding of those events: gender history does not only analyze women's experiences in the spheres they occupy (the family, the private sphere) but "is a primary way of signifying relationships of power." Gender not only describes the culturally imposed attributes of the female sex, but also explains social interaction more generally, so that even areas marked by women's absence – say, high politics – legitimate and define themselves through the celebration of masculine attributes and the exclusion of feminine ones.[17] Gender in this sense is not a descriptive term but a category of analysis: "man" and "woman" are not fixed categories but culturally constructed meanings attributed to sexed bodies that change over time.

The history of sexuality merged with this new approach to the history of women that has by now been extended to explore even political and intellectual history. Since culture prescribed the relationship between gender and sexed bodies, then the relationship between gender and sexuality was culturally constructed rather than timeless and fixed. Thus it was possible to conceive sexual practices as shaped but not determined by gender and to analyze the relationship between them. Since gender not only described sexed bodies but "relationships of power," it described how sexuality was embedded in those relationships. By insisting that sexuality be understood in relationship to gender, then, many historians sought to extend Foucault's insights in new directions as well as to historicize the changing relationship between gender and power neglected by historians who gave women's inequality short shrift. Moreover, the new emphasis on gender proved an important corrective to Foucault, who neglected it entirely. As historians of sexuality increasingly recognized, in so doing he neglected one of the fundamental ways in which sexuality is invested with political and cultural meaning and expresses social status – expresses, for example, women's unequal and subordinate social position. Sexuality, after all, had always been defined in relation to gender in a way that presumed and naturalized social inequities. Dr. Krafft-Ebing gauged normal and perverse sexual behavior by reference to whether or not it signified masculinity in men or femininity in women. Hence sadism was a "normal" male instinct gone awry, and masochism represented the triumph of femininity in men but was an intrinsic part of women's constitution. He also defined homosexuality first and foremost as gender deviance, insisting that men attracted to other men had "feminine" souls and that women who desired women had "masculine" ones. Moreover, female sexuality, as we have seen, was inextricably tied to cultural ideas about women's proper gender role.

Many historians have since taken the relationship between gender and sexuality as their central theme: Jeffrey Weeks argues that the Victorians sought above all to control male lust and male sexuality, asserting that sexual regulation helped consolidate normative constructions of (restrained, self-possessed) masculinity and thus stigmatized so-called gender deviants. John D'Emilio and Estelle Freedman narrate the history of sexuality in the United States as the history of shifting notions of ideal middle-class white masculinity and femininity. In so doing, they shed light on how elites in particular used gender conformity to determine different models of citizenship.[18]

Laqueur's 1990 *Making Sex: Body and Gender from the Greeks to Freud* makes perhaps the most sweeping and important claims about how literate, professional (mostly medical) men constructed the relationship between sexuality and gender to justify male domination. In a study that spans two thousand years of medical discussion about human biology, Laqueur argues that our concept of the body and its pleasures is inseparable from changing notions of masculinity and femininity. He claims that until the eighteenth century, a "one-sex" model predominated in which women's bodies were understood to be inferior versions of men, their genitalia inverted versions of men's own. The female body was less perfect than the male, and this difference illustrated an extracorporeal metaphysical hierarchy. By the end of the eighteenth century, when Enlightenment claims about human liberty and equality did not inherently exclude women, men justified their dominance by turning to nature: the "two-sex" model of gender difference tied ideas about proper modes of sexual expression to women's fundamentally different "nature," leading to the presumption that women were intrinsically more nurturing and less sexually needy than men. As Laqueur puts it: "Sometime in the eighteenth century, sex as we know it was invented." That is, "the two-sex model *was not* manifest in new knowledge about the body and its functions," but "*was* produced through endless microconfrontations over power in the public and private spheres.[19]

In short, historians of sexuality now often seek to understand the formation of sexual norms by reference to changing gender ideals (and increasingly, to ideas about race). They interpret that relationship generally as the history of how different cultures at different historical moments constitute sexual normalcy and deviance and thus narrate it primarily as the history of sexual regulation.

These recent emphases within the history of sexuality (including the relationship between gender and sexuality as well as the nature of Foucault's influence) are developed in subtle and important ways in the growing sub-field of gay and lesbian (or "queer") history. Recall that Foucault suggested that sexual deviance was an important means by which populations were labeled healthy or pathological and thus controlled; sexology and psychoanalysis, he insisted, were two different discourses by which doctors exercised such control. While taking up Foucault's notion that deviance is a form of regulation (rather than an "objective" description of the workings of the mind and body), these historians also reject his insistence that this regulation is all pervasive. Their work links sexuality to power (in this case, to claims about gender), by historicizing the relation between sexuality and gender, but also demonstrates that sexual practices and sexual identities often did not correspond at all to normative gender roles. In an influential 1984 essay about historical shifts in the social organization of sexuality, Gayle Rubin wrested sexual identity away from gender identity, arguing that too often feminist scholars conflated women's sexuality with gender ideals and thus inadvertently reiterated stereotypes of women's intrinsically more "passive" or less forceful sexuality.[20] George Chauncey's recent work on the making of a gay male culture in New York between 1890 and 1940 demonstrates how men used gender roles self-consciously, flexibly, and often with tremendous creativity to define identity and status as well as to ward off public hostility (by presenting themselves as effeminate and unthreatening).[21]

Moreover, such works also show that sexual subcultures offered resistance to social discipline and that deviant sexual identity in particular sometimes became central to *affirmative* definitions of self. Though Foucault had said that sexual identities might become the locus of new self-definitions, he had not really explained how this might be. Most social histories of those condemned for sexual deviance assume implicitly that sexuality is always normatively constituted and thus always socially regulated. Yet they also insist in different ways that sexual deviants use a variety of strategies to combat social marginality and create communities that protect them from the political and psychological consequences of oppression. By putting Foucault's insights into "practice" – by focusing in detailed ways on communities and voices to analyze how individuals constructed and experienced their sexuality – they counter his bleak vision of a world devoid of real historical actors and always in thrall to "power."

Thus historians have written the internal histories of communities – including narratives about how those communities formed, how gay men and lesbians began to identify themselves as such, and how external pressure and discrimination shaped that identification. They demonstrate the existence of vibrant subcultures, clearly constituted within but not absolutely constricted by dominant sexual and political culture. And though such histories tend to be overwhelmingly focused on the late nineteenth and early twentieth centuries, when medical men and legislators first recognized homosexuality as an identity category, historians have increasingly moved into the more distant past. They seek to identify sexual subcultures before the "invention" of homosexuality and to interpret meanings ascribed to sexuality and sexual preference in the premodern period before the self was so inextricably tied to sexual identity.

Starting in the nineteenth century then, historians, writers, medical men and others tied sexuality to self-definition. The histories that trace this development all presume or render problematic that link, assigning it a negative or positive meaning. Since Foucault demonstrated the naïveté implicit in the connection between sexual freedom and human freedom first drawn by anti-Victorians more generally, most historians have found it difficult to celebrate sexual liberation in an unqualified manner. And as historians demonstrated that sexual freedom meant very different things for women and men, they historicized the link between sexual identity, gender identity, and the self – the relationship between sexuality and self was now always a historical product contingent on a wide variety of factors that could never be captured by the opposition between freedom and repression. As historians seek to reconstruct these historical relations in precise terms, within Foucault's conceptual if not methodological framework, they address the tension between sexual regulation and challenges to it. Like Foucault, they reject the notion that sexuality is about human freedom, or that it defines what is most private or most natural about a person; they too believe its centrality to self-identity is an historical phenomenon. But they also celebrate people's use of erotic desire to define identity even as they recognize some of its more problematic social functions – its disciplinary implications, its identity-constraining potential.

Historians of sexuality now address these tensions between positive and negative interpretations of our basic cultural presumption that sexuality is in some fundamental way about selfhood. Debates in the field center implicitly and sometimes explicitly around these tensions, accounting for a deep theoretical split between what might loosely be referred to as the interdisciplinary area of "sexuality studies" faithful to Foucault's vision, and the history of sexuality as written by historians. Notions about selfhood and its relation to sexuality determine distinctions between theoretical approaches: theorists emphasize more the constraints implicit in sexual identity formations, while historians tend to insist on the importance of historical actors' own visions and experiences. But most important, in the thirty odd years since Marcus first made sexuality a respectable area of inquiry, the field has flourished, developing and challenging all the assumptions with which Marcus began. For the history of sexuality, no matter how it is interpreted, is now a history of the generation and regulation of knowledge about gendered human beings; it is about the increasing significance of sex in defining what is most significant, knowable, and discussable about men and women and often defines what constitutes feminine and masculine identities; and it is about how sex symbolizes social order and disorder, in particular anxieties about the erosion of hierarchies based on gender as well as class. Now most inquirers can agree that the link between sexuality and the self is historically contingent and its meaning culturally invested; that sexual identity never exhausts the self and yet always constrains it, that sexuality may express a free or private self and yet is never, in spite of all our illusions, simply free or private.

NOTES

1 The history of gender defines the chronologically and culturally varied construction of male and female identities, of which sexuality is but one important expression. Gender history is thus most often written without reference to sexuality, but the history of sexuality cannot, as we will see, be written without reference to gender.

2 Montgomery Hyde, *The History of Pornography* (New York, 1964), p. 204.

3   Steven Marcus, *The Other Victorians: A Study of Pornography and Sexuality in Mid-Nineteenth Century England* (New York, 1985). The period is dubbed "Victorian" after Queen Victoria of Great Britain, who assumed the throne in 1837 and is usually believed to personify the spirit of that era.

4   Ibid., p. 283.

5   Ibid., p. 2.

6   Ibid., p. 262.

7   Ibid., p. 286.

8   Peter Gay, *The Bourgeois Experience, Victoria to Freud, Volume One: Education of the Senses* (New York: Oxford University Press, 1984), p. 468.

9   Ibid., p. 145.

10 The French title is *La Volonté de savoir* (Paris: Gallimard, 1976). This was the first of a series, of which Foucault completed three volumes before his untimely death in 1984. Hereafter, I quote from the English translation, *The History of Sexuality: An Introduction* (New York: 1981).

11 Ibid., p. 18.

12 Ibid., p. 152.

13 Ibid., p. 157.

14 Ibid.

15 James Grantham Turner, ed. *Sexuality and Gender in Early Modern Europe* (Cambridge: Cambridge University Press, 1993), p. xv.

16 Thomas Laqueur, *Making Sex: Body and Gender from the Greeks to Freud* (Cambridge: Harvard University Press, 1990), p. 11.

17 Reprinted in Joan Scott, *Gender and the Politics of History* (New York: Columbia University Press, 1988), pp. 30, 42.

18 Jeffrey Weeks, *Sex, Politics, and Society: The Regulation of Sexuality since 1800* (London: Longman, 1981); Thomas Laqueur, *Making Sex: Body and Gender from the Greeks to Freud* (Cambridge, MA: Harvard University Press, 1990); John D'Emilio and Estelle D. Freedman, *Intimate Matters: A History of Sexuality in America* (New York: Harper & Row, 1988).

19 Laqueur, *Making Sex*, pp. 149, 192.

20 Gayle Rubin, "Thinking Sex: Notes for a Radical Theory of the Politics of Sexuality," in Carole Vance, ed., *Pleasure and Danger: Exploring Female Sexuality* (Boston: Routledge & Kegan Paul, 1984), pp. 267–319.

21 George Chauncey, *Gay New York: Gender, Urban Culture, and the Making of the Gay Male World, 1890–1940* (New York: Basic Books, 1994).

REFERENCES AND FURTHER READING

Cott, Nancy, *The Bonds of Womanhood: Women's Sphere in New England*, 1780–1835, New Haven: Yale University Press, 1977.

Dean, Carolyn J., *The Frail Social Body: Pornography, Homosexuality, and Other Fantasies in Interwar France*, Berkeley: University of California Press, 2000.

Faderman, Lillian, *Odd Girls and Twilight Lovers: A History of Lesbian Life in Twentieth-Century America*, New York: Penguin, 1991.

Gordon, Linda, *Woman's Body, Woman's Right: Birth Control in America*, Penguin: New York, 1977.

Sedgwick, Eve Kosofky, *Epistemology of the Closet*, Berkeley: University of California Press, 1991.

Merrick, Jeffrey and Bryant T. Ragan, eds. *Homosexuality in Modern France*, Oxford: Oxford University Press, 1997.

Mosse, George, *Nationalism and Sexuality: Respectability and Abnormal Sexuality in Modern Europe*, New York: H. Fertig, 1985.

Roberts, Mary Louise, *Civilization Without Sexes: Reconstructing Gender in Postwar France, 1917–1927*, Chicago: University of Chicago Press, 1994.

Robinson, Paul, *The Modernization of Sex: Havelock Ellis, Alfred Kinsey, William Masters, and Virginia Johnson*, Ithaca: Cornell University Press, 1973.

Smith, Bonnie, *The Gender of History: Men, Women, and Historical Practice*, Cambridge, MA: Harvard University Press, 1999.

CHAPTER NINETEEN

Historicizing Natural Environments: The Deep Roots of Environmental History

Andrew C. Isenberg

At the 1993 meeting of the American Society for Environmental History (ASEH), William Cronon delivered a presidential address that explored the tensions between environmental history and environmental politics. The address came at a pivotal moment: many books published in the 1970s and early 1980s had applauded the past deeds of nature advocates, but by the 1990s, few environmental historians told tidy stories of ecological villains versus ecological saints. Rather, many de-emphasized environmentalists to explain changes to natural environments as complex stories of interaction between people and nature, in which nature was as likely as humanity to contribute to change. The resulting tensions between historians and activists were particularly poignant, Cronon argued, because "like the several other 'new' histories born or reenergized in the wake of the 1960s – women's history, African-American history, Chicano history, gay and lesbian history, and the new social history generally – environmental history has always had an undeniable relation to the political movement that helped spawn it."[1]

While Cronon powerfully asserted the novelty of environmental history, he was careful to allow that the field may not have been born of the political tumult of the 1960s so much as "reenergized" by it. Cronon's qualification was necessary, if for no better reason than moments before he stepped to the podium to deliver his presidential address, the ASEH had awarded him its George Perkins Marsh Prize for his book, *Nature's Metropolis: Chicago and the Great West*. The award is named in honor of the author of *Man and Nature*, a book published in 1864 analyzing the reciprocal relationship between people and the non-human natural environment. The intellectual antecedents of *Nature's Metropolis* included not only Marsh but Frederick Jackson Turner, the nineteenth and early twentieth-century historian of the American West.[2] While, as Cronon attested, the study of the environment was "reenergized" by the environmental movement of the 1960s and 1970s, his own work demonstrated that the roots of environmental history tap deep into the nineteenth century. The environmental movement lent coherence, greater visibility, and a sense of mission to a disparate historiographical tradition, but that historiography reflects the long evolution of historical study of the natural environment.

An awareness of the deep roots of environmental history helps to make better sense of the recent tension between environmental history and environmental politics. From the nineteenth century to the present, a persistent pattern of thought has maintained that nature is cyclic, harmonious, and passive, while human history is linear, dynamic, and active. This view is, in part, a product of romantic thought as it was expressed by Jean-Jacques Rousseau, Johann Wolfgang von Goethe, and Henry David Thoreau, among others. In its ascription of dynamism to human society, it accords with the progressive view common to the scholars who professionalized historical study in the mid-nineteenth century. A certain kind of environmentalism and environmental science – particularly the branch that concerns itself with wilderness preservation and conservation biology – embraces this view, seeing human greed and short-sightedness as responsible for destabilizing the order of nature.

Since the mid-nineteenth century, scholars of the historical relationship between people and nature have repeatedly confronted this dualism between linear, active humanity and cyclic, passive nature. Some historians, particularly those scholars working in the nineteenth and early twentieth century, have embraced the dualism in order to emphasize humanity's transformation of nature. Marsh wrote, "man is everywhere a disturbing agent. Wherever he plants his foot, the harmonies of nature are turned to discords."[3] Others, particularly French historians writing in the 1930s, likewise accepted a largely static notion of an orderly nature as a way to emphasize the slowly changing character of rural life over a long term. As the twentieth century has progressed, however, biologists and ecologists have advanced an increasingly dynamic view of the non-human natural environment.[4] This new science of disequilibrium and disharmony has challenged both environmentalists and environmental historians to conceive of nature not simply as a passive subject of human alteration or as a brake on human historical momentum, but as a dynamic force of change in natural and human history. The evolution of that understanding has been neither direct nor uniform, however. Both scientists and historians have, during the past century, periodically reasserted an understanding of nature as basically orderly and enduring. As a consequence, historical understanding of the relationship between humanity and nature has evolved in complex patterns that variously embrace and reject the idea of a dynamic nature. The tension between historians and activists that Cronon saw in 1993 was a part of that long evolution.

Reciprocity

Until the middle of the nineteenth century, most scholars believed that nature's order transcended historical change. Harmonious, self-regulating, and permanent, the non-human natural world stood apart from a dynamic human history. One of the first significant blows to this intellectual edifice was Charles Lyell's three-volume *Principles of Geology*, published between 1830 and 1833, which suggested the slow but monumental alteration of the planet's land-scapes. Lyell's study influenced the next generation of naturalists, particularly Charles Darwin, whose 1859 *Origin of Species* argued for a natural world in which historical change was paramount. Explicitly rejecting the early nine-teenth-century view of nature as unchanging, Darwin and others advanced the notion that change in the form of the evolution of species was intrinsic to the operations of nature. Nature, in short, was a historical artifact; its constitution at any moment was a product of forces of historical change.

Before the end of the nineteenth century, Marsh and Turner had begun to integrate human agency into the concept of a changing natural environment. Marsh and Turner shared important methodological traits with later environ-mental historians. Both were committed to interdisciplinary study. Moreover, like the French *Annalistes* of the 1920s and 1930s, and the "new social his-torians" of the 1960s, both scholars abhorred history that merely recited the political deeds of great men.

Most important, Marsh and Turner shared a commitment to the concept that the relationship between people and nature is reciprocal. Yet here their approaches to the study of the environment in history diverged. Marsh, taking account of the complex interconnections that make up the natural world, measured the environmental and social costs of human manipulations and alterations of nature. Deforestation and erosion, according to Marsh, aroused nature's wrath, "and she avenges herself upon the intruder, by letting loose upon her defaced provinces destructive energies hitherto kept in check." Marsh's study of past interactions between people and nature, largely in the Mediterranean world, revealed considerable degradation. *Man and Nature*, accordingly, was primarily declensionist and hortatory:

> There are parts of Asia Minor, of Northern Africa, of Greece, and even of Alpine Europe, where the operation of causes set in action by man has brought the face of the earth to a desolation almost as complete as that of the moon. . . . The earth is fast becoming an unfit home for its noblest inhabitant. . . .[5]

In short, human mismanagement of the natural world, according to Marsh, would eventually undermine the environments upon which humanity relied for its existence.

Turner, too, focused on the reciprocal relationship between people and nature. Where Marsh was declensionist, however, Turner was triumphalist. In North America, the progressive transformation of the "wilderness" to "civilization" was, in Turner's analysis, a cause for celebration. Human alteration of the environment produced not suffering but progress. Turner's analytical apparatus was less Darwinian than Lamarckian: settlers' encounter with the wilderness produced the ideal American characteristics of fortitude, ingenuity, and independence; settlers, in turn, bequeathed these characteristics to their descendants. His analysis was also equal parts Lockean. The progress of the frontier of settlement across the continent kept America democratic by virtue of settlers' "continuous touch with the simplicity of primitive society," a concept he inherited from John Locke's notion of "the liberty of the state of Nature."[6]

While asserting the historical significance of the environment, Marsh and Turner regarded environments as passive. Nature was acted upon by people; nature itself was not a historical actor, except in the sense that a degraded landscape impoverished its inhabitants (in Marsh's view) or the taming of the wilderness produced positive social characteristics (in Turner's view).

Geography

In the 1930s and after, Turner's field of western American history inspired several re-conceptions of the relationship between human and natural history. The new views of the West were quite different from Turner's triumphalist paradigm, however. Between the 1880s and the 1930s, the North American Great Plains witnessed a series of environmental and economic catastrophes: the near-extinction of the bison by the early 1880s; the collapse of the free-range cattle industry in the mid-1880s; the agricultural depression of the 1890s; and the "dust bowl" of the 1930s.[7] These disasters, all caused in part by the drought-prone climate of the region, prompted the Texas historian Walter Prescott Webb, in his 1931 study, *The Great Plains*, to declare aridity to be the determining characteristic of the grasslands. While Marsh and Turner had focused on people's transformations of nature, Webb focused on the limitations that nature placed on human endeavors. The relative lack of precipitation in the Great Plains, according to Webb, dictated the underpopulated and underdeveloped character of the region. Toward the end of his career, in 1957, Webb amplified his study of the Great Plains into a new, post-Turnerian paradigm for the history of the American West. "The heart of the West," Webb wrote, "is a desert, unqualified and absolute." Nature determined that the West would be an "oasis society"; owned in large part by a federal government unable to funnel land into private hands; a region of defeated expectations. In the 1980s, Webb's environmental determinism won numerous adherents from the "New Western History" school. His work has been echoed in recent studies of African, Asian, and Australian history.[8]

Webb reflected a broad acceptance by the 1930s of the importance of geographical perspectives in history and the social sciences. At the forefront of this intellectual movement was the geographer Carl Ortwin Sauer, whose "cultural landscape" united geography and culture. "The cultural landscape is fashioned out of a natural area by a cultural group," wrote Sauer in 1925. "Culture is the agent, the natural area is the medium, the cultural landscape the result." Regional environments, according to Sauer, provided opportunities that were seized, missed, or misused by cultural groups to create specific landscapes.[9] Sauer's assertion was an early articulation of what came to be known later as "place theory," exemplified by the geographer Yi-Fu Tuan's 1977 postulation that space plus culture equals place.[10]

Still more influential than Webb and Sauer in integrating geography and history was the work of several French historians, particularly Lucien Febvre and Marc Bloch, the founders, in 1929, of the journal *Annales d'histoire économique et sociale*. The *Annalistes*, like Marsh and Turner before them, rejected positivist, fact- and document-based, event-oriented history in favor of what they called *histoire totale*, which situated the study of history within geography and other theoretically-grounded disciplines. Yet the *Annalistes* did not emerge in the 1920s *sui generis*. Febvre and Bloch had been inspired by a previous generation of French intellectuals, particularly the geographer Paul Vidal de la Blache, whose work emphasized the interaction of people and nature in the creation of regional mentalities.[11]

Like Sauer, the *Annalistes* did not ascribe to simple geographical determinism. Anticipating Sauer's idea of the "cultural landscape," Febvre argued in 1922 that geography was the key to understanding human history, but it did not explain everything. "There is some geography in a wheat field," he wrote, "but a wheat field is not a geographical fact." A field of wheat was also the product of a farmer, seeds, and the implements and techniques of cultivation – forces produced by cultural, not strictly natural history.[12] The *Annalistes* sought not to impose geography as the determining force in history – this approach they disparaged as typical of mere geographers. Rather, they aimed to slow the pace of history, to retreat from the action of politics to what Febvre's student Fernand Braudel called *la longue durée*: "man in his relationship to the environment, a history in which all change is slow, a history of constant repetition, ever-recurring cycles." Not surprisingly, this approach oriented *Annalistes* toward agricultural history, an approach typified by Braudel's student Emmanuel Le Roy Ladurie in his 1966 work, *The Peasants of Languedoc*.[13] Yet the *Annalistes* also contemplated demography and climate, subjects that would become more important in the study of environmental history in succeeding decades.[14]

Webb, Sauer, and the *Annalistes* went beyond the examples of Marsh and Turner in embedding human history in a natural context. Their absorption of geography made their study of the environment more theoretically sophisticated than that of their predecessors. Nature, in their view, if not exactly an agent in human history, nonetheless provided the conditions that permitted certain human possibilities and precluded others.

Ecology

Following rapidly upon the scholars who had been inspired by geography was a group, headed by Aldo Leopold, a one-time forest ranger and a professor of game management at the University of Wisconsin–Madison, inspired by ecology. The subtle differences between these two sources of inspiration were not completely understood by scholars at the time. Eventually, the differences emerged as deterministic. Emphasizing interconnections in a dynamic nature rather than the static, enduring influences of landscape or climate, Leopold and his followers conceived of nature as a process rather than strictly a place. Yet despite their attention to nature's dynamism, they ultimately argued for an inherent order in nature that human societies altered at their own peril.

In North America, some members of this group of scholars focused on Native Americans' relationships to the land. Taking their cue from a Rousseauian ideal of the noble savage, and influenced in no small part by the conservation movement that Marsh had helped to inspire, scholars depicted Indians as primitive conservationists. As early as the 1910s, the leading authority on the native hunting groups of Canada, the anthropologist Frank Speck, argued that Indians' hunting techniques functioned to conserve game supplies.[15] The Depression-era scholarly search for alternative economic models to capitalism, followed by decolonization in the second half of the twentieth century, fueled this interpretation of pre-colonial land uses as sustainable alternatives to capitalist resource exploitation. By the 1960s and 1970s, this "functionalist" or "structuralist" school of anthropology had come to interpret many aspects of pre-colonial cultures – even or especially aspects that seemed unusual or irrational to Western cultures – as adaptations to regional environments. Thus anthropologists argued that Native American hunting taboos, Islamic proscriptions against pork, and Hindu proscriptions against beef were grounded in environmental conditions.[16] While finding agency and sagacity in pre-colonial cultures in ways that their scholarly predecessors had not, the functionalists shared with them a static conception of the relationships between such cultural groups and nature. They presumed that the purpose of cultural proscriptions on land use was the sustainability of the human relationship with nature. The functionalists often accepted the mere existence of proscriptions as ontological evidence for sustainability.

By the 1930s, some ecologists and wildlife biologists came to believe that non-human nature did not require pre-capitalist societies to act as managers of natural stability. The environment, they argued, could maintain its own stability. In 1935, the British ecologist A. G. Tansley coined the term "ecosystem" to indicate the complex interconnections that functioned to maintain natural stability. By the 1940s, Leopold, by drawing on Tansley and another British ecologist, Charles Elton, had articulated an idea of nature as a self-regulating system. Wolves, for example, kept populations of grazing and browsing species under control. Eliminate wolves – which both private hunters and public authorities in the United States were determined to accomplish in the first half of the twentieth century – and populations of grazing and browsing animals would expand beyond the ability of environments to sustain them. Leopold observed such disastrous eruptions of deer populations in the Kaibab National Forest in Arizona and in the forests of Wisconsin.[17]

To restore functional integrity to these environments, Leopold argued, one must restore wolves. Leopold's wolves functioned like Speck's Indians to conserve resources and maintain environmental stability. Overstocking a range with cattle maximized the productivity of the land, but at the risk of overgrazing. Wolves that preyed on such cattle, Leopold argued, were not manifesting a violent and unpredictable wilderness, but doing their "job of trimming the herd to fit the range."[18] The environmental historian Donald Worster, the chief intellectual proponent of Leopold's view, has likewise argued that "nature constitutes a different and greater kind of order than anything that we, acting as one species alone, can create."[19] According to this view, an event such as the southern plains dust bowl of the 1930s – the subject of Worster's best-known book – was not a climatic anomaly but a reminder, like the Kaibab deer eruption, of the imperative of recognizing and accommodating to the order of nature.

Leopold's view of nature, like Speck's interpretation of Indian hunting, was implicitly critical of capitalist land use strategies. Worster, drawing on a scholarly tradition of Marxist historical materialism, made that critique explicit. In his 1979 study of the dust bowl, he argued that the root of the ecological catastrophe in the southern plains was the quintessentially capitalist view that "Nature must be seen as capital." He wrote, "A business culture attaches no other value to nature than this; the nonhuman world is desanctified and demystified as a consequence."[20] Worster's call for sanctity was instructive. Influenced by Leopold, who before his death articulated a "land ethic" that proscribed actions that harmed the beauty or ecological integrity of the environment, Worster called for a spiritual regard for nature – combined with a communitarian social organization – to reverse the capitalist degradation of the environment. "Ecological harmony," he wrote in one of his essays, "is a non-market value that takes a collective will to achieve."[21]

Populations

Leopold's moral ecology presumed order in a self-regulating non-human nature. His hope was for humanity to discover and abide by nature's laws. Disasters such as the dust bowl or the eruption and subsequent crash of the Kaibab deer population were *a priori* the results of human interference and mismanagement. By the 1950s, however, ecologists and historians had begun to see similar environmental changes emerging from nature itself. These studies focused on population biology, particularly the unpredictable fluctuations of plant and animal (including human) species. Such studies built, to some degree, on the *Annales* school's interest in demography, but they emerged in the second half of the twentieth century fueled by widespread concern for global population growth. Quite in contrast to Leopoldian notions of nature, which implied that environments, while dynamic, were self-regulating in the absence of human meddling, these works emphasized the unpredictability and uncontrollability of nature.

One of the earliest entrants into the field was Hans Zinsser's *Rats, Lice, and History* (1935), which, in the grassroots tradition of Marsh, Turner, and the *Annales* historians, located the determining forces of human history not in the deeds of the powerful, but in the overlooked (and despised) non-human carriers of infectious diseases. The field reached its apogee in William McNeill's *Plagues and Peoples* (1976). McNeill charted the determining role of disease in human history, from the decline of ancient empires in the Mediterranean, India, and China, to the Black Death of fourteenth-century Europe, to the depopulation of the Americas after Columbus. As in Zinsser's book, in McNeill's study microbes, rather than people, were the main actors in history. "We all want human experience to make sense, and historians cater to this universal demand by emphasizing elements in the past that are calculable, definable, and, often, controllable as well," McNeill wrote in a critique of historical methodology dating back to the nineteenth century. "Epidemic disease, when it did become decisive in peace or in war, ran counter to the effort to make the past intelligible."[22]

To make sense of disease, McNeill and others borrowed models from the environmental sciences. Biologists' concept of "niche" was crucial to the development of this school of thought. Charles Elton, whose work had powerfully influenced Leopold, had been one of the first proponents in the 1920s of the concept of ecological niches. An animal population, he argued, tended to expand until it reached the limit of its environment to sustain it. This tendency had inspired Leopold to argue for the conservation of predators, in order to keep other animal populations in check. Certain kinds of diseases found niches, too; "crowd diseases" such as smallpox and measles were endemic to Old World cities. Epidemics occurred when a host transmitted a microbe to a previously unexposed population. In a sense, the relationship between microbes and people mirrored the Leopoldian relationship between wolves and deer: diseases, like predators, functioned to keep populations in check. Yet they did not function perfectly; humans not only acquired immunities to certain diseases but built cultural bulwarks against their spread.

By the second half of the twentieth century, demographers had come to think that industrialization and medical advances had eliminated the poverty and disease that had once restrained the growth of the human population. While they certainly applauded the eradication of deadly diseases, they nonetheless feared that vaccines had rendered the concept of niche irrelevant for human beings – or, perhaps, had made the entire planet into the human niche. In 1968, Paul Ehrlich, a Stanford University population biologist whose research centered on butterfly populations, argued in his neo-Malthusian jeremiad, *The Population Bomb*, that human population growth would inevitably result in the exhaustion of resources. People thus needed not only to manage populations of wildlife but to control their own numbers as well.[23] In more recent years, however, historians and social anthropologists have complicated Ehrlich's simple model by paying greater attention to land use, arguing that in many parts of the developing world resource shortages are more the consequence of extractive resource strategies than of overpopulation.

Beginning in 1949, historians and ecologists began to integrate the study of niches and population with the history of human colonialism and expansion. Andrew Clark's 1949 study, *The Invasion of New Zealand by People, Plants, and Animals*, was followed in 1958 by Elton's *The Ecology of Invasions by Animals and Plants*.[24] European chestnut blight and starlings in North America, North American muskrats in Asia, Chinese mitten crabs in northern Europe, and, most famously perhaps, European rabbits in Australia multiplied exponentially in their new environments. The historian Alfred Crosby has made the most compelling analysis of the role of ecological invasions in history in two major works, *The Columbian Exchange* (1972) and *Ecological Imperialism* (1986). While Crosby's first work noted, for instance, that the Spanish conquest of Mexico in the sixteenth century would not have succeeded were it not for an outbreak of smallpox among the Aztecs, by the time of the publication of his second study he had extended this notion to a global scale. Europeans, he argued, possessed irresistible ecological advantages when they colonized temperate regions of the world: Australia, New Zealand, North America, and the southern cone of South America. Europeans' "portmanteau biota" of diseases, animals, and plants overwhelmed indigenous human, animal, and plant species which had no previous exposure to them and thus no means to resist the invaders.[25]

Nature, according to McNeill, Crosby, and others, was both unpredictable and unquestionably in control. Europeans "were seldom masters of the biological changes they triggered," according to Crosby. "They benefited from the great majority of these changes, but benefit or not, their role was less often a matter of judgment and choice than of being downstream of a bursting dam."[26] Crosby's metaphor illustrated both the potentials and the pitfalls of the school of niche, population, and ecological invasion. The school's notion of nature was dynamic but deterministic. Human existence was fundamentally biological; "judgment and choice" mattered for little.

Wilderness

Throughout the evolution of historical writing on the environment, scholars remained faithful to Marsh and Turner's emphasis on the reciprocal relationship between people and nature, but they emphasized different sides of the interaction. McNeill, Crosby, and their adherents had pushed the terms of that relationship in favor of the environment. Other scholars, working at roughly the same time, emphasized cultural factors in the human relationship with nature. In the United States between the 1950s and 1970s, interest in literate views of nature such as those of the nineteenth-century nature writers Henry David Thoreau and John Muir revived. This interest owed itself, in part, to the prevailing preeminence in postwar America of intellectual and cultural history. One of the earliest examples of this type of work was Henry Nash Smith's 1950 study *Virgin Land*, a seminal work in the emerging field of American studies. Smith recast the American West not as Turner's frontier or Webb's desert but as a cultural construct, a mythical garden, a "vast and constantly growing agricultural society." Smith's book, which encompassed Thomas Jefferson, Thoreau, Turner, and nineteenth-century dime novel heroes, removed the emphasis from the land itself and refocused it on Americans' cultural apprehensions of the land.[27]

The publication of Smith's book preceded the resurgence of the environmental movement in the 1960s. Later writers on the subject of nature and culture were more directly influenced by the movement. That influence manifested itself in historians' choices of subject: to a considerable extent, they focused on nature writers whose ideas could be regarded as proto-environmentalist. Often, this meant nineteenth-century romanticists: Thoreau and Ralph Waldo Emerson, for instance. Research focused not only on American notions of nature. The study of cultural apprehensions of nature transcended national boundaries. European intellectuals – Linneaus, Rousseau, Wordsworth, and Goethe – received considerable attention.[28]

Most influential, however, was Roderick Nash's *Wilderness and the American Mind*, which went through three editions between 1967 and 1982. Revisiting "wilderness," the subject that had been central to Turner's concept of Americans' relationship to nature, Nash's book echoed Turner in several respects. According to Nash, a basic fear of wilderness, a legacy of the Dark Ages and Puritanism, animated Americans to raze forests and destroy wildlife in the effort to replace them with farms and domesticated animals. Nash's analysis turned on the same historical moment that had inspired Turner's essay on the frontier in 1893: the seeming near-exhaustion of wilderness by the end of the nineteenth century. By that time, according to Nash, Americans' fears of wilderness had been replaced by an anxiety that they had become overly mechanized, industrialized, and urbanized. Preservation began fitfully, with the creation of Yosemite Park in 1864 and Yellowstone Park in 1872, and culminated with the passage of the Wilderness Act in 1964, an event that Nash celebrated as much or more than Turner had once celebrated the transformation of wilderness to civilization.[29]

Nash lionized preservationists; in his account of twentieth-century preservation, it is sometimes difficult to separate his views from those of the wilderness advocates he discusses. Other historians, however, were more skeptical of the accomplishments of early environmentalists. Earliest among these was Samuel Hays, whose 1957 study, *Conservation and the Gospel of Efficiency*, cast the American Progressive-era conservation movement not as a morally simple tale of "people versus the interests" but as a complex story of technological, business, and political history. Hays was far more circumspect in his assessment of conservationists than Nash had been. The conservationists did some good work, he argued, but they were at times elitist, undemocratic, and monopolistic. Hays' book was followed in more recent years by yet more critical studies of wildlife protection and forestry that have regarded environmentalism as a subject of historical study, rather than an intellectual guide. They argued that people's understandings of nature were as historically contingent as changing environments.[30]

Integration

A series of prize-winning works of environmental history seemed to burst on the scene in the late 1970s and 1980s: Worster's *Dust Bowl* (1979); Richard White's *Land Use, Environment, and Social Change* (1980); Cronon's *Changes in the Land* (1983); and Arthur McEvoy's *The Fisherman's Problem* (1986). To many readers at the time, it seemed as if the field of environmental history had emerged unanticipated, like a geyser erupting from deeply buried groundwaters. Yet the field had recognizable sources above the surface. The field's headwaters were located in the nineteenth century, in the work of Marsh and Turner. The rivulets of thought produced at these sources gathered force in the twentieth century, as historically-minded studies of geography and ecology, by Sauer, Leopold, and Elton, among others, as well as geographically- and ecologically-minded historical studies, by Webb, the *Annalistes*, and others, converged. The confluence of these streams of thought became the rapid current of environmental history.

Environmental historians made explicit the interaction between humanity and the non-human natural environment that was implicit in earlier scholarship. Worster, White, Cronon, and McEvoy reconciled the growing division between materially-based studies such as those by McNeill and Crosby and culturally-grounded ones such as Nash's, and returned to an integrated view of the relationship between nature and human history. White defined the relationship as "reciprocal." Cronon called it "dialectical." Both models, and those of other environmental historians such as McEvoy and Carolyn Merchant, regard both human society and nature as dynamic and interactive agents of historical change. Most environmental historians working in the last two decades ascribe to neither environmental nor cultural determinism. Nor do most regard either environments or cultures as static: environments, even absent human influence, are liable to change; cultures, in their relationship to nature, are equally dynamic.[31] Environmental historians' understanding of culture reflected the sophisticated work of recent cultural historians. Many have sought to integrate considerations of class, ethnicity, and gender into their work.[32] Grounded in a methodology of interaction and change, the field has produced a number of important studies in recent years, of the transition to capitalism in Europe, the environmental context and consequences of the interaction of European colonizers and the colonized in the Americas, Africa, Australia, and New Zealand; the decline of biodiversity; the expansion of European biota; and the formation of environmental ideas.

Much of the labor of environmental historians has been in the tradition of Marsh: understanding the human role in and the social consequences of environmental change. In general, this work has focused on the history of the environment since the rise of industrialism in the nineteenth century. Many of these studies, influenced by the scholarship of historical materialism, are explicitly critical of capitalist resource use. To labor historians' critique of capitalism's effect on workers, environmental historians have added the insight that capitalist resource extraction has, in several instances, proved to be unsustainable. Yet environmental historians who take seriously the recent work in ecology that suggests the inherent dynamism of nature have a much more difficult task than the one that faced Marsh. They must decide whether environmental change is the consequence of human action, natural origin, or, more often, a combination of both. The result has been a reconsideration of many assumptions about the historical relationship between humanity and nature.

For many environmental historians, that reconsideration has meant a critique of the romantic ideas that have influenced the historical study of nature since Marsh's time. Environmental historians have achieved the greatest distance from romantic notions of nature in their examinations of urban environments. Romanticists have long considered cities to be the antitheses of wilderness or bucolic pastoral landscapes. This disregard for cities has allowed environmental historians to study the ecology of urban places unburdened by the notion of nature as pristine, unspoiled, and uninhabited by people. Andrew Hurley's brilliant study of Gary, Indiana, stands out as a model of this type of scholarship. Hurley does not privilege wilderness advocates' definition of environmentalism, but rather contrasts that perspective with that of working-class white and African-American residents of Gary, who were less concerned with wilderness than with cleaning up the urban landscape.[33]

The de-romanticization of historical study of the environment has also influenced the study of the relationship between indigenous or pre-capitalist societies and the land. Working in the tradition of Rousseau and Speck, environmental historians of North America, like many environmentalists, had once confidently assumed that Native American land use strategies were sustainable. Several recent studies, by both historians and anthropologists, have cast considerable doubt on this proposition. They have pointed to the overexploitation of resources such as the beaver, bison, caribou, deer, seal, sea otter, and whale in both the historic and proto-historic periods. The result of these studies is a more contextualized view of Native American resource strategies: where and when Native Americans learned to practice sustainable strategies, according to McEvoy, there "is no reason to presume that it was not a historical process, costly, time consuming, and probably marked by expensive failure."[34] Paralleling the study of environmental crises in the ancient world and in pre-modern Europe, these studies have argued that the over-exploitation of nature has not been exclusively the work of industrial societies.

Many environmental historians have complicated the cultural history of environmentalism by broadening their study beyond its romantic origins in the writings of Rousseau, Goethe, and Thoreau. Richard Grove has argued that the earliest conservationist ideas emerged as a consequence of European colonialism. Seventeenth-century Europeans' encounter with unfamiliar tropical environments spurred their investigations of natural history. Within a generation, such studies turned to the consideration of the impact of European colonialism on the land, and to the development of conservation techniques to sustain European commerce. Other studies, of North America, central Asia, and Africa, have similarly argued that whether twentieth-century conservationism preserved resources or propped up the economic forces that extracted them, it was fundamentally colonial in character.[35]

Altogether, recent work in environmental history has critically reassessed romantic notions of nature and greatly complicated Marsh's causal explanations while remaining essentially true to his set of concerns and basic methodology. Like Marsh and Turner, environmental historians remain committed to interdisciplinary study and to "grassroots history." Unlike them, modern environmental historians have come to understand some environmental changes as the consequence not of human action but inherent to a changing nature. Their aim is not to exculpate industrial societies for their degradation of nature. Rather, their goal is to understand change in the context of a dynamic environment.

This is not to suggest that environmental historians have come to complete agreement on the relationship between humanity and nature. Worster has remained committed to the idea that nature's order transcends human history. "Historians are temperamentally and philosophically inclined to see change instead of stability in the world," Worster wrote in 1990. "Environmental history is for me an exception to this tendency. . . . We are not required, simply because we are historians, to attempt some final historicization of nature, nor because we are mainly students of human society are we required to reduce all landscapes to essentially social or cultural expressions."[36] Worster's view was representative of many historians in the field. In general, these historians rejected the scientific views that had come into vogue in the last third of the twentieth century suggesting that nature is fundamentally dynamic. Their views remain in tension with those environmental historians who have embraced the notion of nature's inherent dynamism.

Those tensions were on display at the ASEH meeting in 2000, when the George Perkins Marsh Prize went to Jay Taylor for his book, *Making Salmon: An Environmental History of the Northwest Fisheries Crisis*. Taylor's book attributed the decline of the salmon fisheries to a complex variety of causes, including aboriginal and industrial fishing, alterations to riverine environments, and ecological changes inherent in nature.[37] Taylor was determined not to cast the decline of the fisheries as a simple moral fable of a pristine Eden first inhabited by Indians practicing sustainable fishing and later destabilized by Euro-American overharvesting. Moments after Taylor received his award, the ASEH's invited speaker, Billy Frank, stepped to the podium. Frank, of the Northwest Indian Fisheries Commission, offered his own version of the history of the decline of the region's fisheries, one that unambiguously and unapologetically blamed commercial Euro-American fishers for the crisis. The assembled environmental historians gave Frank an enthusiastic standing ovation.

The ASEH's endorsement of both Taylor and Frank reveals the heart of the problem of historicizing natural environments. The legacy of Rousseau, Goethe, and Thoreau is a powerful one. Many if not most environmental historians adhere to some part of their vision, just as did their intellectual predecessors Speck, Leopold, and the *Annalistes*. When environmental historians confront assumptions about nature's transcendent harmony they confront their own historiographical traditions and, as often as not, themselves. The environmental movement has set the terms for that confrontation in recent years: historians such as Taylor who argue for the complex origins of environmental change find themselves arguing not only with other environmental historians but with environmentalists. This is a frustrating argument for many environmental historians who often regard themselves as sympathetic to the environmental movement. The tension is unlikely to go away, however, because it reflects the challenges of the longstanding and ongoing effort to incorporate nature into history.

NOTES

1 William Cronon, "The Uses of Environmental History," *Environmental History Review* 17 (1993): p. 2.
2 Cronon, *Nature's Metropolis: Chicago and the Great West* (New York: Norton, 1991); George Perkins Marsh, *Man and Nature; or, Physical Geography as Modified by Human Action*, ed. David Lowenthal (Cambridge, MA: Belknap Press, 1965); Frederick Jackson Turner, "The Significance of the Frontier in American History," American Historical Association *Annual Report* (1893), pp. 199–227.
3 Marsh, *Man and Nature*, p. 36.
4 See Daniel Botkin, *Discordant Harmonies: A New Ecology for the Twenty-first Century* (New York: Oxford University Press, 1990).
5 Marsh, *Man and Nature*, pp. 42–3.
6 Turner, "The Significance of the Frontier."
7 See Andrew C. Isenberg, *The Destruction of the Bison: An Environmental History, 1750–1920* (New York: Cambridge University Press, 2000), pp. 123–63; Worster, *Dust Bowl: The Southern Plains in the 1930s* (New York: Oxford University Press, 1979).
8 Walter Prescott Webb, *The Great Plains* (Boston: Ginn, 1931); Webb, "The American West: Perpetual Mirage," *Harper's Magazine*, 214 (1957), pp. 25–31. See Webb's influence in James L. A. Webb, *Desert Frontier: Ecological and Economic Change Along the Western Sahel, 1600–1850* (Madison: University of Wisconsin Press, 1995).
9 Carl O. Sauer, "The Morphology of Landscape," *University of California Publications in Geography* 2 (1925): 19–53.
10 Yi-Fu Tuan, *Space and Place: The Perspective of Experience* (Minneapolis: University of Minnesota Press, 1977).
11 See Alan R. H. Baker, "Reflections on the Relations of Historical Geography and the *Annales* School of History," in Alan R. H. Baker and D. Gregory, eds., *Historical Geography: Interpretive Essays* (Cambridge: Cambridge University Press, 1984), pp. 1–27.
12 Lucien Febvre, *A Geographical Introduction to History* (1922; New York: Knopf, 1925), p. 46. See also Marc Bloch, *French Rural History: An Essay on its Basic Characteristics* (1931; Berkeley: University of California Press, 1966).
13 Fernand Braudel, *The Mediterranean and the Mediterranean World in the Age of Philip II*, vol. 1 (1949; New York: Harper and Row, 1972), p. 20. Emmanuel Le Roy Ladurie, *The Peasants of Languedoc* (1966; Urbana: University of Illinois Press, 1974).
14 See Le Roy Ladurie, *Times of Feast, Times of Famine: A History of Climate since the Year 1000* (Garden City, NY: Doubleday, 1971).
15 See, for example, Frank Speck, "Mistassini Hunting Territories in the Labrador Peninsula," *American Anthropologist* 25 (1923): 452–71.

16 See Calvin Martin, *Keepers of the Game: Indian-Animal Relationships and the Fur Trade* (Berkeley: University of California Press, 1978); Marvin Harris, *Cows, Pigs, and Witches: The Riddles of Culture* (New York: Random House, 1974), pp. 6–50.

17 Aldo Leopold, *A Sand County Almanac, and Sketches Here and There* (New York: Oxford University Press, 1949), pp. 129–33, 165–226.

18 Leopold, *Sand County Almanac*, p. 132.

19 Worster, *Wealth of Nature*, p. 183.

20 Worster, *Dust Bowl*, p. 6.

21 Worster, *Wealth of Nature*, p. 133.

22 William H. McNeill, *Plagues and Peoples* (Garden City: Anchor, 1976), p. 4. Hans Zinsser, *Rats, Lice, and History* (Boston, 1935).

23 Paul Ehrlich, *The Population Bomb* (New York: Ballantine, 1968), pp. 15–67.

24 Andrew Clark, *The Invasion of New Zealand by People, Plants, and Animals* (New Brunswick, NJ: Rutgers University Press, 1949); Elton, *The Ecology of Invasions by Animals and Plants* (London: Chapman and Hall, 1958), pp. 15–32.

25 Alfred W. Crosby, *Ecological Imperialism: The Biological Expansion of Europe, 900–1900* (New York: Cambridge University Press, 1986); Crosby, *The Columbian Exchange: Biological and Cultural Consequences of 1492* (Westport, CT: Greenwood Press, 1972).

26 Crosby, *Ecological Imperialism*, p. 192.

27 Henry Nash Smith, *Virgin Land: The American West as Symbol and Myth* (Cambridge, MA: Harvard University Press, 1950).

28 Clarence Glacken, *Traces on the Rhodian Shore: Nature and Culture in Western Thought from Ancient Times to the End of the Eighteenth Century* (Berkeley: University of California Press, 1967).

29 Roderick Nash, *Wilderness and the American Mind*, 3rd edn. (New Haven: Yale University Press, 1982).

30 Samuel P. Hays, *Conservation and the Gospel of Efficiency: The Progressive Conservation Movement, 1890–1920* (Cambridge, MA: Harvard University Press, 1957).

31 See Richard White, "American Environmental History: The Development of a New Historical Field," *Pacific Historical Review* 54 (1985): 297–335; Cronon, *Changes in the Land: Indians, Colonists, and the Ecology of New England* (New York: Hill and Wang, 1983), p. 13; Arthur F. McEvoy, "Toward an Interactive Theory of Nature and Culture: Ecology, Production, and Cognition in the California Fishing Industry," in Worster, ed., *The Ends of the Earth: Perspectives on Modern Environmental History* (New York: Cambridge University Press, 1988); pp. 211–29; Carolyn Merchant, "The Theoretical Structure of Ecological Revolutions," *Environmental Review* 11 (1987): 265–74.

32 For gender, see Merchant, *Ecological Revolutions: Nature, Gender, and Science in New England* (Chapel Hill: University of North Carolina Press, 1989). For labor, see White, *The Organic Machine: The Remaking of the Columbia River* (New York: Hill and Wang, 1995).

33 Andrew Hurley, *Environmental Inequalities: Class, Race, and Industrial Pollution in Gary, Indiana, 1945–1980* (Chapel Hill: University of North Carolina Press, 1995).

34   McEvoy, *The Fisherman's Problem: Ecology and Law in the California Fisheries, 1850–1980* (New York: Cambridge University Press, 1986), p. 21.

35   James Fairhead and Melissa Leach, *Misreading the African Landscape: Society and Ecology in a Forest-Savanna Mosaic* (Cambridge: Cambridge University Press, 1996).

36   Worster, "Seeing Beyond Culture," *Journal of American History* 76 (1990): 1147.

37   Joseph E. Taylor, *Making Salmon: An Environmental History of the Northwest Fisheries Crisis* (Seattle: University of Washington Press, 1999), pp. 6–7.

REFERENCES AND FURTHER READING

Cronon, William, *Changes in the Land: Indians, Colonists, and the Ecology of New England*, New York: Hill and Wang, 1983.

Cronon, William, ed., *Uncommon Ground: Toward Reinventing Nature*, New York: Norton, 1995.

Crosby, Alfred W., *Ecological Imperialism: The Biological Expansion of Europe, 900–1900*, New York: Cambridge University Press, 1986.

Dean, Warren, *With Broadax and Firebrand: The Destruction of the Brazilian Atlantic Forest*, Berkeley: University of California Press, 1995.

Dorsey, Kurkpatrick, *The Dawn of Conservation Diplomacy: U.S.–Canadian Wildlife Protection Treaties in the Progressive Era*, Seattle: University of Washington Press, 1998.

Dunlap, Thomas R., *DDT: Scientists, Citizens, and Public Policy*, Princeton, NJ: Princeton University Press, 1981.

Durham, William H., *Scarcity and Survival in Central America: Ecological Origins of the Soccer War*, Stanford, CA: Stanford University Press, 1979.

Fairhead, James, and Melissa Leach, *Misreading the African Landscape: Society and Ecology in a Forest-Savanna Mosaic*, Cambridge: Cambridge University Press, 1996.

Grove, Richard H., *Green Imperialism: Colonial Expansion, Tropical Island Edens and the Origins of Environmentalism, 1600–1860*, New York: Cambridge University Press.

Hurley, Andrew, *Environmental Inequalities: Class, Race, and Industrial Pollution in Gary, Indiana, 1945–1980*, Chapel Hill: University of North Carolina Press, 1995.

Isenberg, Andrew C., *The Destruction of the Bison: An Environmental History, 1750–1920*, New York: Cambridge University Press, 2000.

Kjaergaard, Thorkild, *The Danish Revolution, 1500–1800: An Ecohistorical Interpretation*, Cambridge: Cambridge University Press, 1994.

Krech, Shepard, III, *The Ecological Indian: Myth and History*, New York: Norton, 1999.

McEvoy, Arthur F., *The Fisherman's Problem: Ecology and Law in the California Fisheries, 1850–1980*, New York: Cambridge University Press, 1986.

McNeill, J. R., *Something New Under the Sun: An Environmental History of the Twentieth-Century World*, New York: Norton, 2000.

Taylor, Joseph E., III, *Making Salmon: An Environmental History of the Northwest Fisheries Crisis*, Seattle: University of Washington Press, 1999.

Warren, Louis, *The Hunters's Game: Poachers and Conservationists in Twentieth-Century America*. New Haven: Yale University Press, 1997.

White, Richard, *Land Use, Environment, and Social Change: The Shaping of Island County, Washington*, Seattle: University of Washington Press, 1979.

Worster, Donald. *Nature's Economy: A History of Ecological Ideas*, 2nd edn., New York: Cambridge University Press, 1994.

Worster, Donald, *The Wealth of Nature: Environmental History and the Ecological Imagination*, New York: Oxford University Press, 1993.

PART IV

Challenges to the Boundaries of Western Historical Thought

CHAPTER TWENTY

The New World History

JERRY H. BENTLEY

The term *world history* means different things to different people. To some it brings to mind a basic survey of all the world's past. To others it means foreign history – the history of lands other than one's own. To a few it retains a metaphysical scent, recalling the efforts of Oswald Spengler, Arnold J. Toynbee, and others to distill philosophical significance from the historical record. To many it carries strong macrosociological connotations, reflecting the influence of dependency economics and world-system analysis across the boundary lines of several scholarly disciplines.

As understood by a growing constituency, however, the term *world history* suggests yet a different approach to the past. It does not imply that historians must deal with the entire history of all the world's peoples, and certainly not all at the same time. It refers instead to historical scholarship that explicitly compares experiences across the boundary lines of societies, or that examines interactions between peoples of different societies, or that analyzes large-scale historical patterns and processes that transcend individual societies. This kind of world history deals with historical processes that have not respected national, political, geographical, or cultural boundary lines, but rather have influenced affairs on transregional, continental, hemispheric, and global scales. These processes include climatic changes, biological diffusions, the spread of infectious and contagious diseases, mass migrations, transfers of technology, campaigns of imperial expansion, cross-cultural trade, the spread of ideas and ideals, and the expansion of religious faiths and cultural traditions. In combination, these processes have left quite a mark on the world's past. But national states and individual societies, which are the most common analytical units of historical scholarship, make inadequate frameworks for the study of these processes, which call instead for large-scale comparative, cross-cultural, and systematic analyses.

Quite apart from bringing processes of cross-cultural interaction into historical focus, a principal concern of most contemporary world history is to construct alternatives to Eurocentric understandings of the past. Here Euro-centrism refers to assumptions widely shared since the nineteenth century among European and Euro-American peoples that their lands have been the sites of genuine historical development, hence that their experiences consti-tute a standard against which it is possible to measure the development of other societies. Constructing alternatives to Eurocentric approaches does not mean denying the significance of Europe in world history. To the contrary, a great deal of recent scholarship in world history seeks precisely to explain the prominence of Europe in the modern world. Yet recent approaches to world history reject teleological assumptions that European forms of political orga-nization (such as the national state) or economic development (such as indus-trialization) are either natural or inevitable. This scholarship also rejects arguments that credit European peoples with superior rationality, creativity, industriousness, or aggressiveness compared to other peoples, since historians have discovered the same or similar qualities in many other societies.

This essay begins by discussing the emergence of world history and efforts to theorize the global past. It then turns to recent scholarship on several themes that are especially important for global historical analysis – cross-cultural trade, biological diffusions and exchanges, cultural encounters and exchanges, imperialism and colonialism, and migrations and diasporas – focus-ing special attention on efforts to subject large-scale processes to historical analysis and to reconsider Eurocentric understandings of the past. The essay concludes by raising some critical questions about the larger world history project.

National History and World History

World history in some sense of the term has been prominent for a very long time. Herodotus, Sima Qian, and Juvaini all looked beyond their own soci-eties (classical Greece, Han-dynasty China, and Mongol-dominated Persia, respectively) and took the larger world into account. During the Enlighten-ment, Voltaire undertook his famous cross-cultural history of customs, while the Göttingen historians Johann Cristoph Gatterer and August Ludwig Schlözer worked to establish an analytical "universal history." Global conflicts of the twentieth century prompted reflections on world history from a remark-ably diverse group of thinkers (most of them not professional historians), including H. G. Wells, Oswald Spengler, Arnold J. Toynbee, and Jawaharlal Nehru, among others.

After history became a field of professional scholarship in the nineteenth century, however, historians largely turned away from large-scale approaches to the past in favor of studies focusing on individual societies, especially national communities in Europe. The explanation for this narrowing of historians' focus lies in the political and social environment of nineteenth-century Europe. Like sociology, anthropology, economics, and political science, history emerged as a professional field of study in a Europe that had embarked on processes of dynamic state-building, rapid industrialization, and global imperialism. This political and social context profoundly influenced the development of history and the social sciences. Under the spell of the powerful national states that were taking shape around them, European scholars focused their attention on national communities, which they took as natural units of historical and social analysis. In light of industrialization and imperialism, they construed Europe as the site of genuine historical development, as opposed to other regions that they considered stagnant and unchanging, and they based their models of social change and historical development exclusively on European experience.

By the late nineteenth century, European scholars had adopted a global division of academic labor that reflected this view of the world: historians dealt with past political experiences of the ancient Mediterranean and Europe, including European expansion in the larger world; sociologists, economists, and political scientists examined contemporary European societies; orientalists studied the complex and literate but supposedly unchanging societies of Mesopotamia, Egypt, Persia, India, and China; and anthropologists took responsibility for the unlettered peoples of Africa, southeast Asia, America, and Oceania, who supposedly lacked any proper history.

By the mid-twentieth century, scholars were working to breach the artificial boundary lines separating these scholarly disciplines. Historians drew inspiration from Karl Marx, Max Weber, Emile Durkheim, and other social theorists in developing new approaches to economic and social history. When they looked beyond literary, religious, and philosophical texts, historians and orientalists discovered that Asian societies had indeed undergone change and historical development. Historians and anthropologists also began a process of *rapprochement*: it became clear that the supposedly isolated and primitive societies studied by anthropologists were in fact the products of interaction with Europeans and other peoples, and historians realized that modern industrial society itself had a cultural dimension that they could best study using the insights and vocabulary of anthropologists.

While freely trespassing artificial boundary lines between disciplines, historians and social scientists continued to respect equally artificial borders between individual societies. Since the nineteenth century, for example, professional historians have viewed the past almost exclusively through the optic of a world divided into national states. They have treated history as a property attaching to national communities, presenting it as French history, Chinese history, Mexican history, and the like. They have taken cultural distinctiveness, exclusive identities, local knowledge, and the experiences of individual societies as the principal concerns of their studies. When dealing with eras before the emergence of modern national states, historians have generally studied the development of ostensibly coherent societies such as "imperial China" or "medieval Germany," thereby construing the past through the lenses of a world divided into national communities.[1] While addressing themes quite different from those of traditional political and diplomatic history, social historians and feminist scholars have also cast their studies within the framework of national communities. The metanarratives informing labor history and feminist history clearly suggest that class and gender are portable constructs of near-universal significance, but historians have rarely explored issues of class or gender in contexts larger than national states.[2] Even when they have issued scorching critiques of patriotic narratives, historians have assumed that national states are the natural units of historical analysis.[3] Indeed, in many ways, professional historical scholarship since the nineteenth century has been an artifact of the national-state era of world history.

National states are undoubtedly important units of historical analysis. They make pertinent contexts for the examination of many historical problems of enormous significance. They also are important for the understanding of the world beyond national communities themselves. Some of them have played large roles on the world stage, and the organization of peoples into national communities has itself become a supremely important global political process during the past two centuries.

Yet historical experience is the product not only of developments that take place within individual societies, but also of many large-scale processes that transcend national, political, geographical, and cultural boundary lines. It is certainly possible and useful to explore the influence of these processes in local contexts – to study the effects of Mongol imperialism in China, for example, or the results of epidemic smallpox in Mexico. But in the quest for historical meaning, it is also desirable to investigate the dynamics of the larger processes themselves, as well as the interactions of different peoples and societies that fueled the processes and felt their effects. For these purposes it is necessary to adopt frames of reference much larger than national communities or individual societies and to develop comparative, transregional, continental, hemispheric, oceanic, and global approaches to the past.

By the mid-twentieth century, several developments encouraged some historians to push their analyses beyond the national, political, geographical, and cultural boundary lines conventionally observed by scholars and to venture beyond the concerns that have dominated historical scholarship since the nineteenth century – cultural distinctiveness, exclusive identities, local knowledge, and the experiences of individual societies. First, historians and area specialists generated a tremendous body of knowledge about peoples and societies beyond Europe. Although often tainted by imperialist interests, basic information about Asia, Africa, the pre-Columbian Americas, and Oceania was an indispensable foundation for efforts to think about broader patterns of his-

torical experience. Furthermore, global empires, global wars, and global economic depression made it clear that national states and individual societies did
not determine their own fates in isolation. Rather, all states and societies participated in larger networks of power and exchange that profoundly influenced
the fortunes of all peoples on planet earth. Moreover, scholarly specialization
produced such fragmentation of knowledge that it discouraged efforts to seek
larger meaning in the past. Scholars, teachers, public officials, and the general
public all called for the reintegration of historical knowledge and the development of fresh perspectives on the past. Motivated by this desire and
equipped with a growing understanding of the larger world, historians and
other scholars began to probe the dynamics of large-scale processes in times
past.

Credit for placing large-scale processes on the agenda of professional historians is due principally to Marshall G. S. Hodgson, L. S. Stavrianos, William
H. McNeill, and Philip D. Curtin. Hodgson sharply criticized the kind of
Eurocentric scholarship that measured the world's societies against the standard of European experience, and he called for comparative, transregional,
hemispheric, and global approaches to the past.[4] Stavrianos tirelessly promoted
the teaching of world history and insisted on the need to analyze the human
past from a global point of view.[5] McNeill recognized that individual societies
are not the only sites of historical development, that historical processes take
place between and among societies as well as within individual societies, and
he developed this insight into a dynamic vision of the global past. By analyzing encounters, interactions, and exchanges between peoples of different societies, he sought to understand some of the most powerful processes of world
history. He articulated his vision of the past most fully in his book *The Rise
of the West: A History of the Human Community*, which emphasized diffusions
of ideas and technological skills as driving forces of world history.[6] Curtin preferred not to write about the world as a whole, but he developed an influential method of illuminating crucial global themes through comparative case
studies. He also pioneered graduate education and supervised scores of students who helped establish comparative world history as a distinctive approach
to the global past.[7]

Theorizing the Global Past

Most professional historians incline toward empirical research rather than theoretical analysis. Yet all historical scholarship rests on theoretical, philosophical, or ideological assumptions about the world and the dynamics governing
its development. The emergence of world history as a distinctive approach to
the past brought a need to articulate these assumptions and express them in
coherent theoretical terms. In recent years, historical sociologists have been

most active in constructing theoretical frameworks for world history, though professional historians themselves have also begun to take theoretical issues under consideration. Four theoretical schools are most prominent in current debates about world history. Two of them have long been staples of theoretical scholarship in history and the historical social sciences. The other two have emerged only recently, but they seem poised to wield considerable influence in future historical studies. A principal concern of all of these theoretical efforts is the explanation of European and Euro-American dominance in the modern world through imperialism, industrialization, and economic development, but the theories all have implications for the understanding of world history over the long term as well as in modern times.

One theoretical school derives from the comparative sociology of Max Weber, who sought to understand the distinctiveness of modern capitalist Europe through comparison with other societies. Weber argued that Europeans had developed certain cultural traits, including rationality, inquisitiveness, and a strong work ethic, that favored capitalism and economic development. His followers modified and revised Weber's thought in many ways, but a recognizably Weberian approach to the past is identifiable in a great deal of historical and sociological scholarship. Weber's influence is particularly obvious in modernization theory, which views economic development largely as a function of the internal policies and cultural values of individual societies. Modernization theory reached the height of its influence in the 1950s and 1960s, but it continues to inspire scholarship in some quarters. The modernization approach has deeply influenced historians like E. L. Jones and David S. Landes, who view European economic development as the result of cultural traits that favor innovation, social organization that rewards hard work, and governments that encourage initiative rather than stifling it through excessive taxation or regulation. Since the key to historical development from this perspective is the internal organization of individual societies, the especially effective organization of European society becomes the principal explanation for European economic development and world dominance. Because of its emphasis on Europe as the principal site of historical development, the modernization school offers a fundamentally Eurocentric explanation of modern world history. Indeed, this approach also implies a Eurocentric understanding of the larger global past, since some scholars have sought to trace Europe's supposed distinctiveness to deep historical roots.[8]

A Marxist response to the modernization approach takes the form of world-system analysis, which holds that European dominance was due not so much to hard work and discipline as to imperialism and exploitation of other societies. World-system analysts agree with Karl Marx that economic circumstances within every society generate class divisions that produce social conflicts and drive historical development. World-system analysis goes further, however, to explore relations between and among societies, holding that strong "core" societies force weak "peripheral" societies to participate in unequal exchange relationships that enrich the core and hinder economic development in the periphery. As formulated by Immanuel Wallerstein, world-system analysis posits the emergence of a modern, capitalist, European-dominated world system in the sixteenth century. Like the modernization school, world-system theory reflects a kind of Eurocentrism in that it makes European peoples the agents of modernity, although here the explanation for European world dominance is aggressiveness rather than industriousness, exploitation of other societies rather than hard work developing domestic economies. Like modernization theory again, the world-system approach has implications for premodern as well as modern times, as several scholars have recently argued that the principles of world-system theory extend deep into the past.[9]

Disenchantment with the Eurocentrism of both modernization and world-system schools has led recent critics to formulate a third theoretical approach that explains European economic development and world dominance not as a product of special European qualities but rather as a result of chance developments. Other societies were just as industrious and disciplined as the Europe that modernization analysts describe, so these critics argue, just as aggressive and imperialist as the Europe that world-system analysts depict. Thus Europe enjoyed no significant political, military, economic, social, or cultural advantages over Chinese, Indian, Ottoman, or many other societies until the nineteenth century, when industrialization vastly increased European power. Andre Gunder Frank explains industrialization as a result of efforts to supplement scarce labor with mechanical devices, while R. Bin Wong considers it the outcome of an unpredictable burst of technological innovation, and Kenneth Pomeranz emphasizes windfall gains from overseas colonies and the fortuitous proximity of coal resources to manufacturing centers. In any case, European industrialization and world dominance were not natural or inevitable outgrowths of long-term conditions so much as unpredictable and accidental results of chance circumstances.[10]

A fourth theoretical approach draws inspiration from geographical, ecological, and environmental analysis rather than political economy in seeking to account for the larger course of world history. Alfred W. Crosby argues that European plants, animals, diseases, and human populations mutually reinforced one another as they ventured into the larger world and created "neo-Europes" in several of the world's temperate zones. Jared Diamond looks to the deep past in explaining the development of powerful, complex societies in Eurasia as the result of global biological endowments as of 10,000 years ago. Most of the world's domesticable plant and animal species were natives to southwest Asia, and they traveled readily across much of the Eurasian landmass. By contrast, sub-Saharan Africa, the Americas, and Oceania harbored many fewer species susceptible to domestication. Thus Eurasian lands were unusually hospitable environments for the emergence of agriculture, densely populated societies, writing, technology, and powerful social organization.[11] While they do not necessarily contradict the other three theories, and indeed complement them in some ways, these geographically, ecologically, and environmentally grounded theories make different assumptions about the dynamics driving historical development. They insist particularly on the need to take the natural world seriously and understand historical development in light of human relationships with the natural world.

Cross-Cultural Trade

Working implicitly or explicitly with reference to one or more of these theories, world historians have recently devoted considerable attention to processes of cross-cultural interaction. Among the most prominent topics of recent scholarship on world history is cross-cultural trade. Throughout history, cross-cultural trade and commercial exchanges have profoundly influenced the development of individual societies and the world as a whole by bringing about systematic interaction between sometimes distant regions. Indeed, as Philip D. Curtin has suggested, they have been "perhaps the most important external stimuli to change, leaving aside the immeasurable and less-benign influence of military conquest."[12] Thus, cross-cultural trade lends itself readily to the analysis of transregional and global integration.

Much of the scholarship on cross-cultural trade reflects debates about the nature of the modern, European-dominated world economy. Some scholars writing from both liberal and Marxist perspectives have adopted a somewhat Eurocentric view in arguing that cross-cultural trade in premodern times was so small as to have only limited economic and social significance. From this viewpoint, it was only after European mariners linked the world regions into an interdependent global economy that cross-cultural trade became important. Others seeking alternatives to Eurocentric views have recognized considerable significance in premodern trade. Granting that premodern trade was less voluminous than modern and contemporary trade, recent studies have shown that it nevertheless deeply influenced all societies involved in cross-cultural exchange. It has become clear, for example, that premodern trade often involved large cargoes of bulk commodities as well as luxury goods and that it helped to shape the economies and societies of peoples participating in cross-cultural trade. Even when it involved small volumes of luxury goods, premodern trade had important cultural and political implications, since expensive and exotic items from afar often served as prestige goods consumed by elite classes in trading societies. Furthermore, the establishment of trade networks facilitated biological, technological, and cultural as well as commercial exchanges.[13]

Since quantitative data is quite rare for early times, studies of premodern trade have focused mostly on the organization of trade. In contrast to an earlier generation of scholarship, which viewed premodern trade as largely a function of political interests, recent studies have emphasized merchants' orientation to the market by showing that they paid close attention to prices and the availability of commodities. In contrast to earlier assumptions that premodern merchants were basically small-scale peddlers, recent studies have shown that they devised an array of financial instruments to facilitate their ventures and a variety of partnerships to minimize risks to their investments. They maintained large expatriate colonies ("trade diasporas") in foreign lands, and they frequently organized convoys of ships to discourage the attention of pirates.[14] A rich cache of documents discovered in the old synagogue in Cairo has enabled scholars to reconstruct the organization and activities of trading firms, mostly composed of family members and friends, that operated throughout the Mediterranean region, southwest Asia, and the Indian Ocean basin during the period from about 1000 to 1250 CE. Studies based on these documents have confirmed the sophistication of premodern merchants engaged in cross-cultural trade.[15]

Apart from organizational matters, recent scholarship has also focused usefully on the routes and networks of premodern trade. The silk roads and other land routes have attracted attention, but the most prominent spaces featured in recent studies are maritime regions organized around sea and ocean basins. In light of Fernand Braudel's analysis of the Mediterranean, it is clear that many bodies of water, such as the Baltic Sea, the China seas, and the Indian Ocean basin, also served to integrate surrounding lands in premodern times. The most extensive studies of premodern trade in maritime regions are those of K. N. Chaudhuri, who portrayed the Indian Ocean basin as the commercial heart of Asia. For more than a millennium, from the rise of Islam to the establishment of British hegemony in India, Chaudhuri's Indian Ocean basin pulsated to the rhythms of commercial agriculture, industrial production, and maritime trade.[16]

Taken together, recent studies suggest that premodern trade was a very sophisticated affair that relied on techniques similar to those supporting much more voluminous trade in modern times. Premodern merchants were not mere peddlers hawking miscellaneous wares from one village to the next. Rather they were savvy, market-oriented entrepreneurs who calculated their risks and moved sizable quantities of trade goods across long distances. This pattern, observable throughout much of the eastern hemisphere, suggests that western European businessmen enjoyed no advantage over others with respect to commercial skills or organization. Indeed, the Christian merchants of western Europe were latecomers who largely adopted the commercial practices of their Jewish, Muslim, and Byzantine counterparts. Thus recent studies point to the need for alternatives to Eurocentric visions of world economic and commercial history. Long before the emergence of Europe as a global commercial power, merchants from other lands had knit much of the eastern hemisphere into a large trading world that influenced the development of societies and economies throughout the region.

The voyages of European mariners had profound implications for cross-cultural trade, and they helped inaugurate a new era of world history by bringing all the world's regions into sustained interaction in modern times. As in the case of premodern trade, the issue of Eurocentrism looms large in the analysis of cross-cultural trade in the early modern world. Many scholars from both modernization and world-systems schools portray an aggressive and dynamic western Europe as the dominant power of the modern world from the sixteenth century forward. Driven by a ruthless energy, European merchants and adventurers supposedly sailed into the larger world, deploying superior technology and military prowess in their quest for trade and empire. In the process, by these accounts, they created the modern world and established themselves as its masters.

The stunning conquests of Mexico and Peru certainly established Spain as the dominant power in the western hemisphere, and the organization of plantation societies in the Caribbean, Brazil, and North America soon offered profitable opportunities for Portugal, England, France, and other lands as well. Triangular trades and plantation agriculture served as foundations of a larger Atlantic economy that linked the fortunes of all peoples of the Atlantic Ocean basin.[17] Furthermore, European merchants founded large joint-stock trading companies that enabled them to profit handsomely from trade links that spanned the globe, so there is no question that beginning in the sixteenth century, European peoples played a more prominent role on the world stage than ever before.

Yet until the mid-nineteenth century, Europeans hardly dominated the eastern hemisphere. They conquered geographically important coastal regions of the Philippines and Indonesia, where they established new entrepôts like Manila and Batavia, and Dutch merchants subdued many of the important spice-bearing islands of southeast Asia. But Europeans were unable to force their way into the largest markets: in India they had to compete alongside merchants from other lands, while in China and Japan local authorities permitted them to trade only on a limited basis.

Recent studies of global trade have pointed toward a more balanced understanding of the early modern world.[18] European merchants avidly sought opportunities to trade in valuable Asian commodities, but they had little to offer that their Asian counterparts found appealing. The earliest European merchants to visit Asian markets sold small quantities of textiles, firearms, and manufactured items, but only with bullion and profits from intra-Asian trade were they able to purchase enough goods to satisfy European demands for silk, porcelain, pepper, and spices. By the mid-sixteenth century, large supplies of American silver were flowing into Europe. Since demand for silver was extraordinarily strong in China, where authorities were seeking to base the imperial economy on silver, European merchants were able to exchange American treasure for Asian goods. By this account, it was not only European demand for Asian commodities that drove the early-modern world economy, but also Asian and especially Chinese demand for silver and other precious metals.[19] Thus while recognizing the prominent role of Europe in the larger world, recent scholarship does not portray European peoples as the only or principal agents of historical development in early modern times. By considering European experience in global context, it moves beyond Eurocentric visions of the past and yields richer understanding of both Europe and the larger world.

Biological Diffusions and Exchanges

Some of the most dramatic and powerful processes of cross-cultural interaction have involved biological diffusions and exchanges – the spread of microorganisms and disease pathogens, the spread of food and industrial crops, and transfers of livestock and other animal species. Throughout history and into the present day, these kinds of biological diffusions and exchanges have mocked national, political, geographical, and cultural boundary lines. Historians' attention to these processes reflects the general influence of environmental concerns in modern society since the 1950s and the development of environmental history since the 1970s.

Environmental history has demonstrated that human agents do not drive history strictly on their own powers, but rather work in interaction with the natural environment and under its constraints. Human actors have certainly altered the natural environment, but the environment has also presented human beings with surprises, some of them as unpleasant as they were unpredictable. When human beings began to cultivate crops and domesticate animals, for example, they concentrated plants in fields and animals in herds. Little did they realize that they were creating ideal habitats for pathogens and pests that preyed on their crops and flocks. Even less did they realize that some of these pathogens and pests could thrive on human as well as animal hosts.

Historical epidemiology has taken this latter-day awareness and extended it to explain the dynamics of infectious and contagious diseases, many of which originated in animal herds and then adapted to human hosts. Within an individual society, pathogens such as the viruses that cause smallpox and measles can become endemic if the population is large enough to enable the viruses to find constant supplies of fresh hosts who do not possess inherited or acquired immunities. In those cases, the diseases become childhood diseases that exact a regular but limited toll in human lives. But if a society has insufficient population to support the diseases on an endemic basis, or if a society has never been exposed to a given pathogen, then few if any individuals will possess immunities. If a particularly virulent pathogen like the smallpox virus should find its way into such a society, it can touch off massive and destructive epidemics.

World history has seen many such epidemics, some of which have drastically altered the fortunes of human societies. Studies in historical epidemiology by scholars like William H. McNeill and Alfred W. Crosby show that epidemics have been most destructive when pathogens have made their way to societies with large, previously unexposed populations. This has happened frequently when individuals from an infected society have had dealings with others from unexposed societies. During the third century CE, for example, merchants introduced exotic pathogens to societies along the silk roads and caused epidemics in Han China, the Roman empire, and probably other societies as well. After the fourteenth century, bubonic plague traveled the trade routes and ravaged societies throughout much of the eastern hemisphere. From the sixteenth to the nineteenth centuries, a massive transfer of biological species took place following the European voyages of exploration that inaugurated sustained interaction between the peoples of the eastern hemisphere, the western hemisphere, and Oceania. As a part of this larger "Columbian exchange," epidemic smallpox, measles, diphtheria, and other diseases exacted a devastating toll from indigenous peoples in the Americas and Oceania. Indeed, these massive transoceanic epidemics may have caused more deaths than any other agent in human history.[20]

Until very recently, human beings have been able to exercise little control over disease pathogens. They have helped pathogens find new hosts by creating networks of transportation, communication, and exchange, but they have provided these services unwittingly. They have had more conscious influence over the spread of plant and animal species, although these species too have often escaped human supervision and established independent footholds for themselves. Like the diffusion of disease pathogens, the spread of plants and animals has had a profound impact on human societies, and world historians have been able to chart the movements and effects of some species with tolerable precision.

A few species migrated to new lands even before the appearance of human beings on the earth: birds and bats flew to new habitats, and a few land mammals colonized new territories by crossing land bridges, swimming, or drifting across bodies of water. But the arrival of humans greatly facilitated the spread of biological species, particularly after the domestication of plants and animals some 10,000 years ago.[21] Cultivators introduced wheat to temperate lands throughout Eurasia and north Africa, for example, and spread rice throughout tropical and subtropical Asia. Horses, cattle, sheep, goats, camels, swine, and other animals also found their ways to new lands with human aid. These diffusions all had social, economic, and environmental implications in the lands they affected, and they clearly merit attention in historical scholarship.

Beyond the general significance of plant and animal diffusions, historians have made it clear that some rounds of exchange have had especially deep effects. During the first few centuries after the establishment of Islam, for example, Muslim merchants, missionaries, soldiers, diplomats, and administrators traveled throughout much of Eurasia and north Africa, from Morocco to India and later to Indonesia as well. During their journeys they noticed food and industrial crops that they thought might flourish in other Islamic lands, and they initiated a large-scale transfer of crops to new lands: hard wheat, sorghum, eggplant, melons, citrus fruits, cotton, and indigo all took root in new lands as a result of this conscious effort to spread crops. A similar round of transplantation took place on an even larger scale after the sixteenth century. The Columbian exchange resulted in the spread of American foods like maize, potatoes, manioc, tomatoes, peanuts, and peppers to other world regions and the introduction of wheat, rice, vegetables, fruits, horses, cattle, sheep, goats, swine, and other species to the western hemisphere. By adding calories and variety to diets, both the Islamic transfer of crops and the Columbian exchange fueled massive population increase in several world regions. In the absence of these processes, it would be impossible to understand either the development of individual societies or the larger course of world history.[22]

Cultural Encounters and Exchanges

Throughout history, cross-cultural travel and communication have facilitated cultural and religious as well as commercial and biological exchanges. Study of the world religions and their spread is a venerable enterprise among historians and theologians, whose studies have often provided lucid analyses of religious missions. More recently, anthropological and ethnohistorical inspiration has helped generate a large and growing body of scholarship on encounters and interactions between peoples from different societies and cultural traditions.

The study of these encounters and interactions is a highly problematic venture, since all parties, including latter-day scholars, inevitably reflect their own cultural assumptions and preferences. Since the publication of Edward Said's *Orientalism*, a spirited postcolonial critique has attacked the imperialist, ethnocentric, and racist assumptions that often undergirded earlier generations of scholarship.[23] Granting that scholars cannot entirely escape their own cultural inheritance, might there at least be some way to deal responsibly with other peoples and their societies? Or does historical analysis of other peoples inevitably say more about the observer than the observed?

While undoubtedly reflecting the perspectives of their own societies, many scholars have worked conscientiously to understand cultural encounters and exchanges that have sometimes had deep and lasting historical effects. Most of the resulting studies have dealt with interactions in specific regions, but they have often sought to illuminate larger historical patterns from local experiences. In any case, rather than viewing individual cultural traditions as coherent and self-sufficient systems, they have emphasized the roles of encounters, interactions, and exchanges in shaping cultural traditions. One strand of recent scholarship views cross-cultural interactions as functions of power relations. Greg Dening examined the destruction of Marquesan society under the pressure of European political, military, economic, and cultural power, for example, while Jean and John Comaroff portrayed Christian missions in nineteenth-century Africa as cultural expressions of European imperialism.[24] While also placing cultural interactions in larger political, social, and economic contexts, another strand of recent research emphasizes conscious cultural borrowing or reciprocal exchanges between peoples of different cultural traditions rather than the domination or displacement of one tradition by another. Thus it has become clear that ancient Greeks drew inspiration from their Egyptian and Semitic contemporaries – indeed that cultural exchanges flowed in all directions in the ancient Mediterranean basin – and that Spanish conquests in the Americas and Philippines did not lead so much to the blanket imposition of European Christianity as to the formation of syncretic traditions that made a place for indigenous interests and preserved pre-Christian cultural elements.[25]

Even more than for cross-cultural trade and biological diffusions, it has proved difficult to study cultural encounters and exchanges on large scales, partly because scholars lack a common vocabulary or set of conceptual tools for comparative cultural analysis. Yet Mary W. Helms has probed the political and cultural significance of long-distance travel, and I have argued in my own work that despite local differences, several patterns of cross-cultural conversion, conflict, and compromise are recognizable over the long term.[26] Further explorations of large-scale cultural interactions would make welcome additions to scholarship in world history.

Imperialism and Colonialism

Imperialism and colonialism have long been staples of historical scholarship. Until recently, historians generally treated them as deliberate ventures or unpremeditated operations of individual expansive societies rather than cross-cultural processes calling for larger analytical perspectives. Yet imperialism and colonialism clearly are themes of prime significance for any historian seeking to understand processes of cross-cultural interaction. Indeed, several scholars have taken imaginative broad-gauged approaches to these themes. Daniel Headrick, for example, has explored the role of technology in the building and maintenance of European empires by examining the various military, transportation, communication, and even pharmaceutical technologies that enabled Europeans to establish themselves in distant lands, and also by probing political and cultural obstacles to the transfer of technological expertise from European to colonized peoples.[27] Michael Adas has investigated the cultural dimensions of imperial and colonial relations by studying several cases of millenarian rebellion against European colonial rule, and also by showing that European observers formed ideologies of dominance on the basis of their convictions that other peoples were technologically inferior.[28] Christopher A. Bayly has insightfully studied the rise of the second British empire as a global process of cross-cultural interaction: just as historians of cross-cultural trade considered European commerce in global context, Bayly examined the emerging British empire in light of political and social developments in Asian, American, African, and European lands.[29] Jürgen Osterhammel has surveyed a vast scholarly literature and offered a comprehensive comparative analysis of modern colonialism, colonial states, and their political, social, economic, and cultural effects in colonized lands.[30]

Most recent scholarship on imperialism and colonialism has focused more narrowly on the activities of the imperialists, the experiences of the colonized, or interaction between the two in particular contexts. Many recent studies have deepened and enriched the understanding of imperialism and colonialism – by highlighting their cultural dimensions, for example, or by treating them as complex interactive processes involving conflict, negotiation, and often cooperation between various parties rather than the simple imposition of foreign rule on subject peoples.[31] Postcolonial scholarship and the subaltern school have drawn attention to methodological and analytical problems that complicate efforts to study imperialism and colonialism: drawing on post-modern critiques of knowledge, postcolonial and subaltern scholars have argued that reliance on European categories of thought and knowledge regimes inevitably leads to distorted, Eurocentric interpretations.[32] Taken together, these recent studies yield a complicated picture of imperialism and colonialism. They effectively dispose of any lingering notions that expansive European imperialists simply marched in as the agents of historical development and established colonial rule over passive foreign subjects. Rather they portray imperialism and colonialism as messy processes in which all parties were historical agents, even if the agency of some parties has proved difficult to recover from surviving records.[33]

Yet national and ethnic identities remain such strong concerns in scholarship on imperialism and colonialism that large-scale issues have not come into such clear historical focus as they have for processes like cross-cultural trade or biological diffusions and exchanges. It is neither mysterious nor surprising that identity concerns should figure so prominently in scholarship on imperialism and colonialism: one of the prime purposes of historical scholarship over the millennia has been to recount the experiences and understand the development of peoples and their societies through time. In some ways, however, emphasis on identities in recent scholarship has resulted in missed opportunities. It has created the impression that modern imperialist ventures of western European and Euro-American peoples were utterly unique projects without deeper historical context in the form of premodern imperialism, for example, and it has also deflected attention from imperial and colonial projects of Russian, Chinese, Japanese, Indonesian, and other peoples in modern times.

Migrations and Diasporas

Like imperialism and colonialism, migrations and diasporas are crucial themes for the analysis of cross-cultural interactions. From the movements of *Homo ergaster* and *Homo erectus* that established human communities in the world beyond Africa, to the long-range migrations of Indo-European, Bantu, Austronesian, and other peoples, to the massive flows of settlers, laborers, and refugees in modern and contemporary times, migrations and diasporas have profoundly influenced the development of individual societies and the world as a whole. As in the case of imperialism and colonialism, however, interests of contemporary identity have driven recent scholarship on migrations and diasporas to the point that large-scale issues have rarely come into clear focus. There is a vast scholarly literature on the experiences of particular groups who migrated to specific places. Much less attention has gone to the large-scale analysis of migrations and the political, social, and economic conditions under which they have taken place.

The exceptions to this rule, however, make fundamental contributions to the understanding of world history.[34] A particularly rich literature deals with the Atlantic slave trade and the African diaspora. Some large-scale dimensions of these topics have to do with the organization of plantation agriculture by European colonists in the Americas, the emergence of triangular trades in the Atlantic Ocean basin, the recruitment and transport of about twelve million involuntary African laborers, and the establishment of African-American societies in the western hemisphere, all of which have received considerable attention since the 1960s. Philip D. Curtin in particular has contributed to the understanding of slavery and African migration, first by placing studies of the slave trade on a solid quantitative foundation, then by understanding slavery in the context of the "plantation complex" that became such a prominent feature of the Atlantic Ocean basin during the seventeenth and eighteenth centuries.[35] Working within this general framework, other scholars have thrown new light on developments that would be difficult or impossible to understand in the context of national communities or supposedly coherent individual societies: Patrick Manning studied the social and economic effects of slave trading in Africa as well as lands that received slave populations, for example, while John Thornton called attention to the survival of African social and cultural traditions in the Americas, and Richard Price examined the formation of maroon societies by runaway slaves.[36]

A smaller but growing body of scholarship deals with indentured labor and other labor migrations during the century following the end of slave trading and the abolition of slavery. These migrations actually involved many more people than did the Atlantic slave trade, and their effects are readily visible in many parts of the contemporary world inhabited by descendants of the migrants. Demand for workers came initially from planters who could no longer make use of slave labor and later from industrialists as well. During the nineteenth and early twentieth century to 1914, some fifty million European migrants made their way to the Americas, Australia, New Zealand, southern Africa, and other destinations, some as indentured laborers but most as free agents, while smaller numbers of indentured laborers from Africa, India, China, Japan, and other lands moved to tropical and subtropical regions to work on plantations or in mines. Recent scholarship has explicitly and usefully emphasized the connections of these vast migratory flows to imperialism and capitalism.[37]

Meanwhile, in recent years the category of diaspora has emerged conspicuously as a rival or at least as a supplement to earlier analytical approaches to migrations. In contrast to the political, economic, and demographic issues that loom largest in scholarship on migration, diaspora studies focus attention more on the social and cultural dimensions of large-scale migrations, and particularly on the experiences of expatriate communities and their descendants in relation to both homelands and host societies. The associations of diaspora studies with contemporary identity politics are clear, and they have sometimes led diaspora scholars into unnecessary debates – founded on a dubious politics of inclusion and exclusion – concerning which groups qualify for diaspora status. Nevertheless, the diaspora perspective has brought insight to processes of social and cultural interaction through deployment of concepts like syncretism, hybridity, creolization, and transculturation to problematize popular assumptions concerning assimilation and conversion.[38]

Caveats and Concerns

Global historical analysis calls many of the received categories of professional historical scholarship into question. While recognizing the significance of national states in modern times, for example, recent world history rejects the national state as the default category of historical analysis. Instead, it focuses attention on processes that unfold on transregional, continental, hemispheric, oceanic, and global scales. It deals not so much with the experiences and internal organization of individual, ostensibly coherent societies as with processes that work their effects across the national, political, geographical, and cultural boundary lines conventionally observed in historical scholarship. Yet the categories discussed in this essay – cross-cultural trade, biological diffusions and exchanges, cultural encounters and exchanges, imperialism and colonialism, migrations and diasporas – are no more absolute than those they displace. Even from the brief discussion here, it is clear that these categories overlap in all imaginable ways: commercial, biological, and cultural exchanges generally take place all at the same time, and often in the context of imperialism or migration or both. Thus, new approaches to world history do not yield a simple picture of the world. To the contrary, they depict a messy and complicated world. To that extent, of course, they perhaps capture an important dimension of global historical reality.

Yet questions remain concerning the construction of global perspectives themselves. One question has to do with ideology: To what extent does world history represent particular political or economic interests? From early times to the present, desire to know the larger world has been most prominent among expansive imperial and commercial powers such as the Roman empire, Han China, the Abbasid caliphate, Tang China, the Mongol empire, the British empire, and the United States. Efforts to know the larger world inevitably mirror some kind of interest in the larger world. In the form of area studies as well as world history, some of those efforts have clearly reflected immediate political and economic interests. It does not follow, however, that global historical analysis is necessarily an ideological tool of imperialism or global capitalism, any more than historical scholarship on Adolf Hitler necessarily valorizes Nazi ideology. Indeed, any critical approach to world history necessarily recognizes that global processes have produced fragmentation as well as integration, misery as well as prosperity.

A reservation that is perhaps more serious has to do with the lenses through which world historians view the larger world. Leaving aside Eurocentric, orientalist, racist, and other varieties of aggressively ethnocentric perspectives, which inevitably taint representations of other peoples and societies, the problem remains that even the most cosmopolitan approach comes from some perspective that complicates efforts to understand other peoples, societies, and cultural traditions. Indeed, some argue that professional historical scholarship is itself a Eurocentric project that takes the modern European national state both as a historical norm and as its principal subject, even when it deals with the world beyond Europe.[39] Granting that absolute analytical purity is a noble dream akin to perfect objectivity, a self-reflective awareness that questions regimes of intellectual and cultural domination might nevertheless support improved practical understandings of the world and the cross-cultural interactions that have shaped it throughout human history.[40]

Although unquestionably problematic, world history is also a necessary project. Over the course of a few decades, global historical analysis has demolished assumptions that history is a property attaching exclusively to national states or other ostensibly coherent individual societies. While recognizing that cultural distinctiveness, exclusive identities, local knowledge, and the experiences of individual societies are perfectly valid interests, it has gone beyond these traditional concerns of professional historical scholarship and brought large-scale processes into clear historical focus. In doing so, it has demonstrated that various transregional, continental, hemispheric, oceanic, and global frameworks make appropriate contexts, alongside national states and individual societies, for the analysis of many historical processes. Furthermore, global historical analysis has offered opportunities to move beyond Eurocentrism and other ethnocentric approaches to the past by understanding the experiences of all the world's peoples in larger historical context, rather than viewing some of them as totally exceptional, incomparable, and unrelated to the experiences of others. Thus, recent scholarship in world history has not only contributed to the understanding of the world as a whole, but also has constructed contexts for the better understanding of individual regions and their relationships with the larger whole.

NOTES

1 See Prasenjit Duara, *Rescuing History from the Nation: Questioning Narratives of Modern China* (Chicago, 1995).

2 See, for example, E. P. Thompson, *The Making of the English Working Class* (Harmondsworth, 1968); and Carol Berkin and Mary Beth Norton, *Women of America: A History* (Boston, 1979).

3 See for example William Appleman Williams, *The Tragedy of American Diplomacy*, rev. edn. (New York, 1988); or Howard Zinn, *A People's History of the United States*, rev. edn. (New York, 1995).

4 Marshall G. S. Hodgson, The *Venture of Islam: Conscience and History in a World Civilization*, 3 vols. (Chicago, 1974); and *Rethinking World History: Essays on Europe, Islam, and World History*, ed. by Edmund Burke, III (Cambridge, 1993). See also Edmund Burke, III, "Marshall G. S. Hodgson and the Hemispheric, Interregional Approach to World History," *Journal of World History* 6 (1995): 237–50.

5 L. S. Stavrianos, *Global Rift: The Third World Comes of Age* (New York, 1981); and *Lifelines from Our Past: A New World History* (New York, 1989). See also Gilbert Allardyce, "Toward World History: American Historians and the Coming of the World History Course," *Journal of World History* 1 (1990): 23–76.

6   William H. McNeill, *The Rise of the West: A History of the Human Community* (Chicago, 1963). See also McNeill's reflective essay, "*The Rise of the West* after Twenty-Five Years," *Journal of World History* 1 (1990): 1–21; his volume of collected essays, *Mythistory and Other Essays* (Chicago, 1986); and Allardyce, "Toward World History."

7   Philip D. Curtin, *Cross-Cultural Trade in World History* (Cambridge, 1984); *The Rise and Fall of the Plantation Complex: Essays in Atlantic History*, 2nd edn. (Cambridge, 1998); *The World and the West: The European Challenge and the Overseas Response in the Age of Empire* (Cambridge, 2000). See also Craig A. Lockard, "The Contributions of Philip Curtin and the 'Wisconsin School' to the Study and Promotion of Comparative World History," *Journal of Third World Studies* 11 (1994): 180–223.

8   E. L. Jones, *The European Miracle: Environments, Economies and Geopolitics in the History of Europe and Asia*, 2nd edn. (Cambridge, 1986); *Growth Recurring: Economic Change in World History* (Oxford, 1988); and David S. Landes, *The Wealth and Poverty of Nations: Why Some Are So Rich and Some So Poor* (New York, 1998). For recent efforts to seek origins of European distinctiveness in pre-modern times, see Michael Mann, *The Sources of Social Power*, vol. 1 (Cambridge, 1986); John A. Hall, *Powers and Liberties: The Causes and Consequences of the Rise of the West* (Oxford, 1985); and Alfred W. Crosby, *The Measure of Reality: Quantification and Western Society, 1250–1600* (Cambridge, 1997). For a critique of modernization studies, see Craig Lockard, "Global History, Modernization, and the World-Systems Approach: A Critique," *The History Teacher* 14 (1981): 489–515.

9   Immanuel Wallerstein, *The Modern World-System*, 3 vols. to date (New York, 1974–); Eric R. Wolf, *Europe and the People Without History* (Berkeley, 1982). For studies extending world-system analysis to premodern times, see Janet L. Abu-Lughod, *Before European Hegemony: The World System, A.D. 1250–1350* (New York, 1989); Andre Gunder Frank and Barry K. Gills, eds., *The World System: Five Hundred Years or Five Thousand?* (London, 1993); and Christopher Chase-Dunn and Thomas D. Hall, *Rise and Demise: Comparing World-Systems* (Boulder, 1997).

10 Andre Gunder Frank, *ReORIENT: Global Economy in the Asian Age* (Berkeley, 1998); R. Bin Wong, *China Transformed: Historical Change and the Limits of European Experience* (Ithaca, 1997); Kenneth Pomeranz, *The Great Divergence: Europe, China, and the Making of the Modern World Economy* (Princeton, 2000). See also Jack Goldstone, "The Problem of the 'Early Modern' World," *Journal of the Economic and Social History of the Orient* 41 (1998): 249–84; and "The Rise of the West – Or Not? A Revision to Socio-economic History," *Sociological Theory*, forthcoming.

11 Alfred W. Crosby, *Ecological Imperialism: The Biological Expansion of Europe, 900–1900* (Cambridge, 1986); Jared Diamond, *Guns, Germs, and Steel: The Fates of Human Societies* (New York, 1997). For a sketch of an even larger project that places human history in the context of universal history since the big bang, see David Christian, "The Case for 'Big History,'" *Journal of World History* 2 (1991): 223–38.

12 Curtin, *Cross-Cultural Trade in World History*, p. 1.

13 Jerry H. Bentley, "Cross-Cultural Interaction and Periodization in World History," *American Historical Review* 101 (1996): 749–70; and "Hemispheric Integration, 500–1500 C.E.," *Journal of World History* 9 (1998): 237–54.

14 Curtin, *Cross-Cultural Trade in World History*.

15 S. D. Goitein, *A Mediterranean Society: The Jewish Communities of the Arab World as Portrayed in the Documents of the Cairo Geniza*, 6 vols. (Berkeley, 1967–93).

16 K. N. Chaudhuri, *Trade and Civilisation in the Indian Ocean: An Economic History from the Rise of Islam to 1750* (Cambridge, 1985); *Asia before Europe: Economy and Civilisation of the Indian Ocean from the Rise of Islam to 1750* (Cambridge, 1990). See also Jerry H. Bentley, "Sea and Ocean Basins as Frameworks of Historical Analysis," *Geographical Review* 89 (1999): 215–24.

17 Curtin, *The Rise and Fall of the Plantation Complex*.

18 For samples of recent scholarship, see James D. Tracy, ed., *The Rise of Merchant Empires: Long-Distance Trade in the Early Modern World, 1350–1750* (Cambridge, 1990); and *The Political Economy of Merchant Empires: State Power and World Trade, 1350–1750* (Cambridge, 1991).

19 See especially the works of Dennis O. Flynn and Arturo Giráldez: "China and the Manila Galleons," in A. J. H. Latham and Heita Kawakatsu, eds., *Japanese Industrialization and the Asian Economy* (London, 1994), pp. 71–90; "Arbitrage, China, and World Trade in the Early Modern Period," *Journal of the Economic and Social History of the Orient* 38 (1995): 29–48; and "Born with a 'Silver Spoon': The Origin of World Trade in 1571," *Journal of World History* 6 (1995): 201–21. See also Richard von Glahn, *Fountain of Fortune: Money and Monetary Policy in China, 1000–1700* (Berkeley, 1996); and John E. Wills, Jr., "Maritime Asia, 1500–1800: The Interactive Emergence of European Domination," *American Historical Review* 98 (1993): 83–105.

20 William H. McNeill, *Plagues and Peoples* (Garden City, NY, 1976); Alfred W. Crosby, *The Columbian Exchange: Biological and Cultural Consequences of 1492* (Westport, CT, 1972); and *Ecological Imperialism: The Biological Expansion of Europe, 900–1900* (Cambridge, 1986).

21 David A. Burney, "Historical Perspectives on Human-Assisted Biological Invasions," *Evolutionary Anthropology* 4 (1996): 216–21.

22 Andrew M. Watson, *Agricultural Innovation in the Early Islamic World: The Diffusion of Crops and Farming Techniques, 700–1100* (Cambridge, 1983); Crosby, *The Columbian Exchange*.

23 Edward W. Said, *Orientalism: Western Representations of the Orient* (New York, 1978).

24 Greg Dening, *Islands and Beaches: Discourses on a Silent Land – Marquesas, 1774–1880* (Honolulu, 1980); Jean and John Comaroff, *Of Revelation and Revolution: Christianity, Colonialism, and Consciousness in South Africa*, 2 vols. (Chicago, 1991–7).

25 On the ancient Mediterranean, see Martin Bernal, *Black Athena: The Afroasiatic Roots of Classical Civilization*, 2 vols. to date (New Brunswick, 1987–); and Walter Burkert, *The Orientalizing Revolution: Near Eastern Influence on Greek Culture in the Early Archaic Age* (Cambridge, MA, 1992). On Spanish conquests

and syncretic Christianity, see Jacques Lafaye, *Quetzalcóatl and Guadalupe: The Formation of Mexican National Consciousness, 1531–1813*, trans. B. Keen (Chicago, 1976); Sabine MacCormack, *Religion in the Andes: Vision and Imagination in Early Colonial Peru* (Princeton, 1991); and Vicente Rafael, *Contracting Colonialism: Translation and Christian Conversion in Tagalog Society under Early Spanish Rule* (Ithaca, 1988).

26   Mary W. Helms, *Ulysses' Sail: An Ethnographic Odyssey of Power, Knowledge, and Geographical Distance* (Princeton, 1988); and Jerry H. Bentley, *Old World Encounters: Cross-Cultural Contacts and Exchanges in Pre-Modern Times* (New York, 1993).

27   Daniel Headrick, *The Tools of Empire: Technology and European Imperialism in the Nineteenth Century* (New York, 1981); and *The Tentacles of Progress: Technology Transfer in the Age of Imperialism, 1850–1940* (New York, 1988).

28   Michael Adas, *Prophets of Rebellion: Millenarian Protest Movements against the European Colonial Order* (Cambridge, 1987); and *Machines as the Measure of Men: Science, Technology, and Ideologies of Western Dominance* (Ithaca, 1989).

29   Christopher A. Bayly, *Imperial Meridian: The British Empire and the World, 1780–1830* (New York, 1989).

30   Jürgen Osterhammel, *Colonialism: A Theoretical Overview*, trans. S. Frisch (Princeton, 1997).

31   On cultural dimensions, Bernard Cohn, *Colonialism and Its Forms of Knowledge: The British in India* (Princeton, 1996); on interaction and negotiation, Richard White, *The Middle Ground: Indians, Empires, and Republics in the Great Lakes Region, 1650–1815* (Cambridge, 1991).

32   Said, *Orientalism*; Dipesh Chakrabarty, *Provincializing Europe: Postcolonial Thought and Historical Difference* (Princeton, 2000); Ranajit Guha and Gayatri Chakravorty Spivak, eds., *Selected Subaltern Studies* (New York, 1988); Gyan Prakash, "Subaltern Studies as Postcolonial Criticism," *American Historical Review* 99 (1994): 1475–90; Florencia E. Mallon, "The Promise and Dilemma of Subaltern Studies: Perspectives from Latin American History," *American Historical Review* 99 (1994): 1491–1515; Frederick Cooper, "Conflict and Connection: Rethinking Colonial African History," *American Historical Review* 99 (1994): 1516–45.

33   Michael Geyer and Charles Bright, "World History in a Global Age," *American Historical Review* 100 (1995): 1034–60.

34   William H. McNeill and Ruth S. Adams, eds., *Human Migration: Patterns and Policies* (Bloomington, 1978); Wang Gungwu, ed., *Global History and Migrations* (Boulder, 1997).

35   Philip D. Curtin, *The Atlantic Slave Trade: A Census* (Madison, 1969); *The Rise and Fall of the Plantation Complex*.

36   Patrick Manning, *Slavery and African Life: Occidental, Oriental, and African Slave Trades* (Cambridge, 1990); John Thornton, *Africa and Africans in the Making of the Atlantic World*, 2nd edn., (Cambridge, 1998); Richard Price, *First-Time: The Historical Vision of an Afro-American People* (Baltimore, 1983); and *Alabi's World* (Baltimore, 1990).

37   Hugh Tinker, *A New System of Slavery: The Export of Indian Labour Overseas,*

1830–1920, 2nd edn. (London, 1993); David Northrup, *Indentured Labor in the Age of Imperialism, 1834–1922* (Cambridge, 1995); Pieter C. Emmer, ed., *Colonialism and Migration: Indentured Labor before and after Slavery* (Dordrecht, 1986).

38 Robin Cohen, *Global Diasporas: An Introduction* (Seattle, 1997); Paul Gilroy, *The Black Atlantic: Double-Consciousness and Modernity* (Cambridge, MA, 1993); James Clifford, "Diasporas," in his *Routes: Travel and Translation in the Late Twentieth Century* (Cambridge, MA, 1997), pp. 244–77; and Khachig Tölölyan, "Rethinking *Diaspora*(s): Stateless Power in the Transnational Moment," *Diaspora* 5 (1996): 3–36.

39 Chakrabarty, *Provincializing Europe*.

40 Peter Novick, *That Noble Dream: The "Objectivity Question" and the American Historical Profession* (Cambridge, 1988); Edward W. Said, "Orientalism Reconsidered," in Francis Barker, Peter Hulme, Margaret Iverson, and Diana Loxley, eds., *Europe and Its Others*, 2 vols. (Colchester, 1985), 1: 14–27; and Said, *Culture and Imperialism* (New York, 1993).

REFERENCES AND FURTHER READING

Abu-Lughod, Janet L., *Before European Hegemony: The World System*, A.D. *1250–1350*, New York, 1989.

Adas, Michael, *Machines as the Measure of Men: Science, Technology, and Ideologies of Western Dominance*, Ithaca, 1989.

Bentley, Jerry H., *Old World Encounters: Cross-Cultural Contacts and Exchanges in Pre-Modern Times*, New York, 1993.

——, *Shapes of World History in Twentieth-Century Scholarship*. Washington, DC, 1996.

Chaudhuri, K. N., *Trade and Civilisation in the Indian Ocean: An Economic History from the Rise of Islam to 1750*, Cambridge, 1985.

Crosby, Alfred W., *The Columbian Exchange: Biological and Cultural Consequences of 1492*, Westport, CT, 1972.

——, *Ecological Imperialism: The Biological Expansion of Europe, 900–1900*, Cambridge, 1986.

Curtin, Philip D., *Cross-Cultural Trade in World History*, Cambridge, 1984.

——, *The Rise and Fall of the Plantation Complex: Essays in Atlantic History*, 2nd edn. Cambridge, 1998.

——, *The World and the West: The European Challenge and the Overseas Response in the Age of Empire*, Cambridge, 2000.

Frank, Andre Gunder, *ReORIENT: Global Economy in the Asian Age*, Berkeley, 1998.

Headrick, Daniel, *The Tools of Empire: Technology and European Imperialism in the Nineteenth Century*, New York, 1981.

——, *The Tentacles of Progress: Technology Transfer in the Age of Imperialism, 1850–1940*, New York, 1988.

Helms, Mary W., *Ulysses' Sail: An Ethnographic Odyssey of Knowledge, Power, and Geographical Distance*, Princeton, 1988.

Hodgson, Marshall G. S., *Rethinking World History: Essays on Europe, Islam, and World History*, ed. Edmund Burke, III, Cambridge, 1993.

Jones, E. L., *The European Miracle: Environments, Economies, and Geopolitics in the History of Europe and Asia*, 2nd edn., Cambridge, 1986.

——, *Growth Recurring: Economic Change in World History*, Oxford, 1988.

McNeill, William H., *The Rise of the West: A History of the Human Community*, Chicago, 1963.

——, *Plagues and Peoples*, Garden City, NY, 1976.

Pacey, Arnold, *Technology in World Civilization: A Thousand-Year History*, Oxford, 1990.

Pomeranz, Kenneth, *The Great Divergence: Europe, China, and the Making of the Modern World Economy*, Princeton, 2000.

Wallerstein, Immanuel, *The Modern World-System*, 3 vols. to date, New York, 1974– .

Wolf, Eric. R., *Europe and the People Without History*, Berkeley, 1982.

Wong, R. Bin, *China Transformed: Historical Change and the Limits of European Experience*, Ithaca, 1997.

CHAPTER TWENTY-ONE

Postcolonial History

PRASENJIT DUARA

Postcolonialism is not a theory. It presents no systematic alternative to that which it critiques. Rather it is an insight or a perspective that is extraordinarily fertile simply because it provides a point of view from outside the modernizing perspective of Enlightenment rationality that has fostered so much of our modern historical thinking. In other words, it is a perspective which views many of the rationalizing and modernizing forces in the world not only as trends that develop naturally from our historical conditions of existence, but just as much as a powerful ideology or worldview of dominant Westernizing forces in the world, whether in the West or in the new nation-states of the non-West. Historiographically, the postcolonial perspective has sought to deconstruct the grand narratives of imperial and national histories deriving often from an Enlightenment vision of a progressive history, in order to reveal or point to suppressed, defeated, or negated histories and stories.

Precisely because postcolonialism is not a well developed theory but a perspective and, perhaps, a tool-kit for exploring alternative histories, historians who have been inspired or influenced by this perspective have come from diverse intellectual backgrounds and possess different historical objectives whether conservative or radical, humanistic or social scientific. Some of the ones I will discuss in this essay possibly do not even think of themselves as postcolonial historians, and most of them do not see themselves as criticizing all Enlightenment ideals or modernity *in toto*. But I do believe they share in common the critique of the idea of the all-knowing modern subject or actor in history – whether this be the individual or the nation-state – gaining rational mastery over irrationalities of nature and culture, past and present. A stronger or weaker version of this idea informed much of the historical writings of nineteenth-century imperial powers and the nation-states of the twentieth century.

Within the diversity, two features seem to characterize historians writing from a postcolonial perspective. Whether from the country or simply studying the region, they are scholars who study the non-Western world, in particular those regions where European imperialism had been active until the mid-twentieth century. Second, they have been influenced by the paradigm of cultural studies which gives priority to discourse and identity issues in understanding society. For the historian, this has meant that the assumptions underlying the selection of what slice of reality appears as the historical record – regardless among historical actors of the time or among historians past and present – are as important as political or economic analysis of the event or period. Ideally, of course, most of these historians believe that the two – cultural and political-economic analysis – ought to be combined, and in the best of these studies, they are skillfully integrated.

Postcolonial scholarship has been shaped by several intellectual influences, but Edward Said's 1977 work, *Orientalism*, was a landmark event in its history. Said brought to bear the critical insights of French post-structuralist philosophers like Michel Foucault upon the older problem of colonial power. He argued that Western colonial power (in Egypt and the Middle East, in his case) was based not only on economic and political domination, but upon a vast and powerful apparatus of knowledge production of the "Orient," or the world of the colonized, which in turn was undergirded by claims to rationality and detached objectivity. In other words, colonial systems of power-knowledge produced the colonized subjects as objects of scientifically true knowledge, for instance, through categories of "the science of races," in a way that would advance or reproduce colonial domination. Soon after the publication of Said's *Orientalism*, other scholars began to observe that the colonized subjects often reproduced these very categories as ways of understanding the self, as when colonized intellectuals began to look down on extended families as "tribal" or popular religion as "unenlightened." Partha Chatterjee's influential *Nationalism: A Derivative Discourse* explored the problem in relation to nationalism. He argued that nationalism reproduced many of the categories and goals of colonial capitalism in its underlying assumptions. At the same time he tried to show that Indian nationalism, particularly under Gandhi, also sought and experimented with alternative visions of community. In the end, however, these visions went unrealized as the nation-state conformed closely to the norms and imperatives of global capitalism propagated in the name of enlightenment and freedom.[1]

Chatterjee's work did not exist in isolation. It reflected a ferment in Indian historical studies from the late 1970s, generated by the Subaltern Studies group whose participants were historians both in India and in the West. Led by the distinguished radical scholar, Ranajit Guha, the Subaltern Studies group followed a basically Marxist historiographical model. However, its Marxism was one which sought to capture the difference between the orthodox

Marxism of mature capitalist societies and the conditions of colonial society where the subject of history was not the fledgling working class of the modern industrial sector, but the vast majority and variety of the oppressed or subaltern classes. Drawing on Marxist innovators such as Mao Zedong and Antonio Gramsci, the subaltern historians of the early 1980s wrote creative counter-histories exploring silent tracks of subaltern resistance within what Guha described as "the prose of counter-insurgency." As they increasingly encountered the ideas of cultural studies, particularly in their critique of bourgeois *nationalism*, certain methodological differences began to appear both within the group and from their earlier studies. This was perhaps dramatized by the question posed by the deconstructionist literary critic, Gayatri Spivak: Can the subaltern speak? Can the historian find the true voice of the oppressed in the language and texts of the Other? Even more, is the search for the subject of history – for the class or group that will make the historical future – not after all chimerical when the oppressed can also be the oppressor, the exploited worker also the petty patriarch?[2] Faced with such intractable questions, some subaltern historians turned to question History itself as a problematic universalization of a recent European mode of dealing with the past. Putting it bluntly, Dipesh Chakrabarty stated, "in so far as the academic discourse of history – that is, 'history' as a discourse produced at the institutional site of the university – is concerned, 'Europe' remains the sovereign, theoretical subject of all histories, including the ones we call 'Indian,' 'Chinese,' 'Kenyan,' and so on. There is a peculiar way in which all these other histories tend to become variations on a master narrative that could be called 'the history of Europe.'" Hence Chakrabarty's call to provincialize the history of Europe.[3]

Questioning Enlightenment History

Meanwhile, by the early 1990s, the questioning of History itself as a purely objective mode of inquiry began to appear among non-Western historians working outside the Indian sub-continent both independently – often drawing from post-structuralism and anthropology – and in conjunction with the subaltern studies. G. W. Hegel's *The Philosophy of History* became for several of these scholars the prototype of linear, progressive and teleological history – history with a capital H – which by differentiating societies according to whether or not they possessed a linear, forward-moving conception of the nation-in-time, articulated the new hierarchies between civilized and barbarian, advanced and backward, the West and the non-West.[4] These scholars of the non-West began to explore the close connections – indeed mutual production – of linear, progressive history and the modern nation at the turn of the twentieth century. History was no longer seen simply as a neutral mode or science of understanding the past, but as a political worldview and a political instrument. It had become a principal means of claiming sovereignty in the emerging system of nation-states.

Sometime by the late nineteenth century in Europe, and thenceforth in much of the rest of the world, a discourse of rights emerged involving a three-way relationship between a people, a territory, and a history. This relationship became the means of creating a historical agent or (often juridical) subject capable of making claims to sovereign statehood. A people with an alleged self-consciousness – recognizable only in the mirror of a written history – developed a sovereign *right* to the territory they allegedly originally and/or continuously occupied. This historical subject was prefigured in Hegel's conception of spirit evolving into self-consciousness. Without the record of history, there could be no self-consciousness, and without self-consciousness, no progress. While Hegel's spirit manifested itself over a variety of spaces and times, his teleology assured its ultimate realization in the spacetime of Prussia. In the late nineteenth-century nationalist narratives, such a historical subject not only had the right to national sovereignty, but also the right to conquer and colonize those who could not yet articulate the relationship between territorial sovereignty and historical nationhood. Thus it is easy to see why colonizing nations might seek to create categories of knowledge that conserved their colonies as non-nations, and why non-nations had to reconstitute themselves as historical nations simply in order to survive. Moreover, participation in a progressive history also revealed to these would-be nations the mechanism to get ahead. Since the conception of time in linear history was a propulsive one, if they could refashion themselves into sleek homogenized national bodies, they could position themselves to race competitively into modernity.[5]

More than any other non-Western political formation in the nineteenth century, it was the Japanese political leadership – the last to encounter Western imperialism – which succeeded in averting imperialist dominance of their society by transforming it into a modern nation and simultaneously into an imperialist power. Stefan Tanaka has shown the role of the new conception of history in enabling the Japanese to produce a vision of the past that would not only shape it into a nation but also grant it rights over others.[6] Influenced equally by Said's *Orientalism* and Chatterjee's "derivative discourse," *Japan's Orient: Rendering Pasts into History* is a highly illuminating formulation of the distinctive, if not unique, ambivalence in the ideology of Japanese nationalism and imperialism. Tanaka's book focuses on the late nineteenth-century Japanese production of *toyoshi* (East Asian history, or, literally, history of the eastern seas) which allowed the new nation-state to write its history as an enlightened, modern nation, but also as a culture which had its roots in a great Asiatic tradition that could challenge Western claims of superiority. In this way, modern Japanese historical writing was derivative of the Western Enlightenment history of linear progress. Such a mode of historical writing where the nation was not only seen as a coherent geo-body (see below), but also as advancing in time – or advanced – was a necessary condition for Japan to join the club of (imperialist) nations. It thus also generated Japan's own Orientalism which depicted Chinese and other Asians as inferior. At the same time, however, Japanese opposition to Western imperial powers and glorification of Asianism generated a rhetoric of a deep kinship of blood and culture with these same Orientalized Asians – a particularly curious rhetoric given the recentness of its appearance. As this dualistic formulation was disseminated in the popular media, it facilitated the emergence of a Japanese pan-Asianism in which Japan regarded itself as modern and "advanced," but was also "obliged" to help its "backward" Asiatic brethren. Thus, pan-Asianism appeared to naturalize what would later be seen as the cataclysmic Japanese intervention in Asia during World War II.

Although not explicitly identified with a postcolonial perspective, Thongchai Winichakul's *Siam Mapped: A History of the Geo-Body of a Nation* presents an extraordinarily clear grasp of the linear teleology of national histories.[7] By introducing the neologism of the "geo-body," Thongchai shows how nationalists sought to view the history of a nation, here Thailand, as a given territorial entity. The geo-body is different from the actual historical entities that occupied the space of today's Thailand, not only in their geographical shape and extent, but more importantly in their conceptions of space and sovereignty. By writing national histories as the evolution of the original geo-body, these histories make claims on areas, peoples, and cultures that are in fact historically *unverifiable* because such people and cultures did not associate sovereignty with territorial boundedness. The conditions that made possible the geo-body and its history, according to Thongchai, were the new conditions of knowledge-production, in particular the discourse and technology of scientific geography and map-making which displaced, or rather, conquered premodern geographical discourse.

Thongchai's most powerful insights reveal the effects of the territorial transformation of Thailand and its accompanying historical claims upon the different polities, cultures, and people on the frontiers of the traditional Thai polity. Historically in the kingdoms of Southeast Asia, as in most other parts of the world, territorial boundaries as lines of demarcation were nonexistent. Rather there were shifting boundaries and zones, occupied often by petty rulers and tributaries subject to multiple and changing overlords. With the advent of imperialism and the idea of bounded territories – doubtless a result of the relationship between capitalism and geographical knowledge which both enabled and necessitated global mastery – modern empires and nations scrambled to define their geo-bodies. England and France, with empires to the west and east of Siam respectively, in seeking to clarify (and expand) the extent of their territories ended up denying local chiefs and overlords any sovereignty claims in these zones. Maps, after all, do not deal very well with a hierarchy of status claims over territory. As the new Siamese nation caught on to the European game, they moved rapidly to use their traditional overlordship or cultural affinity with border polities to claim territorial sovereignty over them. Often the peoples of these areas did not realize the novelty of the new territorial conception. But when they were suddenly barred from visiting relatives or seeking their livelihood on the other side of the "national" boundary and when they began to be incorporated into a different culture and economy as the backward co-nationals, its significance became all too clear. Thongchai's analysis of the new science of geography, deployed first for purposes of imperialist expansion and containment, and later appropriated by the Thai state to transform itself into a modern nation-state and homogenize its claimed territory at the expense of other peoples, clarified the power of European science in the self-image of indigenous societies. In this way, although Thongchai does not dwell on the philosophical critique of Enlightenment historical writing, the idea of national history as a projection backwards in time of the present geo-body is one of the most lucid demonstrations of its teleological character.

Writing Alternative Histories

Much of this writing has been critical or deconstructive of the linear, progressive form of history. Indeed, as Dipesh Chakrabarty himself wrote, "The project of provincializing 'Europe' refers to a history that does not yet exist; . . .".[8] But one cannot say that there has been no effort to write alternative histories. To be sure, postcolonial scholarship is sufficiently kin to deconstruction and textual analysis (the reading of historical sources is, among other things, decidedly a form of textual analysis) to recognize that there are no pure alternatives uncontaminated by the powers that usually produce historical records. This, we will recall, is the point of departure from the earlier model of subaltern studies and the effort to recover the voice of the true subaltern. Shahid Amin, perhaps the most thoroughly archival of the subaltern historians, shows us in his book, *Event, metaphor, memory: Chauri Chaura, 1922–1992*, that there is a lot to recover in writing an alternative history even when he "fails" to find the true alternative story of Chauri Chaura.[9] In this work, Amin explores the history and memory of the event: a violent storming of a police station in the country town of Chauri Chaura in 1922 by a crowd supposedly committed to the non-violent nationalist movement of Mahatma Gandhi. Gandhi himself called off the movement to protest this violent turn and the very name Chauri Chaura has come to represent a shameful blot in the narrative of the national movement. Amin, who spent much of his childhood in a town not far from Chauri Chaura, combed through all the available sources – in dusty local archives as well as in the India Office library in London – in order to reconstruct both the event itself and the ways it was remembered nationally and locally. In addition, he spent many weeks doing what he calls "historical fieldwork" talking to "the inheritors of historic events at the present site of past actions." It is at the level of sources that Amin achieves his greatest success. He employs an experimental format where the length of his chapters – sometimes two pages long – often conforms to the fragmentary nature of his sources. With a critical sensitivity to the story behind the archival document, Amin shows how the historical source – that ultimate touchstone of truthfulness – was itself produced. Much of the evidence used by the British colonial courts to judge the event as a criminal event (rather than political) was legally truthful. Behind it, however, was the complex interrogation procedure of the approver, a participant who agreed to give testimony in return for immunity, which channeled the narrative to yield the legal truth. And while he is able to evoke, by exploring the economic and cultural spaces and practices, the possible meanings of the event at the time in 1922, through his historical fieldwork, he is able to stretch the meaning of the event itself to include its present meanings in and of that historical space. Whether he is discussing the process of criminal law or the linguistic registers in which the event is recalled, Amin is remarkably sensitive to the dispersal of the meaning of an event over space and time. Thus while Amin will not produce an alternative narrative, his layered investigations produce many stories at an angle from the established narratives.

My own book, *Rescuing History from the Nation*, which probed the close nexus between history and the nation in early twentieth-century China, also sought out suppressed histories within or in the shadow of dominant narratives, often by exploring linguistic transformations in the sources.[10] Although China was not formally or fully colonized, from the end of the nineteenth century, imperialism had a deep impact on the consciousness of the Chinese intelligentsia who began increasingly to view the world through the prevalent social Darwinian conceptions of the period. In this discourse, a linear, progressive history of the Chinese nation was not simply necessary in order to make claims on the past. The creation – or the "awakening," as the nationalist rallying cry would have it – of a national historical subject was necessary for competitive survival (against both imperialism and the slide into barbarism) in the present and the future. History now became a political force in the efforts of modernizing nationalists to either appropriate, subsume or delegitimate popular conceptions and practices of the old society. Thus, for instance, revolutionary nationalists sought to enlist the support of the secret societies which were, in their commitment to restoring a previous dynasty, actually backward looking and often diametrically opposed to the revolutionary conception. Yet by skillful manipulation of the older conceptions and language of these societies the nationalists re-wrote the histories of these societies to reflect revolutionary views.

I also examined some counter-narratives of the nation, narratives inspired both by historical, premodern visions of community as well as by the emancipatory rhetoric of the Enlightenment, which were ultimately defeated or suppressed. In particular, I tried to show how the meanings of certain words from the older Confucian vocabulary were transformed with significant political effects when they were absorbed by the new narrative of progressive history. Thus for instance, the older Confucian word for feudalism "*fengjian*" contained a rather positive meaning in the imperial Chinese system as an ideal of local autonomy directed against an aggrandizing and centralizing imperial power. We may think of it as an indigenous Chinese critique of autocracy. During the very last years of the dynasty before the Republican revolution of 1911, this political tradition of *fengjian* was often invoked to advocate modern, local self-government and was even married to ideas of civil society. But such a recourse to history did not last for long because as the new ideas of a progressive history began to flood the Chinese intellectual scene mainly from Japan during this same period, *fengjian* or feudalism began to be construed in the Enlightenment mode as the other of modernity – as the symbol of darkness and medievality. Indeed, the idea of local autonomy began rapidly to be construed as a hindrance to the emergence of a strong nation-state among many nationalists and the new meaning of *fengjian* with all its negative connotations was deployed against those who supported local autonomy. In a chapter on the federalist movement of the early 1920s, I show how the movement for provincial autonomy was delegitimated significantly by this transformed meaning of *fengjian*.

While many of the alternative histories have emerged from historians of Asia, the postcolonial perspective has had some impact as well on historians of Africa, the Caribbean, and to a lesser extent, of Latin America. The major themes that emerge in these and other recent works is the recovery of agency of the colonized *within colonial categories* and the related idea of the mutual constitution of colonizer and colonized. A volume edited by Gyan Prakash entitled *After Colonialism: Imperial Histories and Postcolonial Displacements*, reveals this theme in several non-Asian colonial histories. The goal of the volume is to explore how, in the aftermath of colonialism, "the history of colonialism and colonialism's disciplining of history can be shaken loose from the domination of categories and ideas it produced – colonizer and colonized; white, black and brown; civilized and uncivilized; modern and archaic, cultural identity; tribe and nation."[11] The book promises to recognize "another history of agency and knowledge alive in the dead weight of the colonial past" by tracking not only colonialism's history of domination and resistance, but those (subaltern) positions and knowledges that were normalized by colonial categories. Its principal methodology is to study the ways in which self-constituting and self-serving colonial narratives and truths were estranged and re-interpreted in the colonial setting. Thus for instance, the entanglement of the rhetoric of the Rights of Man with the practice of slavery in the French colonies reveals the limits of ideology invisible in France.

Departing from the stark opposition between colonizer and colonized in some early postcolonial critiques, heterogeneity, hybridity, the ways in which colonizer and colonized, Paris and Havana made each other, are the common themes in this volume. An author like Joan Dayan who has written on the Haitian revolution of 1791, clearly believes that one has to break with the notion of a coherent historical narrative in order to show how apparently separate processes in different places and times can be meaningful only when related to each other. The revolutionary process in Haiti derives its meaning as much from internal class and racial struggles and indigenous practices such as voodoo as it does from the French Revolution; and she shows in a moment of biting clarity how the meanings of French history itself derive from French understandings of nineteenth-century Haitian developments. Dayan's anti-narrative deliberately scrambles chronology as it seeks to juxtapose different slices of the Haitian revolution with other events spread over a century or more. The essay celebrates the incapacity of any narrative to master these developments, although, ironically, the research is steeped in the historical archive. Most historians, however, seem to want to follow their discipline's urge for coherence-making. Steven Feierman's "Africa in History," in the same volume edited by Prakash, explores, with consummate skill, the variety of narrative forms, including historical African ones as well as contemporary scholarly ones, through which an event could be understood. He thus confronts the indeterminacy and the heterogeneity of the historical event, but in a way in which the openness seems finite. The next stage then can be presented, not with a closure, but with coherent leads which offer avenues for exploration.

Some of the most interesting recent writing on the problems of Japanese colonialism and nationalism also attend to how Japanese identity was shaped by the relationship with Other on the periphery. The work of Ichiro Tomiyama and Alan Christy focus not on the colonies per se, but on Okinawa. Historically the Okinawan islands were not strictly a part of a Japanese polity or empire until the Meiji period when they were annexed and Okinawa was made a prefecture of Japan in 1879. As such, like Hokkaido which also became a part of the Japanese geo-body only in the Meiji period, these territories were regarded as different from the colonies or occupied regions such as Korea or Manchuria. At the same time, they also occupied a status of not quite Japanese. Tomiyama, who writes principally in Japanese, has shown how Okinawa truly problematizes the idea of a colony as always having to be outside the nation. In a series of books and essays he has argued that Okinawa must be thought of as a place that is neither a colony nor not a colony. A colony is by geographical definition, outside the nation, and thus, as he says, the geographical definition displaces the universal form of colonialism. Okinawa was

historically closer to the colonial domains or what the Japanese called the
"outer territories" and economically, too, it was incorporated much like a
colony. However, since it was geographically and administratively part of the
nation, it could not be dealt with rhetorically and politically as a colony. As
neither colony nor quite of the nation, Okinawa was produced as a place in
need of welfare and relief from the benevolent national center in Tokyo. This,
of course, reproduced the stereotypes associated with such a dependent status
within the national culture.

In the 1920s, when Okinawa was devastated by the recession that hit its
relatively vulnerable and underdeveloped export-based economy, the image of
Okinawans as the symbol of backwardness intensified. Not only were their
problems blamed on their own laziness and backwardness, they were also
blamed for the poor image of Japanese (the *kanaka* Japanese) in colonies like
Taiwan. Alan Christy extends this mode of cultural-economic inquiry to argue
that Okinawan elites deployed cultural metaphors to gain advantage for
Okinawa, but ended up strengthening the stereotypes of the Japanese core.
Okinawan elites appealed to the pre-war period "family state" model of the
emperor as Father and Okinawa as a child and urged the father to extend
special dispensations to this late developing child. As Christy makes clear, the
not unambiguous attitude of Okinawans towards assimilation into Japaneseness stemmed from the elites' recognition of the reality that not to be Japanese in the situation was to be automatically relegated to the status of the
colonized (remarkably like Japan itself in relation to the West). Yet, the appeal
to the image of the late developing child contributed all the more to the idea
that Okinawa was not quite Japanese and not deserving of full citizenship.
Christy's most salient argument, however, is that Japaneseness itself was being
generated – from the reality of diverse practices and identities within the
national core – as culturally homogeneous when it was invoked as the standard against which the Okinawan was measured. Thus the anomalous status
of Okinawa as both part of the nation and yet not truly of it or of its contemporary modernity was a necessary part of creating the homogenous and
loyal Japanese citizen that was such a crucial development of the Meiji state-
building process.

I believe these studies of Okinawa advance the postcolonial perspective in
several ways: first, they seek to explore the problem of the nation not simply
in those aspects which reproduce the imperialist project, but in those aspects
of nationalism which reveal new or different problems. Within its territorial
boundaries, the nation-state of the twentieth century seems to have been
bound to follow a logic towards peripheral peoples that could not simply
reproduce such people as different in the way that imperialist states could. Yet
this relationship cannot be understood – or resolved – without grasping the
nation-state's links with capitalism and imperialism. Second, and related, their
analysis of colonialism is attentive to the economic dimension which is com-

bined with the analysis of discourse and identity, arguing consistently that attention to culture and identity among the historical subjects served to obscure critical issues of economic domination.[12]

Departures and Critiques

Criticism of the postcolonial perspective appeared perhaps as early as the perspective itself, but interestingly, it has not come from the defenders of the mission of Western civilization. These defenders are much more critical of multiculturalism which I believe is in significant ways different from postcolonialism since the latter critiques the idea of a coherent, historical subject – whether it be national or ethnic. I suspect the right wing in the West does not yet see the relevance of postcolonialism to Western society in the way in which it is impossible not to see the multicultural challenge to Western hegemony in the West. Rather most of the criticism has come from sources that share the critique of imperialism and capitalism. Within this camp, however, there are the friendlier critics who insist on the diversity of the impact of imperialism and nationalism; this diversity cannot be fully grasped by the origins of the perspective in colonial heartlands of South Asia or the middle east. There is also a much more hostile group deriving from a Marxist or radical persuasion – often from the ex-colonies themeselves – who denounce what they allege is the postcolonial abandonment of foundationalism (that there is a correct or rational foundation to judge historical narratives), of class – both as a product and subject of history, and of revolutionary change. Let me first turn to the relatively friendly criticism.

The field of Chinese history has seen some efforts to modify the postcolonial perspective to adapt to the unusual situation of China which had a semi-colonial status from the nineteenth century until 1945, or we might say, imperialism without colonialism. Tani Barlow, the feminist historian of China who also edits the journal *positions*, where much of the writing inspired by postcolonialism and other critical theories appears, developed the notion of "colonial modernity under the sign of erasure." [13] This is a deconstructive idea expressed in the icon of the signifier as struck out, as in ~~colonial~~. She argues, in other words, that postwar Western, particularly US, scholarship of China and East Asia in general sought to preemptively deny the imperialist or semi-colonial conditions of pre-war China in order to deflect or forswear any possible connection between the imperialist past and the neo-imperialism of the US in the region during the Cold War and through the Vietnam War. Thus, she argues, it is impossible to think of modernity without colonialism especially in East Asia where this false assumption has guided much past scholarship. At the same time, Barlow finds postcolonial scholarship not quite adequate to grasp Chinese conditions where the semi-colonial condition did not reproduce the Manichaean opposition between colonizer and colonized but rather a great many variations. She also objects to the tendency of post-colonial scholarship to privilege the "native" speech and to the expectation of finding an emancipatory postcolonial lexicon applicable to all.

This kind of objection to the stark opposition of colonizer and colonized is a common critique of post-colonial writing that is made by various scholars. Another relatively sympathetic critic, Frederick Cooper, brings up the issue of complicity among the colonized elites who often embraced Western ideas and the need to recognize that Orientalist categories were jointly produced by colonizers and native elites. In an *American Historical Review* forum on subaltern studies, he proposed that that the categories of colonialism and nationalism be treated with more flexibility and sensitivity to their context. Thus not only should notions of modernity, citizenship, liberalism, equality, etc., be seen in their changing context, but subaltern agency can perhaps be found in the ways that "natives" often disassemble these categories and make something else of them.[14] Several of these comments are useful, but I see them more as enriching the project since the basic point – the assumption of a stark opposition between colonizer and colonized – is applicable, if at all, only to an early version of postcolonial writing, as for instance, in Said's *Orientalism* and the early subaltern historical writings. In truth, in the last ten years or so, postcolonial writing has become full of such terms as hybridity, heterogeneity, and that favorite expression of literary theorists: catachresis, defined by Gayatri Spivak as "reversing, displacing, and seizing the apparatus of value-coding."

Ironically, the radical and hostile criticism of postcolonialism makes the opposite point: that the proliferation and celebration of all kinds of difference, the relative inattention to political economy and to the more tangible, institutionalized relations of production and domination, and the dispersion of historical subjectivity in textual analysis and the prison-house of language have robbed postcolonialism of its radical, transforming potential. In the same AHR forum on subaltern studies, a sympathizer, Florencia Mallon, writing on the influence of subaltern studies on Latin American historiography, protested that the Latin Americanists tended to flatten the tension between the radicalism of Gramsci and the poststructuralist emphasis on "difference" which had been in productive tension within subaltern studies. Their analysis of the subaltern, complained Mallon, amounted to no more than a version of postmodernism which allegedly celebrates difference for its own sake, whereas she herself proposed that critical post-structuralism be put to the service of a Gramscian commitment to a class-based emancipation.[15] Other radical critics have not been so generous.

Two of the fiercest critics of postcolonialism are the Indian literary critic Aijaz Ahmad and the intellectual historian of the Chinese revolution, Arif Dirlik. Although the alternatives they propose appear to be different, Dirlik elaborates many of the points that were first made by Ahmad. However, I will attend to his critique because as a historian he is more attentive to the historical issues involved.[16] Dirlik believes it is important to understand the identity of postcolonial intellectuals in order to understand postcolonial discourse. According to Dirlik, postcolonialism is the product of Third-World scholars, most particularly Indian scholars, who have arrived in the academic strongholds of the West. It is an expression of their new-found power and is complicit with the system because it does not criticize capitalism. Needless to say, the whole mode of argumentation which reduces intellectual positions to a social location is a highly dangerous and futile one. It invites the responder to trace the critic's position, in turn, to his own background, and since much of this exchange takes place within a highly elitist transnational academic system, the competition to stake a more radical position on the basis of social location can scarcely be productive. Surely our positions can best be understood by how we view the research field and how we identify the underlying conditions of the objects of our research.

Dirlik's second argument refers to the identity of postcolonial discourse itself. In forsaking the structural analyses of capitalism, postcolonialism is weakened and can be allegedly appropriated by all kinds of conservative forces – such as transnational capitalism and fascism – which reify and celebrate identities in order to conceal their structural origins in capitalism. How exactly postcolonial analysis, which is committed to deconstructing identity, has been useful for fascism or some other entity committed to the reification and glorification of national, ethnic or cultural identity is not easy to grasp. What this confusion reflects, I believe, is the impasse faced by critical historians in the world today. Critical historiography which had found its inspiration in Marxist or socialist-inspired social theory has encountered a world in which the possibilities of non-capitalist emancipation have receded and one where the revolutionary states have been discredited. At the same time, capitalist globalization continues to widen the gap between the powerful and the powerless while the erosion of a national society itself unleashes a reaction which results in still more violent and exclusive reifications of nation, race or culture.

While some scholars like Aijaz Ahmad still subscribe to a revolutionary view of a working-class revolution and liberation, most scholars in America, including Dirlik are much less sanguine and have themselves disavowed the alternative of revolution. They, however, hold to the idea that historical analysis must continue to study the capitalist system as a totality. I am sympathetic to the observation that the postcolonial perspective should return to study the relationships between discourse, identity and political economy, although there are methodological problems here that have yet to be fully grasped. However, since even a critic like Dirlik admits the difficulty of a return to foundational categories and the revolutionary subject of history, it is important to clarify what our historical goals might be. One of the greatest dangers in the postcolonial world is the growth of right-wing nationalism and fascist tendencies which are often in the business of re-writing histories to objectify nation and race. The postcolonial toolkit, with its instruments of discourse and identity analysis, has probably done more to foreground the nation as an object of historical analysis than any other historical approach. When combined intelligently with the political economy approach, the critical historian, it seems to me, can become well-positioned to both historicize these efforts and combat them.

NOTES

1   Edward Said, *Orientalism* (New York, Pantheon, 1978); Partha Chatterjee, *Nationalist Thought and the Colonial World: A Derivative Discourse* (London: Zed Books, 1986).
2   Ranajit Guha and Gayatri Spivak, eds., *Selected Subaltern Studies* (New York: Oxford, 1988).
3   Dipesh Chakravarty, "Postcoloniality and the Artifice of History: Who Speaks for the 'Indian' Pasts?" *Representations* 37 (Winter 1992): 1.
4   Georg W. F. Hegel, *The Philosophy of History*, trans. J. Sibree (New York: Dover Publications, 1956).
5   A fuller version of these ideas can be found in Prasenjit Duara, *Rescuing History from the Nation: Questioning Narratives of Modern China* (Chicago: University of Chicago Press, 1995), ch. 1.
6   Stefan Tanaka, *Japan's Orient: Rendering Pasts into History* (Berkeley: University of California Press, 1993).
7   Thongchai Winichakul, *Siam Mapped: A History of the Geo-Body of a Nation* (Honolulu: University of Hawaii Press, 1994).
8   Chakravarty, "Postcoloniality and the Artifice of History: Who Speaks for the 'Indian' Pasts?": 20.
9   Shahid Amin, *Event, metaphor, memory: Chauri Chaura, 1922–1992* (Berkeley: University of California Press, 1995).
10 Prasenjit Duara, *Rescuing History from the Nation*.
11 Gyan Prakash, *After Colonialism: Imperial Histories and Postcolonial Displacements* (Princeton: Princeton University Press, 1995).
12 Ichiro Tomiyama, "Colonialism and the Sciences of the Tropical Zone: The Academic Analysis of Difference in 'the Island Peoples,'" in Tani E. Barlow, ed., *Formations of Colonial Modernity in East Asia* (Durham: Duke University Press, 1997), pp. 199–222; Alan S. Christy "The Making of Imperial Subjects in Okinawa" in ibid, pp. 141–70.
13 Tani E. Barlow, "Colonialism's Career in Postwar China Studies" in Barlow ed. Ibid, pp. 373–412.
14 Frederick Cooper, "Conflict and Connection: Rethinking Colonial African History," *American Historical Review* 99/5 (December 1994), pp. 1516–45.

15 Florencia E. Mallon, "The Promise and Dilemma of Subaltern Studies: Perspectives from Latin American History" in *American History Review*, pp. 1491–1515.

16 Arif Dirlik, "The Postcolonial Aura: Third World Criticism in the Age of Global Capitalism," in Arif Dirlik, ed., *The Postcolonial Aura: Third World Criticism in the Age of Global Capitalism* (Boulder: Westview, 1997); see also Arif Dirlik, "How the Grinch Hijacked Radicalism: Further Thoughts on the Postcolonial," in *Postcolonial Studies* 2/2 (July 1999).

REFERENCES AND FURTHER READING

AHR Forum *American Historical Review* 99/5 (December 1994), pp. 1475–1645. Includes contribution of Gyan Prakash, "Subaltern Studies as Postcolonial Criticism," pp. 1475–90; Florencia E. Mallon, "The Promise and Dilemma of Subaltern Studies: Perspectives from Latin American History," pp. 1491–1515; "Conflict and Connection: Rethinking Colonial African History," pp. 1516–45.

Amin, Shahid, *Event, metaphor, memory: Chauri Chaura, 1922–1992*, Berkeley: University of California Press, 1995.

Barlow, Tani E., ed., *Formation of Colonial Modernity in East Asia*, Durham: Duke University Press, 1997.

Chakrabarty, Dipesh, *Provincializing Europe*, Princeton, NJ: Princeton University Press, 2000.

Chatterjee, Partha, *Nationalist Thought and the Colonial World: A Derivative Discourse*, London, Zed Books, 1986.

Dirlik Arif, ed., *The Postcolonial Aura: Third World Criticism in the Age of Global Capitalism*, Boulder, Westview, 1997.

Duara, Prasenjit, *Rescuing History from the Nation: Questioning Narratives of Modern China*, Chicago: University of Chicago Press, 1995.

Guha, Ranajit, and Gayatri Spivak, eds., *Selected Subaltern Studies*, New York: Oxford University Press, 1988.

Prakash, Gyan, *After Colonialism: Imperial Histories and Postcolonial Displacements*, Princeton: Princeton University Press, 1995.

Said, Edward, *Orientalism*, New York, Pantheon, 1978.

Tanaka, Stefan, *Japan's Orient: Rendering Pasts into History*, Berkeley: University of California Press, 1993.

Winichakul, Thongchai, *Siam Mapped: A History of the Geo-Body of a Nation*, Honolulu: University of Hawaii Press, 1994.

Chapter Twenty-two

The Multicultural History of Nations

Donna R. Gabaccia

At least since the eighteenth century, concepts of national homogeneity have been central to state-building and to the histories of modern nations.[1] A shared national language or religion, descent from a common ancestor or shared experiences, or a political ideology chosen and held in common justified demands for national self-determination in Europe and the Americas in the eighteenth and nineteenth centuries. For Europe's "ethnic nationalists," nations resembled family or (in the age of Darwin) "racial" groups, rooted in shared biological descent. In the Americas, nationalists more often argued that individuals of diverse origins should choose citizenship and representation by a particular government; their "civic nationalism" has been associated with democratic government since the American and French revolutions. Embrace of a shared political ideology provided the basis for homogeneity in such nations. In the twentieth-century, and during two world wars, American liberals such as Woodrow Wilson and Franklin Roosevelt argued further that a world composed of national groups ruled by their own freely-chosen nation-states could guarantee global harmony.

Still, carving modern nation-states out of the empires of the past was never a simple matter. Whether in Asia, the Americas, Africa, or the Mediterranean, the empires of the pre-Columbian world were a hodge-podge of religions, languages, and identities. Empire-building dynasts had secured the loyalties of peoples culturally unlike themselves with a complex mix of special privileges, personal charisma, and military might. New European empire-builders after 1450 depended even more on technical superiority and brute force to maintain control over heterogeneous peoples and cultures. The conquest of native populations and the transport to the colonies of slave laborers from Africa and Asia and indentured servants from Europe and Asia made the new European empires as culturally diverse ("multi-ethnic") as the older ones. All modern imperial systems required cultural narratives as well as military force to establish some measure of institutional coherence and power.

The same would be true of modern nation-states. Whether defined by civic or ethnic nationalism, most modern nation-states have in fact been culturally diverse. Not only did they inherit the diversity of the empires that spawned them; the age of nation-building was also an era of vast international and intercontinental migrations. New nations that gained their independence from Great Britain, Spain, and Portugal typically abolished slavery but then sought new immigrants as workers and settlers. European nations faced the challenge of peasant localism and – in some cases – religious or ethnic diversity, while industrial growth also required many to seek laborers outside their national territories. There was in fact much diversity within every modern nation, both in Europe and in all of the former European colonies.

Yet a reader might never learn of cultural diversity in the histories of Western nations written in the nineteenth and early twentieth centuries. The nation has long been an important unit in historical writing, and historical scholarship has often helped to foster a belief in national homogeneity. Over the past fifty years, however, and in both Europe and in the neo-Europes created by its empires around the world, earlier histories of homogeneous nations have given way to explorations of relations between national states and their diverse populations. Some of these "multicultural" histories acknowledge that nations are multi-ethnic; that is, they recognize that nations include people who speak different languages or worship and live in quite diverse ways. Other multicultural histories focus on the diversity of cultural identities among citizens who have origins in other countries or who have experienced various forms of religious, racial or ethnic persecution.

Unsurprisingly, this transition from homogeneous national to multicultural histories occurred differently in Europe, Latin America, and the English-speaking world. The collapse of scientific racism and of Europe's empires, the waning of the Cold War, and the waxing of world markets could scarcely have had uniform scholarly consequences. Still, Nathan Glazer's resigned comment "we are all multiculturalists now" – while meant mainly to summarize a transition in national self-understanding within the United States – is increasingly applicable to the Western world as a whole.[2]

Nation-Building and Historical Scholarship

Historians have frequently assumed important roles as nation-builders, and it is significant that history became a distinct profession during the age of nationalism. In Europe, historians played especially important roles in imagining and fostering national homogeneity, while in the Americas, social scientists – with their supposed expertise on racial difference – often contributed more to early accounts of national identities. But whether influenced by romanticism, revolutionary traditions or racial science, the writing of history in the West produced many triumphalist narratives of homogeneous nations, tracing a people's heroic evolution toward political autonomy as nation-states.

The scholarly discovery of national communities proceeded along different paths and at a different pace in Europe, Latin America, and the English-speaking world. In Western Europe, colonial expansion, conflicts with other European empires, and labor migrations from Eastern and Southern Europe made the nineteenth century a period of intense scrutiny of national history. But many of these histories looked always for internal unities rather than differences. In republican histories of France, for example, civic nationalism rendered cultural difference invisible among citizens. Jews, colonized Africans and immigrant Italians alike joined the French nation when they acquired citizenship, learned French, and lived on French soil; subsequent differences of culture or identity were of no interest to the state and of little interest to historians, although sociologists sometime explored their significance. Germans from Herder onward simply excluded from their national histories those lacking German "blood" while ignoring sharp phenotypic, cultural, and even linguistic differences among German-speakers.

In new nations that were formed from the multi-ethnic European empires during the nineteenth and twentieth centuries, differing conceptions of race, descent, and color defined nation-building. Emerging from the British Empire, first the US, and then Australia, South Africa and Canada, viewed their new nations as "settler colonies" – descendants of a racially and culturally superior English (or "Anglo-Celtic"), imperial nation. These "herrenvolk" or white supremacist democracies excluded Native Americans, Africans (whether slave or free), and Asian immigrants from their nations. Institutionally, racial segregation was the rule: "Jim Crow" laws and the exclusion or restriction of immigration in the US, "apartheid" in Africa. In the scholarly world, national histories simply ignored the excluded minorities. In the first half of the century, it was sociologists at the University of Chicago who first offered compelling accounts of the assimilation of European immigrants into the mainstream of consensual citizenship.[3] Building on their work after World War II, "consensus historians" tried to describe the cultural consensus that defined citizenship and membership in the American nation; they focused on economic opportunity as much as political democracy as foundations for national unity.[4] But even histories of the US as a "melting-pot" nation or a "nation of immigrants" focussed on the transformation of the European "many" into the national "one."[5] Dismissing any possibility of cultural diversity among whites, histories simultaneously preserved older notions of the US as a white nation by ignoring the different history of Americans of African and Asian descent.

In early twentieth-century Latin America, social scientists often generated the earliest influential accounts of national unity. But in contrast to the North

American narratives, racial amalgamation was more important in forming the nation than white supremacy, political democracy, or economic prosperity. Latin American countries did not institutionalize racial segregation when they abolished slavery. They welcomed immigration and the "whitening" (or "civilizing") of multi-ethnic populations through inter-marriage (legally prohibited as miscegenation in much of the US) and through the natives' acquisition of European culture. In the twentieth century, sociologist Gilberto Freyre imagined Brazil as a racially hybrid nation in which peoples of African, European and Native American origin enjoyed equal places, and in which African cultural traits also had a place. Responding to Mexico's revolution, philosopher Jose Vasconcelos also traced the emergence of a new, mixed "cosmic race" of Mexicans. In Argentina, however, scholars such as sociologist Gino Germani developed national narratives that resembled the US histories by focusing on the successful melding of European immigrants of many backgrounds into a single, unitary, if culturally hybrid new Argentina.[6] Histories of a mestizo Mexico, Brazilian "racial democracy" or the Argentine "melting pot" may also have consolidated support for new populist, nationalist and authoritarian rulers like Brazil's Getulia Vargas, Mexico's Institutional Revolutionary Party (PRI), and Argentina's Juan Peron.

But such histories also self-consciously proclaimed the superiority of Latin nations over their more powerful but still racially segregated neighbor, the United States. Just as France's history presented its revolutionary and republican experiment with civic nationalism as a better model for Europe than Germany's ethnic nationalism, Brazil claimed its history of racial amalgamation provided a better model for national unity than the system of white supremacy in the United States. If the histories of most European nations ignored cultural diversity, the multi-racial history of Brazil and the civic nationalisms of France and the United States offered different models for the emergence of what would later be called "multicultural history," although this history, too, developed along diverse, national paths.

Hyphenated English-Speakers

Beginning in the 1950s in the United States, and then with gathering momentum in Canada, Australia and South Africa in the 1970s and 1980s, the turn toward multicultural history was evident throughout the English-speaking world by the 1990s. In the United States, first a "hot" war against fascism and then a "cold" war against communism cast troubling shadows over celebratory histories of a nation understood to be essentially white, democratic, contented, and united by a shared Anglo-American culture. The country's harsh treatment of those of African descent made African-American scholars among the earliest critics of the US's celebratory and homogenizing historical narratives and also early practitioners of a new multicultural history.[7] New histories of America's "peculiar institution," slavery, preceded an even larger historical movement to make African-American history both an integral component of a national history of the US, and a critique of it. Civil rights and immigration legislation passed in 1965 to end legal discrimination on the basis of race, color, and national origins, unleashed revisionist energies in historical scholarship, much of it focused on the persistence and importance of racial and ethnic diversity and conflict.

The revisionist historians of the 1970s and much of the 1980s wrote histories of racial minorities and of white (or "unmeltable") "ethnics" descended from European immigrants, often showing relatively little concern with the extent to which these histories formed part of a wider national history.[8] Histories of minorities now legally recognized as such by the nation-state – "Black," "Hispanic," "Native-American," "Asian" – also uncovered the considerable cultural diversity within these groups. By the 1990s, historians of the many groups considered "white ethnics" or "Asian-Americans" also began to ask how and under what conditions the immigrant national identities of groups such as Sicilians or Chinese had been transformed into the pan-ethnic "white" or "Asian" racial identities of the United States.[9] Predictably, critics of the new multicultural histories argued that this work was "disuniting" the American nation.[10]

Already in the 1980s, however, scholars such as Ronald Takaki and Lawrence Fuchs were redefining the American nation as a multi-ethnic "mosaic," "kaleidoscope," or "salad," and rejecting older historical accounts of a unified nation. But did all ethnic groups have an equal place in this mosaic or in American civic nationalism? Having eliminated legal discrimination on the basis of race, the US now more resembled its Latin American neighbors, but its new histories nevertheless emphasized racial diversity rather than cultural amalgamation. Some writers of the new multicultural histories continued to describe membership in the American nation as voluntary while insisting that affirmations of an ethnic (or racial) identity were a sign of national inclusion and membership. In the past, whites had always been free to inter-marry, and as a result a substantial proportion of the descendants of European immigrants found they could choose among several "ethnic options" to supplement their national identities as Irish-, Italian- or Jewish-Americans. As barriers against inter-racial marriage fell after 1965, wider choices for defining one's own identity also opened for peoples "of color," and demands arose for census categories that acknowledged the existence of peoples with multi-racial identities. Other observers suggested that when all Americans, regardless of skin color, could choose their own ethnic identities, rather than having outsiders label them racially, the US might, as a nation, evolve "beyond ethnicity."[11] But still others, the so-called "hard multi-culturalists," and notably the Afrocentrists among them, were less interested in revising understanding of the American nation than in exploring pan-African or pan-Asian racial formation across national boundaries.[12]

Elsewhere in the former British Empire, the writing of multicultural histories emerged in somewhat similar form, but shaped by differing national contexts. In South Africa, as in the US, movements to end apartheid challenged national understanding of itself as a "white nation" at its very roots. Comparative histories of the US and South Africa (or the US, South Africa, and Brazil) by George Fredrickson and Anthony Marx explored the origins of systems of white supremacy and suggested that the earlier exclusion of non-whites from the public life of the nation had resolved sharp and violent conflicts between whites (the Civil War; the Boer War). In Canada, multicultural histories emerged less from a critique of racial discrimination against those of African descent and more from political struggles over bi-lingualism, responding both to discontent among the country's French-speaking minority and the arrival of a huge new immigrant population since World War II. As its new histories show, Canada shared with the US a long history of excluding Asians and Natives from the nation, while finding legal and extra-legal ways to restrict immigration from southern and eastern Europe and Latin America.[13] In Australia, the exclusion of Asians and indigenous peoples from the nation coupled with significant postwar migrations link the issues of the new multicultural histories of this country to those of both the US and Canada.[14] Despite their democratic political institutions, all three countries used race and ethnicity to define national "insiders" and "outsiders" – a cultural and political pattern that new multicultural histories have brought to prominence. Comparisons of the US to Canada and Australia have lagged behind those of the US and South Africa, however, and similarities between the multicultural histories of these nations are less often explored.

New multicultural histories of Great Britain and of its worldwide empire may help us to understand why histories of "hyphenated identities" rather than of racial or cultural amalgamation have characterized the English-speaking world. Somewhat unique among the European empires of the early-modern world, Britain actively encouraged migration to its colonies not only by British but also by non-national Protestants, yet it also legally discouraged them from inter-marrying with colonized natives or with African slaves. In the nineteenth century, Britain treated colonies dominated by white settlers of European origin differently from others, though it also led abolitionism worldwide, discouraged the new "coolie" trade, and avoided overt and systematic institutionalized racial discrimination (like that in the US). In the postwar period, as its empire dissolved into a commonwealth of independent nations, these differences persisted, affecting Britain's willingness to welcome immigrants from nonwhite Jamaica and Pakistan or white Canada or Australia or Ireland and to incorporate them into their imperial nation at home.[15]

Hyphen-less Latin Americans

With the decline and end of military dictatorships in much of Latin America, critics there also began to question the populist and nationalist histories that had focused on racial democracy, and that had celebrated nations produced through miscegenation, acculturation and immigrant amalgamation. Nowhere was this more obvious than in Brazil. The country's racial democracy attracted critical attention from multi-national UN observers already in the 1950s; later, in the 1960s and 1970s, Brazilian critics, like Florestan Fernandes and the Sao Paulo school of social science defied the country's military rulers and sometimes fled into exile after questioning the nationalist myth of racial peace and equality.[16] The restoration of democracy and the emergence of a small Afro-Brazilian movement for racial equality now support Brazilian efforts to revise Gilberto Freyre's earlier, optimistic historical narrative of racial harmonies. Histories of Afro-Brazilians, Native Americans, and European immigrants from Germany, Italy, Spain and Portugal have also proliferated since the 1980s. Still, most Brazilian studies of its multi-ethnic population continue to emphasize racial and cultural hybridity and the importance of a national identity shared by Brazilians across racial and ethnic lines. Economic development, most still predict, will eliminate what appear as signs of racial inequality.[17]

A very substantial part of the multicultural history of Brazil has been written in English by authors from North America. While not limited to studies of Afro-Brazilian life, outsiders offer the harshest critiques of Brazilian racial democracy as history and practice. Is it possible, outsiders ask, that the main legacy of racial democracy has been to leave Afro-Brazilians without identities that can support political solidarity or an attack on racial prejudice? While Brazilian scholars tend to attribute the obstacles Afro-Brazilians face to their poverty, North Americans tend to see their poverty as a consequence of racism.[18] In both accounts, however, the story of a unified racial democracy has been giving way to a new emphasis on internal differences and diversity.

In Argentina in the 1980s, scholars associated with the journal *Latin American Studies of Migration* began to revisit the histories of that country's sizeable immigrant populations. Histories of Italian, Spanish, German, and eastern European Jewish immigrants in Argentina identified the formation of ethnic communities in the late nineteenth and early twentieth centuries. Scholars from Europe and North America explicitly compared the formation of ethnic groups in Argentina and the United States, but they also went beyond Argentine historians by focusing also on native racial minorities of Indian and African origin.[19] Whether written by native or outsider, however, these new multicultural histories of Argentina have generally failed to consider the fate of ethnic minorities and the children of immigrants (the so-called second generation) under the impact of populist nationalism in the 1930s and 1940s. In most accounts of Argentine history, ethnic and racial identities continue to be portrayed as transitory, with little long-term historical significance.

In Mexico, where the continuous domination of the PRI since the 1930s has only recently ended, the development of a new multicultural history that would revise the national history of the country's "cosmic race" remains tentative. A substantial social scientific and anthropological literature on the country's large native populations has established their cultural isolation and minority status without, however, challenging traditional historical national narratives of racial and cultural hybridization and equality. It may be the case that Mexico's Chiapas rebels and the widespread attention they have garnered outside Mexico will generate critiques of the history of Mexico's cosmic race from the margins and from outside, as has been the case in many other Latin American countries.

Multicultural Europe?

Re-interpreting the legacy of imperial conquest, slavery, and immigration restriction has fueled the writing of multicultural histories in the Americas, South Africa, and Australia. But the writing of multicultural history has not been limited to the "new Europes" formed during European empire building in the early-modern era and the nineteenth century. Historically, Europeans ruled their empires and their colonized, multi-ethnic populations from afar and the issue of cultural diversity could be viewed as a probem for colonial administrators. Ethnic nationalism within European nations, by contrast, was often seen as a crucial source of historical unity. Within Europe, ethnic identities were sufficiently intense and the desire for national homogeneity sufficiently developed that linkages between ethnic culture and nation-states seemed almost primordial. Yet even here, where the nation-state was arguably born, revulsion with fascism, a postwar economic boom in western Europe, divisions between communist and democratic Europe, and the formation of a new European "community" have allowed scholars to discover a multi-ethnic past and diverse identities buried within national histories.

The brutal history of Fascism reminded Europeans in particularly poignant ways of the danger in making historical linkages between race and nation even among peoples viewed (from the Americas) as uniformly "white." Yet Germany's ethnic nationalism, with its emphasis on blood and descent as the foundation for citizenship and membership in the nation was widely – although not universally – shared in Europe, even in places that had never embraced Fascism. After the war, communism discouraged expressions of nationalism on one side of the "iron curtain" and the "Berlin wall," while "guest worker" migrations and the gradual construction of a more united Europe raised troubling historical questions about nations, national identities, and citizenship on the other side. Western European social scientists on the left first rejected ethnic nationalism as a form of racism and then called for an exploration of its historical consequences in the lives of immigrant workers.[20]

In Germany, historians subsequently discovered a long national history – reaching back into the nineteenth century – of depending on foreign labor to fuel the national economy yet excluding those laborers from the nation, defined through blood ties among ethnic Germans. Germans in the communist East saw continuities between forced and slave labor programs under Fascism and the huge guest worker migrations to western Germany from southern and Eastern Europe and Turkey in the era after World War II. In the Federal Republic, by contrast, Germans during the 1970s explored the troubling question of whether Germany – which had long viewed itself as a nation of emigrants (to the Americas in the nineteenth century) – should not instead consider itself a "nation of immigrants" like the immigrant societies of the Americas.[21] While often critical of guest worker programs, new histories of postwar Germany focused positively on the country's unions and on state welfare programs that created arenas of equal protection under the law for citizens and immigrant "denizens" (without citizenship) alike. At the same time, scholars working with Dirk Hoerder's Labor Migration project at the University of Bremen moved beyond the traditional themes of German national history. They suggested instead that continuous migrations had shaped "sending" and "receiving" areas in Europe and the Americas alike, and they argued that such migrations challenged modern nationalism in both its civic and ethnic forms.[22]

If Germany could scarcely avoid questions about the linkage of racism and nationalism in its history and in its contemporary denial of full citizenship to "guest workers" and their children, other European nations seemed to avoid these questions with surprising ease. Switzerland, for example, was a self-consciously multi-ethnic nation yet it also remained unapologetically xenophobic in its policies toward immigration and citizenship. Its dependence on foreign labor and its levels of foreign residents had far surpassed those of Germany as early as 1900, but Switzerland produced little multicultural history. Only a few outsiders were willing to tackle the historical task.[23] It is therefore not surprising that the regulations governing Swiss citizenship have remained relatively unchanged and citizenship remains relatively inaccessible to foreign-born workers while opportunities for guest workers and denizens to acquire German citizenship have improved in recent years.

France, of course, had long ago defined its own version of civic nationalism as a form of cultural assimilation. In an interesting twist on Latin American histories of racial democracy and cultural amalgamation, France also insisted that citizenship and the acquisition of French culture eliminated race or ethnicity as sources of identity and difference among its citizens. As the numbers of migrants from France's former empire rose after World War II, however, cultural tensions between the metropolitan French and those of Vietnamese, Algerian, and Caribbean origin were neither invisible nor trivial. Although some French historians have adapted the models of the English-speaking world to explore a multicultural history, and to speak of a French mosaic that tolerates some cultural diversity among immigrants, most defend republican assimilation. In the latter formulation, the expectation of a culturally united and homogeneous French nation emerging from the French melting pot remained firm.[24] As multicultural histories proliferated in the English-speaking world, French intellectuals sometimes responded with horror to the vision of liberal institutions like universities or governmental agencies tolerating, encouraging, and even insisting (through census check-off boxes) that citizens embrace an ethnic or racial identity.

Most of Europe's new multicultural history thus emerged from the economically powerful nations of western Europe that had long drawn migrant labor across European boundaries. But the recognition of migration as an element in national histories, and an exploration of its implications for nation-building, also affected history-writing in the "sending" countries of southern and eastern Europe. Italian historians, for example, increasingly focused on the construction of an imagined Italian community that emerged out of the extreme linguistic and regional diversity that had characterized the peninsula since the collapse of the Roman Empire. Italy's population had also been among the most active participants in both European and American migration systems throughout the century after its political unification. Where Italian historians had, for one hundred years, struggled to create loyalty to a homogeneous, united Italian nation, the new multicultural history broke the nation into a regional mosaic of local communities that served as centers for diasporic networks of migratory "Italians of the world."[25]

By the 1990s, the gradual consolidation of the European Union and the collapse of communism in central and eastern Europe seemed to push the writing of history in somewhat differing directions. Multicultural histories of France, Germany and Italy all argued – if in differing ways – for a recognition of diverse cultural identities within national boundaries and for more emphasis on the significant historical connections (through migration and diplomacy) among European nations. Rather ironically, they promoted pluralist identities at the same time that Europe was being unified from above through new European community economic and political institutions. The collapse of communism, meanwhile, seemed to unleash again the powers of ethnic nationalism as the preferred foundation for nation-building. What harsher symbol could be found of these divergent understandings of nations than the direct military confrontations of Serbian and NATO forces in the Balkans during the last years of the twentieth century?

Multicultural Histories as a New Kind of Nation-building

Because it occurred alongside rising awareness of economic globalization, the final collapse of the European empires, and a new period of major international migration, the writing of multicultural history might be taken for a sign of the declining importance of nation-states in today's world. Many who write multicultural histories do so as critics of their nations and of their nation-states. Some multiculturalists in the US see little political value in an American nation whose historical grounds for unity – herrenvolk democracy – deserve rejection. Many of the works that seek to re-write national histories from a multicultural perspective have also been inspired by post-modernist scholarship on phenomena like postcolonialism, diasporas, and trans-nationalism – historical themes that challenge the significance of nations as the shapers of human identity and human interaction.

Still, it seems likely that most new multicultural histories are actually scholarly efforts to re-imagine the meaning of nations and to describe new grounds for national unity. In the English-speaking world, multicultural histories acknowledge and even celebrate the presence and contributions of those once excluded from the nation, notably racial minorities, in order to include them in a broader narrative of national history. Historians of immigration, for example, have repeatedly argued that foreigners "became American" by acquiring hyphenated ethnic identities along with a national one; in multicultural histories, Native-, African-, Asian- and Latino-Americans also, arguably, find their place in the nation, along with their hyphens. Multicultural histories of the United States, at least, seem to offer to create new grounds for national belonging; they do not always ignore the nation as a category of historical analysis of understanding.

Thus, it should surprise no one to learn that multicultural history has proved more controversial and has generated less revisionist power in those parts of the West (notably France and much of Latin America) where nations had long been imagined as racially or culturally inclusive. The different ways of linking nation-building, racial or cultural unity, and the forms of national government in Latin America (with its frequent interludes of authoritarian regimes) and France (with its tension between republican and more culturally pluralist theories of civic nationalism) surely deserve more comparison than they have received. If comparisons of the United States and South Africa have shed light on the origins and varieties of white supremacy as a form of segregated nation-building, so too comparisons of Argentina and Brazil and France might help us understand the other end of a continuum that stretches through amalgamation to assimilation. These strategies for creating internal unity have also been forms of nation-building which a new multicultural perspective might help us to understand better.

Even the most extensive multicultural literatures – those of the English-speaking world – fail to offer thorough revisions of national histories and sometimes they also ignore sources of national unity that are obvious only to outsiders. As critics have noted, the use of "culture" by multiculturalists in the US is both exceedingly narrow and surprisingly vague. Multicultural histories are almost always histories of discrete racial and ethnic groups. Other powerful markers of culture – notably religion, class, language, region, and gender – may be noted, but they are rarely considered central. Few multicultural histories consider the significance of the multiple components of individual identities, or the fact that race and ethnicity are only two of the many ways that Americans describe themselves. Ethnic groups, like nations, are constructed and imagined communities; they are no more natural than nations and ethnic communities are by no means the only influence on the identities of individual citizens.

Multicultural histories too often simply ignore the persistence of nationalism and national identities in the contemporary world. Many seem to suggest that individual North Americans share little beyond a common legal–political system, the English language, and intense awareness of color distinctions. Multicultural histories can therefore shed little light on the fact that 91 percent of the respondents in a recent US poll agreed that "being an American is a big part of who I am." The economic and global political power of the United States has scarcely diminished as multicultural history has grown in popularity, and national unity has remained a key theme of American political life. To the casual observer from outside, multicultural American nationalism seems no less intense than the unifying nationalism of the French, who insist that citizens choose French culture along with French citizenship.

Brazil, France, and the US have long vied as self-conscious exemplars of differing models of nation-building, and the rise of multicultural history has not eliminated this national competition so much as transformed it. Foreign scholars, especially English speakers, have played an increasing role in describing the national histories of other nations. Is it, for example, problematic that North American scholars have written so much of the multicultural history of Brazil, Argentina or Europe? It is surely an exaggeration to claim that the writing of "hyphenated" multicultural history is an intellectual product of the US, now exported along with hamburgers or liberal enthusiasms for free trade and markets. But scholars in France and Brazil might justifiably complain about cultural "blindspots" when North American racial and cultural categories are used to discuss the multicultural history of their own nations.

It is also worth noting that international perspectives on multicultural histories less frequently travel in the opposite direction. Few historians of the US regularly read histories of their own nation written by Europeans or Latin Americans. Is it because their "English-only" nationalism discourages them from learning the national languages in which they are written? Or do

American scholars ignore foreign historians because their analytical assumptions do not fit into current American conceptions of multicultural history? French criticism of multiculturalism as a potentially racist obsession with descent and ascribed status, and the French preference for individual rather than group rights and for cultural assimilation are surely alternatives worth considering in a country that prides its own republican roots. It is also important to note that inter-marriage, culinary exchange, and other types of blending and cultural amalgamation that are highlighted in Latin American histories deserve a larger place than they have had in multicultural histories of the United States.

Finally, the role of historians as nation-builders, regardless of background, continues to deserve critical scrutiny. Histories that homogenize and those that celebrate diversity, like national histories and comparative or global ones, all carry their own conceptual dangers. Historians who venture abroad to write the histories of other nations often bring fresh insights precisely because they are less emotionally and intellectually influenced by the nationalist scholarly assumptions of the countries to which they belong. For this very reason, however, those who specialize in the histories of nations not their own need to be particularly aware of how the writing of history – its categories, genres and sensibilities – still varies considerably across national borders, and how these differences reflect national self-understanding. In all these respects, the new multicultural histories of nations bear the mark and carry the burden of the special relation of history, nation-building, and nationalism in the West, and a simplistic account of multicultural diversity can be as distorting as a simplistic account of national unity.

NOTES

1 Benedict Anderson, *Imagined Communities: Reflections on the Origin and Spread of Nationalism* (New York: Verso, 1983).
2 Nathan Glazer, *We are All Multiculturalists Now* (Cambridge, MA: Harvard University Press, 1997).
3 See, for example, Louis Wirth, *The Ghetto* (Chicago: University of Chicago Press, 1928).
4 David Morris Potter, *People of Plenty: Economic Abundance and the American Character* (Chicago: University of Chicago Press, 1954).
5 Louis Adamic, *A Nation of Nations* (New York: Harper, 1945); Oscar Handlin, *The Uprooted: The Epic Story of the Great Migration that Made the American People* (Boston: Little, Brown, 2nd edn., 1973, 1951).
6 Gilberto Freyre, *Brazil, an Interpretation* (New York: A. A. Knopf, 1947); José Vasconcelos, *The Cosmic Race: A Bilingual Edition* (Baltimore, MD: Johns Hopkins University Press, 1997); Gino Germani, "Mass Immigration and Mod-

ernization in Argenina," *Studies in Comparative International Development* 2/11 (1966): 165–82.

7 For an early example, that has remained in print in subsequent editions for more than half a century, see John Hope Franklin, *From Slavery to Freedom: A History of American Negroes*, 1st edn., New York: A. A. Knopf, 1947).

8 John E. Bodnar, *The Transplanted: A History of Immigrants in Urban America* (Bloomington: Indiana University Press, 1985); Ronald T. Takaki, *Strangers from a Different Shore: A History of Asian Americans* (Boston: Little, Brown, 1989).

9 David Roediger, *The Wages of Whiteness: Race and the Making of the American Working Class* (London, New York: Verso, 1991); Yen Le Espiritu, *Asian American Panethnicity: Bridging Institutions and Identities* (Philadelphia: Temple University Press, 1992).

10 Arthur M. Schlesinger, Jr., *The Disuniting of America* (New York: Norton, 1992).

11 David A. Hollinger, *Postethnic America: Beyond Multiculturalism* (New York: BasicBooks, 1995).

12 Molefi K. Asante, *The Afrocentric Idea* (Philadelphia: Temple University Press, 1987).

13 Richard J. F. Day, *Multiculturalism and the History of Canadian Diversity* (Toronto: University of Toronto Press, 1999).

14 Stephen Castles et al., *Mistaken Identity: Multiculturalism and the Demise of Nationalism in Australia* (Sydney: Pluto, 1988).

15 Kathleen Paul, *Whitewashing Britain: Race and Citizenship in the Postwar Era* (Ithaca, N.Y.: Cornell University Press, 1997); Robin Cohen, *Frontiers of Identity: The British and the Others* (London, New York: Longman, 1994).

16 See Fernandes, *The Negro in Brazilian Society* in the references and further reading section below. Also useful is Magnus Morner, *Race Mixture in the History of Latin America* (Boston: Little, Brown, 1967); Carl N. Degler, *Neither Black nor White: Slavery and Race Relations in Brazil and the United States* (Madison, WI: University of Wisconsin Press, 1986, 1971); Robert Brent Toplin, *Freedom and Prejudice: The Legacy of Slavery in the United States and Brazil* (Westport, CT: Greenwood Press, 1981).

17 Besides the work of Thomas Skidmore, in the references and further reading section below, see Jeff Lesser, *Negotiating National Identity: Immigrants, Minorities, and the Struggle for Ethnicity in Brazil* (Durham, NC: Duke University Press, 1999).

18 Kim D. Butler, *Freedoms Given, Freedoms Won: Afro-Brazilians in Post-Abolition Sao Paulo and Salvador* (New Brunswick, NJ: Rutgers University Press, 1998); George Reid Andrews, *Blacks and Whites in São Paulo, Brazil, 1888–1988* (Madison: University of Wisconsin Press, 1991).

19 George Reid Andrews, *The Afro-Argentines of Buenos Aires, 1800–1900* (Madison: University of Wisconsin Press, 1980); Samuel L. Baily, *Immigrants in the Land of Promise: Italians in Buenos Aires and New York, 1870–1914* (Ithaca: Cornell University Press, 1999).

20 Stephen Castles and Godula Kosack, *Immigrant Workers and Class Structure in Western Europe* (London and New York: Institute of Race Relations, London, by Oxford University Press, 1973).

21 Klaus J. Bade, *Vom Auswanderungsland zum Einwanderungsland?: Deutschland 1880–1980* (Berlin: Colloquium, 1983).

22 Dirk Hoerder, ed., *Labor Migration in the Atlantic Economies: The European and North American Working Classes During the Period of Industrialization* (Westport, CT: Greenwood Press, 1985).

23 Madelyn Holmes, *Forgotten Migrants: Foreign Workers in Switzerland before World War I* (Rutherford, NJ and London: Fairleigh Dickinson University Press and Associated University Presses, 1988).

24 Besides Nancy Green, "Le 'Melting Pot': Made in America, Produced in France," in the references and further reading section, see Gerard Noiriel, *The French Melting Pot: Immigration, Citizenship, and National Identity* (Minneapolis: University of Minnesota Press, 1996); Donald L. Horowitz and Gerard Noiriel, eds., *Immigrants in Two Democracies: French and American Experience* (New York: New York University Press, 1992).

25 Donna R. Gabaccia, *Italy's Many Diasporas* (London and Seattle: University College of London Press and University of Washington Press, 2000).

REFERENCES AND FURTHER READING

Appiah, Anthony, "The Multiculturalist Misunderstanding," *New York Review of Books*, October 9, 1997, pp. 30–6.

Fernandes, Florestan, *The Negro in Brazilian Society*, New York: Atheneum, 1971.

Fredrickson, George M., *White Supremacy: A Comparative Study in American and South African History*, Oxford: Oxford University Press, 1981.

Fuchs, Lawrence H., *The American Kaleidoscope: Race, Ethnicity, and the Civic Culture*, Middletown, CT: Wesleyan University Press, 1990.

Green, Nancy, "Le 'Melting Pot': Made in America, Produced in France," *Journal of American History* 86/3 (December 1999): 1188–208.

Mann, Arthur, *The One and the Many: Reflections on the American Identity*, Chicago: University of Chicago Press, 1979.

Marx, Anthony W., *Making Race and Nation: A Comparison of South Africa, The United States and Brazil*, Cambridge: Cambridge University Press, 1998.

Skidmore, Thomas E., *Black into White: Race and Nationality in Brazilian Thought*, New York: Oxford University Press, 1974.

Takaki, Ronald, *A Different Mirror: A History of Multicultural America*, Boston: Little, Brown and Company, 1993.

CHAPTER TWENTY-THREE

New Technologies and Historical Knowledge

JAMES M. MURRAY

Nearly twenty years ago members of the history faculty of Stanford University became the more or less willing subjects in an experiment that would have been impossible even a decade before. With sponsorship from computer and software firms, each of them received a brand new IBM personal computer equipped with word processing software (on floppy disks). What made the "Tiro Project" doubly unusual, however, was the systematic instruction each of them received in basic computer operation and wordprocessing (using a program called Wordstar). By all accounts the project was a resounding success; articles in the campus newspaper quoted middle-aged professors, who never thought they would use computers, extolling the new technology. The articles went on to suggest that computers might be the means to at last bridge the gap between the humanities and sciences as portrayed by C. P. Snow, for at last historians and scientists had something to talk about as they plied the buffet table of the Stanford Faculty club.

The topos of the awestruck humanist gratefully embracing computers is at best a half-truth and caricature, whether the setting is Stanford of the early 1980s or any university in the 2000s. For many historians had used computers and recognized their potential value for historical research as early as the 1950s. And in fact the greatest challenge of the Tiro project for a group of mostly junior faculty was to convert their data into IBM compatible format. Thus not only computers but also personal or micro computers were well known to at least a part of the history faculty prior to the project. There was also a self-mocking slyness about the name given to the project itself. Tiro was, of course, Cicero's personal secretary and slave, famous for his skill and credited by legend with the invention of a system of shorthand – Tironian notes. As chief scribe for an important statesman and author, Tiro advanced beyond mere dictation to supervise the editing, copying, and storage of the finished "rolls" containing his master's writings. So influential and indispensable did he become to Cicero, the story goes, that he extorted his freedom in exchange for the return of original and unique manuscripts held hostage. Faced with the destruction of his literary oeuvre, Cicero capitulated, becoming if not the first, surely the most famous early victim of technology.

As technological naifs and veterans, masters and victims, scoffers and evangelists, historians have played many roles as new technologies have rushed into their discipline. But by now no one can deny that technology has changed the way we research, teach, and communicate. This essay therefore addresses the problem of historical change: how profoundly have technological changes altered historical work in recent years, and how profound are the changes yet to come? Navigating perilously along the line between history and prophecy, I will argue that we have entered a revolutionary era in which the very basis of our work as historians is being transformed. Two essential criteria will serve as the bellwethers of change: historians' relationship with sources, and the relationship of professional historians with students, the general public, and each other. Judged according to these measures, the potential for change in the way history is written and distributed is at least as great as that we have witnessed in economic sectors such as retailing and printing, and in other professions such as technical and architectural drafting and the law.

Having made what some may consider a bold statement, I must add that I am not writing as a technological zealot, for like most historians I have adopted what I found useful for my own work as a medieval European historian and ignored the rest. Yet even this modest technological ambition has led me along unimagined paths from a relatively early (1982) microcomputer user, to early use of a portable computer in archival research (1985), "e-mail" (1988), and designer and maintainer of my department's website (1996). I suspect that many other historians could make similar lists of their own progression through the technological cornucopia of the last decades. Skepticism is also in order, for the revolution we will get in historical studies will almost surely not be the one we expect.

As an example, we can look at the recent past in the history of historians and computers. A generation ago some among us predicted a revolution in the use of the main frame computer and its ability to process large data sets fed to it on punched cards amassed by "cliometricians." So euphoric were these early proponents that no less a figure than Emmanuel Le Roy Ladurie predicted that the next generation of historians would be computer programmers or they would not be historians at all. The revolution we have actually experienced, however, came via the single-user "microcomputer" as it used to be called, which captivated historians not because of its number crunching capabilities, but for its ability to process text. In less than two decades department halls have ceased ringing with the rapid-fire of electric typewriters or the more halting pace of hunt-and-peck manuals. In my own department the last hold-out of the typewriter age has retired, and even he had an e-mail address at the end (though he claimed it was his daughter's).

Historians and Their Computers

The numbers speak for themselves. In a recent survey conducted by the American Association for History and Computing, 485 historians from 101 American colleges and universities described their use of computers. Some 93 percent of them reported using a computer in their research; fully 98 percent had a computer in their office; 91 percent had an Internet connection.[1] Thus in less than a generation historians have made the single greatest change in the technology of their day-to-day professional lives since history became a profession based in the university. And a whole range of ancillary changes accompanied the shift to computers. Departments ceased employing the supernumerary secretaries who once typed manuscripts for faculty. The traditional acknowledgement or dedication to the dutiful spouse or secretary (almost always female) who typed and retyped the book manuscript has disappeared. Who now remembers the once ubiquitous advertisements for thesis/dissertation typing at a dollar per page? Taken together, these mark an interesting change in the sociology of the historical profession.

Yet the real explanation for the rapid adoption of computer technology lies in its clear ability to act as a more-or-less transparent writing tool – a "super typewriter" if you will, which solved a host of related problems. With a computer the dissertation writer could make infinite revisions of the most radical kind with little need to retype. By the mid-1980s the price of dissertation typing services and the cost of a basic computer reached something approaching parity, leading many graduate students (the early adopters) to choose computer purchase as the route to writing their dissertations. Other forces were at work as well: with shrinking budgets departments reduced and eliminated support staff, so that in the 1990s most departments had half the number of secretaries as before. The shrinking real value of academic salaries, as well as broader socio-cultural changes, meant that both partners in the household went to work their own jobs outside the home. Thus computers appeared to solve the problems of historical scholarship while at the same time providing a technological cushion to the diminishing financial resources colleges and universities supply to their humanities faculty and to the changing structure of academic families.

Few historians in the late 1980s, however, subscribed to the idea that computers were about to change the profession as they had known it. Most used the computer as a word processor, few employed it to organize data bases or run statistical programs, fewer still learned to program it. But once again a new technology in the guise of the old – electronic mail – found ready acceptance among historians. Usually imitating colleagues in the sciences and social sciences, historians in steadily increasing numbers learned the value of an electronic network known as Arpanet, the ancestor of the Internet. This string of computers gathered together in clusters (nodes) was originally conceived as a communications system that would withstand partial destruction in the event of a nuclear war. Various transfer programs could send and receive messages and files from any computer linked to a node. Historians learned that the machine they had considered a writing appliance was much more. By the mid-1990s software had evolved to the point that it could send and receive large packets of specially encoded data, sufficient to carry both text, sound and pictures, via the Internet, as it was now known. This became the World Wide Web.

No one could have foreseen that a device to replace the typewriter would serve as the bridge into a digital world with wonderful and troubling possibilities. Network communications that bring together the technologies of libraries, archives, professional societies and academic institutions are now challenging and transforming almost every aspect of the historian's work. These changes appeared so sweeping by 1998 that the University of Pennsylvania classicist, James J. O'Donnell, could write (in a typical summary of the situation) that we stood "at a moment when all the conditions of scholarly discourse are about to be upended by the transformation of electronic technologies."[2] But technology may once again be serving as the medium for change and not simply as the cause of change, for it offers solutions, as word processing once did, to preexisting problems and challenges in the research and writing of history.

Computers in Libraries and Archives

Nowhere is this more true than in the libraries of Europe and North America. Of course the invention of the modern research library with its guarantee of public access, its careful organization of books and documents, and its systematic administration by professionally trained librarians both made possible and accompanied the rise of the academic historian. In their role as repositories of both primary and secondary sources, libraries have traditionally served as the "laboratories" of historians, who must use their materials for their research and writing. Perhaps no other institution better symbolizes the triumph of post-Enlightenment ideas about historical scholarship. Yet libraries and library science are in the midst of the most sweeping changes in their history. Ominously for some historians, libraries are restructuring themselves into information "portals" in which providing books and journals is only one of an ever lengthening list of services. And these services are often provided far beyond the walls of the library building itself.

As with the historian's embrace of the computer, the changes in libraries began with computer-based solutions to problems of scale and expense, which led, in turn, to unexpected possibilities. One of the most costly and time-consuming of the librarian's chores was the physical management of tens of thousands, even millions of items in a library's collection. From acquisition, cataloging, shelving, to circulation, the computer database offered the perfect medium for combining the once separate forms of information generated by each step of the process into a standard and readily accessible format. The enormous technical challenges posed by such a task were largely solved in the 1960s and 1970s, and one by one research libraries ceased updating their card catalogues, gradually shifting from a hybrid to a completely electronic library catalogue. Historians were forced to deal with the consequences, which included confronting the question of whether an "electronic" or "virtual" catalogue was really superior to what it replaced. Struggles often occurred between those who wished to destroy the traditional card catalogue and those who insisted on its preservation. Traditionalists were right at first: the initial software was too clumsy and primitive to replace paper cards, neither could it contain the handwritten additions and corrections often added by generations of users.

By the 1990s these shortcomings were overcome, the struggle subsided, and card catalogues are now preserved (if at all) as rare artifacts. The reasons for this go beyond better software, or even cost savings: the electronic catalogue is simply better in every respect. It is accessible from great distances, even from anywhere in the world (a point to which we will return); and as a guide to the library's collection it is much faster, more flexible and more responsive to the will of the researcher than the old paper catalogue entries. For example, electronic technology conveniently allows the searcher to use the two dominant cataloging systems in US libraries, not to mention those of institutions, like Harvard's Widener Library and foreign libraries, which have unique systems of their own. More information is also available electronically since computer catalogues usually give circulation information about a particular book along with its physical location in a main or remote library. Keyword searches also allow users to construct their own topics freeing researchers from traditional organizing principles. In short, the whole value of a library's collection has been greatly enhanced by computer technology because its contents have become more useful to the researcher without the addition of a single volume.

Here again there were unintended consequences. Through the successful development of electronic catalogues, librarians gained skills in other kinds of large-scale databases. The library's computer system seemed like the natural place to offer this information to patrons, so a wide variety of new electronic resources also became available. Most research libraries offer some access to large databases such as Dialog and Lexis/Nexis and to more specialized resources, such as Medline (on-line medical journal abstracts) and MLA Bibliography, which indexes a huge mass of literary scholarship. Such venerable reference works as the *Oxford English Dictionary* and *Encyclopedia Britannica* are also available electronically, and the list is rapidly growing. Yet perhaps the most useful feature of electronic catalogs and databases is their availability on the Internet. Thus since the mid-1990s most historians have had access from their own computers to the on-line catalogues of most of the great library collections of North America and Europe. By seeking to cut costs and increase efficiency the library has in effect transcended itself and become a new kind of global institution.

The other great nineteenth-century institution crucial to the historical profession, the archive, has been less affected by computers, at least until recently. This is largely due to the lack of standardization in archival materials as opposed to the high degree of uniformity in books. The absence of uniform cataloging systems has forced each archive to develop unique strategies or a series of uncoordinated, arbitrary efforts to make sense of its collections. Many of these efforts went horribly wrong: in the State Archives of Bruges, Belgium, for example, an early archivist decided to organize the vast medieval collection by document type – all charters in one collection, cartularies in another, account books somewhere else – thus destroying the institutional context from which the document was created. Nearly every archive has its own story of errors that became a permanent feature of the collection because the resources necessary to correct them have been judged to be too great. But computer technology is supplying a means to correct such shortcomings.

One increasingly popular aid to the researcher is the posting of information about an archives' collections and operation on a World Wide Web site. In many cases such web sites include listings of a depository's holdings and electronic versions of indexes and guides. Such information allows a researcher to prepare a research trip in advance so that wasted time is kept to a minimum. Sometimes the very fact of creating such a site has caused archives to translate collection information directly from handwritten inventories to web postings, effectively bypassing print altogether.[3] Despite the obvious value of these new resources, however, it is the electronic storage of archival documents that holds the greatest promise of fundamental change in the way historians work. But promise is not yet reality.

Certainly the technology exists to provide an electronic facsimile of nearly any kind of paper or parchment record kept in the traditional archive. A digital Magna Carta is already available from the web sites of the Public Record Office, the British Library, and the US National archives. The oldest public record in the English-speaking world, *Domesday Book*, will soon be available in digital facsimile.[4] This is a significant step forward for researchers, because for many years they could consult only a very uneven photographic copy of the book. There are innumerable other projects, both great and small, that have already placed manuscript and archival materials in the digital realm. Sometimes the results are distributed in the form of a CD-ROM by traditional publishers in partnership with the library or archive in which the material resides. Others are available on the World Wide Web, essentially free for the clicking. In these cases, and in many others, national archives are at last real-izing the dream of free access to significant public records for all.

Digitization also offers other far-ranging possibilities of integration and pre-sentation. One striking example is a CD-ROM/DVD project produced by the Library of Congress, "Eyes of the Nation," whose goal is nothing less than presenting the entire history of the United States through documents selected from the library's special collections. Combining text and images, these disks offer vast, thematically organized windows into American history. The mate-rials available run from manuscript letters to books, photographs, and three hours of full-screen video in the DVD version. Themes are as varied as "Enter-tainment," "Transportation," and the "African-American Experience," and each theme is organized chronologically from colonial times to the present day. Part five of the series gives links to the Library of Congress's American Memory Web site, which provides further access to hundreds of thousands of historical documents. In fact, this project is only part of a major drive to make much of the library's contents available online. The Librarian of Congress, James Billington, recently reported that the library's website had three million items of American cultural history already available, and that number would rise to over five million by the end of the year 2000.[5]

Despite the almost dizzying possibilities of having the contents of archives and libraries on line, some troubling issues remain. For example, who decides which archival or library sources are digitized and made available online? It is highly unlikely that all of the vast archival sources of even a single historical period, like the European Middle Ages, could be made available, so choices will have to be made. Whether historians will have a role in making those choices is unclear. And access to archival and library sources has traditionally been only a part of the experience of doing history. Travel to the archives, res-idence there with rounds of lunches and dinners with colleagues, and the very act of living in the city and country of your subject have been an important formative ritual for many historians. If such travel were to cease, would his-torical writing suffer as a result?

Another unexpected aspect of the new technology appears in its ability to create and disseminate new bodies of historical sources outside the traditional institutions of libraries and archives. One notable example is the Survivors of the Shoah Visual History Foundation, which the director Steven Spielberg created in 1994 after producing his film "Schindler's List" because he was determined to collect testimony of survivors and other eyewitnesses of the Holocaust. In a remarkably short time this group has been able to amass more than 50,000 interviews, whose contents fill some 200,000 videotapes. The foundation's goal is to make these digitized testimonies available to the world's libraries, schools and universities, and to anyone with Internet access. As of now, an interactive CD-ROM and three film documentaries have resulted from the project. To give some idea of the immensity of the task, these interviews occupy eighteen times more electronic storage space than the entire printed collection of the Library of Congress.[6]

It is, however, far too easy to become enraptured about these new resources and thereby lose one's critical perspective. For it remains to be seen whether the craft of the historian will be fundamentally changed by the fact that all United States Census data are now available for the price of a CD-ROM or web connection. The novelist Annie Proulx is an eloquent opponent of the new technology: "I rarely use the Internet for research, as I find the process cumbersome and detestable. The information gained is often untrustworthy and couched in execrable prose. It is unpleasant to sit in front of a twitching screen suffering assault by virus, power outage, sluggish searches, system crashes, the lack of direct human discourse, all in an atmosphere of scam and hustle." Before librarians take comfort from her complaints she goes on to add "Nor do I do much library research these days, though once I haunted the stacks. Libraries have changed. They are no longer quiet but rather noisy places where people gather to exchange murder mysteries . . . One stands in line to use computers not a few down for the count, most with smeared and filthy screens, running on creaky software."[7]

Proulx puts her finger on a number of areas of concern in the developing technology of research and its access. She is correct to point out that users are forced to put up with a level of failure and balky performance that would be simply unacceptable (or dangerous) in such things as automobiles and airplanes. She is also quite right to say that traditional libraries and computers coexist uneasily in many places, where too often researchers are unable to use the library's catalog because all the computers are occupied by players of the latest web-based computer game. And she points out that the traditional quiet of the reading room has given way to the noise of the public computer lab, which in too many cases means the quiet-seeking reader of books is driven out. Yet these problems will be solved as technology matures, and as architects and librarians are able to create better spaces to accommodate the differing needs of twenty-first century library users. But her critique of the information available on the Web is not so easily dismissed, for what is offered is too often execrable, untrustworthy and profit-driven.

The commercial nature of many of the databases and other services offered by research libraries has become a concern for many. Where traditionally a book was either owned or not, was available or not – both facts now easily ascertainable by electronic search of the catalogue – the people who now use a research library are dependent on a continuous business relationship with database vendors, who sell access to a database, not its contents. Thus for many of its electronic resources, the library is forced to become a renter rather than an owner of information, with all the attendant changes such status brings with it. Like it or not, researchers are being forced to accept the fact that research materials are increasingly subject to the vagaries of the market in which vendors may come and go. Access to information often depends on business decisions and marketing considerations, all of which are shot through with change and instability. This means in practice that academic libraries may offer only a limited version of the large commercial databases like Lexis/Nexis or Dialog and that services available today may not be so tomorrow. Researchers will no longer be able to count on unlimited free access via their research library. For many historians, long accustomed to the permanence of libraries and archives, this is a worrying trend.

At present most of the vast resources of the World Wide Web do not belong to fee-charging corporations, which is both the Web's strength and its weakness. The Web exists outside the organizing categories of the library on the one hand, and the fee structures and bottom line considerations of the corporation on the other. Thus there is a wealth of information available, though much of it is of dubious value to the historian, for web-based materials also exist largely outside the peer-review process of critique and correction. There have been many calls for historians and historical organizations to create some kind of institution to review and certify web content. One German plan envisions a "History Online" Institute that would maintain six hierarchically organized and linked modules for different types of resources (dictionaries, newspapers, bibliographies, databases, etc.).[8] Some attempts at organizing such websites have already been made. The Labyrinth based at Georgetown University has since 1994 sought to provide "an organizational structure" to the resources in medieval studies offered on the World Wide Web. These efforts have resulted in a sophisticated menu of available resources, from Anglo-Saxon texts to collections of medieval art on line. Equally important in the view of Labyrinth's creators is the model it provides of collaborative effort by a large number of scholars across many disciplines. Labyrinth's success is demonstrated by statistics, which show a doubling of "hits" between January 1997 and April 2000 and a similar doubling in the number of bytes sent and web pages summarized.[9]

Yet the statistics do not remove concerns about such sites. Institutional and financial support is lacking for many of them, and even the fortunate few with university affiliations, like Labyrinth, are not immune from the whims of university budget cutters. Rigorous review of the content of linked sites is also beyond the capacity of most of these projects, though the quality is usually far superior to what can be obtained through a general search of the Web. Nonetheless, no one pretends that such "master sites" offer anything comparable to the peer-reviewed journal or academic press monograph. It may require the efforts and resources of national groups like the American Historical Association to spearhead a systematic project to bring to the Web the same or similar standards it applies to books and films. No matter who undertakes it, "certifying" the Web for scholars is a formidable task.

The Gains and Losses of Computer Technology

To return to the concerns articulated by Annie Proulx, it may well be asked
whether investing time and money in digitization and scholarly websites is
worth the cost. After all it is abundantly clear that in most academic libraries
money for technology has come from budgets once used to purchase books
and other print materials. Even the most avid technophilic scholar cannot
welcome a new information regime that results in fewer books on his or her
library's shelves. Is there a clear benefit and advantage to be gained by historians in the shift to electronic media?

James J. O'Donnell, who is both a Classics professor and Vice Provost for
Information Systems and Computing at the University of Pennsylvania, delivers a clear and eloquent affirmation of new technologies in his book, *Avatars
of the Word: From Papyrus to Cyberspace*. O'Donnell argues that many aspects
of the World Wide Web are reminiscent of earlier transitions in scholarly technology, particularly those between papyrus roll and parchment codex, and
manuscript book and printed book. In each of those cases, scholars invented
ways of dealing with the "instability" of the text, i.e., the fact that before printing the precise content of discourse could never be fixed. Subtle and effective
technologies like canon tables for manuscripts of the bible, as well as ancestors of the index, concordance, page number, and running head all had their
origins in the manuscript culture of the Middle Ages. The medium of print
added the possibility of relative standardization and with it the illusion of permanence enshrined in copyright. The mid-twentieth century academic library
marked the culmination of mass-produced texts, protected by copyright, and
organized and indexed by powerful and ingenious systems. Yet the Web shows
that there is nothing fixed and permanent about the world of print, any more
than there was in the papyrus roll of Antiquity.

In accepting the essential arbitrariness of our "knowledge systems," O'Donnell sees potential liberation from the structural conformity such systems have
imposed on scholars for centuries. Established categories and interpretations
are the principal villains for O'Donnell. And the scholarly monograph is to
him the logical result, with its "linearity" of single author narrative subsum-
ing and resting upon a rich loam of other linear texts. It is increasingly the
scholarly equivalent of the dinosaur, he alleges, and changes in the publishing
industry have made it an endangered species. What he conceives as a replacement for the monograph is a shift from the single author to the diversity of
many authors and many levels of commentary and interpretation; it will be the
reader rather than the footnote-dropping author who summons up links and
connections across cyberspace in pursuit of the subject. This new heuristic,
according to O'Donnell, abandons the fiction that truth is singular, that any
book can be "definitive," or that categories such as the biography can fully

capture the complexity of even a single human life. His example is Augustine, one of the most richly ambiguous figures in Western History, whose biography has been written by master historians such as Peter Brown, but whose life as he presented it in his *Confessions* remains elusive. No matter how skillful a biographer might be, the biography as a genre cannot overcome a life's elusiveness because of its reliance on the single narrative line to capture its subject. O'Donnell asks us to imagine a biography of Augustine composed in cyberspace, able to display any of the five million words he wrote and to navigate through and around them by drawing on centuries of commentary and scholarship instantly. This could allow tentative and experimental lines of interpretation, more playful than the ponderous seriousness of traditional publication, which could then be critiqued and commented on by others. Subversive of traditional categories and disciplines, O'Donnell believes that this "online Augustine creates a space that belongs more nearly to Augustine, that facilitates navigation more powerfully than any print archive can do, and that encourages systematic and comprehensive questions that generate results from the whole range of a huge oeuvre."[10]

This new genre is thus a peculiar hybrid of complete information (all Augustine's oeuvre and commentary at a keystroke) leading to an incomplete result (a biographical "thread" that might exist only for a moment). Yet does the average reader really desire more information and less coherence? For if the biographer abandons the role of interpreter in favor of that of set designer, will that space, that stage, really "belong" to the historical Augustine? Or will it just be another artificial construction, with a new set of barriers to historical understanding?

Even O'Donnell does not predict the rapid disappearance of the monograph, let alone the book, even if libraries are buying fewer of them. But his vision of a new monograph suggests that innovative future books will not occupy the space between two covers. Given the intense experimentation around the so-called electronic book, there is much debate about the form and structure of books in the future. This question will not directly affect historians in the near term, but it is certain that all the traditional means of scholarly communication will have to adapt to a new environment. This kind of change has already occurred with the adoption of e-mail as a means of accomplishing what a letter once did; and the ability to send articles and book chapters via attached word processing files enables writers to circulate their work from computer to computer before publication.

Internet Sites and the Historian

Computer to computer communication among historians has also developed via the Internet. A new forum for scholars has taken shape around the H-Net site hosted by Michigan State University. Organized as an electronic cooperative, H-Net seeks to sponsor and organize ". . . a diverse readership dedicated to friendly, productive, scholarly communications."[11] These efforts have evolved along several paths, one of the most interesting of which is the rise of discussion lists organized around a particular theme or historical specialty. By 1999 there were more than a hundred such lists with over 60,000 subscribers in some 90 countries. Each network is reminiscent of a scholarly journal with a board of editors, which includes a general editor who is the chief gatekeeper. But unlike a journal the goal of each "list" is to promote an egalitarian "exchange of ideas" that breaks down traditional barriers and hierarchies. Each electronic message is received and edited for content by the editorial board before it is distributed to the list and posted on the list's website or archive. In an interim report on the progress of H-Net, its director, Mark Kornbluh, reported on some of the interesting developments this new form of communication has brought. One important trend, for example, is the large number of subscribers who are not professional historians, but part of a larger educated public interested in history. Kornbluh sees H-Net as a way to reconnect academic scholars with this wider public as well as with institutions like historical societies and state humanities councils.[12]

Two networks deserve special mention for the increasingly central role they have come to play in important areas of academic life. The first is the H-Net's Job Guide that provides a searchable listing of jobs in the Humanities and Social Sciences. With weekly updates, this electronic guide has become important to both departments and job seekers in a remarkably short time. The second resource offered by H-Net also demonstrates the ability of the Internet to overcome limitations of traditional scholarly media, in this case with the electronic publication of book reviews. H-Net Reviews follows the methods and standards of scholarly journals in finding experts to review books in their area of historical expertise. But the fact that such reviews are distributed via e-mail and/or network lists results in a much shorter time between publication and review, and it gives the opportunity for longer reviews of books. The difference can be dramatic, with electronic reviews often appearing within months of a book's publication and allowing the reviewer two or three times the word count of traditional print journals. Moreover, archived reviews are easily searchable across a number of search categories. The number of reviews distributed by this means has grown rapidly, doubling from 500 to 1,000 annually between 1996 and 1998.[13]

The fact that H-Net plans to expand into online journals and has begun developing an interdisciplinary journal to utilize the Web's multimedia and text linking capabilities is a clear sign that scholarly journals are also feeling the effects of the new technologies. The professional journal of course was one of the very earliest creations and creators of history as a profession. Its purpose was to stake a claim to a distinctive occupational identity by publishing articles and reviews that set standards of rigor and accuracy for all historians. It also served the purpose of bundling together information on current directions in one or a variety of fields, with the goal of both informing subscribers and influencing the course of future research. Over decades, some historical journals have acquired a cachet akin to a trademark, so that readers turn to their pages for what they consider to be the best and most authoritative work in that field. It is precisely these functions that electronic publication threatens to assume. As Christopher L. Tomlins has written: "Scholarly journals that do not begin changing now in ways that respond creatively to the online environment will no doubt still be around in ten or fifteen years. But their capacity to perform their key disseminating and authorizing functions efficiently and usefully will be significantly impaired, and their audience will by then be rapidly wasting away. They will have become a fringe technology, a curiosity. They will no longer be in a position to add value to professional discourse."[14]

Tomlins believes that traditional print journals and the electronic newcomers are entering a period of "parallelism and convergence," with the creation of electronic offshoots of print journals on the one hand, and the continuation by both media of the journal's role "in enhancing and authorizing intellectual communication."[15] This may mean that electronic journals operate very much like their paper colleagues, with an established editorial process from peer review through copy editing. It might be that in the future print journals would elect to publish their book reviews online in order to meet the challenge of the electronic reviews and to streamline what everyone admits is an unwieldy process. There are a vast number of other possible combinations and variations on both traditional and new categories, which will no doubt be explored in the future. The disappearance of the print scholarly journal in the short or medium term is highly unlikely, but even such skeptics as Michael Grossberg, editor of the *American Historical Review*, have now thrown in their lot with the new technology. In fact both the American Historical Association and the Organization of American Historians have joined together to form the "History Cooperative" website, which offers full text versions of recent issues of both organization's journals.[16]

Of perhaps greater future concern to historians than the survival of print journals is the question of how journals will be stored and distributed. In recent years private "media" companies, Wolters Kluwer in particular, have through purchase and merger taken control of the publication and distribution of a large number of print journals. Both Kluwer and its merger partner Reed Elsevier have in the past been accused of using a monopoly position to inflate the price of science journals, as well as striking special deals with specific customers. In 1997, for example, the consortium of Ohio university and college libraries (OhioLink) reached agreement with Reed Elsevier to supply electronic versions of 1,000 research journals at a cost estimated to be one-seventh of the price of subscriptions to the print versions of those journals.[17] The not-for-profit JSTOR project has set out to archive electronically and sell access to back issues (usually five years old and older) of a large number of prominent history journals. This organization, funded through the Andrew W. Mellon foundation and subscribers, is itself a curious entity, with a central office in New York, NY, and electronic infrastructure shared among Princeton University, the University of Michigan and the University of Manchester in the UK. Its database gives historians full-text access with electronic searching capability through nearly seventy years of the medieval journal, *Speculum*, for example.[18] Yet there are dangers in consolidation and electronic distribution as well. Kluwer controls not only a vast number of journals, but also Lexis/Nexis, the huge database and data software company, and future takeovers and mergers might well result in further corporate concentration or control of scholarly information. The availability of electronic versions of print journals, both current and past, has also brought into question the need for print "duplicates." Some libraries are moving bound journals to storage as a result, or negotiating discounts, as did OhioLink, for electronic versions of print journals with the clear intent that many member libraries would not receive a hard copy.

While academic journals have the oldest claim to the role of communicator and inculcator of professional values and information, the monograph has been for the last half century the chief vehicle of prestige and professional advancement for the academic historian. Over the last two generations, this form of historical writing has come to shape most scholarly discourse, so that Ph.D. dissertations have become preliminary drafts of an eventual monograph (itself a *sine qua non* for promotion and tenure), and journal articles more-or-less finished versions of book chapters. All the while that professional historians were building careers around the monograph, the economic ground was shifting under their feet. Changes in publishing policies, library acquisition budgets, journal prices and other ancillary areas have resulted in distressingly familiar statistics such as the 60 percent decline in standing-order sales of monographs to academic libraries. This fact alone has caused many university presses to entirely reorient their publishing efforts away from the monograph and into more lucrative areas. It is simply no longer possible to publish an academic book outside a narrow range of "hot" subject areas with an American publisher. As so often in the short history of computers and historians, the new technology is being called upon to solve an economic and intellectual problem.

The most intriguing and promising experimental solution to the monograph crisis is the American Historical Association's Gutenberg-E program. With the support of grants from the Andrew W. Mellon foundation, and under the leadership of Robert Darnton, this initiative combines traditional aspects of the academic fellowship, university press publication and book prize by offering fellowships to six recent recipients of the Ph.D. so that they can convert their dissertations into "genuine electronic books." The awards are made after review and ranking by an expert jury of historians, and the finished products will receive the imprimatur of the Columbia University Press. The competition is not free and open to all, but alternated among "hard to publish" fields such as Africa, colonial Latin America and South Asia in the 1999 competion; Europe before 1800 in the 2000 version; and diplomatic and military history "not primarily of the United States" in 2001.[19]

What the product will look (and sound) like as it evolves is as yet unclear, although publicity releases insist it will be a "true e-book." Robert Darnton envisions this as "a layered electronic palimpsest" allowing different readers to find what they are seeking through the hyperlinked text of the whole rather than provide a single narrative line of the traditional monograph. In describing his own electronic book project, a "multidimensional exploration of the publishing industry in the Age of Enlightenment," Darnton is striving for a monograph of many voices "organized in levels of increasing complexity, so that at its apex it can be read by undergraduates and at its base it can communicate original research to specialists."[20] An electronic version of Darnton's presidential address to the American Historical Assocation gives an idea of these new possibilities. To recapture this "early Internet," the social world of eighteenth-century Paris, there are links to maps of Paris showing important cafés, and there are linked sound files with recordings of popular songs of the time. Others among the first group of Gutenberg-e fellows have less ambitious goals for their e-books. Most plan to include maps and other visual aids; some plan also to have audio resources; others are frankly unsure if the dissertation form can be translated in such a way so as to preserve the essential argument and conclusion of the original study. The experience of William G. Thomas and his "Valley of the Shadow Project" is not reassuring on this score. In this large web-based project providing huge quantities of text and visual information in an attempt to document the Civil War experiences of the populations of a southern and northern county, its organizers have found it impossible to maintain a single, critical argument capable of being sustained across the gigabytes of data.[21] It is quite possible that writers of electronic books will have less and less in common with authors of traditional scholarly monographs. Traditional scholarly books will persist for some time, albeit as James J. O'Donnell predicts, "[in] the way the leather bound edition of the classics now survives, not so much to be read but to make a statement about the book and the owner of the book."[22] This may very well be true, but it is not yet clear what bundle of electronic technology will replace the monograph and whether historians of the present and future will accept it as an authoritative means to publish their research. The Gutenberg-e experiment may well succeed in one of its goals, that being "to change attitudes of academics toward e-books. By making most (sic) of the new media, the program may also contribute to a new conception of the book itself as a vehicle of knowledge."[23] Nowhere is the road ahead hazier than in this aspect of scholarly publishing.

A Computerized Future for Historical Scholarship?

From its beginnings the modern historical profession has rested upon a set of institutions that were largely defined and developed in the course of the nineteenth century. The archive, research library, museum, university, professional society were in turn dependent on technology and a willingness to invest in the production of what some have called social or cultural capital. These institutions and investments have produced the phenomenal growth of historical knowledge through the organization of scholarly meetings and the publication of journals and books, which in turn established norms and standards of scholarship and behavior in the profession. By the late twentieth century, however, the foundations of the historical profession were increasingly called into question by budget cutting and by the struggle to find and hold a new public audience. Technological change is thus as much a symptom as a cause of many of the changes history as a discipline is experiencing.

I have sought in this essay to avoid prophecy and apocalyptism, as I have sought to limit my focus to the crucial issues of how historians will interact with their sources, with each other and with their public (outside the classroom). It is, I believe, in these essentially social processes that one can see the greatest impact of new information technologies. We have already traveled an appreciable distance along the road of change in less than a generation. Where once computers were rare, they are now ubiquitous; where once only archaeologists had "sites" now many historians have them too, albeit of the "web" variety; and a growing number of historians now compose web pages as well as text intended for journals and books. A certain "amphibiousness" is now expected of all historians, professional and amateur alike, as they move between different media or audiences, and we can only expect the challenges of producing for both new and traditional media to grow in the near future.

We cannot predict what forms these challenges will take. The recent past of startling developments like the Internet, and the new capabilities of personal computers to manipulate images and sound – even moving images – as easily as text must caution us against believing that the pace of technological change will slow down. This is particularly true in the institutions that historians have traditionally relied upon for research sources, financial support, and employment. There is no question that the academic library is rapidly becoming an information portal in cyberspace, providing access to information it does not "own" in the traditional sense, to users far distant from its physical location. Universities are in many cases following their libraries by offering "distance" learning as a replacement or supplement to residential programs. Scholarly publishing is searching for a role and presence both in print and in cyberspace, either through creating a parallel "electronic" version of their print offerings, or by seeking to create new kinds of "Web" scholarship as envisioned by Darnton and O'Donnell or as yet undreamed of. In all these cases change is likely to be evolutionary, leaving intact the familiar print journal, academic monograph and professional society. How quickly these traditions are forced to the margins by economic and technological change remains to be seen.

Meanwhile, hints about the historian's future world are becoming visible today. The success of websites created by historians suggests that a much broader audience might be attracted via the Web than through textbook, article or monograph. Professional and amateur historians of the future may well use this new medium to gain a more central place for themselves in the public discussion and understanding of the past. This connection to the public, however, may come at the cost of losing the security of the professional historian's traditional mooring place – the university – especially given the permanent shortage of faculty positions. Advanced skills in organizing and criticizing large amounts of information may give increasing numbers of historians employment as "Information Officers" or "Knowledge Managers" in corporate settings. One example of such changes can be seen in the career of Brook Manville, who holds a Ph.D. in Classics and Ancient History from Yale University and who left a teaching position at Northwestern University to enter business. After stints as an analyst and writer, he was hired by the business consultancy firm, McKinsey and Co., where he invented the position of Director of Knowledge Management. During his time at McKinsey, Manville was featured in a book by the management guru, Tom Peters, who called him McKinsey's "secret weapon" in the company's quest to capture and use the accumulated experience of its consultants. His system harnessed the corporate archives as source and repository of ideas, set up "practice" centers enlisting teams of consultants around a particular specialty to pool knowledge, and coordinated a rigorous review of the written results of consultants' experiences in order to identify "core" knowledge. He then made certain that this "core" was readily available to consultants and clients in both printed and electronic form, with careful attention to a writing style that would be accessible to the intended audience. Manville's conclusion from this experience, as quoted by Peters, is illuminating: "Knowledge is not the technical accumulation of information . . . The crucial factors are the format . . . credibility . . . zippiness and instant availability."[24] Clearly this is doing history by another name, though the emphasis on "zippiness" and "instant availability" may sound alien to traditional historians. In any event, more historians may be employed outside the academy in the future, and no historian may be able to rest comfortably in a stable and linear career free of the job changing turbulence of the rest of the economy.

Many will find much to fear in all this. There are still fundamental questions that are unresolved, including how technology will change teaching, which I have left out of this essay. Fear is a natural response to certain change; yet on balance I think there is much more reason to be optimistic, even excited, rather than afraid of the technological prospects of the twenty-first century. Historians will certainly have a different relationship with their sources and with their colleagues, and they will probably communicate the results of their research in different ways. That is all in the nature of things, and in any event how could a profession whose subject is the ineluctability of change over time expect to be an exception?

NOTES

1   Dennis A. Trinkle, "Computers and the Practice of History: Where are We? Where are We Headed?" *Perspectives* 37/2 (February 1999): 31.
2   James J. O'Donnell, *Avatars of the Word: From Papyrus to Cyberspace* (Cambridge, MA: Harvard University Press, 1998), p. 133.
3   Some examples are the sophisticated web site of the Netherlands Royal archives (http://www.archiefnet.nl/); the Archives nationales of France (http://www.archivesdefrance.culture.gouv.fr/CHAN/CHANmain.htm), of Britain (http://www.pro.gov.uk), and the United States (http://www.nara.gov).
4   See the "Web" exhibition at http://learningcurve.pro.gov.uk/millennium/.
5   *New York Times*, April 24, 2000; The Library of Congress's American Memory Site is at http://memory.loc.gov/; the National Archives also sponsor a web site designed to bring primary documents into the classroom. It is at http://www.nara.gov/education/teaching/teaching.html.
6   Information about the project is available at http://www.vhf.org/. A good introduction with interviews was published in *The Wall Street Journal*, March 22, 1999.
7   *New York Times*, May 10, 1999.
8   Andreas Ohrmund/Paul Tidemann. *Internet für Historiker. Eine praxisorientierte Einführung* (Darmstadt, 1999), p. 167.
9   These numbers are available at http://www.georgetown.edu/labyrinth/stats/.
10 O'Donnell, *Avatars of the Word*, p. 136.
11 The H-net homepage is http://h-net2.msu.edu/.
12 Mark Lawrence Kornbluh, "H-Net: Humanities and Social Sciences OnLine," *Perspectives* 37/2 (February 1999): 6.
13 Kornbluh, *Perspectives*, p. 48.
14 Christopher L. Tomlins, *Wave of the Present: The Scholarly Journal on the Edge of the Internet*, ACLS occasional paper, No. 43 (1990), 5.
15 Tomlins, *Wave*, p. 12.

16 The site is at http://www.historycooperative.org/.
17 OhioLink is at http://www.ohiolink.edu/.
18 JSTOR is at http://www.jstor.org/jstor/.
19 The program is fully described at http://www.theaha.org/prizes/gutenberg/.
20 *Perspectives* 38/5 (May 2000): 7. Robert Darnton's articles on the intersection of his own work and the internet are the multimedia, "An Early Information Society: News and Media in Eighteenth-century Paris," *American Historical Review* 105/1 (2000): 1–35 and an electronic version at http://www.indiana.edu/~ahr/darnton/. A slightly abridged version appeared as "Paris: The Early Internet," in the *New York Review of Books*, June 29, 2000.
21 William G. Thomas, "Fax Me Everything You Have on the Civil War! A Look at Web Audiences in the Valley of the Shadow Project," *Perspectives* 37/2 (February 1999): 36–37.
22 O'Donnell, *Avatars*, p. 59; and see his Web page at http://ccat.sas.upenn.edu/jod/jod.html.
23 http://www.theaha.org/prizes/gutenberg/
24 Thomas J. Peters, *Liberation Management: necessary disorganization for the nanosecond nineties* (New York: A. A. Knopf, 1992), pp. 389–90.

REFERENCES AND FURTHER READING

Darnton, Robert, "An Early Information Society: News and Media in Eighteenth-Century Paris," *American Historical Review* 105/1 (2000): 1–35, and at http://www.indiana.edu/~ahr/darnton.
Gershenfeld, Neil A., *When Things Start to Think*, New York: Henry Holt, 1999.
Greenstein, Daniel I., *A Historian's Guide to Computing*, New York: Oxford University Press, 1994.
Higgs, Edward, *History and Electronic Artefacts*, Oxford: Clarendon Press; New York: Oxford University Press, 1998.
Kilgour, Frederick G., *The Evolution of the Book*, New York: Oxford University Press, 1998.
Lanham, Richard A., *The Electronic Word: Democracy, Technology, and the Arts*, Chicago: University of Chicago Press, 1993.
O'Donnell, James J., *Avatars of the Word: From Papyrus to Cyberspace*, Cambridge, MA: Harvard University Press, 1998.
Trinkle, Dennis A., *The History Highway 2000: A Guide to Internet Resources*, Armonk, NY: M.E. Sharpe, 2000.

CHAPTER TWENTY-FOUR

The Visual Media and Historical Knowledge

ROBERT A. ROSENSTONE

The impulse to tell the past in moving images on a screen no doubt long precedes the invention of the motion picture. Less than four years after the first public screening in Paris in December, 1896 by the Lumière brothers of films made on their new *cinematograph*, their countryman, George Méliès, was staging recent historical scenes such as *The Dreyfus Affair* for the camera. Within a decade, films set in the past – *The Assassination of the Duc of Guise* (1908) from France, *The Last Days of Pompeii* (1908) and *The Capture of Rome* (1905) from Italy, or *Uncle Tom's Cabin* (1903) from the United States – were common. In countries as diverse as Japan, Russia, England, and Denmark, some of the earliest dramatic films (often based upon stage plays) involved the depiction of historical events and characters. Long before cinema reached its twentieth birthday, the "historical" was a regular part of screen fare.

The real question for those who care about history is whether such telling of the past, or any telling of the past on the screen counts as "historical thinking" or contributes to "historical understanding." One could easily imagine a *Companion to Historical Thought* that would wholly ignore the visual media, but such a volume would be short sighted for doing so. For now, at the beginning of the twenty-first century, it must be clear to even the most academic of historians that the visual media have become (perhaps) the chief conveyor of public history, that for every person who reads a book on a historical topic about which a film has been made (such as *Gandhi*, 1982; *The Return of Martin Guerre*, 1983; *Born on the Fourth of July*, 1989; *Schindler's List*, 1993; *Saving Private Ryan*, 1998; *The Patriot*, 2000), many millions of people are likely to encounter that same past on the screen. Rather than dismissing such works – as many professional historians and journalists do – as mere "fiction" or "entertainment," or lamenting their obvious "inaccuracies," we who care about historical consciousness would do better to investigate exactly how films work to create a historical world. This means focusing on their rules of engagement with the traces of the past, and investigating the codes and conventions by which they bring history to the screen.

In order to do so, some background is in order, as are some analytical distinctions. The early dramatic "historicals" were not, it is clear, very serious about the kinds of questions that concern historians. Rather than attempting to understand or explain events or movements or people, they were romances, "costume dramas" such as *Gone With the Wind* (1940), that used (and misused) the past as a mere setting for tales of adventure and love. Not only has this kind of "historical" been part of every national cinema, it has created a tradition, or genre, that continues up to this day. Yet alongside these costume dramas there has grown another sort of historical film, one that does not hesitate to pose serious questions of and make serious interpretations about the meaning of the past. Without contesting questions of precedence or insisting on a precise lineage, let me suggest that among the first of these, certainly in the United States, was David Wark Griffith's *Birth of a Nation* (1915).

Today one must be cautious in writing of this film because it is so overtly racist, so overflowing with vicious stereotypes of African Americans as savage, uneducated, and uncultured. Yet its depiction of the Civil War and Reconstruction, its exaltation of the Ku Klux Klan as heroes in a race war, and its dreadful stereotypes, are reflections of the major historical interpretations of the era in which it was produced – not just the beliefs of the citizen in the street but the wisdom of the most powerful school of American historians of that era. At the time the film was made, former historian Woodrow Wilson happened to be sitting in the White House, and on February 18, 1915, *Birth of a Nation* was screened in the Presidential mansion. A Southerner by birth, the President was deeply moved by the film and his response to it – quoted secondhand but accepted by historians as more or less authentic – both suggests something about the prevailing historical wisdom and proved prophetic for the future role of the historical film: "It's like writing history with Lightning. And my only regret is that it is all so terribly true."

A decade after Griffith's morally and politically regressive masterpiece, Russian filmmaker Sergei Eisenstein began to use the historical film to provide the fledgling Soviet Union with its own history and foundation myths – the two notions being in Russia, as in all countries, closely intertwined. In an effort to create a new and revolutionary theory and practice of filmmaking for a new and revolutionary regime, Eisenstein brilliantly utilized montage to construct epic works that promoted the twin-edged theme of the masses entering history and history entering the masses, works that feature no heroes or even individual characters, save for the few who (as in a written narrative history) rise out of the crowd for a moment to articulate an idea or symbolize an event. The first of these films, *Battleship Potemkin* (1925), leaned a long way towards myth as it took a minor incident from the Revolution of 1905, a mutiny on a Black Sea battleship, and turned it into a stunning metaphor to show how the proletariat can overturn oppression and make a revolution. Three years later, *October* (1928) – for all its invented interludes, such as the storming of the Winter Palace – stayed close to the details of the so-called Ten Days of the Bolshevik Revolution, even as it downplayed the contribution of both Lenin and his party. Though some of its tropes might be unusual in a historical work – humor, repetition, visual metaphor, the poetry of movement – *October* provided an overall interpretation that can still stack up against those argued by the major historians of the revolution.

The same revolution also provided the topic for what is probably the first of the important historical documentaries, Esfir Shub's compilation film, *The Fall of the Romanov Dynasty* (1927). Desiring to depict the birth of the new regime in which she lived, Shub painstakingly exhumed and catalogued the extensive home movies of Czar Nicolas, then intercut sequences of royal boating parties, croquet matches, and religious rituals with actuality (newsreel) footage of farm labor, factories, politicians, cavalry on parade, soldiers marching, artillery firing, and revolutionary street demonstrations. Emphasizing these images were inter-titles – a close shot of a munitions assembly line followed by: "The hands of workers preparing the death of their brothers," a comment that can be interpreted as either propagandistic or historical, but is really both at the same time.

Taken together, Griffith, Shub, and Eisenstein may be considered the originators of the three types of arguably serious historical films that have been produced ever since: the mainstream drama (and its longer sibling the television miniseries or docudrama), the compilation documentary, and the experimental or innovative history. In *Birth of a Nation*, Griffith created what we might call the "standard" work of history on film, the "realistic" (melo) drama that depicts the plight of heroes, heroines and villains caught up in the sweep of huge historical events, men and women whose stories show both the impact of such events on individual lives and, through the figure we know as synechdoche, serve to exemplify larger historical themes – in this case how Northern carpetbaggers manipulated ignorant ex-slaves to oppress and exploit the conquered South, which was happily saved from destruction by the bravery of the Ku Klux Klan. Shub is equally "realistic," editing together footage of actual historical moments to create a sense of the past "as it really was," or at least as moments looked through the lens of a camera from a particular point of view. Eisenstein, by contrast, produced the first of what we might call "experimental" or "innovative" works of history on film. *October* makes no attempt at realism, the pretense that the screen is a direct window onto a past reality. On the contrary, through its refusal to focus on individuals, its radical editing (four times as many cuts as in the standard film of the time), and its overt visual metaphors (a screen full of raised sickles represents the peasantry; turning wheels mean a motorcycle brigade; a statue being torn down indicates the fall of the Czar; the same statue reassembling itself suggests the Provisional

Government has taken over the role of Czar), *October* clearly reveals that it is constructing a particular vision of the past.

With their varying approaches to putting history on the screen, each of these types of film makes somewhat different assumptions about historical reality, about what is important for us to know of the past. These assumptions do not change with the improving technology of the medium itself. Adding spoken dialogue and sound effects, moving from black and white to color film, enlarging and widening the screen, introducing surround sound, digitalizing the image or shrinking it to fit the size of a television monitor in a living room – none of these changes does much if anything to alter the kind of historical thinking we encounter in the visual media. The real differences lie between the three kinds of historical films. All insist, as they must, on the primacy of the image, but each utilizes images in a different way to create historical meaning.

The dramatic feature film, directed by the descendants of Griffith, has been and continues to be, in terms of audience and influence, the most important form of history in the visual media. Everywhere in the world, movies mean dramatic feature films, with the documentary consigned to a marginal status and the innovative film hardly recognized at all, except among small circles of devotees. This pattern certainly holds true for the "historical." Dramatic features such as *Schindler's List, Born on the Fourth of July, The Return of Martin Guerre, Gandhi, Saving Private Ryan, Lily Marlene* (1980), *The Night of the Shooting Stars* (1983), *Underground* (1998) are the kinds of film that reach a wide audience and sometimes become the focus of public debate about history, a debate that often swirls around the issue of whether or not the film got the facts right. As I shall soon argue, the accuracy of fact is hardly the first or even most important question to ask about the kind of historical thinking that takes place on the screen.

Whether the mainstream drama focuses on documented people or creates fictional characters and sets them amidst some important event or movement (most films contain both actual and invented characters), the historical thinking involved is much the same: individuals (one, two, or a small group) are at the forefront of the historical process. Through their eyes and lives and, usually, loves, we see strikes, invasions, revolutions, dictatorships, ethnic conflict, scientific experiments, legal battles, political movements, holocausts. But we do more than see: we feel as well. Using image, music, and sound effect along with the spoken (and shouted, whispered, hummed, and cooed) word, the dramatic film aims directly at the emotions. It doesn't simply provide an image of the past, it wants you to feel strongly about that image – specifically, about the characters involved in the historical situations that it depicts. Portraying the world in the present tense, the dramatic feature plunges you into the midst of history, attempting to destroy the distance between you and the past and to obliterate – at least while you are watching – your ability to think about what you are seeing. Film does more than want to teach the lesson that history hurts; it wants you, the viewer, to experience the hurt (and pleasures) of the past.

The major way we experience – or imagine we experience – the past on the screen is obviously through our eye. We see bodies, faces, landscapes, buildings, animals, tools, implements, weapons, clothing, furniture, all the material objects that belong to a culture at a given historical period, objects that are used and misused, ignored and cherished, objects that sometimes can help to define livelihoods, identities, and destinies. Such objects, which the camera demands in order to make a scene look "real," and which written history can easily and usually does ignore, are part of the texture and the factuality of the world on film. What in written history Roland Barthes once called "reality effects," and dismissed as mere notations, achieve on the screen a certain, important "thingness." Because they tell us much about the people, processes, and times, "reality effects" in film become facts under description, important elements in the creation of historical meaning.

The desire to elicit strong, immediate emotion and the emphasis on visual, even tactile reality, are no doubt the practices that most clearly distinguish the historical film from academic history in our time. By focusing on the experience of individuals or small groups, film may situate itself closer to biography or microhistory or popular narrative history than to traditional narrative, and while each of these genres has occasionally been criticized as not sufficiently "historical" by some of the professoriat, each has also won enough supporters to qualify as an accepted genre that makes some contribution to our understanding of the past. Other aspects of the dramatic film seem much closer to the common practice of historians. Like the academic, the filmmaker tells a story with a beginning, a middle, and an end, and a strong moral flavor. Like the academic, the filmmaker tells a story almost always embedded in a progressive view of the past, and this is true even with such unlikely subjects as slavery, the Holocaust, or the mass atrocities of the Khmer Rouge. Like the academic, the filmmaker can maintain such a viewpoint only through the very act of telling the past: whatever humanity has lost – runs the implicit message – is now redeemed by the creation of this work, by the witnessing of the historical wrongs that this film allows us to share.

The documentary film, considered as a mode of historical understanding, shares a great deal with the dramatic feature: it tells a linear and moral story, often deals (especially in recent years) with large topics through the experience of a small group of participants, spends a good deal of time on the thingness of objects, and aims to stir the emotions not only through the selection, framing, and juxtaposition of still and moving images, but also by employing a soundtrack overflowing with language, sound effects, and music of the era being depicted. Unlike the dramatic film, the majority of its images are not staged for the camera, but are gathered from museums and from photo and film archives – the exception being the Talking Heads, contemporary interviews with participants in the historical events or experts, often professors of history, whose words are used to give shape to and create the broader meaning of the past.

The claim of the documentary is that it somehow gives us direct access to history. That its historical images, through their indexical relationship to people, landscapes, and objects, can provide an unmediated experience of the past – certainly more direct than the created past of the feature film. But this is no more than a mystification. Except in its contemporary interviews, the documentary, unlike the dramatic feature, speaks not in the present tense but in a specifically visual tense we can dub "nostalgia," a tense whose emotional appeal can pull in a huge audience, such as that which followed Ken Burns' PBS series, *The Civil War*. Old photos and actuality footage, and clips from old feature films – by their original aesthetic, their deterioration over the years, and their reminder of what once was or wasn't there, all come bathed in a warm feeling about how times have changed, how much we have gained, how much we have lost. The people in those photos and film clips did not find – as we do – each other's hair or clothing styles quaint, or the furniture they sit on, the buildings they front, the tools and weapons they hold, old fashioned or outmoded. What such images can never do is bring a direct experience of history, for the intervening years intrude too much upon the viewer's consciousness.

The experimental or innovative historical film constitutes a baggy category, one that contains a wide variety of theories, ideologies, and aesthetic approaches with both potential and real impact upon historical thought. These are largely works of opposition, consciously created to contest the seamless stories of heroes and victims that make up the mainstream feature and the standard documentary. They are, at the same time, part of a search for a new vocabulary in which to render the past on the screen, an effort to make history (depending upon the film) more complex, interrogative, and self conscious, a matter of tough, even unanswerable questions rather than of slick stories. The best of these films propose new strategies for dealing with the traces of the past, strategies that point towards new forms of historical thought, forms that need not be limited to the screen, but might, with necessary alterations due to the medium, be carried back to the printed page.

So diverse and hidden (since few are popular) are these kinds of films, that here I can do no more than point to a few and suggest how they attempt to rethink history on the screen. Eisenstein has had a few heirs, filmmakers (mostly from the Third World) who create dramatic features which place the collective or the masses rather than the individual at the center of the historical process. Brazil's Carlos Diegues does this and then something even more radical in *Quilombo* (1984), a history of Palmyra, a long-lived seventeenth-century runaway slave society, which is portrayed in song and dance (samba) by actors costumed as if partaking in Carnival. This attack on a "realistic" portrayal of historical events has been pursued by other filmmakers – Ousmane Sembene in *Ceddo* (1977), a highly stylized story of religious and tribal upheaval in Senegal; Luis Valdes in *Zoot Suit* (1980), which uses song and dance and a mythical central character, El Pachuco, the spirit of the Barrio, to portray Anglo-Mexican tensions and conflict in World War Two Los Angeles; Alex Cox, in his anachronism-laden (Mercedes automobiles, helicopters, and computer terminals in the 1850s) black comedy, *Walker* (1987). Other critiques of the "period look" of film have come in documentaries – Claude Lanzmann's *Shoah* (1985), a history of the Holocaust that contains no images from the 1940s, or Hans Jurgen Syberberg's *Hitler, a Film from Germany* (1977), which uses puppets, sets, historical objects, actors, and back-projection to create the Third Reich on what is overtly a sound stage.

Such staples of film as the dramatic story and the heightening of emotion have also been called into question. In a series of consciously dedramatized works – among them *The Age of Iron* (1964), *The Rise of Louis XIV* (1966), and *The Age of the Medici* (1972) – Roberto Rossellini uses non-actors to haltingly deliver lines which are far closer in form to lectures than dialogue, and lets the "reality effect" of sumptuous costumes and settings carry the argument for his highly materialist interpretation of the past. History as a single story with a clear (moral) conclusion can also be contested. In *Far From Poland* (1984), a work that mixes documentary and drama, director Jill Godmilow presents a history of the Solidarity Movement through competing voices and images that refuse to coalesce into a single story or meaning. Using a similar mixture of genres, Trinh T. Min-ha, in *Surname Viet Given Name Nam* (1989) dispenses with linear story in favor of incident, pastiche, rumination; the very form of the film is historically unsettling, a kind of theme and variation that is signaled in the opening sequence, a dance in which a group of women combine and recombine in patterns that repeat and vary in endless combinations.

The works of Godmilow and Trinh, along with Syberberg's *Hitler* (and a number of other films I have examined elsewhere) properly belong to a small but growing body of films about the past which, more than almost anything done on the printed page, would properly fit into a category labeled Post-modern History – at least as defined by theorists of the postmodern.[1] These are histories which do some or all of the following: foreground their own construction; tell the past self-reflexively and from a multiplicity of viewpoints; forsake normal story development, or problematize the stories they recount; utilize humor, parody, and absurdist images as modes of presenting the past; refuse to insist on a coherent or single meaning of events; indulge in fragmentary or poetic knowledge; and never forget that the present moment is the site of all past representation. By using such offbeat tropes and techniques, these films issue a sharp challenge to both the practices of the mainstream drama and documentary and the traditional claims of empirical history – a challenge parallel to that issued by post-structuralist theorists, only here the challenge is embodied (or envisioned) in works which combine both a new theory and a practice of history.

Filmmakers create films, not theories about film, let alone theories about history. (Which means it is to their finished productions rather than their stated intentions that we usually must go to understand the historical thinking we find on the screen.) To this general rule, there are some exceptions. Eisenstein, a major theorist, does occasionally invoke the Marxist dialectic in reference to history, but only in passing; clearly more interested in notions of montage or what he called "intellectual" cinema, the Russian never does any sustained explication of the relationship between his historical works and the past events they evoke or describe. Roberto Rossellini, whose twelve plus films about the past may be the most sustained historical oeuvre of any director, provides contradictory ideas about his portrayal of history without ever bothering to resolve them. On the one hand, he invokes notions of the didactic film, one which can objectively describe the past and create a direct, unmediated vison; on the other, he insists that his works are based upon a moral vision, without admitting that such a moral vision inevitably creates a point of view which cannot be objective. More recent directors concerned with history have overtly admitted its subjective components. Rainer Werner Fassbinder, director in the seventies of several films dealing with the Third Reich and its legacy, did not hesitate to explain, "we make a particular film about a particular time from our point of view." Oliver Stone, who in half a dozen films has charted aspects of American society from the Vietnam war into the eighties, initially claimed to be creating history but then retreated under attacks from the press, particularly about *JFK* (1991) and *Nixon* (1998), to an extreme subjectivist position, asking: "What is history? Some people say it's a bunch of gossip made up by soldiers who passed it around a campfire."[2]

For any sustained thinking about history and film, one must turn to the work of a mere handful of professional historians, since all but a few academics have considered the topic outside the pale of their interests or duties. Most historians would like to turn Oliver Stone's words against historical films – and see them as a bunch of (mostly untrue) stories that directors put upon the screen. The distaste for film has been possible because for most of the twentieth century historians saw their own work as an empirical undertaking, a human science that properly made certain kinds of truth claims about the past, claims that could hardly be matched by the costume dramas, swashbucklers, and romances that were regularly turned out by studios around the world. So rarely did historians comment upon the topic that Robert Novick's book, *That Noble Dream*, a lengthy survey of American historical practice in the twentieth century, contains but a single reference to motion pictures. In a 1935 letter that is highly revealing about professional attitudes, Louis

Gottschalk of the University of Chicago wrote the president of Metro-Goldwyn-Mayer: "If the cinema art is going to draw its subjects so generously from history, it owes to its patrons and its own higher ideals to achieve greater accuracy. No picture of a historical nature ought to be offered to the public until a reputable historian has had a chance to criticize and revise it."[3]

Factors other than the quality of films kept historians from considering motion pictures a serious way of understanding the past. Clearly the visual media fell on the wrong side of the once enormous wall that separated high culture and low (or mass) culture, which meant that films could not be taken seriously until that wall collapsed – as it began to do in the sixties. More important: for at least the first half of the century academics were secure in the belief that their kind of knowledge of past politics, economic, social and cultural life was "true" knowledge, and certain that the culture at large accepted the truths about the past that professional historians could provide. But after mid century, as the claims of traditional history and its Euro-centered metanarratives increasingly began to be called into question from a variety of disciplines and quarters – by feminists, ethnic minorities, postcolonial theorists, anthropologists, narratologists, philosophers of history, deconstructionists, and postmodernists – a climate developed that allowed academics to look more closely at the relationship between film and historical knowledge.

Sometime in the 1970s, the number of historians interested in film reached enough of a critical mass to begin producing conferences, essays, journals, and books. The first of the latter was *The Historian and Film* (1976), a collection of essays by (mostly) British historians which focused upon questions of newsreel, movies in the classroom, and how to evaluate films as historical evidence. Conferences on history and film in 1977 and 1979 at the University of Bielefeld's Center for Interdisciplinary Research drew scholars from Germany, Denmark, France, the Netherlands, the UK, and the US, and led indirectly to a volume entitled *Feature Films as History* (1981). Here the emphasis was largely on how the analysis of dramatic features, particularly groups of them, could lead to an understanding of particular ideologies or climates of opinion (anti-Semitism, liberalism, the Popular Front, national consciousness in Germany and France in the 1920s). A single essay – "*Battleship Potemkin* – Film and Reality" by D. J. Wenden – wrestled with the question of how a film might work to interpret, even illuminate something in the past. In trying to weigh Eisenstein's account of the ship's mutiny against written data and evidence, the author suggests – in what may be the first instance of a historian understanding that film must necessarily create a different history from what we find on the page – that rather than creating a literal reality, the filmmaker made "brilliant use of the ship's revolt as a symbol for the whole revolutionary effort of the Russian people in 1905" (p. 40).

Two French historians in the same period moved more directly towards the notion of film as historical discourse. Marc Ferro, whose occasional pieces on the topic were gathered into *Cinema et histoire* (1977), advances the thesis that film, even the dramatic feature, can like any cultural artifact through careful analysis be made to reveal a great deal about the period in which it is made.[4] Only in the book's final essay does Ferro face a more problematic question: can there be "a filmic writing of history" (pp. 158–64)? At first he seems doubtful. Filmmakers, he argues, do no more than incorporate either a national or oppositional ideology into their works, which means the historical film is usually no more than a transcription "of a vision of history which has been conceived by others" (p. 161). But then he allows for possible exceptions. Some directors in some works (he names Russia's Andrei Tarkovsky, Senegal's Ousmane Sembene, Germany's Hans Jurgen Syberberg, Italy's Luchino Visconti) are strong enough to separate themselves from ideological forces and create an interpretation of history which is not a reconstitution of someone else's vison, but "really an original contribution to the understanding of past phenomena and their relation to the present" (p. 163).

Pierre Sorlin, who devotes all of *The Film in History* (1980) to the question of how the dramatic feature "restages the past," never goes as far as Ferro in accepting history on the screen. The closest he comes is with regard to *October*, first dismissed as "propaganda," then resuscitated as not propaganda but as a view of the revolution independent of Bolshevik ideology. Sorlin insists that "Historical films are all fictional," and explains: "even if they are based on records, they have to reconstruct in a purely imaginary way the greater part of what they show" (p. 21). Suspicious of film's simplicity, he writes off the historical film as a "dissertation about history which does not," as good historians should, "question its subject." Yet he does detail how such films fit into a larger discourse; specifically, how works about the French Revolution, the Italian Risorgimento, the American Civil War, and the Russian Revolution are like written histories insofar as they must be judged not against some current knowledge of their topic but with regard to the prevailing historical understanding at the time.

The last two decades of the century saw an eruption of interest in history and film. Historians, journalists, and the general public in the United States and Europe became embroiled in the controversies surrounding such works as *JFK* and *Schindler's List* and their attendant issues: does a grand conspiracy lie at the heart of American government, and what is the morality of using a single good German and those he saved to represent the horrors of the Holocaust? Within academia, courses on history and film sprouted up in many universities, panels and conferences on the visual media and history became commonplace, and not only were two journals wholly devoted to the topic (*History and Film*, US; *Film Historia*, Spain), but most major historical publications began to run reviews of or articles on motion pictures – and this includes journals in the US, France, Italy, the UK, Spain, Australia. Yet most of this activity consisted of no more than a kind of ad hoc analysis of individual films. When it came to a more theoretical understanding of how the screen might be used to tell the past, almost nobody went beyond the brief hints made by Wenden, Ferro, and Sorlin.

What kept and continues to keep historians from fully coming to grips with film as history is our traditional reflex: empiricism. However much we might enjoy a dramatic feature set in the past, the specialist of the period represented is bound at many points to cry "foul" – and to argue that a particular scene, a character, a moment, a bit of dialogue, or a whole sequence of events is not an accurate reflection of the sources, but only an invention. Such judgments are not mistaken. Settings, actors, costumes, gestures, dialogue, music, and other elements on the screen – all of necessity, as Sorlin pointed out twenty years ago – partake of a good deal of the imaginary. Certainly the screen provides no clear window onto a vanished past; the best it can do is to provide a construction of proximate realities to what once was. Here we face the larger point, the more fundamental issue raised but never fully explored by Sorlin: if the bulk of what historical films show on the screen is fiction, how can we consider them to be History?

Maybe one should not insist upon the word – at least not in its capitalized form. The best and more serious kind of historical film does "history" only insofar as it attempts to make meaning out of something that has occurred in the past. Like written history, it utilizes traces of that past, but its rules of engagement with them are structured by the demands of the medium and the practices it has evolved – which means that its claims will be far different from those of history on the page. To give but a few examples: The basic element of the medium, the camera, is a greedy mechanism which, in order to create a world, must show more precise details – arrangements of furniture, the way tools are handled, stances or gestures, the exact locations of warriors in a landscape or strikers before a factory – than historical research could ever fully provide. The dramatic structure, which means the need for plausible characters and psychic tension, and the limitations on screen time, ensures that dialogue will have to be created, events and characters condensed, compressed, altered – even invented. However counter intuitive it may seem, what we see on the screen is – and in this sense precisely like written history – not a window onto the past but a construction of a simulated past, not a literal reality but a metaphoric one.

The notion that written History works as metaphor has been powerfully argued by more than one theorist in recent years. Even those who do not accept the position that metaphor is central to historical understanding have come to realize that works of history cannot literally recreate the past but can only enfold its trace elements into a verbal construction, a text that attempts to explain vanished people, events, moments, and movements to us in the present. Doing so involves much more than the literal. Even the most scholarly histories are, in the words of Robert Berkhofer, "more structures of interpretation than the structures of factuality they purport to be." Indeed, the literary job of historical realism, the only mode of writing Historians recognize as legitimate – and one to which most filmmakers slavishly adhere – is to "make the structure of interpretation appear to be (the same as) the structure of factuality."[5] What this suggests is that both written history and films invoke the authenticity (or reality) that comes from using those traces, that documentary evidence we call "facts," and then go on to employ a literary or filmic vocabulary to create "history."

Whatever they share in terms of interpretive structure, the relationship of data to discourse, historical books and films divide on one crucial issue: invention. The most radical theorists may talk of the fictive qualities of all narrative, but however metaphoric, historical narrative is always built on blocks of verifiable data. The dramatic film, by contrast (and here is where it parts company most sharply with the documentary and gets closest to the historical novel), indulges in the invention of characters, dialogue, incidents, and events; indeed, some historical films are made up of wholly invented characters placed into a documented setting or situation. This practice of invention may be enough to remove from the dramatic film the word "history," but certainly not the ideas of historical "thinking" or "understanding." Not if by that phrase we mean coming to grips with the issues from the past that trouble and challenge us in the present – questions of social change, gender relations, individual and group identity, class, ethnicity, war, colonialism, revolution, ideology, and nationalism.

It is just these kinds of major social and cultural issues that are explored in what one might call "the new historical," a film with roots in the past – Eisenstein's *October* or Carl Dreyer's *Joan of Arc* (1928) are among the forbears – which has become increasingly common in the last thirty years. The breakup of the Hollywood studio system, the creation of film capabilities in newly-independent Third World countries, the activism of the sixties, the collapse of the Soviet Bloc, the creation of lightweight, less expensive film and video equipment, the vast expansion of television channels and cable systems – such factors no doubt underlie, but don't exactly explain, the flourishing of this genre of dramatic motion pictures (which has a counterpart in the proliferation of documentaries, sponsored by television channels) that downplay or eschew traditional romance and attempt to deal seriously with the meaning of the past.

The term, "new historical," may seem to imply a movement, but it would be more accurately described as a tendency, and a diffuse one at that. Individual examples of such films have been produced just about everywhere movies are made, but they also tend to appear in two sorts of clusters: as either several works by a single director (Andrzej Wajda, Poland; Oliver Stone, US; Theo Angelopolous, Greece; Ousemane Sembene, Senegal) or several films in a single country in a brief period of time (the New German Cinema or the Cinema Nuovo of Brazil, both in the seventies; Cuban film in the sixties). Attempts to pinpoint the cause of such clusters can be no more than speculation. Financial and business considerations must certainly be involved, yet such movies tend to appear at moments when nations are undergoing some kind of cultural or political stress, change or upheaval – the attempt to come to grips with the trauma of Vietnam (Oliver Stone); the corruption and internal conflicts that presaged the end of Communism (Wajda); terrorism, repression, and the legacy of the Third Reich (New German Cinema); the breakup of a nation (the cinema of the former Yugoslavia in the nineties); the desire to find (or create) a heritage for a postcolonial country (Sembene, Cinema Nuovo, Australia in the eighties); or to justify a revolutionary change of regimes (Cuba).

Clusters of films (and those listed above are suggestive rather than comprehensive) do more than point to the recurrent vitality of the historical. To investigate them is to see the roles such works can play in historical thinking. One way to conceptualize this is to say that films Vision, Contest, and Revision History – and while individual works may lean more towards one of these tasks, any film probably undertakes all three. To *Vision History* is, obviously, to provide some idea of how events and people of the past looked (and sounded), not as literal, not through a clear window, but as (on the page) a construction, an approximation, but one that yet can reveal things with an experiential quality alien to the word: say great physical exertion, the fear, courage, and movement of men on battlefields full of weapons, explosions, bombs (*Saving Private Ryan*). To *Contest History* is to question the metanarratives that structure historical knowledge or the smaller historical truths and unquestioned, received notions, to show, say, the ambiguity of the benefits of modernization (Satyajit Ray, *The Home and the World*, 1984), or to undercut the Italian myth of widespread resistance to fascism (the Taviani brothers, *Night of the Shooting Stars*), or to question the personnel and motivations that make up the accepted history of the founding of a modern state (Shohei Imamura, *Eijanaika*, 1981). To *Revision History* is to contest that naive "realism" which, on the screen or page, tries to show the world "as it is," and instead to use expressive modes of representation that expand the vocabulary of the historian and match aesthetics to moral judgment – by utilizing surrealism to express the surreality of the Stalin purges (Tengiz Abuladze, *Repentance*, 1986); black comedy for the exasperating recurrence of American invasions of Nicaragua (Alex Cox, *Walker*); post-modern pastiche for the disjuncture between image and ideology in the Third Reich (Alexander Kluge, *Die Patriotin*, 1979).

This Visioning, Contesting, and Revisioning all take place in motion pictures which are, we must never forget, largely works of fiction. But admitting the role of fiction does not mean to admit that such films can say anything at all or make up anything they wish about the past. At least not if such works wish to be seen as a serious contribution to our understanding. For we who take the past seriously to consider a film a "historical" rather than a "costume drama," it must – no matter what its inventions or style or subject matter – engage the discourse of history, the already existing body of writing, arguments, debates, memories, images, moral positions and – as important – data surrounding the topic with which it deals. The film's metaphors, compressions, alterations and inventions must grow out of that discourse and add something to it. The true historical film does not, any more than the written word, aim to deny or even alter a larger sense of history – its aim rather is to evoke and comment upon the past by using the tools and practices that the medium has developed.

For the traditionalist historian, such an argument may smack of sophistry, perhaps even dimwittedness. But to those historians with faces set towards the future, it may seem more like common sense. Even if the film could deliver traditional data as well as the written word (which it cannot, as a practical matter, do very well), what would be the point? We already have books. To attend the cinema, or to watch a television screen, is to undergo an experience far different from that of reading words on a page. That difference lies at the heart of the historical film. However we define, measure, and analyze that difference – and none of this has yet been undertaken very convincingly, perhaps because of the great slippage involved in translating a multimedia experience into linear words – we can at least understand that the experience is different enough to let us think that ultimately the historical film takes us back to the most basic questions: What do we want from the past? Why do we want to know it? What else might we want to know that we don't already know? To learn by example? To feel (or think we feel) what others (may have) felt in given situations? To experience, if only distantly, what others experienced in war, revolution, political crisis, times of troubles and times of plenty? Or perhaps, as in the history once practiced by the Greeks, to be inspired into ethical or aesthetic contemplation of the human condition?

It may seem counterintuitive, even downright insulting to suggest the film as a new form of historical thinking. Yet in this increasingly visual age, we must be prepared to at least entertain such a notion. For visual thinking of the past, metaphor and symbol may become far more important than amassing data or creating a logical argument. Theorist Frank Ankersmit has already argued that even with regard to written history, "the metaphorical dimension . . . is more powerful than the literal or factual dimensions," and has broached the notion that in the future we need to focus less on the past itself than on the language we use for speaking about the past.[6] This at least suggests that we might judge historians less by their data and more by the aptness of their metaphors. In a world of film, these would be visual metaphors – or perhaps something we can simply call Vision. Here is a major point shared by both films and books –

each is more than the sum of its parts. A written work is based upon data, but the totality of its words transcend the data and launch into a realm of moral argument and metaphor. Film also utilizes data, if in a rather more casual way, before it too launches into the same realm. Vision, metaphor, overall argument or moral is precisely the point at which film and written history come the closest to each other. The details of the past are necessary, interesting, even fascinating, but what we really want to know is how to think about them, what they mean. The printed page and film are both ready to tell us.

Perhaps a century from now, when people are writing a future companion to historical thought, history as we today practice it on the page will have come to seem a quaint or antiquarian endeavor – as we now think of chronicle. Or maybe it will be seen as religious endeavor, practiced by a priesthood who cares about explicating the truth of sacred texts. It is possible that the historiographers of such a world, one in which the visual media ever more dominate realities, will find themselves returning to study the strategies of historical representation that are found in the kinds of films mentioned in this essay, strategies painfully developed during the first century of motion pictures, a period when a goodly number of filmmakers struggled, consciously, semiconsciously, and (yes) unconsciously, to create upon the screen a new version of historical thought and understanding.

NOTES

1 See my essays, "Revisioning History: Contemporary Filmmakers and the Construction of the Past," and "Film and the Beginnings of Postmodern History," both in *Visions of the Past: The Challenge of Film to Our Idea of History* (Cambridge, MA: Harvard University Press, 1995), pp. 169–224.

2 Quoted in Oliver Stone, "Stone on Stone's Image," in Robert Brent Toplin, editor, *Oliver Stone's USA: Film, History, and Controversy* (Lawrence, KS: University of Kansas, 2000), p. 47. Stone in his essay does not disavow the quotation but makes it clear he is not happy with its use: "I was speaking to a reporter who printed that sentence as a snappy sound bite. It certainly makes me look like I disdain historians, which I do not . . ."

3 Quoted in Peter Novick, *That Noble Dream: The "Objectivity Question" and the American Historical Profession* (New York: Cambridge University Press, 1988), p. 194.

4 Ferro's notion of film as cultural artifact that can be used, like novels or paintings, to illuminate historical topics or periods, was one of the first works in what is by now something between a tendency and a sub field of history. At least the last twenty-five years has seen a proliferation of essays and books in which historians and scholars in cinema studies, utilizing the approach of cultural history, focus upon the relationship between particular bodies of film and some historically significant

subject. Good examples include (but are not limited to) Marsha Kinder, *Blood Cinema: The Reconstruction of National Identity in Spain* (Berkeley, CA: University of California Press, 1993), Eric Rentschler, *The Ministry of Illusion: Nazi Cinema and its Afterlife* (Cambridge, MA: Harvard University, 1996); Heide Fehrenbach, *Cinema in Democratizing Germany: Reconstructing National Identity After Hitler* (Chapel Hill, NC: University of North Carolina Press, 1995); Angela Dalle Vache, *The Body in the Mirror: Shapes of History in Italian Cinema* (Princeton, NJ: Princeton University Press, 1992).

5   Robert Berkhofer, *Beyond the Great Story: History as Text and Discourse* (Cambridge, MA: Harvard University Press, 1995), p. 60.

6   Frank Ankersmit, "Historiography and Postmodernism," *History and Tropology: The Rise and Fall of Metaphor* (Berkeley, CA: University of California Press, 1994).

REFERENCES AND FURTHER READING

Burgoyne, Robert, *Film Nation: Hollywood Looks at U.S. History*, Minneapolis: University of Minnesota Press, 1997.

Dallet, Sylvie, ed., *Guerres revolutionnaires: histoire and cinema*, Paris: l'Harmattan, 1984.

Davis, Natalie, *Slaves on the Screen*, Cambridge, MA: Harvard University Press, 2000.

Dolan, Sean B., ed., *Telling the Story: The Media, The Public, and American History*, Boston: New England Foundation for the Humanities, 1994.

Ferro, Marc, *Cinema et histoire*, Paris: Edition Denoel, 1977, translated by Naomi Green as *Cinema and History*, Detroit: Wayne State University Press, 1988.

Grindon, Leger, *Shadows on the Past: Studies in the Historical Fiction Film*, Philadelphia: Temple University Press, 1994.

Kaes, Anton, *From Hitler to Heimat: The Return of History as Film*, Cambridge, MA: Harvard University Press, 1989.

Rosenstone, Robert A., ed., *Revisioning History: Film and the Construction of a New Past*, Princeton, NJ: Princeton University Press, 1995.

Rosenstone, Robert A., *Visions of the Past: The Challenge of Film to Our Idea of History*, Cambridge, MA: Harvard University Press, 1995.

Short, K. R. M., ed., *Feature Films as History*, Knoxville: University of Tennessee Press, 1981.

Sobchack, Vivian, ed., *The Persistence of History: Cinema, Television, and the Modern Event*, New York and London: Routledge, 1996.

Sorlin, Pierre, *The Film in History: Restaging the Past*, Totowa, NJ: Barnes and Noble, 1980.

Consolidated Bibliography

Abrams, M. H., *Natural Supernaturalism: Tradition and Revolution in Romantic Literature*, New York, 1971.

Abu-Lughod, Janet L., *Before European Hegemony: The World System, A.D. 1250–1350*, New York, 1989.

Adamson, Walter L., *Marx and the Disillusionment of Marxism*, Berkeley, 1985.

Adas, Michael, *Machines as the Measure of Men: Science, Technology, and Ideologies of Western Dominance*, Ithaca, 1989.

AHR Forum *American Historical Review* 99/5 (December 1994), pp. 1475–1645. Includes contribution of Gyan Prakash, "Subaltern Studies as Postcolonial Criticism," pp. 1475–90; Florencia E. Mallon, "The Promise and Dilemma of Subaltern Studies: Perspectives from Latin American History," pp. 1491–515; "Conflict and Connection: Rethinking Colonial African History," pp. 1516–45.

Amin, Shahid, *Event, Metaphor, Memory: Chauri Chaura, 1922–1992*, Berkeley, 1995.

Anderson, Benedict R. O'G, *Imagined Communities: Reflections on the Origin and Spread of Nationalism*, 2nd edn., London and New York, 1991.

Appiah, Anthony, "The Multiculturalist Misunderstanding," *New York Review of Books*, October 9, 1997, pp. 30–6.

Ariès, Philippe, *Le Temps de l'Histoire*, Monaco, 1954.

Arrian, *History of Alexander and Indica*, 2 vols. Translated, with introduction and notes by P. A. Brunt, Cambridge, MA, 1976 and 1983.

Auerbach, Erich, *Mimesis The Representation of Reality in Western Literature*, trans. Willard Trask, Princeton, 1953.

Bancroft, George, *History of the United States of America, from the Discovery of the Continent*, six volumes, centenary edition, Boston, 1879.

Bann, Stephen, *The Clothing of Clio: A Study of the Representation of History in Nineteenth-Century Britain and France*, Cambridge, 1984.

Barlow, Tani E., ed., *Formation of Colonial Modernity in East Asia*, Durham, 1997.

Barnes, Harry Elmer, *A History of Historical Writing*, 2nd edn., New York, 1962.

Becker, Carl, *The Heavenly City of the Eighteenth-Century Philosophers*, New Haven, 1932.

Beer, Jeannette M. A., *Narrative Conventions of Truth in the Middle Ages*, Geneva, 1981.

Beiser, Frederick, *Enlightenment, Revolution, and Romanticism: The Genesis of Modern German Political Thought*, Cambridge, MA, 1992.

Bentley, Jerry H., *Old World Encounters: Cross-Cultural Contacts and Exchanges in Pre-Modern Times*, New York, 1993.

——, *Shapes of World History in Twentieth-Century Scholarship*, Washington, DC, 1996.

Berding, Helmut, "Leopold von Ranke," in *Deutsche Historiker*, ed. Hans-Ulrich Wehler, vol. 1, Göttingen, 1971, pp. 7–24.

Berkowitz, Peter, *Nietzsche: The Ethics of an Immoralist*, Cambridge, MA and London, 1995.

Berlin, Isaiah, *Karl Marx: His Life and Environment*, 3rd edn., New York, 1963.

——, *Vico and Herder: Two Studies in the History of Ideas*, London, 1976.

Best, Geoffrey, *War and Law since 1945*, Oxford, 1994.

Biagioli, Mario, ed., *The Science Studies Reader*, New York, 1999.

Blenkinsopp, J., *The Pentateuch: An Introduction to the First Five Books of the Bible*, New York, 1992.

Boedeker, D. (ed.), "Herodotus and the Invention of History," *Arethusa*, 20 (1987).

Borowski, Harry, ed., *The Harmon Memorial Lectures in Military History, 1959–1987*, Washington, DC, 1988.

Bosworth, A. B., *From Arrian to Alexander. Studies in Historical Interpretation*, Oxford, 1988.

Bourdieu, Pierre, *Distinction: A Social Critique of the Judgement of Taste*, trans. R. Nice, Cambridge, MA, 1984.

——, *Practical Reason: On the Theory of Action*, Stanford, 1998.

Brandt, William J., *The Shape of Medieval History Studies in Modes of Perception*, New Haven and London, 1966.

Breisach, Ernest, *Historiography Ancient, Medieval and Modern*, Chicago and London, 1983.

——, *Historiography. Ancient. Medieval. Modern*, Chicago, 1983.

Brothers, Leslie, *Friday's Footprint: How Society Shapes the Human Mind*, New York, 1997.

Brown, Patricia Fortini, *Venice and Antiquity: The Venetian Sense of the Past*. New Haven, 1996.

Browning, Christopher, *Ordinary Men: Reserve Police Battalion 101 and the Final Solution in Poland*, New York, 1993.

Brunt, P. A., "Ciecero and Historiography," in *Philias charin: Miscellanea di studi classici in onore di Eugenio Manni*, vol. 1 (Rome, 1980), pp. 311–40; reprinted in *Studies in Greek History and Thought*, Oxford, 1993, pp. 181–209.

Burgoyne, Robert, *Film Nation: Hollywood Looks at U.S. History*, Minneapolis, 1997.

Burke, Peter, *The Renaissance Sense of the Past*. New York, 1969.

——, *The French Historical Revolution. The Annales School 1929–1989*, London, 1990.

——, *The French Historical Revolution: The Annales School, 1929–1989*, Cambridge, 1990.

Butterfield, Herbert, *Man on His Past. The Study of the History of Historical Scholarship*, Cambridge, 1955.

Canary, Robert H., *George Bancroft*, New York, 1974.

Cassirer, Ernst, *The Philosophy of the Enlightenment*. Trans. Koelln and Pettegrove. Princeton, 1932.

Certeau, Michel de, *The Writing of History*, New York, 1988.

Chakrabarty, Dipesh, *Provincializing Europe*, Princeton, 2000.

Chatterjee, Partha, *Nationalist Thought and the Colonial World: A Derivative Discourse*, London, 1986.

Chaudhuri, K. N., *Trade and Civilisation in the Indian Ocean: An Economic History from the Rise of Islam to 1750*, Cambridge, 1985.

Cochrane, Eric, *Historians and Historiography in the Italian Renaissance*, Chicago, 1981.

Coddington, Edwin B., *The Gettysburgh Campaign: A Study in Command*, New York, 1968.

Coffman, Edward M., *The Old Army: A Portrait of the American Army in Peacetime, 1784–1898*, New York, 1988.

Cohen, G. A., *Karl Marx's Theory of History: A Defence*, Princeton, 1978.

Colby, R., G. N. Cantor, J. R. R. Christy, and M. J. S. Hodge, eds., *Companion to the History of Modern Science*, London, 1990.

Comaroff, Jean and John L. Comaroff, *Of Revelation and Revolution: Christianity, Colonialism, and Consciousness in South Africa*, Chicago, 1991.

——, *Of Revelation and Revolution: The Dialectics of Modernity on a South African Frontier*, Chicago, 1997.

Condorcet, *Selected Writings*. Edited by Keith Michael Baker. Indianapolis, 1976.

Connor, W. R., *Thucydides*, Princeton, 1984.

Cott, Nancy, *The Bonds of Womanhood: Women's Sphere in New England, 1780–1835*, New Haven, 1977.

Cronon, William, *Changes in the Land: Indians, Colonists, and the Ecology of New England*, New York, 1983.

——, ed., *Uncommon Ground: Toward Reinventing Nature*, New York, 1995.

Crosby, Alfred W., *The Columbian Exchange: Biological and Cultural Consequences of 1492*, Westport, 1972.

——, *Ecological Imperialism: The Biological Expansion of Europe, 900–1900*, New York, 1986.

——, *Ecological Imperialism: The Biological Expansion of Europe, 900–1900*, Cambridge, 1986.

Crossley, Ceri, *French Historians and Romanticism: Thierry, Guizot, the Saint-Simonians, Quinet, Michelet*, London and New York, 1993.

Culler, A. Dwight, *The Victorian Mirror of History*, New Haven and London, 1985.

Curtin, Philip D. *Cross-Cultural Trade in World History*, Cambridge, 1984.

——, *The Rise and Fall of the Plantation Complex: Essays in Atlantic History*, 2nd edn., Cambridge, 1998.

——, *The World and the West: The European Challenge and the Overseas Response in the Age of Empire*, Cambridge, 2000.

Dallet, Sylvie, ed., *Guerres révolutionnaires: histoire et cinéma*, Paris: l'Harmattan, 1984.

Darnton, Robert, "An Early Information Society: News and Media in Eighteenth-Century Paris," *American Historical Review* 105/1 (2000): 1–35, and at http://www.indiana.edu/~ahr/darnton.

Davis, Natalie Zemon, "Gender and Genre: Women as Historical Writers, 1400–1820." In *Beyond Their Sex: Learned Women of the European Past*, ed. Patricia A. Labalme, New York, 1980, pp. 153–82.

——, *The Return of Martin Guerre*, Cambridge, MA, 1983.

——, *Fiction in the Archives: Pardon Tales and Their Tellers in Sixteenth-Century France*, Stanford, 1987.

——, *Slaves on Screen*, Cambridge, MA, 2000.

Dean, Carolyn J., *The Frail Social Body: Pornography, Homosexuality, and Other Fantasies in Interwar France*, Berkeley, 2000.

Dean, Warren, *With Broadax and Firebrand: The Destruction of the Brazilian Atlantic Forest*, Berkeley, 1995.

Den Boer, Pim, *History as a Profession. The Study of History in France, 1818–1914*, Princeton, 1998.

Dentan, R. C., ed., *The Idea of History in the Ancient Near East*, New Haven and London, 1955.

Dillery, J. D., *Xenophon and the History of his Times*, London and New York, 1995.

Dirks, Nicholas B. ed., *The Hollow Crown: Ethnohistory of an Indian Kingdom*. Cambridge, 1987.

——, *In Near Ruins: Cultural Theory at the End of the Century*, Minneapolis, 1998.

Dirlik Arif, ed., *The Postcolonial Aura: Third World Criticism in the Age of Global Capitalism*, Boulder, 1997.

Dolan, Sean B., ed., *Telling the Story: The Media, The Public, and American History*, Boston, 1994.

Dorey, T. A., ed., *Latin Historians*, London, 1966.

Dorsey, Kurkpatrick, *The Dawn of Conservation Diplomacy: U.S.–Canadian Wildlife Protection Treaties in the Progressive Era*, Seattle, 1998.

Doughty, Robert A., The *Breaking Point: Sedan and the Fall of France, 1940*, Hamden, CT, 1990.

Duara, Prasenjit, *Rescuing History from the Nation: Questioning Narratives of Modern China*, Chicago, 1995.

Duff, T., *Plutarch's Lives. Exploring Virtue and Vice*, Oxford, 1999.

Dunlap, Thomas R., *DDT: Scientists, Citizens, and Public Policy*, Princeton, 1981.

Durham, William H., *Scarcity and Survival in Central America: Ecological Origins of the Soccer War*, Stanford, 1979.

Eagleton, Terry, *Literary Theory: An Introduction*, 2nd edn., Minneapolis, 1996.

Eckstein, A. M., *Moral Vision in the Histories of Polybius*, Los Angeles and Berkeley, 1995.

Elias, Norbert, *The Civilizing Process: The Development of Manners*, trans. Edmund Jephcott, 1939; New York, 1978.

Elman, Benjamin A., *From Philosophy to Philology. Intellectual and Social Aspects of Change in Late Imperial China*, Cambridge, MA, 1984.

Elster, Jan, *Making Sense of Marx*, Cambridge and New York, 1985.

Faderman, Lillian, *Odd Girls and Twilight Lovers: A History of Lesbian Life in Twentieth-Century America*, New York, 1991.

Fairhead, James, and Melissa Leach, *Misreading the African Landscape: Society and Ecology in a Forest-Savanna Mosaic*, Cambridge, 1996.

Febvre, Lucien, "History and Psychology [1938]," and "Sensibility and History: How to Reconstitute the Emotional Life of the Past [1941]," in Peter Burke, ed., *A New Kind of History and Other Essays*, trans. K. Folca, New York, 1973.

Ferguson, Adam, *An Essay on the History of Civil Society*, edited by Fania Oz-Salzburger. Cambridge, 1995.

Ferguson, Walter, *The Renaissance in Historical Thought*, Boston, 1948.

Fernandes, Florestan, *The Negro in Brazilian Society*, New York, 1971.

Ferro, Marc, *Cinema et histoire*, Paris, 1977, translated by Naomi Green as *Cinema and History*, Detroit, 1988.

Forbes, Duncan, *Hume's Philosophical Politics*, Cambridge, 1975.

Fornara, C. W., *The Nature of History in Ancient Greece and Rome*, Berkeley, 1983.

Frank, André Gunder, *ReORIENT: Global Economy in the Asian Age*, Berkeley, 1998.

Fredrickson, George M., *White Supremacy: A Comparative Study in American and South African History*, Oxford, 1981.

Fuchs, Lawrence H., *The American Kaleidoscope: Race, Ethnicity, and the Civic Culture*, Middletown, CT, 1990.

Galbraith, V. H. *Historical Research in Medieval England*, London, 1951.

Gazi, Effi, *"Scientific" History. The Greek Case of Comparative Perspective (1860–1920)*, New York, 2000.

Gershenfeld, Neil A., *When Things Start to Think*, New York, 1999.

Gilbert, Felix, *Machiavelli and Guicciardini: Politics and History in Sixteenth-Century Florence*, 2nd edn., New York, 1984.

——, *History: Politics or Culture? Reflections on Ranke and Burckhardt*, Princeton, 1990.

Ginzburg, Carlo, *The Cheese and the Worms: The Cosmos of a Sixteenth-Century Miller*, trans. Anne and John Tedeschi, Baltimore, 1980 [orig. 1976].

Goffart, Walter, *The Narrators of Barbarian History Jordanes, Gregory of Tours, Bede and Paul the Deacon (AD 550–800)*, Princeton, 1988.

Gooch, George P., *History and Historians in the Nineteenth Century*, London, 1914.

——, *History and Historians in the Nineteenth Century*, 2nd rev. edn., London and New York, 1952.

Gordon, Linda, *Woman's Body, Woman's Right: Birth Control in America*, New York, 1977.

Gossman, Lionel, *Between History and Literature*, Cambridge, MA, 1990.

——, *Basel in the Age of Burckhardt: A Study in Unseasonable Ideas*, Chicago, 2000.

Gould, J., *Herodotus*, London and New York, 1989.

Grafton, Anthony, *The Footnote: A Curious History*, Cambridge, MA, 1997.

Gramsci, Antonio, *Selections from the Prison Notebooks*, ed. and trans. Q. Hoare and G. Nowell Smith, New York, 1971.

Gransden, Antonia, *Historical Writing in England c.559–c.1307*, Ithaca, 1974.

Gray, V. J., *The Character of Xenophon's Hellenica*, Baltimore, 1989.

Green, Louis, *Chronicle into History: An Essay on the Interpretation of History in Florentine Fourteenth-Century Chronicles*, Cambridge, 1972.

Green, Nancy, "'Le Melting Pot': Made in America, Produced in France," *Journal of American History* 86/3 (December 1999): 1188–208.

Greenstein, Daniel I., *A Historian's Guide to Computing*, New York, 1994.

Grindon, Leger, *Shadows on the Past: Studies in the Historical Fiction Film*, Philadelphia, 1994.

Grove, Richard H., *Green Imperialism: Colonial Expansion, Tropical Island Edens and the Origins of Environmentalism, 1600–1860*, New York, 1995.

Guenée, Bernard, "L'historien par les mots," in Bernard Guenée, ed., *Le Métier d'Historien au Moyen Age: Etudes sur l'historiographie médiévale*, Paris, 1977.

——, *Histoire et Culture Historique dans l'Occident Médiéval*, Paris, 1980.

Guha, Ranajit, ed., *A Subaltern Studies Reader, 1986–1995*, Minneapolis, 1997.

——, and Gayatri Spivak, eds., *Selected Subaltern Studies*, New York, 1988.

Hamburger, Joseph, *Macaulay and the Whig Tradition*, Chicago, 1976.

Hanning, Robert, *The Vision of History in Early Britain*, New York, 1966.

Hartog, F., *The Mirror of Herodotus*, Berkeley, 1988.

Hay, Denys, *Annalists and Historians: Western Historiography from the VIIIth to the XVIIIth Century*, London, 1977.

Hazard, Paul, *The European Mind: the Critical Years, 1680–1715*, trans. J. Lewis May, New Haven, 1953.

Headrick, Daniel, *The Tools of Empire: Technology and European Imperialism in the Nineteenth Century*, New York, 1981.

——, *The Tentacles of Progress: Technology Transfer in the Age of Imperialism, 1850–1940*, New York, 1988.

Hegel, Georg Wilhelm Friedrich, *The Philosophy of History*, trans. J. Sibree, New York, 1956.

——, *Hegel's Philosophy of Right*, trans. T. M. Knox, Oxford, 1972.

Helms, Mary W., *Ulysses' Sail: An Ethnographic Odyssey of Knowledge, Power, and Geographical Distance*, Princeton, 1988.

Herder, Johann Gottfried, *Reflections on the Philosophy of History*, trans. T. O. Churchill, Chicago, 1968.

——, *J. G. Herder on Social and Political Culture*, Trans. F. M. Barnard, Cambridge, 1969.

Herodotus, *The Histories*, trans. R. Waterfield, with introduction and notes by C. Dewald, Oxford, 1998.

Higgs, Edward, *History and Electronic Artefacts*, Oxford, 1998.

Higham, John, Felix Gilbert, and Leonard Krieger, *History*, Englewood Cliffs, 1965.

Hobsbawm, E. J., *Nations and Nationalism since 1780: Programme, Myth, Reality*, Cambridge, 1990.

Hodgson, Marshall, G. S., *Rethinking World History: Essays on Europe, Islam, and World History*, ed. Edmund Burke, III, Cambridge, 1993.

Hornblower, S., *Thucydides*, London, 1987.

——, (ed.), *Greek Historiography*, Oxford, 1994.

Howard, Michael, *The Franco-Prussian War*, New York, 1961.

Hunt, Lynn, *Politics, Culture, and Class in the French Revolution*, Berkeley, 1984.

——, ed., *The New Cultural History*, Berkeley, 1989.

Huppert, George, *The Idea of Perfect History: Historical Erudition and Historical Philosophy in Renaissance France*, Urbana, 1970.

Hurley, Andrew, *Environmental Inequalities: Class, Race, and Industrial Pollution in Gary, Indiana, 1945–1980*, Chapel Hill, 1995.

Ianziti, Gary, *Humanist Historiography under the Sforzas: Politics and Propaganda in Fifteenth-Century Milan*, Oxford, 1988.

Iggers, Georg G., *The German Conception of History: The National Tradition of Historical Thought From Herder to the Present*, Middletown, CT, 1968.

——, *The German Conception of History. The National Tradition of Historical Thought from Herder to the Present*, 2nd. edn., Middletown, CT, 1983.

Immerwahr, H. R., *Form and Thought in Herodotus*, Cleveland, 1966.

Isenberg, Andrew C., *The Destruction of the Bison: An Environmental History, 1750–1920*, New York, 2000.

Jones, E. L., *The European Miracle: Environments, Economies, and Geopolitics in the History of Europe and Asia*, 2nd edn., Cambridge, 1986.

——, *Growth Recurring: Economic Change in World History*, Oxford, 1988.

Kaes, Anton, *From Hitler to Heimat: The Return of History as Film*, Cambridge, MA, 1989.

Kant, Immanuel, *The Contest of the Faculties*, trans. Mary J. Gregor, New York, 1979.

——, *Political Writings*, trans. H. B. Nisbet, Cambridge, 1991.

Keller, Evelyn Fox, *Reflections on Gender and Science*, New Haven, 1985.

Kelley, Donald R., *Foundations of Modern Historical Scholarship: Language, Law, and History in the French Renaissance*, New York, 1970.

——, "Humanism and History," in *Renaissance Humanism: Foundations, Forms, and Legacy*, Vol. 3, *Humanism and the Disciplines*, ed. Albert Rabil, Jr., Philadelphia, 1988, pp. 236–70.

——, *Faces of History Historical Inquiry from Herodotus to Herder*, New Haven and London, 1998.

——, "Renaissance Retrospection," in his *Faces of History: Historical Inquiry from Herodotus to Herder*, New Haven, 1998, pp. 130–61.

Kelly, George A., *Idealism, Politics, and History: Sources of Hegelian Thought*, Cambridge, 1969.

Kenyon, John, *The History Men: The Historical Profession in England since the Renaissance*, Pittsburgh, 1983.

Keylor, William, *Academy and Community. The Foundation of the French Historical Profession*, Cambridge, MA, 1975.

Kidd, Colin, *Subverting Scotland's Past: Scottish Whig Historians and the Creation of an Anglo-British Identity, 1689–c.1830*, Cambridge, 1993.

Kilgour, Frederick G., *The Evolution of the Book*, New York, 1998.

Kjaergaard, Thorkild, *The Danish Revolution, 1500–1800: An Ecohistorical Interpretation*, Cambridge, 1994.

Knudsen, Jonathan, *Justus Möser and the German Enlightenment*, Cambridge, 1986.

Kolakowski, Leszek, *Main Currents of Marxism*, 3 vols., trans. P. S. Falla, Oxford, 1978.

Koselleck, Reinhart, *Futures Past: On the Semantics of Historical Time*, Cambridge, MA, 1985.

Kraus, C. S. and A. J. Woodman, *Latin Historians*, Oxford, 1997.

Kraus, Michael, and Joyce, Davis D., *The Writing of American History*, revised edition, Norman, 1985.

Krech, Shepard, *The Ecological Indian: Myth and History*, New York, 1999.

Krieger, Leonard, *Ranke: The Meaning of History*, Chicago, 1977.

Laistner, M. L. W., *The Greater Roman Historians*, Berkeley and Los Angeles, 1947.

Lanham, Richard A., *The Electronic Word: democracy, technology, and the arts*, Chicago, 1993.

Lateiner, D., *The Historical Method of Herodotus*, Toronto, 1989.

Latour, Bruno, *Science in Action: How to Follow Scientists and Engineers through Society*, Cambridge, MA, 1987.

Le Roy Ladurie, Emmanuel, *Montaillou: The Promised Land of Error*, trans. Barbara Bray, New York, 1978 [orig. 1975].

Lemche, N. P., *The Israelites In History and Tradition*, Louisville, KY, 1998.

Levi, Giovanni, *Inheriting Power: The Story of an Exorcist*, trans. Lydia G. Cochrane, Chicago, 1988.

Lichtheim, George, *Marxism: An Historical and Critical Study*, 2nd edn., New York, 1965.

Luce, T. J., "Tacitus on 'History's Highest Function': *praecipuum munus annalium* (Ann. 3.65)," *Aufstieg und Niedergang der römischen Welt* 2.33.4 (1991), pp. 2904–27.

——, *The Greek Historians*, London, 1997.

Macaulay, Thomas Babington, *History of England from the Accession of James the Second*, 5 vols., London, 1849–61.

——, "History," in *The Works of Lord Macaulay*, 5: 122–61, New York, 1900.

Mah, Harold, *The End of Philosophy, the Origin of "Ideology": Karl Marx and the Crisis of the Young Hegelians*, Berkeley, 1987.

Mallett, Michael, *Mercenaries and the Masters: Warfare in Renaissance Italy*, London, 1974.

Mann, Arthur, *The One and the Many: Reflections on the American Identity*, Chicago, 1979.

Marincola, J., *Authority and Tradition in Ancient Historiography*, Cambridge, 1997.

Marx, Anthony W., *Making Race and Nation: A Comparison of South Africa, The United States and Brazil*, Cambridge, 1998.

McEvoy, Arthur F., *The Fisherman's Problem: Ecology and Law in the California Fisheries, 1850–1980*, New York, 1986.

McGann, Jerome J., *The Romantic Ideology: A Critical Investigation*, Chicago, 1983.

McNeill, J. R., *Something New Under the Sun: An Environmental History of the Twentieth-Century World*, New York, 2000.

McNeill, William H., *The Rise of the West: A History of the Human Community*, Chicago, 1963.

——, *Plagues and Peoples*, New York, 1976.

Meek, Ronald, *Social Science and the Ignoble Savage*, Cambridge, 1976.

Megill, Allan, *Prophets of Extremity: Nietzsche, Heidegger, Foucault, Derrida*, Berkeley, 1985.

Meinecke, Friedrich, *Historism: The Rise of a New Historical Outlook*, Princeton, 1972.

Mellor, R., *The Roman Historians*, London, 1999.

Merrick, Jeffrey and Bryant T. Ragan, eds., *Homosexuality in Modern France*, Oxford, 1997.

Michelet, Jules, *History of France*, 2 vols., trans. G. H. Smith, New York, 1857.

——, *The People*, trans. John P. McKay, Urbana, 1973.

Mommsen, Theodor, "Petrarch's Conception of the 'Dark Ages,'" *Speculum* 17 (1942): 226–42.

Mommsen, Wolfgang J., *Max Weber and German Politics*, Chicago, 1984.

Mosse, George, *Nationalism and Sexuality: Respectability and Abnormal Sexuality in Modern Europe*, New York, 1985.

Muir, Edward and Guido Ruggiero, eds., *Microhistory and the Lost Peoples of Europe*, trans. Eren Branch, Baltimore, 1991.

Mullen, E. T. Jr., *Ethnic Myths and Pentateuchal Foundations: A New Approach to the Formation of the Pentateuch*, Atlanta, 1997.

Noth, M., *The Deuteronomistic History*, JSOT Suppl. 15, Sheffield, 1981 (translated from *Überlieferungsgeschichtliche Studien*, Tübingen, 1957, pp. 1–110).

——, *The Chronicler's History*, translation and introduction by H. G. M. Williamson, JSOT Suppl. 50, Sheffield: JSOT Press (translated from *Überlieferungsgeschichtliche Studien*, pp. 110–80).

Novick, Peter, *That Noble Dream. The "Objectivity Question" and the American Historical Profession*, Cambridge, MA, 1988.

Nye, Russell B., *George Bancroft: Brahmin Rebel*, New York, 1972 [1944].

O'Brien, Karen, *Narratives of Enlightenment: Cosmopolitan History from Voltaire to Gibbon*, Cambridge, 1997.

O'Donnell, James J., *Avatars of the Word: from Papyrus to Cyberspace*, Cambridge, MA, 1998.

Ortner, Sherry B. ed., *High Religion: A Cultural and Political History of Sherpa Buddhism*, Princeton, NJ, 1989.

——, *The Fate of "Culture": Geertz and Beyond*, Berkeley, 1999.

Pacey, Arnold, *Technology in World Civilization: A Thousand-Year History*, Oxford, 1990.

Paret, Peter, ed., *Makers of Modern Strategy from Machiavelli to the Nuclear Age*, Princeton, 1986.

——, *Imagined Battles: Reflections of War in European Art*, Chapel Hill, 1997.

Parker, Geoffrey, *The Army of Flanders and the Spanish Road, 1567–1659*, New York, 1972.

Partner, Nancy, *Serious Entertainments: The Writing of History in Twelfth-Century England*, Chicago, 1977.

Pascal, Roy, *The German Sturm und Drang*, Manchester, 1967.

Pemberton, John, *On the Subject of "Java,"* Ithaca, 1994.

Phillips, Mark, *Francesco Guicciardini: The Historian's Craft*, Toronto, 1977.

Pickering, Andrew, ed., *Science as Practice and Culture*, Chicago, 1992.

Plutarch, *Greek Lives* and *Roman Lives*, trans. R. Waterfield, introduction and notes by P. A. Stadter, Oxford, 1998, 1999.

Pocock, J. G. A., *Barbarism and Religion. Vol. I: the Enlightenments of Edward Gibbon, 1737–1764*, Cambridge, 1999.

——, *Barbarism and Religion. Vol. II: Narratives of Civil Government*, Cambridge, 1999.

Pomeranz, Kenneth, *The Great Divergence: Europe, China, and the Making of the Modern World Economy*, Princeton, 2000.

Porter, Theodore, *Trust in Numbers: The Pursuit of Objectivity in Science and Public Life*, Princeton, 1995.

Prakash, Gyan, *After Colonialism: Imperial Histories and Postcolonial Displacements*, Princeton, 1995.

Rad, G. von, "The Beginnings of Historical Writing in Ancient Israel" (1944), in *The Problem of the Hexateuch and Other Essays*, trans. E. W. T. Dicken, Edinburgh and London, 1966, pp. 166–204.

Rader, Melvin, *Marx's Interpretation of History*, New York, 1979.

Ranke, Leopold von, *The Theory and Practice of History*, ed. Georg G. Iggers and Konrad von Moltke, Indianapolis, 1973.

Reddy, William M., "Against Constructionism: The Historical Ethnography of Emotions," *Current Anthropology* 38 (June 1997): 326–51.

Redlich, Fritz, *The German Military Enterpriser and his Work Force: A Study in European Social and Economic History*, 2 vols., Wiesbaden, 1964–5.

Reill, Peter Hans, *The German Enlightenment and the Rise of Historicism*, Berkeley, 1975.

Revel, Jacques, "Microanalysis and the Construction of the Social," in Jacques Revel and Lynn Hunt, eds., *Histories: French Constructions of the Past*, trans. Arthur Goldhammer et al., New York, 1995, pp. 492–502.

——, ed., *Jeux d'échelles: La micro-analyse à l'expérience*, Paris, 1996.

Ringer, Fritz, *The Decline of the German Mandarins: The German Academic Community 1890–1933*, Cambridge, MA, 1969.

Roberts, Mary Louise, *Civilization Without Sexes: Reconstructing Gender in Postwar France, 1917–1927*, Chicago, 1994.

Robinson, Paul, *The Modernization of Sex: Havelock Ellis, Alfred Kinsey, William Masters, and Virginia Johnson*, Ithaca, 1973.

Rood, T., *Thucydides: a Narratological Approach*, Oxford, 1998.

Roper, Lyndal, *Oedipus and the Devil: Witchcraft, Sexuality and Religion in Early Modern Europe*, London, 1994.

Rosenstone, Robert A., ed., *Revisioning History: Film and the Construction of a New Past*, Princeton, 1995.

——, *Visions of the Past: The Challenge of Film to Our Idea of History*, Cambridge, MA, 1995.

Sabean, David Warren, *Property, Production, and Family in Neckarhausen, 1700–1870*, Cambridge, 1990.

——, *Kinship in Neckarhausen, 1700–1870*, Cambridge, 1998.

Sacks, K., *Polybius on the Writing of History*, Berkeley, 1981.

Sahlins, Marshall, *Historical Metaphors and Mythical Realities: Structure in the Early History of the Sandwich Islands Kingdom*, Ann Arbor, 1981.

——, *Islands of History*, Chicago, 1985.

Said, Edward, *Orientalism*, New York, 1978.

Scardigli, B., ed., *Essays on Plutarch's Lives*, Oxford, 1995.

Schnädelbach, Herbert, *Philosophy in Germany, 1831–1933*, Cambridge, 1984.

Schorske, Carl E., "History as Vocation in Burckhardt's Basel," in *Thinking with History: Explorations in the Passage to Modernism*, Princeton, 1998, ch. 4.

Sedgwick, Eve Kosofky, *Epistemology of the Closet*, Berkeley, 1991.

Seigel, Jerrold, *Marx's Fate: The Shape of a Life*, Princeton, 1978.

Shapin, Steven, *A Social History of Truth: Civility and Science in Seventeenth-Century England*, Chicago, 1994.

——, and Simon Schaffer, *Leviathan and the Air Pump: Hobbes, Boyle, and the Experimental Life*, Princeton, 1985.

Short, K. R. M., ed., *Feature Films as History*, Knoxville, 1981.

Shrimpton, G. S., *History and Memory in Ancient Greece*, Montreal, 1997.

Shy, John W., *A People Numerous and Armed: Reflections on the Military Struggle for American Independence*, New York, 1976.

Skidmore, Thomas E., *Black into White; Race and Nationality in Brazilian Thought*, New York, 1974.

Smith, Bonnie, *The Gender of History: Men, Women, and Historical Practice*, Cambridge, MA, 1999.

Sobchack, Vivian, ed., *The Persistence of History: Cinema, Television, and the Modern Event*, New York and London, 1996.

Sorlin, Pierre, *The Film in History: Restaging the Past*, Totowa, 1980.

Sparks, K. L., *Ethnicity and Identity in Ancient Israel: Prolegomena to the Study of Ethnic Sentiments and their Expression in the Hebrew Bible*, Winona Lake, 1998.

Spiegel, Gabrielle M., *The Chronicle Tradition of Saint-Denis A Survey*, Leiden and Boston, 1978.

——, *Romancing the Past: The Rise of Vernacular Prose Historiography in Thirteenth Century France*, Berkeley, 1993.

——, *The Past as Text: The Theory and Practice of Medieval Historiography*, Baltimore, 1997.

Stadter, P. A., *Arrian of Nicomedia*, Chapel Hill, 1980.

Stein, Peter, *Legal Evolution: the Story of an Idea*, Cambridge, 1980.

Stern, Fritz, ed., *The Varieties of History from Voltaire to the Present*, New York, 1973.

Streuver, Nancy S., *The Language of History in the Renaissance: Rhetoric and Historical Consciousness in Florentine Humanism*, Princeton, 1970.

Takaki, Ronald, *A Different Mirror: A History of Multicultural America*, Boston, 1993.

Tanaka, Stefan, *Japan's Orient: Rendering Pasts into History*, Berkeley, 1993.

Taylor, Charles, *Hegel*, Cambridge, 1975.

Taylor, Joseph E., III, *Making Salmon: An Environmental History of the Northwest Fisheries Crisis*, Seattle, 1999.

Taylor, Mark C., *Deconstruction in Context: Literature and Philosophy*, Chicago, 1986.

Thierry, Augustin, "Autobiographical Preface," in *The Historical Essays, Published under the Title of "Dix ans d'études historiques,"* and *Narratives of the Merovingian Era*, Philadelphia, 1845, pp. 7–24.

Thompson, E. P., *The Making of the English Working Class*, London, 1963.

Thucydides, *The Peloponnesian War*, translated with introduction and notes by S. Lattimore, Indianapolis, 1998.

Toews, John, *Hegelianism: The Path Toward Dialectical Humanism*, Cambridge, 1981.

Trevor-Roper, Hugh, "The Historical Philosophy of the Enlightenment," in *Studies on Voltaire and the Eighteenth Century*, 24 (1963): 1667–88.

Trinkle, Dennis A., *The History Highway 2000: a guide to Internet resources*, Armonk, 2000.

Tuplin, C., *The Failings of Empire: A Reading of Xenophon Hellenica 2.3.11–7.5.27*, Stuttgart, 1993.

Twitchett, Denis, *The Writing of Official History under the T'ang*, Cambridge, 1992.

Van Seters, John, *In Search of History: Historiography in the Ancient World and the Origins of Biblical History*, New Haven, 1983.

——, *Prologue to History: The Yahwist as Historian in Genesis*, Louisville, 1992.

——, *The Life of Moses: The Yahwist as Historian in Exodus–Numbers*, Louisville, 1994.

——, "The Historiography of the Ancient Near East," in Jack M. Sasson, *Civilizations of the Ancient Near East*, vol. 4, New York, 1995, pp. 2433–44.

——, *The Pentateuch: A Social-Science Commentary*, Sheffield, 1999.

Vaughn, Richard, *Matthew Paris*, Cambridge, 1958.

Vitzthum, Richard C., *The American Compromise: Theme and Method in the Histories of Bancroft, Parkman, and Adams*, Norman, OK, 1974.

Vyverberg, Henry, *Historical Pessimism in the French Enlightenment*, Cambridge, MA, 1958.

Walbank, F. W., *Polybius*, Berkeley, 1972.

Wallerstein, Immanuel. *The Modern World-System*, 3 vols. to date, New York, 1974–.

Wang, Q. Edward, *Inventing China Through History: The May Fourth Approach to Historiography*, Albany, 2001.

Warren, Louis, *The Hunters's Game: Poachers and Conservationists in Twentieth-Century America*, New Haven, 1997.

Weber, Marianne, *Max Weber: A Biography*, trans. Harry Zohn, introduction by Guenther Roth, New Brunswick and Oxford, 1988.

Weiss, Roberto, *The Renaissance Discovery of Classical Antiquity*, 2nd edn. Oxford, 1988.

Wellhausen, J., *Prolegomena to the History of Israel* (1883), New York, 1957.

White, Hayden, *Metahistory: The Historical Imagination in Nineteenth-Century Europe*, Baltimore and London, 1973.

White, Richard, *Land Use, Environment, and Social Change: The Shaping of Island County, Washington*, Seattle, 1979.

Wilcox, Donald J., *The Development of Florentine Humanist Historiography in the Fifteenth Century*, Cambridge, MA, 1969.

Winichakul, Thongchai, *Siam Mapped: A History of the Geo-Body of a Nation*, Honolulu, 1994.

Wiseman, T. P., *Clio's Cosmetics*, Leicester, 1979.

——, "Practice and Theory in Roman Historiography," in *History* 66 (1981): 375–93; reprinted in *Roman Studies: Literary and Historical*, Liverpool, 1987, pp. 244–62.

Wolf, Eric. R., *Europe and the People Without History*, Berkeley, 1982.

Wong, R. Bin, *China Transformed: Historical Change and the Limits of European Experience*, Ithaca, 1997.

Woodman, A. J., *Rhetoric in Classical Historiography*, London, 1988.

Woolf, D. R., *A Global Encyclopedia of Historical Writing*, 2 vols., New York, 1998.

——, *The Idea of History in Early Stuart England*, Toronto, 1990.

Worster, Donald, *The Wealth of Nature: Environmental History and the Ecological Imagination*, New York, 1993.

——, *Nature's Economy: A History of Ecological Ideas*, 2nd edn., New York, 1994.

Xenophon, *A History of My Times*, trans. R. Warner, introduction and notes by G. Cawkwell, Harmondsworth, 1979.

Index

Aaron, 27
ab Urbe Condita (Livy), 62
Abraham, 23, 24, 26, 28
Abrams, M. H., 325
Absalom, 21
absolute monarchies, 126, 134
"abstract thought," 210
Abu-Lughod, Lila, 288, 292
Abuladze, Tengiz, 478
Académie des Inscriptions et des Belles Lettres, 226
Academy of Sciences (France), 303
Achaean Federation, 51, 52
Achilles, 36
Acton, Lord, 231
Acts of the Apostles, 38
Adam, 25, 28, 82
Adams, Henry, 232
Adas, Michael, 407
Adorno, Theodor, 219
aemulatio, 67
affectivity, 281
Africa, professionalization of historical studies, 232
African diaspora, 408
African-Americans, 435–6, 467
After Colonialism: Imperial Histories and Postcolonial Displacements, 424–5
The Age of Iron, 472
The Age of Louis XIV (Voltaire), 133, 134, 145, 246
The Age of the Medici, 472
agency, 330, 424
Agesilaus, 48
Agilram, 92
Agnadello, 102
Agricola (Tacitus), 63, 66, 72, 73
agricultural depression, 375
agricultural history, 376, 399–400, 403, 404–5
Agrippa, Henricus Cornelius, 110, 111
Ahab, 22
Ahaz, 29
Ahijah, 29
Ahmad, Aijaz, 428–9
Aimoin of Fleury, 93

air-pump, 312–13
Akademie der Wissenschaften, 256–7
Alabama, 270
alchemy, 299, 303
d'Alembert, Jean le Rond, 125–6, 136
Alexander the Great, 38, 53–4, 84, 156
Alexander Severus, 64
alienation
    Hegelian philosophy, 155, 159, 161; Herder's German historicism, 144, 154–5, 160; Kantian philosophy, 155; Marx, 207
Alombert, Charles, 250
"Also a Philosophy of History for the Cultivation of Humanity" (Herder), 145–7, 148, 150
American Association for History and Computing, 449
American Historical Association, 230, 455, 459, 460–1
American Historical Review, 230, 365, 428, 459
American Indians, 377, 384
American Society for Environmental History (ASEH), 372, 385
Amin, Shahid, 422–3
Ammianus Marcellinus, 64
Ammon, 23
Amnon, 21
Anabasis (Arrian), 53–4
Anabasis (Xenophon), 48, 50
anarchism, 196
Anatomy of Criticism (Frye), 330
The Ancient Constitution and the Feudal Law (Pocock), 126
Anderson, Benedict, 185
Anderson, Michael, 283
Anderson, Perry, 141
Andrew W. Mellon foundation, 460
Angelopolous, Theo, 477
Anglicanism, 139
Anglo-Saxon Chronicle, 93
Anglo-Saxons, rise of, 88, 90–1
animal diffusions, 404–5
Ankersmit, Frank, 479
Annales, 237, 262, 341, 348, 376

Annales Maximi, 60
Annales school, 341
  demography, 376, 379; environmental history,
    374, 376, 377, 379, 382, 385; history of
    mentalities, 264, 343; integration of
    geography and history, 376, 377, 382;
    total/micro history, 262, 263, 264, 265–6,
    272
Annalists, 60
Annals (Camden), 107–8
*Annals of the German Empire under the House of
  Saxony*, 229
Annals (Tacitus), 63–4, 68, 73
Annotations on the New Testament (Valla), 103
anomie, 345
anthropology
  armed power, 256, 257; history of culture,
    277–93; microhistory, 271; post-structuralism,
    286, 287–9; postcolonial history, 419;
    psychocultural, 292; relations to history, 9,
    237, 256, 277–8, 290–3, 320, 337, 395;
    sovereignty of culture, 278–81; structuralism,
    322; *see also* cultural anthropology
antiquarian historiography, 125–6
antiquarianism, Renaissance historiography, 114–
  15
Antonines, 138
Antony, 54
apartheid, 434, 437
Apollo, 175
Apollonius, 67
appearance–essence dichotomy, 209–10
Appian, 38, 39, 65
Arabs, 23
Aram, 23
Aramaic documents, 31
archaeology, Thucydides, 45
The Archaeology of Knowledge (Foucault), 327
Archias, 41
Archidamus, 47
archives
  and computers, 452–3; Macaulay, 194; military,
    248, 249; national historiography, 188, 194,
    234–5; opening of state archives, 140, 229
Argentina, 435, 438–9, 442
aridity, 375
Ariès, Philippe, 232, 264–5
Aristobulus, 53
aristocratic families, medieval genealogies, 94
Aristotle, 101
ark of the covenant, 19
armed power *see* war historiography
L'Armée et ses problèmes au XVIII Siècle (Léonard),
  253
Aronowitz, Stanley, 314
Arpanet, 449
Arrian, 35, 38, 39, 53–4, 57
art history, 320
The Art of Verifying Dates (Mabillon), 125
Art of War (Machiavelli), 245
Artaxerxes I, 30
artifacts, 320
  Renaissance historiography, 99, 104
artisanship, 217
Artists and Warfare in the Renaissance (Hale), 257

Aryan physics, 307
ASEH, 372, 385
Asia
  professionalization of historical studies, 225;
    trade, 402–3
Asianism, 420–1
The Assassination of the Duc of Guise, 466
associations, 230
Assyrian historiography, 15, 20, 32
Astell, Mary, 109
astronomy, 304
Athens
  Herodotus, 40, 41; Thucydides, 43–4, 45, 46,
    47; Xenophon, 49
Atlantic Ocean basin, 402, 408
atomic bomb, 311
auctores, 80
Auerbach, Erich, 84, 87, 90
August Wilhelm, Prince of Prussia, 247
Augustine, Saint, 88, 457
  City of God, 70, 82–3; and Petrarch, 99; and
    Sallust, 70, 75
Augustus, 62, 64, 133
Auslander, Leora, 277
Austin, John, 329
Australia, 434, 437
Austria, 167, 169
authorship, 326
autism, 352
autonomy, moral and rational, 152, 153, 155, 156,
  158
Avatars of the Word (O'Donnell), 456
Aztecs, 380

Babylonia
  end of Jewish exile, 28, 31; origins of life, 22
Babylonian historiography, 15, 32
  chronology of the world, 25; king-lists, 25–6;
    legend of Sargon the Great, 24, 33*n*
Babylonian Talmud, 83
Bacchylides, 67
Bach, Johann Sebastian, 175
Bacon, Francis, 114, 195, 305, 306
Baden, 167, 176
Bahktin, Mikhail, 322, 325
Bali, 85, 280
Balkan peninsula, 37
Bancroft, George, 186, 198–200, 201, 232
barbarian histories, 88–92
barbarian societies, 130, 131, 132
Barbarism and Religion (Pocock), 123–4
Barlow, Tani, 427–8
Baron, Hans, 104
Barraclough, Geoffrey, 233
Barth, Fredrik, 272
Barthes, Roland, 322, 323–4, 328, 332, 347, 470
Basel, 171, 180
Basel in the Age of Burckhardt (Gossmann), 180
Bateson, Gregory, 280
Bathsheba, 21
Battista di Montefeltro, 102, 109
Battleship Potemkin, 467–8
"*Battleship Potemkin* – Film and Reality"
  (Wenden), 474
Baudouin, François, 115

Bay, Edna G., 288
Bayle, Pierre, 125
Bayly, Christopher A., 407
Beard, Charles, 232, 237
Beard, Mary, 232
Beauvaisis, 265
Becker, Carl, 127
Bede, 82, 83, 88, 89, 90–1, 92, 93
Bell Laboratories, 262
Bell Telephone, 305
Bembo, Pietro, 102
Benedict, Ruth, 280
Benedict, St., 92
Benedictine Maurist Order, 125
Benedictines, 229
Benevento, 92
Benjamin, Walter, 219
Benoît of Saint-Maur, 93
Berkhofer, Robert, 477
Berlin University, 228
Berr, Henri, 233, 236–7
Bertrande de Rols, 271
Bevir, Mark, 330
Bible
  as basis for medieval chronological schemes, 83;
    medieval typological interpretation, 84–5
biblical chronology, 299
biblical historiography, 15–32
biblical texts, analysis of, 227, 321
Big Bang, 262
Bildung, 228
Billington, James, 453
biodiversity, 383
biography
  Arrian's *History of Alexander the Great*, 53–4;
    and computer technology, 456–7;
    establishment of genre, 8; Greek
    historiography, 35, 53–6, 57; medieval
    historiography, 81; Plutarch's *Parallel Lives*,
    54–6, 57; psychobiographies, 338; Renaissance
    historiography, 108; scientists, 303–4, 311–12;
    Suetonius' *Lives of the Caesars*, 64
biological diffusions, 393, 403–5, 410
biology, 315
Biondo, Flavio, 103
biota, 383
Birth of the Asylum (Foucault), 180
Birth of a Nation, 467, 468
The Birth of The Clinic (Foucault), 327
The Birth of Tragedy (Nietzsche), 175
Bismarck, Prince Otto Edward Leopold von, 175
bison, 375
Black Death, 379
Blake, William, 265
Blanc, Louis, 188, 196, 232
Bloch, Ernest, 176
Bloch, Iwan, 364
Bloch, Joseph, 214–15
Bloch, Marc, 82, 227, 237, 341, 376
Bloch, Maurice, 285
Boccaccio, Giovanni, 105, 108–9, 110
Bodin, Jean, 112, 113–14
body, 347, 353, 367
Bollandists, 227, 229
Bolshevik Revolution, 216, 468

The Book of the City of Ladies (Christine de Pizan),
  109
*Book of the Deeds and Good Manners of the Learned
  King Charles V* (Pizan), 109
Book in Praise of Women (Bisticci), 108
book reviews, 458
Born on the Fourth of July, 466, 469
Bossuet, Jacques Bénigne, 125, 199
Boulainvilliers, Henri, Comte de, 126
Bourdieu, Pierre, 217–18, 219, 284, 348
bourgeoisie, Marx, 209
Boyle, Robert, 312–13
Bracciolini, Poggio, 105, 245
brain chemistry, 341
brain lesions, 351
Braudel, Fernand, 141, 267, 301
  comparison to Le Roy Ladurie, 265; man's
    relationship to the environment, 376; *The
    Mediterranean*, 263, 264, 401; total history,
    263
Brazil, 435, 438, 442, 443, 478
breviare, 80
Brewster, David, 303–4
Britain
  bureaucracy, 227–8; Christianity, 90–1; growth
    of popular historical writing, 185; higher
    education, 227–8; historical journals, 230;
    history workshop movement, 239; Hume's
    History of Great Britain, 134; market
    economy, 227; multiculturalism, 437; national
    historiography, 193–7; official campaign
    histories, 251; professional disillusionment,
    267; professionalization of historical studies,
    231; reactions to French Revolution, 193; war
    historiography, 253; *see also* England; Scotland
Britannia (Camden), 107
British Empire, 407
Britons, fall of, 88, 90–1
Brodie, Bernard, 254
Brown, Judith, 269
Brown, Peter, 457
Brucker, Gene, 269, 270–1
Bruni, Leonardo, 102–3, 104, 109, 111, 245
Brutus, 54
bubonic plague, 404
Buckle, Henry Thomas, 232, 233, 254
Bulgaria, 236
Burckhardt, Jacob, 100, 171–4, 180, 182
bureaucracy, 227–8
Burke, Edmund, 234
Burke, Peter, 101
Burns, Ken, 471
Burton, John Hill, 197
Bush, Vannevar, 307
Bynum, Caroline, 353
Byzantium, 88

Caesar, Julius
  continuation or works by anonymous authors,
    64; drive to power, 156; influence on
    Renaissance historiography, 101–2, 107;
    Plutarch's *Parallel Lives*, 54; poetry, 65; and
    Sallust, 61, 70, 71; war historiography, 61, 244
Caferro, William, 256
calculus, 299

Caligula, 62, 63
Callicratidas, 49
Cambodia, 267
Cambridge University, 231
Cambyses, 40
Camden, William, 107–8
La Campagne de 1800 en Allemagne (Alombert and Colin), 250
Canaan, conquest of, 20
Canaanite peoples, 23
Canada
    Indian hunting techniques, 377; multiculturalism, 437; settler colony, 434
cannibalism, 344
canon tables, 82
Capetian France, 94
Capital (Marx), 210, 212–14, 219
capitalism
    colonialism, 418; environmental history, 383; land use strategies, 378, 383; Marx, 210, 212–14, 217; postcolonialism, 429; Weber, 177–8, 181, 309, 398
capitalist mode of production, 212–13, 215
The Capture of Rome, 466
Carl von Clausewitz: Politik und Krieg (Rothfels), 253
Carlini of Vellano, Benedetta, 269
Carlyle, Thomas, 232
carnivals, 322
Carolingian Empire, 92
Carolingian France, 94
Cartesian epistemology, 128
Carthage, 51, 52, 70
Cassirer, Ernst, 123, 125, 127
Cassius Dio, 38
catachresis, 428
Catilina, Lucius Sergius, 61, 70, 74
Cato the Elder, 62, 66
Cato the Younger, 54, 61, 70, 71
cattle industry, 375
causal primacy, 130
causality, divine intervention, 18, 19, 20–1
The Causes of War (Howard), 258
CD-ROMs, 452, 453
Ceddo, 472
Cellarius, 125
Celtic peoples, 168
censorship, 358
Centre d'études d'histoire de la Défense, 255, 257
Cereta, Laura, 119*n*
Cerutti, Simona, 272
Chakrabarty, Dipesh, 419, 422
chance developments, 399
Changes in the Land (Cronon), 382
Charlemagne, 84, 86, 92, 102
Charles I, King of England, 134
Charles XII, King of Sweden, 133
charters, Renaissance historiography, 115
Chartism, 193, 196, 286, 287
Châtelet, Emilie de, 133
Chatterjee, Partha, 418, 420
Chaudhuri, K. N., 401
Chauncey, George, 367–8
Chauri Chaura, 422–3
The Cheese and the Worms (Ginzburg), 268–9

Chiesa, Giulio Cesare, 272
childhood, 264–5
childhood sexual feelings, 339, 340
China
    postcolonial scholarship, 423–4, 428–9; professionalization of historical studies, 225, 231; science, 316; trade, 402, 403
Christian Coalition, 314
Christianity
    and ancient Rome, 88; Anglicanism, 139; Augustine's *City of God*, 70, 82–3; barbarian histories, 88–92; biblical typological interpretation, 84–5; in Britain, 90–1; French national historiography, 191; Gibbon's *Decline and Fall*, 138; God's operation within history, 81; loss of influence, 125; nature of time, 81–2; notions of God, 155; patristic historians, 88; Voltaire, 133; *see also* Protestantism
Christy, Alan, 425, 426
Chronica Majora (Matthew of Paris), 93
Chronicle (Eusebius), 82
chronicles
    Israelite historiography, 16; medieval historiography, 79, 80–1, 94, 95; Near East historical genres, 16; Renaissance historiography, 105–7
Chronicles, Books of, 17, 27–32
chronicus, 80
chronographus, 80
chronology, Renaissance historiography, 114–15
Churchill, Winston, 232
Cicero
    definition of history, 79, 80; function of history, 232; influence on medieval historiography, 79, 80, 81; influence on Renaissance historiography, 101, 113; and Livy, 66; *Orator*, 66, 67, 68, 79, 101; and Petrarch, 99; and Plutarch, 54, 55; rhetorical tradition, 79, 81; and Tiro, 447–8
Cimabue, Giovanni, 101
cinema *see* visual media
Cinema et histoire, 475
Cinema Nuovo, 478
cinematograph, 466
circumcision rites, 26, 27
cities, 22, 383–4
City of God (Augustine), 70, 82–3
civic humanism, 131
civic nationalism, 432, 434, 435, 440–1
civil society, 127–8, 216
The Civil War, 471
The Civil War in France (Marx), 215
civilization
    Elias, 342–3; Enlightenment historiography, 130–9; Freud, 342
Civilization and its Discontents (Freud), 338, 342
The Civilization of the Renaissance in Italy (Burckhardt), 100, 172–3, 180
The Civilizing Process (Elias), 342–3
Clark, Andrew, 380
class composition, 286
class consciousness, 287
class relations
    Bourdieu, 218; environmental history, 383;

Gramsci, 216; Marx, 201, 205, 213, 214, 398; Sabean's study, 290–1; Thompson, 217; universal significance, 396; Weber, 179
The Class Struggles in France (Marx), 215
classical texts, analysis of, 227
Claudius, 62, 63
Claudius (Suetonius), 66
Clausewitz, Carl von, 246, 247, 249–50, 252
Cleopatra, 54
climate
Annalistes, 376; Montesquieu, 129
climatic changes, 393
clinical psychology, 292
cognitive science, 341
Cold War, 162, 309
Colin, Jean, 250, 251
Collection des documents inédits sur l'histoire de France, 229
Collier, Jane Fishburne, 288–9
colligere, 80
colonialism, 406–8, 410, 421–2
Enlightenment historiography, 136–7; environmental history, 380, 383, 384; impact of culture, 291; power and domination, 418; *see also* imperialism; postcolonial history
Columbia University Press, 461
Columbian exchange, 405
The Columbian Exchange (Crosby), 380
Columbus, Christopher, 106
Comaroff, Jean, 289–90, 291, 406
Comaroff, John, 289–90, 291, 406
Commentaries on the Deeds of Francesco Sforza (Simonetta), 112
commerce, as force behind European expansion, 137
commercial civilization, 130–1
"The Commissary and his Significance in General" (Hintze), 252–3
commodity form, 212
common sense, 187
communism, 205, 207, 213, 254, 266–7
The Communist Manifesto (Marx and Engels), 209
compilare, 80
computers, 447–64
and archives, 452–3; Internet, 450, 452, 454, 457–62; in libraries, 450–2, 453, 454–5, 456, 460, 462–3; use by historians, 449–50
Conant, James B., 307–8
Concerning Famous Women (Boccaccio), 108–9
"concrete" life, 210, 211
"concrete in the mind," 210, 211
Condillac, Etienne Bonnot de, 187
Condorcet, Marie Jean Antoine Nicholas de Caritat, Marquis de, 124, 132
Confessions (Augustine), 457
conflict
culture's inability to deal with, 283; post-structuralism, 288
conjectural history, 124, 130–2, 139–41
consciousness
Hegel's spirit, 156; neuroscience, 351
conservation biology, 373
Conservation and the Gospel of Efficiency (Hays), 382
conservation movement, 377, 382

Considerations on the Causes of the Grandeur of the Romans and of their Decadence (Montesquieu), 129
Constantine the Great, 82, 84, 88
Constantius, 64
The Content of the Form (White), 331
contraception, 357
contradictions, Hegelian philosophy, 159, 161
Cook, Captain, 285
Cooper, Frederick, 428
cooperation, 211
Corbaccio (Boccaccio), 108, 110
Corbin, Alain, 271
Corcyra, 47
Cordus, Cremutius, 63
Corinth, 51
Corinthians, 44
Cosimo I, 113
cosmology, Israelite historiography, 24–5
costume dramas, 467
The Course in General Linguistics (Saussure), 323, 346
Covenanters, 196
Cowper, William, 195
Cox, Alex, 472, 478
Crane, Susan, 277
Crassus, 54
creation accounts
Israelite historiography, 22, 23, 24–5; Mesopotamian historiography, 22
Creationists, 314
creativity, 207, 208, 214
critical theory, 219
Critique of Political Economy (Marx), 213, 221
Critique of Practical Reason (Kant), 151, 152, 154, 155
Critique of Pure Reason (Kant), 151
Croce, Benedetto, 232
Croesus, 37, 40, 41, 42, 47
Cronon, William, 372–3, 382, 383
Crosby, Alfred, 380–1, 383, 399, 404
cross-cultural interactions, 3, 405–6, 410
cross-cultural trade, 393, 400–3, 410
crowd action, 282
crowd diseases, 379
The Crowd in History (Rudé), 344
The Crowd (Le Bon), 344
crowd psychology, 343–5
Cuba, 478
cult of the hero, 174
cultural anthropology, 11, 172, 174, 181, 217, 269
cultural capital, 218
cultural change, 284, 285
cultural codes, 218
cultural criticism, Nietzsche, 174–6
cultural determinism, 383
cultural difference, 6, 281
cultural exchanges, 3, 405–6, 410
cultural hegemony, 216–17
cultural history, 277–93, 337
and psychology, 281, 283, 345, 346; science as, 312–14; social constructionism, 346; and social history, 239, 281–3
cultural individuality, 146–7, 149

cultural landscape, 376
cultural nationalism, 144
cultural sciences, 226
cultural studies, 418, 419
cultural turn, 218
culture
  anthropologists' disquiet, 283–4; Bourdieu, 217–18; Burckhardt, 171–4, 180; colonial and postcolonial societies, 291; distinctiveness of, 6; environmental determinism, 383; ethnographer relations, 283, 286; framing of social reality, 346; gender and sexuality, 366; Gramsci, 216–17, 218; historians discover, 281–3; historicizing of, 283–7; inability to deal with diversity and conflict, 283; Marx, 205; microhistory, 271–2; modern historiography stress on, 238–9; origins and invention of, 22; psychocultural anthropology, 292; sexuality, 363; sovereignty of, 278–81; synchronic character, 283, 284; Thompson, 217, 218; Weber, 177, 238; see also historicism; historicism, German; multiculturalism
Curtin, Philip D., 397, 400, 408
custom
  Herodotus, 42–3; and language, 321; medieval society, 85; Voltaire's cross-cultural history of, 394
Cynoscephalae, Battle of, 72
Cyropaideia (Xenophon), 48
Cyrus the Great, 28, 30, 31, 37, 40, 48
Cyrus the prince, 48, 49

Dahomey, 288
Damasio, Antonio R., 351
Dämonie der Macht (Ritter), 170
Daniel, Book of, 83
Darius, 40
Darnton, Robert, 271, 460, 461, 463
Darwin, Charles, 298, 299, 308, 310, 311, 374
Daston, Lorraine, 313
databases, 451–2, 454–5
Dati, Goro, 105
dating system, 82
David, 18–19, 21–2, 28, 30, 84
David, royal house of, 28
"David Strauss, the Confessor and the Writer" (Nietzsche), 175
Davis, Natalie Z., 181, 234, 286
  crowd violence, 345; Martin Guerre, 269, 271; "The Reasons of Misrule," 282; "The Rites of Violence," 282
Dayan, Joan, 425
de Bolla, Peter, 331
de Thou, Jacques-August, 113
death, history of, 342, 343
Decalogue, laws of the, 17
Decameron (Boccaccio), 105
decision making, 351–2
Declamation on the Nobility and Preeminence of the Female Sex (Agrippa), 110
deconstruction, 325–6, 422
deeds, medieval historiography, 80
deforestation, 374
Degler, Carl, 360, 361

degradation, 373
deity see God
Delambre, Jean-Baptiste-Joseph, 304
Delbrück, Hans, 251–2
Della Casa, Giovanni di ser Lodovico, 269
Delphi, 47
deMause, Lloyd, 338–9
D'Emilio, John, 366
democracy, 170, 344
Democracy in America (Tocqueville), 170
Democratic Subjects (Joyce), 287
demography, 238, 376, 379–81
Demos, John, 270, 271
Demosthenes, 55
Dening, Greg, 406
Denis, St., 89
Denmark, historical journals, 230
dependency economics, 393
dependency theory, 285
Derrida, Jacques, 325, 327, 328, 329
desires, 152, 153, 155
despotism
  in Montesquieu, 129, 133, 137; in Raynal and Diderot, 137; in Rousseau, 131; in Voltaire, 133, 137
Deuteronomistic History (DtrH), 16–22, 24, 28, 31
Das Deutsche Reich und der zweite Weltkrieg, 250
development theories, Enlightenment historiography, 127–32
Dialog database, 451, 455
Dialogue on Orators (Tacitus), 63
Diamond, Jared, 399
diasporas, 27, 408–9, 410
Diceto, Ralph, 93
Dictionary of Scientific Biography, 311–12
Dictionnaire biographique, 304
didactic histories, 35, 49, 51
Diderot, Denis, 132, 136–7, 139
Diegues, Carlos, 471–2
difference, 428
digitization, 453
Dilthey, Wilhelm, 226, 321
Dio Cassius, 65
Diodorus of Sicily, 38, 39
Dionysius of Halicarnassus, 38, 65
Dionysus, 175
diphtheria, 404
diplomatics, 227
Dirks, Nicholas, 291
Dirlik, Arif, 428–9
Discipline and Punish (Foucault), 180, 327
discourse, 279, 286–9, 322, 326–8, 418
Discourse on the Origin and Foundations of Inequality Among Men (Rousseau), 131
Discourse on Universal History (Bossuet), 125
discussion lists, 458
disease, 379–80, 393, 403–4
dissertations, 230, 449
diversity
  culture's inability to deal with, 283; post-structuralism, 287, 288
divine will, 199
Dix ans d'études historiques (Thierry), 189
doctoral dissertations, 230, 449

documentation, 8, 320
  legal, 31, 115; microhistory, 262; Middle Ages,
    456; official campaign histories, 250–1; and
    professionalization, 226–32; Renaissance
    historiography, 99, 103, 104, 112–13, 115;
    war historiography, 248, 249
Domesday Book, 452
Dominic, St., 95
Domitian, 63
Donation of Constantine, 103, 114
Dreyer, Carl, 477
The Dreyfus Affair, 466
Driver, Tom, 85
Droysen, J. G., 226, 233, 235, 255
drug therapies, 341
drug trials, 315
DtrH *see* Deuteronomistic History (DtrH)
Du Bois, W. E. B., 240
Du Pont, 305
du Tilh, Armand, 271
Duby, Georges, 233
Dudo of Saint-Quentin, 93
Duhem, Pierre, 306
Dulcinea in the Factory (Farnsworth-Alvear),
    289
Dunning School, 235, 240
Durkheim, Emile, 236–7, 263, 265, 271, 278,
    279, 282, 345, 395
dust bowl, 375, 378
Dust Bowl (Worster), 382
DVDs, 453
dynastic chronicles, medieval historiography, 81

e-books, 457, 460–2
e-mail, 449–50, 457
Eadmer, 93
Eagleton, Terry, 324
ecclesiastical history, 38
Ecclesiastical History of the English People (Bede),
    88, 90–1, 92
Ecclesiastical History (Eusebius), 82, 88, 90
Ecole des Chartes, 230–1
Ecole normale supérieure, 228
Ecole Pratique des Hautes Etudes, 231
ecological harmony, 378
Ecological Imperialism (Crosby), 380
ecological invasions, 380
ecological niches, 379
ecology, 377–8, 382, 383, 399–400
The Ecology of Invasions by Animals and Plants
    (Elton), 380
economic capital, 218
economic determinism, 205, 208, 213, 215, 216
economic history, 238, 264, 337
economic primacy, 214–15, 216
economics, 9, 237, 337, 395
Economy and Society (Weber), 176
ecosystem, 378
écriture, 325
Edinburgh Review, 194, 195, 196, 230
Edinburgh school, 310
Edison, Thomas, 311
Edom, 23
Edwards, Jonathan, 199
ego, 350–1

Egypt
  Herodotus, 41, 42; Israelites in, 24; as part of
    Persian Empire, 37
Egyptian historiography, 15, 18, 20, 32
Ehrlich, Paul, 380
The Eighteenth Brumaire of Louis Napoleon (Marx),
    215
Eijanaika, 478
Einstein, Albert, 298, 299, 307, 311
Eisenstein, Sergei, 467–9, 471, 473, 474, 477
Elagabalus, 76
electoral behavior, 238
electro-magnetism, 299
electronic books, 457, 460–2
electronic journals, 458–60
electronic mail, 449–50, 457
Elias, Norbert, 342–3, 349
Elijah, 83
Elizabeth I, Queen of England, 111
Elkins, 279
Ellis, Havelock, 360
éloges, 302–3, 304
Elohim, 26
Elton, Charles, 378, 379, 380, 382
Elton, Geoffrey, 233
Emerson, Ralph Waldo, 199, 381
emotional constructionism, 349
emotionology, 349
emotions
  Elias, 342–3, 349; Febvre, 349; Geertz, 292;
    Lévi-Strauss, 279; and reason, 351–2; Reddy,
    349; selfhood, 351–2; Thucydides, 47; Turner,
    280–1, 292
emotives, 349
Encyclopedia Britannica, 451
Encyclopedia (Diderot and D'Alembert), 136
Engels, Friedrich, 205, 211
  call for more Marxist history, 218; *The
    Communist Manifesto*, 209; gender inequality,
    288; *The German Ideology*, 206; influence on
    Marx, 207; letters from Marx, 213; materialist
    conception of history, 214–15; study of
    historical events, 220; technique of historical
    writing, 206; war historiography, 254
Engerman, Stanley, 238
England
  Act of Union (1707), 135, 196; Bede's
    Ecclesiastical History of the English People, 88,
    90–1, 92; Catherine Macaulay's *History of
    England*, 135, 193; colonialism, 421–2; crowd
    action, 282, 345; feudalism, 134–5; history of
    science, 303; Hume's *History of England*, 132,
    134–5, 193–4; medieval national
    historiography, 93; Ranke's theory, 168, 171;
    Thomas Babington Macaulay's *History of
    England*, 194–6; vernacular traditions, 107–8
English Historical Review, 230, 231
Enlightenment historiography, 123–41
  colonialism, 136–7; conjectural history, 124,
    130–2, 139–41; four-stages theory, 128, 130,
    136, 137, 139, 196; France, 124, 130, 131–2,
    139, 143, 145–6; German criticism of, 143–4,
    145, 146–7; global narratives, 129, 136–7;
    grand narratives, 127, 139, 141; narrative
    structure, 124, 132, 139; philosophical history,

Enlightenment historiography (*cont'd*)
    123–4, 132–41, 143–4, 145–6, 187; pre-
    Enlightenment traditions, 124–6; progress
    theories, 127, 139, 140, 187–8; property, 128,
    131; reason, 187–8; Scotland, 124, 130–1,
    134–6, 138, 139, 196; total history, 263;
    wars, 244
Enlightenment sensationalism, Kant's critique of,
    151–3
environmental despoilation, 309
environmental determinism, 383
environmental history, 372–86
    Annales school, 374, 376, 377, 379, 382, 385;
    biological diffusions, 393, 403–5, 410;
    colonialism, 380, 383, 384; ecology, 377–8,
    382, 383, 399–400; geography, 375–7, 382;
    integration, 382–6; populations, 379–81;
    reciprocity of people and nature, 374–5, 381;
    wilderness, 381–2
environmental movement, 267, 372–3, 381, 385
Ephorus, 50
epic poetry, 35–7
Epictetus, 53
epidemic disease, 379–80, 393, 403–4
epistemological relativism, 149, 150, 162
Epistles (Pliny), 65, 68
Erasmus, 103
Erikson, Erik H., 338
erosion, 374
erotica, 358
erudite historiography, 125–6, 300
Essay Concerning Human Understanding (Hume),
    193
An Essay on the History of Civil Society (Ferguson),
    130, 131
Essay on Manners (Voltaire), 132, 133–4, 145
Essay on the Study of Literature (Gibbon), 137–8
essence, Marx's view of, 206, 207, 208, 209–10
ether, 299
ethics
    Kant, 151, 152–3, 162; Plutarch, 55
ethnic nationalism, 432, 439–40, 441
ethnicity
    environmental history, 383; Ranke's concerns
    with, 168–9
ethnography, 277, 290–2
    Herodotus, 42, 43; relations of ethnographer
    and subjects, 283, 286; Thucydides, 45
eugenics, 307
Eumaeus, 37
Eurocentrism, 394, 397, 398, 399, 400, 402, 407,
    410
European development, Enlightenment
    historiography, 136–7, 140–1
Eusebius, 82, 88, 90, 102
Evans-Pritchard, Sir Edward Evan, 283
Eve, 82
Event, metaphor, memory: Chauri Chaura (Amin),
    422–3
evolutionary histories, 211–12
evolutionary theory, 299, 308, 374
evolutionary biology, 341
excerpere, 80
exemplar theory of history, 7
    medieval historiography, 79; Roman

historiography, 69–74
existence, 206
Exodus, Book of, 26
experience, 143, 214
exploitation, Marx, 207, 209, 212
"Eyes of the Nation," 453
Ezra, Book of, 17, 30–1
Ezra the scribe, 30, 31

The Fall of the Romanov Dynasty, 468
families, medieval genealogies, 94
family history, 357
Far From Poland, 472
Farge, Arlette, 270
Farnsworth-Alvear, Ann, 289
fascism, 429, 430, 439
Fassbinder, Rainer Werner, 473
fear, Montesquieu, 129
Feature Films as History, 474
Febvre, Lucien, 237, 341–2, 343, 345, 348, 349,
    376
feeling, 143, 281
    see also emotions
Feierman, Steven, 425
femininity, 365, 366, 367
feminism, 267, 283–4, 288–9, 330, 345, 348, 367,
    396
fengjian, 424
Ferguson, Adam, 124, 130, 131, 146
Fernandes, Florestan, 438
Ferro, Marc, 474–5, 476
festivals, 322
fetishism, 364
feudalism
    emergence as socio-economic category, 126; in
    England, 134–5; Herder, 148; Hume, 134–5;
    Montesquieu, 129, 137; Raynal and Diderot,
    137; Robertson, 135–6; Voltaire, 137
Feuerbach, Ludwig, 206
Feyerabend, Paul, 309
Fichte, Johann Gottlieb, 154, 155, 195
Film Historia, 475
The Film in History (Sorlin), 475
films *see* visual media
Fin de Siècle Vienna: Politics and Culture
    (Schorske), 180
Firth, R. W., 279
Fish, Stanley, 320
The Fisherman's Problem (McEvoy), 382
Flamininus, 72
Fleury, 93
Florence, 269
    Bracciolini's *Florentine History*, 105; Bruni's
    Histories of the Florentine People, 102, 103, 104,
    105; Dati's *History of Florence*, 105; literacy,
    105; local chronicles, 105; Machiavelli's
    Florentine Histories, 102, 111, 245
Florentine Histories (Machiavelli), 102, 111, 245
Florentine History (Bracciolini), 105
Florus, 64
Fogel, Robert, 233, 238
Fontenelle, Bernard de, 302
food laws, Jewish, 26, 27
footnotes, 116, 138
forces of production, 213–14

forgeries, medieval political life, 86
Fortescue, John, 251
Foucault, Michel, 182, 418
    The Archaeology of Knowledge, 327; *Birth of the
    Asylum*, 180; *The Birth of The Clinic*, 327;
    chronological organization of his histories, 5;
    Discipline and Punish, 180, 327; discourse,
    289, 326–7, 328; historical continuity, 286;
    History of Sexuality, 181, 346–7, 362–3,
    364–5; knowledge, 180–1, 327; *Madness and
    Civilization*, 327; neglect of gender, 366; New
    Historicism, 163*n*; and Nietzsche, 180–1; *The
    Order of Things*, 327; power, 180–1, 289, 327,
    363, 364, 365, 368; psychoanalysis, 364, 367;
    rejection of psychology, 346–7; sexual
    deviance, 363, 367; sexual identities, 368;
    sexuality as gauge of human freedom, 362,
    368, 369; support from Hayden White, 330
foundationalism, 427
Fournier, Jacques, 268
Fox, Richard, 285
France
    Academy of Sciences, 303; ancient constitution
    debate, 126; archival studies, 234; civic
    nationalism, 432, 434, 435, 440–1;
    colonialism, 421–2, 425; crowd action, 282,
    344, 345; cultural history of labor, 284;
    education, 228, 230–1; emergence after
    collapse of Carolingian Empire, 92;
    Enlightenment historiography, 124, 130,
    131–2, 139, 143, 145–6; erudite
    historiography, 125; genealogically patterned
    chronicles, 94; growth of popular historical
    writing, 185; historical journals, 230; history
    of science, 303; legal tradition, 115; Marx,
    215; medieval national historiography, 93–4;
    Merovingian period, 89, 93, 94; microhistory,
    262, 263, 268, 269–70, 272; multiculturalism,
    434, 440–1, 442, 443, 444; national
    historiography, 93–4, 189–92, 197, 234, 236;
    official campaign histories, 250, 251;
    professional disillusionment, 267;
    professionalization of historical studies, 230–1;
    professionalization and politics, 234, 235, 236;
    Ranke's *History of France*, 249; Ranke's
    theory, 168; royal history, 93–4; total history,
    262, 263–6; universities, 231; vernacular
    traditions, 107; Voltaire's perfected culture of,
    145–6; war with Prussia, 175, 250
Francis, St., 95
Frank, Andre Gunder, 399
Frank, Billy, 385
Frankfurt School, 219
Franks, 87, 88, 89–90, 92
Frazer, James George, 278
fraternity, French national historiography, 192
Frederick II, King of Prussia, 145, 146, 167, 247,
    252
Frederick William, King of Prussia II, 154
Fredrickson, George, 437
Freedman, Estelle, 366
freedom
    American national historiography, 197, 199–200;
    Hegel's spirit, 156, 157, 158; Hume, 193;
    sexuality as gauge to, 362, 368, 369

French Revolution (1789)
    Clausewitz, 249–50; crowd behavior, 344; effect
    on consciousness of history, 277; Hegel, 144,
    158; impact in Britain, 193; impact in
    Germany, 144, 149, 153–4, 155, 158, 168,
    170; justification of private property, 284;
    Kant, 144, 153–4, 155, 158; political
    language, 287; Ranke, 168, 170
French Revolution (1830), 168
Freud, Sigmund, 341, 343, 349, 359, 364
    anti-Freudian writings, 339; *Civilization and its
    Discontents*, 338, 342; dream content, 214;
    ego and superego, 350; feminist criticism of,
    345; *Group Psychology and the Analysis of the
    Ego*, 344; infantile sexual feelings, 339;
    *Leonardo da Vinci and a Memory of His
    Childhood*, 338, 339; psychohistory, 337, 338,
    339, 340; *Totem and Taboo*, 338; unconscious,
    350
Freyre, Gilberto, 435, 438
Freytag, Gustav, 232
From Duty to Desire (Collier), 288–9
Frye, Northrop, 330
Fuchs, Lawrence, 436
functionalism, 377–8
Furet, François, 286, 287
Fustel de Coulanges, 239–40

Gadamer, Hans Georg, 216, 321
Gaimar, 93
Gaius Sallustius Crispus *see* Sallust
Galba, 63
Galbraith, V. H., 78
Galileo, 306
Galison, Peter, 313
Gandhi, 466, 469
Gandhi, Mahatma, 418, 422
Garibaldi, Giuseppe, 254
Gatterer, Johann Cristoph, 227, 394
gay history, 367–8
Gay, Peter, 340, 360–1, 362, 363
Gazi, Effi, 235–6
Gazzaniga, Michael S., 341, 350
Geertz, Clifford, 85, 172, 269, 279, 283, 286
    emotions, 292; empty existential features of life,
    284; feeling, 281; influence of Weber, 181,
    238; *Interpretation of Cultures*, 181;
    orientational requirements, 280; "Person,
    Time, and Conduct in Bali," 280; post-
    structuralist challenge, 287; uniformity of
    cultures, 271
Geist (spirit), 155–9, 206, 207, 420
Gell-Mann, Murray, 262
Gellner, Ernest, 141
"Gender: A Useful Category of Historical Analysis"
    (Scott), 365
gender
    environmental history, 383; feminist insistence
    on importance of, 283–4; historian's
    assumptions about, 7; history of science, 313;
    and power, 366; and psychoanalysis, 345, 346,
    348; and sexuality, 365–7, 369*n*; studies by
    anthropologists and historians, 288–9;
    universal significance, 396; *see also* women's
    history

genealogical chronology
  Greek historiography, 42; Israelite historiography, 23, 25–6, 28; medieval historiography, 94
Genealogies (Hecataeus of Miletus), 37
genealogy, methodological idea of, 181
General Electric, 305
Genesis, Book of, 23, 25, 26, 83
genetic force, 151
genetics, 299–300
geo-body, 421–2
Geoffrey of Monmouth, 93
geography, 9, 237, 264, 375–7, 382
  Herodotus, 42, 43, 56; Montesquieu, 129; world history, 399–400
Georgetown University, 455
Gerald of Wales, 93
German historiography
  Hegelian philosophy of history, 144–5, 151, 154–9, 161, 162; Kantian philosophy of history, 143–4, 151–4, 155, 156, 158, 162; legacies inherited by modern writing, 161–2; nation-state formation, 166–7, 168–70, 175–6; nationalism, 144, 166, 170; primacy of politics, 166–82; *see also* historicism, German; Ranke, Leopold von
German idealism, 155, 187, 199
The German Ideology (Marx), 206, 207, 208, 209, 210, 211
German Reformation, 134, 136, 157, 166, 169
German Romanticism, 154
German Social Democratic Party, 177
Germani, Gino, 435
Germania (Tacitus), 63
Germanus, 89
Germany
  academic freedom, 235; adoption of French Enlightenment standards, 145–6; archival studies, 234–5; aristocratic privilege, 148–9; building of nation-state, 166–7, 168–70, 175–6; economists, 176–7; educated elite, 166–7, 169; education reform, 228; emergence after collapse of Carolingian Empire, 92; estate system, 148–9; ethnic nationalism, 439–40; higher education, 227; historical journals, 230; history as a science, 226; history workshop movement, 239; medieval national historiography, 93, 94; microhistory, 269; multiculturalism, 439–40, 441; national historiographies, 234–5, 236, 434; nationalism, 144; Nazism, 228, 306–7; New German Cinema, 478; official campaign histories, 250, 251; professionalization of historical studies, 227, 228–30, 237–8; professionalization and politics, 234–5, 236; reactions to French Revolution, 144, 149, 153–4, 155, 158, 168, 170; religious identity, 166; teaching of history, 227; tribal past, 148, 160; universities, 227, 228–30; *see also* Prussia
Gervase of Canterbury, 93
gesta, 80
Gesta episcoporum Mettensium (Paul the Deacon), 92
Getica (Jordanes), 88, 89
Gibbon, Edward, 123, 124, 132, 137–9, 140, 187, 225

Giesebrecht, Wilhelm von, 230
Gilbert, Felix, 253
Gildas, 91, 93
Gillispie, Charles C., 312
Ginzburg, Carlo, 233, 268–9, 270, 273
Giotto di Bondone, 101
Giovanni and Lusanna (Brucker), 270–1
Giovio, Paolo, 112–13, 229
Girardet, Raoul, 253
Glazer, Nathan, 433
global narratives, Enlightenment historiography, 129, 136–7
globalization, 10, 397, 429
God
  Augustine's *City of God*, 70, 82–3; Hegel's spirit, 155; Israelite historiography, 15; notion of the "elect Nation," 81; operation within history, 81–2; *see also* YAHWEH
Godmilow, Jill, 472
Goethe, Johann Wolfgang von, 148, 149, 154, 373, 381, 384, 385
Goffart, Walter, 82, 88, 89
Goffman, Erving, 272
Gone With the Wind, 467
Gooch, George P., 229
Goodman, James, 270
Goody, Jack, 285
Gossmann, Lionel, 180
Goths, 88, 89
Göttingen, University of, 227
Gottschalk, Louis, 473–4
Goubert, Pierre, 265
government forms, Montesquieu, 129
Gracchi, 62
grace, 83
Gramsci, Antonio, 216–17, 218, 419, 428
grand narratives, 127, 139, 141, 239
Grandes Chroniques de France (Primat), 93–4
gravity, theory of, 298, 305
gravity waves, 310
great flood, 22, 23, 26
The Great Plains (Webb), 375
Greece, professionalization, 235–6
Greek Cultural History (Burckhardt), 174
Greek historiography, 35–57
  biography, 35, 53–6, 57; epic poetry, 35–7; genealogical chronology, 42; imperialism, 41; influence on Roman historiography, 64–8; Israelite historiography, 30, 32; king-lists, 40; legacy of, 56–7; military leadership, 48–50; myths, 42; nature of time, 81; oral traditions, 36–7, 40, 42, 43, 228; political leadership, 35, 48–50
Greeks, ancient, 23, 174
Green, John Richard, 232
Greenblatt, Stephen, 163*n*
Gregory, Brad, 273, 275*n*
Gregory of Tours, 83, 87, 88, 89–90, 92, 93
Grendi, Edoardo, 271
Griffith, David Wark, 467, 468
Grimm Brothers, 91
Grimoald I, 92
Grimoald III, 92
Gross, Paul R., 314
Grossberg, Michael, 459

Grotius, Hugo, 127
Group Psychology and the Analysis of the Ego
     (Freud), 344
Grove, Richard, 384
Grundrisse (Marx), 210, 211, 212, 215, 221
Guenée, Bernard, 80
Guerre, Martin, 263, 269, 271, 466, 469
Guha, Ranajit, 285, 418
Guicciardini, Francesco, 106–7, 111–12, 113, 114,
     126, 229
Guillaume de Nangis, 93
Guillaume le Breton, 93
Guizot, François, 229, 232
Gunkel, H., 33*n*
Gutenberg-E program, 460–1
Gymnasien, 228

H-Net, 457–8
Habermas, Jürgen, 219
Habilitation, 230
Hadrian, 64
hagiographies, medieval historiography, 81, 83, 91
Haitian revolution, 425
Hale, John, 257
Halicarnassus, 39–40
Hammonds, Barbara, 232
Hammonds, John, 232
Handbook of Social Psychology, 349–50
Hannibal, 52
Hanning, Robert, 91
Haraway, Donna, 313
Hays, Samuel, 382
Hazard, Paul, 125, 126
Headrick, Daniel, 407
heavenly bodies, 25
*The Heavenly City of the Eighteenth-Century
     Philosophers* (Becker), 127
Hecataeus of Miletus, 37, 39
Hegel, Georg Wilhelm Friedrich
     alienation, 155, 159, 161; concept of spirit *Geist*,
          155–9, 206, 207, 420; the "concrete," 210,
          211; consciousness, 156; contradictions, 159,
          161; end of history, 144–5, 159, 160, 162;
          freedom, 156, 157, 158; historical teleology,
          211; influence on postcolonial historians, 419,
          420; *Lectures on the Philosophy of History*,
          156–7, 158, 160, 419; Marx's critique of,
          159, 206–9, 216; philosophy of history,
          144–5, 151, 154–9, 160, 161, 162, 195; *The
          Philosophy of Right*, 158–9
hegemony, 289
Helen, 42
Hellenica (Theopompus), 50
Helms, Mary W., 406
Helvidius, 63
Hempel, Carl Gustav, 339
Henry II, King of England, 93
Henry of Huntington, 93
heraldics, 227
Herder, Johann Gottfried
     alienation, 144, 154–5, 160; "Also a Philosophy
          of History for the Cultivation of Humanity,"
          145–7, 148, 150; historicism, 143, 144,
          145–52, 158, 160, 188; *Ideas For a Philosophy
          of History*, 150, 151, 152; legacy of, 161, 162;

Sturm und Drang movement, 148, 149, 154
heredity, 300
hermeneutics, 227, 321
Herodian, 38, 65
Herodotus, 8, 10, 30, 35, 37, 38, 39–43, 45
     Battle of Marathon, 251–2; comparisons of
          values and actions, 55; custom, 42–3; divine
          intervention, 21; geography, 42, 43, 56;
          influence on Renaissance historiography, 102;
          information sources, 40, 41–3, 56; legacy of,
          56–7; motives of his investigations, 68; Persian
          kings, 22; sense of duty, 73; skepticism, 15,
          74; wise advisers and oracles, 21, 47; world
          history viewpoint, 394; and Xenophon, 49
heroes, 22, 23, 174
Hessen, Boris, 309
heteroglossia, 322, 325
heterosexuality, 364
Hezekiah, 29
Higham, John, 225
Higher Superstition (Gross and Levitt), 314
Hildreth, Richard, 198
Hill, Christopher, 309
Hindu ritual kingship, 291
Hinduism, 377
Hintze, Otto, 251, 252–3
Histoire de France (Michelet), 190, 191
Histoire de la Révolution française (Michelet),
     190
Historia Augusta, 64
Historia Francorum (Aimoin of Fleury), 93
The Historian and Film, 474
historical continuity, 5, 286
Historical and Critical Dictionary (Bayle), 125
historical demography, 238
Historical Discourse (Barthes), 328
*Historical Disquisition concerning the Knowledge
     which the Ancients had of India* (Robertson),
     136
historical ethnography, 277
historical geography, 264
historical ideal types, 208
Historical Library (Vignier), 107
historical materialism, 159, 160, 214–15, 383
historical specificity, 168
historical thought
     actions and social structures, 8; belief in
          recognizable meanings, 5–6; cultural
          contextualism, 10; distinctiveness of cultures,
          6; exemplary models, 7; global understanding,
          10; identity creation, 7; importance of
          verifiable evidence, 8; interdisciplinary
          methods, 9; objectivity, 8–9; and politics, 7–8;
          tradition and themes of, 4–10; universal
          patterns of meaning, 6; widening subjects of,
          9–10
historicism, 6, 286, 301
historicism, German, 140, 143–4
     alienation, 144, 154–5, 160; before 1800,
          145–51; criticism of Enlightenment, 143–4,
          145, 146–7; definition, 143; focus on German
          traditions, 144; German tribalism, 148, 160;
          individuality, 146–7, 149; legacy of, 161–2;
          mythological origins, 148–9, 160; paradoxical
          desire to escape history, 160; relativism,

historicism, German (*cont'd*)
    149–50, 162; *see also* Herder, Johann
    Gottfried; Möser, Justus; Ranke, Leopold von
historicus, 80
Histories (Herodotus), 39–43
Histories (Polybius), 51–2
Histories (Sallust), 61
Histories (Tacitus), 63, 66, 73
Histories of the Florentine People (Bruni), 102, 103,
    104, 105
Histories of His Own Times (Giovio), 112, 113
The Histories of the Latin and Germanic Peoples
    (Ranke), 229
Histories of the Swiss (Müller), 248
historiographus, 80
Historische Zeitschrift, 230
Historisk Tidskrift, 230
Historism (Meinecke), 163*n*
history
    in education curriculum, 117*n*; Hegel's end of,
    144–5, 159, 160, 162; medieval definitions of,
    79; as a science, 226–7, 232, 233, 236–7;
    versus science, 298–302; *see also*
    professionalization
History (Higham), 225
History of the Abbots of Wearmouth-Jarrow (Bede),
    91
History of Alexander the Great (Arrian), 53–4
History of America (Robertson), 132, 136
History of the Art of War, 251
History of the August City of Turin (Tesauro), 115
History of the British Army (Fortescue), 51
History of the Britons (Nennius), 91
History of Charles XII (Voltaire), 133
History of Civilization in England (Buckle), 233
"History Cooperative" website, 459
*The History of the Decline and Fall of the Roman
    Empire* (Gibbon), 132, 138–9
History of Early Rome (Dionysius of Halicarnassus),
    38
History of England (Catherine Macaulay), 135, 193
History of England (Hume), 132, 134–5, 193–4
History of England (Thomas Babington Macaulay),
    194–6
History and Film, 475
History of Florence (Dati), 105
History of France (Ranke), 249
History of the Franks (Gregory of Tours), 87, 88,
    89–90
History from the Decline of the Roman Empire
    (Bondi), 103
History of Great Britain (Hume), 134
History of Greece (Xenophon), 48–50
History of the Inductive Science (Whewell), 304–5
History of Italy (Guicciardini), 106, 112, 113
History of the Jewish People (Josephus), 38
History of the Liberty of the Swiss (Gibbon), 138
History of the Lombards (Paul the Deacon), 88,
    91–2
History of the Modern Fact (Poovey), 287
"History Online" Institute, 455
History of Osnabrück (Möser), 147
History of the Peloponnesian War (Thucydides),
    43–7
History of Pornography (Hyde), 358

History of the Reign of the Emperor Charles V
    (Robertson), 132, 135–6
History of the Reign of King Henry the Seventh
    (Bacon), 114
History of Science Society, 307, 314–15
History of Scotland (Robertson), 135
History of the Seven Years War (Frederick the
    Great), 247
History of Sexuality (Foucault), 181, 346–7, 362–3,
    364–5
History of the Two Indies (Raynal and Diderot),
    132, 136–7
History of the United States (Bancroft), 198,
    199–200
*History of the Warfare of Science with Technology in
    Christendom* (White), 305
history workshop movement, 239
The History of the World (Raleigh), 107
Hitler, Adolf, 76, 338, 344
Hitler, a Film from Germany, 472
Hittites, 15, 20
Hobbes, Thomas, 127, 313
Hobsbawm, Eric, 217
Hodgson, Marshall G. S., 397
Hoerder, Dirk, 440
Hohenstaufen dynasty, 94
Hokkaido, 425
Hollan, Douglas, 292
Holocaust, 331–2, 453–4
Holy Roman Empire, 107, 147, 149, 169
The Home and the World, 478
Homer, 35–6, 37, 39, 45, 47, 67, 69
homosexuality, 363, 364, 366, 367–8
honor, Montesquieu, 129
Horace, 67
Horkheimer, Max, 219
How to Write History (Lucian), 67
Howard, Michael, 258
Hubbard, Ruth, 313
human nature, Thucydides, 46–7
human rights, 188, 420
Humanität, 150, 152
Humboldt, Wilhelm von, 161, 228
Hume, David, 123, 124, 138, 139, 140, 187
    Essay Concerning Human Understanding, 193;
    feudalism, 134–5; *History of England*, 132,
    134–5, 193–4; *History of Great Britain*, 134;
    Treatise of Human Nature, 134
Hunt, Lynn, 283, 329
hunting techniques, 377
Hurley, Andrew, 384
hybridization, 300
Hyde, Montgomery, 358

"Idea for a Universal History With a Cosmopolitan
    Purpose" (Kant), 151, 152, 153, 154, 156
ideal types, 208
Ideas For a Philosophy of History (Herder), 150,
    151, 152
identity
    creation of, 7; and postcolonialism, 418; and
    sexuality, 363–4, 368
identity, corporate
    Israelite historiography, 15, 20, 27, 32; Near
    East historical genres, 15

identity, ethnic
  imperialism and colonialism, 407–8; Israelite
    historiography, 24, 27, 28
identity, national
  imperialism and colonialism, 407–8; Israelite
    historiography, 20, 27
identity, religious, 166
Iliad (Homer), 36, 39, 67
illegitimacy rates, 357
imagination, French national historiography, 190
imagined communities, 185
Imamura, Shohei, 478
Imitation of Christ, 191
imperial chronicles, medieval historiography, 81
imperialism
  Enlightenment historiography, 136; Greek
    historiography, 41; Japan, 420–1;
    multiculturalism, 432–3; postcolonial history,
    418; world history, 393, 395, 406–8, 410; *see
    also* colonialism
impulses, 156, 279, 342
Inca civilization, 211, 288
Incarnation, 81, 82
indentured labor, 409
India, 136, 402, 418, 422–3
Indian Ocean basin, 401
individualism
  Burckhardt, 173; emergence of, 338, 347–8;
    Kant, 153
individuality, 146–7, 149
Indonesia, 402
industrialization, 380, 395, 399
infantile sexual feelings, 339, 340
influence on Renaissance
  historiography, oral traditions, 113, 115
information industries, 315
information sources
  Arrian, 53; Enlightenment historiography, 140;
    expansion of, 140; Herodotus, 40, 41–3, 56;
    idea of original source, 104; Israelite
    historiography, 15, 17, 22, 31; libraries,
    450–2, 453, 454–5, 456, 460, 462–3;
    Macaulay, 194; national historiography, 188;
    Plutarch, 54–5; Polybius, 52; Renaissance
    historiography, 103–4, 112–13, 115–16;
    Roman historiography, 67; status of, 321;
    Thucydides, 45–6, 56; Xenophon, 50; *see also*
    archives; artifacts; documentation
information technologies *see* computers
Inheriting Power (Levi), 272
*An Inquiry into the Nature and Causes of the
  Wealth of Nations* (Smith), 130
instincts, 152, 153, 155, 342
Institutes (Quintilian), 66
intellectual history, science as, 305–9
intellectual history epochs, 132
intellectual property, 316
internalization, 348
Internet, 450, 452, 454, 457–62
Interpretation of Cultures (Geertz), 181
intransitive writing, 332
The Invasion of New Zealand (Clark), 380
investigation, Herodotus, 41–2
Isaac, 23, 28
Isidore of Seville, 80, 90

Isis, 307
Islam, 377, 405
Israel, ancient, Weber, 179
Israelite historiography, 15–32
  chronicles, 16; corporate identity, 15, 20, 27, 32;
    cosmology, 24–5; Court History of David,
    21–2, 28; creation accounts, 22, 23, 24–5;
    Deuteronomistic History (DtrH), 16–22, 24,
    28, 31; eternal covenant, 26; ethnic identity,
    24, 27, 28; genealogical chronology, 23, 25–6,
    28; information sources, 15, 17, 22, 31;
    monarchy, 18–19, 21; myths, 15, 22, 25;
    national identity, 20, 27; patriarchal age, 24;
    priestly cults, 26–7; Priestly History (P),
    16–17, 24–7, 28; relationship to promised
    land, 17, 20, 24, 32; Second Temple period,
    26–7, 28; YAHWEH, 17–18, 19, 20–1, 23, 24,
    26, 27; Yahwist's History (J), 16–17, 22–4,
    25, 26–7
Italy
  historical journals, 230; medieval national
    historiography, 93, 94; microhistory, 262, 263,
    268–9, 270, 272; multiculturalism, 441;
    professional disillusionment, 267;
    professionalization of historical studies, 231;
    see also Renaissance historiography

J *see* Yahwist's History (J)
Jacob, 23, 28
Jacobinism, 286
Japan
  historical journals, 230; nationalism and
    imperialism, 420–1, 425–6; professionalization
    of historical studies, 225, 231;
    professionalization and politics, 235; trade, 402
Japan's Orient (Tanaka), 420
Jaspers, Karl, 176
Jaurès, Jean, 232
Java, 291
Jefferson, Thomas, 75, 381
Jeroboam, 19, 22
Jerome, St., 82, 88
Jerusalem
  as centre of community of Israel, 18, 31–2;
    David's descendants on throne of, 19;
    destruction of, 19; rebuilding of walls by
    Nehemiah, 30, 31
Jerusalem Temple, 19, 28
  rebuilding under Zerubbabel, 30, 31
Jesuit college system, 117*n*
Jesuits, 229
Jesus Christ
  Incarnation, 81, 82; as redeemer, 83
Jewish diaspora, 27
Jewish nation, elected by God, 81
Jewish War (Josephus), 38
JFK, 473, 475
Joachim of Fiore, 83
Joan of Arc, 191
Joan of Arc (film), 477
John of Salisbury, 82
Johns Hopkins University, 231
Johnson, Virginia, 360
Jones, E. L., 398
Jordan of Fantosmes, 93

Jordanes, 88, 89
Joseph story, 24
Josephus, 31, 33*n*, 38, 65
Joshua, 17, 20, 27
Joshua, Book of, 17–18
Josiah, King of Judah, 17, 19, 29
Journal of Psychohistory, 338, 339
journals, 140, 230, 458–60
Joyce, Patrick, 287
JSTOR project, 460
Judah, kingdom of, 28, 29–31
Judaism, 81, 133
judgment, Herodotus, 41–2
Judges, Book of, 18
Jugurthine war, 61
justice, French national
    historiography, 189
Justin, 64, 65, 72
Juvaini, 394

Kagan, Richard, 270
Kant, Immanuel, 143–4, 151–4, 163*n*, 195
    alienation, 155; autonomy, 152, 153, 155, 156,
        158; *Critique of Practical Reason*, 151, 152,
        154, 155; *Critique of Pure Reason*, 151;
        Enlightenment sensationalism, 151–3; ethics,
        151, 152–3, 162; French Revolution (1789),
        144, 153–4, 155, 158; "Idea for a Universal
        History With a Cosmopolitan Purpose," 151,
        152, 153, 154, 156; "thing in itself," 240
Kaplan, Robert D., 260*n*
Keczkemeti, Paul, 254
Keller, Evelyn Fox, 313
Kelvin, Lord, 305
Kepler, Johannes, 304
king-lists
    Babylonian historiography, 25–6; Greek
        historiography, 40; Israelite historiography, 16;
        Mesopotamian historiography, 22; Near East
        historical genres, 16
Kings, Books of, 17, 18, 19, 21, 29
kings, deeds of
    Israelite historiography, 15–16; Near East
        historical genres, 15
kingship
    creation of, 25; French medieval historiography,
        93–4; medieval consecration ceremony, 85; *see
        also* monarchy
Kluge, Alexander, 478
Kluwer, 459, 460
knowledge
    Foucault, 180–1, 327; Marx, 207
knowledge production, 418, 421
knowledge-based economy, 315–16
Korea, professionalization of historical studies, 225,
    231
Kornbluh, Mark, 458
Koyré, Alexandre, 307
Krafft-Ebing, Richard von, 363–4, 366
Kristeller, Paul Oskar, 101
Ku Klux Klan, 467, 468
Kuehn, Thomas, 270–1
Kuhn, Thomas, 308–9, 310
Kulturkampf, 306
Kurosawa, Akira, 270

labor
    cultural history of, 284; indentured, 409; Marx,
        207, 211
labor, division of, 130–1, 211
labor historians, 330, 396
labor migrations, 409
labor militancy, 209
Labrousse, Ernest, 264
Labyrinth, 455
Lacan, Jacques, 322
LaCapra, Dominick, 329
Lagrange, Joseph Louis, Comte de, 304
Lamprecht, Karl, 233, 237
Land Use, Environment, and Social Change
    (White), 382
Landes, David S., 398
Lang, Berel, 332
Langer, William L., 338
language, 239, 286–7, 321, 346; *see also* linguistics
langue, 323, 325
Languedoc, 238, 265–6
Lanzmann, Claude, 472
Laqueur, Thomas, 313, 365, 366–7
The Last Days of Pompeii, 466
Latin America
    multiculturalism, 434–5, 438–9, 442;
        professionalization of historical studies, 231;
        subaltern studies, 428
Latin American Studies of Migration, 438
Latour, Bruno, 312
Lavisse, Ernest, 231
law
    French national historiography, 189–90;
        Hegel's spirit, 157; Macaulay, 195;
        Montesquieu, 129; Renaissance historiography,
        114, 115
Lays of Ancient Rome (Macaulay), 194
Le Bon, Gustave, 344
Le Goff, Jacques, 233
Le Roy Ladurie, Emmanuel, 233, 267, 269
    Montaillou, 268, 270; new technology, 448;
        The Peasants of Languedoc, 238, 265–6,
        376
Leach, Edmund, 279
Lecky, W. E. H., 232
Lectures on the Philosophy of History (Hegel), 156–7,
    158, 160, 419
legal documents, 31, 115
legal historians, 115
legends
    Babylonian legend of Sargon, 24, 33*n*; Israelite
        historiography, 15; medieval political life, 86;
        see also myths
lek, 280
Lenin, Vladimir Ilich, 468
Léonard, Emile G., 253
Leonardo da Vinci, 101, 339
Leonardo da Vinci and a Memory of His Childhood
    (Freud), 338, 339
Leopold, Aldo, 377, 378, 379, 382, 385
Leopold of Austria, 248
lesbian history, 367, 368
Lessing, Gottfried, 163*n*
Letters Concerning the English Nation (Voltaire),
    124, 132

Lettres sur l'histoire de France (Thierry), 189
Levi, Giovanni, 234, 266–7, 271, 272, 273
Lévi-Strauss, Claude, 279, 280–1, 283, 286, 287, 322
Leviathan and the Air-Pump (Shapin and Schaffer), 312–13
Levitical priesthood, 28
Levitt, Norman, 314
Lexis/Nexis database, 451, 455, 460
liberal humanitarianism, 181
liberalism
    national historiography, 188; war historiography, 254
liberty
    French national historiography, 189, 192, 197; Hume, 193; Scottish national historiography, 196–7
libraries, 450–2, 453, 454–5, 456, 460, 462–3
library catalogues, 451–2
Library of Congress, 453
Library of History (Diodorus of Sicily), 38
Libya, as part of Persian Empire, 37
Liebig, Justus, 306
Life of Gregory the Great (Paul the Deacon), 92
Life of Saint Cuthbert (Bede), 91
light, creation of, 25
Lily Marlene, 469
Lingua Franca, 314
linguistic signs, 322–4, 346
linguistics, 9, 256, 257, 292, 319–33
    discourse, 322, 326–8; linguistic turn, 328–30; post-structuralism, 324–6; Renaissance historiography, 103; semiotics, 322–3; structuralism, 322, 323–4; textual analysis, 320–3
Linneaus, Carolus, 381
literacy, ancient Greece, 38
literary criticism, 11, 278, 322
literary studies, 9, 319–33
literature, 232–4, 239
Liu Zhiji, 231
Lives of the Caesars (Suetonius), 64
Lives of Eminent Artists (Vasari), 100–1
Lives of Illustrious Men (Vespasiano), 108
Livy, 61, 62, 64, 65, 67, 68
    influence on Renaissance historiography, 75, 101–2, 103; moral exemplars, 71–2, 73; Niebuhr's studies of, 228; and Petrarch, 99; and Plutarch, 55; skepticism, 74; writing style, 66
Lloyd, Elizabeth, 313
Locke, John, 187, 375
logical positivism, 306, 308
Logiques de la foule (Farge and Revel), 270
Lombards, 88, 91–2
Louis XIV, King of France, 133, 146
Louis XVI, King of France, 155
Louis Napoleon, 191, 209
Louis Philippe, 189
Louis the Pious, 92
Löwith, Karl, 179
Lucian, 67
Lucrecia de Leon, 270
Lucullus, 61
Ludwig, Emil, 232

Luitprand, 92
Lukács, Georg, 176
Luke, St., 38
Lumière brothers, 466
Lusanna di Girolamo, 269
Luther, Martin, 157, 169, 338, 353
Lutz, Catherine, 292
Lydia, 40
Lyell, Charles, 374
Lyotard, Jean-François, 127, 139, 141
Lysander, 49

Mabillon, Jean, 125
Mably, Gabriel Bonnot de, 126
Macaulay, Catharine, 135, 193, 225
Macaulay, Thomas Babington, 186, 194–6, 200, 201, 255
McCrie, Rev. Thomas, 202*n*
Macedonia, 51
McEvoy, Arthur, 382, 383, 384
Mach, Ernst, 306
Machiavelli, Niccolò, 100, 114, 115, 126, 225
    advice literature, 106, 329; *Art of War*, 245; *Florentine Histories*, 102, 111, 245; inspired by Livy, 75; *The Prince*, 106, 245, 329; war historiography, 245
The Machiavellian Moment (Pocock), 126
machine politics, 178
McKinsey and Co., 463
McNeill, William, 141, 379, 380, 381, 383, 397, 404
Macrobius, 70
Madness and Civilization (Foucault), 327
Magna Carta, 452
The Making of the English Working Class (Thompson), 217
Making Salmon (Taylor), 385
Making Sex (Laqueur), 366–7
Malatesta, Battista, 102, 109
Malatesta, Galeazzo, 102
Malinowski, Bronislaw, 279, 282
Mallon, Florencia, 428
Malthusian theory, 299, 310
Man and Nature (Marsh), 372, 374
Mandrou, Robert, 264
Manhattan Project, 307, 311
Manlius Vulso, 71
Mann, Michael, 141
manners, history of, 342–3
Manning, Patrick, 409
Mantinea, 48, 50
manuscripts
    Middle Ages, 456; Renaissance historiography, 99, 104; *see also* documentation
Manville, Brook, 463
Mao Zedong, 419
Marathon, Battle of, 251–2
Marcus, Steven, 358–61, 362, 369
Margaret of Austria, 110
Marinella, Lucrezia, 110–11
maritime regions, 401
Marius, Gaius, 61, 70
Mark Antony, 54
market economy, 227, 228
maroon societies, 409

marriage, 289, 290
Marsh, George Perkins, 372, 373, 374, 375, 377,
    379, 381, 382, 383, 384
Marshall, S. L. A., 258
Martin Guerre (Davis), 269, 271
Martin of Tours, St., 89
martyrs, Gregory of Tours, 90
Marx, Anthony, 437
Marx, Karl, 11, 139, 141, 145, 205–21, 285, 395
    Capital, 210, 212–14, 219; *The Civil War in
    France*, 215; class relations, 201, 205, 213,
    214, 398; *The Class Struggles in France*, 215;
    The Communist Manifesto, 209; conceptions of
    theory and history, 208–16, 219, 220–1;
    critique of Hegel, 159, 206–9, 216; *Critique
    of Political Economy*, 213, 221; critique of
    professionalism, 236; *The Eighteenth Brumaire
    of Louis Napoleon*, 215; essence, 206, 207,
    208, 209–10; exploitation, 207, 209, 212; *The
    German Ideology*, 206, 207, 208, 209, 210,
    211; *Grundrisse*, 210, 211, 212, 215, 221;
    historical transcendence, 161; and later
    Marxist historians, 216–18; Macaulay's
    criticism, 196; materialism, 159, 160, 214–15;
    misunderstandings of, 205–6; opposition of
    national historiography, 188; philosophy, 208,
    209, 220–1; production means/modes, 205,
    208, 211, 212–13, 214, 215; "Theses on
    Feuerbach," 207, 209; thought, 209, 210,
    214; war historiography, 254; and Weber, 179
Marxism, 266–7, 285
    compared with nationalism, 201; critique by
    Weber, 179; critique of postcolonialism, 427;
    lines of causation, 287; linguistic turn, 330;
    revolutions, 218–19; structuralism, 324;
    subaltern studies, 418–19; universalism, 162;
    war historiography, 254
masculinity, 365, 366, 367
masochism, 363, 364, 366
mass culture, 219
mass production, 213
Masters, William, 360
materialism, 159, 160, 187, 214–15, 383
Matthew of Paris, 93
Maurists, 125, 227, 229
Maxwell, James Clerk, 299, 311
Mead, Margaret, 280
measles, 379, 403, 404
Mechanics Institutes, 310
medical advances, 380
*The Medical and Surgical History of the War of the
    Rebellion*, 250
mendicant orders, 95
Medici, Cosimo de', 106, 108
Medici family, 133
Medici, Lorenzo de', 106
medieval government, 85
medieval historiography, 78–96
    barbarian histories, 88–90; biblical chronological
    schemes, 83; biblical typological interpretation,
    84–5; body and self, 353; characteristics of,
    79–87; chronicles, 79, 80–1, 94, 95; diversity
    of forms and practices, 78–9, 80–1; evolution
    of writing, 87–96; exemplar theory of history,
    79; failings of, 78; hagiographies, 81, 83, 91;

influence of Cicero, 79, 80, 81; monastic
    histories, 79, 81; narrative structure, 86–7;
    political utility of history, 85–6; rhetoric, 78,
    79–80, 81; terminology describing
    historians/historical texts, 80; universal
    history, 82–3, 88; wars, 244; weak sense of
    chronology, 85
medieval pedagogy, 78
The Mediterranean (Braudel), 263, 264, 401
Medline, 451
Meek, Ronald, 130, 131
Mehring, Franz, 232
Mein Kampf (Hitler), 344
Meinecke, Friedrich, 150, 163*n*
Melanesia, 282
Meleager, 36
Melian dialogue, 46, 47
Méliès, George, 466
Mellon, Andrew W., Foundation, 460
memory, 292, 351, 352, 353
Memphis, 42
Mendel, Gregor, 299–300
Menocchio, 268–9
mental illness, 327
mentalities, history of, 238, 264, 343
Mercenary Companies and the Decline of Siena
    (Caferro), 256
Merchant, Carolyn, 383
meritocracy, 303
Merovingian France, 89, 93, 94
Merton, Robert K., 309–10
mesmerism, 339
Mesopotamia, 18, 20, 21, 22
Metahistory (White), 328, 330–1
metanarratives, 331
metaphor, 476, 479–80
metaphysics, 144, 154–9, 195
Method for the Easy Comprehension of History
    (Bodin), 113–14
Metz, Bishops of, 92
Mexico, 435, 439
Michelangelo, 101
Michelet, Jules, 185, 193
    archival research, 234; critique by Barthes, 328;
    Histoire de France, 190, 191; *Histoire de la
    Révolution française*, 190; national
    historiography, 186, 190–2, 197, 200; *Le
    peuple*, 190, 191, 192; and Vico, 128; war
    historiography, 255–6
Michelet, Pauline, 191–2
Michelson–Morley experiment, 299
Michigan State University, 457–8
microbes, 379–80
microhistory, 265, 266–74, 291
    of the extraordinary, 269–71, 274; France, 262,
    263, 268, 269–70, 272; Germany, 269; Italy,
    262, 263, 268–9, 270, 272; of the ordinary,
    271–3, 274; problem of generalization, 273–4;
    rejection of large-scale models, 263; United
    States, 263, 270
Middle Ages
    behavior codes, 343; manuscript culture, 456;
    national historiographies, 89, 92–4; *see also*
    medieval historiography
midrash, 27, 30

migrations, 393, 408–9, 410, 433, 441
military history *see* war historiography
military leadership, Greek historiography, 48–50
"Military Organization and the Organization of the State" (Hintze), 252
Mill, John Stuart, 195
Millar, John, 124, 130
Millikan, Robert, 311
Milton, John, 194
Mimnermus, 67
mind, 341
Mintz, Sidney, 285
miracles
    Bede, 91; Gregory of Tours, 90
missionaries, 290, 406
MLA Bibliography, 451
Moab, 23
modernization, 227, 343
modernization theory, 398, 399, 402
Mommsen, Theodor, 233
monarchical governments, Montesquieu, 129
monarchy
    absolute monarchies, 126, 134; Egyptian historiography, 18; Israelite historiography, 18–19, 21; Mesopotamian historiography, 18, 21; *see also* kingship
monastic histories, medieval historiography, 79, 81
monastic houses, French medieval historiography, 93–4
monastic humility, 80
money, 211
Monod, Gabriel, 231
monographs, 456–7, 460–1
Montaigne, Michel Eyquem de, 172
Montaillou (Le Roy Ladurie), 268, 270
Monte Cassino, 92
Montesquieu, Charles de Secondat, 132, 138
    despotism, 129, 133, 137; dispute with Voltaire, 137; feudalism, 129, 137; Herder's criticism of, 146; *On the Spirit of the Laws*, 124, 128–9, 130, 133; *Persian letters*, 124, 129
Monumenta Germaniae historica, 229, 234
monumental inscriptions, Near East historical genres, 15
Moon, Sun, and Witches (Silverblatt), 288
moral agency, 152
moral autonomy, 152, 153
moral conformity, 181
"The Moral Economy of the English Crowd in the Eighteenth Century" (Thompson), 282
moral exemplars, 7, 69–74, 79
moral order, 23
moral philosophy, 198
moral progress, 198
moral relativism, 149–50, 162
Moralia (Plutarch), 54
Mosaic code, 17, 29
Möser, Justus, 143, 144, 147, 148–9, 160, 161
Moses, 17, 24, 26, 27
motion pictures *see* visual media
motivations, 153
Motley, John, 198, 232
movies *see* visual media
Muir, John, 381
Müller, Johannes von, 247–8, 250

multiculturalism, 3, 427, 432–44
    English-speaking world, 435–7, 443–4; Europe, 437, 439–41; France, 434, 440–1, 442, 443, 444; Germany, 439–40, 441; Latin America, 434–5, 438–9, 442; United States, 435–7, 442, 443–4
Muratori, Ludovico, 125, 229
Mussolini, Benito, 217, 344
Mythologies (Barthes), 323
myths
    German historicism, 148–9, 160; Greek historiography, 42; Israelite historiography, 15, 22, 25; medieval political life, 86; *see also* legends

naming systems, 279
Napoleon Bonaparte, 144, 149, 156, 167, 169, 170, 250, 252
Napoleon III, 191, 209
narratives
    different forms of, 5; Enlightenment historiography, 124, 132, 139; global narratives of the Enlightenment, 129, 136–7; grand narratives of the Enlightenment, 127, 139, 141; Israelite historiography, 15; medieval historiography, 86–7; modern historiography, 141
Narratives of Enlightenment (O'Brien), 123–4
Nash, Roderick, 381–2, 383
Nathan, 22
Nation, 230
nation, Ranke's concerns with, 168–70
nation-state, 185, 395
    German historiography, 166–7, 168–70, 175–6; Hegel, 206; multiculturalism, 432–44
national character, notion of, 135
national historiographies, 166, 185–201
    archives, 188, 194, 234–5; Britain, 193–7; France, 93–4, 189–92, 197, 234, 236; Germany, 93, 94, 234–5, 236; Italy, 93, 94; Middle Ages, 89, 92–4; post-Enlightenment intellectuals, 187–9; postcolonialism, 419–22; reason, 187–8, 189–90; romanticism, 186–7; Scotland, 135, 193, 196–7, 202*n*; United States, 197–200, 434; and world history, 394–7, 409–10
national individuality, 146–7, 149
national memory, 292
National Science Foundation, 307
nationalism, 144, 185–6, 201
    German historiography, 144, 166, 170; Japan, 420–1, 425–6; postcolonial history, 418; and professionalization, 234; *see also* civic nationalism; ethnic nationalism
Nationalism: A Derivative Discourse (Chatterjee), 418
Native Americans, 377, 384
natural jurisprudence theory, 127
natural law traditions, 127–8
natural rights theory, 127
natural selection, theory of, 298, 310
natural sociability, 131
nature
    as contributor to change, 372; destabilization of, 373; dynamism of, 373, 385; ecology, 377–8,

nature (*cont'd*)
382, 383, 399–400; humanity's transformation of, 373, 374–5; integration, 382–6; Marx, 207; passivity of, 374, 375; population biology, 379–81; reciprocal relation to people, 374, 375, 381; romantic notions of, 373, 383–4; wilderness, 381–2
Nature's Metropolis (Cronon), 372
Nazism, 306–7, 338
Near East historiography, 15–16, 19–20
necrophilia, 364
Needham, Joseph, 316
needs, material, 206, 207, 208, 213
Nehemiah, 30
Nehemiah, Book of, 17, 30–1
Nehru, Jawaharlal, 394
Nennius, 91, 93
neoclassical historiography, 99–104, 126–7
Nepos, 55
Nero, 63, 64
Nerva, 73
Netherlands, professionalization of historical studies, 231
neuroscience, 341, 349–53
neutrality, 236
New England, 198
New German Cinema, 478
New Historicism, 163*n*
New History school, 236–7, 263, 376
The New Science (Vico), 128
The New York Times, 314
Newton, Isaac, 298, 299, 303–4, 305, 309, 311
Niccoli, Niccolò, 108
Nicholas V, Pope, 103
Niebuhr, Barthold Georg, 123, 228, 229
Nietzsche, Friedrich
    The Birth of Tragedy, 175; critique of professionalism, 236; "David Strauss, the Confessor and the Writer," 175; and Foucault, 180–1; history as cultural criticism, 174–6; influence on Weber, 177, 179; "On the Advantage and Disadvantage of History for Life," 159–60, 175, 236; politics, 175, 180–1, 182; religion, 175; self, 347; *Untimely Meditations*, 175
Nigeria, professionalization of historical studies, 232
The Night of the Shooting Stars, 469, 478
Nixon, 473
Noah, 26
Nobility and Excellence of Women (Marinella), 110
Noiriel, Gérard, 348, 349
noman, 353
Normans, 91
North America
    savage societies, 130, 131; *see also* Canada; United States
North American Review (Bancroft), 198
nostalgia, 471
Novick, Peter, 226, 236, 313
Novick, Robert, 473
nuclear age, 252, 253

objectification, 348
objectivist paradigm, 348

objectivity
    colonial power, 418; history of science, 297–8, 303, 313; as professional ethos, 8–9, 226, 232, 234, 236, 239–40
O'Brien, Karen, 123–4, 133, 139
obscenity, 358
October, 468–9, 475, 477
O'Donnell, James J., 450, 456–7, 461, 463
Odysseus (Homer), 36, 37, 39
OhioLink, 459–60
Okinawa, 425–6
Old Testament, 15–32
Olympiads, 52
Oman, Charles, 251
On Diplomacy (Mabillon), 125
On the Origin of Species (Darwin), 299, 374
"On Raising History to the Level of a Science" (Droysen), 233
On the Ruin and Conquest of Britain (Gildas), 91
On the Spirit of the Laws (Montesquieu), 124, 128–9, 130, 133
On the Study of History (Burckhardt), 171–2
On the Uncertainty and Vanity of the Sciences (Agrippa), 110
"On the Advantage and Disadvantage of History for Life" (Nietzsche), 159–60, 175, 236
On War (Clausewitz), 250
oral traditions
    ancient Greece, 36–7, 40, 42, 43, 228; ancient Rome, 228; Renaissance historiography, 113, 115
Orator (Cicero), 66, 67, 68, 79, 101
The Order of Things (Foucault), 327
Orderic of Vitalis, 93
Organization of American Historians, 459
Orientalism (Said), 405, 418, 420, 428
orientalists, 395
orientational requirements, 280
The Origin of the Distinction of Ranks (Millar), 130
Orosius, 83, 88
Ortner, Sherry, 285
Osnabrück, 147, 148–9
Osterhammel, Jürgen, 407
The Other Victorians (Marcus), 358–61
Otho, 63
Ottoman Empire, 112–13
Oxford English Dictionary, 451
Oxford University, 231

P *see* Priestly History (P)
pain, 152
Paine, Tom, 195
paleography, 227
pan-Asianism, 421
papacy, 103
Papua New Guinea, 353
Parallel Lives (Plutarch), 54–6
parents, 340
Pares, Richard, 253
Parkman, Francis, 198
parole, 323, 325
Parthia, 53
Partner, Nancy, 86
Pasquier, Estienne, 107, 115, 116
passions, 156

Pasteurians, 312
patent rights, 315
Paterculus, Velleius, 64
pathogens, 403–4
patrimonial inheritance, 94
The Patriot, 466
Die Patriotin, 478
patristic historians, 88
Patrizi, Francesco, 111
Paul the Deacon, 88, 91–2
Pausanias, 44–5
The Peasants of Languedoc (Le Roy Ladurie), 238,
	265–6, 376
Peirce, Charles Sanders, 322
Peloponnesian War, 43–7, 48, 74, 244
Pemberton, John, 291
Pentateuch, 16, 28
people's will, 198, 200
perceptions, 151, 152, 177
performances, 284–5
Pericles, 44, 46, 47, 55, 133
"The Perilous Purview of Psychohistory"
	(Schmidt), 339–40
Peron, Juan, 435
Persia, Peloponnesian War, 43
Persian Empire, 37, 40, 53
Persian letters (Montesquieu), 124, 129
Persian Wars, Herodotus, 39, 40–1
"Person, Time, and Conduct in Bali" (Geertz),
	280
personalities, genetic force, 151
personhood, 352–3
pests, 403
Peter I, Emperor of Russia, 133
Peters, Tom, 463
Petrarch, Francesco, 99, 100, 101, 102, 103, 105,
	106, 116
Le peuple (Michelet), 190, 191, 192
Phaeacians, 36
Pharamond, 94
Philip II, King of Spain, 264
Philip II of Macedon, 51
Philip V of Macedon, 72
Philippica (Theopompus), 50–1
Philippine hill people, 284
Philippines, 402
Philistines, 18
philology, 227, 231, 320
Philopoemen, 54
philosophers, as historians of science, 302–3
philosophical history
	Enlightenment historiography, 123–4, 132–41,
		143–4, 145–6, 187; *see also* Gibbon, Edward;
		Hume, David; Robertson, William; Voltaire,
		François Marie Arouet de
philosophy
	Marx, 208, 209, 220–1; replacement by history,
		233; *see also* Hegel, Georg Wilhelm Friedrich;
		Kant, Immanuel
The Philosophy of the Enlightenment, 123
The Philosophy of Right (Hegel), 158–9
Phlius, 49
Phoenician peoples, 23, 32
Phoenix, 36
phrenology, 310, 339

physics, 315
Pizan, Christine de, 109–10
place theory, 376
plague, 404
Plagues and Peoples (McNeill), 379
plant diffusions, 404–5
plantation agriculture, 402, 408
Plataea, 39
pleasure, 152
The Pleasure of the Text (Barthes), 323–4
Pliny, 65, 68
Plutarch, 8, 35, 38, 39, 54–6, 57, 64
Pocock, J. G. A., 123–4, 126, 139, 329, 330, 331
poetics, 279
Poetics (Aristotle), 101
poetry, Greek epics, 35–7
Poggio, 105, 245
polis, 36, 174
political conservatism, 149
political economy, 285
political language, 287
political leadership, Greek historiography, 35,
	48–50
political nationalism, 144
political organization, Hegel, 156–7
political science, 9, 395
politics, 7–8
	Burckhardt, 171–4, 180, 182; German
		historiography, 166–82; Greek historiography,
		38; Marx, 213–14; medieval historiography,
		85–6; Nietzsche, 175, 180–1, 182; and
		professionalization, 234–6; Ranke, 166,
		167–71, 172, 180, 181, 182; Renaissance
		historiography, 102–3, 104–8, 126; and
		science, 306–7; Thucydides, 47; Weber,
		176–9, 181, 182
"Politics as a Vocation" (Weber), 178
Poliziano, Angelo, 104
Poltava, Battle of, 133
Polybius, 35, 38, 50–2, 73–4, 126
	concept of causation, 57; influence on Livy, 72;
		protests against bad history, 30; Punic Wars,
		244; Roman history, 51–2, 64–5, 72
Pomeranz, Kenneth, 399
Pompey, 54, 62
Poni, Carlo, 270
poor, 281–2
Poovey, Mary, 287
Popper, Karl, 306
popular history, 255–6
The Population Bomb (Ehrlich), 380
populations, 379–81
pornography, 358, 359, 360
Porter, Theodore, 313
positions, 427
positivism, 95, 233, 306, 308
The Post-modern Condition (Lyotard), 127, 139
post-structuralism
	cultural historians of science, 312; emotional
		discourse, 292; emphasis on difference, 428;
		influence on anthropology and history, 286,
		287–9; linguistics, 324–6; postcolonial history,
		418, 419, 428; and psychology, 345, 346; self,
		347; social constructionism, 346; total history,
		266

postcolonial history, 330, 407, 417–30
  anthropology, 419; capitalism, 429; criticism of,
    427–30; national historiographies, 419–22;
    post-structuralism, 418, 419, 428; questioning
    of history, 419–22; writing of alternative
    histories, 422–7; *see also* subaltern studies
postcolonial societies, 291
postindustrial societies, 219
postmodern history, 472
postmodernism, 96, 238, 278
power, 7–8
  colonialism, 418; and emotions, 349; Foucault,
    180–1, 289, 327, 363, 364, 365, 368; and
    gender, 366; Herodotus, 41; post-
    structuralism, 287, 289; and sexuality, 363,
    364, 365, 367; Thucydides, 45; Weber, 181
practice theory, 284, 285
Prager, Jeffrey, 341
Prakash, Gyan, 424
pre-capitalist cultures, 377–8, 384
pre-capitalist modes of production, 213
premodern trade, 400–2
Presbyterianism, 135, 139, 196
Prescott, William Hickling, 198, 232
presentation, method of in Marx, 212, 215
preservation, 382
Das Preussische Heer der Befreiungskriege
    (Schwertfeger), 250
Price, Richard, 409
priestly cults, Israelite
    historiography, 26–7
Priestly History (P), 16–17, 24–7, 28
Primat, 93
primitive cultures, 281
The Prince (Machiavelli), 106, 245, 329
Principles of Geology (Lyell), 374
Principles of Sociology (Spencer), 252
print journals, 458–60
printing, 456
probability, Thucydides, 45
Problems of Dostoyevsky's Poetics (Bahktin), 322
production means/modes
    Marx, 205, 208, 211, 212–13, 214, 215; Weber,
    179
productive forces, 213–14
productive relations, 213–14
professionalization, 3, 140, 225–40, 300, 320,
    394–5
  and critical study of documents, 226–32; critique
    of, 236–9; definition, 225; disillusionments,
    267; ethos of objectivity, 8–9, 226, 232, 234,
    236, 239–40; limits and importance of,
    239–40; and literature, 232–4, 239; and
    politics, 234–6
progress, 96
  Bancroft, 198–9; Enlightenment theories, 127,
    139, 140, 187–8; narratives about, 297, 300;
    national historians, 187–8
Prolegomena to Homer (Wolf), 227
proletariat, 207, 209, 213, 214, 219
property
  Enlightenment historiography, 128, 131;
    principle of, 284
prophets, 21, 30
The Protestant Ethic and the Spirit of Capitalism
    (Weber), 177–8, 181

Protestantism, 166, 169, 177–8, 234, 265, 309–
    10
Proulx, Annie, 454, 456
Providence, 199, 200
Prussia
  cultural critique of, 174; economic development,
    177; Hegel, 159, 420; national leadership,
    166, 167, 169, 179; Ranke's belief in, 169,
    171, 179; reforms, 159, 167; war with France,
    175, 250; *see also* Germany
Prussian Academy of Sciences, 145
Prussian School, 234, 235
pseudo-history, 27
pseudo-sciences, 310
psyche *see* self
psychiatry, 327, 341
psychoanalysis, 338–41
  Febvre, 342; feminist critique of, 345, 348;
    Foucault, 364, 367; historians of gender, 345,
    346, 348
psychobiographies, 338
psychocultural anthropology, 292
psychohistory, 337, 338–41
psychology, 9, 11, 256, 337–53
  anthropology, 281, 292; biological foundations
    of, 340; comparative analysis, 322; cultural
    autonomy, 281, 283; ignored by history,
    341–7; origins, 340; self, 337–8, 341, 342–3,
    347–53; *see also* crowd psychology
Psychopathia sexualis (Krafft-Ebing), 363–4
Ptolemy, 53, 304
public archives *see* archives
Pufendorf, Samuel, 127–8, 131
Punic Wars, 244
Puritans, 134, 177–8, 195, 197, 310
Pyrrhonism, 125, 132

Quaderni storici, 270
quantum mechanics, 308
quantum physics, 310
quarks, 262
queer history, 367
Quellenkritik, 231
Quilombo, 471–2
Quintilian, 66, 79, 99
Quintus Fabius Pictor, 60

Rabelais, François, 322
Rabelais and His World (Bahktin), 322
race, Ranke's concerns with, 168–9
race relations, 345, 346
racism, 434–6
  apartheid, 434, 437; Australia, 434, 437;
    Canada, 434, 437; United States, 197, 235,
    240, 434, 435–6, 437; visual media, 467; *see
    also* slavery
Raleigh, Walter, 107
Ranke, Leopold von, 11, 123, 174, 175, 176, 237
  belief in Prussia, 169, 171, 179; broad appeal to
    the public, 233; centrality of power, 181;
    concern with the nation, 168–70; critics of,
    180; dislike of Hegelian philosophy, 157;
    ethnicity, 168–9; French Revolution (1789),
    168, 170; historicism, 147, 149, 160, 161;
    *The Histories of the Latin and Germanic
    Peoples*, 229; *History of France*, 249;

impartiality, 232, 234; nationalism, 234; objectivity, 234, 239; presentation of facts, 232; primacy of politics, 166, 167–71, 172, 180, 181, 182; professionalization, 147, 160, 161, 226, 229, 230; race, 168–9; rejection of chaos, 234; religion, 170, 172; source criticism, 321; task of the historian, 226; use of archives, 229; use of primary sources, 226

Rashomon, 270

rational autonomy, 152, 153, 155, 156, 158

rational self-consciousness, 156, 157

rationality

colonial power, 418; Hegel's spirit, 156, 206; Kant, 153; Weber, 179, 181, 398

Rats, Lice, and History (Zinsser), 379

Ray, Satyajit, 478

Raynal, Abbé Guillaume-Thomas, 132, 136–7, 139

reality, 206, 208, 209–10

reality effects, 470, 472

reason

Bancroft, 198–9; and emotions, 351–2; Enlightenment historiography, 187–8; French national historiography, 189–90; Hegel's spirit, 156, 158; national historiography, 187–8; Thucydides, 47

"The Reasons of Misrule" (Davis), 282

Récits des temps mérovingens précédés de considerations sur l'histoire de France (Thierry), 189

Reddy, William, 349

redemption, 199

redigere, 80

Reed Elsevier, 459–60

Reformation, 134, 136, 157, 166, 169

Rehoboam, 20

relations of production, 213–14

relativism, 149–50, 162

relativity, theory of, 298, 299, 307

religion

Bancroft, 199–200; Burckhardt, 172, 174, 180, 183n; history of, 320; Hume, 193; Macaulay, 195; Michelet, 191; Nietzsche, 175; Ranke, 170, 172; and science, 305–6, 309–10; Scottish national historiography, 196; universal patterns of meaning, 6; Voltaire, 133; Weber, 179, 181

religious exchanges, 405

religious identity, 166

religious riots, 282

Renaissance, Burckhardt, 172–3, 180

Renaissance historiography, 99–117

antiquarianism, 114–15; artifacts, 99, 104; awareness and sense of the past, 100–4; biography, 108; charters, 115; chronicle writing, 105–7; chronology, 114–15; distinctive forms of, 102–4; documentation, 99, 103, 104, 112–13, 115; fascination with Rome, 99–100, 101; historical methodology, 111–17; historical periodization, 116; influence of Caesar, 101–2, 107; influence of Cicero, 101, 113; influence of Livy, 75, 101–2, 103; influence of Sallust, 101–2; influence of Tacitus, 101–2, 103; influence of Thucydides, 102; information sources, 103–4, 112–13, 115–16; law, 114, 115; manuscripts, 99, 104; politics, 102–3, 104–8, 126;

vernacular traditions, 104–8; wars, 244; women's history, 108–11

Repentance, 478

republicanism

Kant, 153–4; Montesquieu, 129

Rescuing History from the Nation (Duara), 423–4

research, 225–32

scientific, 305, 306, 315–16; *see also* archives; artifacts; documentation; information sources

research academies, 227

Researches on France (Pasquier), 107, 116

The Return of Martin Guerre, 263, 466, 469

Revel, Jacques, 270, 272

Revelation, Book of, 83

revolutionary consciousness, 158

revolutions, 209, 213–14, 218–19; *see also* French Revolution (1789); Russian Revolution

Revue des Deux Mondes, 230

Revue Historique, 230

rhetoric, medieval historiography, 78, 79–80, 81

Richardson, 84

Riess, Ludwig, 231

rights, 188, 420

Rigord of Saint-Denis, 80, 93

rinascita, 100

The Rise of Louis XIV, 472

The Rise of the West (McNeill), 397

"The Rites of Violence" (Davis), 282

Ritter, Gerhard, 170

rituals, 174, 280–1

circumcision rites, 26, 27

Rivista storica, 230

Robert of Torigni, 93

Robertson, William, 123, 124, 138, 140

causal primacy, 130; growth of liberty, 196; *Historical Disquisition concerning the Knowledge which the Ancients had of India*, 136; *History of America*, 132, 136; *History of the Reign of the Emperor Charles V*, 132, 135–6; *History of Scotland*, 135; Presbyterianism, 135, 139, 196; rebuke of Voltaire, 132

Robinson, James Harvey, 263, 345

Rolls Series, 229

Roman historiography, 60–76

aemulatio, 67; composition of speeches for characters, 66–7; definition of history, 79; exemplar theory of history, 69–74; Greek legacy, 64–8; information sources, 67; nature of time, 81

Roman History (Mommsen), 233

Roman History (Niebuhr), 228, 229

Romana (Jordanes), 89

Romania, 236

romanticism, 186–7

Rome/Roman Empire

aristocratic culture, 65; break up into two halves, 88; Christian historiography, 88; Gibbon's *Decline and Fall*, 138–9; and the Goths, 89; literary accomplishment, 65; Livy, 62; Montesquieu on, 129; moral decline, 69–73; Niebuhr's studies of, 228; Petrarch's visits, 99; Plutarch's *Parallel Lives*, 54–6; Polybius, 51–2, 64–5, 72; Renaissance historiography, 99–100, 101; rise of, 51; Rousseau's superior social condition of, 148

Romulus, 54
Roosevelt, Franklin, 432
Roper, Lyndal, 348, 349
Rorty, Richard, 329
Rosaldo, Renato, 284
Roseberry, William, 285
Ross, Andrew, 314
Rossellini, Roberto, 472, 473
Rothfels, Hans, 253
Round Hill School, 198
Rousseau, Jean-Jacques, 124, 148, 373, 381, 384, 385
   Discourse on the Origin and Foundations of Inequality Among Men, 131; *The Social Contract*, 153
royal chronicles
   Israelite historiography, 16; medieval historiography, 81; Near East historical genres, 16
Royal Society, 303, 313
royalty *see* kingship; monarchy
Rubin, Gayle, 367
Rucellai, Giovanni, 106
Rudé, George, 344
Runyan, William McKinley, 339
Russia, professionalization of historical studies, 231
Russian Revolution, 216, 468

Sabbath, 25, 26, 27
Sabean, David, 269, 289, 290–1, 353
sacrificial rituals, 174
sadism, 363–4, 366
Sahlins, Marshall, 284, 285
Said, Edward, 405, 418, 420, 428
St. Albans abbey, 93
Saint-Denis, 86, 93, 94
Saint-Germain-des-Près, 93
saints
   Bede, 91; Gregory of Tours, 90
Salamis, 39
Salian dynasty, 94
Sallust, 60–2, 64, 65, 72, 73, 90
   and Caesar, 61, 70, 71; *Histories*, 61; influence on Renaissance historiography, 101–2; revered in Middle Ages, 75; and St. Augustine, 70, 75; and Thucydides, 66; *War against Catiline*, 61, 70–1, 74; *War against Jugurtha*, 61, 66, 70; writing style, 66
salmon fisheries, 385
salvation, 96
Samaria, 29, 31
Samaritans of Mount Gerazim, 29
Samos, 41, 42
Samuel, 18
Samuel, Books of, 18, 21
Sanudo, Marin, 107
Sargon the Great, 24, 33n
Sarton, George, 307
Sauer, Carl Ortwin, 376, 377, 382
Saul, 18, 28
Saussure, Ferdinand de, 322–3, 325, 346
savage societies, 130, 131, 132
Savigny, Carl Friedrich von, 147, 149, 157, 159
Saving Private Ryan, 466, 469, 478
Saxon dynasty, 94

Saxony, 167
Scala, Bartolomeo della, 105
Scaliger, Joseph Justus, 114
Scandza, 89
Schaffer, Simon, 312–13
Schama, Simon, 270
Schelling, Friedrich, 155, 195
Schiebinger, Londa, 313
Schiller, Friedrich, 149, 154
Schindler's List, 453, 466, 469, 475
schizophrenia, 350–1
Schleiermacher, Friedrich, 321
Schlözer, August Ludwig, 394
Schmidt, Casper G., 339–40
Schmoller, Gustav, 176–7
Schneider, David, 279
scholarly monographs, 456–7, 460–1
scholastic compendia, 95
Schorske, Carl E., 180
Schwertfeger, Bernhard, 250, 251
science
   biographical writing, 303–4, 311–12; as cultural history, 312–14; history of, 297–316; as intellectual history, 305–9; laboratory studies, 311, 315; objectivity, 297–8, 303, 313; philosophers as historians of, 302–3; and politics, 306–7; and religion, 305–6, 309–10; research, 305, 306, 315–16; as social history, 309–12; technological development, 305, 309, 311; versus history, 298–302; Weber's writings, 178; and women, 310, 313
science of diplomatics, 300
"Science as a Vocation" (Weber), 178
science wars, 314–15
scientific change, 308–9, 310
scientific community, Kuhn's theory, 308–9
Scipio Africanus the younger, 51
Scotland
   Act of Union (1707), 135, 196; Enlightenment historiography, 124, 130–1, 134–6, 138, 139, 196; national historiography, 135, 193, 196–7, 202n
Scott, James C., 285
Scott, Joan W., 330, 346, 365
Scott, Sir Walter, 190, 194, 196–7
Scottish Common Sense philosophy, 195, 199
Scottish moral philosophy, 187
Scottsboro Boys, 270
scriptores, 80
Scythia, 42
Seceders, 202n
secretaries, 449
secularization, 123, 125
Seeley, John Robert, 231
Segesta, 45
Sejanus, 74
Seleucid kings, 51
self, 8, 337–8, 347–53
   as an illusion, 341; colonized subjects, 418; Elias, 342–3; emotions, 351–2; minimal versus narrative, 350–1; neuroscience, 349–53; and sexuality, 363–4, 368–9
self-alienation, 155
self-conscious awareness, 207
self-consciousness, 156, 157, 420

self-control, 342–3
self-division, 155
self-interests, 152, 153, 155, 156
Sembene, Ousmane, 472, 475, 477, 478
seminars, 229, 231
semiotics, 322–3
Sempach, Battle of, 248
Seneca, 66
Senecio, 63
sensationalist psychology, 151, 152
sense perception, 151, 152, 177
sensibility, study of, 342
"Sensibility and History" (Febvre), 342
Serbia, 201, 236
Seven Books against the Pagans (Orosius), 83
Sewell, William, 284
sex
    link to gender, 313; in the unconscious, 350
sexism, 310
sexology, 363, 364, 367
sexual desire, 363–4
sexual deviance, 363–4, 367, 368
sexual feelings, 339, 340
sexual identity, 363–4, 368
sexual liberation, 358, 360, 368
sexual repression, 358–60
sexuality, 346–7, 357–69
    centrality of male sexuality, 359–60; as gauge of
        human freedom, 362, 368, 369; and gender,
        365–7, 369n; homosexuality, 363, 364, 366,
        367–8; and power, 363, 364, 365, 367
Sforza regime, 112
El Shaddai, 26
shame, 342
Shapin, Steven, 311, 312–13
Shay, Daniel, 200
Sherpa Buddhism, 285
shifters, 328
Shoah, 472
Short Chronicle of the Kings of France, 80
Shorter, Edward, 283
Shub, Esfir, 468
Siam Mapped (Thongchai), 421–2
Siberia, 131
Sicily, 45, 46, 47
Siemens, 305
Siena, 256
signs, 322–4, 346
Silesian weavers' revolt, 209
silk roads, 401
silver, 403
Silverblatt, Irene, 288
Sima Qian, 394
Simiand, François, 263–4, 265
Simonetta, Giovanni, 112
Simonides, 67
sin, 82–3
Sinai covenant, 26
skepticism, 15, 37, 74, 187
*Sketch for a Historical Picture of the Progress of the
    Human Mind* (Condorcet), 132
Skinner, Quentin, 329–30, 331
slavery, 197, 199–200, 408–9, 436
smallpox, 379, 380, 403, 404
Smith, Adam, 124, 130–1

Smith, Henry Nash, 381
Smith-Rosenberg, Carroll, 360
Smyth, William, 194
Snow, C. P., 447
Soboul, Albert, 254
social actors, 177
social coherence, 153
social constructionism, 345–6, 349
social contract, 127
The Social Contract (Rousseau), 153
Social Darwinism, 310
social history, 237, 254, 257, 337, 374
    and cultural history, 239, 281–3; rejection of
        psychology, 345; science as, 309–12
social individuality, 146–7, 149
social interactions, 272, 273–4
social norms, 282
social relations, Marx, 208
Social Science and the Ignoble Savage (Meek), 130
social structure, 8, 127, 205, 281, 283
Social Text, 314
socialism, 196, 344
La Société militaire dans la France contemporaine
    (Girardet), 253
Society for the History of Technology, 311
socio-economic progress, Enlightenment
    historiography, 127, 139, 140, 187–8
sociology, 9, 11, 237, 281, 309–10, 337, 395
Socrates, 48
Sokal, Alan, 314
Les Soldats de l'an deux (Soboul), 254
soldiers, 247, 248
Solidarity Movement, 472
Solomon, 19, 20, 21, 22, 28, 30
Solon, 42, 47, 55
sophrosyne, 175
Sorbonne, 231
Sorlin, Pierre, 475, 476
sources *see* archives; artifacts; documentation;
    information sources
Sources of the Self (Taylor), 348
South Africa, 290, 434, 437, 442
sovereignty, 420
Soviet Union
    Marxism, 179, 219; visual media, 467–8
Spain, professionalization of historical studies, 231
Sparks, Jared, 198
Sparta
    Herodotus, 40, 41, 42; Rousseau's superior
        social condition of, 148; Thucydides, 43–4,
        47; Xenophon, 49, 50
Speck, Frank, 377, 378, 384, 385
Speculum, 460
Speculum Historiale (Vincent of Beauvais), 95
speech, 323
speech act theory, 329
Spence, Jonathan, 270
Spencer, Herbert, 252
Spengler, Oswald, 232, 393, 394
Spielberg, Steven, 453
spirit (*Geist*), 155–9, 206, 207, 420
Spivak, Gayatri, 419, 428
stadial history, 128, 130–2, 136, 137, 139, 196
Stalin, Joseph, 76
Stanford University, 447

state
  cultural hegemony, 216–17; and military
    institutions, 252–3; Montesquieu's
    government forms, 129; *see also* nation-state;
    politics
state archives *see* archives
state development, Hegel, 156–7
state formation
  Burckhardt, 173; Ranke, 167, 168–70
status, 228
Stavrianos, L. S., 397
Stedman Jones, Gareth, 273, 286, 287
Steenkerke, Battle of, 246
Steiner, George, 332
Stewart, Dugald, 131
Stewart, Pamela J., 353
Stone, Oliver, 473, 477, 478, 480*n*
Strathern, Andrew, 353
Strayer, Joseph R., 86
Structural Transformation of the Public Sphere
  (Habermas), 219
structuralism, 322, 323–4, 377
The Structure of Scientific Revolutions (Kuhn), 308
Sturm und Drang movement, 148, 149, 154
subaltern studies, 285, 330, 407, 418–19, 422,
  428
subjectivist paradigm, 348
subjectivity, 125, 281, 347
subsistence modes, 128, 130, 141
Suetonius, 64, 66
Suger, 93
Sulla, 55, 61, 65, 70, 71
Superconducting Supercollider, 314
superego, 350
superstition, 138
superstructures, 213, 214, 217
Surname Viet Given Name Nam, 472
Survivors of the Shoah Visual History Foundation,
  453–4
Sweden, 239
Switzerland, 247–8, 440
Sybel, Heinrich von, 230, 235
Syberberg, Hans Jürgen, 472, 475
Syria, 23

tabernacle, 27
Tacitus, 10, 61, 62–4, 65, 67, 72–3, 74, 126, 225
  Agricola, 63, 66, 72, 73; *Annals*, 63–4, 68, 73;
    Dialogue on Orators, 63; *Germania*, 63;
    Histories, 63, 66, 73; influence on Renaissance
    historiography, 101–2, 103; long-term
    influence of, 75–6; writing style, 66
Taine, Hippolyte, 344
Takaki, Ronald, 436
Tanaka, Stefan, 420
Tang Dynasty, 225
Tansley, A. G., 378
Tarkovsky, Andrei, 475
Taussig, Michael, 285
Taviani brothers, 478
Taylor, Charles, 348
Taylor, Jay, 385
technological development, 208, 213, 305, 309,
  311, 407; *see also* computers
technology transfers, 393

De temporum ratione (Bede), 91
Ten Dialogues on History (Patrizi), 111
tent of meeting, 27
Tesauro, Emanuele, 115
Tetrateuch, 16
textual analysis, 227, 320–3, 422
  definition of text, 320–1
textual conversation, 321
textual criticism, 227, 231, 300
textual deconstruction, 278
Thailand, 421–2
That Noble Dream (Novick), 313, 473
Thebes, 49, 50
Themistocles, 44–5
theocracy, 27
theology, medieval historiography, 78
Theopompus, 50–1
theory
  Marx's interaction with history, 208–16, 219,
    220–1; Ranke's protest against, 168
Thermopylae, 39
"Theses on Feuerbach" (Marx), 207, 209
Theseus, 54
Thierry, Augustin, 189–90, 193, 194, 197
Thirty Years War, 245
Thomas, William G., 461
Thompson, E. P., 217, 218, 266, 282, 285, 286,
  345
Thompson, William, 305
Thongchai Winichakul, 421–2
Thoreau, Henry David, 199, 373, 381, 384, 385
Thornton, John, 409
thought, Marx's materialist view of, 209, 210, 214
Thrace, 43–4
Thrasea Paetus, 64
Thucydides, 35, 37, 38, 43–8, 49, 51, 225
  comparisons of values and actions, 55; history as
    a practical guide, 74; influence on Ranke, 229;
    influence on Renaissance historiography, 102;
    influence on Sallust, 66; legacy of, 56–7;
    objectivity, 9; Peloponnesian War, 43–7, 74,
    244; skepticism, 15, 74
Tiberius, 63, 65, 73
Tilly, Charles, 283, 345
time
  creation of, 25; nature of, 81–2; and selfhood,
    351, 352
Time on the Cross (Fogel and Engerman), 238
Tiro, 447–8
Tiro Project, 447
Titus, 62
Tocqueville, Alexis de, 170, 232
Tokyo Imperial University, 231
Tomiyama, Ichiro, 425–6
Tomlins, Christopher, 459
Torah, 83
total history, 262–6
  disillusionment with, 166–7; history of science,
    304
Totem and Taboo (Freud), 338
totemism, 279
Totemism (Lévi-Strauss), 279
Totila, 102
Toynbee, Arnold J., 232, 393, 394
toyoshi, 420

trade, 393, 400–3, 410
trade unions, 217
tradition, 321; *see also* custom
tragic historians, 51
training, 227
Trajan, Emperor, 53, 54, 73
The Transformations of War (Colin), 251
Treatise of Human Nature (Hume), 134
Treitschke, Heinrich von, 235
Trevelyan, George Macaulay, 254
Trevor-Roper, Hugh, 123, 124, 140
triangular trades, 402, 408
Trinh T. Min-ha, 472
Trobriand Islanders, 282
Troeltsch, Ernst, 176
Trogus, Pompeius, 64
Trojan war, 23, 36
tropes, 328, 330–1
Tropics of Discourse (White), 331
Truth and Method (Gadamer), 321
Tswana peoples, 290
Tuan, Yi-Fu, 376
Tuchman, Barbara, 232
Turgot, Anne Robert Jacques, 124
Turner, Frederick Jackson, 233, 372, 374, 375,
    377, 379, 381, 382, 384
Turner, James Grantham, 365
Turner, Victor, 279, 283, 286
    emotions, 280–1, 292; empty existential features
    of life, 284; post-structuralist challenge, 287;
    rituals, 280–1
Tytler, Patrick Fraser, 197

Ukraine, 37, 42, 201
Ultras, 189
Uncle Tom's Cabin, 466
unconscious, 350
Underground, 469
United States
    academic freedom, 235; African-Americans,
    435–6, 467; bureaucracy, 227–8; civic
    nationalism, 432, 435; environmental
    catastrophes, 375–6; growth of popular
    historical writing, 185; higher education,
    227–8, 230; historical journals, 230;
    microhistory, 263, 270; multiculturalism,
    435–7, 442, 443–4; national historiography,
    197–200, 434; Native Americans, 377, 384;
    official campaign histories, 250; professional
    disillusionment, 267; professionalization and
    politics, 235; racism, 197, 235, 240, 434,
    435–6, 437; science, 307–8; settlers, 375,
    434; universities, 231, 235; visual media, 467;
    war historiography, 253–4; wilderness, 381–2;
    wolf population, 378
universal chronicles, medieval historiography, 79,
    81
universal history, 6, 394
    end of tradition of, 125; Greek historiography,
    50; Herder, 150–1; Israelite historiography,
    23, 25; Kantian philosophy, 143–4, 151–4,
    155, 156, 158, 162; medieval historiography,
    82–3, 88; modern German historiography,
    162; *see also* philosophical history
Universal History Divided into an Ancient,

Medieval and New Period (Cellarius), 125
Universal Law (Vico), 128
universal moral order, 23
universities, 227, 228–31, 235, 239
university chair, 140
The Unredeemed Captive (Demos), 271
Untimely Meditations (Nietzsche), 175
urban chronicles, 95
urban environments, 383–4
Uriah, 21
Ussher, Bishop James, 33*n*

vaccines, 380
Valdes, Luis, 472
Valla, Lorenzo, 103–4, 114
"Valley of the Shadow Project," 461
values, Weber, 177
Vargas, Getulia, 435
Varro, 99
Vasari, Giorgio, 100–1
Vasconcelos, Jose, 435
Vatican Library, 103, 112
Vegetius, 244
vengeance, Greek historiography, 41
Venice, 102, 107
Verdun, Treaty of, 92
Verona, 102
Vespasian, 62, 63
Vespasiano da Bisticci, 108
Vicinus, Martha, 360
Vico, Giambattista, 124, 128, 190, 199
Vidal de la Blache, Paul, 376
Vienna Circle, 306
Vietnam, professionalization of historical studies,
    226
Vietnam War, 309
Vignier, Nicolas, 107
Villani, Giovanni, 105
Vincent of Beauvais, 95
violence, war historiography, 258–9
Virgil, 67
Virgin Land (Smith), 381
virtue, Montesquieu, 129
Visconti, Luchino, 475
visual media, 466–80
    documentary films, 468, 470–1; dramatic feature
    films, 468, 469–70, 477; experimental or
    innovative historical film, 468–9, 471–3; new
    historical films, 477–8
visual plasticity, 87, 90
Vitellius, 63
Volney, Constantin, 187
Voltaire, François Marie Arouet de, 123, 124,
    132–4, 136, 138, 139, 140, 187
    The Age of Louis XIV, 133, 134, 145, 246;
    cross-cultural history of customs, 394;
    despotism, 133, 137; dispute with
    Montesquieu, 137; erudite historiography,
    125–6; *Essay on Manners*, 132, 133–4, 145;
    Herder's criticism of, 146; perfected culture of
    France, 145–6; war historiography, 245–6
von Rad, G., 33*n*

Wace, 93
Wagner, Adolf, 176–7

Wagner, Richard, 175
Waitz, Georg, 230
Wajda, Andrzej, 477, 478
Walker, 472, 478
Wallerstein, Immanuel, 141, 399
War against Catiline (Sallust), 61, 70–1, 74
War against Jugurtha (Sallust), 61, 66, 70
war historiography, 243–59
  Caesar, 61, 244; Clausewitz, 246, 247, 249–50;
    documentation, 248, 249; Frederick the Great,
    247; Herodotus, 39, 40–1; integrative
    histories, 251–3, 255–6;Machiavelli, 245;
    Marxism, 254; Muller, 247–8; new military
    history, 256–8; official histories, 250–1, 255;
    Polybius, 244; Thucydides, 43–7, 74, 244;
    violence, 258–9; Voltaire, 245–6
War and Trade in the West Indies (Pares), 253
Waverly novels (Scott), 190, 194, 196
Webb, Beatrice, 232
Webb, Sidney, 232
Webb, Walter Prescott, 375–6, 377, 381, 382
Weber, Max, 11, 85, 139, 141, 162, 176–9, 182,
    237, 282, 345, 395
  capitalism, 177–8, 181, 309, 398; culture, 177,
    238; distinction between cultural sciences,
    226; *Economy and Society*, 176; historical ideal
    types, 208; politics, 176–9, 181, 182; power,
    181; *The Protestant Ethic and the Spirit of
    Capitalism*, 177–8, 181; rationality, 179, 181,
    398; religion, 179, 181; "Science as a
    Vocation," 178
Weeks, Jeffrey, 366
Wellenkamp, Jane, 292
Wellhausen, J., 33n
Wells, H. G., 232, 394
Welser, Markus, 113
Wenden, D. J., 474, 476
Whewell, William, 304–5
Whiggism, 193–7
White, Andrew Dickson, 305–6
White, Hayden, 239, 240, 319, 328, 330–1, 332
White, Richard, 382, 383
wilderness, 381–2
Wilderness Act (USA), 382
Wilderness and the American Mind (Nash), 381–2
wilderness preservation, 373
Wilhelm II, Emperor of Germany, 177
William of Jumièges, 93
William of Malmesbury, 93
William of Newburgh, 93
William of Poitiers, 93
Williams, Eunice, 271
Wilson, Woodrow, 432, 467

Winckelmann, Johann, 160–1
Wissenschaft, 226
Wives of the Leopard (Bay), 288
Wolf, Eric, 285
Wolf, F. A., 227, 228
Wolters Kluwer, 459, 460
wolves, 378
women, as professional historians, 236
women's history, 181, 238
  Enlightenment historiography, 135; female
    sexuality, 357, 360–2, 366, 367; Herodotus,
    43; Renaissance historiography, 108–11;
    science, 310, 313; *see also* gender
women's liberation, 267
Wong, R. Bin, 399
Woolf, Daniel, 232
word processing, 447, 457
Wordsworth, William, 381
work ethic, 177–8, 398
working class, 213, 217
The World at War, 253
world history, 10, 393–411
  biological diffusions, 393, 403–5, 410; cross-
    cultural trade, 393, 400–3, 410; cultural
    exchanges, 3, 405–6, 410; different meanings
    of, 393; imperialism and colonialism, 393,
    395, 406–8, 410; migrations, 393, 408–9,
    410; and national history, 394–7, 409–10;
    theoretical approaches, 397–400
World War II, 253
World Wide Web, 450, 452–3, 455, 456
world-systems theory, 285, 393, 398–9, 402
Worster, Donald, 378, 382, 383, 385
Writing Degree Zero (Barthes), 324
Wundt, Wilhelm, 340
Würtemburg, 269, 290–1

Xenophon, 35, 38, 48–50, 61
Xerxes, 40, 41, 43, 47

YAHWEH, 17–18, 19, 20–1, 23, 24, 26, 27
Yahwist's History (J), 16–17, 22–4, 25, 26–7
Yellowstone Park, 382
Yosemite Park, 382
Young Hegelians, 159
Young, James, 332
Young Man Luther (Erikson), 338

Zerissenheit, 154, 155
Zerubbabel, 30, 31
Zinsser, Hans, 379
Zoot Suit, 472
Zweig, George, 262